The
Morphology
OF
Biblical
Greek

A Companion to
Basics of Biblical Greek
and
The Analytical Lexicon to the Greek New Testament

William D. Mounce

ZondervanPublishingHouse
Grand Rapids, Michigan

A Division of HarperCollinsPublishers

This text is dedicated to

William Sanford LaSor.

My professor and friend, who always put time
with his students ahead of his own professional
advancement, and who tried to teach me what
inductive language study is all about.

Morphology of Biblical Greek
Copyright © 1994 by William D. Mounce

Requests for information should be addressed to:
Zondervan Publishing House
Grand Rapids, MI 49530

Library of Congress Cataloging in Publication Data

Mounce, William. D
    The morphology of biblical Greek: a companion to the Basics of biblical Greek and
Analytical lexicon to the Greek New Testament / William D. Mounce
        p.   cm.
    Includes index
    ISBN 0-310-41040-1
    1. Greek language, Biblical—Morphology. 2. Greek language, Biblical—
Dictionaries—English. I. Mounce, William D. Basics of biblical Greek. II. Mounce,
William. D. Analytical lexicon to the Greek New Testament. III. Title.
    PA836.M68 1994
    487′.4—dc20   94-34331

                                                                                CIP

The Greek New Testament, edited by Kurt Aland, Matthew Black, Carlo M. Martini, Bruce
M. Metzger, and Allen Wikgren. Fourth Revised Edition. © 1966, 1968, 1975, 1983, 1993 by
the United Bible Societies. Used by permission.

Edited by Verlyn D. Verbrugge

Printed in the United States of America

95 96 97 98 99 / QG / 10 9 8 7 6 5 4 3 2

This edition is printed on acid-free paper and meets the American National Standards
Institute Z39.48 standard.

Table of Contents

The table of contents is not exhaustive; it skips some secondary discussions.

Phonology

Vocalic change

Consonantal change

Verbal Formation

Indicative Tenses

Non-Indicative "Moods"

Noun Paradigms

Adjective Paradigms

Principal Parts

Preface

I hate memorizing words, especially principal parts. But it seems that all I did when I was learning Greek was to memorize, or at least try to memorize. Especially those irregular forms. Question: "Why does the aorist passive of ἀκούω have a σ before the θ (ἠκούσθην)?" Answer: "It's irregular, so memorize it." I hate memorizing!

At seminary I was introduced to Prof. William LaSor and his inductive grammar, and later to the works by Profs. Robert Funk and H.W. Smyth. It was here that I first realized that Greek was a tremendously regular language, if you know the rules. My debt to these three scholars cannot be overestimated.

As I learned these rules, memorization not only became easier but unnecessary in many situations, especially of principal parts. I found that it is essential to think in terms of verbal roots. As we all know, once you know the forms of, ἔρχο-μαι, for example, you know the forms of eighteen other verbs. But more than that, if you can see all the verbs that form their principal parts the same way side by side, there is something about it that helps you remember what they are even without memorization. Having words sorted by category and not alphabetically as they are in this text may be a nuisance at first because you first have to look up their category in the *Index*, but in the long run we feel it is the best arrangement. You do not need to memorize all the categories, or what we call "tags"; it is helpful, however, to learn the basic tags as we have laid them out starting on page xviii.

After many years of working on this text, I had to lay it aside for several years while I taught, worked on other projects, and completed my *Analytical Lexicon* and *Basics of Biblical Greek*, which is based on what I had learned doing the *Morphology*. Both of these works are keyed into the *Morphology* for easy reference. And while I see many areas that I would like to enlarge, it is now ready to be shared with others who dislike memorization as much as I.

MBG is designed primarily as an aid to knowing New Testament Greek. While using the term *Biblical* in the name *Morphology of Biblical Greek* may be a bit of a misnomer since it does not deal heavily with the LXX, *MBG* does incorporate a significant amount of material that goes beyond the New Testament, including variants, the LXX, and Hellenistic Greek in general.

Despite the size and relative uniqueness of this work, it is far from being exhaustive. It does not deal with pure phonology and morphology; the rules listed at the beginning are designed to be a quick reference guide for the rest of the book. It does not delve into word formation (cf *BDF* §108-125, *MH* 267-410, Robertson 143-176, Smyth §822-899). It does not attempt to replace the discussions in *A Greek Grammar of the New Testament and Other Early Christina Literature* (F. Blass, A. Debrunner, R. Funk), *A Grammar of New Testament Greek* (J.H. Moulton, W.F. Howard), or *A Greek-English Lexicon of the New Testament and Other Early Christian Literature* (W. Bauer, W.F. Arndt, F.W. Gingrich, F.W. Danker).

The primary purpose of *MBG* is to categorize all the words in the New Testament, and others, assemble all the rules that govern their inflection, and present that information in a way that the student can understand without first having to learn the entire field of morphology. As such it functions as an introduction to the more detailed analyses of the language by these texts and others.

Of the many things I learned writing this text, two stand out. Students cannot approach Greek as if it were a "dead" language. True, Koine Greek is no longer spoken, but what we have in the New Testament is a snapshot of a language that was alive and changing. Secondly, language study must be descriptive, not pre-scriptive. When I started Greek I thought, for example, that either a word had a second aorist or it didn't. But then you find the three aorist passive forms of ἀνοίγω (ἠνεῴχθην, ἠνοίχθην, ἠνοίγην). Then you realize that the same root can form its present either as ῥήσσω or ῥήγνυμι, and even the compounds to switch back and forth between these two forms of the same verb. The best we can do is describe what we see and allow for the variations that accompany any living lan-guage.

I would be remiss in not mentioning a few people who were instrumental in the writing of the book. William Sanford LaSor, former professor at Fuller Theolog-ical Seminary, was one of the truly great pioneers in inductive language study. It was through his writing and our continuing friendship that the seed was planted and watered that eventually resulted in *MBG*. The three-volume grammar of Robert Funk was also enthralling; anyone familiar with his work will see my indebtedness to him. The monumental work of Hebert Weir Smyth was used as the final authority. These three grammars are heavily cross-referenced for further study, and because I wanted to give credit to whom credit is due. Dr. Walter W. Wessel was also a tremendous help and encouragement, answering my unusual questions at any time, day or night. Among the many students that used and worked on *MBG* I would like to thank especially John Stone, Lester Yamashita, Brad Rigney, Bob Ramsey, and Ian and Kathleen Lopez. Special thanks to Ed van der Maas, Stan Gundry, and Zondervan for publishing a book they felt was of academic importance even though it is not destined for blockbuster sales, and to my editor, Verlyn Verbrugge, for his careful work and many fine suggestions. Thanks also to Scotte Meredith, for shouldering the burden of StarSoft while I finished this text, and to Garland Avenue Alliance Church for their support.

I must also thank my good friend Μῆλον as well as *Gramcord* and *acCordance*, two superb computer programs that were instrumental in writing *MBG*.

But most of my thanks must go to Robin, who has constantly encouraged me to "play with my Greek." If there ever was a wife who supported her husband in all his endeavors, it surely is she, even to the point of encouraging me to quit a secure job and move to Spokane so I could finish this and other writing projects.

What started as a frustration has developed into what I trust will be a useful Greek aid. At the core of this study is a profound reverence for the biblical text and a desire to understand God's word as completely as possible. May this grammar be as much help to you as it has been to me.

Bill Mounce

How to use *MBG*

MBG is unique in its structure. It is worth your time to study the following discussion.

Numbering system

The numbering system is straightforward. The pattern is as follows.

§30

§31

§32.1

§32.2

§32.3a

§32.3b

§32.3c(1)

§32.3c(2)

§32.3c(3a)

§32.3c(3b)

§32.3d

§32.4

§33

Nouns, adjectives, and verbs follow a similar pattern. Nouns are prefaced with "n-," adjectives with "a-," simple verbs with "v-," and compound verbs with "cv-." (Only compound verbs formed with prepositions are listed as "cv-" verbs; compounds formed with other words such as nouns, adverbs, etc. are listed as "v-" verbs. See pp. 248f. for the rationale.)

n-1

n-2

n-3a

n-3b

n-3c(1)

n-3c(2)

n-3c(3a)

n-3c(3b)

n-3c(4)

n-3d

n-4

Nouns are divided into three categories.

n-1	First declension	ὥρα, ὥρας
n-2	Second declension	λόγος, λόγου
n-3	Third declension	σάρξ, σαρκός

It is helpful to learn the basic subdivisons of third declension nouns.

n-3a	Stems ending in a labial	ἄραψ, ἄραβος
n-3b	Stems ending in a velar	σάρξ, σαρκός
n-3c	Stems ending in a dental	ἐλπίς, ἐλπίδος
n-3d	Stems ending in a sibilant	γένος, γένους
n-3e	Stems ending in a semi-vowel	πόλις, πόλεως
n-3f	Stems showing different degrees of ablaut	πατήρ, πατρός
n-3g	Irregular nouns	Ἰησοῦς, Ἰησοῦ

Adjectives are divided into five categories, depending on how many endings are used and from which declension.

a-1	2-1-2	ἅγιος, ἁγία, ἅγιον
a-2	3-1-3	πᾶς, πᾶσα, πᾶν
a-3	2-2	ἁμαρτωλός, ἁμαρτωλόν
a-4	3-3	ἀληθής, ἀληθές
a-5	Irregular and indeclinable roots	δύο; ἕξ

Verbs are divided into v-1 through v-8, depending upon how they modify their verbal root in order to form their present tense stem.

v-1	Present tense = verbal root	*λυ ‣ λύω ‣ ἔλυσα
v-2	Present tense = verbal root + ι̯	*βαλ ‣ βάλλω ‣ ἔβαλον
v-3	Present tense = verbal root + ν	*αὐξα ‣ αὐξάνω ‣ αὐξήσω
v-4	Present tense = verbal root + τ	*βαπ ‣ βάπτω ‣ βάψω
v-5	Present tense = verbal root + σκ	*ἀρε ‣ ἀρέσκω ‣ ἀρέσω
v-6	Athematic (μι) verbs	*δο ‣ δίδωμι
v-7	Verbal roots that undergo ablaut	ἀκούω ‣ ἀκήκοα
v-8	Verbs that use more than one verbal root to form their different tense stems.	ἐσθίω ‣ φάγομαι

It is helpful to learn the basic subdivisons of v-1 verbs.

v-1a	Roots ending in ι̯ or Ϝ	λύω
v-1b	Roots ending in a stop	βλέπω
v-1c	Roots ending in a liquid/nasal	φέρω
v-1d	Roots ending in a vowel	
	v-1d(1) α contracts	ἀγαπάω

v-1d(2)	ε contracts	ποιέω
v-1d(3)	o contracts	πληρόω

MBG uses, as far as possible, linguistically correct terminology such as "dental," "assimilation," etc. While this can be confusing at first, it is important for the student to learn the basic terminology. In the section on rules, you do not actually have to know the terminology; the charts explain what the terminology is saying. The serious student should learn the classification scheme for consonants (§11) and especially the "Square of Stops" (§12). Most find the terminology helpful and automatic after several encounters.

Charts and lists

There are several ways you can use *MBG*. The simplest is to view it as a collection of charts and lists. I would encourage you to page through the text and become familiar with what it contains.

Inductive

In class we use *MBG* inductively. As we are reading through the biblical text and come across a form that doesn't make sense, we check the index to get the word's morphological tag and look it up. Once we see why the word is formed the way it is, it is easier to recognize the form the next time it is encountered. Here are some examples.

1. You have noticed that whenever a consonantal stop (π β φ, κ γ χ, τ δ θ) is followed by a σ, there are consistent changes (such as in the future and aorist). Rather than simply memorizing what happens in each case, you want to learn the basic rules. So you look up in the table of contents, and find that §22 is entitled "Stop + σ." There you will see why σ becomes ψ (βλέψω), ξ (διώξω), or drops out (χάρις).

2. σάββατον is a seemingly regular second declension neuter noun. You know that the dative plural of ἔργον, for example, is ἔργοις and therefore would expect to find σάββατοις. Yet you find σάββασιν thirteen times, an ending you are used to finding on third declension nouns (e.g., χάρισιν). What is happening? You turn to the index, find that σάββατον is a n-2c noun, and look the category up. You find the paradigm and the listing of all the nouns declined like σάββατον.

   In the footnote to σάββατον you read, "Has a dative plural form σάββασιν formed by analogy to third declension neuter nouns with roots ending in τ (n-3c[4,5]): *σαββατ + σι."

3. How does ἀκούω become ἀκήκοα in the perfect? If you turn to the discussion of reduplication (§32), as you skim through you will find that there is something called "Attic Reduplication" (§32.6). There you read that the vowel

and consonant are both reduplicated, and the second vowel is then length-ened. One of the examples is,

ἀκούω   *ακο ▸ ακακο ▸ ἀκήκοα (v-1a[8]).

You could also find this information by looking ἀκούω up in the index, find it is a v-1a(8) verb, look it up in the section on principal parts where the per-fect tense stem ἀκήκοα is listed. There you will see a footnote explaining that in the perfect ἀκούω undergoes "Attic Reduplication," which is discussed at §32.6.

4. You have wondered why there is an iota in the present tense αἴρω but in every other tense it is not there. In the index you find that αἴρω is a v-2d(2) verb. There you find the following introduction.

"The present undergoes significant changes. When ι is added to λ (v-2d[1]), they produce λλ (§26.6). In the other four classes, ι becomes vocalic ι, and the final stem consonant and the ι undergo metathesis (§7.6; §26.7).[1] (ὀφείλω fol-lows the pattern of the latter four classes.) Therefore, when looking at the tenses other than the present, remember that the λλ or the ι is a factor only in the present. It does not have to be accounted for in the other tenses."

You can now skim down to the word and you see its entry.

αἴρω[2]   ἀρῶ   ἦρα   ἦρκα   ἦρμαι   ἤρθην

The principal parts are listed for every word that forms its principal parts just like αἴρω, and the footnotes give you compounds and any further expla-nation necessary to understand the forms of the principal parts. Compound verbs formed with prepositions are footnoted under their simple verb.

The morphological tags for each word can become detailed. Not many will remember what "v-1d(2c)" stands for. What works for us is to memorize the basic divisions listed on pp. xvii - xix. If the word fits in one of the lesser-known categories, follow the tags as they are printed in the header of each page.

Deductive

Many brave souls in my classes use *MBG* deductively, reading through from cover to cover. Of course, there is too much information to memorize, but it gave

---

1   αρι ▸ αιρ; ερι ▸ ειρ; ανι ▸ αιν; ενι ▸ ειν. Smyth (§519) and LaSor (§24.2553) say that the ι drops and the preceding vowel is lengthened to compensate. Funk (§484.40) says in the case of ανι/αρι, ι is inserted (epenthesis) and the ι dropped. In the case of ενι/ερι, the ι is dropped and the preceding vowel is lengthened in compensation. Morphology is not an exact science, and all three explanations achieve the same result.

2   ἀπαίρω, ἐξαίρω, ἐπαίρω (in N.T. only as passive), μεταίρω, συναίρω, ὑπεραίρω. On the augment see §31.5d.

them the feel for the language and the arrangement of the text, both of which were invaluable.

MBG is broken down into eight basic divisions.

§1-§9   **Vowel changes.** Sections §1-§9 discuss the types of changes we see with vowels. If you have a question about contractions, ablaut, etc., this is the place to go.

§10-§28   **Consonantal changes.** Sections §10-§28 discuss the types of changes we see with consonants. Whereas vocalic changes are basically well known, consonantal changes are rarely taught and yet are the key in understanding especially the third declension and principal parts.

§28-§29   **Accents.** Here we look at the rules for accents, and those situations where knowing accents can help translation.

§30-§36   **Verb formation.** Sections §30-§36 contain the rules for augmentation, reduplication, a brief introduction to the formation of tense stems, tense and mood formatives, connecting vowels, personal endings, and movable v.

§40-§96   **Mood and tense formation.** Sections §40-§96 discuss verbal formation. It is broken down between the moods (indicative, subjunctive, optative, imperative), including the infinitive and participle. The indicative is further divided into the different tenses. Here you can find paradigms of almost any verbal form you wish, lists of special formations such as Attic futures, second aorists, verbs inserting σ in their tense stems, etc.

Nouns, adj.   The discussions of nouns and adjectives are straightforward. Nouns are divided into declensions, and adjectives are categorized depending upon how many endings are used in their inflection in different genders.

Principal parts   The discussion of principal parts will probably be the most beneficial aspect of *MBG*. You should read the introduction. If your question has to do with how a principal part is formed, this is the place to go. It does not discuss personal endings (§36).

Referenced Bibliography and Abbreviations

ALGNT *The Analytical Lexicon to the Greek New Testament,* William D. Mounce (Zondervan, 1993).

BAGD *A Greek-English Lexicon of the New Testament and Other Early Christian Literature,* Walter Bauer, William F. Arndt, F. Wilbur Gingrich, Frederick W. Danker (The University of Chicago Press, 1979).

BBG *The Basics of Biblical Greek,* William D. Mounce (Zondervan, 1993).

BDF *A Greek Grammar of the New Testament and Other Early Christian Literature,* F. Blass, A. Debrunner, Robert W. Funk (The University of Chicago Press, 1961).

Carson *Greek Accents: A Student's Manual,* D.A. Carson (Baker, 1985).

Funk *A Beginning-Intermediate Grammar of Hellenistic Greek,* Robert W. Funk (Scholars Press, 1973), 3 vols.

LaSor *Handbook of New Testament Greek,* William Sanford LaSor (Eerdmans, 1973), 2 vols.

LS *A Greek-English Lexicon,* Henry Stuart Jones, Roderick McKenzie, E.A. Barber (Oxford, 1977).

MBG *The Morphology of Biblical Greek,* William D. Mounce (Zondervan, 1994).

MH *A Grammar of New Testament Greek,* James Hope Moulton, Wilbert Francis Howard, vol. 2, *Accidence and Word-Formation* (T. & T. Clark, 1979).

Robertson *A Grammar of the Greek New Testament in the Light of Historical Research,* A.T. Robertson (Broadman, 1934).

Smyth *Greek Grammar,* Herbert Weir Smyth (Harvard University Press, 1920).

ι   Consonantal iota, discussed at §27.

F   Digamma, discussed at §28.

§   Section number in *MBG* and other reference works.

acc   Accusative

dat   Dative

gen   Genitive

nom   Nominative

pl   Plural

sg   Singular

T.R.   Textus Receptus

Phonology

Introduction to Vocalic Change   (§1)

One of the problems with many morphological texts is that they assume that the beginning student understands the basics of the field of morphology. What follows is our attempt to explain, in as simple and untechnical language as possible, what happens to vowels in Greek.

Every language has ways that people like to speak and ways that they do not. Certain sounds appeal to them. Others do not. For example, English speakers do not like the pause that is necessary to pronounce the word "a" when it is followed by another word that begins with a vowel. Since vowels are produced by air flowing out of the mouth, you have to make an unnatural stop after the "a" in order to make the second vowel understandable. Therefore, we use an "a" in front of words beginning with a consonant, and an "an" if the next word begins with a vowel. The "n" makes it so that the speaker does not have to pronounce two vowel sounds in a row. Greek is no different, and in §6 you will see all the ways the Greeks got around this "unnatural stop," which is technically called "hiatus."

There are other considerations that come into play in explaining the behavior of vowels. For example, in all languages, vowels are pronounced differently from one location to another. The "i" in "fire" is pronounced differently in Minnesota, Kentucky, and Texas. Likewise Greek had its different dialects that must be considered. There also is the matter of the influence of foreign speakers on a language.

Morphology (a study of the written form of the language) is directly controlled by **phonology** (how the language was spoken). In other words, what we read was determined by how it was spoken. If one vowel followed another and both could be blended into one sound, they did so (contraction). If not, the word was syllabified between the two vowels. If one word ended in a vowel and the next word began with the vowel, the first vowel could drop out (apocope) to help pronunciation. The changes are not mysterious and irrational. They follow specific rules based upon the nature of the spoken language.

Another thing that is helpful to understand is that the vocalic changes we will be discussing all occurred before the word assumed the shape as we now have it. For example, §2.10 says that when a two-syllable word originally had a vowel-sigma-vowel pattern, the sigma dropped out but the two vowels did not contract. As far as the people of the New Testament times were concerned, the word θεσος never really occurred. The σ had dropped out many years earlier, and nowhere in the New Testament does it ever occur. But at one time the σ was there, and it explains why the ε and ο do not contract to ου in θεός.

This is our point. The changes that we will be discussing are not changes you can see in the New Testament. They are changes that went into making the word appear in the form in which it now does in the New Testament. They are what happened when different suffixes and endings were put on tense stems. They are what happened as the language evolved through influences of various Greek dialects and other languages, as well as the evolution due to the natural simplification process of any language through the years.

Those who have done work in phonology will recognize that this is a simplification, but a simplification that is necessary for those who are first starting out in morphological studies.

Vowel Contractions (§2)

Contractions of Single Vowels

§2.1   **Chart**

	α	ε	η	ι	υ	ο	ω
α	α[3]	α[7]	α[7]	αι[2]	αυ[2]	ω[5]	ω[5]
ε	η[7]	ει[4]	η[3]	ει[2]	ευ[2]	ου[6]	ω[5]
η	η[7]	η[3]	η[3]	ῃ[2]	ηυ[2]	ω[5]	ω[5]
ο	ω[5]	ου[6]	ω[5]	οι[2]	ου[2]	ου[4]	ω[3 5]
ω	ω[5]	ω[5]	ω[5]	ῳ[2]	ωυ[2]	ω[3 5]	ω[3 5]

The superscripts refer to the rule number that discusses that particular contraction (e.g., "3" = §2.3). For a fuller discussion showing long and short vowels, see Smyth §59. See also *MH* 89-92.

The seven vowels are α, ε, η, ι, ο, υ, and ω. ε and ο are always short, η and ω are always long. α, ι, and υ can be either short or long.

§2.2   The basic rule is as follows:

a.   like vowels assimilate to their common long (cf. §2.3).

b.   unlike vowels assimilate, either the second to the first (**progressive assimilation**, e.g., αε ‣ α), or the first to the second (**regressive assimilation**, e.g., εη ‣ η).

c.   If the second vowel is an υ or ι, then the two vowels form a diphthong. If the first vowel is long and the second ι, then the ι subscripts (cf. §2.11-18).

There are two ways to give the vowel contraction rules. The first moves from the uncontracted to the contracted. The second moves from the contracted back to the uncontracted. We list the former as the basic rules (e.g., §2.4) and the latter as sub-rules (e.g., §2.4a). *BBG* follows the sub-rules. Smyth's rules are at §48-59.

§2.3   Two like vowels form their common[1] long.

α + α ‣ α   ε + η ‣ η

ι + ι ‣ ι   η + ε ‣ η

υ + υ ‣ υ   ο + ω ‣ ω

η + η ‣ η   ω + ο ‣ ω

ω + ω ‣ ω

§2.4   Exceptions to §2.3.

ε + ε ‣ ει   ποιε + ετε ‣ ποιεῖτε

ο + ο ‣ ου   φανερο + ομεν ‣ φανεροῦμεν

These diphthongs are "spurious" (§2.14).

§2.4a   ει is formed by εε.

ει ‹ εε   ποιεῖτε ‹ ποιεετε

§2.4b   ου is formed by εο (§2.6), οε (§2.6), and οο.

ου ‹ εο   ποιοῦμεν ‹ ποιεομεν

ου ‹ οε   πληροῦτε ‹ πληροετε

ου ‹ οο   πληροῦμεν ‹ πληροομεν

§2.5   ο or ω overcome α, ε, or η regardless of the order, and form ω.

α + ο ‣ ω   ἀγαπα + ομεν ‣ ἀγαπῶμεν

ο + η ‣ ω   φανερο + ητε ‣ φανερῶτε

§2.5a   ω is formed from almost any combination of omicron or omega with any other vowel, except for §2.4b (also §2.6).

§2.6   Exceptions to §2.5.

ε + ο ‣ ου   ποιε + ομαι ‣ ποιοῦμαι

ο + ε ‣ ου   φανερο + ετε ‣ φανεροῦτε

These diphthongs are "spurious" (§2.14).

---

[1]   ε and η are viewed as common, as are ο and ω.

§2.7 If α comes before ε or η, they will contract to α. If ε or η comes before α, they will contract to η ("progressive assimilation," §2.2).

α + ε ⟩ α   γεννα + ετε ⟩ γεννᾶτε (ind.)

α + η ⟩ α   γεννα + ητε ⟩ γεννᾶτε (subj.)

ε + α ⟩ α

η + α ⟩ α

§2.7a   α is formed from αε.

§2.7b   η is formed from εα.

§2.8 When three vowels come into contact, and if the first two or the last two do not form a diphthong, then the second and third vowels contract first, and the result contracts with the first vowel. In other words, contraction is from the right to the left ("progressive assimilation"; §2.2; Smyth §55). This is especially frequent in contract verbs.

αει ⟩ αι ⟩ ᾳ   ἀγαπαει ⟩ ἀγαπᾷ

εαι ⟩ εᾳ ⟩ ῃ   ποιεσαι ⟩ ποιεαι ⟩ ποιηι ⟩ ποιῇ

§2.9 Sometimes when a long and a short vowel come into contact, they will not contract. This is often due to "analogy" (§3.4; Smyth §57).

§2.10 Sometimes there is a two-syllable word that had the pattern "vowel-sigma-vowel" or "vowel-digamma-vowel," and the intervocalic sigma (§25.5) or digamma (§27.4) has dropped out. In cases like this, those remaining two vowels normally do not contract.

For example, θέος is from the stem *θεσο. The σ dropped out and the ε and o did not contract to ου.

They can contract in polysyllabic forms (θεσός + κῦδος ⟩ θουκυδίδης; Smyth §58)

Contractions with Diphthongs

§2.11 A **diphthong** (δίφθογγυς; "having two sounds") consists of two vowels that produce one sound. The first vowel must be an open vowel (α, ε, η, o, ω), and the second vowel must be a closed vowel (ι, υ) form.[1] "Open" and "closed" refer to the relative shape of the mouth when pronouncing the vowels. Diphthongs are considered "long" for accent purposes except for final αι and οι (except in the optative, where they are considered long).

---

[1]   The only possible exception to this is υ + ι, which can contract to υ (Smyth §51c) or can remain υι.

Possible diphthongs in Greek are αι, ει, οι, αυ, ευ, ου, ηυ, υι. The so-called "improper" diphthongs are ᾳ, ῃ, and ῳ (cf. §2.18).

§2.12   A closed and an open vowel never form a diphthong, and the word is syllabified between the two vowels (e.g., ἀι ὤν).

§2.13   **Contraction chart for diphthongs**

In the following charts, the ει and ου diphthongs are separated depending whether they are "spurious" or "genuine." See §2.14 for definitions and §2.13c for why this distinction is important in understanding vowel contractions. Some of these combinations may be theoretical; it is questionable whether they ever occur.

	αι	ει (spurious)	ει (genuine)	οι
α	ᾳ	ᾳ	ᾳ	ῳ
ε	ῃ	ει	ει	οι
η	ῃ	η	ῃ	ῳ
ο	ῳ	ου	οι	οι
ω	ῳ	ω	ῳ	ῳ

	αυ	ευ	ηυ	ου (spurious)	ου (genuine)
α	αυ	αυ	αυ	ω	ωυ
ε	ηυ	ευ	ηυ	ου	ου
η	ηυ	ηυ	ηυ	ω	ωυ
ο	ωυ	ου	ωυ	ου	ου
ω	ωυ	ωυ	ωυ	ω	ωυ

	υι[1]	ᾳ	ῃ	ῳ
α	αυ	ᾳ	ᾳ	ῳ
ε	ευ	ῃ	ῃ	ῳ
η	ηυ	ῃ	ῃ	ῳ
ο	ου	ῳ	οι	ῳ
ω	ωυ	ῳ	ῳ	ῳ

§2.13a   **Single vowel + diphthong** (beginning with the **same** vowel as the single vowel). When a single vowel is followed by a diphthong that begins with the same vowel as the single vowel, then the two similar vowels combine into one.

---

[1]   Our assumption is that the ι drops out. υι is not listed in Smyth (§59).

If the second vowel in the diphthong is an υ it remains (unless the second vowel of the newly formed diphthong is an υ in which case the two upsilons simplify to one). If the second vowel in the diphthong is an iota, it subscripts under the newly formed diphthong.

α + αι ▸ αι

α + ᾳ ▸ ᾳ

§2.13b **Single vowel + diphthong** (beginning with a vowel **different** from the single vowel). When a single vowel is followed by a diphthong that begins with a vowel different from the single vowel, the single vowel and the first vowel of the diphthong contract according to the regular rules, and then the result of that contraction will contract with the second vowel of the diphthong ("regressive assimilation," §2.2).

If the second vowel in the diphthong is an υ, it remains (unless the second vowel of the newly formed diphthong is an υ in which case the two upsilons simplify to one). If the second vowel in the diphthong is an ι, it subscripts under the newly formed diphthong.

ο + ου ▸ ουυ ▸ ου

α + αι ▸ αι ▸ ᾳ

Exceptions:

ε + οι ▸ οι

ο + ει[1] ▸ οι   πληροεις ▸ πληροῖς[2]

ο + η ▸ οι   φανερο + η ▸ φανεροῖ

§2.13c When ει or ου are spurious (§2.14), the diphthong is regarded as simple ε or ο (i.e., the final vowel of the diphthong is dropped; cf. Smyth §59).

α + ει ▸ αι ▸ α

ε + ει ▸ειι ▸ει

η + ει ▸ ηι ▸ η

ο + ει ▸ ουι ▸ου

α + ου ▸ ωυ ▸ω

ε + ου ▸ ουυ ▸ου

ο + ου ▸ουυ ▸ου

---

[1] When ει is genuine, the contraction forms οι. When ει is spurious the contraction forms ου.

[2] In the present active of omicron contract verbs, οει ▸ ου (e.g., δηλοῦν).

§2.14   εɩ and ου are called **spurious** (or "apparent") diphthongs when they are formed as the result of a contraction (e.g., εε, εο, οε, οο) or compensatory lengthening (§3.5; Smyth §6). They are called **genuine** diphthongs when they are formed by the combining of ε + ɩ and ο + υ.

See §2.13c for how this affects contraction. The New Testament does not always follow this distinction.

§2.15   **Diphthongization** is when two independent vowels form a diphthong. (In other words, it is when two distinct sounds are blended into one.)

§2.16   **Monophongization** is when a diphthong is reduced to a single vowel. (In other words, the long sound of a diphthong is reduced to the sound of one singular vowel.)

§2.17   **Diaresis.** It is possible for two successive vowels that normally form a diphthong not to do so. In this case a diaresis (¨) is written over the second vowel. (The term is from the Greek διάρεσις, meaning "separation.")

We often find a diaresis over a foreign word that has been transliterated into Greek. Although Greek would form a diphthong, the original language did not, and to remain true to the word's actual pronunciation the diaresis indicates that the two vowels are pronounced separately. For example: Μωϋσῆς. We also find it in words where the two vowels originally had been separated by a sigma or digamma, which by the Hellenistic period had dropped out.

§2.18   The **iota subscript** is the result of a change in the Greek language that happened many years before the time of the New Testament. In the diphthongs αɩ, ηɩ, and ωɩ, the Greeks stopped pronouncing the ɩ. But the ɩ would not drop out of the writing, and it was written under the vowels α, η, and ω when those vowels were written as small letters (ᾳ, ῃ, ῳ), and after the vowels when they were written as a capital (Αɩ, Ηɩ, Ωɩ), called **iota adscript**. The Greeks began not to write the iota starting around 100 B.C., but we still find it as late as the 1100s A.D. (cf. Smyth §51, but see also LaSor §11.56).

Quantitative Vowel Gradation (§3)

§3.1   For various reasons, a vowel can shift its quantity from long to short, or from short to long. In "quantitative" vowel gradation (pronounced *gra da´ tion*), a vowel is lengthened or shortened to its *corresponding* long or short vowel. In "qualitative" vowel gradation (§4), the vowel is altered to a totally different vowel. Smyth's rules are at §27-33.

We use the term **ablaut** to describe any type of vowel change, whether it is quantitative or qualitative (§4). Some (e.g., LaSor) use the term "ablaut" only for qualitative vowel gradation.

§3.2   The terms "short" and "long" apply to the relative length of time it requires to pronounce the vowel. ε and o are always short. η and ω are always long. α, ι, and υ can be either short or long. This means that whether α, ι, or υ are long or short, they will look the same.

§3.3   Quantitative vowel gradation normally follows this pattern (for both lengthening and shortening). η and ω always remain long.

α	↔	α
α	↔	η	γεννάω › γεννήσω
ε	↔	η	ποιέω › ποιήσω; πατήρ › πατέρα
ι	↔	ι	κυλίω › κυλίσω
o	↔	ω	φανερόω › φανερώσω; ἄρχων › ἄρχοντος
υ	↔	υ	λύω › λύσω

§3.3a   α will lengthen to long α if ε, ι, or ρ comes immediately before it. If not, α will lengthen to η. (This is a peculiarity of the Attic dialect that was carried over into the Koine; Smyth, §31). There are some exceptions; cf. n-1a nouns.

§3.3b   Vowels can be altered in slightly different patterns (cf. §3.5). Variation centers mainly on the ε and o.

Lengthening of a Short Vowel

§3.4   **Analogic lengthening.** Different types of words have different patterns. For example, third declension nouns with stems ending in μα form their dative plural with σι. Second declension nouns such as σάββατον form their dative plural with -οις. But because the third declension is a familiar pattern, we can find examples of second declension nouns that form their dative plurals sometimes as second declension nouns (e.g., σάββατοις, a form that does not occur in the NT) and sometimes as third declension nouns (σάββασι; occurring 13 times in the NT, always with a movable ν). We say that σάββασι is formed by "analogy" to the pattern of third declension nouns whose stems end in μα.

In the same manner, we find words whose vowels are lengthened "by analogy to" patterns in other classes of words. This is "analogic lengthening" or "lengthening by analogy."

§3.5   **Compensatory lengthening.** When a consonant is dropped out of
a word for phonetic reasons, the preceding vowel is often lengthen
in order to "compensate" for that loss (cf. Smyth §37; LaSor §15.2;
Funk §914). The vowel is lengthened in a pattern similar to that in
§3.3 except for ε and o.

α ▸ α	παντσ ▸ πᾶς
α ▸ η	
ε ▸ ει	δέρω ▸ ἔδειρα
η ▸ η	
ι ▸ ι	κρινῶ ▸ ἔκρινα
o ▸ ου	*λυονσι ▸ λυοσι ▸ λύουσι
υ ▸ υ	δεικνυντς ▸ δεικνύς
ω ▸ ω	

§3.5a   α will lengthen to α if ε, ι, or ρ comes immediately before
it. If not, α will lengthen to η (§3.3a). This is a characteristic of the Attic dialect. In Ionic α always lengthens to η
(Smyth §30D2).

§3.5b   α will lengthen to η in the first aorist of liquid and nasal
stems, unless preceded by if ι or ρ (ε φαν σα ▸ ἔφηνα;
Smyth §37b; Funk §9140).

§3.5c   This is seen especially in third declension nouns ending
in ντ (n-3c[5]), the third person plural personal ending
νσι, and in the formation of v-2d verbs.

§3.5d   ει and ου formed through compensatory lengthening
are considered spurious (§2.14).

§3.5e   In Doric and Aeolic, α always lengthened to α (Smyth
§534D).

§3.6   If the second element of a compound word begins with a short
vowel, that short vowel can lengthen in the formation of a compound.

§3.7   A short vowel that has undergone metathesis will often be lengthened. ("Metathesis" is when two sounds within a word exchange
places; cf. §17.)

Reduction of a Long Vowel

§3.8   When two long vowels come into contact, the first may reduce to its
corresponding short vowel. See pattern in §3.3.

§3.9 Reduction of a long vowel is frequent when the following letters occur between a long vowel and a consonant: ι, υ, λ, ρ, μ, ν (Smyth §40).

Qualitative Vowel Gradation (§4)

§4.1 **Qualitative vowel gradation** is when a vowel or diphthong is altered for some reason. It occurs due to inflection and word formation. In English, an example would be "sing, sang, sung." The stem vowel is altered to form the various tenses (cf. Smyth §35-36, §476-486; *BDF* §22-28; Robertson, 181-203).

We use the term **ablaut** to describe any type of vowel change, whether it is quantitative or qualitative (§4).

§4.2 The change is qualitative: the vowel is not just lengthened or reduced to its corresponding vowel as it is in quantitative vowel gradation (§3). The vowel is actually changed to a *non-corresponding* vowel. Smyth (§35a) gives the following words, all from the same stem, as examples of ablaut: φέρω; φόρος; φώρ; φαρέτρα; δίφρος. The shift is normally an ε ‣ o shift (Smyth, §35d).

§4.3 Discussions in the grammars of ablaut are notoriously complicated. Part of the confusion is because very few spend the time to explain for the novice what is going on. Another problem is the variation in terminology: like syntactical studies, morphological grammarians cannot agree on standard terminology for morphology.

BAGD uses "strong, weak, and zero." In verbs, Funk speaks of strong and weak, including the zero form under "weak" (§911-912). In nouns he speaks of strong, middle, and weak. Smyth likewise joins weak and zero (§35a). LaSor separates weak and zero (§15.41; §24.315).

The terms "strong, weak," and "zero" seem to us to best describe what is happening, because in the zero grade there is no vowel present (§4.4e). We will use the same terms for both nouns and verbs.

§4.3a The basic shifts are ε ‹ › o and a long vowel ‹ › α/ε/o (Smyth §35d).

§4.3b Funk gives a large chart of all forms of ablaut found in the New Testament (§911.1-7). Smyth has a similar list (§36, §476-86). If a verb stem shows ablaut, it tends to show the strong grade in the present tense (LaSor

§24.2223). Following is a summary; # stands for the zero form.

ε/ο	‹›	α/#		α	‹›	#
ει/οι	‹›	ι		ω	‹›	ο
ευ	‹›	υ/ε/#		ου/αυ	‹›	ο/α
η/ει	‹›	α/ε				

§4.4   **Strong; weak; zero**

§4.4a   To say that a vowel undergoes **strong** vowel gradation means that the vowel has been altered to one of the possible strong vowels (e.g., ἀνήρ).

§4.4b   To say that a vowel undergoes **weak** vowel gradation means that the vowel has been altered to one of the possible weak vowels (e.g., ἄνερ).

§4.4c   To say that a vowel is reduced to its **zero** form means that the vowel has dropped out of the word altogether (e.g., ἀνδρός). Zero gradation also describes the loss of a single vowel in a diphthong. The zero form can be difficult to see, especially if a sonant consonant has produced a vowel (§5).

Syncope (§7.2) can produce the same result as the zero grade; the vowel is absent.

§4.4d   For example, πατήρ (η) is the strong form. πατέρες (ε) is the weak form. πατρός (-) is the zero form.

§4.4e   Although it has problems, it is helpful at first to associate "strong" with the long vowels, "weak" with the short vowels, and "zero" with the absence of the vowel. The problem is that as we will see below, there are short vowels in the strong vowel gradation pattern.

§4.5   Sometimes the zero grade is obscured by a vocalic consonant (§5; e.g., εστλκα › εσταλκα). See Smyth for further discussion (§35).

§4.6   ι/υ often drop out when followed by a vowel (βοῦς › βοός; Smyth §43).

§4.7   There are often multiple ways of explaining the same form. For example, how do you explain the shift in βάλλω? *βαλ › βλη › βέβληκα. You can say the α drops out due to ablaut (§4) or syncope (§7.2). You can also postulate metathesis (*βαλ › βλα; §7.6) and then the α lengthens (› βλη).

There also is the subject of multiple verb roots. The verb πίνω has the perfect active form πέπωκα. Some say there are two roots, *πι and *πο (lengthened to πω), while others say it is the same vowel that has been changed due to ablaut. We find somewhat the same situation in δίδωμι, which has the long vowel in the present singular and the short vowel in the plural (δίδομεν). Is this to be explained with postulating two stems or a vowel that changes its length?

While these types of discussions can be interesting and important in certain respects, they are beyond the scope of this text.

Vocalic Consonants (§5)

§5.1

For various reasons such as vowel gradation and inflection, a liquid (λ ρ) or nasal (μ ν) can occur between two consonants, and the resulting consonant cluster is unpronounceable. In some cases one of the consonants will "develop" a vowel immediately preceding or following itself. At other times the consonant will totally assimilate to the vowel.

These consonants are called **vocalic consonants**, or **sonants** (because the vowel produces an additional sound), or **syllabics** (because the vowel forms an additional syllable). In grammars, syllabic consonants are often written with a little circle at their base below the line (ρ̥; cf. Funk §906; §913; Smyth §35b-c, §482).

λ ⸱ αλ or λα

ρ ⸱ αρ or ρα

μ ⸱ α

ν ⸱ α   *αυτομντ ⸱ αὐτόματον; *ὀνομν ⸱ ὄνομα

§5.2

English also has vocalic consonants. Many people pronounce the word "film" as "filem" because the "lm" combination is difficult. Likewise, some pronounce the word "bottle" as "bottele" to help with the "tl" cluster. We would say that the "l" and the "t" both "develop" an "e."

§5.3

A clear example in Greek is πατήρ. The word undergoes zero vowel gradation in the dative plural whereby losing the η after the ρ (*πατηρ ⸱ πατρσι). Because the ρ between two consonants is difficult to pronounce, the ρ develops an α (⸱ πατράσι).

§5.4

The zero form of ablaut often creates the need for a syllabic vowel. The example in §5.3 shows this.

Avoidance of Successive Vowels (§6)

§6.1   **Haitus**. Greek, especially the Attic dialect, avoided pronouncing two vowel sounds in immediate succession, whether it be two vowels in a word, or two words where the first ends in a vowel and the second begins with a vowel (see Introduction, §1; *MH* 62-63). In order to distinguish the two vowel sounds, the speaker would have to make an unnatural pause between the two vowels. The pause is called "haitus" and was avoided in Greek through various means. Funk calls this the "euphony" of vowels (§916).

Within One Word

§6.2   **Contraction**. Whenever two vowels that can contract come into immediate contact, they contract (§2.1-10).

§6.3   **Diphthong**. Whenever two vowels that can form a diphthong come into immediate contact, they form a diphthong (§2.6,11).

Between Two Words

§6.4   **Crasis**. If two words occur in which the first ends in a vowel or a diphthong and the second begins with a vowel, the two words can be joined and the vowels contract, thus avoiding hiatus. A coronis (') is written over the point of contraction.[1] The following combinations form a crasis in the New Testament. The number of times it occurs is given in the third column. Cf. *BDF* §18; *MH* 63-64; Robertson, 208.

κἀγώ	καὶ ἐγώ	76
κἀκεῖ	καὶ ἐκεῖ	10
κἀκεῖθεν	καὶ ἐκεῖθεν	10
κἀκεῖνος	καὶ ἐκεῖνος	7
κἀμέ	καὶ με	3
κἀμοί	καὶ ἐμοί	5
κἄν	καὶ ἄν and καὶ ἐάν	17
τοὐναντίον	τὸ ἐναντίον	3
τοὔνομα	τὸ ὄνομα	1

---

[1]   From κορωνίς, meaning "hook." The term "crasis" is from the Greek κρᾶσις, meaning "mingling."

There are other words that were originally formed through crasis but in our texts can be written as its own word or as two words.

ἐάνπερ	καίγε	καίτοιγε
μενοῦνγε	μήγε	μήπου
μήπως		

§6.4a   Crasis occurs with words that are frequently found together. It is somewhat like a contraction in English. See Smyth §62-69 for the general rules, and *BDF* §18 for discussion.

§6.4b   Crasis was much more common in Classical Greek, especially in poetry (e.g., with the article [οἱ ἄνδρες › ἄνδρες], relative pronoun). In Koine Greek it occurs primarily with καί.

§6.5   **Elision.** In order to avoid hiatus, a word ending in a short vowel often drops that vowel when the next word begins with a vowel. (Smyth §70-75; Funk §918; *BDF* §17; *MH* 61-62. See Smyth §76 also for "aphaeresis" or "inverse elision.")

§6.5a   Normally an **apostrophe** (’) marks where an elision has occurred (e.g., ἀπ’ αὐτοῦ). But if the elision is due to the formation of a compound word in which the first element is a preposition, then the elision is not marked (e.g., ἀπέρχομαι).

§6.5b   ἀλλά, ἀπό, διά, ἐπί, παρά, and μετά regularly elide.

§6.5c   ἀντί elides only when followed by ὧν. (ἀνθ’ ὧν occurs four times in the New Testament.)

§6.5d   περί elides only when followed by a word beginning with ι. There are no examples in the NT.[1]

§6.5e   The following are not elided: πρό; ὅτι; monosyllables (unless they end in ε); the ι in the dative endings; words ending in υ; words that can take a movable ν or movable ς (LaSor §15.534; Smyth §72b).

§6.5f   When a vowel has been elided, if the final consonant of the first word is a stop (§12), and if the following word begins with a rough breathing, it is common for the stop to aspirate to its corresponding aspirated stop.

μετά + ὧν › μετ’ ὧν › μεθ’ ὧν

---

[1]   If the verb begins with a rough breathing, the ι stays (e.g., περιίστημι).

§6.6   **Movable ν.** The general rule is that a ν is added to certain forms ending in ι or ε when the next word begins with a vowel. In grammars it is usually written in brackets: ουσι(ν).

This is the basic rule. But in Koine Greek the ν appears to be used somewhat erratically, being added even when the following word begins with a consonant, thus deserving the name **irrational ν.**

See §36.9 for more specifics, and see Smyth (§134) for a discussion of the rules in Classical Greek (also *MH* 113; Funk §920; *BDF* §20).

§6.7   **Movable ς.** Sometimes a ς is used in the same way as is the movable ν (§6.6; *BDF* §21; Smyth §136D; *MH* 112-113). It is almost always found on οὕτως (204t, 4t without) but rarely on ἄχρις (Rom 11:25; 1 Cor 11:26; Gal 3:19; Heb 3:13; 46t without) and μέχρις (Mk 13:30; Gal 4:19; Heb 12:4; 14t without).

§6.7a   Smyth (§136) and Funk (§921) say that ἔξ uses a movable ς; see §19.3c for LaSor's explanation.

§6.7b   εὐθύ (from εὐθύς) and εὐθύς (adverb) are two different words.

Various Vocalic Changes (§7)

§7.1   **Apocope.** (ἀποκοπή; *a cutting off*) When a word ends in a short vowel and the following word begins with a consonant, the final short vowel can be dropped. This can be done for euphony, poetic structure, or other reasons (Smyth §75D).

§7.2   **Syncope.** (συνκοπή, *cutting up*) When a short vowel occurs between two consonants, neither consonant being in a cluster, the short vowel can drop out, i.e., it goes to its zero grade (§4.4c; Smyth §476a; *MH* 92-93). When there are multiple ways of explaining the same form (cf. §4.7), Smyth often speaks of syncope (e.g., §493) but only in reference to short vowels (§476a).

*θαν › τέθνηκα   *σεχ › ἔσχον

*πετ › πτήσομαι   πατερος › πατρός

§7.2a   If a vowel is dropped out due to syncope, and as a result a liquid (λ ρ) is immediately followed by a nasal (μ ν), then an epenthetic letter may be inserted between the two consonants (§18).

§7.3   **Hyphaeresus.** (ὑφαίρεσις, *omission*) An ε followed by a vowel may drop out (Smyth §44a).

ἑορτή › ὀρτή
ἀδεέως › ἀδεῶς

§7.4 **Prothesis.** (Also "prosthesis"; LaSor §15.8) If a word begins with a consonant cluster, a vowel may be placed before the cluster (e.g., χθές › ἐχθές). The vowel is called a "pro(s)thetic" vowel. (πρόθεσις, "a placing before.") Cf. *MH* 89; Robertson, 205-206.

  §7.4a It is especially common to find prothetic α, ε, or ο before an initial λ, μ, ρ, or ϝ (Smyth §41, LaSor §15.81). Funk (915) says it is an initial short vowel followed by λ, μ, or ρ. For example, it can be seen in the formation of the two cognate words λίπος and ἀλείφω.

  §7.4b In English grammar "prothesis" is defined as "the addition of a letter, syllable, or phoneme to the beginning of a word, as of *be-* in *beloved, a-* in *ahead*" (Webster).

§7.5 **Harmony.** A vowel in one syllable can be totally assimilated to the vowel in the following syllable.

  *βυβλιο › βιβλίον

§7.6 **Metathesis.** Metathesis is when two sounds within a word exchange places (LaSor §13.4). Both vowels and consonants can undergo metathesis. See fuller discussion in §17 and *MH* 100f.

  §7.2 points out that what can be explained with metathesis can also be explained other ways. For example, the shift from *βαλ › βλα › βλη › βέβληκα can be explained through metathesis, or through ablaut and the insertion of an η (*βαλ › βλ › βλη › βέβληκα).

§7.7 **Transfer of quality.** Sometimes a short and a long vowel, or conversely a long and a short vowel, alter their lengths so that the long becomes short and the short becomes long. The transfer patterns are ηο ‹› εω and ηα ‹› εα (Funk §909, Smyth §34).

  πόληος › πόλεως. The η and ο switch so the long η becomes its short ε, and the short ο becomes its long ω.

  *βασιληα (short final α) › βασιλέα (long final α).

§7.8 The ι and υ of diphthongs often drop out if followed by a vowel. Actually, they were consonantal iota and digamma (§26-27; Smyth §43).

§7.9 **Epenthesis.** Cf. §18.

§7.10 **Aphesis.** Aphesis (ἄφησις) is the dropping of a short, initial, unaccented vowel, such as in the English "esquire" › "squire".

§7.11   **Synizesis.** (συνίζησις) In poetry, when two vowels or a vowel and
a diphthong occur in successive syllables, the two vowels/diph-
thong can be pronounced as one sound while still written as two
(Smyth §60-61).

Introduction to
Consonantal Change (§10)

In "Introduction to Vocalic Changes" (§1), we said that the written form of the
word was the result of how the language was spoken. Vowels are changed
because the Greeks did not like certain combinations of sounds or some such reason. The same holds true for changes in consonants. Certain consonantal sounds
do not naturally follow other consonantal sounds, and therefore usually the first
consonant is modified so the combination of the two is easier to pronounce.

There are, of course, many other reasons why consonants change. For example,
there used to be two additional letters in the Greek alphabet, ι (consonantal iota)
and Ϝ (digamma). At some time prior to Koine Greek, both these letters dropped
out of use, but the fact that they used to be part of the language will affect some
words' forms. For example, ι was added to the verbal base of some verbs in order
to form their present tense stem: *βαλ + ι + ω. But when λ and ι occur side by side,
they would modify and form geminate λ (βάλλω). What this means is that in the
tenses other than the present, we only have to account for one λ (such as in the
aorist ἔβαλον) because the ι was used only in the present.

The whole field of consonantal phonetics may be a bit frightening at first because
it will be new to most. But like many things, the fear is mostly because it is new
and not because it is difficult. As was the case with vowels, consonantal changes
are pretty much common sense, and we have tried to write the rules so that you
can understand any one of them without having to understand everything about
phonetics. We would strongly encourage you to make use of the charts. The
explanations use the technical language, and eventually you will understand the
terminology. But the key is the charts. Just follow the arrows and all should make
sense.

As was the case with vowels, the changes we will be discussing are for the most
part theoretical. For example, the theoretical form συνλαμβάνω never existed.
When the compound was originally created, the ν on συν was changed to a λ,
resulting in συλλαμβάνω, because the Greek tongue did not want to say the νλ
combination. So we say, "When a ν is immediately followed by a λ, the ν assimilates to a λ."

Or we talk about the root *θε. To form the present stem it reduplicates the initial
consonant and separates the two with an ι, lengthens the stem vowel to a η, and
uses the alternate personal ending μι: θε ‣ θιθε ‣ θιθη ‣ θιθημι. But the Greeks did

not like to pronounce two consecutive syllables beginning with an "aspirate," a sound made by a continual passage of air between the roof of the mouth and the tongue that is pressed upwards, such as a theta. Therefore, the θ is "deaspirated" to its corresponding deaspirated stop, which is τ: θιθημι ‣ τίθημι.

Two final examples will suffice. ἀνήρ looses the η in the genitive and develops a δ before the ρ: ανηρ ‣ ἀνδρός. Why a δ and not some other consonant, or why develop any consonant at all? Say the word "ανρ" outloud, and be sure to form the ρ sound on the end of your tongue like you do in English, and not in the back of your throat as you would in the German. Say it several times outloud, quickly if necessary. If you still cannot hear it, trill the ρ sound a little like you would in Spanish. What do you hear? You hear a δ sound, don't you, automatically being said before the ρ. Why? That is just the way an English-speaking mouth forms its letters. When the η drops out, it is unnatural to pronounce νρ. What our tongues almost expect is to find a δ sound before the ρ. When it is not there, the tongue does it anyway. So we say that an "epenthetic" δ is inserted between the ν and ρ (§18.3).

λαμβάνω is always a good illustration. The root is *λαβ. It is in a class of verbs that adds αν to the verbal root to form the present stem: λαβ ‣ λαβαν + ω. But a subclass of this division inserts a ν before the β: λαβανω ‣ λανβανω. Now pronounce this word. Can you feel how the tongue goes from being pressed to the top of the mouth with the mouth open when it says the ν, to the tongue dropping down a bit and the mouth closing to say the β? Instead of making the ν sound so distinct, try pronouncing it, but while you are doing so start to close your lips in preparation for the β sound. In fact, start to make the β sound before you are done with the ν sound. What are you saying? The ν has become a μ. But this is a totally natural movement. You are saying "vvvvv" but the mouth is getting ready to say "β." As the mouth closes and the tongue drops in preparation for the β, it affects the pronunciation of the ν such that it become a μ: λανβανω ‣ λαμβάνω.

Here is what these examples are trying to show. All the changes that we will be discussing came about for very common sense reasons. That is the beauty of language. Their form is controlled by their use, and if the word is hard to pronounce, it is modified. There are other reasons for consonantal modification, but this is one of the most obvious.

Our challenge is this. As you study the rules below, say the words you are reading in their various stages. Listen to yourself and see if you can hear why the changes are made. After some practice, you should be able almost to guess what is going to happen.

Greek is not an irregular language. It is tremendously regular; the trick is to develop an ear for how the Greeks liked to speak and for which sounds they found difficult to pronounce. Then realize that all those "irregularities" that you may have been forced to memorize in Beginning Greek class are really not irregular but perfectly regular.

Classification of Consonants   (§11)

§11.1   Whereas vowels are the basic sounds of a language, consonants are the interruption and restriction of those sounds (LaSor §10.41). Consonants are formed through a combination of three factors:

1. whether or not the vocal cords are used;
2. to what extent the flow of air is restricted;
3. what part of the mouth is used.

§11.2   No consonant is formed by just one of these factors, but by a combination usually of all three. For every consonant the vocal cords either are or are not used, the air flow is to some degree restricted, and a certain part of the mouth is used (although the latter factor only comes into real consideration on the six stops and three aspirates). For example, β uses the vocal cords, the air flow is completely stopped, and the lips are closed. β is therefore a voiced consonant, a stop, and a labial.

§11.3   As is usually the case with grammarians, every one seems to use a different set of terms. We have adopted the terminology that we feel best describes what is actually happening in the pronunciation of the consonant, and the terminology that is linguistically correct. For more discussion see LaSor (§12) and Smyth (§15-21).

First scheme: Use of vocal cords

§11.4   We have classified consonants according to the three different factors described in §11.1. The first scheme distinguishes between consonants that use the vocal cords and those that do not. To understand the difference, put your finger tips against your voice box, pronounce β, and then pronounce θ. The vibration of the voice box while the β is said shows that the voice is being used. But during the θ there is no vibration because the voice box is not being used. This is the difference between a voiced and a voiceless consonant.

§11.5   **Voiceless.**   The voice is not used in the pronunciation of the consonant (also called "unvoiced," "smooth," "surd," "silent").

θ, κ, ξ, π, σ, τ, φ, χ, ψ, ῥ

§11.6   **Voiced.**   The voice is used in the pronunciation of the consonant (also called "middle," or "sonant," which means "having sound"). (All vowels are voiced sounds.)

β, γ, δ, ζ, λ, μ, ν, ρ (except ῥ), ɪ, Ϝ, γ-nasal

§11.7 Smyth arranges the consonants "according to the increasing degree of noise" (§15c), beginning with the vowels, then nasals, semivowels, liquids, sibilants, stops, and double consonants.

Second scheme: Part of the Mouth

§11.8 The second scheme classifies consonants according to what part of the mouth is used to form the consonants. Labials, velars, and dentals are called "stops" (cf. §12.1; *MH* 108-112).

§11.9 **Labial.** The lips are used to pronounce the consonant.

π voiceless labial

β voiced labial

φ labial aspirate

μ labial nasal (also called "labio-nasal"). *BAGD* refers to μ primarily as a nasal.

ψ labial affricate. *MBG* refers to ψ primarily as a double consonant.

ϝ labial fricative

§11.9a The term "lingual" refers to those consonants requiring the tongue in their pronunciation: λ ρ v. *MBG* does not use this term.

§11.10 **Velar.** The soft palate is used to pronounce the consonant. "Velar" is the adjective form of the noun "velum," which is another name for the soft palate. The soft palate is the soft area right in back of the hard part of the roof of the mouth. In the pronunciation of these consonants, the back of the tongue comes up against this area of the roof of the mouth and the air flows over the top of the tongue. Some grammarians use the term "palatal" instead of "velar."

κ voiceless velar

γ voiced velar

χ velar aspirate

ξ velar affricate. *MBG* refers to ξ as a double consonant.

§11.11 **Dental.** The teeth are used to pronounce the consonant. This is the way the description is normally given, although it is not actually correct. The tongue does not actually touch the teeth. (If it does you need braces.) Rather, the tongue clicks against the alveolar ridge, which is right behind the teeth, hence some use the term "alveolar." Say a "t" sound and feel where the tongue touches (also called "linguals").

τ   voiceless dental

δ   voiced dental

θ   dental aspirate

ζ   dental affricate. When *MBG* refers to "dentals," ζ is not included.

§11.12   **Guttural.**   A letter that is pronounced solely in the throat.

'   The rough breathing is also a voiceless fricative (cf. §11.15; LaSor §12.44).

Scheme three: Air flow

§11.13   The third scheme classifies consonants according to how the air flow is restricted in the pronunciation of the consonant.

§11.14   **Stop.**   In the pronunciation of the consonant, the air flow is completely stopped (also called "mutes" and "plosives").

β, γ, δ   (voiced)

π, κ, τ   (voiceless)

§11.14a   The aspirates (φ χ θ) are sometimes called stops. They actually are not, because the air flow does not stop during their pronunciation. But the stops and aspirates do work together in an orderly pattern, as illustrated by the "Square of Stops" (§12.1). Therefore, when discussing the "Square of Stops," because it makes instruction so much easier, we will refer to aspirates as stops. When not discussing the "Square of Stops," we will not call aspirates stops (§12.5).

§11.15   **Fricative.**   In the pronunciation of the consonant, the air flow is not stopped completely although its flow is impeded. Whereas the time required to pronounce a stop is by definition very short, a fricative can be pronounced for a long time, until the speaker runs out of breath. θ, φ, χ, ϝ, and ι were originally fricatives (also called "spirant," "continuant").

γγ   γ-nasal. A gamma that is followed immediately by a velar (κ γ χ, including the velar double consonant ξ) is a gamma-nasal. It is pronounced like a v. Smyth gives the following examples that show how the pronunciation was carried over into Latin and English: ἄγκυρα (*ancora*; anchor), ἄγγελος (*angelus*; angel), σφίγξ (English: sphinx).

λ   liquid fricative

μ   nasal fricative (sometimes called a liquid fricative)

ν   nasal fricative (sometimes called a liquid fricative)

ρ   liquid fricative

σ   sibilant fricative

῾   gutteral fricative. The rough breathing is included at §11.12 because the location of the sound in the mouth is partially responsible for its pronunciation. But like the sibilant, most of its pronunciation is due to the tongue pressing upward so that when the air is forced over it the friction produces the sound of the rough breathing. The friction of the sibilant is up near the front of the mouth while the friction of the gutteral is in the back of the throat (cf. §11.12,17).

§11.16   **Affricate.**   An affricate is the combination of a stop and a fricative. We will usually call affricates **double consonants**, since the term is more widely used.

ψ   labial affricate (which can be formed through the combination of a labial [π β φ] and a sibilant)

ξ   velar affricate (which can be formed through the combination of a velar [κ γ χ] and a sibilant)

ζ   dental affricate (which is a combination of σδ, δσ, or δι).

    §11.16a   **Assibilate.** An assibilate is the combination of a stop and a sibilant. In Greek, all double consonants are assibilates, since the only fricative used to form double consonants is the sibilant.

    §11.16b   When a word ends in a stop and a sibilant is added (for example, in the dative plural or in the future or aorist tenses), the affricate that results is not actually a change in sound (and therefore not a true phonetic change). A π and a σ are pronounced exactly the same as a ψ. The change is merely orthographic, i.e., ψ is a way of writing πσ, βσ, or φσ (cf. §22.1).

§11.17   **Aspirate.**   An aspirate is the combination of a stop and aspiration. "Aspiration" is the result of letting the air flow come out of the mouth unrestricted. For example, aspiration is what makes a τ into a θ (cf. §14.7).

φ   labial aspirate   θ   dental aspirate

χ   velar aspirate   ῾   rough breathing; cf. §11.15.

    §11.17a   **Spirantization** is the development of a stop or aspirate into a fricative. Eventually all the Greek aspirates underwent spirantization (LaSor §12.323).

§11.18   **Liquid**.   The tip of the tongue is pressed against the front of the roof of the mouth, and the air is allowed to flow around the tongue without friction (thus "liquid").

λ   Also called "lateral."

ρ   Initial ρ always has rough breathing.

> **§11.18a**   μ and ν are sometimes classified as "liquid" consonants because they are formed somewhat the same way and share many of the same characteristics. We will use the term "liquid" only for λ and ρ. However, "liquid" verbs are those verbs ending in a liquid or a nasal.

§11.19   **Nasal**.   Like the liquids, the tongue is pressed against the front of the roof of the mouth. But unlike the true "liquids," the air flows only through the nasal cavity (thus "nasal") and not around the tongue and out the mouth. Try to pronounce one of the nasals with your nose pinched shut.

μ   labial nasal

ν   dental nasal

γ-nasal   velar nasal (formed with any velar preceded by γ.)

§11.20   **Sibilant**.   A sibilant is pronounced by letting the air flow over the top of the tongue, which at the same time is pressing up near the roof of the mouth, thus producing friction as the air flows over it. (This is opposed to the liquids in which the air goes around the tongue with no friction, and the nasals in which the air goes up through the nasal cavity.) Also called "spirant."

σ   The sigma is the only true sibilant in Greek.

ζ ξ ψ   The three double consonants are formed by adding δ (or ι), a velar, or a dental, respectively, to a sigma (§11.16).

ι ͷ   The semi-consonants also functioned as sibilants before they dropped out of use.

Miscellaneous

§11.21   **Sonant**.   A sonant is a consonant that produces a vowel sound either immediately before it or after it in order to aid pronunciation; cf. §5.

§11.22   **Semivowel**.   (Also called "semiconsonant," because they shared characteristics of both a vowel and a consonant.) There are two in Greek: "consonantal iota" written in grammars as ι; and "digamma" represented as ͷ or ͹. These two consonants were a part of the Greek alphabet, but for various reasons were no longer used by the time of Koine Greek. In other words, you will not see either of these letters anywhere in the New Testament. However, the fact that they used to be in certain words will explain the present form of that word. (Actually, consonantal upsilon dropped out of use and was replaced by the digamma. When the digamma dropped out of use it was either ignored (as in Attic) or replaced by upsilon [cf. Funk §905].)

For example, if the semivowel did not drop out altogether, the ι will show itself as an iota and the ϝ as an upsilon. The υ in βασιλεύς is really an ϝ, and the ι in κυλίω is really an ι. That is why the υ and the ι will not contract with the ω, which you would expect if it had been a simple upsilon or iota.

Also, there are many verbs that form their present tense stem by adding a ι to their verbal base stem, and the ι changes the stem. For example, there is a verbal root *βαλ. Thus, the perfectly regular second aorist is ἔβαλον. But to form the present tense stem a ι is added to the verbal root (*βαλι), and λ + ι form λλ, giving us βάλλω. How the semivowels affect other words will become apparent throughout our discussion, especially in §26, §27, and class v-2 verbs.

§11.23 The following chart summarizes the preceding (cf. Smyth §22).

Divisions	Voiced	Labial	Velar	Dental
Nasals	Voiced	μ	γ-nasal	ν
Semivowels	Voiced	ϝ	ι	
Liquids	Voiceless Voiced		ρ̇ λ, ρ̇	
Spirants	Voiceless		σ	
Stops	Voiceless Voiced Aspirate	π β φ	κ γ χ	τ δ θ
Double consonants	Voiced Voiceless	ψ	ξ	ζ

Not pictured are the fricatives: γγ, λ, μ, ν, ρ, σ, ' (cf. §11.15). The aspirates (except for rough breathing) are listed with the stops.

Square of Stops (§12)

§12.1

		Orders			
		voiceless	*voiced*	*aspirate*	
	labial	π	β	φ	
Classes	velar	κ	γ	χ	*(cognate)*
	dental	τ	δ	θ	

(coordinate)

The voiceless stops are also called "surd" (e.g., LaSor). Funk (§904.1) and Smyth (§16) use the terminology "smooth," "middle," and "rough" for "voiceless," "voiced," and "aspirate."

§12.2   The rough breathing is also an aspirate (§11.17). You may want to write it immediately below the θ.

§12.3   The **orders** are determined by how the air flow is restricted in the pronunciation of the consonant, and if the voice is used. The three orders are "voiceless" (§11.4), "voiced" (§11.4), and "aspirate" (§11.17). Three consonants belonging to one order are **coordinate**.

§12.4   The **classes** are determined by what part of the mouth is used in the pronunciation of the consonant. The three classes are "labial" (§11.9), "velar" (§11.10), and "dental" (§11.11). Three consonants belonging to one class are said to be **cognate**.

§12.4a   There are mnemonic devices for remembering these nine stops. Some may seem a little silly; but it seems that the sillier the mnemonic, the easier they are remembered. For example, "the pie (π) went bye (β) with a φ (i.e., sound of rushing wind)." "The cat (κ) at the gardener (γ) went χ (i.e., sound of a cat hissing)." "The top (τ) of the door (δ) went thud (θ)."

§12.5   The aspirates (φ χ θ) are sometimes classified as stops. They actually are not because the air flow does not stop during their pronunciation. But the stops and aspirates do work together in an orderly pattern as illustrated by the "Square of Stops" (§12). Therefore, when discussing the "Square of Stops," because it makes instruction so much easier, we will refer to aspirates as stops. When not discussing the "Square of Stops," we will not call aspirates stops (§11.14a).

For a discussion of the changes experienced by stops see §20-§22 below (cf. Smyth §82-84).

Assimilation / Dissimilation (§13)

§13.1   **Assimilation.** When two consonants that do not have similar sounds come into contact, the resulting combination was often undesirable to pronounce (§10). One consonant can be changed to another consonant that sounds similar to the other consonant. This is called "assimilation" ("to become similar, alike"). Assimilation is the opposite of "dissimilation" (§13.2). This assimilation is either "total" or "partial" (cf. LaSor §13.1; *BDF* §19).

>   **§13.1a**   **Total** assimilation is when one consonant actually becomes the same as the other consonant. For example, a word ending in π, such as *κρυπ (› κρύπτω), will show a total assimilation of the final π to a μ (§21.1) in the first person singular, perfect middle/passive: κε + *κρυπ + μενος › κεκρυμμένος. μμ is easier to pronounce than πμ.

>   **§13.1b**   **Partial** assimilation is when one consonant modifies to become somewhat like the other consonant, but it does not actually become the same as the other consonant. For example, a word ending in γ such as *στηριγ (› στηρίζω) will show a partial assimilation of the final γ to a κ (§20.2) in the third person singular, perfect middle/passive: ε + *στηριγ + ται › ἐστήρικται (γτ › κτ).

>   **§13.1c**   If the first consonant is changed, it is termed **regressive assimilation**. If the second consonant is changed, it is termed **progressive assimilation**.

>   **§13.1d**   Smyth uses the term "assimilation" for vowels (#45; e.g., βυβλίον › βιβλίον; cf. βύβλος).

§13.2   **Dissimilation.** When two vowels that have a similar sound come into contact, it is possible for one of the consonants to be changed to another consonant whose sound is different from the former. This is called "dissimilation," which means "to become dissimilar, unlike, different." Dissimilation is the opposite of assimilation (§13.1).

For example, when there are two lambdas in the same word, one λ can dissimilate to a ρ (ἀλγαλεος › ἀργαλέος; Smyth §129).

§13.3   Usually, the first consonant will assimilate to the second consonant, as in the cases above. Rarely, the second will assimilate to the first, as in the following in which the ν totally assimilates to the λ: *ολνυ › ὄλλυμι.

§13.4   Patterns of assimilation and dissimilation have been organized in §14-§27 according to the consonants that most commonly undergo assimilation or dissimilation. Below is one that did not fit neatly into our organization.

§13.4a   λ ‣ ρ.   If a word has two λλ, the first λ can totally dissimilate to ρ (cf. Smyth §129).

Aspiration   (§14)

§14.1   Aspiration is the process by which a voiceless stop (π κ τ) is partially assimilated to the aspirate (φ χ θ) of its same class (i.e., it is made coordinate). For example, a stop followed by a rough breathing is aspirated; cf. §14.7, *MH* 97-100.

π + ΄ ‣ φ ΄   ἀπὸ οὗ ‣ ἀφ᾽ οὗ

κ + ΄ ‣ χ ΄   οὐκ ὁ ‣ οὐχ ὁ

τ + ΄ ‣ θ ΄   ἀντὶ οὗ ‣ ἀνθ᾽ οὗ

§14.2   As discussed in §11.17, aspiration is the result of letting the air flow out of the mouth unrestricted. It is what makes a τ into a θ. In a sense, it is as if you added a "h" to the transliterated form of the stop. It is the opposite of deaspiration (§15).

p (π) + h ‣ ph (φ)

k (κ) + h ‣ kh (χ)

t (τ) + h ‣ th (θ)

§14.3   Aspiration is especially common in cases of elision, crasis, and in the formation of compounds. It is also frequent when a preposition is followed by a relative pronoun (§6.5f)

ἀπὸ οὗ   ‣ ἀφ᾽ οὗ

ἀπό + ἵημι   ‣ ἀπίημι (elision, §6.5) ‣ ἀφίημι

μετὰ οὗ   ‣ μεθ᾽ οὗ.

§14.4   **labial + θ.**   When a labial stop (π β) is immediately followed by a θ, the first stop is aspirated.

π + θ ‣ φθ   *βλαπ + θηναι ‣ βλαφθῆναι

β + θ ‣ φθ   *συντετρίβ + θαι ‣ συντετρῖφθαι

ψ + θ ‣ φθ   γεγραφ + σθε ‣ γεγραψθε ‣ γέγραφθε

§14.5   **velar + θ.**   When a velar stop (κ γ) is immediately followed by a θ, the first stop is aspirated. Compounds with ἐκ resist this assimilation.

κ + θ ‣ χθ   διώκω ‣ ἐδιώχθην

γ + θ ‣ χθ   ἄγω ‣ ἤχθην

ξ + θ ‣ χθ   δεδιωκ + σθε ‣ δεδιωξθε ‣ δεδίωχθε

§14.6   **Transfer of aspiration.** In words with a voiceless stop and an aspirate, it is possible that the aspiration will be passed from the aspirate to the voiceless stop. In other words, the aspirate is deaspirated, and the stop is aspirated. (The aspirate will be deaspirated to its cognate voiceless stop, and the voiceless stop will be aspirated to its cognate aspirate: φ ‹‣ π; χ ‹‣ κ; θ ‹‣ τ. See Smyth §124; Funk §928.4.)

*παθ + σκ ‣ πατσχω ‣ πάσχω (§22.3)

*θαπ ‣ θάπτω ‣ ἐτάφην

§14.7   **Voiceless stop + ʽ.** When a word ends in a voiceless stop, and the next word begins with a vowel and rough breathing, the stop is aspirated to its cognate aspirate.

π + ʽ ‣ φʽ   ἐπι + ἵστημι ‣ ἐπίστημι (§6.5b) ‣ ἐφίστημι

κ[1] + ʽ ‣ χʽ

τ + ʽ ‣ θʽ   κατα + ἱημι ‣ κατίημι (§6.5) ‣ καθίημι

§14.7a   Aspiration can occur in word formation (e.g., προ + ὁρος ‣ φροῦδος; Smyth §124a).

Deaspiration   (§15)

§15.1   Deaspiration is the process by which an aspirate (φ χ θʽ) is partially assimilated to the voiceless stop (π κ τ) of its same class (i.e., it is made cognate).

φ ‣ π   φεφιληκα ‣ πεφίλκα

χ ‣ κ   χεχωρηκα ‣ κεχώρηκα

θ ‣ τ   θιθημι ‣ τίθημι

§15.2   Deaspiration is the opposite of aspiration (§14.2). Instead of letting the air flow freely out of the mouth as it does in the pronunciation of an aspirate, the air flow is stopped as it forms its corresponding

---

[1]   Notice that in the compound ἐκ + ἵστημι, it forms ἐξίστημι rather than ἐχίστημι as this rule suggests. Remember that ἵστημι is really *στα that reduplicates to form the present tense stem (‣ σιστημι), but then the initial σ is changed to a rough breathing. However, when it is compound, the reduplicated σ is not the initial letter and is therefore not replaced with a rough breathing, and so the κ of the preposition joins with σιστημι. This is also a good illustration of how the morphological rules are not mutually exclusive. There are often several rules working together.

voiceless stop. It is what makes a θ into a τ. In a sense, deaspiration is the same as taking the "h" out of the transliterated form of the aspirate.

ph (φ) minus h = p (π)

kh (χ) minus h = k (κ)

th (θ) minus h = t (τ)

§15.3   Normally the first of the two aspirates will deaspirate, although at times it is the second that is changed.

*θε   ›   θιθημι   ›   τίθημι

*θαφ   ›   θάπτω   ›   ἐτάφην

*θη   ›   θεθηθι   ›   τέθητι

> **§15.3a**   The aorist passive imperative ending is really θι. It will deaspirate to a τ when preceded by the θ of the first aorist passive: *λυ + θη + θι › λύθητι (cf. §71).

§15.4   Deaspiration normally occurs when two aspirates are brought into close proximity, especially when two successive syllables begin with aspirates. The further apart the aspirates, the less the chance that one will deaspirate.

§15.5   **Reduplication.**   If a word begins with an aspirate, when it reduplicates the reduplicated aspirate will deaspirate (cf. §32.2a). In fact, aspirates can never even be geminate (cf. §16; Smyth §81).

φ › φεφ › πεφ   φανερόω   ›   πεφανέρωμαι

χ › χεχ › κεχ   χαρίζομαι   ›   κεχάρισμαι

θ › θεθ › τεθ   θεραπεύω   ›   τεθεραπευμένον

§15.6   **Stem aspirates.**   Some words originally had two aspirates in the stem. The first aspirate will have deaspirated (as is seen in the lexical form). However, when the second aspirate is lost, the first aspirate will return (LaSor §13.24, §13.245; Funk §928.2).

θρίξ is from the stem *θριχ. In the genitive the θ deaspirates to τ because of the χ (› τρίχος). But in the dative plural (τριχσι), the χ is lost because it is joined with the σ and written as a ξ (τριξι). The original θ therefore returns in the dative plural (θριξί; cf. ταχύς; Smyth §125f).

τρέφω is from the stem *θρεφ. In the present tense, the θ deaspirates to τ because of the φ (› τρέφω). But in the future the φ is lost because it is joined with the σ and is written as a ψ (τρέψω). The original θ therefore returns in the future (θρέψω).

§15.7 **' + aspirate.** The rough breathing is an aspirate (§11.17). Therefore, when a word begins with a rough breathing and also contains another aspirate, the rough breathing can deaspirate to a smooth breathing (Smyth §125e).

*σεχ is a good example. The initial σ is replaced by a rough breathing (ἐχ; §25.6a). Because χ is an aspirate, the rough breathing deaspirates to a smooth breathing (ἐχ). When the χ is lost, as it does for example in the future, the rough breathing remains (ἕξω).

§15.8 **θ (aorist passive).** If a stem has an aspirate, and if it adds θ to form the aorist passive, then the stem aspirate may deaspirate.

θύω ‣ εθυθην ‣ ἐτύθην

*θε ‣ εθεθην ‣ ἐτέθην

§15.8a Aspirates can resist this deaspiration (cf. Smyth §125N).

ἐφάνθην

§15.9 **Aorist imperative passive.** The aorist imperative passive morpheme is actually θι that normally deaspirates after the θ of the tense formative (λυ + θη + θι ‣ λυθηθι ‣ λύθητι). The morpheme is still visible in certain forms (γνῶθι, γράφηθι).

Gemination / Reduction (§16)

§16.1 When a vowel is doubled through lengthening, the double vowels are called **geminate**. The process of doubling is called **gemination** (e.g., "σσ" is a "geminate σ"; cf. LaSor §13.3).

§16.1a An example of gemination is a word beginning with ρ that can double the consonant when the word is augmented (§31.2b), or when it is the second element in a compound word (ῥήγνυμι ‣ ἔρρηξεν).

§16.2 Reduction can be *partial* if the geminate is reduced to a single consonant, or it can be *total* if the geminate drops out altogether.

§16.3 A voiced stop can never be geminate (ββ, δδ, γγ).

§16.4 In earlier forms of Greek, a word with an initial ρ doubled the ρ when it was used as the second element in a compound word or when an inflectional morpheme was added (περί + ῥήγνυμι ‣ περιρρήγνυμι). This doubling is almost always ignored in Koine Greek (περιρήγνυμι). Sometimes a lexicon will indicate this by placing parentheses around the first ρ (περι(ρ)ρήγνυμι; cf. LaSor §13.34, Smyth §80).

Metathesis   (§17)

§17.1   Metathesis is when two sounds within a word exchange places. This is not the same thing as vocalic consonants. Words sometimes explained with metathesis can be explained other ways as well; cf. §4.7.

§17.2   Smyth specifies that metathesis applies to the exchange of a vowel and a consonant (§128). For example: *τκ ‣ τιτκω ‣ τίκτω (infinitive: τεκνεῖν).

§17.3   If a short vowel undergoes metathesis, it is often lengthened.

Epenthesis   (§18)

§18.1   **Epenthesis** (e pen ´ the sis) is when a consonant is inserted into a word to help with pronunciation. Smyth calls this "development" (§130). We use the term "epenthesis" for the insertion of both a consonant or a vowel (cf. §5). Epenthesis often occurs in conjunction with metathesis (§17) and syncope (§7.2). See LaSor §13.5. See also movable ν (§6.6) and movable ς (§6.7).

§18.2   **Epenthetic β.** When μλ or μρ occurs, a β can be inserted between the two consonants (cf. §23.3).

μ + λ ‣ μβλ   μεμλωκα ‣ μέμβλωκα

μ + ρ ‣ μβρ   μεσημρια ‣ μεσημβρία

§18.2a   If a μ is the first letter in the word, it will be dropped.

§18.3   **Epenthetic δ.** When νρ occurs, a δ can be inserted between the two consonants.

ν + ρ ‣ νδρ   *ανη ‣ ανηρος ‣ ανρος (§4.4) ‣ ἄνδρος

§18.4   **Epenthetic μ.** When a **labial** stop is followed by a λ or a σ, an epenthetic μ is sometimes added before the labial.

π + λ /σ ‣ μπλ /σ   πιπλημι ‣ πίμπλημι

β + λ /σ ‣ μβ /σ /σ

ψ + λ /σ ‣ μψλ /σ   ληψομαι ‣ λήμψομαι

§18.5   **Epenthetic ν.** In the present tense of class 3a(2b) verbs, an epenthetic ν is added.

*μαθ + αν ‣ μανθάνω

§18.5a Often this ν will in turn undergo further changes according to the standard rules.

*λαβ + αν ‣ λανβανω ‣ λαμβάνω (§24.1)

*τυχ + αν ‣ τυνχανω ‣ τυγχάνω (§24.2)

§18.6 **Epenthetic σ.** Some verbs add an epenthetic σ before the endings in the perfect middle/passive (κλείω ‣ κέκλεισμαι; §46.5) and before the tense formative in the aorist passive (κλείω ‣ ἐκλείσθην; §46.5). All examples in the New Testament are listed at §46.5 (cf. Smyth, §489).

§18.7 An ε can be inserted before the tense formative in the perfect active (βάλλω ‣ βέβληκα; §45.3) and aorist passive (‣ ἐβλήθην; §47.7). It is then usually lengthened to η.

Dropping of Final Consonants   (§19)

§19.1 Only vowels and certain consonants (ν ρ σ ξ ["ks"] ψ ["ps"]) can stand at the end of a word. If a word ends in any other consonant, that consonant will be dropped. (On ἐκ and οὐκ see §19.3-4.)

When a final consonant is dropped, the stem vowel will often lengthen in compensation.

For example, The stem of ὄνομα is actually *ονοματ. There is no ending for the nominative singular for this class noun, and therefore you are left with the bare stem. But since a τ cannot stand at the end of a word, it is dropped, leaving us with ὄνομα. When there is an ending such as -ος in the genitive singular, the τ will not be dropped (‣ ὀνόματος).

§19.2 In order to remain true to their actual pronunciation, some foreign words are allowed to retain their final consonants. For example: Ἰσραήλ, Δαυίδ (cf. n-3g(2)).

§19.3 ἐκ is really ἐξ (i.e., "eks"). The σ drops out if the following word begins with a consonant (i.e., interconsonantal σ: §25.4b; cf. LaSor §13.35, Smyth §133a [but see §136] contrary to Funk). If the following word begins with a vowel, the σ stays. In compound verbs formed with ἐκ, the κ returns to the original ξ when the verb is augmented (ἐκβάλλω ‣ ἐξέβαλον).

Because the κ is the result of phonetic change, it rarely changes in those circumstances where κ is normally changed (e.g., §20.2).

§19.4   oὐ is really oὐκ. The κ drops out if the following word begins with a consonant (e.g., oὐ δύναται). The κ aspirates to a χ if the following word begins with a rough breathing (oὐχ ὑμεῖς, but oὐκ ἐγίνωσκεν; §14.7; LaSor §13.3511).

§19.5   If a word ends in a vowel and a μ, the μ can be assimilated to a ν (Smyth §133c).

*ιππομ › ἵππον

*εμ › ἔν .

Stop + Dental   (§20)

§20.1   **Labial** + dental.   The labial is made coordinate (i.e., the labial is partially assimilated to the labial of the same order as the dental). In other words, the labial must be of the same order (§12.3) as the dental. If the dental is voiceless, the labial is altered to the voiceless labial (π); if voiced, to the voiced labial (β); if aspirate, to the aspirate labial (φ).

π + τ   *κρυπ › κεκρύπται (› κρύπτω)
β + τ › πτ   *συντριβ › συντέτριπται
φ + τ   *γράφ › γέγραπται

π + δ
β + δ › βδ
φ + δ

π + θ   *βλαπ › βλαφθῆναι (› βλάπτω)
β + θ › φθ   *συντρίβ › συντετρίφθαι
φ + θ   *ἐξαλείφ › ἐξαλειφθῆναι

§20.2   **Velar** + dental.   The velar is made coordinate (i.e., the velar is partially assimilated to the velar of the same order as the dental). In other words, the velar must be of the same order (§12.3) as the dental. If the dental is voiceless, the velar is altered to the voiceless velar (κ); if voiced, to the voiced velar (γ); if aspirate, to the aspirate velar (χ).

κ + τ
γ + τ › κτ   *στηριγ › ἐστήρικται (› στηρίζω)
χ + τ   *δέχ › δέδεκται (› δέχομαι)

κ + δ
γ + δ › γδ
χ + δ

κ	+	θ	*διωκ ‣ ἐδιώχθην
γ	+	θ ‣ χθ	*ανοιγ ‣ ἀνεῴχθην
χ	+	θ	*δεχ ‣ ἐδέχθην

§20.2 The κ in ἐκ is not assimilated in compounds (e.g., ἐκτελέω; ἐκδικέω; ἐκθαμβέω).

§20.3 **Dental + dental.** The first dental dissimilates to a sibilant.

τ	+	τ	
δ	+	τ ‣ στ	*αγιαδ ‣ ἡγίασται (‣ ἁγιάζω)
θ	+	τ	
τ	+	δ	
δ	+	δ ‣ σδ	
θ	+	δ	
τ	+	θ	
δ	+	θ ‣ σθ	*θαυμαδ ‣ ἐθαυμάσθη (‣ θαυμάζω)
θ	+	θ	*πείθ ‣ ἐπείσθησαν

§20.3 ττ, if formed by κ ̯ or χ ̯ (§26.3), will sometimes remain due to the influence of the Attic dialect. (Cf. κρείττων; ἐλάττων; Smyth §78,83a; Funk §925.2.)

Stop + μ   (§21)

§21.1 **Labial + μ.** The labial totally assimilates to a μ (Smyth §85).

π	+	μ	*κρυπ ‣ κεκρυμμένος (‣ κρύπτω)
β	+	μ ‣ μμ	*θλίβ ‣ τεθλιμμένη
φ	+	μ	*γράφ ‣ γέγραμμαι

§21.1a If this would result in a triple cluster (e.g., μμμ), then one μ is dropped (LaSor §13.1211; Smyth §85b).

*πεμπ ‣ πεπεμμμαι ‣ πέπεμμαι

§21.2 **Velar + μ.** The velar is partially assimilated to the voiced velar (γ).

κ	+	μ	*διώκ ‣ δεδιωγμένοι
γ	+	μ ‣ γμ	*ἀνοίγ ‣ ἠνεῳγμένη
χ	+	μ	*δέχ ‣ δέδεγμαι

§21.2a In the formation of nouns, this assimilation can be resisted; cf. δραχμή, ἀκμή; Smyth §85a.

§21.2b Compounds with ἐκ resist this assimilation (cf. ἐκμάσσω).

§21.2c   κμ and χμ can sometimes be retained, especially when it
is the result of a phonetic change (καμ ‣ κέκμηκα) or
word formation (ἐκμάσσω; δραχμή; Smyth §85a; LaSor
§13.1231; Funk §926.2).

§21.3   **Dental + μ.**   The dental is usually totally assimilated to σ in the
perfect middle (Funk §926.3).

τ + μ

δ + μ ‣ σμ   *ἀγιαδ ‣ ἡγιασμένη (‣ ἀγιάζω)

θ + μ   *πείθ ‣ πεπείσμεθα

Stop + σ   (§22)

§22.1   **Labial + σ.**   The labial and the σ are written as a ψ. This is not assimilation because πσ and ψ are pronounced the same. The change is
merely orthographic (§11.16b; §22.2). Funk uses the term "coalesce"
(§926.3)

π + σ   *βλεπ + σω ‣ βλέψω

*λαιλαπ + σ ‣ λαῖλαψ

β + σ ‣ ψ   *διατριβ + σα ‣ διέτριψα

*Αραβ + σ ‣ Ἄραψ

φ + σ   ε + *γραφ + σα ‣ ἔγραψα

§22.1a   Technically, the β and φ are first changed to a π, and then
written as a ψ.

§22.2   **Velar + σ.**   The velar and the σ are written as a ξ. This is an orthographic and not a phonetic change (cf. §11.16b; §22.1).

κ + σ   *διωκ + σω ‣ διώξω

*σαρκ + σι ‣ σάρξι

γ + σ ‣ ξ   *φευγ + σονται ‣ φεύξονται

*σαλπιγγ + σ ‣ σάλπιγξ

χ + σ   *αρχ + σομαι ‣ ἄρξομαι

*τριχ + σ ‣ θρίξ

§22.2a   In compound words where ἐκ is joined with a word
beginning with a σ, the κ and the σ will not be written
as a ξ.

§22.2b   With class v-5 verbs, the χ drops out before the σ, and
the σ and κ are not written as a ξ (cf. *δαχ ‣ διδαχσκω ‣
διδασκω

§22.2c   Technically, the γ and the χ are first changed to a κ, and
then written as a ξ.

§22.2d   On ἐκ see §19.3.

§22.3   **Dental + σ.**   The dental assimilates to a σ, and then the geminate σ
is simplified.

τ + σ   *χαριτ + σ ‣ χάρις (χάριτος)

δ + σ ‣ σσ ‣ σ   *βαπτιδ + σω ‣ βαπτίσω
                              *ελπιδ + σ ‣ ἐλπίς

θ + σ   *πειθ + σω ‣ πείσω
                              *ορνιθ + ς ‣ ὄρνις

§22.3a   Technically, the dental first assimilates to τ and then to
σ (Smyth §98a).

μ   (§23)

§23.1   **Stop + μ.**   §23.1 is an abbreviation of §21. See there for more details.

§23.1a   labial + μ.   The labial assimilates to a μ.

π + μ   *κρυπ ‣ κεκρυμμένος (‣ κρύπτω)
β + μ ‣ μμ   *θλίβ ‣ τεθλιμμένη
φ + μ   *γράφ ‣ γέγραμμαι

§23.1b   velar + μ.   The velar is partially assimilated to the
voiced velar (γ).

κ + μ   *διώκ ‣ δεδιωγμένοι
γ + μ ‣ γμ   *ἀνοίγ ‣ ἠνεῳγμένη
χ + μ   *δέχ ‣ δέδεγμαι

§23.1c   dental + μ.   The dental is usually assimilated to a σ.

τ + μ
δ + μ ‣ σμ   *αγιαδ ‣ ἡγιασμένη (‣ ἁγιάζω)
θ + μ   *πείθ ‣ πεπείσμεθα

§23.2   **ν/ψ + μ.**   When ν or ψ come into contact with μ, they totally assimilate to μ (Smyth §94).

ν + μ ‣ μμ   ἐν + μένω ‣ ἐμμένω (‣ ἐνέμεινα)
ψ + μ ‣ μμ

§23.3   **μλ / μρ.**   When either of these combinations occur, a β can be inserted between the two. The following is an abbreviation of §18.2; see there for more details.

μ + λ › μβλ   μεμλωκα › μέμβλωκα

μ + ρ › μβρ   .   μεσημ(ε)ρια › μεσεμβρία

§23.4   **Labial + λ/σ.**   When a labial stop is followed by a λ or a σ, an epenthetic μ is sometimes added before the labial. This is an abbreviation of §18.4. See there for more details.

π + λ/σ › μπλ/σ   πιπλημι › πίμπλημι

β + λ/σ › μβλ/σ

φ + λ/σ › μφλ/σ

ψ + λ/σ › μψλ/σ   ληψομαι › λήμψομαι

§23.5   **σ + μ/ν.**   When a σ comes into contact with μ or ν, the σ drops out. This is an abbreviation of §25.8. See there for more details.

σ + μ › μ   *εσ + μι › εμι › εἰμί (§3.5)

σ + ν › ν   *εσ + νυμι › ἔννυμι

ν   (§24)

§24.1   **ν + labial.**   The ν partially assimilates to a μ (Smyth §91).

ν + π › μπ   σύν + παθέω › συμπαθέω › συνεπάθησα

ν + β › μβ   σύν + βαίνω › συμβαίνω › συνέβαινον

ν + φ › μφ   σύν + φέρω › συμφέρω › συνέφερον

ν + ψ › μψ   συν + ψηφίζω › συμψηφίζω › συνεψήθισα

§24.2   **ν + velar.**   The ν partially assimilates to γ-nasal. (This assimilation is only orthographic; it does not affect the pronunciation of the consonant cluster; cf. Smyth §92.)

ν + κ › γκ   ἐν + καινίζω › ἐγκαινίζω › ἐνεκαίνισα

ν + γ › γγ   ἐν + γράφω › ἐγγράφω › ἐνέγραψα

ν + χ › γχ   ἐν + χρίω › ἐγχρίω › ἐνέχρισα

ν + ξ › γξ   συν + ξύω › συγξύω

§24.2a   Similar to this is the fact that a γ followed by a velar (i.e., a γ-nasal) will assimilate to a ν in pronunciation, but not orthographically. In other words, the γ is pronounced like a ν, but it will still be written as a γ.

§24.2b This phonetic dissimilation can be seen in some Greek words borrowed by Latin. Smyth gives the following examples: ἄγκυρα ‣ *ancora*; ἄγγελος ‣ *angelus* (angel); σφίγξ ‣ *sphinx*.

§24.2c In many NT manuscripts the ν remains (LaSor §13.1321).

§24.3 **ν + dental.** A ν will not be altered if followed by a dental. (Smyth points out that this ν may itself be the result of the assimilation of a μ to a ν (§93), and it therefore resists further modification.)

§24.3a When a dental occurs between a ν and σ, the dental assimilates to σ. The geminate σσ simplifies, the ν drops out, and the preceding vowel undergoes compensatory lengthening.

λυοντσι ‣ λυονσσι ‣ λυονσι ‣ λυοσι ‣ λύουσι

παντσι ‣ πανσσι ‣ πανσι ‣ πασι ‣ πᾶσι

ὀδοντσι ‣ οδονσσι ‣ οδονσι ‣ οδοσι ‣ ὀδοῦσι

§24.3b The ντσ combination is common. However, in the dative plural of n-3c(5) nouns there is no compensatory lengthening (Smyth §250).

§24.4 **ν + σ.** The ν will usually drop out, and the vowel immediately before the ν will undergo compensatory lengthening (§3.3; cf. §25.3).

§24.4a This change is frequent in third declension nouns with stems ending in ν (n-3f[1]; e.g., αιων + σι ‣ αἰῶσι; *ποιμεν + σι ‣ ποιμέσι) but without lengthening (Smyth §96a, 250N).

§24.4b ἐν can resist this assimilation (e.g., ἐνσείω, ἐνσκευάζω; cf. §24.13).

§24.5 **σύν + σ or vowel.** When σύν is added to a word beginning with σ or vowel, the ν may totally assimilate to a σ (LaSor §13.1342; Smyth §101).

συν + σ ‣ συσσ   συσσῴζω

§24.5a If the word begins with a consonant cluster, the geminate σ will simplify.

σύν + στρατιώτης ‣ συσστρατιωτης ‣ συστρατιώτης

§24.5b If the word does not begin with a consonant cluster, the geminate σ remains. There are no examples of this in the New Testament (e.g., σύσσημον, σύσσωμος).

§24.6   **σύν + consonant.**   When σύν is added to a word beginning with a consonant, especially ζ, the ν totally assimilates to a σ and is then simplified (cf. *BDF* §19, Smyth §101a).

σύν + ζητέω ‣ συσζητεω ‣ συζητέω (‣ συνεζήτουν)

§24.7   **ν + liquid.**   The ν may be totally assimilated to the liquid (Smyth §95).

ν + λ ‣ λλ   σύν + λαλέω ‣ συλλαλέω ‣ συνελάλουν

ν + ρ ‣ ρρ   σύν + ρέω ‣ συρρέω

§24.7a   When ἐν forms a compound with a word beginning with a liquid, the ν resists this assimilation (cf. §24.13).

§24.8   **ν + μ.**   The ν may totally assimilate to the μ.

σύν   + μοροφίζω   ‣   συμμοροφίζω

ἐν   + μετερος   ‣   ἔμμετερος

κε + κλιν + μαι   ‣   κέκλιμμαι

§24.8a   Some verbs appear to assimilate their final ν to a σ in the perfect middle/passive (μαι, μεθα); the ν shows before the other personal endings. But as Smyth points out (§489h), the σ is borrowed by analogy from the verbs ending in a dental, which therefore form a σ in the perfect mid/pas (cf. §24.12).

§24.9   **λν ‣ λλ.**   *ολνυ undergoes reverse assimilation in which the ν totally assimilates to the preceding λ (cf. §13.3; Smyth §90).

*ολνυ ‣ ὄλλυμι

§24.10   **βν / φν.**   In these two clusters, the labial usually assimilates to a μ (Smyth §88).

βν ‣ μν   σεβνος ‣ σεμνός

φν ‣ μν   στυφνος ‣ στυμνός

§24.11   **Final ν dropped.**   The final ν is dropped in some verbs before the:

a.   κ of the first perfect active (κρίνω ‣ κέκρικα).

b.   endings of the perfect middle/passive stem (κρίνω ‣ κέκριμενα).

c.   θ of the aorist passive (κρίνω ‣ ἐκρίθη).

§24.12   **Final ν ‣ σ.**   The final ν in some words appears to have assimilated to a σ before the perfect middle/passive endings. Actually, the ν was dropped (§24.11) and the σ added by analogy to verbs ending in a dental stem (Smyth §489h; cf. §24.8a).

φαιν ‣ πέφασμαι

This change may occur only with endings beginning with μ. If the ending begins with a dental, there will be no change (§24.3).

§24.13   ἐν does not loose its ν before ρ, σ, or ζ (ἐνσείω, ἐνσκευάζω; §24.7a, Smyth §101a).

σ   (§25)

§25.1   σ + σ.   When a geminate σ results from inflection or some phonetic change, it will usually reduce to a single σ.

σ + σ ‣ σσ ‣ σ

§25.1a   If the geminate σ is the result of a velar + ι (§26.3a), then it will not reduce. This is common in the present tense of v-2b verbs (κηρυγι ‣ κηρύσσω).

§25.1b   When σσ is the Attic form of ττ, it will not simplify (cf. §26.5).

§25.2   **stop + σ.**   The following is an abbreviation of §22. See there for more details.

labial + σ	A labial and the σ are written as a ψ.

π	+	σ			*βλεπ + σω ‣ βλέψω
β	+	σ	‣	ψ	*διατριβ + σα ‣ διέτριψα
φ	+	σ			*γραφ + σω ‣ ἔγραψα

velar + σ	A velar and the σ are written as a ξ.

κ	+	σ			*διωκ + σω ‣ διώξω
γ	+	σ	‣	ξ	*φευγ + σονται ‣ φεύξονται
χ	+	σ			*αρχ + σομαι ‣ ἄρξομαι

dental + σ	A dental assimilates to a σ, and then the geminate σ simplifies.

τ	+	σ			*χαριτ + σ ‣ χάρις
δ	+	σ	‣	σσ ‣ σ	*βαπτιδ + σω ‣ βαπτίσω
θ	+	σ			*πειθ + σω ‣ πείσω

§25.3   ν + σ.   The ν will usually drop out, and the vowel immediately before the ν will undergo compensatory lengthening (§3.5; §24.4).

§25.4   **Interconsonantal σ.**   A σ that occurs between two consonants often drops out (Funk §930.1).

γράφω ‣ γέγραφσθε ‣ γέγραφθε

§25.4a   If the σ is the first letter in the second element of a compound word, it will not drop out (Smyth §103a).

§25.4b   On ἐκ see §19.3.

§25.5   **Intervocalic σ.**   A σ occurring between two vowels will usually become the gutteral fricative (i.e., rough breathing) and drop out. The two vowels that then come into contact will usually contract (LaSor §13.361; Smyth §120; Funk §930.2).

§25.5a   This loss is frequent in:

1. second singular middle endings (λυεσαι ‣ λυῃ; ελυεσο ‣ ἐλύου), except in perfect (λέλυσαι) and pluperfect (ἐλέλυσο) of ω verbs and the present (τίθεσαι) and imperfect (ἐτίθεσο) of μι verbs.

2. future of liquid verbs (μενεσω ‣ μενεω ‣ μενῶ).

3. aorist (active/middle) of liquid verbs (μένω ‣ ἔμεινα). Smyth (§121), LaSor (§13.363), and Funk (§930.5) say that the σ disappears due to the liquid and the preceding vowel is lengthened to compensate (§3.5). Others teach that the tense formative is α.

4. third declension nouns with stems ending in σ (*γενεσ + ι [γένος] ‣ γενεσι ‣ γένει [n-3d]).

5. third declension adjectives with stems ending in ης/ες (*ἀληθες + ι [ἀληθής] ‣ ἀληθεσι ‣ ἀληθεῖ [a-4a]).

§25.5b   The σ of the personal ending is retained:

1. in the future (δώσω) and first aorist (ἔστησεν) of μι verbs.

2. in σαι (ἵστασαι), σο (ἐδίδοσο), and σι (τίθησι) endings for μι verbs.

3. if the σ is the result of a geminate σ being reduced.

4. if it is the result of a phonetic change.

§25.5c   If an interconsonantal σ drops out of a two-syllable word, the two vowels will not contract. For example, the proper stem of θέος is *θεσο. The σ dropped out, but the vowels do not contract to ου.

§25.6 **Initial σ + vowel.** Initial sigmas followed by a vowel are often lost with subsequent changes.

§25.6a If the word originally began with a σ followed by a vowel, the σ usually was replaced with a rough breathing (Smyth #119; cf. the word "seven" in Greek, ἑπτά, and in Latin, *septem*).

For example, the original stem of ἔχω was *σεχ. The σ was replaced by a rough breathing (ˌ ἐχω). In the present, the rough breathing was deaspirated because of the χ (ˌ ἔχω; §15.7). The rough breathing returns in the future since the aspirate χ is written as a ξ because of the σ of the future (ˌ ἕξω).

§25.6b If a word begins with a σ, when it is reduplicated the reduplicated σ may dissimilate to a rough breathing (LaSor §13.23).

For example, the stem of ἵστημι is *στα. To form the present stem, the σ is reduplicated, the stem vowel lengthened, and the alternate ending is used (*στα ˌ σιστημι). The first σ is then replaced with a rough breathing (ˌ ἵστημι). Cf. ἵημι (v-6a).

This rule is not always followed. The perfect of σπείρω is ἔσπαρμαι, and the perfect of σῴζω is σέσωκα.

§25.6c If a reduplicated σ is not dissimilated to a rough breathing (§25.6b), the original σ may be intervocalic and it may drop out. The ε that separated the two sigmas may or may not contract with the first stem vowel.

§25.6d If a word begins with a σ that is itself the result of phonetic change, it will not dissimilate to a rough breathing.

§25.6e When the cluster σμ or σν begins a word, the σ usually drops out and the vowel will undergo compensatory lengthening (§3.5) (unless the μ or ν begins a sufformative; cf. LaSor §13.365-6).

§25.7 **Liquid + σ.** The σ may drop out, and the preceding vowel undergoes compensatory lengthening (§3.5).

λ + σ ˌ λ			*αγγελσα ˌ ηγγελσα ˌ ἤγγειλα
μ + σ ˌ μ			τρέμω ˌ ετρεμσα ˌ ἔτρειμα
ν + σ ˌ ν			μένω ˌ ἐμενσα ˌ ἔμεινα
ρ + σ ˌ ρ			δέρω ˌ ἔδερσα ˌ ἔδειρα

§25.8   σ + μ / ν.   When σ is followed by μ or ν, the σ is often lost. The preceding vowel can undergo compensatory lengthening (cf. §23.5; Smyth §105).

σ + μ › μ   *εσ + μι › εμι › εἰμί
σ + ν › ν   *εσ + νυμι › ἔννυμι

§25.8a   If the μ begins a suffix, the σ will not drop out.

§25.9   σδ.   When σ and δ are combined "in adverbs denoting motion towards," they can produce ζ (Smyth §106).

§25.10   For the ν + dental + σ combination, see §24.3a.

Consonantal Iota (ι̯) (§26)

§26.1   Greek had several letters that over the course of the centuries dropped out of use. Like the digamma (§27), consonantal iota dropped out of use by the time of Koine Greek. Although it never actually shows up in our texts, it is responsible for the forms of many words (Funk §932; LaSor §13.16). It can be seen in Latin cognates as "i," and in Greek as "ι" and "ζ." It roughly corresponds to the English "y," sounding like the "y" in "yet" (Smyth §20a; Funk §150).

§26.2   γ(γ)/δ + ι̯   When γι̯, γγι̯, or δι̯ is preceded by a vowel, or when γι̯ is preceded by a consonant, they form ζ or δ respectively.

vowel + γι̯   ›   ζ   *ἁρπαγ + ι̯ › ἁρπάζω (cf. ἁρπαγή)
vowel + γγι̯   ›   ζ   *κλαγγ + ι̯ › κλάζω
vowel + δι̯   ›   ζ   *ελπιδ + ι̯ › ἐλπίζω
consonant + γι̯ ›   δ   *εργ + ι̯ › ἔρδω

§26.3   velar + ι̯.   The velar and ι̯ assimilate to a geminate σ.

κ + ι̯ › σσ   *κηρυκ + ι̯ › κηρύσσω (cf. κῆρυξ)
γ + ι̯ › σσ   *ταγ + ι̯ › τάσσω (cf. ταγή)
χ + ι̯ › σσ   *ταραχ + ι̯ › ταράσσω (cf. ταραχή)

§26.3a   The geminate σ will not reduce; cf §25.1a.

§26.3b   In the Attic dialect, these combinations formed ττ. In Ionic and most of the other dialects, they form σσ (cf. Smyth §78, §112). The Koine did not follow the Attic here (θάλασσα vs θάλαττα; κρείσσων vs κρείττων; φυλάσσω vs φυλάττω).

§26.4   **τ/θ +ι ‣ σσ.**   When τ or θ come into immediate contact with ι, if the τ/θ is preceded by a short vowel, the ι dissimilates to σ, and the dental (τ θ) assimilates to σ and simplifies (§22.3).

If the τ/θ is preceded by anything else (e.g., long vowel, diphthong, or consonant), it merely becomes σ (Smyth §113).

This is not the same phenomena as in §26.3b; i.e., this σσ does not develop as ττ in the Attic dialect (; LaSor §13.161).

τ + ι ‣ σσ (‣ σ)   *πλατ + ι ‣ πλατσ ‣ πλάσσω
                        *παντ + ι ‣ παντσ ‣ πανσσ ‣ πανσ ‣ πᾶσα

θ + ι ‣ σσ (‣ σ)   *Μελιθ + ι ‣ Μελιθσ ‣ Μέλισσα
                        *μεθ + ι ‣ μεθσ ‣ μεσσος ‣ μέσος

§26.5   **τ/θ +ι ‣ ττ.**   When the τ or θ come into immediate contact with ι, they can become ττ, which is then open to the σσ shift in the Ionic dialect (Smyth §114, but see §26.4). If they become ττ in Attic, σσ was used in Koine Greek (LaSor §13.1612). This change is by analogy to κι ‣ ττ (§26.3).

τ + ι ‣ ττ   *μελιτ + ι ‣ μέλιττα (cf. μέλι, μέλιτος)

θ + ι ‣ ττ   *κορυθ + ι ‣ κορύττω (cf. κόρυς)

§26.6   **λ +ι.**   When λ and ι come into immediate contact, the ι assimilates to a λ (LaSor §13.163; Smyth §110).

λ + ι ‣ λλ   *βαλ + ι ‣ βάλλω
                        *αγγελ + ι ‣ ἀγγέλλω
                        ἀλι ‣ ἄλλος (Latin alius)

§26.7   **Metathesis.**   In the following combinations, the consonantal iota becomes vocalic iota and undergoes metathesis (§17; cf. v-2 verbs; Funk §932.6; LaSor §13.164; Smyth §111, 128).

αν + ι ‣ ανι ‣ αιν   *φαν + ι ‣ φανιω ‣ φαίνω ‣ ἔφανα

ον + ι ‣ ονι ‣ οιν

αρ + ι ‣ αρι ‣ αιρ   *χαρ + ι ‣ χαριω ‣ χαίρω ‣ ἐχάρην

ορ + ι ‣ ορι ‣ οιρ   *μορ +ι ‣ μοριω ‣ μοῖρα

§26.7a   Smyth calls this "epenthesis," but then qualifies it by adding that it "is more exactly a partial assimilation of the preceding vowel sound to the following consonantal ι" (§111).

§26.8   **Dropping of ι.**   In the following combinations, the consonantal iota drops out, and the vowel undergoes compensatory lengthening (§3.5; LaSor §13.1641; Funk §932.7; 484.4-5; 2361).

εν + ι › εν › ην

ερ + ι › ερ › ηρ   *εγερ + ι › ἐγείρω (aorist passive: ἠγέρθην)

ιν + ι › ιν › ιν

ιρ + ι › ιρ › ιρ

υν + ι › υν › υν

υρ + ι › υρ › υρ

§26.8a   LaSor and Funk differ somewhat on how they treat this
phenomena; cf. Smyth §37a.

§26.9   **labial + ι › labial + τ**

Verbs whose present tense stems end in πτ (e.g., καλύπτω) are
formed from roots ending in a labial (π β φ). To form the present
tense stem, ι is added to the root, and the labial + ι combination
formed πτ.

*καλυπ + ι › καλύπτω › ἐκάλυψα

§26.10   **τ + final ι.** When a stem ends in τι, the τι form σι (Smyth §115).

τι › σι   τιθητ + ι › τίθησι, πλουτ + ι › πλούσιος (cf. πλοῦτος)

Digamma (Ϝ)   (§27)

§27.1   Like the consonantal iota (§26), digamma dropped out of use before
the Koine period. It is written in grammars as Ϝ or ϝ. (*MH* uses an
italicized *w*.) Its name is "Ϝαυ," or "vau," was also called digamma
because of its shape (i.e., two gammas). It was pronounced "w." It
originally came between ε and ζ in the alphabet (Funk §150). It was
still written as late as 200 B.C. in the Boeotian dialect, although for
the most part it had dropped out elsewhere, and out of all dialects
by the Koine period (cf. Smyth §3). Although it was no longer used
in the Koine period, the fact that it used to be in certain words
explains their present form. (It is classified as a "semiconsonant" or
"semivowel"; §11.22.)

§27.2   **Initial Ϝ.** Certain verbs used to begin with a digamma (§31.5).
Although it is no longer there, the verb will augment or reduplicate
as if it still were (cf. Funk §933.2).

For example, the root of εἶδον is *Ϝιδ. It therefore uses the syllabic
augment because digamma would be treated as a consonant (› εϜιδ).
When the intervocalic digamma dropped out, the word became
εἶδον. If there had been no digamma, it would have used the temporal augment instead, since the word would have begun with a vowel
(› ἶδον).

Another example is ὁράω. The imperfect is ἑώρων and not ὥρων as you would expect. The root is *Ϝορα. It therefore receives the syllabic augment (› εϜορα), the intervocalic Ϝ dropped out (› εορα; §27.4), and the ο was lengthened (› ἑώρων; perfect: ἑώρακα). Other examples are εϜεργαζομαι › εἰργάσθην and ϜεϜοικα › ἔοικα.

§27.3   **Initial σϜ.**   In some words, initial σϜ was dropped.

For example, the stem of the relative pronoun is *σϜο-. The σϜ dropped out and was replaced by a rough breathing (› ὅς). The Latin retained the σϜ in its relative pronoun: "suus" (Smyth 123).[1]

§27.4   **Intervocalic Ϝ.**   Intervocalic digamma usually drops out. The two vowels that are therefore brought into contact may diphthongize or may contract.

ε + *Ϝιδ › εἶδον

§27.4a   This is especially frequent in the perfect of verbs that originally began with a digamma (in which the digamma is followed by a single vowel).

*Ϝορα › ϜεϜορα › ἑώρακα

*Ϝ(ο)ιδ › ϜεϜοιδα › Ϝεοιδα › εοιδα › οἶδα

§27.5   **Interconsonantal Ϝ.**   When a Ϝ originally occurred between two consonants, it could drop out.

§27.6   **Verbs in εϜ.**   Verbs whose stems end in εϜ will undergo various changes depending on whether the digamma is followed by a consonant or a vowel (LaSor §13.373).

§27.6a   If the digamma is followed by a consonant:

1.   Ϝ becomes υ, and the ε will diphthongize with the υ.

2.   the subsequent ευ diphthong will not contract with the connecting vowel in the present tense (although sometimes they do by analogy to contract verbs) nor with the inflectional endings that begin with a vowel.

3.   the word will undergo strong vowel gradation.

§27.6b   If the digamma is followed by a vowel:

a.   Ϝ will drop out.

b.   ε will not contract with the following connecting

---

[1]   ἡδύς (Latin: *sua(d)vis*); οὗ; οἱ; ἔθος; ἦθος (Latin: *suetus*).

vowel (although sometimes it does by analogy to contract verbs).

c.   the word will undergo weak vowel gradation.

*πλεϝ › πλέω (present) › πλεύσομαι (future)

*πνεϝ › πνέω (present) › ἔπνευσα (aorist)

*ῥεϝ › ῥέω (present) › ῥεύσομαι (future)

§27.7   **Nouns in α/ε/οϝ.**   3rd declension nouns ending in αϝ (n-3e[2]; νηϝος › ναῦς), εϝ (n-3e[3]), or οϝ (n-3e[4]; e.g., νοῦς) follow the same pattern as in §27.6. If the case ending begins with a consonant, the ϝ becomes an υ. If the case ending begins with a vowel, the ϝ drops out (Funk §933.1).

For example, the stem of βασιλεύς is *βασιληϝ. Since the nominative singular ending is σ, it forms βασιλεύς. The genitive singular ending is ος. This forms βασιλέως in which the digamma drops out altogether, and the ο is lengthened in compensation.

§27.8   Sometimes the ϝ will reappear in other forms (Funk §933.3).

*πνεϝ › πνέω › ἔπνευσα (v-1a[7])

*ρεϝ › ῥέω › ῥεύσω (v-1a[7])

*κλαϝι › κλαίω › κλαύσω (v-2c)

Accents   (§28)

§28.1   **Introduction.**   Following are the basic rules of accents (§28). Examples that show why knowing accents can help in parsing are given in §29.

The following rules are based on those given by LaSor (§16-§17), clarified by Wallace, and cross-referenced to Carson, *Greek Accents*, for further study. We refer to Carson's rules with his nomenclature (GR: general rules; VR: verb rules; NR: noun rules; IWR: indeclinable word rules; AR: adjective rules; EPR: enclitic and proclitic rules; PR: pronoun rules). For an excellent summary of the rules, with examples, see E.V.N. Goetchius, *The Language of the New Testament* (Charles Scribner's Sons, 1965) pp. 317-400 (also *MH* 51-60). Rules pertaining to μι verbs are given throughout our discussion.

The basic noun rules (§28.12) tell us what accent may or may not fall on what syllable. They do not necessarily tell us what syllable must be accented. The basic verb rule (§28.15) is more helpful at showing which syllable should be accented.

§28.2 **Three accents**. There are three accents, the acute (´), grave (`), and circumflex (ˆ).

§28.3 **Stress**. Originally an accent indicated a change in pitch, either a higher pitch (´), lower pitch (`), or a rise and fall in pitch (ˆ; cf. Smyth §151). At some time they came to indicate which syllable received the stress in pronunciation.

> **§28.3a** The grave was originally a drop in pitch. Smyth says, "The acute marks syllables pronounced in a raised tone. The grave is a low-pitched tone as contrasted with the acute. The circumflex combines acute and grave" (§150). The question then becomes: Is the grave low-pitched relative to the normal speaking tone, or merely lower than the acute, which could place it at normal speaking tone?

> **§28.3b** Carson argues that the grave indicated no change in pitch (i.e., the absence of an acute or circumflex) and therefore, theoretically, could be placed on any unaccented syllable. Eventually it was dropped except in one special situation (see §28.10). Accordingly, Carson argues that the grave was pronounced lower in relation to the acute, i.e., at normal speaking tone. For a short background on the rules see Carson, *Accents*, pp. 13-18.

§28.4 **Placement**. Every word has one and only one accent that is placed over a vowel, not a consonant (except see §28.24d).

> **§28.4a** Accents can only stand on one of the last three syllables in a word (θάνατος, ἀγάπη, ἀδελφός).

> **§28.4b** If the word begins with a capital single vowel, the breathing and accent are placed before the vowel (Ἕλλην).

> **§28.4c** Accents on a diphthong are over the second vowel (Αἴγυπτος) unless the word is all capital letters (ΆΙΡΩ).

> **§28.4d** The acute and grave are placed after the breathing (ἄδικος); the circumflex is placed over the breathing (αἷμα).

> **§28.4e** Enclitics (§28.23-24) and proclitics (§28.25) create exceptions to this rule (δύναταί τι).

§28.5 **Long and short vowels**. ε and ο are always short, η and ω are always long, and α, ι, and υ can be either short or long. While it may be tempting to think of long and short as descriptive of the sound of the vowel, it is best to see them merely as categories (see Carson, *Accents*, 13-14).

§28.5a   Diphthongs are normally considered long for accent purposes (but see §28.17a).

§28.5b   Diphthongs with iota subscripts are always considered long. While α can be long or short, ᾳ is always long, as are ῃ and ῳ.

§28.5c   Smyth marks the vowels in his paradigms as to whether they are long or short.

§28.6   **Long and short syllables.**   A syllable is considered long for the purpose of accent if the vowel or diphthong in the syllable is long.

§28.6a   When the diphthongs αι and οι occur at the end of a word (with no consonant after them), they are considered short for accent purposes (ἄν-θρω-ποι), except in the optative where they are considered long.

λῦσαι   first aorist active infinitive, or
          second singular first aorist middle imperative
λύσαι   first aorist active optative.

§28.6b   A syllable with a short vowel that is followed by two consonants is actually long (Smyth §144), but for accent purposes it is viewed as short.

§28.6c   If a short vowel is followed by a stop and a liquid, then the syllable may be viewed as short (Smyth §145).

§28.6d   In some third declension noun classes, the endings εως and εων are viewed as short (πό-λε-ως).

§28.7   **Terminology.**   In numbering syllables (e.g., "first") in discussions about accents, we start at the right end of the word and work to the left.

	antepenult	penult	ultima
acute	proparoxytone θέ-λη-σις	paroxytone ἀν-θρώ-που	oxytone θε-ός θε-ὸς
circumflex		properispomenon ζῶν-τα	perispomenon πα-θεῖν

§28.7a   The ultima is the last syllable in a word (ός in θε-ός).

§28.7b   The penult is the second from the last syllable in a word (θρώ in ἀν-θρώ-που). It is also called the "penultima."

§28.7c   The antepenult is the third from the last syllable in a word (θέ in θέλη-σις). It is also called the "antepenultima."

§28.7d   An "oxytone" is a word that has an acute on the ultima (θεός).

A word that has a grave on the ultima is also classified as an oxytone (θεὸς). This is because accents are discussed for a word in isolation, as if there were no following words. If you refer to a word that in the text has a grave, you change the grave to an acute in your discussion.

§28.7e   A "paroxytone" is a word that has an acute on the penult (ἀνθρώπου).

§28.7f   A "proparoxytone" is a word that has an acute on the antepenult (θέλησις).

§28.7g   A "perispomenon" is a word that has a circumflex on the ultima (παθεῖν).

§28.7h   A "preperispomenon" is a word that has a circumflex on the penult (ζῶντα).

§28.7i   These terms originally described the accented syllable, but now are used to describe the entire word.

§28.7j   A word that is not accented on the ultima is called a "barytone."

§28.8   **Eight basic rules.** Following is a summary of the basics. References are given to the following discussions of the specifics. The "Notes" draw out implications from the rules; they do not add to it.

1.	*The acute can stand on any of the last three syllables, the circumflex on either of the last two (only if they are long), and the grave on the last syllable.*
	Note A: a long ultima prevents the antepenult from being accented.
	Note B: a circumflex can stand only on a long vowel or diphthong.
	Note C: the ultima can have an acute or grave and, if it is long, a circumflex.

2.	If the ultima is long and the penult is accented, it must use the acute (αἴρω).
	Note D: this does not require the penult to be accented. It says that *if* the penult is accented and the ultima is long, then it will use the acute (cf. ἀκοή).
3.	If the ultima is short and the long penult is accented, it must use the circumflex (αἷμα).
	Note E: this does not require the penult to be accented.
	Note F: if both the ultima and penult are short and the penult is accented, it must use an acute since a circumflex cannot stand on a short vowel (λόγος).
4.	If the ultima has an acute and is followed directly by another word (except an enclitic), the acute becomes a grave (πρὸς τὸν θεόν; §28.10).
5.	Nouns tend to have a persistent accent (§28.12).
6.	Verbs tend to have a recessive accent (§28.5).
7.	Enclitics are viewed as being part of the preceding word (§28.23-24).
8.	Proclitics have no accent and are pronounced with the following word (§28.25).

Position of accent	Long ultima	Short ultima
Ultima	´ ` ˆ	´ `
Short penult	´	´
Long penult	´	ˆ
Antepenult	none	´

§28.8a   Except for rule §6, these rules do not tell us what syllable must be accented. They only tell us what accents are eligible for which syllables.

§28.8b   John 9:40-41 illustrates all the different breathings, accents, and punctuation, and includes examples of proclitics and enclitics.

Ἤκουσαν ἐκ τῶν Φαρισαίων ταῦτα οἱ μετ' αὐτοῦ ὄντες καὶ εἶπον αὐτῷ, Μὴ καὶ ἡμεῖς τυφλοί ἐσμεν; εἶπεν αὐτοῖς ὁ Ἰησοῦς, Εἰ τυφλοὶ ἦτε, οὐκ ἂν εἴχετε ἁμαρτίαν· νῦν δὲ λέγετε ὅτι Βλέπομεν, ἡ ἁμαρτία ὑμῶν μένει.

§28.9   **Acute.** An acute accent (´) can be placed on any of the last three syllables.

ἐ-γώ   λό-γος   ἄν-θρω-πος

§28.10   **Grave.** A grave accent (`) can stand only on the last syllable (i.e., the ultima).

Ἀρχὴ τοῦ εὐαγγελίου

> **§28.10a**   A grave occurs only when the rules call for an acute on the ultima (i.e., an oxytone), but the word is immediately followed by another accented word (i.e., not a punctuation mark or an enclitic). In this case the acute becomes a grave (cf. §28.24a).
>
> **§28.10b**   If the word is followed by punctuation, major or minor, the acute remains (πρὸς τὸν θεόν).
>
> **§28.10c**   If the word is followed by an enclitic (§28.24a), the acute remains (ἡ σάρξ μου).
>
> **§28.10d**   The acute accent on the interrogative particle (τίς) is never changed to a grave (τίς δὲ ἐξ ὑμῶν).
>
> **§28.10e**   Sometimes a grave is placed on the ultima of the indefinite pronoun (e.g., τινὸς), which is an enclitic.

§28.11   **Circumflex.** A circumflex accent (ˆ) can stand on the last two syllables (ultima or penult).

Ἀρχὴ τοῦ εὐαγγελίου

φωνὴ βοῶντος ἐν τῇ ἐρήμῳ

> **§28.11a**   A circumflex can stand only on a long syllable.

§28.12   **Nouns.** The general rule for nouns is that the accent is **persistent**. This means that the accent tries to stay on the same syllable as is accented in the nominative singular form (NR.1).

> **§28.12a**   It can never go further "back" from the ultima than it is in the nominative singular. For example, if the nominative singular has an accent on the penult, the accent will never move back to the antepenult. (n-3e[5b] nouns appear to be an exception; see there.)
>
> **§28.12b**   Accents on the nominative singular forms of nouns and adjectives must be memorized. The rules will not tell you which syllable is accented.

§28.12c   If the ultima shifts in length, you will often see a change in accent (ἄνθρωπος ‣ ἀνθρώπου).

§28.12d   Most of the following rules help you decide whether an α is long or short. Many of the rules are drawn from Carson and Goetchius.

§28.12e   **First declension**

1.   The final α in first declension feminine nouns ending in εα, ια, or ρα is long.

2.   In the genitive and dative singular, an α in the ultima of a feminine noun is long (ὥρας, ὥρᾳ; NR.8).

3.   The genitive plural must have a circumflex on the ultima, regardless of which syllable is accented in the nominative singular (ὡρῶν ; NR.5). (ων is actually a contraction of εων.) But cf. §28.13a.

     However, feminine adjectives and participles in ος accent as if they were masculine and neuter (cf. Smyth §209).

4.   In the accusative plural, an α in the ultima is long (ὥρας; NR.6).

     Goetchius states the rule that the α in the ending -ας is always long (§394.2c).

5.   "In first declension nouns ending in α or ας, whether the α in the ultima is long or short in the nominative singular, it is the same in the vocative and the accusative singular" (NR.7; cf. Goetchius §394.2a).

6.   "The final α in the vocative of first declension masculine nouns is considered short, unless there is a long -ας ultima in the nominative singular, in which instance it is long" (NR.9).

§28.12f   **First and second declension**

1.   First and second declension words that have an acute on the ultima in the nominative singular (i.e., oxytone; e.g., ἀγαθή) will have a circumflex on the ultima in the genitive (ἀγαθῆς) and dative (ἀγαθῇ), both singular and plural. Elsewhere they will have an acute (NR.2).

     Machen gives the rule a little differently: if the ultima is accented, it will have a circumflex in the genitive and dative (singular and plural) and an acute elsewhere (§40).

2. If the ultima of the nominative singular form has a circumflex, all other singular forms will also have the circumflex on the ultima (Μανασσῆς, Μανασσῆ; NR. 3).

3. The α in the ultima of the nominative or accusative plural of neuter nouns is short (δῶρα; NR.4).

§28.12g **Third declension**

1. The normal noun rules apply to third declension nouns: the accent is persistent. But realize that in nouns that have an additional syllable in the genitive (e.g., ἀστήρ, ἀστέρος), "same" is computed from the left side of the word and not the right as we normally do. Therefore, ἀστήρ and ἀστέρος are accented on the "same" syllable. Cf. NR.11.

2. Third declension monosyllables (i.e., words with only one syllable) in the genitive and dative (singular and plural) accent the ultima with an acute (i.e., are oxytone). The genitive plural will have a circumflex on the ultima (σάρξ, σαρκός, σαρκῶν). γυνή follows this rule even though it is disyllabic. πᾶς and a few others are exceptions.

3. "Third declension nouns whose stems end in -αντ, and whose dative plural therefore has a penult which could be long or short, will always reckon that syllable long if it has an accent" (NR.12).

4. "Third declension neuter nouns of the second (-ες) type adhere, in all inflections except the nominative/accusative singular, to VR.2" (NR.13), which are the rules governing contractions (§28.21).

5. Nouns like πόλις, πόλεως allow the antepenult to be accented in the genitive (singular and plural), even though the ultima is long (NR.14).

6. The α in the ultima is short in the following situations:

   • Accusative singular and plural, masculine and feminine.

   • Nominative and accusative plural neuter (NR.4).

§28.13 **Adjectives.** For the most part, adjectives are accented as nouns.

§28.13a In adjectives and participles that follow the 3-1-3 pattern (e.g., πᾶς, πᾶσα, πᾶν), the genitive plural uses a circumflex on the ultima (πασῶν, not πάσων), i.e., they follow the noun rules (§28.12e-3) and not the adjective (AR.5).

§28.13b   First and second declension adjectives ending in εα, ια, or ρα have a long α in the singular forms (AR.2).

§28.13c   "Third declension adjectives adopt accent patterns like those laid down for nouns in NR.1, NR.4, and NR.10" (AR.3).

§28.13d   "Third declension adjectives of the second (-ες) type adhere, in all inflections except the nominative masculine/feminine singular, to VR.2" (AR.4).

§28.13e   "Verbal adjectives in τός are oxytone; those in τερος are paroxytone" (LaSor §17.76, Smyth §425c).

§28.13f   Contract adjectives always have a circumflex on their ultima (διπλοῦς).

§28.14   **Pronouns.**   For the most part, pronouns are accented as adjectives (PR.1).

§28.14a   The interrogative pronoun τίς is always accented with an acute on the first syllable (PR.2).

§28.15   **Verbs.**   The general rule for finite verbs is that the accent is **recessive**. This means the accent moves as close to the antepenult as the rules allow (VR.1). Because this rule is for finite verbal forms, it does not necessarily apply to participles, as we will see below. This rule can be regularly violated by certain forms (below).

§28.15a   Liquid futures, active and middle, are accented like ε contract verbs in the present.

§28.15b   The α in the tense formatives σα and κα is short (ἔλυσα, λέλυκα; VR. 5).

§28.15c   In the present active and second aorist active subjunctive of μι verbs, there is a circumflex on the long vowel (VR. 16.1).

§28.16   **Subjunctive.**   Verbs in the subjunctive are normally recessive.

§28.16a   In the thematic conjugation the singular forms of contract verbs could have an acute, but rather they have circumflex.

§28.16b   The aorist passive is not recessive. It always uses a circumflex on the contracted syllable (λυθῶ, λυθῶμεν).

§28.17   **Optative.**   Verbs in the optative are recessive.

§28.17a   Final αι and οι are considered long πλεονάσαι; (cf. §27.5a).

§28.18   **Imperative**. Imperatives are generally recessive (e.g., λυέτωσαν).

§28.18a   Second aorist imperatives generally have a recessive accent. However, the second singular middle uses a circumflex on the ultima (i.e., is perispomenon, λαβοῦ; VR. 10.

There are irregular accents on verbs corresponding to λέγω (including εἶπον) and ἔρχομαι. They are oxytone (VR.7). Compound forms are recessive.

εἰπέ, εἰπόν, ἐλθέ, ἰδέ, λαβέ

Monosyllabic second aorist middle imperatives in -οῦ from μι verbs, when compounded with monosyllabic prepositions, retain the circumflex (προδοῦ). If it is a disyllabic preposition, the accent becomes recessive (ἀπόδου).

§28.18b   ἰδού is properly an aorist imperative and should therefore be accented ἰδοῦ. But in Koine Greek it is viewed as an interjection and is oxytone (Carson, p. 78).

§28.19   **Infinitives**. Infinitives are generally recessive in the present (λύεσθαι; VR.4) and future (λύσειν).

§28.19a   The present active infinitive is accented with an acute on the penult (λύειν; VR. 16.2).

§28.19b   The aorist infinitive is generally accented with an acute on the penult (ἐτοιμάσαι), except in the following two situations.

§28.19c   The first aorist middle infinitive is recessive (γένεσθαι; VR.10).

§28.19d   The second aorist active infinitive is accented with a circumflex on the ultima (εἰπεῖν; VR. 8).

§28.19e   The perfect infinitive is accented with an acute on the penult (λελυκέναι; VR. 11).

§28.19f   The aorist passive infinitive is accented with a circumflex on the penult (λυθῆναι; VR. 12).

§28.19g   εἶναι is not enclitic.

§28.20   **Participle**. Participles are accented as adjectives and not as verbs.

§28.20a   The following participles have a recessive accent (AR.8).

      1.   Present middle/passive (λυόμενος).

      2.   Aorist middle (λυσάμενος, γενόμενος).

      3.   Present of δύναμαι (δυνάμενος).

§28.20b   The nominative masculine/neuter singular participle ending in any consonant except ς in the nominative singular is oxytone (λιπών, λιπόν).

§28.20c   The genitive plural feminine follows noun rules, not adjective. This means the genitive plural will always have a circumflex over the ultima.

§28.20d   Second aorist active participles are accented on the first syllable of the inflected ending (εἰπών, εἰπόντες, cf. the present forms λέγων, λέγοντες).

             Carson states the rule another way. Second aorist active participles are accented like the present participle of εἰμί (AR.7).

§28.20e   The aorist passive in the nominative singular is not recessive.

§28.20f   Perfect active participle has an acute on the first syllable of the inflected ending (like second aorist active participle and imperatives): λελυκώς, εἰπέ, εἰπών.

§28.20g   Perfect middle/passive participle is always accented on the μέν (the penult). This becomes a significant parsing clue if the ultima is short, since normally the accent would move to the antepenult.

§28.20h   In the present active and second aorist participle of athematic verbs, the accent is not recessive (διδούς; VR. 16.3). ἵστημι has a first and second aorist form, and neither is recessive.

§28.21   **Contraction.** To understand the accent on a contracted form, you need to look at it in its uncontracted form (e.g., ἀγαπᾶτε ‹ ἀγα-πά-ε-τε).

If either syllable that undergoes contraction has the accent in its uncontracted form, then the contracted syllable must receive the accent. This is why, for example, the present tense contract verbs are always accented on the contracted syllable.

If either syllable did not have the accent before contraction, the word accents according to the usual rules (i.e., the contracted syllable will not have the accent).

§28.21a   If the accent is on the antepenult, it will have the acute (as usual).

§28.21b If the accent is on the penult, the normal rules apply (VR.2.1).

1. If the ultima is short, a contracted penult will have a circumflex (φιλέουσι ‣ φιλοῦσι).

2. If the ultima is long, a contracted penult will have an acute (φιλεόντων ‣ φιλούντων).

§28.21c If the accent is on the ultima, it will take a circumflex (λαβεῖν).

However, if the ultima is contracted and the verb originally was oxytone (i.e., had an acute on the ultima), the contracted form will take the acute (e.g., ὑψωθείς).

§28.21d Carson gives the following two variations on his normal rules (pp. 24f., cf. Goetchius §397.2-3).

"If the first of the two contracting syllables, before contraction, has the acute, then the acute combines with the unwritten grave accent on the other contracting syllable to form the circumflex."[1]

"If the second of two contracting syllables, before contraction, has the acute accent, then the contracted syllable also has the acute, since clearly ` ´ will not combine to generate ´ ` = ˆ."

§28.21e "In -αω contract verbs, if the contracted syllable centers on an α or an ą, that syllable is long" (VR.14).

§28.21f In -οω verbs, final αι/οι are long because they are the result of contraction (φανεροῖ; VR.15).

§28.22 **Verbal compounds.** Carson states the rules as follows: "In all verbs compounded with a preposition, the accent of the verb cannot fall farther back than one syllable before the verb proper" (VR.17), thus allowing for ἐπίθες.

§28.22a When a verbal forms "forgets" that it was originally compound, this rule can be ignored.

§28.23 **Enclitics.** Enclitics are monosyllables or disyllables that have no accent of their own and are viewed as if they were a part of the preceding word. Enclitics "lean upon" (ἐγκλίνω) the preceding word.

As far as accents are concerned, think of the two words as being one word and apply the normal rules. This will handle most situations (cf. Machen §93).

---

[1] It is possible to think of the grave as being placed on every unaccented syllable (cf. §27.3b).

The following are enclitics.

Personal pronoun: μου, μοι, με, σου, σοι, σε

Indefinite pronoun: τις, τι (in all inflected forms)

Particles: γε, τε, τοι, περ

Indefinite adverbs: που, ποτε, πω, πως

Pres ind. of εἰμι: except second singular (εἶ)

Pres ind. of φημι: except second singular (φῇς)

§28.23a   Sometimes the disyllabic forms of enclitics are accented (τινός).

1. When the preceding word has an acute on the penult (ὥρα ἐστίν).

2. When the enclitic is emphasized (e.g., when the author is making a contrast).

3. When the enclitic begins a clause.

§28.23b   Interrogative pronouns are never enclitic; the indefinite pronoun is enclitic.

§28.24   Because an enclitic is viewed as part of the preceding word, it affects the accent rules. The following rules and examples come mostly from LaSor (§17.822-825; cf. Carson, *Accents*, 47-52; Smyth §181-187).

§28.24a   An oxytone preceding an enclitic does not change its acute to a grave (ἡ σάρξ μου; EPR.1; cf. §27.10a).

§28.24b   "If the word preceding an enclitic has a circumflex accent on the ultima, then both monosyllabic and disyllabic enclitics normally lose their accent" (EPR.4).

§28.24c   "If the word preceding an enclitic has an acute on the penult, then:

• a disyllabic enclitic retains its accent

• a monosyllabic enclitic loses its accent" (EPR.3, cf. Goetchius §400.4b).

§28.24d   The enclitic adds an additional accent on the ultima of the preceding word under either of the following conditions (EPR.2).

1. The preceding word has a circumflex on the penult (i.e., properispomenon; ἡ γλῶσσά μου).

2. The preceding word has an acute on the antepenult (i.e., proparoxytone; τοῦ πνεύματός μου).

§28.24e   When you have a series of enclitics, each enclitic passes its accent to the previous enclitic, and the last enclitic is unaccented (εἴ τίς τί σοί φησιν, citing Smyth §185).

"If the word before an enclitic is itself a proclitic (except οὐ, οὐκ, οὐχ) or an enclitic, it has an acute accent on the ultima" (EPR.5; cf. Machen §92). μάρτυς γάρ μού ἐστιν ὁ θεός (Rom 1:9).

§28.24f   Sometimes enclitics are written as if they actually were part of the preceding word (ᾧτινι, οἵδε, μήτε). In that case, the compound word is usually accented as if the enclitic were still a separate word (EPR.9).

§28.24g   Enclitics can be accented under the following circumstances (EPR.6).

1. There is emphasis on the enclitic.

2. The enclitic is the first word in the clause.

3. The enclitic is preceded by the negation οὐ (οὐκ, οὐχ).

4. The disyllabic enclitic is followed by a word that has an acute on the penult.

§28.24h   ἐστί changes to ἔστι in the following situations (cf. EPR.8).

1. When it expresses existence (πιστεῦσαι ... ὅτι ἔστιν; Heb 11:6).

2. When it follows certain particles (οὐ, οὐκ, μή, εἰ, ὡς, καί, ἀλλά, τοῦτο (e.g., τοῦτ᾽ ἔστιν; Smyth §187).

3. When it is the first word in the clause.

ἔστιν γὰρ ὥρα τρίτη τῆς ἡμέρας (Acts 2:15).

§28.25   **Proclitics.** Proclitics are monosyllables that have no accent of their own. They "lean forward" (προκλίνω) to the following word. Proclitics do not affect accents as do enclitics. The following are proclitics.

Article	ὁ, ἡ, οἱ, αἱ (masculine and feminine definite article, nominative singular and plural)
Prepositions	εἰς, ἐξ (ἐκ), ἐν
Conjunctions	εἰ, ὡς
Negation	οὐ, οὐκ, οὐχ

§28.25a   Proclitics can take an accent under certain circumstances.

• If the following word is an enclitic (§28.13; EPR.5; ἕν τε, ὅ τε)

• If the proclitic (especially the negation) stands at the end of a clause (EPR.7; τὸ ναὶ ναὶ καὶ τὸ οὒ οὔ; James 5:12).

§28.26   **Elision**.   Prepositions and conjunctions that have an acute on their ultima (i.e., oxytones) lose the accent when the final vowel elides (κατὰ ὑμῶν › καθ᾽ ὑμῶν; IWR.2).

§28.27   **Crasis**.   In the formation of a crasis, the first word loses its accent (καὶ ἐγώ › κἀγώ).

§28.28   **Indeclinable words**.   Indeclinable words follow normal accent rules, but which syllable is accented must be memorized (IWR.1).

ὥστε appears to violate the normal rules, except that it originally was two words–ὡς + the enclitic τε (cf. ὥσπερ, οὔτε).

For adverb rules see Carson, pp. 109f.

§28.29   The two most common places you will see changes in noun accents is when the ultima changes its length due to inflection and when an enclitic or proclitic is involved.

§28.30   **Inconsistences**.   While these are the basic rules, there are many irregularities as you might expect of a living and dynamic language.

Accents and Parsing   (§29)

§29.1   There are several places where noticing the accent (and breathings) will help you parse a word.

§29.2   Accents can help distinguish between otherwise identical forms. See Jay (pp. 278-9) for a few others.

1.	αἱ	article
	αἵ	relative pronoun
2.	ἀλλά	particle
	ἄλλα	neuter plural, nom. and acc. of ἄλλος
3.	ἄρα	particle meaning "therefore"
	ἀρα	inferential particle (Luke 18:8; Acts 8:30; Gal 2:17)
	ἀρά, ἡ	"curse" (Rom 3:14)
4.	αὐταί	from αὐτός
	αὗται	from οὗτος
5.	αὐτή	from αὐτός (form never occurs in the NT)
	αὕτη	from οὗτος

6. δώῃ   aorist subjunctive of δίδωμι
    δῴη   aorist optative of δίδωμι

7. εἰ   particle
    εἶ   present active indicative second sg. of εἰμί

8. εἰς   preposition
    εἷς   masculine adjective of εἷς, μία, ἕν

9. ἐν   preposition
    ἕν   neuter adjective of εἷς, μία, ἕν

10. ἔξω   adverb
    ἕξω   future of ἔχω

11. ἡ   article
    ἤ   particle
    ἥ, ᾗ,   relative pronoun
    ᾖ   present active subjunctive third sg. of εἰμί

12. ἥν   relative pronoun
    ἦν   imperfect third sg. of εἰμί
    ἤν   a contracted form of ἐάν

13. ἧς   relative pronoun
    ἦς   imperfect second sg. of εἰμί
    ᾖς   present active subjunctive second sg. of εἰμί

14. ὁ   article
    ὅ   relative pronoun

15. οἱ   article
    οἵ   relative pronoun

16. ὄν   present active participle neuter sg. of εἰμί
    ὅν   relative pronoun

17. οὐ   negation
    οὗ   relative pronoun

18. πότε   interrogative adverb meaning "when"
    ποτέ   enclitic particle meaning "once"

19. πού   enclitic particle meaning "somewhere"
    ποῦ   interrogative adverb meaning "where"

20. πῶς   interrogative particle meaning "how"
    πώς   enclitic particle meaning "in any way"

21. τίς   interrogative pronoun
    τις   indefinite pronoun

22. ὤ   interjection (also written ὦ)

   ὦ   present subjunctive first sg. of εἰμί[1]

   ᾧ   relative pronoun

   Ὦ   the letter omega

23. ὤν   present active participle of εἰμί

   ὦν   relative pronoun, genitive pl.

24. Liquid futures   e.g., κρινῶ is future; κρίνω is present

§29.3   Perfect middle/passive participles are always accented on the μέν participle morpheme. If the ultima is short, this is a valuable parsing guide.

§29.4   Second aorist (active and passive) participles always accent the first inflected syllable.

Verb Formation

Introduction   (§30)

Sections §31-39 discuss how the verb is formed, beginning with the left and working right. It deals with augmentation, reduplication, formation of the tense stem, tense formative, thematic vowel, personal endings, and movable ν. If your questions are about how the verbal root is altered to form the tense stem, this is discussed in the discussion on principal parts.

The lists we have compiled are quite exhaustive in terms of the vocabulary of the New Testament. All the words in the UBS (4th edition) text are included, along with many of the variants.

On the next page is an overview of the formation of verbs. When we list verbs as examples in §30-§36, we will not describe all the morphological changes that occur in the formation of the tense stem.

At the end (§96), we have listed partial paradigms of εἰμί, οἶδα, ἀφίημι, and γινώσκω.

---

[1]   These first two forms are identical and accent does not help.

Master Verb Chart

Tense	Aug/ Redup	Tense stem	Tense form.	Conn. vowel	Personal endings	1st sing paradigm
Present act		pres		o/ε	prim act	λύω
Present mid/pas		pres		o/ε	prim mid/pas	λύομαι
Imperfect act	ε	pres		o/ε	sec act	ἔλυον
Imperfect mid/pas	ε	pres		o/ε	sec mid/pas	ἐλυόμην
Future act		fut act	σ	o/ε	prim act	λύσω
Liquid fut act		fut act	εσ	o/ε	prim act	κρινῶ
Future mid		fut act	σ	o/ε	prim mid/pas	ἐλεύσομαι
1st future pas		aor pas	θησ	o/ε	prim mid/pas	λυθήσομαι
2nd future pas		aor pas	ησ	o/ε	prim mid/pas	ἀποσταλήσομαι
1st aorist act	ε	aor act	σα		sec act	ἔλυσα
Liquid aorist act	ε	aor act	α		sec act	ἔμεινα
2nd aorist act	ε	aor act		o/ε	sec act	ἔλαβον
1st aorist mid	ε	aor act	σα		sec mid/pas	ἐλυσάμην
2nd aorist mid	ε	aor act		o/ε	sec mid/pas	ἐγενόμην
1st aorist pas	ε	aor pas	θη		sec act	ἐλύθην
2nd aorist pas	ε	aor pas	η		sec act	ἐγράφην
1st perfect act	λε	perf act	κα		prim act	λέλυκα
2nd perfect act	λε	perf act	α		prim act	γέγονα
Perfect mid/pas	λε	perf pas			prim mid/pas	λέλυμαι
1st pluperf act	(ε)λε	perf act	κ	ει	sec act	ἐλελύκη
2nd pluperf act	(ε)λε	perf act	-	ει	sec act	ἐγεγόνη
pluperf mid/pas	(ε)λε	perf pas			sec pass	ἐλελύμην

For further general rules governing this chart and the verbal system, see *BBG*, pp. 345-348.

Augment and Vocalic Reduplication   (§31)

§31.1   **Introduction.** Since the rules for augmenting in the aorist and vocalic reduplication in the perfect are basically the same, both will be discussed together.

In *BBG* we use the term "vocalic reduplication" for what is sometimes called "augment" in the perfect tense. Although augmentation and vocalic reduplication have a similarity, in the perfect vocalic reduplication sometimes behaves differently from augmentation and has a different significance.

Augments appear in secondary tenses (imperfect, aorist, pluperfect), although they can be omitted in the pluperfect.

§31.2   **Syllabic Augment.** If the word begins with a consonant, the syllabic augment ε is added before the initial consonant. (It is called "syllabic" because it adds another syllable to the word.) In the pluperfect the augment, when it is used, appears before the reduplication (cf. *BDF* §66).

λύω ‣ ἔλυσα ‣ ἐλελύκειν

§31.2a   Sometimes there is an η (temporal augment; §31.3) where we would expect to find an ε (syllabic augment). This is usually because the word began with a consonant (σ and ϝ especially; see §31.5) that dropped out of use. See *BDF* §66.3; *MH* 188f. Smyth adds that η could be used as the syllabic augment (§433).

θέλω (*εθελ) augments to ἤθελον (v-1d[2c]). δύναμαι (v-6b) can augment with ε (ἐδύνατο) and η (ἠδύνατο) as does μέλλω (ἔμελλον; ἤμελλον; v-1d[2c]). See the discussions of their principal parts for further discussion.

§31.2b   **Initial ρ.** Verbs beginning with ρ sometimes double the ρ before the augment (cf. *BDF* §11.1, 68; *MH*, 101f., 193). Some of the older texts write a smooth breathing over the first ρ and a rough breathing over the second (e.g., ἔῤῥηξεν). We have included only those principal parts that occur in the New Testament.[1]

λέγω, -, -, -, -, ἐρρέθην[2]   v-1b(2)

ῥαντίζω, -, ἐρράντισα, -, -, -   v-2a(1)

ῥήγνυμι (ἐρρήσσετο), -, ἔρρηξα,[3] -, -, -   v-3c(2)

---

[1]   ἔρρανα is a first aorist occurring as a v.l. in Rev 19:13, from ῥαίνω (v-2d[4]).

[2]   Uses *ϝρε for its aorist passive stem.

[3]   The compound προσρήσσω forms its aorist with a single ρ (προσέρηξα).

ῥίπτω, -, ἔρριψα, -, -, -   v-4

ῥύομαι, -, ἐρρυσάμην, -, -, ἐρρύσθην   v-1a(4)

In the New Testament, ῥαπίζω always occurs with a single ρ. ῥιζόω, ῥιπίζω, ῥυπαίνω, and ῥώννυμι (and compounds) do not occur in an augmented form.

§31.2c   **Consonant cluster.** If the verb begins with a consonant cluster or double consonant, in the *perfect* the verb will undergo vocalic rather than consonantal reduplication (i.e., what most call "augment"; cf. §32.3; Funk §3430.2).

βδελύσσομαι	ἐβδέλυγμαι	v-2b
μνηστεύω	ἐμνήστευμαι	v-1a(6)
ξυράω	ἐξύρημαι	v-1d(1a)
στέλλω	ἔσταλκα	v-2d(1)
φθέγγομαι	ἐφθεγξάμην	v-1b(2)

This does not apply to verbs beginning with a consonant cluster composed of a stop and a liquid (cf. §32.3).[1]

κράζω	κέκραγα	v-2a(2)
θνῄσκω	τέθνηκα	v-5a
κάμνω	*κμη ‣ κέκμηκα	v-3a(1)
τέμνω	*τμη ‣ τέτμηκα	v-3a(1)

Exceptions to §31.2c:

κτάομαι	κέκτημαι	v-1d(1a)
μιμνῄσκομαι	*μνη ‣ μέμνημαι	v-5a
πίπτω	*πτω ‣ πέπτωκα	v-1b(3)

§31.2d   Sometimes words beginning with λ undergo vocalic reduplication in the perfect using ει instead of reduplication (Smyth §440a; LaSor 24.3144).

λαμβάνω	*λαβ ‣ εἴληφα	v-3a(2b)

§31.2e   Sometimes words beginning with βλ or γλ undergo vocalic reduplication in the perfect instead of consonantal reduplication (Smyth §440a; LaSor 24.3145). There are no examples in the New Testament.

βλαστάνω	ἐβλάστηκα[2]
γλύφω	ἔγλυφα

---

[1] If the verb begins with three consonants, and the last two are a stop and a liquid, then §31.2c does apply (στρωννύω ‣ ἔστρωμαι [v-3c(1)]; σφραγίζω ‣ ἐσφράγισμαι [v-2a(1)]).

[2] But usually βεβλάστηκα.

§31.2f   Words beginning with γν always undergo vocalic reduplication in the perfect instead of consonantal reduplicate (Smyth §440a; LaSor 24.3145).

γινώσκω   *γνο ‣ ἔγνωκα   v-5a
γνωρίζω   *γνωριδ ‣ ἐγνώρικα   v-2a(1)

§31.3   **Temporal Augment.** Verbs with an initial single vowel are augmented by lengthening that vowel (*BDF* §67).

α ‣ η   ἀγαπάω ‣ ἠγάπησα
ε ‣ η   ἐγείρω ‣ ἤγειρα
ο ‣ ω   ὀνομάζω ‣ ὠνόμασα
η ‣ η   ἡγέομαι ‣ ἡγήσατο
ι ‣ ι   ἰσχύω ‣ ἴσχυσα
υ ‣ υ   ὑστερέω ‣ ὑστέρησα
ω ‣ ω   ὠφελέω ‣ ὠφελήσεν

§31.3a   When the vowel is long, you will not see the augment
(e.g., ἡγήσατο).

§31.4   **Initial Diphthong.** Verbs with an initial diphthong lengthen the
first vowel according to the pattern in §31.3. If the second vowel of
the diphthong is an υ, it will remain. If the second vowel is an ι, it
will subscript (*MH* 191-192).

αυ ‣ ηυ   αὐξάνω ‣ ηὔξανεν
ευ ‣ ηυ   εὐλαβέομαι ‣ ηὐλαβήθην
αι ‣ ῃ   αἰτέω ‣ ᾐτήσατο
ει ‣ ῃ   There is no example in the New Testament.[1]
οι ‣ ῳ   οἰκοδομέω ‣ ᾠκοδόμησεν

§31.4a   Initial diphthongs often are not augmented. ου is never
augmented (because an initial ου at the beginning of a
word is never a pure diphthong; Smyth §437) and ευ
only rarely (εὑρίσκω ‣ εὕρισκον; cf. *BDF* 67.1).

ἤμην, from εἰμί, is from the stem *εσ and is therefore not
an exception to this rule.

§31.4b   Some words with an initial diphthong vary between
augmenting and not augmenting.[2]

οἰκοδομέω   οἰκοδομήθην ᾠκοδομήθην   v-1d(2a)

---

[1]   The only augmented form of a verb beginning in ει is εἴξαμεν (‣ εἴκω; §31.4a). The
stem of εἰμί is *εσ, and therefore its imperfect ἤμην is not an exception.

[2]   In Classical Greek, βούλομαι could do both (Smyth §430), but in the N.T. it always
augments.

§31.5   **Initial σ and ϝ.** There are words that originally began with a σ or
ϝ, but by the time of Koine Greek these initial consonants had
dropped out of use. However, the words can augment as if the σ or
ϝ were still there.[1]

The verb will look like it begins with a vowel (e.g., ἔχω), and therefore one would expect the temporal augment (e.g., ἦχω). But instead
the augment is syllabic (εἶχον, from the root *σεχ). What has happened is the initial letter, in this case σ, has dropped out (§25.5; §27.4)
and the ε of the syllabic augment contracts with the first stem vowel
that followed the σ or ϝ (unless the second vowel is long, in which
case they will not). ε + *σεχ ▸ εεχ ▸ εἶχον.

§31.5a   Initial σ

αἱρέω	*ἑ-ἑλ[2] ▸ εἶλον	v-1d(2a)
ἐάω	*σεϝα ▸ εἴασα	v-1d(1b)
ἐθίζω	*σϝεθιδ ▸ εἴθισα	v-2a(1)
ἑλκύω	*σελκυ ▸ εἵλκυσα	v-1a(4)
ἔχω	*σεχ ▸ εἶχον	v-1b(2)
ἵημι	*σε ▸ σισε ▸ ἱσε ▸ ἱε ▸ ἵημι ▸ ἦκα[3]	v-6a
συνέπομαι	συν + *σεπ ▸ συνειπόμην	cv-1d(3)

§31.5b   Initial ϝ

ἄγνυμι	*ϝαγ ▸ ἔαξα	v-3c(2)
ἁλίσκομαι	*ϝαλ ▸ ἑάλων	v-5b
ἀνοίγω	αν + *ϝοιγ ▸ ἀνέῳξα	cv-1b(2)
ἐργάζομαι	*ϝεργαδ ▸ εἰργασάμην	v-2a(1)
λέγω	*ϝεπ ▸ εἶπον	v-1b(2)
λέγω	ϝερ ▸ εἴρηκα / εἴρημαι	v-1b(2)
ὁράω	*ϝορα ▸ ἑώρακα[4]	v-1d(1a)
ὁράω	ϝιδ ▸ εἶδον	v-1d(1a)
ὠθέω	*ϝωθε ▸ ἔωσα	v-1b(4)
ὠνέομαι	*ϝωνε ▸ ἐωνήθην	v-1d(2a)

Cf. also ἀνδάνω, ἕζομαι, ἐλίττω, ἕπτομαι, ἕρπω, ἑστιάω
(Smyth §431).

---

[1]   Smyth §431; Funk §3371, §3430.4 (for similar effect in reduplication). Smyth comments that in Homer a syllabic augment before a vowel is "sure proof of initial ϝ"
(§431D).

[2]   Smyth (§431) lists it this way without specifying the initial consonant.

[3]   See Smyth §431.

[4]   Includes a double augment.

§31.5c   Sometimes the evidence of an initial Ϝ can be lost.

*Ϝοικε › ᾤκουν

*Ϝωθεω › ἐώθουν (Classical) and ὤθουν (Koine)

*Ϝωνε › ἐωνησάμην (Classical) and ὠνησάμην (Koine)

§31.5d   Sometimes augments may appear irregular, but there
are other factors. For example, αἴρω augments to ἦρα,
appearing to lose the ι. However, the root is *αρ and the
ι was added to form the present tense stem (v-2d[2]; cf.
§31.9).

§31.6   **Compound verbs.**   Compound verbs augment the verbal part of
the compound. This makes sense since the augment indicates past
time and the non-verbal element of the compound cannot express
time (*BDF* §67.2; *MH* 192).

ἐνεργέω › ἐνήργηκα

§31.6a   Some compounds are treated as if they are not compounds, and therefore the augment will affect the first
part of the word. This is especially true if the compound
is formed with a noun (and not a preposition, e.g.,
οἰκοδομέω from οἰκοδόμος) or with δυσ. This same phenomena is found with reduplication (§32.5a).

ἀπειλέω › ἠπείλησα (cv-1d[2a])

ψευδομαρτυρέω › ἐψευδομαρτύρησα (v-1d[2a])

§31.6b   Some compound verbs appear to receive two augments, one for each element of the compound (cf.
§31.8).

§31.6c   If a compound is formed with a preposition ending in a
vowel and a verb beginning with a consonant, the final
vowel of the preposition will be dropped and the verb
will receive the syllabic augment (apocope; §7.1). (This
is true for all prepositions except περί and πρό.)

§31.6d   This means that there is no contraction if the verbal part
of the compound begins with a vowel. The final vowel
of the preposition will already have dropped out and
the initial vowel of the verbal part of the compound will
receive the temporal augment. (As above, περί and πρό
do not elide; §6.5d,e).

§31.6e   When a preposition has undergone some morphological change in the formation of a compound verb such as
elision or assimilation, when the augment is added the

morphological change on the preposition is often reversed.

A good example is a compound using ἐκ. The preposition is properly ἐξ (i.e., "eks"). When the following word begins with a consonant, the σ in the ξ becomes interconsonantal and drops out (e.g., ἐκβάλλω; §27.5). But when the verbal part of the compound is augmented, the σ is no longer interconsonantal and therefore remains ἐξ (e.g., ἐξέβαλον).

Two other good examples are compounds formed with ἐν and συν. The final ν is liable to all sorts of changes depending upon the initial consonant of the verbal element of the compound (§24). But when the verb is augmented, the ν returns to ν (e.g., συλλέγω ‣ συνέλεξα).

§31.7   **Lack of augment.** In certain circumstances it is not unusual to find a word in an augmented tense without an augment (*MH* 190f.).

     §31.7a   Words beginning with a diphthong frequently do not augment. Verbs with initial ει rarely augment and verbs with ου never augment; cf. §31.4.

     §31.7b   Compound verbs can lose the augment (cf. list of verbs in *BDF* §67.2; §69).

         δια + ἑρμήνευω ‣ διερμήνευσα

     §31.7c   The pluperfect frequently has no augment (especially in compound verbs; cf. *BDF* §66.1, Smyth §451). See the list of all pluperfects in the New Testament at §45.6c, §46.7.

     §31.7d   Remember that the vowels ι and υ can be either long or short. This means that ὑστέρηκα, the perfect of ὑστερέω, has vocalic reduplication; short υ has been lengthened to long υ.

§31.8   **Double augment.** Some verbs appear to receive a double augments (see §32.6b; Smyth §451; *MH* 189; Robertson, 367-368).

     ἀντικαθίστημι ‣ ἀντεκατέστητε (cv-6a)

     ἀποκαθίστημι ‣ ἀπεκατέστη (cv-6a)

     ἀνοίγω (ἀνέῳγα; cv-1b[2]) and ὁράω (ἑώρων; v-1d[1a]) may have a double augment in the perfect. See v-1d(1a).

§31.9   **Irregularities.** Sometimes what appears to be an irregular augment is really the result of the formation of the present tense stem from the verbal root.

For example, αἴρω augments to ἦρα, making it appear that the ι has been lost. Actually, the verbal root is *αρ and thus the formation of the aorist is perfectly regular. The ι was added after the ρ in the formation of the present tense stem, and the ρ and ι switched places (i.e., metathesis, §7.6).

*αρ + ι › αριω › αἴρω

Consonantal Reduplication   (§32)

§32.1 **Introduction.**   Consonantal reduplication is primarily a characteristic of the perfect tense (including the pluperfect and future perfect tenses). Yet it is found in the present (v-5a, v-6) and even twice in the aorist (§44.5d). We use the term "vocalic reduplication" to describe what is sometimes called "augment" in the perfect tense; §31.1.

In the present, v-6a verbs[1] reduplicate the initial consonant of their verbal root to form their present tense stem. A verb that is formed thus can also reduplicate in the perfect, but the vowel in between the reduplicated consonants will be different: ι in the present (e.g., δίδωμι); ε in the perfect (e.g., δέδωκα).

§32.2 **Single consonant.**   If a word begins with a single consonant, that consonant is reduplicated and separated from the original with a vowel. If it is the perfect (including the pluperfect and future perfect), the vowel is ε; if present it is an ι.

*λυ › λέλυκα

*δο › δίδωμι

> **§32.2a** If the reduplicated consonant is an aspirate, it will deaspirate (§15.5).
>
> φ › φεφ › πεφ   φανερόω › πεφανέρωμαι
>
> χ › χεχ › κεχ   χαρίζομαι › κεχάρισμαι
>
> θ › θεθ › τεθ   θεραπεύω › τεθεράπευμαι

§32.3 **Consonant cluster in the perfect.**   If a verb begins with a consonant cluster composed of a stop + λ or ρ, the stop is usually reduplicated and the two stops are separated with an ε.

γράφω › γέγραφα

κλίνω › κέκλικα

---

[1] Also a few other isolated examples such as some v-5a verbs, γίνομαι, πίπτω, τίκτω.

§32.3a Words beginning with any other cluster will not reduplicate to form the perfect but will have a vocalic reduplication (e.g., στρέφω ‣ ἔστραμμαι; §31.2c).

§32.4 **Consonant cluster in the present.** If the word begins with a cluster and reduplicates to form the present tense stem, the first consonant of the cluster will reduplicate and be separated with an ι.

We have listed the aorist below to make the reduplication in the present clear. We have listed all verbs that reduplicate their verbal root in the formation of the present tense stem except for μι verbs, which reduplicate as a rule. Most are v-5 verbs (which add [ι]σκ in the formation of the present tense stem).

*βρω	βιβρω ‣ βιβρώσκω ‣ ἐβρώθην	v-5a
*γεν	γεν ‣ γν ‣ γιγν ‣ γιν ‣ γίνομαι	v-1c(2)
*γνο	γιγνο ‣ γιγνώσκω ‣ γινώσκω ‣ ἔγνων	v-5a
*μνη	μιμνη ‣ μιμνήσκομαι ‣ ἔμνησα	v-5a
*πρα	πιπρα + σκω ‣ πιπράσκω ‣ ἐπράθην	v-5a
*πετ	*πετ ‣ πτ ‣ πιπτ ‣ πίπτω ‣ ἔπεσον	v-1b(3)

In Classical Greek cf. also διδράσκω (*δρα ‣ ἔδραν) and τιτρώσκω (*τρω ‣ ἔτρωσα).

§32.5 **Compound verbs.** Compound verbs normally reduplicate the verbal element of the compound.

ἐκβάλλω ἐκ + *βαλ ‣ ἐκβέβληκα

ἐγγράφω ἐν + γράφω ‣ ἐγγέγραφα

§32.5a Some compounds became viewed as simple verbs and therefore reduplicate the beginning of the first element. This can also apply to compounds formed with nouns (e.g., ἀγαθοποιέω ‣ ἠγαθοποίησα), adverbs, and certain prefixes (e.g., δυσ). This same phenomena is seen in augmentation (§31.6a; *BDF* §69.1).

§32.6 **Attic reduplication.** This is a special form of reduplication that applies only to certain words in the perfect.[1] If one of these verbs began with α, ε, or ο followed by a single consonant, the vowel and consonant were both reduplicated, and the original stem vowel was then lengthened (α ‣ η). In other words, the word underwent both a reduplication and a lengthening. Cf. Smyth §446, Funk §344.[2]

---

[1] This name was given by the Greek grammarians, but "Attic" reduplication is found in Homer and other dialects (Smyth §446a). Cf. §44.5d for reduplication in the aorist.

[2] Cf. also ἀγείρω, ὀρύττω.

ἀκούω	*ακου ‣ ακακου ‣ ἀκήκοα	v-1a(8)
ἐγείρω	*εγερ ‣ εγεγερμαι ‣ ἐγήγερμαι	v-2d(3)
ἐλαύνω	*ελα ‣ ελελακα ‣ ἐλήλακα	v-3c(2)
ἐλέγχω	*ελεγ ‣ ελελεγ ‣ ἐλήλεγμαι	v-1b(2)
ἔρχομαι	*ελευθ ‣ ελελυθα ‣ ἐλήλυθα	v-1b(2)
ὄλλυμι	*ολ ‣ ολολα ‣ ὀλῶλα	v-3c(2)
ὄμνυμι	*ομ ‣ ομομνυ ‣ ὀμώμοκα	v-3c(2)
φέρω	*ενεκ ‣ ενενοχ ‣ ἐνήνοχα	v-1c(1)

§32.7 **Initial σ / Ϝ.** If a verb originally began with σ or Ϝ, the reduplicated σ or Ϝ may dissimilate to a rough breathing (§27.6b; cf. §31.5).

| *στα | σιστημι ‣ ἵστημι | v-6a |
| *Ϝορα | ϜεϜωρακα ‣ ἐϜωρακα ‣ ἑώρακα | v-1d(1a) |

§32.8 **Exceptions.** Following are the exceptions to the rules as stated above that occur in the New Testament.

βδελύσσομαι	ἐβδελυγμένος	v-2b
θνῄσκω	τέθνηκα	v-5a
κάμνω	κέκμηκα	v-3a(1)
κτάομαι	κέκτημαι	v-1d(1a)
μνηστεύω	μεμνηστευμένη (ἐμνηστευμένη)	v-1a(6)
σπείρω	‣ ἔσπαρμαι	v-2d[3]
σῴζω	*σωδ ‣ σέσωκα	v-2a[1]
τέμνω	*τμη ‣ τέτμηκα ‣ τετμημένος	v-3a[1]

Formation of the Tense Stem   (§33)

§33.1 Some texts divide verbs based on whether the verb is thematic uncontracted, contracted, or athematic. Others (Funk, LaSor, Smyth) divide based on how the verbal root is modified to form the present tense stem, and secondly by whether they are thematic on athematic.

We follow the latter with a few modifications. The terminology (e.g., v-1a) is our own.

§33.2 Because the lexical form uses the present tense of the verb, it is often assumed that the present tense is the base form of the verb and all other tenses are formed from it. This is wrong. The present tense is, in fact, the most "irregular" of all the tenses and the second aorist is one of the most "regular" (cf. *BBG* §20.1-20.5).

§33.3 The **verbal root** of a verb is the base form of the verb.[1] (It is indicated in *MBG* with an *.) The root can often be seen in cognate words (e.g., *κηρυγ › κηρύσσω › κήρυγμα). Sometimes the root is hypothetical in that it never is seen in any word.[2]

The **tense stem** is the form the verbal root takes in a specific tense. In some cases the present tense stem and the verbal root will be identical (e.g., *λυ › λύω; *αγαπα › ἀγαπάω). In other situations the verbal root has been modified in the formation of the present tense stem (e.g., *βαλ › βάλλω › ἔβαλον).

Therefore, if you really want to understand how a verb's principal parts are formed, you must start with the verbal root.

Grammars are not always clear whether they view the augment/reduplication, tense formative, and connecting vowel as part of the tense stem or not. In other words, is the aorist verbal stem of ἔβαλον ἔβαλο (without the personal ending), ἔβαλ (without the connecting vowel), or βαλ (without the augment)? Funk (§355) includes everything except the personal ending as part of the tense stem. While there does not appear to be a "right" or "wrong" answer to this question, we have found it helpful to think of the tense stem as just the verb form itself without the prefixes and suffixes (e.g., *βαλ).

§33.4 We classify verbs by how the verbal root is modified in order to form the present tense stem (cf. Smyth §496). Following are five of the six basic categories:

v-1 Present tense = verbal root[3]   *λυ › λύω › λύσω

v-2 Present tense = verbal root + ι   *βαλ › βάλλω › βαλῶ

v-3 Present tense = verbal root + ν[4]   *αὐξα › αὐξάνω › αὐξήσω

v-4 Present tense = verbal root + τ   *βαπ › βάπτω › βάψω

v-5 Present tense = verbal root + σκ[5]   *ἀρε › ἀρέσκω › ἀρέσω

§33.5 v-6 Athematic (μι) verbs. The sixth category is composed of athematic verbs, mostly μι verbs. These stems follow the athematic conjugation, use the alternate personal endings, and some of them reduplicate their verbal roots to form their present tense stems.

---

[1] Smyth also uses the terms "verb stem" and "theme." Others speak of the "verbal base."

[2] See Smyth §371-2 on primitive and denominative verbs.

[3] If a verbal root undergoes ablaut, it will generally use the strong form in the present tense.

[4] If the stem ends in a consonant, αν is added.

[5] If the stem ends in a consonant, ισκ is added.

v-3c(1) and v-3c(2) verbs also use the alternate μι endings, but they do not reduplicate in the present tense.

§33.6 These are the six basic categories. But many of the verbs within these categories also show other types of modifications. Verbs in almost all categories change in their stem vowel in the formation of their principal parts. Many of the verbs also use more than one verbal root in forming their different tense stems. Therefore, out of these six categories we have drawn all these verbs, and have repeated them in v-7 and v-8.

v-7 Verbal roots that change their stem vowel

v-8 Verbs that use more than one verbal root to form their different tense stems.

§33.7 Verbs are also classified as to whether they are weak or strong. **Weak** verbs are those verbs that form their principal parts according to the regular pattern with no change in the stem itself. In English, we would call these the regular verbs, such as "study, studied, have studied."

§33.8 **Strong** verbs form their principal parts by altering the stem. For example, the present βάλλω is a modification of the verbal root *βαλ. Therefore, βάλλω is a strong verb.

In English we would call these the "irregular" verbs, such as "write, wrote, have written." In Greek they modify their stem.

No verb in the New Testament has all strong principal parts, and only nine of those listed in *BAGD* have two strong principal parts (Funk §350). Usually, a verb will have mostly weak forms except in one or two of the tenses.

"Irregular" forms are actually the result of the simplification process that is continually at work in any spoken language. These verbs were altered because the original speakers found these other modification patterns simpler. It therefore holds that the more a word is used, the more "irregular" it becomes. This is why the verb "to be" is the most irregular verb in any language.

The above is of course a simplification of the situation, but as a general description it is helpful.

Tense and Mood Formatives (§34)

§34.1 **Introduction**. In between the stem and the personal endings, we find tense formatives, connecting vowels, and mood formatives.

When tense formatives are added, issues relating to the final stem vowel may also become significant.

The grammars can be confusing at this point. Take, for example, the tense formative σα used in the aorist active of "weak" verbs. Is the α part of the tense formative or is it a connecting vowel? Also, what about the ω/η used in the subjunctive? Are these lengthened connecting vowels or mood formatives? We made our decisions on these issues based on what we think is correct and on what is didactically most sound, i.e., what helps the student the most.

LaSor speaks of these morphemes as "infixes" when they are inserted into the middle of a word.

§34.2   **Final stem consonant.** If the word's stem ends in a consonant, and the next element in the inflectional form of the word begins with a consonant, the final stem consonant frequently is modified. These types of changes are especially evident in the future and first aorist where the σ is added to the stem, and the perfect middle/passive where the endings are added directly to the stem without a connecting vowel. Our discussions in §21 - §27 cover all these types of changes that occur in the New Testament.

§34.3   **Final stem vowel.** If the stem of a word ends in a vowel, that vowel will be lengthened before all of the tense formatives, and before the personal endings in the perfect middle/passive, according to the pattern in §3.3.

§34.4   **Tense formatives.** The following suffixes are added in the formation of these different tenses. (See the disclaimer in §34.1 above.) For accent purposes you should note that the α is always short.

future (act/mid)	σ	λύσω
1 future (pas)	θησ	λυθήσομαι
2 future (pas)	ησ	γραφήσομαι
1 aorist (act/mid)	σα[1]	ἔλυσα
1 aorist (pas)	θε[2]	ἐλύθην
2 aorist (pas)	ε[3]	ἐγράφην
1 perfect (act)	κα[4]	λέλυκα

---

[1]   σα becomes σε in the third person singular in order to distinguish it from the first person singular. It actually is a "relic of the personal ending" (Smyth §455N).

[2]   θε often lengthens to θη (ἐλύθην).

[3]   ε often lengthens to η (ἐγράφην).

[4]   κα becomes κε in the third person singular in order to distinguish it from the first person singular.

2 perfect (act)	α^1	γέγραφα
1 pluperfect (act)	κ^2	(ἐ)λελύκειν

§34.5   **Mood formatives.** The optative adds the mood formative ι between the stem and the secondary personal endings. A connecting vowel is used in the present and second aorist. When joined with connecting vowels and tense formatives we find the following (cf. Smyth §459-61).

οι	All tenses except those below	λύοιμι; βάλοιμι^3
αι	First aorist (act/mid)	λύσαιμι^4
ιη	First aorist passive	λυθείην

LaSor (§24.431) thinks of αι and οι as connecting vowels.

§34.5a   The subjunctive uses lengthened connecting vowels (ω/η) that function as if they were mood formatives, but we view them as lengthened connecting vowels (cf. Smyth §378).

§34.5b   In the optative, final οι is considered long for accent purposes.

Thematic and Athematic
Conjugations (§35)

§35.1   Most verbs use a thematic vowel immediately before the personal endings ("thematic" conjugation). The "thematic" vowel is also called a "connecting" or "variable" vowel. Other verbs join the personal endings directly to the stem ("athematic" = α privative + "thematic").

§35.1a   A verb that uses the athematic conjugation in a certain tense will use that conjugation consistently throughout

---

1   α becomes ε in the third person singular in order to distinguish it from the first person singular.

2   Smyth (§455) lists the tense formatives and thematic vowels for the first pluperfect as κη (from κεα), κει (from κεε) and κε. He lists the second pluperfect connecting vowels as η, ει, and ε while saying that there is no tense formative in the "second perfect and pluperfect." Funk lists κει as the tense formative for the first pluperfect and ει for the second. We will view ει as connecting vowels. The distinction may be merely academic.

3   ο is a connecting vowel.

4   α is part of the tense formative.

that tense. But a verb can alternate between thematic and athematic conjugations from tense to tense.

§35.1b The athematic conjugation was in the process of dropping out of use in Hellenistic Greek. We even find the same verb in multiple conjugations (e.g., ἵστημι, ἱστάνω).

§35.2 **Thematic.** In the indicative of some formations of the present, imperfect, second aorist (active/middle), and all futures, a connecting vowel is inserted between the stem (or tense formative) and the personal ending.

§35.2a In the indicative, o is used with personal endings beginning with μ or ν and ε is used elsewhere. In the optative, o is used everywhere.

§35.2b In the subjunctive, the connecting vowels are lengthened so that ω is used with personal endings beginning with μ or ν. η is used elsewhere.

§35.2c In the pluperfect Smyth says ει are the connecting vowels. Funk says they are part of the tense formative.

§35.2d It is easy to confuse the vowel in the aorist (σα) and perfect (κα) tense formative with a connecting vowel. Although it is certainly not necessary, it is helpful to keep tense formatives and connecting vowels separate.

§35.3 **Athematic conjugation.** Some verbs add the personal endings directly to their stems (or tense formatives). These words will use the alternate personal endings (§36).

§35.3a Athematic conjugations are found in some present, imperfect, and second aorist constructions, and in all perfect (middle/passive), pluperfect (middle), and aorist (passive, where the η is part of the tense formative) constructions. It is also found in a few second perfect and pluperfect (active) constructions.

Personal Endings   (§36)

§36.1   Before studying the following discussion, be sure you understand connecting vowels (discussed in §35). In order to make the verb structure simple for beginners, many teachers teach that the connecting vowel and the personal ending together form the personal ending. Even if this is necessary at first, it must eventually be refined. Following is a technically correct discussion of the personal endings (albeit with a few simplifications, as any student of Classical Greek will realize). If you wish even further discussion, see Smyth §463-464, Funk §318-319, and *BBG* §16.5, 6, 11.

§36.2   The endings are divided between primary and secondary. This is a helpful distinction for parsing; if you can tell whether a verb uses primary or secondary endings, you have narrowed down the possible tenses. The personal ending helps to define person, number, and voice (allowing for deponents and the use of active personal endings in the aorist passive).

§36.3   The **primary** endings are used on the unaugmented tenses. In the indicative these are the present, future, and perfect. In the subjunctive it is all tenses.

§36.4   The **secondary** endings are used on the augmented tenses. In the indicative these are the imperfect, aorist, and pluperfect. In the optative it is all tenses (even though the optative is not augmented).

§36.5   **Indicative.**   The endings given in the "regular" column are those most commonly found; those under "alternate" are found on isolated forms, mostly on μι verbs.

| | primary active | | secondary active | |
	regular	alternate	regular	alternate
1 sg	-[1]	μι	1 sg ν[2]	
2 sg	ς[3]		2 sg ς[4]	
3 sg	ι[5]	σι(ν)[6]	3 sg - (ν)[7]	
1 pl	μεν		1 pl μεν	
2 pl	τε		2 pl τε	
3 pl	νσι(ν)[8]	ασι(ν)[9]	3 pl ν[10]	σαν[11]

[1] - indicates that no ending is used. The ω that stands at the end of the first person singular of verbs in the thematic conjugation is really the lengthened connecting vowel ο (e.g., λύω).

[2] The ending was originally μ. It assimilates to ν when preceded by a vowel (sonant, §5). When it is preceded by a consonant it assimilates to an α (μ › μ › α; e.g., ἔλυσα; Smyth §133c, 464a; Funk §3190.1).

   In the optative, if the tense formative is ιη then the ending is ν; otherwise it is μι.

[3] The ending is actually σι. When added to the connecting vowel, the σ became intervocalic (§25.5) and dropped out. In the present tense this left, e.g., λυει, which then added a final σ (λυεσι › λυει › λύεις). The subjunctive also adds σ by analogy to the indicative. In the perfect σ (not σι) is the ending (Smyth §463b.2). Funk (§3670.2) says the ει is inexplicable. Didactically it helps to think of the ending as ες.

   There is an old alternate ending θα (derived from σθα), used only rarely.

[4] There is an old alternate ending σθα used rarely (Smyth §462; Funk §3190.2). Originally it was a perfect ending that came to be used in the imperfect.

[5] The third singular ending is difficult. Smyth lists τι as the only ending (used for example by ἐστί) that was changed to σι (as seen in the μι verbs, e.g., τίθησι). He adds that ει (e.g., λύει) cannot be derived from it (§463c). Many times no ending is used, and if the connecting vowel is ε, a movable ν may be added. Funk (§3670.2) says the ει in εις is inexplicable. The ι is short for accent purposes.

[6] The ending actually is τι, and in Attic Greek τ was changed to σ.

[7] - indicates that no ending is used. If the connecting vowel is ε, then a movable ν may be added. The ending originally was τ, which was subsequently dropped (§19).

   In the aorist and perfect active, the tense formatives σα/κα shift to σε/κε to differentiate the ending from the first person singular.

[8] In every case the initial ν will drop out because of the σ (§24.4). What happens to the preceding stem vowel varies from case to case. Usually it will undergo compensatory lengthening (λυονσι › λυοσι › λύουσι; §3.5).

   The ending actually was ντι as can be seen in the Doric (e.g., λύοντι; Smyth §462). τ shifted to σ in Attic and therefore Koine Greek.

[9] The ending was αντι (short α). The τ became σ (αντι › ανσι), and when ν dropped out (§24.4), the α was lengthened to ασι (long α) (e.g., τιθέασι). The ι is short for accent purposes. See Smyth §463d.

[10] The ending is actually ντ, but the τ drops out because it cannot stand at the end of a word (§19).

[11] This alternate ending developed by analogy to the σα + ν ending in the aorist (ἔλυσαν). It is used in the imperfect and second aorist of μι verbs, the aorist passive, pluperfect, and optative, where the mood formative is ιη (cf. §60). See BDF §84.

primary middle/passive		*secondary middle/passive*	
1 sg	μαι	1 sg	μην
2 sg	σαι[1]	2 sg	σο[2]
3 sg	ται	3 sg	το
1 pl	μεθα	1 pl	μεθα
2 pl	σθε	2 pl	σθε
3 pl[3]	νται	3 pl	ντο

Changes in the second person singular (active and middle/passive) and the third person plural active are summarized in §40.2, and §40.2 will be referred to throughout the rest of the paradigms.

§36.6   **Subjunctive**. The subjunctive uses lengthened connecting vowels and primary endings. Exactly the same endings are found everywhere, regardless of tense. As usual, the aorist passive uses active endings.[4]

The endings are formed as if the long connecting vowel is contracting with the form of the personal endings that you see in the indicative, and this is how we will list the endings in the paradigm.

active subjunctive

1 sg	ω	+	ω	‣	ω
2 sg	η	+	εις	‣	ης
3 sg	η	+	ει	‣	η
1 pl	ω	+	ομεν	‣	ωμεν
2 pl	η	+	ετε	‣	ητε
3 pl	ω	+	ουσι	‣	ωσι

---

[1]   The ending is properly σαι. When the connecting vowel ε precedes it, the σ becomes intervocalic (§25.5) and drops out. Contraction differs from case to case.

     The σ does not drop out of the perfect middle/passive in the thematic conjugation (λέλυσαι) or the present of μι verbs (e.g., δίδοσαι).

[2]   The ending is properly σο. When the connecting vowel ε precedes it, the σ becomes intervocalic (§25.5) and drops out (except in the athematic conjugation, e.g., ἐδίδοσο). Neither is it lost in the pluperfect (e.g., ἐλέλυσο). Contraction differs from case to case.

[3]   In Classical Greek, if the stem ended in a consonant, the ν became sonant (§5) and assimilated to α (νται ‣ γται ‣ αται; ντο ‣ γτο ‣ ατο).

[4]   In first aorist passive, the η of the tense formative is absorbed (λυθῇς).

middle/passive subjunctive

1 sg	ω	+	μαι	›	ωμαι
2 sg	η	+	σαι	›	ῃ
3 sg	η	+	ται	›	ηται
1 pl	ω	+	μεθα	›	ώμεθα
2 pl	η	+	σθε	›	ησθε
3 pl	ω	+	νται	›	ωνται

§36.7   **Optative**.   The optative does make any distinction between primary and secondary tenses when assigning personal endings.

	active	*middle/passive*
1 sg	μι	μην
2 sg	ς	σο[1]
3 sg	-	το
1 pl	μεν	μεθα
2 pl	τε	σθε
3 pl	εν	ντο

§36.8   **Imperative**.   Following are the imperative endings (Smyth §469).

	active	*middle*
2 sg	θι,[2] -,[3] ε,[4] ς[5]	σο[6]
3 sg	τω	σθω
2 pl	τε	σθε
3 pl	τωσαν	σθωσαν
	ντων	σθων

In all the paradigms of the imperative we will list two sets of endings for the third person plural imperative. The first was used in Koine (e.g., τωσαν), the second in Classical (e.g., ντων). A few times you will see verbal forms in Koine Greek using the classical endings.

---

[1] When the σ is intervocalic it will drop out (λύοιο).

[2] In the aorist passive, the θ of the imperatival ending deaspirates to τ (λυθηθι › λύθητι; §15.3a). Smyth (§466c) says λῦσον and λῦσαι are "obscure in origin." θι is used in the aorist active of ἵστημι › στῆθι, but not in the other μι verbs.

[3] No ending is used in the present and second aorist active (λῦε, βάλε).

[4] μι verbs often use ε in the second person singular present (διδοε › δίδου, τιθεε › τίτει, ιστηε › ἵστη).

[5] The second aorist active of μι verbs often uses σ and not θι (δός, θές, but στῆθι).

[6] The σ is retained in the perfect (λέλυσο) and the present of μι verbs (τίθεσο). Elsewhere the intervocalic sigma drops out and the vowels contract to ου.

§36.9   **Movable v.**   The general rule is that a v is added to certain forms ending in ι or ε when the next word begins with a vowel (see our discussion at §6.6). However, we often find movable v when the following word begins with a consonant, thus deserving the name "irrational v." In Koine Greek it is used most of the time on the following forms.

- the dative plural of third declension words (σαρξίν).

- third person ending -σι (λύουσιν, δίδωσιν, εἰσίν)

- third person singular -ε (ἔλυεν)

- ἐστίν

It is best to page through the paradigms and see when it is used, and when it is not used, since we have assigned movable v based on New Testament usage.

§36.9a   **Movable ς** is not found on verbs; cf. §6.7.

Introduction to Verbs   (§40)

The preceding sections (§30-§36) dealt with the individual elements of the verbs. Pp. 248ff. deal with the formation of the tense stems for each of the principal parts. Sections §41-§93 show how those two elements are combined.

Sections §41 through §95 are broken down into the moods (including the infinitive and the participle). Each mood is broken into tenses. Each tense subdivision will be started with a short outline of its contents. It is then generally broken down into thematic conjugation (consonant stems, contracts, liquids) and athematic conjugation, with special sections as needed (e.g., verbs inserting σ in the aorist passive).

Questions pertaining to augment, reduplication, final stem changes, personal endings, and the like will not be discussed here. They are covered in §30 – §36. Be sure to have a thorough knowledge of those discussions before proceeding.

Sample Paradigm   (§40.1)

On the following page is a sample paradigm. Each paradigm has a title, a description line (in italics), and then the paradigm. Following the label (e.g., "1 sg") is listed the true personal ending (see §36 for details) and then the actual verb form. Changes to personal endings that will be seen in all the verbs in that category will be footnoted in the paradigm. Any changes that are peculiar to a verb will be footnoted with the word itself in the principal parts listing. As we discussed in §36, what we have listed as the personal ending may be a slight simplification of what that ending really is. Our intention here is to help students learn Greek, and didactic concerns sometimes override purely academic concerns.

Thematic Stems   (§41.1)

tense stem + connecting vowel + primary ending

		present active		**present middle/passive**
1 sg	-	λύω	μαι	λύομαι
2 sg	ς[1]	λύεις	σαι	λύη[2]
3 sg	ι	λύει	ται	λύεται
1 pl	μεν	λύομεν	μεθα	λυόμεθα
2 pl	τε	λύετε	σθε	λύεσθε
3 pl	νσι[3]	λύουσι(ν)	νται	λύονται

---

[1]   You can think of the ending as ες, which contracts with the connecting vowel to form εις. Cf. §40.2.

[2]   Intervocalic σ drops out (§25.5) and the vowels contract (ε + σαι › εαι › ηι › η). Cf. §40.2.

[3]   The ν drops out because of the σ (§24.4), and the preceding stem vowel lengthens in compensation (§3.5). Cf. §40.2.

Normal Changes   (§40.2)

Three primary endings and one secondary ending will regularly be modified. They are discussed in §36.5 and reviewed here for emphasis. In the paradigms that follow we will reference this section.

1.   The second person singular primary active ending is actually σι (λύεις). It undergoes significant changes when the σ drops and is then added back by analogy (λυ + ε + σι › λυει › λύεις).

    There are advantages to thinking of the ending as ες. This is what we find in the secondary when we join the connecting vowel to the ending (e.g., ἔλυες), and the consistency might help you remember. Also, you can think of the ε as contracting with the connecting vowel, forming εις (e.g., λυ + ε + ες › λύεις).

2.   The third plural primary active ending is actually ντι (λύουσι). In Attic the τ became σ, and the ν always drops out because of the σ (§24.4). The final stem vowel lengthens to compensate (§3.5; e.g., λυ + ο + ντι › λυονσι › λυοσι › λύουσι).

3.   The second person singular primary passive ending is σαι (λύη). When it is preceded by a vowel the σ becomes intervocalic and drops out (§25.5), and the vowels contract regularly (e.g., λυ + ε + σαι › λυεαι › λυηι › λύη).

4.   The second person singular secondary ending is σο. When it is preceded by a vowel the σ becomes intervocalic, drops out (§25.5), and the vowels contract regularly (e.g., ε + λυ + σα + σο › ελυσαο › ἐλύσω).

Contract Verbs   (§40.3)

In the present and imperfect, contract verbs combine with the personal endings as if the endings were what is visible in λύω.

present		*imperfect*	
ω	φανερο + - › φανερῶ	ον	ε +γεννα + ον › ἐγέννων
εις	γεννα + εις › γεννᾷς	ες	ε + ποιε + ε + ες › ἐποίεις
ει	ποιε + ει › ποιεῖ	ε	ε + φανερο + ε › ἐφανέρου
ομεν	γεννα + ο + μεν › γεννῶμεν	ομεν	ε + γεννα + ομεν › ἐγεννώμεν
ετε	ποιε + ε + τε › ποιεῖτε	ετε	ε + ποιε + ετε › ἐποιεῖτε
ουσι	φανερο + ουσι › φανεροῦσι	ον	ε + φανερο + ον › ἐφανέρουν

However, this is not true for the second singular middle/passive in the present. In this situation the verb contracts with σαι. γεννα + ε + σαι › γενναεαι › γενναει › γενναι › γεννᾳ.

When we list the personal endings in the paradigms for contract verbs, we will list the personal endings as seen on λύω except for the second singular middle/ passive secondary, where we list σαι (e.g., ω, εις, ει, ομεν, ετε, ουσι; ον, ες, ε, ομεν, ετε, ον).

When a contract verb is followed by a tense formative, its final stem vowel lengthens (future, aorist). γεννάω › γεννήσω. ποιέω › ἐποίησα. The final stem vowel also lengthens in the perfect middle/passive, even though there is no tense formative. φανερόω › πεφανέρωμαι.

Athematic (μι) Verbs   (§40.4)

The athematic conjugation (otherwise known as the μι verbs) is so named because these verbs do not use a thematic vowel between their stem and the personal ending. ("Athematic" is a compound of the alpha-privative and the word "thematic".) They have several peculiarities that, if remembered, make recognition quite easy (cf. BBG §34.6-§34.10; MH 201-207; Smyth §717-799).

1. μι verbs reduplicate their initial stem letter to form the present, and separate the reduplicated consonant with an iota (δο › διδο › δίδωμεν).

2. μι verbs do not ordinarily use a connecting (i.e., "thematic") vowel in the indicative. Their personal ending is added directly to the stem. However, the stem does end in a vowel (διδω + μι › δίδωμι).

There are three classes of μι verbs, based on their final stem vowel: α (ἵστημι), ε (τίθημι), and ο (δίδωμι). δείκνυμι, formed with a root ending in υ, is viewed as a μι verb in the present (and imperfect), but in other tenses it follows the regular formation patterns using the root *δεικ (e.g., ἔδειξα). As is true of all v-3c verbs, νυ was added to form the present tense stem and νυ is therefore lacking in the other tenses. We will list the paradigms of δεικνύμι only in the present and imperfect. To see the full paradigm see Smyth §418, §422.

3. μι verbs employ three different personal endings in the present active, μι (first singular), σι (third singular), and ασι (third plural; ἵστημι, ἵστησι, ἱστᾶσι).

   As opposed to the thematic conjugation, the intervocalic σ of the σι and σαι endings does not drop out (e.g., δίδωσι, δίδοσαι).

4. The stem vowel of μι verbs can lengthen (δίδωμι) or shorten (δίδομεν). For recognition purposes it is not essential to know when these changes will occur. If you want to know, study the paradigms.

5. Most of the μι verbs use κα as their tense formative in the aorist (ἔδωκα). These are called "kappa aorists."

   ἵστημι has both a first and second aorist, but it never occurs in the aorist middle. The other μι verbs have kappa aorists in the active. In the aorist passive they all have first aorists (ἐστάθην, ἐτέθην, ἐδόθην).

Regular μι verbs are classified as v-6 verbs. They are also called the "root class." v-3c(1-2) verbs also use the alternate μι endings but do not follow the other formation rules (e.g., ζώννυμι, ῥήγνυμι). They add (ν)νυ to the verbal root to form their present tense stem (and therefore the imperfect). The other tenses are formed regularly.

All μι verbs are defective. Not one of them, even in Classical Greek, occurs in all forms (Smyth §415). μι verbs were also in the process of moving over to the thematic conjugation during the Koine period (*BDF* §92). That is why we find, e.g., τίθεις instead of the classical τίθης, δεικνύεις and not δείκνυς. It is also why we see the same verbal root being used as a μι verb (ἵστημι; v-6) and in other formations (ἱστάνω; v-3a[1]; cf. *BDF* §93-94). There are no μι verbs in Modern Greek.

Present Indicative   (§41)

Thematic Stems   (§41.1)

tense stem + connecting vowel + primary ending

		present active		present middle/passive
1 *sg*	-	λύω	μαι	λύομαι
2 *sg*	ς[1]	λύεις	σαι[2]	λύη
3 *sg*	ι	λύει	ται	λύεται

---

[1]   You can think of the ending as ες, which contracts with the connecting vowel to form εις. Cf. §40.2.

[2]   Intervocalic σ drops out (§25.5) and the vowels contract. ε + σαι › εαι › ηι › η. Cf. §40.2.

1 pl	μεν	λύομεν	μεθα	λυόμεθα
2 pl	τε	λύετε	σθε	λύεσθε
3 pl	νσι[1]	λύουσι(ν)	νται	λύονται

Contract Stems (§41.2)

tense stem + connecting vowel + modified primary ending (§40.3)

present active

		*γεννα	*ποιε	*φανερο
1 sg	ω	γεννῶ	ποιῶ	φανερῶ
2 sg	εις	γεννᾷς	ποιεῖς	φανεροῖς[2]
3 sg	ει	γεννᾷ	ποιεῖ	φανεροῖ[2]
1 pl	ομεν	γεννῶμεν	ποιοῦμεν	φανεροῦμεν
2 pl	ετε	γεννᾶτε	ποιεῖτε	φανεροῦτε
3 pl	ουσι	γεννῶσι	ποιοῦσι	φανεροῦσι

present middle/passive

		γεννῶμαι	ποιοῦμαι	φανερούμαι
1 sg	μαι	γεννῶμαι	ποιοῦμαι	φανεροῦμαι
2 sg	σαι[3]	γεννᾷ	ποιῇ[4]	φανεροῖ
3 sg	ται	γεννᾶται	ποιεῖται	φανεροῦται
1 pl	μεθα	γεννώμεθα	ποιούμεθα	φανερούμεθα
2 pl	σθε	γεννᾶσθε	ποιεῖσθε	φανεροῦσθε
3 pl	νται	γεννῶνται	ποιοῦνται	φανεροῦνται

---

[1]   The ν drops out because of the σ (§24.4), and the preceding stem vowel lengthens in compensation (§3.5). Cf. §40.2.

[2]   On the irregular contraction see §2.13b.

[3]   Intervocalic σ drops out (§25.5) and the vowels contract. Cf. §40.2.

[4]   Classical Greek allowed ποιῇ and ποιεῖ.

Athematic Stems (§41.3)

reduplicated tense stem + alternate primary ending

		* *στα[1]	**θε[2]	**δο	**δεικνυ[3]
present active					
1 sg	μι	ἵστημι	τίθημι	δίδωμι	δείκνυμι
2 sg	ς	ἵστης	τίθης	δίδως	δείκνυς
3 sg	σι(ν)	ἵστησι(ν)	τίθησι(ν)	δίδωσι(ν)	δείκνυσι(ν)
1 pl	μεν	ἵσταμεν	τίθεμεν	δίδομεν	δείκνυμεν
2 pl	τε	ἵστατε	τίθετε	δίδοτε	δείκνυτε
3 pl	ασι(ν)	ἱστᾶσι(ν)[4]	τιθεῖσι(ν)[5]	διδοῦσι(ν)[6]	δεικνύασι(ν)
present middle/passive					
1 sg	μαι	ἵσταμαι	τίθεμαι	δίδομαι	δείκνυμαι
2 sg	σαι[7]	ἵστασαι	τίθεσαι	δίδοσαι	δείκνυσαι
3 sg	ται	ἵσταται	τίθεται	δίδοται	δείκνυται
1 pl	μεθα	ἱστάμεθα	τιθέμεθα	διδόμεθα	δεικνύμεθα
2 pl	σθε	ἵστασθε	τίθεσθε	δίδοσθε	δείκνυσθε
3 pl	νται	ἵστανται	τίθενται	δίδονται	δείκνυνται

---

[1] **στα reduplicates to σιστα. Since Greek avoids successive syllables beginning with σ, the first σ is replaced by rough breathing. See §25.6b.

[2] **θε reduplicates to θιθε, but since Greek avoids successive syllables beginning with an aspirate (θ), the first θ is deaspirated to τ. See §15.3, 5.

[3] See §40.4. For the full paradigm of δείκνυμι see Smyth §418, §422.

[4] Contraction of ἱστάασι(ν).

[5] In Classical Greek we find the uncontracted form τιθέασι. The contraction here appears to be with ουσι and not ασι. εουσι ⟩ ειυσι ⟩ εισι.

[6] In Classical Greek we find the uncontracted form διδόασι in the third plural. The contraction here appears to be with ουσι and not ασι. οουσι ⟩ ουυσι ⟩ ουσι.

[7] Intervocalic σ does not drop out (§40.4[3]).

Imperfect Indicative   (§42)

Thematic Stems   (§42.1)

augment + tense stem + connecting vowel + secondary ending

		imperfect active		imperfect middle/passive
1 sg	ν	ἔλυον	μην	ἐλυόμην
2 sg	ς	ἔλυες	σο[1]	ἐλύου
3 sg	- (ν)	ἔλυε(ν)	το	ἐλύετο
1 pl	μεν	ἐλύομεν	μεθα	ἐλυόμεθα
2 pl	τε	ἐλύετε	σθε	ἐλύεσθε
3 pl	ν	ἔλυον	ντο	ἐλύοντο

Contract Stems   (§42.2)

In Attic and Koine Greek, movable ν was not added to the third singular imperfect form of contracts (Smyth §399). For accent purposes, contracted vowels are long.

augment + tense stem + connecting vowel + modified secondary ending (§40.3)

imperfect active

1 sg	ν	ἐγέννων	ἐποίουν	ἐφανέρουν
2 sg	ς	ἐγέννας	ἐποίεις	ἐφανέρους
3 sg	ε	ἐγέννα	ἐποίει	ἐφανέρου
1 pl	μεν	ἐγεννῶμεν	ἐποιοῦμεν	ἐφανεροῦμεν
2 pl	τε	ἐγεννᾶτε	ἐποιεῖτε	ἐφανεροῦτε
3 pl	ν	ἐγέννων	ἐποίουν	ἐφανέρουν

imperfect middle/passive

1 sg	μην	ἐγεννώμην	ἐποιούμην	ἐφανερούμην
2 sg	σο[1]	ἐγεννῶ	ἐποιοῦ	ἐφανεροῦ
3 sg	το	ἐγεννᾶτο	ἐποιεῖτο	ἐφανεροῦτο
1 pl	μεθα	ἐγεννώμεθα	ἐποιούμεθα	ἐφανερούμεθα
2 pl	σθε	ἐγεννᾶσθε	ἐποιεῖσθε	ἐφανεροῦσθε
3 pl	ντο	ἐγεννῶντο	ἐποιοῦντο	ἐφανεροῦντο

---

[1]   Intervocalic σ drops out and the vowels contract. ε + σο › εο (§25.5) › ου. Cf. §40.2.

Athematic Stems (§42.3)

The forms followed with an * show how the μι verbs were shifting over to the thematic conjugation (ετιθες ‣ ἐτίθεις, εδιδοον ‣ ἐδίδουν; cf. §40.2). Stems in ε could have endings like λύω, and stems in ο could have endings like φανερόω. The same changes are present in Classical Greek.

augment + reduplicated tense stem + alternate secondary ending

imperfect active indicative

1 sg	ν	ἵστην	ἐτίθην	ἐδίδουν*	ἐδείκνυν
2 sg	ς	ἵστης	ἐτίθεις*	ἐδίδους*	ἐδείκνυς
3 sg	-	ἵστη	ἐτίθει*	ἐδίδου*	ἐδείκνυ
1 pl	μεν	ἵσταμεν	ἐτίθεμεν	ἐδίδομεν	ἐδείκνυμεν
2 pl	τε	ἵστατε	ἐτίθετε	ἐδίδοτε	ἐδείκνυτε
3 pl	σαν	ἵστασαν	ἐτίθεσαν	ἐδίδοσαν	ἐδείκνυσαν

imperfect middle/passive indicative

1 sg	μην	ἱστάμην	ἐτιθέμην	ἐδιδόμην	ἐδεικνύμην
2 sg	σο	ἵστασο	ἐτίθεσο	ἐδίδοσο	ἐδείκνυσο
3 sg	το	ἵστατο	ἐτίθετο	ἐδίδοτο	ἐδείκνυτο
1 pl	μεθα	ἱστάμεθα	ἐτιθέμεθα	ἐδιδόμεθα	ἐδεικνύμεθα
2 pl	σθε	ἵστασθε	ἐτίθεσθε	ἐδίδοσθε	ἐδείκνυσθε
3 pl	ντο	ἵσταντο	ἐτίθεντο	ἐδίδοντο	ἐδείκνυντο

Future Active/Middle Indicative (§43)

The only variation in the future is how the tense formative affects the verbal stem. Once the future stem is formed, words are conjugated basically like the present.

The future has a "defective" paradigm. This means that the future does not occur in all moods. It does not occur in the imperative or subjunctive, and it is rare in the optative (in indirect discourse after a secondary tense).

Originally future forms in σ were derived from first aorist subjunctive forms. If the stem undergoes ablaut, the future tends to use the strong form.

On the future in general see *MH* 218-220.

Thematic Stems   (§43.1)

tense stem + tense formative (σ) + connecting vowel + primary ending

		future active		**future middle**
1 sg	-	λύσω	μαι	λύσομαι
2 sg	ς[1]	λύσεις	σαι[2]	λύσῃ
3 sg	ι	λύσει	ται	λύσεται
1 pl	μεν	λύσομεν	μεθα	λυσόμεθα
2 pl	τε	λύσετε	σθε	λύσεσθε
3 pl	νσι(ν)[3]	λύσουσι(ν)	νται	λύσονται

Contract Stems   (§43.2)

Contract verbs lengthen their final stem vowel before the σ of the future. Other than this, they are identical to the uncontracted forms. v-1d(2b) verbs may or may not lengthen their final ε before the σ (καλέω ‣ καλέσω).

tense stem (lengthened final vowel) + tense formative (σ) + connecting vowel + modified primary ending (§.40.3)

future active indicative

		*γεννα	*ποιε	*φανερο
1 sg	-	γεννήσω	ποιήσω	φανερώσω
2 sg	ς[1]	γεννήσεις	ποιήσεις	φανερώσεις
3 sg	ι	γεννήσει	ποιήσει	φανερώσει
1 pl	μεν	γεννήσομεν	ποιήσομεν	φανερώσομεν
2 pl	τε	γεννήσετε	ποιήσετε	φανερώσετε
3 pl	νσι(ν)[3]	γεννήσουσι(ν)	ποιήσουσι(ν)	φανερώσουσι(ν)

---

[1] You can think of the ending as ες, which contracts with the connecting vowel to form εις. Cf. §40.2.

[2] Intervocalic σ drops out and the vowels contract. ε + σαι ‣ εαι (§25.5) ‣ ηι ‣ ῃ. Cf. §40.2.

[3] The ν drops out because of the σ (§24.4), and the preceding stem vowel lengthens in compensation (§3.5). Cf. §40.2.

future middle indicative

1 sg	μαι	γεννήσομαι	ποιήσομαι	φανερώσομαι
2 sg	σαι[1]	γεννήσῃ	ποιήσῃ	φανερώσῃ
3 sg	ται	γεννήσεται	ποιήσεται	φανερώσεται
1 pl	μεθα	γεννησόμεθα	ποιησόμεθα	φανερωσόμεθα
2 pl	σθε	γεννήσεσθε	ποιήσεσθε	φανερώσεσθε
3 pl	νται	γεννήσονται	ποιήσονται	φανερώσονται

Liquid Stems (§43.3)

Verbs whose verbal roots end in a liquid (λ ρ) or a nasal (μ ν) are called "liquid verbs." They form their future by adding not σ but εσ and then the thematic vowel. The σ is therefore always intervocalic and drops out (§25.5), and the ε of the tense formative and the connecting vowel contract (cf. LaSor §24.2555; Funk §376; Smyth §535). Liquid verbs are therefore conjugated and accented (cf. Carson, VR.9) in the future just as if they were ε contract verbs in the present.

Smyth explains them differently (§544). He says the σ of the future is simply lost, and the preceding vowel is lengthened in compensation. On liquids in general see Smyth §614-620.

In the following paradigm we have listed the tense formative, connecting vowels, and personal endings in the first column.

tense stem + tense formative (εσ) + connecting vowel + primary ending

	future active		**future middle**	
1 sg	εσο	κρινῶ	εσομαι	κρινοῦμαι
2 sg	εσες[2]	κρινεῖς	εσεσαι[3]	κρινῇ
3 sg	εσε	κρινεῖ	εσεται	κρινεῖται
1 pl	εσομεν	κρινοῦμεν	εσομεθα	κρινούμεθα
2 pl	εσετε	κρινεῖτε	εσεσθε	κρινεῖσθε
3 pl	εσονσι(ν)[4]	κρινοῦσι(ν)	εσονται	κρινοῦνται

---

[1]　Intervocalic σ drops out and the vowels contract. ε + σαι ‣ εαι (§25.5) ‣ ηι ‣ ῃ. Cf. §40.2.

[2]　You can think of the ending as ες (εσ + ες), intervocalic σ drops out, and εε contract to ει; cf. §40.2.

[3]　Intervocalic σ drops out (§25.5) and the vowels contract. εσ + ε + σαι ‣ εεαι ‣ εηι ‣ εη ‣ ῃ. Cf. §40.2. In Classical Greek both μενεῖ and μενῇ were possible. A search of the N.T. for second singular future middle forms shows the following: 31 forms, all are indicative, all use the ending ῇ except for the uncontracted φάγεσαι (ἐσθίω) and πίεσαι (πίνω) in Luke 17:8.

[4]　The ν drops out because of the σ (§24.4), and the preceding stem vowel lengthens in compensation (§3.5). Cf. §40.2.

Following is a list of all liquid futures (active/middle) of words occurring in the
New Testament. Compound verbs are listed as their simple verb form.

ἀγγέλλω	ἀγγελῶ	v-2d(1)
αἱρέω	ἑλῶ[1]	v-1d(2a)
αἴρω	ἀρῶ	v-2d(2)
βάλλω	βαλῶ	v-2d(1)
ἐγείρω	ἐγερῶ	v-2d(3)
θνῄσκω	θανοῦμαι	v-5a
κλίνω	κλινῶ	v-1c(2)
κρίνω	κρινῶ	v-1c(2)
κτείνω	κτενῶ	v-2d(5)
λέγω	ἐρῶ[2]	v-1b(2)
μένω	μενῶ	v-1c(2)
ὄλλυμι	ὀλῶ[3]	v-3c(2)
πικραίνω	πικρανῶ	v-2d(4)
πληθύνω	πληθυνῶ	v-1c(2)
πλύνω	πλυνῶ	v-1c(2)
ποιμαίνω	ποιμανῶ	v-2d(4)
σκληρύνω	σκληρυνῶ	v-1c(2)
στέλλω	στελῶ	v-2d(1)
τείνω	τενῶ	v-2d(5)
τέλλω	τελῶ	v-2d(1)
φαίνω	φανοῦμαι	v-2d(4)
φθείρω	φθερῶ	v-2d(3)
χαίρω	χαροῦμαι[4]	v-2d(2)
ψάλλω	ψαλῶ	v-2d(1)

The following words have liquid futures, but they do not appear in the New
Testament. ξαίνω (v-2d[4]), μεγαλύνω (v-1c[2]), μιαίνω (v-2d[4]), ὀξύνω (v-1c[2]),
πληθύνω (v-1c[2]), ῥαίνω (v-2d[4]), τίλλω (v-2d[1]).

Three liquid stems use the regular formation patterns, γίνομαι (γενήσομαι;
v-1c[2]), οἰκτίρω (οἰκτιρήσω; v-2d[3]), χαίρω (χαρήσομαι; v-2d[2]).

φέρω is a liquid stem but uses a different non-liquid root for the future stem: οἴσω
(v-1c(1); *οι).

---

[1]   From the verbal root *ελ. In the N.T. αἱρέω uses the future αἱρήσομαι (Phil 1:22), but
       it can use ἑλῶ in compounds (ἀνελεῖ).

[2]   From the root *Ϝερ.

[3]   Also ὀλέσω (e.g., ἀπολέσει).

[4]   Also χαρήσομαι.

Athematic Stems   (§43.4)

μι verbs form their future with just their verbal root; there is no reduplication as there is in the present. The stem vowel is always long and their conjugation is regular.

tense stem + tense formative (σ) + primary ending

future active

1 sg	-	στήσω	θήσω	δώσω
2 sg	ς[1]	στήσεις	θήσεις	δώσεις
3 sg	ι	στήσει	θήσει	δώσει
1 pl	μεν	στήσομεν	θήσομεν	δώσομεν
2 pl	τε	στήσετε	θήσετε	δώσετε
3 pl	νσι(ν)[2]	στήσουσι(ν)	θήσουσι(ν)	δώσουσι(ν)

future middle

1 sg	μαι	στήσομαι	θήσομαι	δώσομαι
2 sg	σαι[3]	στήση	θήση	δώση
3 sg	ται	στήσεται	θήσεται	δώσεται
1 pl	μεθα	στησόμεθα	θησόμεθα	δωσόμεθα
2 pl	σθε	στήσεσθε	θήσεσθε	δώσεσθε
3 pl	νται	στήσονται	θήσονται	δώσονται

Stems Ending in a Stop   (§43.5)

(π β φ, κ γ χ, τ δ θ)

Labial   If a stem ends with a π, β, or φ, the final consonant and the σ will be written as a ψ (§22.1; v-1b[1]).

*βλεπ	+ σ	+ ω	▸	βλέψω
*θλιβ	+ σ	+ ω	▸	θλίψω
*γραφ	+ σ	+ ω	▸	γράψω

Velar   If a stem ends with a κ, γ, or χ, the final consonant and the σ will be written as a ξ (§22.2; v-1b[2]).

---

1   You can think of the ending as ες, which contracts with the connecting vowel to form εις. Cf. §40.2.

2   The ν drops out because of the σ (§24.4), and the preceding stem vowel lengthens in compensation (§3.5). Cf. §40.2.

3   Intervocalic σ drops out (§25.5) and the vowels contract. ε + σαι ▸ εαι ▸ ηι ▸ η. Cf. §40.2.

                *διωκ   + σ + ω   › διώξω

                *οἰγ   + σ + ω   › οἴξω

                *αρχ   + σ + ομαι › ἄρξομαι

Dental   If a stem ends with a τ, δ, or θ, the final consonant becomes a σ, joins with the other σ, and then the double σ simplifies to one σ (§22.3; v-1b[3]).

                *πετ   + σ + ομαι › πεσσουμαι › πεσοῦμαι

                *αειδ   + σ + ομαι › αεισσομαι › ἀείσομαι

                *πειθ   + σ + ω   › πεισσω › πείσω

Words Ending in αζω or ιζω   (§43.6)

The verbal stems in these categories really end in δ (v-2a(1)) or γ (v-2a[2]). In order to form the present stem, ι is added to the verbal root. But δ or γ added to ι form ζ (§26.2), thus making it appear that the verb actually ends in ζ. Therefore, what we described in §43.5 above concerning dentals and velars applies also to these words. (The original δ or γ reappear in the other tenses, only to be modified for other reasons.)

                *βαπτιδ + ι + ω   › βαπτίζω   present

                *βαπτιδ + σ + ω   › βαπτισσω › βαπτίσω   future

                *κραγ   + ι + ω   › κράζω   present

                *κραγ   + σ + ω   › κράξω   future

Attic Future   (§43.7)

§43.7a   In Attic, Homeric, and several other dialects, the future was formed differently. Smyth (§538-9) says that "verbs in -ιζω of more than two syllables drop σ and insert ε, thus making -ι(σ)έω, -ι(σ)έομαι, which contract to -ιῶ and -ιοῦμαι." He gives a further description that applied to Classical Greek but not to Koine, including verbs in -αννυμι, -εννυμι, and a few in -αζω.[1]

           Funk (§3760; Smyth §539e) says Attic futures are used on stems ending in δ or θ (dentals), which are then lost because of the following σ in the tense formative. These futures add σε, the σ drops out, and the

---

[1]   In Classical Greek the Attic future was used with stems ending in a short α or ε where the vowel is not preceded by a long syllable. σ is dropped and αω and εω contract to ῶ. If there is an ι before σ, ισεω contracted to ιῶ. This allows for other Attic futures not found in the N.T. such as καλῶ (καλέω), τελῶ (τελέω), ἐλῶ (ἐλαυνω), σκεδῶ (σκεδάννυμι), βιβῶ (βιβάζω). See Smyth for his list of words. *BDF* say that the Attic future "is, in general, missing from Hellenistic Greek" (§74).

ε contracts with the following connecting vowel. Attic futures are therefore conjugated like liquid verbs (§43.3; BDF §74.1).[1]

Some verbs (e.g., καθίζω) alternate between a Koine future (καθίσω) and an Attic future (καθιῶ). (All -αζω verbs regularly form their future in -άσω.)

§43.7b   Following are all the Attic futures in the New Testament. Remember, ιζω verbs really have stems ending in a dental. All of these listed except for ἐκχέω (cv-1a[7]) are v-2a(1) verbs.

present	future	inflected NT form
ἀφορίζω	ἀφοριῶ[2]	ἀφοριοῦσιν, ἀφορίσει
ἐκχέω	ἐκχεῶ	ἐκχεῶ
ἐγγίζω	ἐγγιῶ	ἐγγιεῖ
ἐδαφίζω	ἐδαφιῶ	ἐδαφιοῦσιν
ἐλπίζω	ἐλπιῶ	ἐλπιοῦσιν
καθαρίζω	καθαριῶ	καθαριεῖ
κομίζω	κομιοῦμαι[3]	κομιεῖσθε, κομίσεται
μακαρίζω	μακαριῶ	μακαριοῦσιν
μετοικίζω	μετοικιῶ	μετοικιῶ
παροργίζω	παροργιῶ	παροργιῶ

γνωρίζω and στηρίζω have regular futures.

See also ἀκουτίζω, καθίζω,[4] κατατίζω, μερίζω, ὁμαλίζω, ῥαντίζω, φωτίζω, χρονίζω.

Miscellaneous (§43.8)

Following are some other peculiarities of futures found in the New Testament.

§43.8a   The **Doric Future** is another way of forming the future peculiar to the Doric dialect. They are future middles with an active meaning. Instead of adding just σ, they add σε,[5] but unlike Attic futures they are not limited to dental stems. The ε then contracts with the connecting vowels ο/ε (σέομαι ‣ σοῦμαι). Smyth adds that most of these

---

1   Normally a stem ending in a dental would lose the dental but keep the σ; *βαπτιδ + σω ‣ βαπτίσω.

2   Also ὁρίσω.

3   Also κομίσομαι.

4   Has an Attic future καθιῶ, but in the N.T. it uses only a Koine future, καθίσει (Mt 25:31).

5   Liquid futures add εσ.

words also have a regularly formed future in Classical Greek (§540; cf. Funk §3761).

Their inflectional pattern is as follows.

1 sg	-σῶ	-σοῦμαι
2 sg	-σεῖς	-σῇ
3 sg	-σεῖ	-σεῖται
1 pl	-σοῦμεν	-σούμεθα
2 pl	-σεῖτε	-σεῖσθε
3 pl	-σοῦσι	-σοῦνται

The only Doric form in the N.T. is the future of πίπτω (πεσοῦμαι; v-1b[3]). It is from the strong grade of the root *πετ. It adds σε, the τ drops out and the vowels contract. πετ + σε + ομαι ‣ πεσσεομαι ‣ πεσεομαι ‣ πεσοῦμαι.[1]

§43.8b **Contract Future** is a general category encompassing any future that is formed through contraction, including Attic and Doric futures. In addition, Funk (§3762) lists πάσχω[2] and χέω ‣ χεῶ (which occurs in the compound ἐκχέω).

§43.8c **No indication.** Some verbs show no indication in the formation of their future (cf. Smyth §541; BDF §74.2; Attic futures; Liquid futures).

πίνω has a future πίομαι (*πι; v-3a[1])

ἐσθίω has two future forms, φάγομαι (*φαγ; four times) and ἔδομαι (not in the New Testament), both from different stems.

§43.8d **Insert η after the tense formative.** In most the tenses there are examples of stems that insert η after the tense stem and before the tense formative. There are five examples of this in futures in the New Testament, and one in which ε is used rather than η.[3]

---

1   κλαίω (κλαυσοῦμαι) and φεύγω (φευξοῦμαι) can have Doric futures, but not in the N.T. κλαύσουσιν (Rev 18:9) is accented as a regular future, and φεύξονται (John 10:5) and φεύξεται (Jas 4:7) do not show contraction.

   The futures of πλέω (πλευσοῦμαι), πνέω (πνευσοῦμαι), and πυνθάνομαι (πευσοῦμαι) do not occur in the N.T., but they are Doric futures.

   νέω (νευσοῦμαι) and χέζω (χεσοῦμαι) do not occur in the N.T. at all.

2   πάσχω is from the stem *παθ, which in the future inserts an ε before the connecting vowel and personal ending (ται) and then contracts. παθ + ε + ο + μαι ‣ πεθεομαι ‣ παθεῖται. Occurs in 2 Clem 7:5.

3   χαίρω (v-2d[2]) also inserts an η in its future (χαρήσομαι), but its future does not appear in the N.T.

ἁμαρτάνω	ἁμαρτήσω	*αμαρτ	v-3a(2a)
ἀπόλλυμι	ἀπολέσω	*ολ	cv-3c(2)
γίνομαι	γενήσομαι	*γεν	v-1c(2)
εὑρίσκω	εὑρήσω	*ευρ	v-5b
οἶδα	εἰδήσω	*Ϝιδ	v-1b(3)
οἰκτίρω	οἰκτιρήσω	*οικτιρ	v-2d(3)

§43.8e   **Augment**. καταγνύμι (v-3c[2]) is improperly augmented in the future (κατά + Ϝαγνυμι › κατεάξω; Funk §3372.3; *BDF* 66.2).

Aorist Active/Middle Indicative   (§44)

Contrary to how most beginning grammars describe it, the aorist is not the irregular tense. The present tense is the real culprit. The tense stem in the aorist, whether it be first or second aorist, is most likely the closest stem to the actual verbal root. If you can train yourself to think this way, Greek morphology will become much easier to understand.

The α in the first aorist tense formative is short for accent purposes (ἔλυσα).

First Aorist   (§44.1)

Thematic stems   (§44.1a)

Note that the α is not a thematic vowel but part of the tense formative. Except for technical discussions, this fact will not come into play very much.

augment + tense stem + tense formative (σα) + secondary ending

	first aorist active		**first aorist middle**	
1 sg	-[1]	ἔλυσα	μην	ἐλυσάμην
2 sg	ς	ἔλυσας	σο[2]	ἐλύσω
3 sg	-(ν)[3]	ἔλυσε(ν)	το	ἐλύσατο

---

[1]   Contrary to the normal pattern, the first person singular active uses no personal ending.

[2]   The σ of the personal ending is intervocalic and drops out, and the α and ο contract to ω (§25.5a). Cf. §40.2.

[3]   The third person singular active uses no personal ending, but in order to avoid confusion with the first singular, it alters the vowel in the tense formative toε by analogy to the imperfect.

1 pl	μεν	ἐλύσαμεν	μεθα	ἐλυσάμεθα
2 pl	τε	ἐλύσατε ₋	σθε	ἐλύσασθε
3 pl	ν	ἔλυσαν	ντο	ἐλύσαντο

Contract Stems   (§44.1b)

Contract verbs are regular in the aorist. They lengthen their final stem vowel before the tense formative. Cf. 40.3.

augment + tense stem (lengthened final vowel) + tense formative (σα)+ secondary ending

first aorist active indicative

		*γεννα	*ποιε	*φανερο
1 sg	-[1]	ἐγέννησα	ἐποίησα	ἐφανέρωσα
2 sg	ς	ἐγέννησας	ἐποίησας	ἐφανέρωσας
3 sg	-(ν)[2]	ἐγέννησε(ν)	ἐποίησε(ν)	ἐφανέρωσε(ν)
1 pl	μεν	ἐγεννήσαμεν	ἐποιήσαμεν	ἐφανερώσαμεν
2 pl	τε	ἐγεννήσατε	ἐποιήσατε	ἐφανερώσατε
3 pl	ν	ἐγέννησαν	ἐποίησαν	ἐφανέρωσαν

first aorist middle indicative

		*γεννα	*ποιε	*φανερο
1 sg	μην	ἐγεννησάμην	ἐποιησάμην	ἐφανερωσάμην
2 sg	σο[3]	ἐγεννήσω	ἐποιήσω	ἐφανερώσω
3 sg	το	ἐγεννήσατο	ἐποιήσατο	ἐφανερώσατο
1 pl	μεθα	ἐγεννησάμεθα	ἐποιησάμεθα	ἐφανερωσάμεθα
2 pl	σθε	ἐγεννήσασθε	ἐποιήσασθε	ἐφανερώσασθε
3 pl	ντο	ἐγεννήσαντο	ἐποιήσαντο	ἐφανερώσαντο

---

[1] Contrary to the normal pattern, the first person singular active uses no personal ending.

[2] The third person singular active uses no personal ending, but in order to avoid confusion with the first singular, it alters the vowel in the tense formative τοε by analogy to the imperfect.

[3] The σ of the personal ending is intervocalic and drops out (§25.5a), and the tense formative vowel and ο contract to ω (ε + γεννα + σα + σο ‹ εγεννησασο ‹ εγεννησαο ‹ ἐγεννήσω). Cf. §40.2.

Liquid Stems (§44.1c)

Verbs whose verbal roots end in a liquid (λ ρ) or a nasal (μ ν) are called "liquid verbs." They form their aorist by adding α (not σα) and by modifying their stem vowel (cf. §25.5a).

augment + tense stem + tense formative (α) + secondary ending

		aorist active			**aorist middle**
		*φην			*αμην
1 sg	-[1]	ἔμεινα	μην		ἐμεινάμην
2 sg	ς	ἔμεινας	σο[2]		ἐμείνω
3 sg	-(ν)[3]	ἔμεινε(ν)	το		ἐμείνατο
1 pl	μεν	ἐμείναμεν	μεθα		ἐμεινάμεθα
2 pl	τε	ἐμείνατε	σθε		ἐμείνασθε
3 pl	ν	ἔμειναν	ντο		ἐμείναντο

Most of the liquid aorists come from the v-2d category. In addition to those, these are the remaining liquid aorists that occur in the New Testament. Some compounds are listed under their simple verb.

ἀμύνομαι	ἠμυνάμην	v-1c(2)
βαθύνω	ἐβάθυνα	v-1c(2)
γαμέω	ἔγημα[4]	v-1d(2a)
δέρω	ἔδειρα	v-1c(1)
διαμαρτύρομαι	διεμαρτυράμην	v-1c(1)
εὐθύνω	εὔθυνα	v-1c(2)
κερδαίνω	ἐκέρδανα[5]	v-3d
κλίνω	ἔκλινα	v-1c(2)
κρίνω	ἔκρινα	v-1c(2)
μένω	ἔμεινα	v-1c(2)
μολύνω	ἐμόλυνα	v-1c(2)
πλύνω	ἔπλυνα	v-1c(2)
σκληρύνω	ἐσκλήρυνα	v-1c(2)

---

[1] Contrary to the normal pattern, the first person singular active uses no personal ending (cf. the imperfect ἔλυον).

[2] The σ of the personal ending is intervocalic and drops out, and the α and ο contract to ω (εμειν + α + σο ‣ εμειναο ‣ ἐμείνω; §25.5a). Cf. §40.2.

[3] The third person singular active uses no personal ending, but in order to avoid confusion with the 1st singular, it alters the vowel in the tense formative to ε by analogy to the imperfect.

[4] Normally uses a regular first aorist in the N.T., ἐγάμησα.

[5] Liquid aorist is used once (1 Cor 9:21); elsewhere it uses a first aorist, ἐκέρδησα (fourteen times).

The following words have liquid aorists, but the aorist forms do not occur in the New Testament: βαρύνω (v-1c[2]), πληθύνω (v-1c[2]), σύρω (v-1c[1]). γίνομαι has a liquid stem, but its aorist is a second aorist (ἐγενόμην; v-1c[2]).

κ aorists (§44.1d)

Three μι verbs (v-6) form their aorist active indicative with κα instead of σα as the tense formative.

In the middle μι verbs are conjugated athematically as root aorists, so we have classified them as second aorists (§44.2b). ἵστημι never occurs in the New Testament as a κ aorist. The final κ in ἤνεγκα (‹ φέρω) is part of the verbal stem and therefore not a κ aorist.

In Classical Greek, the aorist active singular was formed as below. However, the aorist active plural was almost always formed as a second aorist: ἔθεμεν, ἔδομεν, etc. (§44.2b; Smyth §755). In the non-indicative moods the second aorist is used exclusively.

Smyth lists κ aorists as second aorists, but didactically it is helpful to think of the κα as a tense formative and therefore first aorist (cf. LaSor §24.4722). Funk (§412) classifies them as weak verbs since they use weak (i.e., first aorist) endings.

aorist active	*η[1]	*θε	*δο
1 sg	-	ἀφῆκα	ἔθηκα	ἔδωκα
2 sg	ς	ἀφῆκας	ἔθηκας	ἔδωκας
3 sg	-(ν)	ἀφῆκε(ν)	ἔθηκε(ν)	ἔδωκε(ν)
1 pl	μεν	ἀφήκαμεν	ἐθήκαμεν	ἐδώκαμεν
2 pl	τε	ἀφήκατε	ἐθήκατε	ἐδώκατε
3 pl	ν	ἀφῆκαν	ἔθηκαν	ἔδωκαν

Athematic stems (§44.1e)

ἵστημι (*στα) has a first (below) and second (§44.2b) aorist. It is the only μι verb to do so.

1 sg	-	ἔστησα
2 sg	ς	ἔστησας
3 sg	-(ν)	ἔστησε(ν)
1 pl	μεν	ἔστημεν
2 pl	τε	ἔστητε
3 pl	σαν	ἔστησαν

---

[1]   ἀφίημι is a compound of ἀπό and ἵημι. In the formation of the present stem, the o elides (§6.5) and the π aspirates to a φ (§14.3). The η therefore represents the stem vowel. See v-6a for a discussion of ἵημι.

Second Aorist (§44.2)

As we have said before, it is not the second aorist that is irregular; the present alters the verbal root most dramatically. By and large, the stem of the second aorist is in fact the verbal root of the word. A verb that has a second aorist will *always* have a different stem than it has in the present and can therefore be distinguished from the imperfect. (This is not true in the second perfect, e.g., γράφω ‣ γέγραφα.) If a verb undergoes ablaut, the second aorist tense stem–and hence the verbal root–tend to show the weak grade. See *MH* 208-214; Smyth §546-554.

Thematic stems (§44.2a)

augment + tense stem + connecting vowel + secondary ending

		aorist active		aorist middle
1 sg	ν	ἔβαλον	μην	ἐβαλόμην
2 sg	ς	ἔβαλες	σο[1]	ἐβάλου
3 sg	-(ν)	ἔβαλε(ν)	το	ἐβάλετο
1 pl	μεν	ἐβάλομεν	μεθα	ἐβαλόμεθα
2 pl	τε	ἐβάλετε	σθε	ἐβάλεσθε
3 pl	ν	ἔβαλον	ντο	ἐβάλοντο

All the second aorists of words occurring in the New Testament are listed at §44.5e.

Athematic Stems (§44.2b)

Verbs that follow the athematic conjugation are also "root aorists" (cf. §44.2c) since the personal ending is added directly to the verbal root without an intervening connecting vowel. δύνω (v-3a[1]) and πέτομαι (v-1b[3]) also have root aorists but they are not μι verbs. In the New Testament there are three μι verbs with root aorists.

ἵστημι does not have an aorist middle. We have substituted ἐπριάμην (Smyth §415, §416).

The aorist active of τίθημι is first aorist (κ aorist; §44.1d). The aorist middle is a root aorist (below).

The aorist active and middle of δίδωμι is first aorist (κ aorist; §44.1d). It has a regular first aorist in the subjunctive (§52.4).

The aorist active of ἀφίημι is first aorist (κ aorist; §44.1d). ἀφίημι has a root aorist in the middle but it does not occur in the New Testament.

---

1   The σ of the personal ending is intervocalic and drops out, and the o and o contract to ου (§25.5a). Cf. §40.2.

The forms in parentheses do not occur in the New Testament; we have included them for completeness.

augment + tense stem + secondary ending

		*στα	*θε	*δο

aorist active

1 *sg*	ν	ἔστην	(ἔθην)	(ἔδων)
2 *sg*	ς	ἔστης	(ἔθης)	(ἔδως)
3 *sg*	-	ἔστη	(ἔθη)	(ἔδω)
1 *pl*	μεν	ἔστημεν	(ἔθεμεν)	(ἔδομεν)
2 *pl*	τε	ἔστητε	(ἔθετε)	(ἔδοτε)
3 *pl*	σαν	ἔστησαν	(ἔθεασαν)	(ἔδοσαν)

aorist middle

1 *sg*	μην	ἐπριάμην¹	ἐθέμην	(ἐδόμην)
2 *sg*	σο²	ἐπρίω	ἔθου	(ἔδου)
3 *sg*	το	ἐπρίατο	ἔθετο	(ἔδοτο)
1 *pl*	μεθα	ἐπριάμεθα	ἐθέμεθα	(ἐδόμεθα)
2 *pl*	σθε	ἐπρίασθε	ἔθεσθε	ἔδοσθε
3 *pl*	ντο	ἐπρίαντο	ἔθεντο	ἔδοντο

Root aorists   (§44.2c)

When the personal ending is added directly to the verbal stem in the aorist, it is called a "root aorist." μι verbs in the active and middle are root aorists (e.g., ἵστημι › ἔστην), as are βαίνω (*βα › ἔβην; v-3d), γίνωσκω (*γνο › ἔγνων; v-5a), δύω (*δυ › ἐδύην; v-1a[4]), and ἐπιπέτομαι (*πετ › ἔπτην; v-1b[3]).³ Cf. Funk §411 and §44.5e. Root aorists are easily confused with second aorists, which however use a connecting vowel.

aorist active

1 *sg*	ν	ἔβην	ἔγνων	ἔστην
2 *sg*	ς	ἔβης	ἔγνως	ἔστης
3 *sg*	-	ἔβη	ἔγνω	ἔστη

---

¹   If ἵστημι did occur in the aorist middle, its forms would be ἐστάμην, ἔστω, ἔστατο, ἐστάμεθα, ἔστασθε, and ἔσταντο.

²   The intervocalic σ drops off (§25.5) and the vowels contract. Cf. §40.2.

³   εἰμί may appear to have a root aorist, but ἤμην is an imperfect.

1 pl	μεν	ἔβημεν	ἔγνωμεν	ἔστημεν
2 pl	τε	ἔβητε	ἔγνωτε	ἔστητε
3 pl	ν	ἔβησαν	ἔγνωσαν	ἔστησαν

δύω (v-1a[4]) appears as ἔδυ in Mark 1:32, a third singular aorist active from the alternate form δύω and as such a root aorist. It has a first aorist, ἔδυσα. ἐπιπέτομαι (v-1b[3]) also has a root aorist ἐπέπτην, which does not occur in the New Testament (Funk §411). Cf. χέω, ἔχεα for a similar construction (§44.5e).

Stems Ending in a Stop (§44.3)

(τ δ θ, π β φ, κ γ χ)

As is the case in the future (§43.5), if a stem ends with a stop the final consonant can be changed.

Labial If a stem ends with a π, β, or φ, the dental will be dropped (§22.1).

ε + *βλεπ + σα › ἔβλεψα

ε + *θλιβ + σα › ἔτριψα

ε + *γραφ + σα › ἔγραψα

Velar If a stem ends with a κ, γ, or χ, the final consonant and the σ will be written as a ξ (§22.2).

ε + *διωκ + σα › ἐδίωξα

ε + *πνιγ + σα › ἔπνιξα

ε + *δεχ + σαμην › ἐδεξάμην

Dental If a stem ends with a τ, δ, or θ, the final consonant becomes a σ, joins with the other σ, and then the double σ simplifies to one σ (§22.3).

ε + *ψευδ + σαμην › εψευσσαμην › ἐψευσάμην

ε + *πειθ + σα › επεισσα › ἔπεισα

Words Ending in αζω or ιζω (§44.4)

§44.4 The verbal stems in these categories really end in δ (v-2a[1]) or γ (v-2a[2]). In order to form the present stem, ι is added to the verbal root. But δ or γ added to ι form ζ (§26.2), thus making it appear that the verb actually ends in ζ. Therefore, what we described in §43.3 above concerning dentals and velars applies also to these words. (The original δ or γ reappear in the other tenses, only to be modified for other reasons.)

*βαπτιδ + ι + ω › βαπτίζω   present

*βαπτιδ + σα › βαπτισσα › ἐβάπτισα   aorist

*κραγ	+ ι + ω	‣ κράζω	present
*κραγ	+ σα	‣ ἔκραξα	aorist

Miscellaneous (§44.5)

§44.5a   **Second aorists.** Following are listed all verbs in the New Testament that have a second aorist (active/middle). Some compounds are listed under the simple verb. Very similar to second aorists are root aorists (§44.2c).

present	*aorist*	*root*	*tag*
ἄγω	ἤγαγον	*αγ	v-1b(2)
αἱρέω	εἱλόμην[1]	*Ϝελ	v-1d(2a)
αἰσθάνομαι	ἠσθόμην	*αισθ	v-3a(2a)
ἅλλομαι	ἡλόμην[2]	*αλ	v-2d(1)
ἁμαρτάνω	ἥμαρτον[3]	*αμαρτ	v-3a(2a)
ἀναθάλλω	ἀνέθαλον	ἀνά + *θαλ	cv-2d(1)
ἀνακράζω	ἀνέκραγον[4]	ἀνά + *κραγ	cv-2a(2)
ἀποθνῄσκω	ἀπέθανον[5]	ἀπό + *θαν	cv-5a
ἀπόλλυμι	ἀπωλόμην[6]	*απ + ολ	cv-3c(2)
βάλλω	ἔβαλον	*βαλ	v-2d(1)
γίνομαι	ἐγενόμην	*γεν	v-1c(2)
ἔρχομαι	ἦλθον	*ελθ	v-1b(2)
ἐσθίω	ἔφαγον	*φαγ	v-1b(3)
εὑρίσκω	εὗρον	*ευρ	v-5b
ἔχω	ἔσχον	*σεχ	v-1b(2)
θιγγάνω	ἔθιγον	*θιγ	v-3a(2b)
ἱκνέομαι	ἱκόμην	*ικ	v-3b
κάμνω	ἔκαμον	*καμ	v-3a(1)
λαγχάνω	ἔλαχον	*λαχ	v-3a(2b)
λαμβάνω	ἔλαβον	*λαβ	v-3a(2b)
λανθάνω	ἔλαθον	*λαθ	v-3a(2b)

---

[1]   Occurs at Heb 11:25 as ἑλόμενος, and at 2 Thess 2:23 as a first aorist, εἵλατο.

[2]   The compound ἐφάλλομαι has a second aorist. The simple verb uses a first aorist, ἡλάμην (Acts 14:10).

[3]   Also has a first aorist form, ἡμάρτησα, used only in non-indicative forms.

[4]   ἀνακράζω occurs once as a second aorist (ἀνέκραγον) and four times as a first aorist. κράζω always uses a first aorist (ἔκραξα).

[5]   Also συναποθνῄσκω.

[6]   The compound συναπόλλυμι occurs with a second aorist, συναπωλόμην. ὄλλυμι has a first aorist, ὤλεσα, which does not occur in the N.T.

λέγω	εἶπον	Ϝιπ	v-1b(2)
λείπω	ἔλιπον	*λιπ	v-1b(1)
μανθάνω	ἔμαθον	*μαθ	v-3a(2b)
ὁράω	εἶδον	*Ϝιδ	v-1d(1a)
ὀφείλω	ὤφελον	*οφ	v-2d(1)
πάσχω	ἔπαθον	*παθ	v-5a
περιτέμνω	περιέτεμον	περι + *τεμ	cv-3a(1)
πέτομαι	ἐπτόμην[1]	*πετ	v-1b(3)
πίνω	ἔπιον	*πι	v-3a(1)
πίπτω	ἔπεσον	*πετ	v-1b(3)
πυνθάνομαι	ἐπυθόμην	*πυθ	v-3a(2b)
τέμνω	ἔτεμον	*τεμ	v-3a(1)
τίκτω	ἔτεκον	*τεκ	v-1b(2)
τρέχω	ἔδραμον	*δραμ	v-1a(2)
τυγχάνω	ἔτυχον	*τυχ	v-3a(2b)
φεύγω	ἔφυγον	*φυγ	v-1b(2)

Cf. ἱκνέομαι (v-3b), φέρω (v-1c[1]), χέω (§44.5e).

§44.5b There are several second aorist stems that use first aorist endings in the New Testament. Some alternate between first and second aorist endings: εἴπατε, εἴδαμεν, ἀνεῖλαν, ἐλθάτω, ἐξείλατο, εὑράμενος et al. See *BDF* §81 for a list.

Funk (§4122) discusses this process. He says that since the first aorist distinguishes between first singular (σα) and third plural (σαν), the first aorist endings were moving over to the second aorist.

- Second aorists can be found with first aorist endings (ἦλθαν, ἤνεγκα, εἶπας, εἶλα, ἔβαλαν).

- Second aorist like ἔπεσον (where σ is part of the stem) were viewed as first aorists (ἔπεσα).

- Some second aorists where developing different forms that were fully first aorist (ἁμαρτάνω › ἥμαρτον and ἁμαρτάω › ἡμάρτησα).

In Modern Greek there is only one set of endings (α, ες, ε(ν), αμεν, ετε and ατε, αν). Cf. *BDF* §81.

§44.5c In several aorists, a letter can be inserted between the tense stem and the tense formative, just like the insertion of η in the other tenses (§45.3).

---

[1] Also has a root aorist (§44.2c).

ἁλίσκομαι	ἥλωσα	*ἁλ (inserts ω)	v-5b
βλαστάνω	ἐβλάστησα	*βλαστ (inserts η)	v-3a(2a)
ὄλλυμι	ὤλεσα	*ολ (inserts ε)	v-3c(2)
ὀμνύω	ὤμοσα	*ομ (inserts ο)	v-3c(2)

§44.5d   There are two examples of reduplication in the aorist (Smyth §448).

ἄγω	*αγ ‣ αγαγ ‣ ἤγαγον	v-3c(2)
φέρω	*ενεκ ‣ ενκ ‣ ενενκ ‣ ενεγκ ‣ ἤνεγκα	v-3c(2)

§44.5e   χέω has a non-sigmatic first aorist, ἔχεα (v-1a[7]).

Perfect Active Indicative   (§45)

First Perfect   (§45.1)

Two things of special note happen in the perfect active. Several times a final stem ν will drop out because of the following κ of the tense formative (§45.4). Also, several times the final stem consonant, if it is a labial (π β) or a velar (κ γ), will aspirate to φ and χ respectively. There are also a substantial number of examples of ablaut (§4). The α in the tense formative is short for accent purposes (λέλυκα). On the perfect active see *MH* 220-221.

The third plural sometimes borrows ν from the aorist active: λέλυκαν instead of λελύκασι (*BDF* §83). On Attic reduplication cf. §32.6.

Thematic Stems (§45.1a)

reduplication + tense stem + tense formative (κα) + primary active ending

1 sg	-[1]	λέλυκα	1 pl	μεν	λελύκαμεν
2 sg	ς[2]	λέλυκας	2 pl	τε	λελύκατε
3 sg	-(ν)[3]	λέλυκε(ν)	3 pl	ασι(ν)	λελύκασι(ν)

---

[1]   No ending is used. α replaces the connecting vowel (Smyth §463a). We prefer to think of κα as the tense formative.

[2]   In the perfect, the real ending is ς, not σι (cf. §36.5).

[3]   The third person singular active uses no personal ending, but in order to avoid confusion with the first singular, it alters the vowel in the tense formative to ε.

Contract Stems   (§45.1b)

Contract verbs form their perfect forms regularly. The final stem vowel is lengthened before the tense formative.

reduplication + tense stem (lengthened final vowel) + tense formative (κα)+ primary active ending

		*γεννα	*ποιε	*φανερο
1 sg	-	γεγέννηκα	πεποίηκα	πεφανέρωκα
2 sg	ς	γεγέννηκας	πεποίηκας	πεφανέρωκας
3 sg	-(ν)[1]	γεγέννηκε(ν)	πεποίηκε(ν)	πεφανέρωκε(ν)
1 pl	μεν	γεγεννήκαμεν	πεποιήκαμεν	πεφανερώκαμεν
2 pl	τε	γεγεννήκατε	πεποιήκατε	πεφανερώκατε
3 pl	ασι(ν)	γεγεννήκασι(ν)	πεποιήκασι(ν)	πεφανερώκασι(ν)

Athematic Stems   (§45.1c)

μι verbs form their perfect tense stem just like a thematic verb. An ε is used to separate the reduplicated initial consonant and not an ι as in the present tense. In the singular, μι verbs use the first perfect. In the plural (and dual in Classical) some use the second perfect (Smyth §417). We have listed all the first perfect forms. For the second perfect see §45.2b.

reduplication + tense stem (lengthened final vowel) + tense formative (κα)+ primary active ending

		*στα	*τε	*δο
1 sg	-	ἕστηκα	τέθεικα	δέδωκα
2 sg	ς	ἕστηκας	τέθεικας	δέδωκας
3 sg	-(ν)[1]	ἕστηκε(ν)	τέθεικε(ν)	δέδωκε(ν)
1 pl	μεν	ἑστήκαμεν	τεθείκαμεν	δεδώκαμεν
2 pl	τε	ἑστήκατε	τεθείκατε	δεδώκατε
3 pl	ασι(ν)	ἑστήκασι(ν)	τεθείκασι(ν)	δεδώκασι(ν)

Second Perfect   (§45.2)

The second perfect is like the first perfect except that it uses α and not κα as the tense formative. Most verbs show a stem change from the present tense. All second perfects in the New Testament are listed at §45.5b. See Smyth §561-573.

---

[1] The third person singular active uses no personal ending, but in order to avoid confusion with the first singular, it alters the vowel in the tense formative to ε.

Thematic Stems   (§45.2a)

reduplication + tense stem + tense formative (α) + primary active ending

1 sg	-	γέγονα	1 pl	μεν	γεγόναμεν
2 sg	ς	γέγονας	2 pl	τε	γεγόνατε
3 sg	-(ν)[1]	γέγονε(ν)	3 pl	ασι(ν)	γεγόνασι(ν)

Athematic Stems   (§45.2b)

Only ἵστημι has a second perfect form. (The other μι verbs have first perfect forms.) The singular tends to be first perfect and the plural second perfect as in the paradigm below. In the New Testament we only find the first perfect indicative of ἵστημι in the singular. However, non-indicative plural forms can be found (ἑστῶτες).

reduplication + tense stem+ tense formative (κα) + primary active ending

		*στα	*θε	*δο
1 sg	-	ἕστηκα
2 sg	ς	ἕστηκας
3 sg	-(ν)[1]	ἕστηκε(ν)
1 pl	μεν	ἕσταμεν
2 pl	τε	ἕστατε
3 pl	ασι(ν)	ἑστᾶσι(ν)

Insertion of an η   (§45.3)

Smyth (§485) discusses the insertion of an epsilon as a general rule, as well as the insertion of α and ο (§486), a σ (§489), and a θ (§490), as well as related changes.

There are multiple ways of describing the same verbal form. For example, *βαλ goes to βέβληκα in the perfect middle/passive. One way to look at it is to say the stem vowel reduces to the zero state due to ablaut (› βλ) and an η is inserted (› βλη). Another way is to state that the α and λ undergo metathesis (› βλα) and then the α lengthens (› βλη; cf. θνήσκω, καλέω, κάμνω, and τέμνω). Since the primary emphasis of this text is to help students identify forms, we have limited our technical discussions on these kinds of issues. We will attempt to describe the change in a way that makes sense in light of the basic phonetic rules.

Ten words in the New Testament insert an η between the verbal root and the perfect active tense formative. A similar insertion occurs in the other stems (cf. §46.6, §47.7).

---

[1]   The third person singular active uses no personal ending, but in order to avoid confusion with the first singular, it alters the vowel in the tense formative to ε.

ἁμαρτάνω	ἡμάρτηκα	*αμαρτ	v-3a(2a)
βάλλω	βέβληκα	*βαλ	v-2d(1)
εὑρίσκω	εὕρηκα	*ευρ	v-5b
μανθάνω	μεμάθηκα	*μαθ	v-3a(2b)
μένω	μεμένηκα	*μεν	v-1c(2)

Cf. ἔχω (ἔσχηκα), which can be due to metathesis (*σεχ ‣ σχε ‣ σχη ‣ ἔσχηκα), and καλέω (κέκληκα; v-1d[2b]). See also θνῄσκω (τέθνηκα; v-5a), κάμνω (κέκμηκα; v-3a[1]), and τέμνω (τέτμηκα; v-3a[1]), although these perfects do not occur in the New Testament. εἴρηκα is from *Ϝρη and therefore the η is not inserted (v-1b[2]).

πίπτω inserts an ω (*πετ ‣ πτ ‣ πεπτ ‣ πέπτωκα; v-1b[3]).

Dropping the Final Stem ν   (§45.4)

Some verbs drop the final ν of their stem in the formation of the perfect tense stem (cf. Smyth §491, Funk §482.30, 24.11; cf. §46.5). This change can also be observed in the perfect middle/passive and the aorist passive. This change should not be confused with v-3 verbs that add ν to form their present tense stem, and therefore the ν is not present in the other tenses.

κλίνω	κέκλικα	v-1c(2)
κρίνω	κέκρικα	v-2d(6)

Miscellaneous   (§45.5)

§45.5a   **ὄμνυμι** inserts ο before the tense formative. *ομ ‣ ὄμνυμι ‣ ὤμοσα ‣ ὀμώμοκα. See §45.3 for a general discussion.

§45.5b   **List of second perfects.**   Below are listed all the second perfects that appear in the New Testament. Some compound verbs are listed under their simple form. For more extra-biblical second perfects see Smyth §704.

ἀκούω	ἀκήκοα	*ακο	v-1a(8)
ἀνοίγω	ἀνέῳγα	*οιγ	cv-1b(2)
γίνομαι	γέγονα	*γεν	v-1c(2)
γράφω	γέγραφα	*γραπ	v-1b(1)
διατάσσω	διατεταχα	δια + *ταγ	cv-2b
ἐκφεύγω	ἐκπέφευγα	*φευγ	v-1b(2)
εἴκω	ἔοικα		v-1b(2)
ἔρχομαι	ἐλήλυθα	*ελευθ	v-1b(2)
κράζω	κέκραγα	*κραγ	v-2a(2)
λαμβάνω	εἴληφα	*ᵉελεπ	v-3a(2b)

-	οἶδα	*οιδ	v-1b(3)
ὄλλυμι	ὄλωλα	*ολ	v-3c(2)
πάσχω	πέπονθα	*πονθ	v-5a
πείθω	πέποιθα	*ποιθ	v-1b(3)
πράσσω	πέπραχα	*πραχ	v-2b
προσφέρω	προσενήνοχα	*ενοχ	v-1c(1)
σήπω	σέσηπα	*σηπ	v-1b(1)
τυγχάνω	τέτυχα	*τυχ	v-3a(2b)

Cf. δείκνυμι (v-3c[2]), λείπω (v-1b[1]), πέμπω (v-1b[1]), ῥήγνυμι (v-3c[2]), τάσσω (v-2b), and φυλάσσω, πεφύλαχα (v-2b).

§45.5c   οἶδα is actually a perfect that is used in Koine Greek as a present. For a fuller paradigm see §96.

	Koine Greek		*Classical Greek*
1 sg	οἶδα	1 sg	οἶδα
2 sg	οἶδας	2 sg	οἶσθα
3 sg	οἶδε(ν)	3 sg	οἶδε
1 pl	οἴδαμεν	1 pl	ἴσμεν
2 pl	οἴδετε	2 pl	ἴστε[1]
3 pl	οἴδασι(ν)	3 pl	ἴσασι[2]

§45.5d   **No present form**. There are two perfects that have lost their present form. εἴωθα (v-1b[3]) is from ἔθω, and ἔοικα (used impersonally as ἔοικεν) is from εἴκω (v-1b[2]).

Pluperfect Active (§45.6)

The pluperfect active is formed from the fourth principal part. There are twenty-two verbs in the New Testament that appear as a pluperfect, occurring a total of eighty-six times (seventy-nine being active, see list below). As is the case with the perfect, a first pluperfect is formed with the tense formative (κ), while the second pluperfect has none. Following the tense formative are the connecting vowels ει.[3] Preceding the reduplication can be an augment, although this is not necessary. This is why the augment is often placed in parentheses in paradigms. On the pluperfect see *MH* 221-224.

---

[1]   Heb 12:17; Jas 1:19

[2]   Acts 26:4

[3]   Funk (§415) views κει as the tense formative of the first pluperfect, ει as the tense formative in the second pluperfect. See our discussion at §34.4 and *BDF* §86.

(augment +) reduplication + tense stem + tense formative (κ) + connecting vowel (ει) +
secondary active ending

		1 pluperfect active	**2 pluperfect active**

Thematic stems   (§45.6a)

1 sg	ν	(ἐ)λελύκειν	(ἐ)γεγράφειν
2 sg	ς[1]	(ἐ)λελύκεις	(ἐ)γεγράφεις
3 sg	-	(ἐ)λελύκει	(ἐ)γεγράφει
1 pl	μεν	(ἐ)λελύκειμεν	(ἐ)γεγράφειμεν
2 pl	τε	(ἐ)λελύκειτε	(ἐ)γεγράφειτε
3 pl	σαν[2]	(ἐ)λελύκεισαν	(ἐ)γεγράφεισαν

In Classical Greek the pluperfect followed a slightly different pattern. The η in
the first and second person singular was formed through contraction (‹ εσα; ‹
εσας). Eventually the κει in the third singular spread to the other forms (Smyth
§467).

1 sg	-	(ἐ)λελύκη
2 sg	ς	(ἐ)λελύκης
3 sg	-	(ἐ)λελύκει
1 pl	μεν	(ἐ)λελύκεμεν
2 pl	τε	(ἐ)λελύκετε
3 pl	σαν	(ἐ)λελύκεσαν

Athematic stems   (§45.6b)

ἵστημι has a first pluperfect form. In Classical Greek ἵστημι could have a second
perfect in the plural, but a first perfect in the singular. ἵστημι does not occur in
the New Testament in a middle/passive form. ἵστημι occurs fourteen times in the
perfect, all being third person (singular and plural).

		Koine	**Classical**
1 sg	-	εἱστήκη	(εἱστήκη)
2 sg	ς	εἱστήκης	(εἱστήκης)
3 sg	-	εἱστήκει	(εἱστήκει)

---

[1]   You can think of the ending as ες, which contracts with the connecting vowel to form
      εις. Cf. §40.2.

[2]   If the verb's stem ends in a consonant, the third plural will always be formed peri-
      phrastically (with ἦσαν and the perfect participle of the verb in the nominative plural
      masculine).

1 pl	μεν	εἱστήκειμεν	ἕσταμεν
2 pl	τε	εἱστήκειτε	ἕστατε
3 pl	σαν	εἱστήκεισαν	ἕστασαν

List of all pluperfects (§45.6c)

Following is a list of all active pluperfects occurring in the New Testament (except periphrastic forms).

βάλλω	βεβλήκειν	v-2d(1)
γίνομαι	(ἐ)γεγόνειν	v-1c(3)
γινώσκω	ἐγνώκειν	v-5a
δίδωμι	(ἐ)δεδώκειν	v-6a
(εἴωθα)	εἰώθειν	v-1b(3)
ἐπιπείθω	ἐπεποίθειν	v-1b(3)
ἔρχομαι	ἐληλύθειν	v-1b(2)
ἵστημι	(ε)ἱστήκειν	v-6a
κρίνω	κεκρίκειν	v-1c(3)
λέγω	εἰρήκειν	v-1b(2)
μένω	μεμενήκειν	v-1c(3)
οἶδα	ᾔδειν	v-1b(3)
ὁράω	ἑωράκειν	v-1d(1a)
πιστεύω	πεπιστεύκειν	v-1a(6)
ποιέω	πεποιήκειν	v-1d(2a)
συναρπάζω	συνηρπάκειν	v-2a(1)

ἵστημι occurs fifteen times, ἔρχομαι eleven times, and οἶδα thirty- three times. There are five more verbs that occur in the pluperfect middle/passive; cf. §46.7. Following are all the verbs that occur as pluperfect actives in the New Testament, except for verses with ᾔδειν (thirty- three times).

Matt 12:7   εἰ δὲ **ἐγνώκειτε** τί ἐστιν· ἔλεος θέλω καὶ οὐ θυσίαν, οὐκ ἂν κατεδικάσατε τοὺς ἀναιτίους.

Matt 12:46   Ἔτι αὐτοῦ λαλοῦντος τοῖς ὄχλοις ἰδοὺ ἡ μήτηρ καὶ οἱ ἀδελφοὶ αὐτοῦ **εἱστήκεισαν** ἔξω ζητοῦντες αὐτῷ λαλῆσαι.

Matt 13:2   καὶ συνήχθησαν πρὸς αὐτὸν ὄχλοι πολλοί, ὥστε αὐτὸν εἰς πλοῖον ἐμβάντα καθῆσθαι, καὶ πᾶς ὁ ὄχλος ἐπὶ τὸν αἰγιαλὸν **εἱστήκει**.

Matt 27:15   Κατὰ δὲ ἑορτὴν **εἰώθει** ὁ ἡγεμὼν ἀπολύειν ἕνα τῷ ὄχλῳ δέσμιον ὃν ἤθελον.

Mark 10:1   Καὶ ἐκεῖθεν ἀναστὰς ἔρχεται εἰς τὰ ὅρια τῆς Ἰουδαίας [καὶ] πέραν τοῦ Ἰορδάνου, καὶ συμπορεύονται πάλιν ὄχλοι πρὸς αὐτόν, καὶ ὡς **εἰώθει** πάλιν ἐδίδασκεν αὐτούς.

Mark 14:44   **δεδώκει** δὲ ὁ παραδιδοὺς αὐτὸν σύσσημον αὐτοῖς λέγων· ὃν ἂν φιλήσω αὐτός ἐστιν, κρατήσατε αὐτὸν καὶ ἀπάγετε ἀσφαλῶς.

Mark 15:7   ἦν δὲ ὁ λεγόμενος Βαραββᾶς μετὰ τῶν στασιαστῶν δεδεμένος οἵτινες ἐν τῇ στάσει φόνον **πεποιήκεισαν**.

Mark 15:10 ἐγίνωσκεν γὰρ ὅτι διὰ φθόνον **παραδεδώκεισαν** αὐτὸν οἱ ἀρχιερεῖς.

Mark 16:9 Ἀναστὰς δὲ πρωῒ πρώτῃ σαββάτου ἐφάνη πρῶτον Μαρίᾳ τῇ Μαγδαληνῇ, παρ' ἧς **ἐκβεβλήκει** ἑπτὰ δαιμόνια.

Luke 8:2 καὶ γυναῖκές τινες αἳ ἦσαν τεθεραπευμέναι ἀπὸ πνευμάτων πονηρῶν καὶ ἀσθενειῶν, Μαρία ἡ καλουμένη Μαγδαληνή, ἀφ' ἧς δαιμόνια ἑπτὰ **ἐξεληλύθει.**

Luke 8:29 παρήγγειλεν γὰρ τῷ πνεύματι τῷ ἀκαθάρτῳ ἐξελθεῖν ἀπὸ τοῦ ἀνθρώπου. πολλοῖς γὰρ χρόνοις **συνηρπάκει** αὐτὸν καὶ ἐδεσμεύετο ἁλύσεσιν καὶ πέδαις φυλασσόμενος καὶ διαρρήσσων τὰ δεσμὰ ἠλαύνετο ὑπὸ τοῦ δαιμονίου εἰς τὰς ἐρήμους.

Luke 8:38 ἐδεῖτο δὲ αὐτοῦ ὁ ἀνὴρ ἀφ' οὗ **ἐξεληλύθει** τὰ δαιμόνια εἶναι σὺν αὐτῷ· ἀπέλυσεν δὲ αὐτὸν λέγων....

Luke 11:22 ἐπὰν δὲ ἰσχυρότερος αὐτοῦ ἐπελθὼν νικήσῃ αὐτόν, τὴν πανοπλίαν αὐτοῦ αἴρει ἐφ' ᾗ **ἐπεποίθει** καὶ τὰ σκῦλα αὐτοῦ διαδίδωσιν.

Luke 19:15 καὶ ἐγένετο ἐν τῷ ἐπανελθεῖν αὐτὸν λαβόντα τὴν βασιλείαν καὶ εἶπεν φωνηθῆναι αὐτῷ τοὺς δούλους τούτους οἷς **δεδώκει** τὸ ἀργύριον, ἵνα γνοῖ τί διεπραγματεύσαντο.

Luke 22:13 ἀπελθόντες δὲ εὗρον καθὼς **εἰρήκει** αὐτοῖς καὶ ἡτοίμασαν τὸ πάσχα.

Luke 23:10 **εἱστήκεισαν** δὲ οἱ ἀρχιερεῖς καὶ οἱ γραμματεῖς εὐτόνως κατηγοροῦντες αὐτοῦ.

Luke 23:35 Καὶ **εἱστήκει** ὁ λαὸς θεωρῶν. ἐξεμυκτήριζον δὲ καὶ οἱ ἄρχοντες λέγοντες· ἄλλους ἔσωσεν, σωσάτω ἑαυτόν, εἰ οὗτός ἐστιν ὁ χριστὸς τοῦ θεοῦ ὁ ἐκλεκτός.

Luke 23:49 **Εἱστήκεισαν** δὲ πάντες οἱ γνωστοὶ αὐτῷ ἀπὸ μακρόθεν καὶ γυναῖκες αἱ συνακολουθοῦσαι αὐτῷ ἀπὸ τῆς Γαλιλαίας ὁρῶσαι ταῦτα.

John 1:35 Τῇ ἐπαύριον πάλιν **εἱστήκει** ὁ Ἰωάννης καὶ ἐκ τῶν μαθητῶν αὐτοῦ δύο

John 4:8 οἱ γὰρ μαθηταὶ αὐτοῦ **ἀπεληλύθεισαν** εἰς τὴν πόλιν ἵνα τροφὰς ἀγοράσωσιν.

John 6:17 καὶ ἐμβάντες εἰς πλοῖον ἤρχοντο πέραν τῆς θαλάσσης εἰς Καφαρναούμ. καὶ σκοτία ἤδη **ἐγεγόνει** καὶ οὔπω **ἐληλύθει** πρὸς αὐτοὺς ὁ Ἰησοῦς,

John 7:30 Ἐζήτουν οὖν αὐτὸν πιάσαι, καὶ οὐδεὶς ἐπέβαλεν ἐπ' αὐτὸν τὴν χεῖρα, ὅτι οὔπω **ἐληλύθει** ἡ ὥρα αὐτοῦ.

John 7:3 Ἐν δὲ τῇ ἐσχάτῃ ἡμέρᾳ τῇ μεγάλῃ τῆς ἑορτῆς **εἱστήκει** ὁ Ἰησοῦς καὶ ἔκραξεν λέγων· ἐάν τις διψᾷ ἐρχέσθω πρός με καὶ πινέτω.

John 8:20 Ταῦτα τὰ ῥήματα ἐλάλησεν ἐν τῷ γαζοφυλακίῳ διδάσκων ἐν τῷ ἱερῷ· καὶ οὐδεὶς ἐπίασεν αὐτόν, ὅτι οὔπω **ἐληλύθει** ἡ ὥρα αὐτοῦ.

John 11:13 **εἰρήκει** δὲ ὁ Ἰησοῦς περὶ τοῦ θανάτου αὐτοῦ, ἐκεῖνοι δὲ ἔδοξαν ὅτι περὶ τῆς κοιμήσεως τοῦ ὕπνου λέγει.

John 11:19 πολλοὶ δὲ ἐκ τῶν Ἰουδαίων **ἐληλύθεισαν** πρὸς τὴν Μάρθαν καὶ Μαριὰμ ἵνα παραμυθήσωνται αὐτὰς περὶ τοῦ ἀδελφοῦ.

John 11:30 οὔπω δὲ **ἐληλύθει** ὁ Ἰησοῦς εἰς τὴν κώμην, ἀλλ' ἦν ἔτι ἐν τῷ τόπῳ ὅπου ὑπήντησεν αὐτῷ ἡ Μάρθα.

John 11:57 **δεδώκεισαν** δὲ οἱ ἀρχιερεῖς καὶ οἱ Φαρισαῖοι ἐντολὰς ἵνα ἐάν τις γνῷ ποῦ ἐστιν μηνύσῃ, ὅπως πιάσωσιν αὐτόν.

John 18:5 ἀπεκρίθησαν αὐτῷ· Ἰησοῦν τὸν Ναζωραῖον. λέγει αὐτοῖς· ἐγώ εἰμι. **εἱστήκει** δὲ καὶ Ἰούδας ὁ παραδιδοὺς αὐτὸν μετ' αὐτῶν.

John 18:16 ὁ δὲ Πέτρος **εἱστήκει** πρὸς τῇ θύρᾳ ἔξω. ἐξῆλθεν οὖν ὁ μαθητὴς ὁ ἄλλος ὁ γνωστὸς τοῦ ἀρχιερέως καὶ εἶπεν τῇ θυρωρῷ καὶ εἰσήγαγεν τὸν Πέτρον.

John 18:18 **εἱστήκεισαν** δὲ οἱ δοῦλοι καὶ οἱ ὑπηρέται ἀνθρακιὰν πεποιηκότες, ὅτι ψῦχος ἦν, καὶ ἐθερμαίνοντο· ἦν δὲ καὶ ὁ Πέτρος μετ' αὐτῶν ἑστὼς καὶ θερμαινόμενος.

John 19:25 **Εἱστήκεισαν** δὲ παρὰ τῷ σταυρῷ τοῦ Ἰησοῦ ἡ μήτηρ αὐτοῦ καὶ ἡ ἀδελφὴ τῆς μητρὸς αὐτοῦ, Μαρία ἡ τοῦ Κλωπᾶ καὶ Μαρία ἡ Μαγδαληνή.

John 20:11 Μαρία δὲ **εἱστήκει** πρὸς τῷ μνημείῳ ἔξω κλαίουσα. ὡς οὖν ἔκλαιεν, παρέκυψεν εἰς τὸ μνημεῖον ....

Acts 1:10   καὶ ὡς ἀτενίζοντες ἦσαν εἰς τὸν οὐρανὸν πορευομένου αὐτοῦ, καὶ ἰδοὺ ἄνδρες
            δύο **παρειστήκεισαν** αὐτοῖς ἐν ἐσθήσεσι λευκαῖς ....

Acts 4:22   ἐτῶν γὰρ ἦν πλειόνων τεσσεράκοντα ὁ ἄνθρωπος ἐφ' ὃν **γεγόνει** τὸ σημεῖον τοῦτο
            τῆς ἰάσεως.

Acts 7:44   Ἡ σκηνὴ τοῦ μαρτυρίου ἦν τοῖς πατράσιν ἡμῶν ἐν τῇ ἐρήμῳ καθὼς διετάξατο ὁ
            λαλῶν τῷ Μωϋσῇ ποιῆσαι αὐτὴν κατὰ τὸν τύπον ὃν **ἑωράκει** ....

Acts 8:27   καὶ ἀναστὰς ἐπορεύθη. καὶ ἰδοὺ ἀνὴρ Αἰθίοψ εὐνοῦχος δυνάστης Κανδάκης
            βασιλίσσης Αἰθιόπων, ὃς ἦν ἐπὶ πάσης τῆς γάζης αὐτῆς, ὃς **ἐληλύθει**
            προσκυνήσων εἰς Ἰερουσαλήμ ....

Acts 9:7   οἱ δὲ ἄνδρες οἱ συνοδεύοντες αὐτῷ **εἱστήκεισαν** ἐνεοί, ἀκούοντες μὲν τῆς φωνῆς
            μηδένα δὲ θεωροῦντες.

Acts 9:21   ἐξίσταντο δὲ πάντες οἱ ἀκούοντες καὶ ἔλεγον· οὐχ οὗτός ἐστιν ὁ πορθήσας εἰς
            Ἰερουσαλὴμ τοὺς ἐπικαλουμένους τὸ ὄνομα τοῦτο, καὶ ὧδε εἰς τοῦτο **ἐληλύθει**
            ἵνα δεδεμένους αὐτοὺς ἀγάγῃ ἐπὶ τοὺς ἀρχιερεῖς;

Acts 14:23 χειροτονήσαντες δὲ αὐτοῖς κατ' ἐκκλησίαν πρεσβυτέρους, προσευξάμενοι μετὰ
            νηστειῶν παρέθεντο αὐτοὺς τῷ κυρίῳ εἰς ὃν **πεπιστεύκεισαν**.

Acts 19:32 ἄλλοι μὲν οὖν ἄλλο τι ἔκραζον· ἦν γὰρ ἡ ἐκκλησία συγκεχυμένη καὶ οἱ πλείους
            οὐκ **ᾔδεισαν** τίνος ἕνεκα **συνεληλύθεισαν**.

Acts 20:16 **κεκρίκει** γὰρ ὁ Παῦλος παραπλεῦσαι τὴν Ἔφεσον, ὅπως μὴ γένηται αὐτῷ
            χρονοτριβῆσαι ἐν τῇ Ἀσίᾳ· ἔσπευδεν γὰρ εἰ δυνατὸν εἴη αὐτῷ τὴν ἡμέραν τῆς
            πεντηκοστῆς γενέσθαι εἰς Ἰεροσόλυμα.

Acts 20:38 ὀδυνώμενοι μάλιστα ἐπὶ τῷ λόγῳ ᾧ **εἰρήκει**, ὅτι οὐκέτι μέλλουσιν τὸ πρόσωπον
            αὐτοῦ θεωρεῖν. προέπεμπον δὲ αὐτὸν εἰς τὸ πλοῖον.

1 John 2:19 ἐξ ἡμῶν ἐξῆλθαν ἀλλ' οὐκ ἦσαν ἐξ ἡμῶν· εἰ γὰρ ἐξ ἡμῶν ἦσαν, **μεμενήκεισαν** ἂν
            μεθ' ἡμῶν· ἀλλ' ἵνα φανερωθῶσιν ὅτι οὐκ εἰσὶν πάντες ἐξ ἡμῶν.

Rev 7:11   Καὶ πάντες οἱ ἄγγελοι **εἱστήκεισαν** κύκλῳ τοῦ θρόνου καὶ τῶν πρεσβυτέρων καὶ
            τῶν τεσσάρων ζῴων καὶ ἔπεσαν ἐνώπιον τοῦ θρόνου ἐπὶ τὰ πρόσωπα αὐτῶν καὶ
            προσεκύνησαν τῷ θεῷ.

§45.6d **ᾔδειν.** ᾔδειν is actually a pluperfect form that functions as the aorist
            of οἶδα, which of course is actually a perfect (cf. §45.5c). Following is
            its paradigm. See also §96.

	Koine Greek		*Classical Greek*
1 sg	ᾔδειν	1 sg	ᾔδη or ᾔδειν
2 sg	ᾔδεις	2 sg	ᾔδησθα or ᾔδεισθα
3 sg	ᾔδει	3 sg	ᾔδ or ᾔδειν
1 pl	ᾔδειμεν	1 pl	ᾖσμεν
2 pl	ᾔδειτε	2 pl	ᾖστε
3 pl	ᾔδεισαν	3 pl	ᾖσαν or ᾔδεσαν

Future Perfect Active   (§45.7)

There are no future perfect active forms in the New Testament. The future perfect is normally middle/passive in form and passive in meaning. It describes a "future state resulting from a completed action" (Smyth §1955, cf. §359, §581-4, §600).

The future perfect is formed from the first perfect active tense stem. It uses a σ as the tense formative, and primary personal endings. The only true future perfect active forms Smyth reports are ἑστήξω (ἵστημι) and τεθνήξω (θνῄσκω). Normally in Classical Greek it is formed periphrastically, using the perfect active participle and future of εἰμί (e.g., γεγραφὼς ἔσομαι). The future perfect is almost exclusively limited to the indicative.

There are four periphrastic future perfects in the New Testament, but they are all middle/passive (cf. §46.8).

Perfect Middle/Passive Indicative   (§46)

The perfect middle/passive is built on the fifth principal part. There is no difference in the stem between the perfect active and the middle/passive except that the middle/passive does not use the tense formative. The middle/passive is also distinguished by a different set of endings.

In the perfect middle/passive, the σ of the personal ending σαι does not drop out.

If the stem of the verb ends in a consonant (including stems that insert a θ), the third person plural is formed periphrastically (Smyth §405). The periphrastic perfect uses the perfect middle participle and indicative forms of εἰμί.

Thematic Stems   (§46.1)

reduplication + tense stem + primary middle/passive ending

1 sg	μαι	λέλυμαι	1 pl	μεθα	λελύμεθα
2 sg	σαι	λέλυσαι	2 pl	σθε	λέλυσθε
3 sg	ται	λέλυται	3 pl	νται	λέλυνται

Contract Stems   (§46.2)

		*γεννα	*ποιε	*φανερο
1 sg	μαι	γεγέννημαι	πεποίημαι	πεφανέρωμαι
2 sg	σαι	γεγέννησαι	πεποίησαι	πεφανέρωσαι
3 sg	ται	γεγέννηται	πεποίηται	πεφανέρωται
1 pl	μεθα	γεγεννήμεθα	πεποιήμεθα	πεφανερώμεθα
2 pl	σθε	γεγέννησθε	πεποίησθε	πεφανέρωσθε
3 pl	νται	γεγέννηνται	πεποίηνται	πεφανέρωνται

Athematic Stems   (§46.3)

		*στα	*θε	*δο
1 sg	μαι	ἕσταμαι	τέθειμαι	δέδομαι
2 sg	σαι	ἕστασαι	τέθεισαι	δέδοσαι
3 sg	ται	ἕσταται	τέθειται	δέδοται
1 pl	μεθα	ἑστάμεθα	τεθείμεθα	δεδόμεθα
2 pl	σθε	ἕστασθε	τέθεισθε	δέδοσθε
3 pl	νται	ἕστανται	τέθεινται	δέδονται

Stems ending in a Stop   (§46.4)

(π β φ, κ γ χ, τ δ θ)

Because there is no connecting vowel or tense formative in the perfect middle/passive, the personal endings are added directly to the stem. When the stem ends in a consonant this will usually produce consonantal change.

μ	μαι / μεθα	labial[1]	+	μ	›	μμ	(§21.1)
		velar[2]	+	μ	›	γμ	(§21.2)
		dental	+	μ	›	σμ	(§21.3)
σ	σαι / σθε	labial	+	σ	›	ψ	(§22.1)
		velar	+	σ	›	ξ	(§22.2)
		dental	+	σ	›	σ	(§22.3)
τ	ται	labial	+	τ	›	πτ	(§20.1)
		velar	+	τ	›	κτ	(§20.2)
		dental	+	τ	›	στ	(§20.3)

---

[1] Stems in μπ drop the π before μ but retain it elsewhere (Smyth §409a).

[2] Stems in γχ change to geminate γ before μ and then simplify (γχ + μ › γγμ › γμ; ἐλήλεγκμαι › ἐλήλεγμαι) but keep the two gammas before other consonants (ἐλήλεγξαι; Smyth §409c).

If you take the rules above and apply them in paradigm form, this is how they will be put into effect.

		labial (*γραφ)	*velar* (*διωκ)	*dental* (*πειθ)
1 sg	μαι	γέγραμμαι	δεδίωγμαι	πέπεισμαι[1]
2 sg	σαι	γέγραψαι	δεδίωξαι	πέπεισαι
3 sg	ται	γέγραπται	δεδίωκται	πέπεισται
1 pl	μεθα	γεγράμμεθα	δεδιώγμεθα	πεπείσμεθα
2 pl	σθε	γέγραφθε[2]	δεδίωχθε[3]	πέπεισθε
3 pl		εἰσὶ γεγραμμένοι	εἰσὶ δεδιωγμένοι	εἰσὶ πεπεισμένοι

Insertion of a σ (§46.5)

This same phenomena is found in the aorist passive (§47.6). A σ is inserted after the stem and before the personal ending. See the general discussion of vowel insertion at §45.3.

This insertion is by analogy to verbs whose stems end in σ, and to verbs whose stems end in a dental (τ δ θ), including v-2 verbs (αζω, ιζω; cf. Smyth §404). The latter will have a σ before a ending beginning with μ (μαι; μεθα) because a dental assimilates to a σ when immediately followed by a μ (§22.3). Smyth (§404) also has a detailed discussion and a set of rules for when this happens (§489a).

Some verbs insert σ in both the perfect middle/passive and the aorist passive, and some insert it in only one or the other. This insertion was happening increasingly in Classical Greek. See Smyth for more details.

Following is the list of the words in the New Testament that insert σ in the perfect middle/passive and the aorist passive tenses. This list does not include stems ending in σ or stems that develop a σ under normal phonetic change. Some compounds are listed under the simple verb.

present	*perfect mid/pas*	*aorist passive*	*classification*
ἀκούω	-	ἠκούσθην	v-1a(8)
ἀμφιέννυμι	ἠμφίεσμαι	-	v-3c(1)
ἀρκέω	-	ἠρκέσθην	v-1d(2b)
γινώσκω	ἔγνωσμαι	ἐγνώσθην	v-5a
ζώννυμι	ἔζωσμαι	-	v-3c(1)
θλάω	-	ἐθλάσθην	v-1d(1b)
θραύω	τέθραυσμαι	-	v-1a(5)

---

[1] Smyth has a different explanation; cf. §409b.

[2] The σ is interconsonantal and therefore drops out (§25.4). γεγραφ + σθε ‣ γέγραφθε.

[3] The σ is interconsonantal and therefore drops out (§25.4). Then the stop (κ) aspirates to a χ (§14.1). δεδιωκ + σθε ‣ δεδιωκθε ‣ δεδίωχθε.

ἱλάσκομαι	-	ἱλάσθην	v-5a
κεράννυμι	κεκέρασμαι	-	v-3c(1)
κλάω	-	ἐκλάσθην	v-1d(1b)
κλείω	κέκλεισμαι	ἐκλείσθην	v-1a(3)
κορέννυμι	κεκόρεσμαι	ἐκορέσθην	v-3c(1)
κρεμάννυμι[1]	-	ἐκρεμάσθην	v-3c(1)
κυλίω	κεκύλισμαι	-	v-1a(1)
λούω	λέλουσμαι[2]	-	v-1a(8)
μεθύσκω	-	ἐμεθύσθην	v-5a
μιμνήσκομαι	-	ἐμνήσθην	v-5a
μνάομαι	μέμνησμαι	-	v-1d(1a)
πίμπλημι	πέπλησμαι	ἐπλήσθην	v-6a
πρίω[3]	-	ἐπρίσθην	v-1a(1)
πτύω	-	ἐπτύσθην	v-1a(4)
ῥύομαι	-	ἐρρύσθην	v-1a(4)
σείω	-	ἐσείσθην	v-1a(3)
σπάω	-	ἐσπάσθην	v-1d(2a)
χαλάω	-	ἐχαλάσθην	v-1d(1b)

τελέω may appear to insert a σ (τετέλεσμαι, ἐτελέσθην), except that the σ is part of the stem that reappears here (*τελεσ). See also ἀγαλλιάω (v-1d[1b]), ἁρπάζω (v-2a[2]), δύναμαι (v-6b), ἑλκύω (v-1a[4]), μιαίνω (v-2d[4]), ὀμνύω (v-3c[2]), πίμπρημι (v-6a), ῥαίνω (v-2d[4]), σβέννυμι (v-3c[1]), χρίω (v-1a[1]).[4]

Insertion of an η   (§46.6)

As in the other tenses, words may insert an η into this principal part between the tense stem and the personal endings (§18.7). See the general discussion of letter insertion at §45.3, especially its discussion of using metathesis to explain some of these forms.[5]

---

1   Also κρέμαμαι (v-1d[2a]).

2   Occurs once in the N.T. with the inserted σ (Heb 10:22) and once without it (Jn 13:10).

3   Some prefer the lexical form πρίζω, in which case the σ is not inserted but is there as the result of normal morphological changes.

4   In Classical Greek, for an insertion of the σ in the perfect middle/passive see also ἄγαμαι, αἰδέομαι, βυνέω, δράω, ἔννυμι, ἐράω, ἐρύω, ἠδύνω, θλάω, κνα(ί)ω, κολούω, ναίω, νάω (*spin*), ξέω, ξύω, ὀδύσσομαι, ὀπυίω, περαίνω, πτίττω, σκεδάννυμι, στόρνυμι, παλαίω, περαίνω, τανύω, ὕω, φλάω, φλεύω, χόω, χρῴζω. This insertion may be more due to dialect differences and later development (Smyth §489h).

    Smyth also lists the following as inserting a σ in the aorist passive: ἄγαμαι, ἀκέομαι, ἀλέω, ἀρύω, ἄχθομαι, βυνέω, δαίνυμι, δράω, εἰλύω, ἐλύω, ἔραμαι (ἐράω), ἔρυμαι (ἐρύω), λαύω, λεύω, λόω, νέω, ξέω, ὀδύσσομαι, ὀίω, ὄνομαι, σάω, στόρνυμι.

5   Related to this is ὄλλυμι (*ολ), which inserts an ε into its perfect (middle/passive) ἀπολώλεκα, but this form does not occur in the N.T. The stem of οἴχμαι (v-1d[2c]) is *οιχε, so the form ᾤχημαι also does not apply to this list.

βάλλω	βέβλημαι	v-2d(1)
γίνομαι	γεγένημαι	v-1c(2)
τέμνω	τέτμημαι	v-3a(1)

ἵημι inserts an ω (ἕωμαι; v-6a).

Pluperfect Middle/Passive   (§46.7)

The middle passive of the pluperfect follows the same pattern as the active, except that there is no tense formative, no connecting vowels, and uses middle/passive endings. If the stem of the verb ends in a consonant (including stems that insert a θ), the third person plural is formed periphrastically (Smyth §405). The periphrastic pluperfect middle/passive uses the perfect middle/passive participle and ἦσαν.

(augment +) reduplication + tense stem + secondary middle/passive ending

1 sg	μην	(ἐ)λελύμην	1 pl	μεθα	(ἐ)λελύμεθα
2 sg	σο[1]	(ἐ)λέλυσο	2 pl	σθε	(ἐ)λέλυσθε
3 sg	το	(ἐ)λέλυτο	3 pl	ντο	(ἐ)λέλυντο

As is true in the perfect middle/passive, when a verbal stem ending in a stop comes directly into contact with the personal ending, the stop and initial consonant of the personal ending may undergo changes. See §46.4 for a list of the rules governing the changes.

		labial (*γραφ)	*velar* (*διωκ)	*dental* (*πειθ)
1 sg	μην	(ἐ)γεγράμμην	(ἐ)δεδίωγμην	(ἐ)πεπείσμην
2 sg	σο[2]	(ἐ)γέγραψο	(ἐ)δεδίωξο	(ἐ)πέπεισο
3 sg	το	(ἐ)γέγραπτο	(ἐ)δεδίωκτο	(ἐ)πέπειστο
1 pl	μεθα	(ἐ)γεγράμμεθα	(ἐ)δεδιώγμεθα	(ἐ)πεπείσμεθα
2 pl	σθε[2]	(ἐ)γέγραφθε	(ἐ)δεδίωχθε	(ἐ)πέπεισθε
3 pl		ἦσαν γεγραμμένοι	ἦσαν δεδιωγμένοι	ἦσαν πεπεισμένοι

Following are all the verbs in the New Testament that have a pluperfect middle/passive form. The verbs occurring in the active are listed at §45.6c.

βάλλω	ἐβέβλητο	v-2d(1)
ἐπιγράφω	ἐπεγέγραπτο	v-1b(1)

---

[1] This is one of the few places where the σ does not drop out.

[2] The interconsonantal σ drops out first, and then the final stem stop may change because of the θ.

ἐπικαλέω	ἐπεκέκλητο	v-1d(2b)
θεμελιόω	τεθεμελίωτο	v-1d(3)
οἰκοδομέω	ᾠκοδόμητο	v-1d(2a)
περιδέω	περιεδέδετο	v-1d(2b)
συντίθημι	συνετέθειντο	v-6a

Here are the seven New Testament verses in which we find pluperfect middle/passive forms.

Matt 7:25   καὶ κατέβη ἡ βροχὴ καὶ ἦλθον οἱ ποταμοὶ καὶ ἔπνευσαν οἱ ἄνεμοι καὶ προσέπεσαν τῇ οἰκίᾳ ἐκείνῃ, καὶ οὐκ ἔπεσεν, **τεθεμελίωτο** γὰρ ἐπὶ τὴν πέτραν.

Luke 4:29   καὶ ἀναστάντες ἐξέβαλον αὐτὸν ἔξω τῆς πόλεως καὶ ἤγαγον αὐτὸν ἕως ὀφρύος τοῦ ὄρους ἐφ᾽ οὗ ἡ πόλις **ᾠκοδόμητο** αὐτῶν ὥστε κατακρημνίσαι αὐτόν ....

Luke 16:20   πτωχὸς δέ τις ὀνόματι Λάζαρος **ἐβέβλητο** πρὸς τὸν πυλῶνα αὐτοῦ εἱλκωμένος ....

John 9:22   ταῦτα εἶπαν οἱ γονεῖς αὐτοῦ ὅτι ἐφοβοῦντο τοὺς Ἰουδαίους· ἤδη γὰρ **συνετέθειντο** οἱ Ἰουδαῖοι ἵνα ἐάν τις αὐτὸν ὁμολογήσῃ χριστόν, ἀποσυνάγωγος γένηται.

John 11:44   ἐξῆλθεν ὁ τεθνηκὼς δεδεμένος τοὺς πόδας καὶ τὰς χεῖρας κειρίαις καὶ ἡ ὄψις αὐτοῦ σουδαρίῳ **περιεδέδετο**. λέγει αὐτοῖς ὁ Ἰησοῦς· λύσατε αὐτὸν καὶ ἄφετε αὐτὸν ὑπάγειν.

Acts 17:23   διερχόμενος γὰρ καὶ ἀναθεωρῶν τὰ σεβάσματα ὑμῶν εὗρον καὶ βωμὸν ἐν ᾧ **ἐπεγέγραπτο**· Ἀγνώστῳ θεῷ. ὃ οὖν ἀγνοοῦντες εὐσεβεῖτε, τοῦτο ἐγὼ καταγγέλλω ὑμῖν.

Acts 26:32   Ἀγρίππας δὲ τῷ Φήστῳ ἔφη· ἀπολελύσθαι ἐδύνατο ὁ ἄνθρωπος οὗτος εἰ μὴ **ἐπεκέκλητο** Καίσαρα.

Future Perfect Middle/Passive   (§46.8)

See the general discussion at §45.7 and Smyth §580-584. The future perfect middle/passive is built on the perfect middle/passive tense stem. The periphrastic form uses the perfect middle/passive participle and the future of εἰμί (ἐψευσμένος ἔσομαι).

reduplication + tense stem + tense formative (σ) + connecting vowel + primary middle/passive ending

1 sg	μαι	λελύσομαι	1 pl	μεθα	λελυσόμεθα
2 sg	σαι[1]	λελύσῃ	2 pl	σθε	λελύσεσθε
3 sg	ται	λελύσεται	3 pl	νται	λελύσονται

There are seven future perfects in the New Testament, and one that occurs as a variant. Six are periphrastic.

Matt. 16:19   δώσω σοι τὰς κλεῖδας τῆς βασιλείας τῶν οὐρανῶν, καὶ ὃ ἐὰν δήσῃς ἐπὶ τῆς γῆς **ἔσται δεδεμένον** ἐν τοῖς οὐρανοῖς, καὶ ὃ ἐὰν λύσῃς ἐπὶ τῆς γῆς **ἔσται λελυμένον** ἐν τοῖς οὐρανοῖς.

Matt 18:18   Ἀμὴν λέγω ὑμῖν· ὅσα ἐὰν δήσητε ἐπὶ τῆς γῆς **ἔσται δεδεμένα** ἐν οὐρανῷ, καὶ ὅσα ἐὰν λύσητε ἐπὶ τῆς γῆς **ἔσται λελυμένα** ἐν οὐρανῷ.

---

[1]   Intervocalic σ drops out (§25.5) and the vowels contract. ε + σαι › εαι › ῃι › ῃ. Cf. §40.2.

Luke 12:52 ἔσονται γὰρ ἀπὸ τοῦ νῦν πέντε ἐν ἑνὶ οἴκῳ **διαμεμερισμένοι**, τρεῖς ἐπὶ δυσὶν καὶ δύο ἐπὶ τρισίν.
Luke 19:40 Λέγω ὑμῖν, ἐὰν οὗτοι σιωπήσουσιν, οἱ λίθοι **κεκράξονται**.[1]
Heb 8:11 Γνῶθι τὸν κύριον, ὅτι πάντες **εἰδήσουσίν** με ἀπὸ μικροῦ ἕως μεγάλου αὐτῶν.
Heb 2:13 καὶ πάλιν, Ἐγὼ **ἔσομαι πεποιθὼς** ἐπ᾽ αὐτῷ, καὶ πάλιν, Ἰδοὺ ἐγὼ καὶ τὰ παιδία ἅ μοι ἔδωκεν ὁ θεός.

Aorist Passive Indicative (§47)

The aorist passive is built from the sixth principal part. The future passive is also built from this unaugmented stem. The aorist passive was originally an active athematic conjugation that was brought over to the aorist passive to distinguish it from the aorist middle (Smyth §802ff.). That is why the aorist passive uses active endings, does not have a connecting vowel, and uses σαν in the third plural, just like μι verbs in the imperfect.

First Aorist Passive (§47.1)

Thematic Stems (§47.1a)

augment + tense stem + tense formative (θη) + secondary active ending

1 sg	ν	ἐλύθην	1 pl	μεν	ἐλύθημεν
2 sg	ς	ἐλύθης	2 pl	τε	ἐλύθητε
3 sg	-	ἐλύθη	3 pl	σαν	ἐλύθησαν

Contract Stems (§47.1b)

augment + tense stem (lengthened final vowel) + tense formative (κα)+ secondary active ending

		*γεννα	*ποιε	*φανερο
1 sg	ν	ἐγεννήθην	ἐποιήθην	ἐφανερώθην
2 sg	ς	ἐγεννήθης	ἐποιήθης	ἐφανερώθης
3 sg	-	ἐγεννήθη	ἐποιήθη	ἐφανερώθη
1 pl	μεν	ἐγεννήθημεν	ἐποιήθημεν	ἐφανερώθημεν
2 pl	τε	ἐγεννήθητε	ἐποιήθητε	ἐφανερώθητε
3 pl	σαν	ἐγεννήθησαν	ἐποιήθησαν	ἐφανερώθησαν

---

[1] κεκράξονται is a v.l. to the accepted κράξουσιν.

Athematic Stems   (§47.1c)

augment + tense stem + tense formative (θη) + secondary active ending

		*στα	*θε[1]	*δο
1 sg	ν	ἐστάθην	ἐτέθην	ἐδόθην
2 sg	ς	ἐστάθης	ἐτέθης	ἐδόθης
3 sg	-	ἐστάθη	ἐτέθη	ἐδόθη
1 pl	μεν	ἐστάθημεν	ἐτέθημεν	ἐδόθημεν
2 pl	τε	ἐστάθητε	ἐτέθητε	ἐδόθητε
3 pl	σαν	ἐστάθησαν	ἐτέθησαν	ἐδόθησαν

Second Aorist Passive   (§47.2)

The second aorist passive is identical to the first aorist passive except that it uses η and not θη as the tense formative. All second aorist passives in the New Testament are list at §47.8.

augment + stem + tense formative (η) + secondary active ending

1 sg	ν	ἐγράφην	1 pl	μεν	ἐγράφημεν
2 sg	ς	ἐγράφης	2 pl	τε	ἐγράφητε
3 sg	-	ἐγράφη	3 pl	σαν	ἐγράφησαν

First Future Passive (§47.3)

The future passive is formed from the unaugmented tense stem of the aorist passive. Its tense formative is θησ and it uses middle/passive endings, unlike the aorist passive that uses active endings.

Thematic Stems   (§47.3a)

tense stem + tense formative (θησ) + connecting vowel + primary middle/passive ending

1 sg	μαι	λυθήσομαι	1 pl	μεθα	λυθησόμεθα
2 sg	σαι[2]	λυθήσῃ	2 pl	σθε	λυθήσεσθε
3 sg	ται	λυθήσεται	3 pl	νται	λυθήσονται

---

[1]   The θ deaspirates to a τ before the θ of the tense formative (§15.3). θε › θη + ν › ἐτέθην.

[2]   Intervocalic σ drops out and the vowels contract. ε + σαι › εαι (§25.5) › ηι › ῃ. Cf. §40.2.

Contract Stems   (§47.3b)

tense stem (lengthened final vowel) + tense formative (θησ)+ connecting vowel +
primary middle/passive ending

		*γεννα	*ποιε	*φανερο
1 sg	μαι	γεννηθήσομαι	ποιηθήσομαι	φανερωθήσομαι
2 sg	σαι[1]	γεννηθήσῃ	ποιηθήσῃ	φανερωθήσῃ
3 sg	ται	γεννηθήσεται	ποιηθήσεται	φανερωθήσεται
1 pl	μεθα	γεννηθησόμεθα	ποιηθησόμεθα	φανερωθησόμεθα
2 pl	σθε	γεννηθήσεσθε	ποιηθήσεσθε	φανερωθήσεσθε
3 pl	νται	γεννηθήσονται	ποιηθήσονται	φανερωθήσονται

Athematic Stems   (§47.3c)

tense stem + tense formative (θησ) + connecting vowel + primary middle/passive ending

		*στα	*θε[2]	*δο
1 sg	μαι	σταθήσομαι	τεθήσομαι	δοθήσομαι
2 sg	σαι[1]	σταθήσῃ	τεθήσῃ	δοθήσῃ
3 sg	ται	σταθήσεται	τεθήσεται	δοθήσεται
1 pl	μεθα	σταθησόμεθα	τεθησόμεθα	δοθησόμεθα
2 pl	σθε	σταθήσεσθε	τεθήσεσθε	δοθήσεσθε
3 pl	νται	σταθήσονται	τεθήσονται	δοθήσονται

Second Future Passive (§47.4)

tense stem + tense formative (ησ) + connecting vowel + primary middle/passive ending

1 sg	μαι	γραφήσομαι	1 pl	μεθα	γραφησόμεθα
2 sg	σαι[1]	γραφήσῃ	2 pl	σθε	γραφήσεσθε
3 sg	ται	γραφήσεται	3 pl	νται	γραφήσονται

For a list of verbs occurring in the New Testament with a second future passive see §47.8.

---

[1]   Intervocalic σ drops out and the vowels contract. ε + σαι › εαι (§25.5) › ηι › ῃ. Cf. §40.2.

[2]   The θ deaspirates to a τ before the θ of the tense formative (§15.3).

Stems Ending in a Stop   (§47.5)

(π β φ, κ γ χ, τ δ θ)

When a verbal root ends in a stop, it will change when placed next to the θ of the tense formative. Labials (π β) and velars (κ γ) aspirate to φ and χ respectively. Dentals (τ δ θ) plus the θ of the tense formative become σ.

A **labial** is aspirated (§20.1)

π	+	θ	*βλαπ ‣ ἐβλάφθην
β	+	θ ‣ φθ	*συντρίβ ‣ συνετίφθην
φ	+	θ	*ἐξαλείφ ‣ ἐξηλείφθην

A **velar** is aspirated (§20.2).

κ	+	θ	*διωκ ‣ ἐδιώχθην
γ	+	θ ‣ χθ	*ανοιγ ‣ ἀνεῴχθην
χ	+	θ	*δεχ ‣ ἐδέχθην

A **dental** dissimilates to σ (§20.3).

τ	+	θ	
δ	+	θ ‣ σθ	*θαυμαδ ‣ ἐθαυμάσθην
θ	+	θ	*πείθ ‣ ἐπείσθην

Insertion of a σ   (§47.6)

As is the case in the perfect middle/passive, some words insert a σ between the stem of the word and the θη of the aorist (and future) passive. See §46.5 for the list and Smyth §489 for further discussion.

Insertion of an η   (§47.7)

As is the case in other tenses, some stems insert an η between the tense stem and the θη tense formative (§18.7). (εὑρίσκω adds ε.) See the general discussion of letter insertion at §45.3.

βάλλω	ἐβλήθην	*βαλ	v-2d(1)
γίνομαι	ἐγενήθην	*γεν	v-1c(2)
δέρω	ἐδάρην	*δαρ	v-1c(1)
εὑρίσκω	εὑρέθην	*ευρ	v-5b
τέμνω	ἐτμήθην	*τμ	v-3a(1)

Second Aorist/Future Passives   (§47.8)

Below is a list of the verbs in the New Testament that have second aorist forms. Forms followed by an asterisk also have a first aorist. Some compounds are listed under their simple verb.

present	aorist passive	future passive	classification
ἀγγέλλω	ἠγγέλην	-	v-2d(1)
ἄγνυμι	ἐάγην	-	v-3c(2)
ἀλλάσσω	ἠλλάγην	ἀλλαγήσομαι	v-2b
ἀνοίγω	ἠνοίγην	ἀνοιγήσομαι	cv-1b(2)
ἁρπάζω	ἡρπάγην*	ἁρπαγήσομαι	v-2a(2)
γράφω	ἐγράφην	-	v-1b(1)
δέρω	-	δαρήσομαι	v-1c(1)
θάπτω	ἐτάφην	-	v-4
καίω	ἐκάην*	καήσομαι	v-2c
κόπτω	ἐκόπην	κοπήσομαι	v-4
κρύπτω	ἐκρύβην	-	v-4
νύσσω	ἐνύγην	-	v-2b
παύω	-	πάησομαι*	v-1a(5)
πλέκω	ἐπλάκην	-	v-1b(2)
πλήσσω	ἐπλήγην	-	v-2b
πνίγω	ἐπνίγην	-	v-1b(2)
ῥέω	ἐρύην	-	v-1a(7)
σπείρω	ἐσπάρην	-	v-2d(3)
στέλλω	ἐστάλην	-	v-2d(1)
στρέφω	ἐστράφην	στραφήσομαι	v-1b(1)
σφάζω	ἐσφάγην	-	v-2a(2)
τάσσω	ἐτάγην*	ταγήσομαι*	v-2b
τρέπω	ἐτράπην	τραπήσομαι	v-1b(1)
τρέφω	ἐτράφην	-	v-1b(1)
τρίβω	-	τριβήσομαι	v-1b(1)
φαίνω	ἐφάνην	φανήσομαι	v-2d(4)
φθείρω	ἐφθάρην	φθαρήσομαι	v-2d(3)
φράσσω	ἐφράγην	φραγήσομαι	v-2b
φύω	ἐφύην	-	v-1a(4)
χαίρω	ἐχάρην	χαρήσομαι	v-2d(2)
ψύχω	-	ψυγήσομαι	v-1b(2)

The following words occur in the New Testament, have second aorist/future passive forms, but those forms do not occur in the New Testament: δύνω (v-3a[1]), θλίβω (v-1b[1]), κλέπτω (v-4), μάσσω (v-2b), μίγνυμι (v-3c[2]), ὀρύσσω (v-2b), ῥήγνυμι (v-3c[2]), ῥίπτω (v-4), σκάπτω (v-4), σφάλλω (v-2d[1]), τήκω (v-1b[2]). Cf. also τίλλω (v-2d[1]), πείρω (v-2d[3]).

There are 289 future passive indicatives in the New Testament. Of those there are thirty second future passives.

Matt 7:7   Αἰτεῖτε καὶ δοθήσεται ὑμῖν, ζητεῖτε καὶ εὑρήσετε, κρούετε καὶ **ἀνοιγήσεται**
              ὑμῖν·

Matt 7:8   πᾶς γὰρ ὁ αἰτῶν λαμβάνει καὶ ὁ ζητῶν εὑρίσκει καὶ τῷ κρούοντι **ἀνοιγήσεται**.

Matt 21:37   ὕστερον δὲ ἀπέστειλεν πρὸς αὐτοὺς τὸν υἱὸν αὐτοῦ λέγων· **ἐντραπήσονται** τὸν
              υἱόν μου.

Matt 24:12   καὶ διὰ τὸ πληθυνθῆναι τὴν ἀνομίαν **ψυγήσεται** ἡ ἀγάπη τῶν πολλῶν.

Matt 24:30   καὶ τότε **φανήσεται** τὸ σημεῖον τοῦ υἱοῦ τοῦ ἀνθρώπου ἐν οὐρανῷ, καὶ τότε
              κόψονται πᾶσαι αἱ φυλαὶ τῆς γῆς καὶ ὄψονται τὸν υἱὸν τοῦ ἀνθρώπου
              ἐρχόμενον ἐπὶ τῶν νεφελῶν τοῦ οὐρανοῦ μετὰ δυνάμεως καὶ δόξης πολλῆς·

Mark 12:6   ἔτι ἕνα εἶχεν υἱὸν ἀγαπητόν· ἀπέστειλεν αὐτὸν ἔσχατον πρὸς αὐτοὺς λέγων ὅτι
              ἐντραπήσονται τὸν υἱόν μου.

Mark 13:9   Βλέπετε δὲ ὑμεῖς ἑαυτούς· παραδώσουσιν ὑμᾶς εἰς συνέδρια καὶ εἰς συναγωγὰς
              δαρήσεσθε καὶ ἐπὶ ἡγεμόνων καὶ βασιλέων σταθήσεσθε ἕνεκεν ἐμοῦ εἰς
              μαρτύριον αὐτοῖς.

Luke 1:14   καὶ ἔσται χαρά σοι καὶ ἀγαλλίασις καὶ πολλοὶ ἐπὶ τῇ γενέσει αὐτοῦ
              χαρήσονται.

Luke 10:6   καὶ ἐὰν ἐκεῖ ᾖ υἱὸς εἰρήνης, **ἐπαναπαήσεται** ἐπ' αὐτὸν ἡ εἰρήνη ὑμῶν· εἰ δὲ μή
              γε, ἐφ' ὑμᾶς ἀνακάμψει.

Luke 11:9   Κἀγὼ ὑμῖν λέγω, αἰτεῖτε καὶ δοθήσεται ὑμῖν, ζητεῖτε καὶ εὑρήσετε, κρούετε καὶ
              ἀνοιγήσεται ὑμῖν·

Luke 11:10   πᾶς γὰρ ὁ αἰτῶν λαμβάνει καὶ ὁ ζητῶν εὑρίσκει καὶ τῷ κρούοντι **ἀνοιγ[ήσ]εται**.

Luke 12:47   Ἐκεῖνος δὲ ὁ δοῦλος ὁ γνοὺς τὸ θέλημα τοῦ κυρίου αὐτοῦ καὶ μὴ ἑτοιμάσας ἢ
              ποιήσας πρὸς τὸ θέλημα αὐτοῦ **δαρήσεται** πολλάς·

Luke 12:48   ὁ δὲ μὴ γνούς, ποιήσας δὲ ἄξια πληγῶν **δαρήσεται** ὀλίγας. παντὶ δὲ ᾧ ἐδόθη
              πολύ, πολὺ ζητηθήσεται παρ' αὐτοῦ, καὶ ᾧ παρέθεντο πολύ, περισσότερον
              αἰτήσουσιν αὐτόν.

Luke 20:13   εἶπεν δὲ ὁ κύριος τοῦ ἀμπελῶνος· τί ποιήσω; πέμψω τὸν υἱόν μου τὸν ἀγαπητόν·
              ἴσως τοῦτον **ἐντραπήσονται**.

John 16:20   ἀμὴν ἀμὴν λέγω ὑμῖν ὅτι κλαύσετε καὶ θρηνήσετε ὑμεῖς, ὁ δὲ κόσμος **χαρήσεται**·
              ὑμεῖς λυπηθήσεσθε, ἀλλ' ἡ λύπη ὑμῶν εἰς χαρὰν γενήσεται.

John 16:22   καὶ ὑμεῖς οὖν νῦν μὲν λύπην ἔχετε· πάλιν δὲ ὄψομαι ὑμᾶς, καὶ **χαρήσεται** ὑμῶν
              ἡ καρδία, καὶ τὴν χαρὰν ὑμῶν οὐδεὶς αἴρει ἀφ' ὑμῶν.

Acts 2:20   ὁ ἥλιος **μεταστραφήσεται** εἰς σκότος καὶ ἡ σελήνη εἰς αἷμα, πρὶν ἐλθεῖν ἡμέραν
              κυρίου τὴν μεγάλην καὶ ἐπιφανῆ.

Rom 11:22   ἴδε οὖν χρηστότητα καὶ ἀποτομίαν θεοῦ· ἐπὶ μὲν τοὺς πεσόντας ἀποτομία, ἐπὶ δὲ
              σὲ χρηστότης θεοῦ, ἐὰν ἐπιμένῃς τῇ χρηστότητι, ἐπεὶ καὶ σὺ **ἐκκοπήσῃ**.

1 Cor 3:15   εἴ τινος τὸ ἔργον **κατακαήσεται**, ζημιωθήσεται, αὐτὸς δὲ σωθήσεται, οὕτως δὲ ὡς
              διὰ πυρός.

1 Cor 15:28   ὅταν δὲ ὑποταγῇ αὐτῷ τὰ πάντα, τότε [καὶ] αὐτὸς ὁ υἱὸς **ὑποταγήσεται** τῷ
              ὑποτάξαντι αὐτῷ τὰ πάντα, ἵνα ᾖ ὁ θεὸς [τὰ] πάντα ἐν πᾶσιν.

1 Cor 15:51   ἰδοὺ μυστήριον ὑμῖν λέγω· πάντες οὐ κοιμηθησόμεθα, πάντες δὲ **ἀλλαγησόμεθα**,

1 Cor 15:52   ἐν ἀτόμῳ, ἐν ῥιπῇ ὀφθαλμοῦ, ἐν τῇ ἐσχάτῃ σάλπιγγι· σαλπίσει γὰρ καὶ οἱ νεκροὶ
              ἐγερθήσονται ἄφθαρτοι καὶ ἡμεῖς **ἀλλαγησόμεθα**.

2 Cor 11:10   ἔστιν ἀλήθεια Χριστοῦ ἐν ἐμοὶ ὅτι ἡ καύχησις αὕτη οὐ **φραγήσεται** εἰς ἐμὲ ἐν
              τοῖς κλίμασιν τῆς Ἀχαΐας.

Phil 1:18 Τί γάρ; πλὴν ὅτι παντὶ τρόπῳ, εἴτε προφάσει εἴτε ἀληθείᾳ, Χριστὸς καταγγέλλεται, καὶ ἐν τούτῳ χαίρω. Ἀλλὰ καὶ **χαρήσομαι,**

1 Thess 4:17 ἔπειτα ἡμεῖς οἱ ζῶντες οἱ περιλειπόμενοι ἅμα σὺν αὐτοῖς **ἁρπαγησόμεθα** ἐν νεφέλαις εἰς ἀπάντησιν τοῦ κυρίου εἰς ἀέρα· καὶ οὕτως πάντοτε σὺν κυρίῳ ἐσόμεθα.

2 Tim 4:4 καὶ ἀπὸ μὲν τῆς ἀληθείας τὴν ἀκοὴν ἀποστρέψουσιν, ἐπὶ δὲ τοὺς μύθους **ἐκτραπήσονται.**

Heb 1:12 καὶ ὡσεὶ περιβόλαιον ἑλίξεις αὐτούς, ὡς ἱμάτιον καὶ **ἀλλαγήσονται·** σὺ δὲ ὁ αὐτὸς εἶ καὶ τὰ ἔτη σου οὐκ ἐκλείψουσιν.

Heb 12:9 εἶτα τοὺς μὲν τῆς σαρκὸς ἡμῶν πατέρας εἴχομεν παιδευτὰς καὶ ἐνετρεπόμεθα· οὐ πολὺ [δὲ] μᾶλλον **ὑποταγησόμεθα** τῷ πατρὶ τῶν πνευμάτων καὶ ζήσομεν;

2 Pet 2:12 Οὗτοι δὲ ὡς ἄλογα ζῷα γεγεννημένα φυσικὰ εἰς ἅλωσιν καὶ φθορὰν ἐν οἷς ἀγνοοῦσιν βλασφημοῦντες, ἐν τῇ φθορᾷ αὐτῶν καὶ **φθαρήσονται**

Rev 14:13 Καὶ ἤκουσα φωνῆς ἐκ τοῦ οὐρανοῦ λεγούσης· γράψον· μακάριοι οἱ νεκροὶ οἱ ἐν κυρίῳ ἀποθνῄσκοντες ἀπ᾽ ἄρτι. ναί, λέγει τὸ πνεῦμα, ἵνα **ἀναπαήσονται** ἐκ τῶν κόπων αὐτῶν, τὰ γὰρ ἔργα αὐτῶν ἀκολουθεῖ μετ᾽ αὐτῶν.

Subjunctive (§50)

The subjunctive is easy to learn.

1. It occurs only in the present, aorist, and the perfect.[1]

2. The connecting vowel is lengthened to η or ω and behaves almost as a mood formative. Even the μι verbs use the same endings, appearing to be thematic, so ω/η are essential for recognition

3. All tenses use primary personal endings. The lengthened connecting vowel contracts with the personal endings as seen on a verb like λύω, just as they do with contract verbs (§40.3). We therefore list the endings as ω, ῃς, ῃ, ωμεν, ητε, and ωσι.

   We will not document the normal changes to the personal endings (cf. §40.2) except for a few second singular contractions that are difficult.

4. The aorist subjunctive is not augmented, as is true of all non-indicative moods. For the stem changes that occur due to the θ of the tense formative, see the aorist indicative (§44.3).

5. μι verbs with stem vowels in o (e.g., δίδωμι) show ω throughout.

6. Outside of the New Testament we find a few by-forms in the second and third person singular of μι verbs (e.g., διδοῖς for διδῷς, διδοῖ for διδῷ; cf. Funk §444.2).

---

[1] Except for οἶδα, which is a perfect with a present meaning, all perfect subjunctives in the N.T. are formed periphrastically (cf. §53).

Present Subjunctive   (§51)

Thematic Stems   (§51.1)

	present active		**present middle/passive**	
1 sg	ω	λύω	ωμαι	λύωμαι
2 sg	ης	λύης	η	λύη
3 sg	η	λύη	ηται	λύηται
1 pl	ωμεν	λύωμεν	ωμεθα	λυώμεθα
2 pl	ητε	λύητε	ησθε	λύησθε
3 pl	ωσι(ν)	λύωσι(ν)	ωνται	λύωνται

Contract Stems   (§51.2)

In the present, when the connecting vowel is ω, there will be no difference between a contract verb and a thematic verb except for accent, which is always on the contracted syllable.

Due to the rules of contractions, α contract verbs will appear to have replaced η with α wherever η is a connecting vowel. ε contract verbs show no variation from the thematic conjugation except for accent. o contracts have some peculiarities. In the second and third person singular active, the endings have been altered by analogy to the indicative.[1]

present active subjunctive

1 sg	ω	γεννῶ	ποιῶ	φανερῶ
2 sg	ης	γεννᾷς[2]	ποιῆς	φανεροῖς[3]
3 sg	η	γεννᾷ	ποιῇ	φανεροῖ[3]
1 pl	ωμεν	γεννῶμεν	ποιῶμεν	φανερῶμεν
2 pl	ητε	γεννᾶτε	ποιῆτε	φανερῶτε
3 pl	ωσι(ν)	γεννῶσι(ν)	ποιῶσι(ν)	φανερῶσι(ν)

---

[1]   "The present subjunctive of verbs in -όω has been assimilated to the indicative, on the analogy of verbs in -άω, although a few 'Attic' forms occur, i.e. -ω- where -ου- occurs in the indicative" (Funk §441.1).

[2]   It appears that the contraction is from αεις and not ηεις.

[3]   On the irregular contraction see §2.13b.

present middle/passive subjunctive

1 sg	ωμαι	γεννῶμαι	ποιῶμαι	φανερῶμαι
2 sg	ῃ	γεννᾷ[1]	ποιῇ	φανεροῖ[2]
3 sg	ηται	γεννᾶται	ποιῆται	φανερῶται
1 pl	ωμεθα	γεννώμεθα	ποιώμεθα	φανερώμεθα
2 pl	ησθε	γεννᾶσθε	ποιῆσθε	φανερῶσθε
3 pl	ωνται	γεννῶνται	ποιῶνται	φανερῶνται

Athematic Stems   (§51.3)

present active subjunctive

		*στα	*θε	*δο[3]
1 sg	ω	ἱστῶ	τιθῶ	διδῶ
2 sg	ῃς	ἱστῇς	τιθῇς	διδῷς
3 sg	ῃ	ἱστῇ	τιθῇ	διδῷ
1 pl	ωμεν	ἱστῶμεν	τιθῶμεν	διδῶμεν
2 pl	ητε	ἱστῆτε	τιθῆτε	διδῶτε
3 pl	ωσι(ν)	ἱστῶσι(ν)	τιθῶσι(ν)	διδῶσι(ν)

present middle/passive subjunctive

1 sg	ωμαι	ἱστῶμαι	τιθῶμαι	διδῶμαι
2 sg	ῃ	ἱστῇ	τιθῇ	διδῷ
3 sg	ηται	ἱστῆται	τιθῆται	διδῶται
1 pl	ωμεθα	ἱστώμεθα	τιθώμεθα	διδώμεθα
2 pl	ησθε	ἱστῆσθε	τιθῆσθε	διδῶσθε
3 pl	ωνται	ἱστῶνται	τιθῶνται	διδῶνται

Aorist Active/Middle Subjunctive   (§52)

The α of the tense formative σα has been absorbed by the lengthened connecting vowels.

---

[1]   It appears that the contraction is from ασαι and not ησαι.

[2]   On the irregular contraction see §2.13b.

[3]   The ω dominates throughout (§50.5). Some forms can appear uncontracted (e.g., διδοῖς, διδοῖ).

Thematic Stems   (§52.1)

		first aorist	*second aorist*

aorist active subjunctive

1 *sg*	ω	λύσω	λίπω
2 *sg*	ῃς	λύσῃς	λίπῃς
3 *sg*	ῃ	λύσῃ	λίπῃ
1 *pl*	ωμεν	λύσωμεν	λίπωμεν
2 *pl*	ητε	λύσητε	λίπητε
3 *pl*	ωσι(ν)	λύσωσι(ν)	λίπωσι(ν)

aorist middle subjunctive

1 *sg*	ωμαι	λύσωμαι	λίπωμαι
2 *sg*	ῃ	λύσῃ	λίπῃ
3 *sg*	ηται	λύσηται	λίπηται
1 *pl*	ωμεθα	λυσώμεθα	λιπώμεθα
2 *pl*	ησθε	λύσησθε	λίπησθε
3 *pl*	ωνται	λύσωνται	λίπωνται

Contract Stems   (§52.2)

aorist active subjunctive

1 *sg*	ω	γεννήσω	ποιήσω	φανερώσω
2 *sg*	ῃς	γεννήσῃς	ποιήσῃς	φανερώσῃς
3 *sg*	ῃ	γεννήσῃ	ποιήσῃ	φανερώσῃ
1 *pl*	ωμεν	γεννήσωμεν	ποιήσωμεν	φανερώσωμεν
2 *pl*	ητε	γεννήσητε	ποιήσητε	φανερώσητε
3 *pl*	ωσι(ν)	γεννήσωσι(ν)	ποιήσωσι(ν)	φανερώσωσι(ν)

aorist middle subjunctive

1 *sg*	ωμαι	γεννήσωμαι	ποιήσωμαι	φανερώσωμαι
2 *sg*	ῃ	γεννήσῃ	ποιήσῃ	φανερώσῃ
3 *sg*	ηται	γεννήσηται	ποιήσηται	φανερώσηται
1 *pl*	ωμεθα	γεννησώμεθα	ποιησώμεθα	φανερωσώμεθα
2 *pl*	ησθε	γεννήσησθε	ποιήσησθε	φανερώσησθε
3 *pl*	ωνται	γεννήσωνται	ποιήσωνται	φανερώσωνται

Liquid Stems (§52.3)

	aorist active subjunctive		**aorist middle subjunctive**	
1 sg	ω	κρίνω	ωμαι	κρίνωμαι
2 sg	ης	κρίνης	η	κρίνη
3 sg	η	κρίνη	ηται	κρίνηται
1 pl	ωμεν	κρίνωμεν	ωμεθα	κρινώμεθα
2 pl	ητε	κρίνητε	ησθε	κρίνησθε
3 pl	ωσι(ν)	κρίνωσι(ν)	ωνται	κρίνωνται

Athematic Stems   (§52.4)

No μι verbs in the New Testament occur in the first aorist middle subjunctive.

first aorist active subjunctive

		*στα	*θε	*δο
1 sg	ω	στήσω	θήσω	δώσω
2 sg	ης	στήσης	θήσης	δώσης
3 sg	ηται	στήση	θήση	δώση
1 pl	ωμεν	στήσωμεν	θήσωμεν	δώσωμεν
2 pl	ητε	στήσητε	θήσητε	δώσητε
3 pl	ωσι(ν)	στήσωσι(ν)	θήσωσι(ν)	δώσωσι(ν)

first aorist middle subjunctive

		*στα	*θε	*δο
1 sg	ωμαι	στήσωμαι	θήσωμαι	δώσωμαι
2 sg	η	στήση	θήση	δώση
3 sg	ηται	στήσηται	θήσηται	δώσηται
1 pl	ωμεθα	στησώμεθα	θησώμεθα	δωσώμεθα
2 pl	ησθε	στήσησθε	θήσησθε	δώσησθε
3 pl	ωνται	στήσωνται	θήσωνται	δώσωνται

second aorist active subjunctive

		*στα	*θε	*δο[1]	ἀφίημι[2]
1 sg	ω	στῶ	θῶ	δῶ	ἀφῶ
2 sg	ῃς	στῇς	θῇς	δῷς	ἀφῇς
3 sg	ῃ	στῇ	θῇ	δῷ[3]	ἀφῇ
1 pl	ωμεν	στῶμεν	θῶμεν	δῶμεν	ἀφῶμεν
2 pl	ητε	στῆτε	θῆτε	δῶτε	ἀφῆτε
3 pl	ωσι(ν)	στῶσι(ν)	θῶσι(ν)	δῶσι(ν)	ἀφῶσι(ν)

second aorist middle subjunctive

		πρίωμαι[4]		
1 sg	ωμαι	πρίωμαι	θῶμαι	δῶμαι
2 sg	ῃ	πρίῃ	θῇ	δῷ
3 sg	ηται	πρίηται	θῆται	δῶται
1 pl	ωμεθα	πριώμεθα	θώμεθα	δώμεθα
2 pl	ησθε	πρίησθε	θῆσθε	δῶσθε
3 pl	ωνται	πρίωνται	θῶνται	δῶνται

Perfect Subjunctive   (§53)

Thematic Stems   (§53.1)

The only perfect subjunctive forms in the New Testament are from οἶδα (cf. *BBG* §31.18).

1 sg	ω	εἰδῶ	*1 pl*	ωμεν	εἰδῶμεν
2 sg	ῃς	εἰδῇς	*2 pl*	ητε	εἰδῆτε
3 sg	ῃ	εἰδῇ	*3 pl*	ωσι(ν)	εἰδῶσι(ν)

The perfect subjunctive is otherwise formed periphrastically.[5] It will use the subjunctive of εἰμί and the perfect participle. If a verb has a second perfect, then the

---

1 δίδωμι is crossing over to the -όω pattern (*BDF* §95.2; *MBG* §40.4).

2 ἀφίημι does not occur in the aorist middle subjunctive in the N.T.

3 Mark 8:37 shows the uncontracted form δοῖ, and in Eph 1:17 it is δώῃ (not to be confused with the optative form δῴη). δῷ occurs six times in the N.T.

4 If ἵστημι occurred in the aorist middle subjunctive, it would have these forms: στῶμαι, στῇ, στῆται, στώμεθα, στῆσθε, στῶνται. Smyth substitutes ἐπρίαμην.

5 See Buist M. Fanning, *Verbal Aspect in New Testament Greek* (Clarendon Press, Oxford: 1990) pp. 396-7.

participle will be formed as a second perfect and everything else will be the same.

active subjunctive			middle/passive subjunctive		
1 sg	ω	λελυκὼς ὦ	1 sg	ω	λελυμένος ὦ
2 sg	ῃς	λελυκὼς ᾖς	2 sg	ῃς	λελυμένος ᾖς
3 sg	ῃ	λελυκὼς ᾖ	3 sg	ῃ	λελυμένος ᾖ
1 pl	ωμεν	λελυκότες ὦμεν	1 pl	ωμεν	λελυμένοι ὦμεν
2 pl	ητε	λελυκότες ἦτε	2 pl	ητε	λελυμένοι ἦτε
3 pl	ωσι(ν)	λελυκότες ὦσι(ν)	3 pl	ωσι(ν)	λελυμένοι ὦσι(ν)

Athematic Stems   (§53.2)

The following forms of ἵστημι do not occur in the New Testament but they are used in Classical Greek (Smyth §417).

second perfect active subjunctive

1 sg	ω	ἑστῶ	1 pl	ωμεν	ἑστῶμεν
2 sg	ῃς	ἑστῇς	2 pl	ητε	ἑστῆτε
3 sg	ῃ	ἑστῇ	3 pl	ωσι(ν)	ἑστῶσι(ν)

Aorist Passive Subjunctive   (§54)

Thematic Stems (§54.1)

		first aorist passive	second aorist passive
1 sg	ω	λυθῶ	γραφῶ
2 sg	ῃς	λυθῇς	γραφῇς
3 sg	ῃ	λυθῇ	γραφῇ
1 pl	ωμεν	λυθῶμεν	γραφῶμεν
2 pl	ητε	λυθῆτε	γραφῆτε
3 pl	ωσι(ν)	λυθῶσι(ν)	γραφῶσι(ν)

Athematic Stems (§54.2)

μι verbs have first aorist forms in the passive, regardless of whether they have first or second aorist forms in the active/middle.

first aorist passive subjunctive

		*στα	*θε	*δο	ἀφίημι
1 sg	ω	σταθῶ	τεθῶ	δοθῶ	ἀφεθῶ
2 sg	ης	σταθῇς	τεθῇς	δοθῇς	ἀφεθῇς
3 sg	ῃ	σταθῇ	τεθῇ	δοθῇ	ἀφεθῇ
1 pl	ωμεν	σταθῶμεν	τεθῶμεν	δοθῶμεν	ἀφεθῶμεν
2 pl	ητε	σταθῆτε	τεθῆτε	δοθῆτε	ἀφεθῆτε
3 pl	ωσι(ν)	σταθῶσι(ν)	τεθῶσι(ν)	δοθῶσι(ν)	ἀφεθῶσι(ν)

Optative (§60)

There are sixty-eight examples of the optative in the New Testament.

1. It is found only in the present (continuous aspect; twenty-three times) and aorist (undefined aspect; forty-five times) in the biblical texts. It occurs twenty-eight times in Luke -Acts and thirty-one times in Paul. εἴη occurs twelve times and γένοιτο seventeen times, fifteen of which are the Pauline phrase μὴ γένοιτο, "God forbid!" The optative was declining in use in Hellenistic Greek.

2. Because the optative can have no real time significance, it does not augment.

3. The thematic vowel is o.

4. The tense formative for the aorist active/middle is σα, which contracts with the mood formative so that all forms have σαι.

    The tense formative for the aorist passive in θε and the mood formative is ιη, which results in θειη in all aorist passive forms.

5. The mood formative in the thematic conjugation is normally ι (except in the aorist passive where it is ιη), and in the athematic conjugation it is ιη (Smyth §393). The ι will never subscript.

    However, ιη could be used as the mood formative and was more common in the singular; ι is more common in the dual and plural. ιη occurs only in the active. It is found on contract verbs, future liquids, μι verbs, and the aorist passive.

    With the two different tense formatives there were two possible endings in the first person singular and third person plural.

tense formative	first singular	third plural
ι	μι λύοιμι	εν λύοιεν
ιη	ν ἱσταιην	σαν ἱσταίησαν

The active endings could therefore be οιμι, οις, οι, οιμεν, οιτε, οιεν, or οιην, οιης, οιη, οιημεν, οιητε, οιησαν. All the optatives occurring in the New Testament are listed at §66.

6. The optative uses secondary personal endings except in the first person singular active, where it uses μι (cf. §36.7 for a fuller discussion).

7. For accent purposes, the final αι/οι are considered long (cf. Carson, p. 125).

8. Classical Greek could show uncontracted forms of μι verbs, but usually they showed the contracted form. We list both below.

9. Only four μι verbs occur in the optative in the New Testament. There are no contract verbs in the New Testament occurring as optatives. See CS p. 308 for the paradigm of the present contract optative.

Present Optative   (§61)

Thematic Stems   (§61.1)

		present active	present middle	
1 sg	μι	λύοιμι	μην	λυοίμην
2 sg	ς	λύοις	σο[1]	λύοιο
3 sg	-	λύοι	το	λύοιτο
1 pl	μεν	λύοιμεν	μεθα	λυοίμεθα
2 pl	τε	λύοιτε	σθε	λύοισθε
3 pl	εν	λύοιεν	ντο	λύοιντο

Athematic Stems   (§61.2)

In μι verbs the mood formative is ιη. Three μι verbs occurs in the present optative. εἰμί (εἴη, third singular; 12 times), δίδωμι (δῷη, third singular, once), and ὀναίμην (ὀνίνημι; first singular, once). If you consider δύναμαι a μι verb since it is athematic, then it should be noted that it occurs three times in the optative (δυναίμην, first singular, twice; δύναιντο, third plural, once).

---

[1]   Intervocalic σ is lost (οισο ▸ οιο; §40.2).

		*στα		*θε	*δο	εἰμί

present active optative

1 sg	ν	ἱσταίην	τιθείην	διδοίην	εἴην
2 sg	ς	ἱσταίης	τιθείης	διδοίης	εἴης
3 sg	-	ἱσταίη	τιθείη	διδοίη	εἴη
1 pl	μεν	ἱσταῖμεν	τιθεῖμεν	διδοῖμεν	εἶμεν
2 pl	τε	ἱσταῖτε	τιθεῖτε	διδοῖτε	εἶτε
3 pl	εν	ἱσταῖεν	τιθεῖεν	διδοῖεν	εἶεν

Less commonly in the plural.

1 pl	μεν	ἱσταίημεν	τιθείημεν	διδοίημεν	εἴημεν
2 pl	τε	ἱσταίητε	τιθείητε	διδοίητε	εἴητε
3 pl	σαν	ἱσταίησαν	τιθείησαν	διδοίησαν	εἴησαν

present middle optative

1 sg	μην	ἱσταίμην	τιθείμην	διδοίμην
2 sg	σο[1]	ἱσταῖο	τιθεῖο	διδοῖο
3 sg	το	ἱσταῖτο	τιθεῖτο	διδοῖτο
1 pl	μεθα	ἱσταίμεθα	τιθείμεθα	διδοίμεθα
2 pl	σθε	ἱσταῖσθε	τιθεῖσθε	διδοῖσθε
3 pl	ντο	ἱσταῖντο	τιθεῖντο	διδοῖντο

Future Active/Middle Optative   (§62)

There are no examples of the future optative in the New Testament.

		active optative			**middle optative**
1 sg	μι	λύσοιμι	μην		λυσοίμην
2 sg	ς	λύσοις	σο[1]		λύσοιο
3 sg	-	λύσοι	το		λύσοιτο
1 pl	μεν	λύσοιμεν	μεθα		λυσοίμεθα
2 pl	τε	λύσοιτε	σθε		λύσοισθε
3 pl	εν	λύσοιεν	ντο		λύσοιντο

---

[1]   Intervocalic σ is lost (αισο › αιο; §40.2).

Aorist Active/Middle Optative (§63)

The aorist active optative occurs twenty-one times in the New Testament (cf. §66). The aorist middle optative occurs nineteen times, seventeen of them being in the form (μὴ) γένοιτο, the third singular of γίνομαι. εὐχαίμην is first singular from εὔχομαι (Acts 26:29). ὀναίμην is first singular from ὀνίνημι (Phlm 20).

Thematic Stems (§63.1)

		first aorist	*second aorist*
aorist active optative			
1 sg	μι	λύσαιμι	βάλοιμι
2 sg	ς	λύσαις	βάλοις
3 sg	-	λύσαι[1]	βάλοι
1 pl	μεν	λύσαιμεν	βάλοιμεν
2 pl	τε	λύσαιτε	βάλοιτε
3 pl	εν	λύσαιεν[2]	βάλοιεν
aorist middle optative			
1 sg	μην	λυσαίμην	βαλοίμην
2 sg	σο[3]	λύσαιο	βάλοιο
3 sg	το	λύσαιτο	βάλοιτο
1 pl	μεθα	λυσαίμεθα	βαλοίμεθα
2 pl	σθε	λύσαισθε	βάλοισθε
3 pl	ντο	λύσαιντο	βάλοιντο

Athematic Stems (§63.2)

		*στα	*θε	*δο
second aorist active optative				
1 sg	ν	σταίην	θείην	δοίην
2 sg	ς	σταίης	θείης	δοίης
3 sg	-	σταίη	θείη	δοίη

---

[1] In Classical Greek the ending was -ειε(ν); cf. *BDF* §85.
[2] Can also be λύσειαν (Acts 17:27; Rom 5:17; 2 Cor 10:15; Jas 1:21).
[3] After the intervocalic σ drops out there is no further contraction (§40.2).

1 pl	μεν	σταῖμεν	θεῖμεν	δοῖμεν
2 pl	τε	σταῖτε	θεῖτε	δοῖτε
3 pl	εν	σταῖεν	θεῖεν	δοῖεν

Less commonly in the plural.

1 pl	μεν	σταίημεν	θείημεν	δοίημεν
2 pl	τε	σταίητε	θείητε	δοίητε
3 pl	σαν	σταίησαν	θείησαν	δοίησαν

second aorist middle optative

1 sg	μην	πριαίμην[1]	θείμην	δοίμην
2 sg	σο[2]	πρίαιο	θεῖο	δοῖο
3 sg	το	πρίαιτο	θεῖτο[3]	δοῖτο
1 pl	μεθα	πριαίμεθα	θείμεθα	δοίμεθα
2 pl	σθε	πρίαισθε	θεῖσθε	δοῖσθε
3 pl	ντο	πρίαιντο	θεῖντο	δοῖντο

Smyth lists alternate forms for τίθημι.

1 pl	μεθα		θοίμεθα
2 pl	σθε		θοῖσθε
3 pl	ντο		θοῖντο

Perfect Optative   (§64)

There is no example of the simple form of the perfect optative in the New Testament. Generally, periphrastic forms are used for the perfect optative in Classical and Hellenistic Greek, formed with the perfect active participle and the optative of εἰμί. The simple forms are rare. All ιη forms are attested as are the third singular and first/third plural for ι forms (Smyth §694-6).

---

[1]   If ἵστημι occurred in the aorist middle it would have the forms σταίμην, σταῖο, σταῖτο, σταίμεθα, σταῖσθε, σταῖντο.

[2]   After the intervocalic σ drops out there is no further contraction (§40.2).

[3]   Occurs also as θοῖτο.

Thematic Stems   (§64.1)

		perfect active[1]			perfect middle/passive		
1 sg	μι	λελύκοιμι[2]	λελυκὼς	εἴην	λελυμένος εἴην		
2 sg	ς	λελύκοις	λελυκὼς	εἴης	λελυμένος εἴης		
3 sg	-	λελύκοι	λελυκὼς	εἴη	λελυμένος εἴη		
1 pl	μεν	λελύκοιμεν	λελυκότες	εἴημεν	λελυμένοι εἶμεν	(εἴημεν)	
2 pl	τε	λελύκοιτε	λελυκότες	εἴητε	λελυμένοι εἶτε	(εἴητε)	
3 pl	εν	λελύκοιεν	λελυκότες	εἴησαν	λελυμένοι εἶεν	(εἴησαν)	

Athematic Stems   (§64.2)

Smyth lists a second perfect optative only for ἵστημι, not for the other μι verbs.

1 sg	μι	ἑσταίην	1 pl	μεν	ἑσταῖμεν
2 sg	ς	ἑσταίης	2 pl	τε	ἑσταῖτε
3 sg	-	ἑσταίη	3 pl	εν	ἑσταῖεν

Less commonly in the plural.

1 pl	μεν	ἑσταίημεν
2 pl	τε	ἑσταίητε
3 pl	σαν	ἑσταίησαν

Aorist Passive Optative   (§65)

In the aorist passive the mood formative becomes ιη. The aorist passive optative occurs five times in the New Testament, all of them being the form πληθυνθείη.

Thematic Stems   (§65.1)

1 sg	ν	λυθείην	1 pl	μεν	λυθεῖμεν
2 sg	ς	λυθείης	2 pl	τε	λυθεῖτε
3 sg	-	λυθείη	3 pl	εν	λυθεῖεν

Less commonly in the plural.

1 pl	μεν	λυθείημεν
2 pl	τε	λυθείητε
3 pl	σαν	λυθείησαν

---

[1]   The first column is the simple form, the second the periphrastic.

[2]   If the mood formative is ιη you find the following forms: λελυκοίην, λελυκοίης, λελυκοίη, λελυκοίημεν, λελυκοίητε, λελυκοίησαν.

Athematic Stems   (§65.2)

first aorist passive optative

1 sg	ν	σταθείην	τεθείην	δοθείην
2 sg	ς	σταθείης	τεθείης	δοθείης
3 sg	-	σταθείη	τεθείη	δοθείη
1 pl	μεν	σταθεῖμεν	τεθεῖμεν	δοθεῖμεν
2 pl	τε	σταθεῖτε	τεθεῖτε	δοθεῖτε
3 pl	εν	σταθεῖεν	τεθεῖεν	δοθεῖεν

Less commonly in the plural.

1 pl	μεν	σταθείημεν	τεθείημεν	δοθείημεν
2 pl	τε	σταθείητε	τεθείητε	δοθείητε
3 pl	σαν	σταθείησαν	τεθείησαν	δοθείησαν

All Optatives in the New Testament   (§66)

Following are all the verses with verbs in the optative in the New Testament, except for those with μὴ γένοιτο (Luke 20:16; Rom 3:4, 6, 31; 6:2, 15; 7:7, 13; 9:14; 11:1; 1 Cor 6:15; Gal 2:17; 3:21; 6:14) and εἴη (Luke 1:29; 3:15; 8:9; 9:46; 15:26; 18:36; 22:23; John 13:24; Acts 8:20; 10:17; 20:16; 21:33).

Mark 11:14   καὶ ἀποκριθεὶς εἶπεν αὐτῇ· μηκέτι εἰς τὸν αἰῶνα ἐκ σοῦ μηδεὶς καρπὸν **φάγοι**. καὶ ἤκουον οἱ μαθηταὶ αὐτοῦ.

Luke 1:38   εἶπεν δὲ Μαριάμ· ἰδοὺ ἡ δούλη κυρίου· **γένοιτό** μοι κατὰ τὸ ῥῆμά σου. καὶ ἀπῆλθεν ἀπ' αὐτῆς ὁ ἄγγελος.

Luke 1:62   ἐνένευον δὲ τῷ πατρὶ αὐτοῦ τὸ τί ἂν θέλοι καλεῖσθαι αὐτό.

Luke 6:11   αὐτοὶ δὲ ἐπλήσθησαν ἀνοίας καὶ διελάλουν πρὸς ἀλλήλους τί ἂν **ποιήσαιεν** τῷ Ἰησοῦ.

Acts 5:24   ὡς δὲ ἤκουσαν τοὺς λόγους τούτους ὅ τε στρατηγὸς τοῦ ἱεροῦ καὶ οἱ ἀρχιερεῖς, διηπόρουν περὶ αὐτῶν τί ἂν **γένοιτο** τοῦτο.

Acts 8:31   ὁ δὲ εἶπεν· πῶς γὰρ ἂν **δυναίμην** ἐὰν μή τις ὁδηγήσει με; παρεκάλεσέν τε τὸν Φίλιππον ἀναβάντα καθίσαι σὺν αὐτῷ.

Acts 17:11   οὗτοι δὲ ἦσαν εὐγενέστεροι τῶν ἐν Θεσσαλονίκῃ, οἵτινες ἐδέξαντο τὸν λόγον μετὰ πάσης προθυμίας καθ' ἡμέραν ἀνακρίνοντες τὰς γραφὰς εἰ **ἔχοι** ταῦτα οὕτως.

Acts 17:18   τινὲς δὲ καὶ τῶν Ἐπικουρείων καὶ Στοϊκῶν φιλοσόφων συνέβαλλον αὐτῷ, καί τινες ἔλεγον· τί ἂν **θέλοι** ὁ σπερμολόγος οὗτος λέγειν; οἱ δέ· ξένων δαιμονίων δοκεῖ καταγγελεὺς εἶναι, ὅτι τὸν Ἰησοῦν καὶ τὴν ἀνάστασιν εὐηγγελίζετο.

Acts 17:27   ζητεῖν τὸν θεόν, εἰ ἄρα γε **ψηλαφήσειαν** αὐτὸν καὶ **εὕροιεν**, καί γε οὐ μακρὰν ἀπὸ ἑνὸς ἑκάστου ἡμῶν ὑπάρχοντα.

Acts 24:19   τινὲς δὲ ἀπὸ τῆς Ἀσίας Ἰουδαῖοι, οὓς ἔδει ἐπὶ σοῦ παρεῖναι καὶ κατηγορεῖν εἴ τι **ἔχοιεν** πρὸς ἐμέ.

Acts 25:16 πρὸς οὓς ἀπεκρίθην ὅτι οὐκ ἔστιν ἔθος Ῥωμαίοις χαρίζεσθαί τινα ἄνθρωπον πρὶν ἢ ὁ κατηγορούμενος κατὰ πρόσωπον **ἔχοι** τοὺς κατηγόρους τόπον τε ἀπολογίας **λάβοι** περὶ τοῦ ἐγκλήματος.

Acts 25:20 ἀπορούμενος δὲ ἐγὼ τὴν περὶ τούτων ζήτησιν ἔλεγον εἰ **βούλοιτο** πορεύεσθαι εἰς Ἱεροσόλυμα κἀκεῖ κρίνεσθαι περὶ τούτων.

Acts 26:29 ὁ δὲ Παῦλος· **εὐξαίμην** ἂν τῷ θεῷ καὶ ἐν ὀλίγῳ καὶ ἐν μεγάλῳ οὐ μόνον σὲ ἀλλὰ καὶ πάντας τοὺς ἀκούοντάς μου σήμερον γενέσθαι τοιούτους ὁποῖος καὶ ἐγώ εἰμι παρεκτὸς τῶν δεσμῶν τούτων.

Acts 27:12 ἀνευθέτου δὲ τοῦ λιμένος ὑπάρχοντος πρὸς παραχειμασίαν οἱ πλείονες ἔθεντο βουλὴν ἀναχθῆναι ἐκεῖθεν, εἴ πως **δύναιντο** καταντήσαντες εἰς Φοίνικα παραχειμάσαι λιμένα τῆς Κρήτης βλέποντα κατὰ λίβα καὶ κατὰ χῶρον.

Acts 27:39 Ὅτε δὲ ἡμέρα ἐγένετο, τὴν γῆν οὐκ ἐπεγίνωσκον, κόλπον δέ τινα κατενόουν ἔχοντα αἰγιαλὸν εἰς ὃν ἐβουλεύοντο εἰ **δύναιντο** ἐξῶσαι τὸ πλοῖον.

Rom 15:5 ὁ δὲ θεὸς τῆς ὑπομονῆς καὶ τῆς παρακλήσεως **δῴη** ὑμῖν τὸ αὐτὸ φρονεῖν ἐν ἀλλήλοις κατὰ Χριστὸν Ἰησοῦν,

Rom 15:13 Ὁ δὲ θεὸς τῆς ἐλπίδος **πληρώσαι** ὑμᾶς πάσης χαρᾶς καὶ εἰρήνης ἐν τῷ πιστεύειν, εἰς τὸ περισσεύειν ὑμᾶς ἐν τῇ ἐλπίδι ἐν δυνάμει πνεύματος ἁγίου.

1 Cor 14:10 τοσαῦτα εἰ **τύχοι** γένη φωνῶν εἰσιν ἐν κόσμῳ καὶ οὐδὲν ἄφωνον·

1 Cor 15:37 καὶ ὃ σπείρεις, οὐ τὸ σῶμα τὸ γενησόμενον σπείρεις ἀλλὰ γυμνὸν κόκκον εἰ **τύχοι** σίτου ἤ τινος τῶν λοιπῶν·

1 Th 3:11 Αὐτὸς δὲ ὁ θεὸς καὶ πατὴρ ἡμῶν καὶ ὁ κύριος ἡμῶν Ἰησοῦς **κατευθύναι** τὴν ὁδὸν ἡμῶν πρὸς ὑμᾶς·

1 Th 3:12 ὑμᾶς δὲ ὁ κύριος **πλεονάσαι** καὶ **περισσεύσαι** τῇ ἀγάπῃ εἰς ἀλλήλους καὶ εἰς πάντας καθάπερ καὶ ἡμεῖς εἰς ὑμᾶς,

1 Th 5:23 Αὐτὸς δὲ ὁ θεὸς τῆς εἰρήνης **ἁγιάσαι** ὑμᾶς ὁλοτελεῖς, καὶ ὁλόκληρον ὑμῶν τὸ πνεῦμα καὶ ἡ ψυχὴ καὶ τὸ σῶμα ἀμέμπτως ἐν τῇ παρουσίᾳ τοῦ κυρίου ἡμῶν Ἰησοῦ Χριστοῦ **τηρηθείη**.

2 Th 2:17 **παρακαλέσαι** ὑμῶν τὰς καρδίας καὶ **στηρίξαι** ἐν παντὶ ἔργῳ καὶ λόγῳ ἀγαθῷ.

2 Th 3:5 Ὁ δὲ κύριος **κατευθύναι** ὑμῶν τὰς καρδίας εἰς τὴν ἀγάπην τοῦ θεοῦ καὶ εἰς τὴν ὑπομονὴν τοῦ Χριστοῦ.

2 Th 3:16 Αὐτὸς δὲ ὁ κύριος τῆς εἰρήνης **δῴη** ὑμῖν τὴν εἰρήνην διὰ παντὸς ἐν παντὶ τρόπῳ. ὁ κύριος μετὰ πάντων ὑμῶν.

2 Tim 1:16 **δῴη** ἔλεος ὁ κύριος τῷ Ὀνησιφόρου οἴκῳ, ὅτι πολλάκις με ἀνέψυξεν καὶ τὴν ἅλυσίν μου οὐκ ἐπαισχύνθη,

2 Tim 1:18 **δῴη** αὐτῷ ὁ κύριος εὑρεῖν ἔλεος παρὰ κυρίου ἐν ἐκείνῃ τῇ ἡμέρᾳ. καὶ ὅσα ἐν Ἐφέσῳ διηκόνησεν, βέλτιον σὺ γινώσκεις.

2 Tim 4:16 Ἐν τῇ πρώτῃ μου ἀπολογίᾳ οὐδείς μοι παρεγένετο, ἀλλὰ πάντες με ἐγκατέλιπον· μὴ αὐτοῖς **λογισθείη**·

Phlm 1:20 ναί ἀδελφέ, ἐγώ σου **ὀναίμην** ἐν κυρίῳ· ἀνάπαυσόν μου τὰ σπλάγχνα ἐν Χριστῷ.

Heb 13:21 **καταρτίσαι** ὑμᾶς ἐν παντὶ ἀγαθῷ εἰς τὸ ποιῆσαι τὸ θέλημα αὐτοῦ, ποιῶν ἐν ἡμῖν τὸ εὐάρεστον ἐνώπιον αὐτοῦ διὰ Ἰησοῦ Χριστοῦ, ᾧ ἡ δόξα εἰς τοὺς αἰῶνας [τῶν αἰώνων], ἀμήν.

1 Pet 1:2 κατὰ πρόγνωσιν θεοῦ πατρὸς ἐν ἁγιασμῷ πνεύματος εἰς ὑπακοὴν καὶ ῥαντισμὸν αἵματος Ἰησοῦ Χριστοῦ, χάρις ὑμῖν καὶ εἰρήνη **πληθυνθείη**.

1 Pet 3:14 ἀλλ' εἰ καὶ **πάσχοιτε** διὰ δικαιοσύνην, μακάριοι. τὸν δὲ φόβον αὐτῶν μὴ φοβηθῆτε μηδὲ ταραχθῆτε,

1 Pet 3:17 κρεῖττον γὰρ ἀγαθοποιοῦντας, εἰ **θέλοι** τὸ θέλημα τοῦ θεοῦ, πάσχειν ἢ κακοποιοῦντας.

2 Pet 1:2   χάρις ὑμῖν καὶ εἰρήνη **πληθυνθείη** ἐν ἐπιγνώσει τοῦ θεοῦ καὶ Ἰησοῦ τοῦ κυρίου ἡμῶν.

Jude 1:2   ἔλεος ὑμῖν καὶ εἰρήνη καὶ ἀγάπη **πληθυνθείη**.

Jude 1:9   Ὁ δὲ Μιχαὴλ ὁ ἀρχάγγελος, ὅτε τῷ διαβόλῳ διακρινόμενος διελέγετο περὶ τοῦ Μωϋσέως σώματος, οὐκ ἐτόλμησεν κρίσιν ἐπενεγκεῖν βλασφημίας ἀλλὰ εἶπεν· **ἐπιτιμήσαι** σοι κύριος.

Imperative   (§70)

The imperative occurs in the New Testament in the present, aorist, and perfect. In the present, the connecting vowel ε is used. In the aorist, the endings are added directly onto the tense formative. There will be no augment in the aorist, since the imperative cannot indicate absolute time but only aspect.

The alternate third plural forms that we list are the Classical forms. For a discussion of the personal endings see §36.8.

Present Imperative   (§71)

Thematic Stems   (§71.1)

active			middle/passive	
2 *sg*	ε	λῦε	σο[1]	λύου
3 *sg*	τω	λυέτω	σθω	λυέσθω
2 *pl*	τε	λύετε	σθε	λύεσθε
3 *pl*	τωσαν	λυέτωσαν	σθωσαν	λυέσθωσαν
	ντων	λυόντων	σθων	λυέσθων

Contract Stems   (§71.2)

present active imperative

2 *sg*	ε	γέννα	ποίει	φανέρου
3 *sg*	τω	γεννάτω	ποιείτω	φανερούτω
2 *pl*	τε	γεννᾶτε	ποιεῖτε	φανεροῦτε
3 *pl*	τωσαν	γεννάτωσαν	ποιείτωσαν	φανερούτωσαν
	ντων	γεννώντων	ποιούντων	φανερούντων

---

[1]   λυ + ε + σο › λυεο › λύου. The intervocalic σ drops outs and the vowels contract (§40.2).

present middle/passive imperative

2 sg	σο[1]	γεννῶ	ποιοῦ	φανεροῦ
3 sg	σθω	γεννάσθω	ποιείσθω	φανερούσθω
2 pl	σθε	γεννᾶσθε	ποιεῖσθε	φανεροῦσθε
3 pl	σθωσαν	γεννάσθωσαν	ποιείσθωσαν	φανερούσθωσαν
	σθων	γεννάσθων	ποιείσθων	φανερούσθων

Athematic Stems (§71.3)

		*ꞌστα	*θε	*δο	*δείκνυ

present active imperative

2 sg	ε	ꞌστη[2]	τίθει	δίδου	δείκνυ[3]
3 sg	τω	ἱστάτω	τιθέτω	διδότω	δεικνύτω
2 pl	τε	ꞌστατε	τίθετε	δίδοτε	δείκνυτε
3 pl	τωσαν	ἱστάτωσαν	τιθέτωσαν	διδότωσαν	δεικνύτωσαν
	ντων	ἱστάντων	τιθέντων	διδόντων	δεικνύντων

present middle/passive imperative

2 sg	σο[4]	ꞌστασο	τίθεσο	δίδοσο	δείκνυσο
3 sg	σθω	ἱστάσθω	τιθέσθω	διδόσθω	δεικνύσθω
2 pl	σθε	ꞌστασθε	τίθεσθε	δίδοσθε	δείκνυσθε
3 pl	σθωσαν	ἱστάσθωσαν	τιθέσθωσαν	διδόσθωσαν	δεικνύσθωσαν
	σθων	ἱστάσθων	τιθέσθων	διδόσθων	δεικνύσθων

---

[1] The intervocalic σ drops out and the vowels contract regularly (§40.2).
γεννα*σο ‣ γεννα*ο ‣ γεννα*ω ‣ γεννῶ. ποιε*σο ‣ ποιε*ο ‣ ποιοῦ. φανερο*σο ‣ φανερο*ο ‣ φανεροῦ.

[2] ꞌστημι lengthens its stem vowel and it does not use an ending.

[3] Like ꞌστημι, no ending is used.

[4] Notice how the intervocalic σ does not drop out (§25.5).

Aorist Active/Middle Imperative   (§72)

Thematic Stems   (§72.1)

first aorist   *second aorist*

aorist active imperative

2 sg	ε	λῦσον[1]	βάλε
3 sg	τω	λυσάτω	βαλέτω
2 pl	τε	λύσατε	βάλετε
3 pl	τωσαν	λυσάτωσαν	βαλέτωσαν
	ντων	λυσάντων	βαλόντων[2]

aorist middle imperative

2 sg	σο	λῦσαι[1]	βαλοῦ
3 sg	σθω	λυσάσθω	βαλέσθω
2 pl	σθε	λύσασθε	βάλεσθε
3 pl	σθωσαν	λυσάσθωσαν	βαλέσθωσαν
	σθων	λυσάσθων	βαλέσθων

Contract Stems   (§72.2)

aorist active imperative

2 sg	-[1]	γέννησον	ποίησον	φανέρωσον
3 sg	τω	γεννήσατω	ποιήσατω	φανερώσατω
2 pl	τε	γεννήσατε	ποιήσατε	φανερώσατε
3 pl	τωσαν	γεννησάτωσαν	ποιησάτωσαν	φανερωσάτωσαν
	ντων	γεννησάντων	ποιησάντων	φανερωσάντων

aorist middle imperative

2 sg	-[1]	γέννησαι	ποίησαι	φανέρωσαι
3 sg	σθω	γεννησάσθω	ποιησάσθω	φανερωσάσθω
2 pl	σθε	γεννήσασθε	ποιήσασθε	φανερώσασθε
3 pl	σθωσαν	γεννησάσθωσαν	ποιησάσθωσαν	φανερωσάσθωσαν
	σθων	γεννησάσθων	ποιησάσθων	φανερωσάσθων

---

[1]   There is no obvious reason for the endings in these second singular imperatives.
[2]   Notice that the connecting vowel is o.

Liquid Stems   (§72.3)

		aorist active		aorist middle
2 sg	-[1]	φῆνον	-[1]	φῆναι
3 sg	τω	φηνάτω	σθω	φηνάσθω
2 pl	τε	φήνατε	σθε	φήνασθε
3 pl	τωσαν	φηνάτωσαν	σθωσαν	φηνάσθωσαν
	ντων	φηνάντων	σθων	φηνάσθων

Athematic Stems   (§72.4)

In the aorist, ιη is added to the verbal root (with a short stem vowel).

second aorist active imperative

2 sg	θι or ς	στῆθι	θές	δός	ἄφες
3 sg	τω	στήτω	θέτω	δότω	ἀφέτω
2 pl	τε	στῆτε	θέτε	δότε	ἄφετε
3 pl	τωσαν	στήτωσαν	θέτωσαν	δότωσαν	ἀφέτωσαν
	ντων	στάντων	θέντων	δόντων	ἀφέντων

γινώσκω has a root aorist like δίδωμι except that in the second singular it uses θι: γνῶθι, γνώτω, γνῶτε, γνώτωσαν.

second aorist middle imperative

The only second aorist middle imperatives in the New Testament are from τίθημι.

2 sg	σο	στῶ	θοῦ	δοῦ
3 sg	σθω	στάσθω	θέσθω	δόσθω
2 pl	σθε	στάσθε	θέσθε	δόσθε
3 pl	σθωσαν	στάσθωσαν	θέσθωσαν	δόσθωσαν
	σθων	στάσθων	θέσθων	δόσθων

Perfect Imperative   (§73)

In Classical and Koine Greek the perfect imperative is usually formed periphrastically with the perfect participle and the present imperative of εἰμί. There is no

---
[1] There is no obvious reason for the endings in these second singular imperatives.

example of the simple form in the classical Attic writers (Smyth §697). Below we list the simple and then the periphrastic forms.

The only active form in the New Testament is ἴστε (Eph 5:5; Jas 1:19) from οἶδα, which is perfect in form but present in meaning. There are only two middle/passive forms: πεφίμωσο (second singular from φιμόω, Mk 4:39); ἔρρωσθε (second plural from ῥώννυμι, Acts 15:29). On the second perfect see Smyth §698.

active imperative			**middle/passive imperative**	
2 sg	ε	λέλυκε	σο	λέλυσο
3 sg	τω	λελυκέτω	σθω	λελύσθω
2 pl	τε	λελύκετε	σθε	λέλυσθε
3 pl	τωσαν	λελυκέτωσαν	σθωσαν	λελύσθωσαν

periphrastic

2 sg	λελυκὼς ἴσθι
3 sg	λελυκὼς ἔστω
2 pl	λελυκότες ἔστε
3 pl	λελυκότες ἔστωσαν

Aorist Passive Imperative   (§74)

The second singular ending is θι. It deaspirates to τ because of the preceding θ in the tense formative.

Thematic Stems   (§74.1)

		first aorist	*second aorist*
2 sg	θι	λύθητι[1]	γράφηθι
3 sg	τω	λυθήτω	γραφήτω
2 pl	τε	λύθητε	γράφητε
3 pl	τωσαν	λυθήτωσαν	γραφήτωσαν
	ντων	λυθέντων	γραφέντων

---

[1] When added to the tense formative θη, the θ in the imperatival ending deaspirates to τ (§15.3a). There is no θ in the second aorist form, so the imperatival morpheme does not deaspirate.

Athematic Stems   (§74.2)

	*στα	*θε	*δο

first aorist passive imperative

		*στα	*θε	*δο
2 sg	θι[1]	στάθητι	τέθητι	δόθητι
3 sg	τω	σταθήτω	τεθήτω	δοθήτω
2 pl	τε	στάθητε	τέθητε	δόθητε
3 pl	·τωσαν	σταθήτωσαν	τεθήτωσαν	δοθήτωσαν
	ντων	σταθέντων	τεθέντων	δοθέντων

Infinitive   (§80)

There are three active infinitive morphemes and one middle/passive morpheme. The active morphemes are εν, ι, and ναι. The middle/passive morpheme is σθαι. The infinitive morpheme in the aorist active for μι verbs is εναι (Smyth §760).

They are added to the tense stem (without augment); when used, the connecting vowel is always ε. In the New Testament the infinitive occurs in the present, future, aorist, and perfect.

The infinitives are arranged in the following order:
thematic, contract (α, ε, ο), liquid
athematic (second line).

Summary

Following is an overview of the infinitival system. It lists the tense formative (if used), connecting vowel (if used), infinitive morpheme, and final form. The μι form is indicated when different.

tense	active				middle/passive			
present		ε	εν	‣ ειν			ε	σθαι ‣ εσθαι
(athematic)			ναι	‣ ναι				
future	σ	ε	εν	‣ σειν	σ		ε	σθαι ‣ σεσθαι
1st future passive					θησ		ε	σθαι ‣ θησεσθαι
2nd future passive					ησ		ε	σθαι ‣ ησεσθαι
1st aorist	σα		ι	‣ σαι	σα			σθαι ‣ σασθαι

---

[1]   The θ deaspirates to τ because of the tense formative; cf. §15.3.

2nd aorist		ε	εν ‣ ειν		ε	σθαι ‣ εσθαι
(athematic)			εναι ‣ εναι			
1st aorist passive				θη		ναι ‣ θηναι
2nd aorist passive				η		ναι ‣ ηναι
1st perfect	κε	ναι ‣ κεναι				σθαι ‣ σθαι
2nd perfect	ε	ναι ‣εναι				σθαι ‣σθαι

Present Infinitive   (§81)

μι verbs will always have a short stem vowel.

present active infinitive

λυείν	γενναν	ποιεῖν	φανεροῦν	κρίνειν
ἱστάναι	τιθέναι	διδόναι	δεικνύναι	εἶναι

present middle/passive infinitive

λύεσθαι	γεννασθαι	ποιεῖσθαι	φανεροῦσθαι	κρίνεσθαι
ἵστασθαι	τίθεσθαι	δίδοσθαι	δείκνυσθαι	

Future Active/Middle Infinitive   (§82)

future active infinitive

λύσειν	γεννήσειν	ποιήσειν	φανερώσειν	κρινεῖν
στήσειν	θήσειν	δώσειν		

future middle infinitive

λύσεσθαι	γεννήσεσθαι	ποιήσεσθαι	φανερώσεσθαι	κρινεῖσθαι
στήσεσθαι	θήσεσθαι	δώσεσθαι		ἔσεσθαι

Aorist Active/Middle Infinitive   (§83)

first aorist active infinitive

λῦσαι	γέννησαι	ποίησαι	φανέρωσαι	κρῖναι
στῆσαι				

second aorist active infinitive

βαλεῖν

στῆναι   θεῖναι   δοῦναι

first aorist middle infinitive

λύσασθαι   γεννήσασθαι   ποιήσασθαι   φανερώσασθαι   κρίνασθαι
στήσασθαι

second aorist middle infinitive

βαλέσθαι

στάσθαι   θέσθαι   δόσθαι

Perfect Infinitive   (§84)

perfect active infinitive

λελυκέναι[1] γεγεννηκέναι   πεποιηκέναι   πεφανερωκέναι
ἑστηκέναι[2] τεθηκέναι   δεδωκέναι

perfect middle/passive infinitive

λελῦσθαι   γεγεννῆσθαι   πεποιῆσθαι   πεφανερῶσθαι
ἑστάσθαι   τεθεῖσθαι   δεδόσθαι

Aorist Passive Infinitive   (§85)

Contract verbs lengthen their final stem vowel before the tense formative. μι
verbs lengthen their final stem vowel in various ways.

first aorist passive infinitive

λυθῆναι   γεννηθῆναι   ποιηθῆναι   φανερωθῆναι   φανῆναι
σταθῆναι   τεθῆναι   δοθῆναι

second aorist passive infinitive

βαλῆναι

---

[1]   Future perfect passive is λελύσεσθαι (cf. Funk §300.2). The second perfect active is
    formed as γεγονέναι.

[2]   Its second perfect is ἑστάναι.

Participle   (§90)

There are only four participle morphemes:

ντ	active (except perfect) and aorist passive
μεν	middle/passive (future passive included but not aorist passive)
οτ	masculine/neuter perfect active[1]
υσ	feminine in the perfect active (Funk §468.2)

The participle appears in the New Testament in the present, future, aorist, and perfect. Even in Classical Greek the future perfect participle was rare.

ντ is the morpheme for all active participles (except the perfect), and for the aorist passive participle. In the present, the participle is preceded by the connecting vowel ο, making the participle appear to be οντ. In the aorist active it is preceded by the tense formative σα, forming σαντ. In the aorist passive it is preceded by θε, forming θεντ.

When ντ is used for a feminine form, the participle morpheme is altered by adding ια to ντ (Smyth §633, §671; Funk §4271.3, §248).

* οντια contract to form ουσα in the present.
* σαντια contract to form σασα in the aorist.
* υσια contract to form κυια in the perfect.

In the following paradigms we list and discuss in detail the paradigms for thematic and athematic forms of the present active and middle/passive, first aorist active, first perfect active, and the first aorist passive. Other paradigms are given in the nominative and genitive singular forms only. On participles see Funk (§246-250). The vocative of participles is always the same as the nominative (Smyth §302).

---

[1]   Technically the participle morpheme started with a digamma: Ϝοτ (Smyth §301c).

Present Participle   (§91)

Thematic Stems   (§91.1)

The present active participle follows the pattern in a-2; the middle/passive follows the pattern from a-1a(2a).

present active participle

nom sg	λύων[1]	λύουσα[2]	λῦον[3]
gen sg	λύοντος	λυούσης	λύοντος
dat sg	λύοντι	λυούσῃ	λύοντι
acc sg	λύοντα	λύουσαν	λῦον
nom pl	λύοντες	λύουσαι	λύοντα
gen pl	λυόντων	λυουσῶν[4]	λυόντων
dat pl	λύουσι(ν)[5]	λυούσαις	λύουσι(ν)
acc pl	λύοντας	λυούσας	λύοντα

present middle/passive participle

nom sg	λυόμενος	λυομένη	λυόμενον
gen sg	λυομένου	λυομένης	λυομένου
dat sg	λυομένῳ	λυομένῃ	λυομένῳ
acc sg	λυόμενον	λυομένην	λυόμενον
nom pl	λυόμενοι	λυόμεναι	λυόμενα
gen pl	λυομένων	λυομένων	λυομένων
dat pl	λυομένοις	λυομέναις	λυομένοις
acc pl	λυομένους	λυομένας	λυόμενα

---

[1] No ending is used. Since τ cannot stand at the end of a Greek word it is dropped, and the preceding vowel is lengthened in compensation (§19.1). (Notice that o is lengthened to ω and not ου; it is perhaps better to call the lengthening of o to ω a form of ablaut (§4). λυοντ ‣ λυον ‣ λύων

[2] The feminine is formed by adding ια to the stem. τι form σ (§26.10), the ν drops out when followed by the σ, and the preceding vowel is lengthened in compensation (§24.4). οντ + ια ‣ ονσα ‣ οσα ‣ ουσα.

[3] No ending is used. Since τ cannot stand at the end of a Greek word it is dropped (§19.1) without any compensation in the preceding vowel.

[4] Unlike adjectives, the accent stays on the ultima as it does with first declension nouns.

[5] ν drops out when followed by σ, and the preceding vowel is lengthened in compensation (§24.4). Notice the difference in compensatory lengthening here and in the nominative singular masculine; cf. §3.5.

Contract Stems (§91.2)

present active participle

| nom sg | πλανῶν | πλανῶσα | πλανῶν |
| gen sg | πλανῶντος | πλανώσης | πλανῶντος |

| nom sg | λαλῶν | λαλοῦσα | λαλοῦν |
| gen sg | λαλοῦντος | λαλούσης | λαλοῦντος |

| nom sg | πληρῶν | πληροῦσα | πληροῦν |
| gen sg | πληροῦντος | πληρούσης | πληροῦντος |

present middle/passive participle

| nom sg | πλανώμενος | πλανωμένη | πλανώμενον |
| gen sg | πλανωμένου | πλανωμένης | πλανωμένου |

| nom sg | λαλούμενος | λαλουμένη | λαλούμενον |
| gen sg | λαλουμένου | λαλουμένης | λαλουμένου |

| nom sg | πληρούμενος | πληρομένη | πληρούμενον |
| gen sg | πληρουμένου | πληρομένης | πληρουμένου |

Athematic Stems (§91.3)

The final stem vowel is short for the participles of μι verbs. They are otherwise declined like a thematic stem.

present active participle

| nom sg | ἱστάς | ἱστᾶσα | ἱστάν |
| gen sg | ἱστάντος | ἱστάσης | ἱστάντος |

| nom sg | τιθείς | τιθεῖσα | τιθέν |
| gen sg | τιθέντος | τιθείσης | τιθέντος |

| nom sg | διδούς | διδοῦσα | διδόν |
| gen sg | διδόντος | διδούσης | διδόντος |

| nom sg | δεικνύς | δεικνῦσα | δεικνύν |
| gen sg | δεικνύντος | δεικνύσης | δεικνύντος |

present middle/passive participle

nom sg	ἱστάμενος	ἱσταμένη	ἱστάμενον
gen sg	ἱσταμένου	ἱσταμένης	ἱσταμένου
nom sg	τιθέμενος	τιθεμένη	τιθέμενον
gen sg	τιθεμένου	τιθεμένης	τιθεμένου
nom sg	διδόμενος	διδομένη	διδόμενον
gen sg	διδομένου	διδομένης	διδομένου
nom sg	δεικνύμενος	δεικνυμένη	δεικνύμενον
gen sg	δεικνυμένου	δεικνυμένης	δεικνυμένου

Future Active/Middle Participle (§92)

There are nine future active participles (σώσων, παραδώσων, προσκυνήσων [twice], συναντήσοντα, ἄξων, ποιήσων, ἀποδώσοντες, κακώσων) and two future middle participles (ἐσόμενον, γενησόμενον) in the New Testament. Contract participles are formed regularly. There are no liquids future participles in the New Testament; γίνομαι inserts an η after its final stem ν and forms its participles as if it were a contract verb: γενησόμενον.

Thematic Stems (§92.1)

active	*nom sg*	λύσων	λύσουσα	λῦσον
	gen sg	λύσοντος	λυσούσης	λύσοντος
middle	*nom sg*	λυσόμενος	λυσομένη	λυσόμενον
	gen sg	λυσομένου	λυσομένης	λυσομένου

Athematic Stems (§92.2)

future active participle

nom sg	στήσων	θήσων	δώσων
gen sg	στήσοντος	θήσοντος	δώσοντος

future middle participle

nom sg	στησόμενος	θησόμενος	δωσόμενος
gen sg	στησομένου	θησομένου	δωσομένου

Aorist Active/Middle Participle   (§93)

The aorist participle uses the same participle morpheme as does the present (ντ)
even though this is not obvious at first glance. There is no augment. The active
and middle follow the third declension in the masculine and neuter and the first
declension in the feminine (3-1-3). The feminine morpheme is altered by adding
ια to ντ; cf. §90.

First Aorist: Thematic Stems   (§93.1)

first aorist active participle

nom sg	λύσας[1]	λύσασα[2]	λῦσαν[3]
gen sg	λύσαντος	λυσάσης	λύσαντος
dat sg	λύσαντι	λυσάσῃ	λύσαντι
acc sg	λύσαντα	λύσασαν	λῦσαν
nom pl	λύσαντες	λύσασαι	λύσαντα
gen pl	λυσάντων	λυσασῶν[4]	λυσάντων
dat pl	λύσασι(ν)[5]	λυσάσαις	λύσασι(ν)
acc pl	λύσαντας	λυσάσας	λύσαντα

first aorist middle participle

nom sg	λυσάμενος	λυσαμένη	λυσάμενον
gen sg	λυσαμένου	λυσαμένης	λυσαμένου

---

[1] λυσαντ + σ ‚ λυσανσ ‚ λυσας. Whereas the present participle uses no ending in the
     nominative singular, these participles use a σ. ντ drop out when followed by σ
     (§24.4c).

[2] The feminine is formed by adding ι to the stem. τι form σ (§26.10), the ν drops off
     when followed by σ (§24.4).

[3] No ending is used, and the τ drops off because it cannot stand at the end of a Greek
     word (§19.1).

[4] Unlike adjectives, the accent stays on the ultima as it does with first declension
     nouns.

[5] λυσαντ + σι ‚ λυσανσι ‚ λυσασι. When the consonant cluster ντ is immediately fol-
     lowed by σ, it will drop out and the preceding vowel will be lengthened in compen-
     sation (§24.4c).

First Aorist: Liquid Stems (§93.2)

aorist active participle

nom sg	κρίνας	κρίνασα	κρίναν
gen sg	κρίναντος	κρινάσης	κρίναντος

aorist middle participle

nom sg	κρινάμενος	κριναμένη	κρινάμενον
gen sg	κριναμένου	κριναμένης	κριναμένου

Second Aorist (§93.3)

second aorist active participle

nom sg	βαλών	βαλοῦσα	βαλόν
gen sg	βαλόντος	βαλούσης	βαλόντος

second aorist middle participle

nom sg	βαλόμενος	βαλομένη	βαλόμενον
gen sg	βαλομένου	βαλομένης	βαλομένου

Athematic Stems (§93.4)

first aorist active participle

nom sg	στήσας[1]	στήσασα	στῆσαν
gen sg	στήσαντος	στησάσης	στήσαντος

first aorist middle participle

nom sg	στησάμενος	στησαμένη	στησάμενον
gen sg	στησαμένου	στησαμένης	στησαμένου

second aorist active participle

nom sg	στάς	στᾶσα	στάν
gen sg	στάντος	στάσης	στάντος

nom sg	θείς	θεῖσα	θέν
gen sg	θέντος	θείσης	θέντος

nom sg	δούς	δοῦσα	δόν
gen sg	δόντος	δούσης	δόντος

---

[1] ἵστημι occurs six times in the N.T. as an aorist active participle. In all cases it uses a second aorist form.

second aorist middle participle

nom sg	στάμενος	σταμένη	στάμενον
gen sg	σταμένου	σταμένης	σταμένου

nom sg	θέμενος	θεμένη	θέμενον
gen sg	θεμένου	θεμένης	θεμένου

nom sg	δόμενος	δομένη	δόμενον
gen sg	δομένου	δομένης	δομένου

Perfect Participle   (§94)

The perfect participle morpheme (masculine and neuter) is οτ.[1] It is otherwise very much like the aorist.

The feminine morpheme is υσ, to which is added ͅα. The σ becomes intervocalic and drops out (§25.5), and ͅ becomes vocalic ι, resulting in υια. υσ + ͅα ‣ υͅα ‣ υια; cf. §90.

The middle/passive adds the participle directly onto the stem with no tense formative. The case endings are the same as λυόμενος, λυομένη, λυόμενον, although accents are not identical in all forms.

The only difference between first and second perfects is that first perfects include the tense formative κ while the second perfect does not (γεγονώς, γεγονυῖα, γεγονός).

Thematic Stems   (§94.1)

perfect active participle

nom sg	λελυκώς[2]	λελυκυῖα[3]	λελυκός[4]
gen sg	λελυκότος	λελυκυίας	λελυκότος
dat sg	λελυκότι	λελυκυίᾳ	λελυκότι
acc sg	λελυκότα	λελυκυῖαν	λελυκός

---

[1] Technically the morpheme is Ϝοτ; cf. §90.

[2] Whereas the present participle uses no ending here, the perfect active uses σ. The τ has dropped out and the ο has lengthened to ω (§4).

[3] See the discussion above the paradigm.

[4] This form is somewhat difficult. The stem is still probably οτ as seen in the genitive and dative. If a σ were added to form the nominative and accusative, this would explain how the τ dropped out (§22.3). But σ is not a proper ending for the neuter; only the masculine. Funk (§249.2) says that the nominative and accusative neuter use an alternate morpheme οσ.

nom pl	λελυκότες	λελυκυῖαι	λελυκότα
gen pl	λελυκότων	λελυκυιῶν	λελυκότων
dat pl	λελυκόσι(ν)[1]	λελυκυίαις	λελυκόσι(ν)
acc pl	λελυκότας	λελυκυίας	λελυκότα

perfect middle/passive participle

nom sg	λελυμένος	λελυμένη	λελυμένον
gen sg	λελυμένου	λελυμένης	λελυμένου

Athematic Stems   (§94.2)

first perfect active participle

nom sg	ἑστηκώς	τεθεικώς[2]	δεδωκώς
gen sg	ἑστηκότος	τεθεικότος	δεδωκότος

second perfect active participle

nom sg	ἑστώς	ἑστῶσα	ἑστός
gen sg	ἑστότος	ἑστώσης	ἑστότος

perfect middle/passive participle

nom sg	ἑσταμένος	τεθειμένος	δεδομένος
gen sg	ἑσταμένου	τεθειμένου	δεδομένου

---

[1]   A dental (τ) drops out when immediately followed by σ (§22.3). οτ + σι › οσι.

[2]   In Classical Greek the form is τεθηκώς.

Aorist Passive Participle   (§95)

The aorist passive uses the tense formative θε. The aorist passive participle is formed on the aorist passive stem without the augment.

Thematic Stems   (§95.1)

first aorist passive participle

nom sg	λυθείς[1]	λυθεῖσα[2]	λυθέν[3]
gen sg	λυθέντος	λυθείσης	λυθέντος
dat sg	λυθέντι	λυθείσῃ	λυθέντι
acc sg	λυθέντα	λυθεῖσαν	λυθέν
nom pl	λυθέντες	λυθεῖσαι	λυθέντα
gen pl	λυθέντων	λυθεισῶν	λυθέντων
dat pl	λυθεῖσι(ν)[4]	λυθείσαις	λυθεῖσι(ν)
acc pl	λυθέντας	λυθείσας	λυθέντα

second aorist passive participle

nom sg	γραφείς	γραφεῖσα	γραφέν
gen sg	γραφέντος	γραφείσης	γραφέντος

first future passive participle

nom sg	λυθησόμενος	λυθησομένη	λυθησόμενον
gen sg	λυθησομένου	λυθησομένης	λυθησομένου

second future passive participle

nom sg	γραφησόμενος	γραφησομένη	γραφησόμενον
gen sg	γραφησομένου	γραφησομένης	γραφησομένου

---

[1]   λυθεεντ + σ › λυθεενσ › λυθεεσ › λυθείς. Whereas the present participle uses no ending in the nominative singular, these participles use a σ. ντ drop out when followed by σ, and the aorist passive shows compensatory lengthening as the ε lengthens to ει (§24.4c).

[2]   θεντια › θενσα › θεσα › θεισα. The feminine is formed by adding ι to the morpheme. τι form σ (§26.10), the ν drops off when followed by σ, and the preceding vowel may show its compensatory lengthening (§24.4).

[3]   No ending is used, and the τ drops off because it cannot stand at the end of a Greek word (§19.1).

[4]   λυθεντ + σι › λυθενσι › λυθεσι › λυθεῖσι. When the consonant cluster ντ is immediately followed by σ, it will drop out and the preceding vowel will be lengthened in compensation (§24.4c).

Athematic Stems (§95.2)

first aorist passive participle

nom sg	σταθείς	σταθεῖσα	σταθέν
gen sg	σταθέντος	σταθείσης	σταθέντος
nom sg	τεθείς	τεθεῖσα	τεθέν
gen sg	τεθέντος	τεθείσης	τεθέντος
nom sg	δοθείς	δοθεῖσα	δοθέν
gen sg	δοθέντος	δοθείσης	δοθέντος

Special Verbs (§96)

Following are partial paradigms of εἰμί, οἶδα, ἀφίημι, and γίνομαι.

εἰμί

	present	*imperfect*[1]	*future*
Indicative			
1 sg	εἰμί[2]	ἤμην	ἔσομαι[2]
2 sg	εἶ	ἦς, ἦσθα[3]	ἔσῃ
3 sg	ἐστί(ν)	ἦν	ἔσται
1 pl	ἐσμέν	ἦμεν, ἤμεθα	ἐσόμεθα
2 pl	ἐστέ	ἦτε	ἔσεσθε
3 pl	εἰσί(ν)	ἦσαν	ἔσονται

Non-indicative present active

	subjunctive	*imperative*	*infinitive*[4]	*optative*
1 sg	ὦ		εἶναι	εἴην
2 sg	ᾖς	ἴσθι		εἴης
3 sg	ᾖ	ἔστω		εἴη

---

[1] Switches between active and middle/passive endings.
[2] The root is *εσ.
[3] An old ending.
[4] Future middle infinitive is ἔσεσθαι.

1 pl	ὦμεν		εἶμεν	(εἴημεν)
2 pl	ἦτε	ἔστε	εἶτε	(εἴητε)
3 pl	ὦσι(ν)	ἔστωσαν	εἶεν	(εἴησαν)

Present participle

	masc	fem	neut		masc	fem	neut
nom sg	ὤν	οὖσα	ὄν	nom pl	ὄντες	οὖσαι	ὄντα
gen sg	ὄντος	οὔσης	ὄντος	gen pl	ὄντων	οὐσῶν	ὄντων
dat sg	ὄντι	οὔσῃ	ὄντι	dat pl	οὖσι(ν)	οὔσαις	οὖσι(ν)
acc sg	ὄντα	οὖσαν	ὄν	acc pl	ὄντας	οὔσας	ὄντα

οἶδα

	perfect		pluperfect

Indicative

1 sg	οἶδα[1]		ᾔδειν[2]
2 sg	οἶδας		ᾔδεις
3 sg	οἶδε(ν)		ᾔδει
1 pl	οἴδαμεν	(ἴσμεν)	ᾔδειμεν
2 pl	οἴδατε	(ἴστε)	ᾔδειτε
3 pl	οἴδασι(ν)	ἴσασι[3]	ᾔδεισαν

Non-indicative perfect

	subjunctive	imperative	active infinitive
1 sg	εἰδῶ		εἰδέναι
2 sg	εἰδῇς	ἴσθι	
3 sg	εἰδῇ	ἴστω	
			active participle
1 pl	εἰδῶμεν		εἰδώς, εἰδυῖα, εἰδός
2 pl	εἰδῆτε	ἴστε	
3 pl	εἰδῶσιν(ν)	ἴστωσαν	

---

[1] Cf. §45.5c.

[2] Cf. §45.6d.

[3] Classical forms (cf. Acts 26:4).

ἀφίημι

	pres. active	*pres. mid/pas*	*future act.*	*aorist act.*[1]	*perfect mid/pas*
Indicative					
1 sg	ἀφίημι	ἀφίεμαι	ἀφήσω	ἀφῆκα	
2 sg	ἀφιεῖς	ἀφίεσαι	ἀφήσεις	ἀφῆκας	
3 sg	ἀφίησι(ν)	ἀφίεται	ἀφήσει	ἀφῆκε(ν)	
1 pl	ἀφίομεν	ἀφιέμεθα	ἀφήσομεν	ἀφήκαμεν	
2 pl	ἀφίετε	ἀφίεσθε	ἀφήσετε	ἀφήκατε	
3 pl	ἀφίουσι(ν)	ἀφίενται	ἀφήσουσι(ν)	ἀφῆκαν	ἀφέωνται

Non-indicative

	present act. subj.[2]	*aorist active subj.*	*aorist passive subj.*
1 sg	ἀφιῶ	ἀφῶ	ἀφεθῶ
2 sg	ἀφιῇς	ἀφῇς	ἀφεθῇς
3 sg	ἀφιῇ	ἀφῇ	ἀφεθῇ
1 pl	ἀφιῶμεν	ἀφῶμεν	ἀφεθῶμεν
2 pl	ἀφιῆτε	ἀφῆτε	ἀφεθῆτε
3 pl	ἀφιῶσι(ν)	ἀφῶσι(ν)	ἀφεθῶσι(ν)

	pres. act. imperative	*aorist act. imperative*	*present active infinitive*
			ἀφιέναι
2 sg	ἀφίει	ἀφές	*aorist active infinitive*
3 sg	ἀφιέτω	ἀφέτω	ἀφεῖναι
2 pl	ἀφίετε	ἄφετε	*aorist participle*
3 pl	ἀφιέντων	ἀφέτωσαν	ἀφείς, ἀφεῖσα, ἀφέν

Aorist of γινώσκω

	indicative	*subjunctive*	*imperative*[3]	*infinitive*	*participle*
1 sg	ἔγνων	γνῶ		γνῶναι	γνούς, γνοῦσα, γνόν
2 sg	ἔγνως	γνῷς	γνῶθι		
3 sg	ἔγνω	γνῷ / γνοῖ	γνώτω		
1 pl	ἔγνωμεν	γνῶμεν			
2 pl	ἔγνωτε	γνῶτε	γνῶτε		
3 pl	ἔγνωσαν	γνῶσιν	γνόντων / γνώτωσαν		

---

[1] The one aorist passive indicative in the N.T. is ἀφέθησαν.

[2] Does not occur in the N.T.

[3] Third singular, aorist passive imperative, γνωσθήτω.

Introduction to Nouns

As is the case with verbs, much of what we learned in our beginning Greek classes about nouns was a necessary simplification. It is much easier to teach that the genitive singular masculine ending is ου added onto a stem ending in a consonant than it is to teach that the stem really ends in ο, the ending is ο, and the omicrons contract to ου. Easier at first, but not accurate, and not helpful in the long run. It is therefore necessary to relearn some basics about noun formation.

Nouns of the first and second declension are stems that end in a vowel. First declension nouns end in α; second declension nouns end in ο. This is why they are called the "vowel" declensions. Third declension nouns are stems that end in a consonant; thus, the "consonant" declension. Vowel stems have one set of endings and consonant stems another, although there is much similarity. One of the major benefits of learning case endings properly is that the similarities are much easier to see (along with the satisfaction of knowing that these really are the proper endings).

We use the term "root" to refer to the theoretical base of a word group. The term "stem" will be used for the root's basic form in a particular instance. For example, the root "δικ" has many forms: δίκαιος, δικαιόω, δικαιοσύνη, etc. (Metzger provides a very nice listing of basic Greek roots and their different forms: *Lexical Aids for Students of New Testament Greek*, pp.49-72.) The stem of δίκαιος is *δικαιο.

When the nominative and vocative are the same form (as it is always is in the plural), we will use the label "*n/v*." Otherwise the vocative will be on a separate line.

In the listings of words in each category, the alphabetizing runs horizontally, not vertically.

Outline

Case Endings

A dash means that no case ending is used. The underline means that the case ending has joined with the final stem vowel (cf. rule 5). The case endings for the masc/fem in the third declension are repeated for the sake of clarity, even though in several cases they are the same as in the first and second declensions.

Notice that the third declension case endings are not substantially different from those used for the first and second declensions. Because third declension stems end in a consonant, there are more changes than in the first and second declension words.

	first/second declension			third declension	
	masc	*fem*	*neut*	*masc/fem*	*neut*
nom sg	ς	-	ν	ς [1]	[2]
gen sg	υ[3]	ς	υ	oς[4]	oς
dat sg	ι[5]	ι	ι	ι[6]	ι
acc sg	ν	ν	ν	α[7]/ν[8]	-
voc sg	α η	α	α	stem[9]	-
n/v pl	ι	ι	α	ες	α[10]
gen pl	ων	ων[11]	ων	ων	ων
dat pl	ις[12]	ις	ις	σι(ν)[13]	σι(ν)
acc pl	νς[14]	ς	α	ας[15] ες[16]	α

[1] Noun stems in ν, ρ, σ, and οντ use no ending in the nominative singular, with the preceding vowel frequently lengthening (ε ‣ η, ο ‣ ω; Smyth §242, Funk §1540.1).

[2] Be prepared for the final stem letter to undergo changes (rule 8, Smyth §244).

[3] The ending is o (LaSor §21.312), which contracts with the final stem vowel and forms oυ (rule 5). It is listed in *BBG* as υ as a simplification. Smyth lists it as ιo.

[4] In certain situations, oς can lengthen to ως (Smyth §214D).

[5] The vowel lengthens (rule 5) and the iota subscripts (rule 4).

[6] Because third declension stems end in a consonant, the iota cannot subscript as it does in the first and second declensions. It remains on the line ("iota adscript").

[7] α is actually the ν ending. When preceded by a consonant, ν can become sonant (§7.7) and become α (Funk §1540.2).

[8] As a general rule, stems ending in a consonant use α. Stems ending in ι or ϝ use ν (Smyth §246). Smyth adds, "Barytone stems of two syllables ending in ιτ, ιδ, ιθ usually drop the dental and add ν" (§247).

[9] Third declension masculine and feminine nouns usually use the bare noun stem for the vocative, often with some vowel change. See Smyth §249 for more.

[10] As opposed to the first and second declensions, this α is an actual case ending and not a changed stem vowel. α replaces the stem vowel. This is also true in the acc. plural.

[11] The ων ending in first declension feminine nouns is always the result of contraction, e.g., εων, αων (LaSor §21.21).

[12] The case ending actually is ισι in the first declension (Smyth §212) and ις or ιοι in the second (Smyth §229).

[13] The ν is a movable ν. Notice that the ending σι is a flipped version of ις, found in the first and second declensions. LaSor lists the morpheme as ισι (§21.216).

[14] The actual case ending for the first and second declension is νς, but the ν drops out because of the following σ. In the first declension the α joins with the σ (ωρα + νς ‣ ὥρας), but in the second declension the final stem o lengthens to oυ (rule 5; λογονς ‣ λογος ‣ λόγους).

Another way to look at is that the ν becomes sonant (§5.1) and develops into α. It is listed in *BBG* as νς as a simplification.

[15] As opposed to the first declension (e.g. ὥρα), the α here is part of the case ending.

[16] ες can be borrowed from the nom. pl. for the acc. pl. (e.g., βασιλεῖς). Smyth §251b.

The Basic Rules Governing Case Endings

1. *Stems ending in α or η are in the first declension, stems in o are in the second, and consonantal stems are in the third.*

2. *All neuter words are the same form in the nominative and accusative* (Smyth §204).

3. *Almost all neuter words, in the nominative and accusative plural, end in α.*

   - In the second declension the α is the changed stem vowel; in the third it is the case ending.

4. *In the dative singular, the ι subscripts if possible.*

   - Because an ι can subscript only under a vowel (in which case the vowel lengthens), it subscripts only in the first and second declensions.

5. *Vowels often change their length ("ablaut").*

   - "Contraction" occurs when two vowels meet and form a different vowel or diphthong.

     λογο + ις › λόγοις

     λογο + ο › λόγου

     γραφη + ων › γραφῶν

   - "Compensatory lengthening" occurs when a vowel is lengthened to compensate for the loss of another letter.

     λογο + νς › λόγος › λογους

6. *In the genitive and dative, the masculine and neuter will always be identical.*

7. *The Square of Stops*

Labials	π	β	φ
Velars	κ	γ	χ
Dentals	τ	δ	θ

   - Labials + σ form ψ; velars plus σ form ξ; dentals plus σ form σ.
   - The ντ combination drops out when followed by σ (παντ + ς › πᾶς).
   - Whatever happens in the nominative singular third declension also happens in the dative plural. σαρκ + σ › σαρξ. σαρκ + σι › σάρξι.

8. *A τ cannot stand at the end of a word and will drop off.*[1]

   - No case ending is used in stems ending in ματ. The τ then drops out.

     ὀνοματ + - › ὀνοματ › ὄνομα.

---

[1] Only ν, ρ, σ (including ξ, ψ) can stand at the end of a word (Funk §155.2).

Vocative

Summary

- In the plural, the vocative is always identical to the nominative plural (ἄνθρωποι).
- In the feminine singular first declension, the vocative is the same as the nominative (ἀδελφή).
- In the singular second declension, the vocative ending is usually ε (ἄνθρωπε).
- In the singular third declension, the vocative is usually the bare stem of the word, sometimes with the stem vowel being changed (πάτερ).

Neuter nouns

The vocative and the nominative/accusative are always identical, in both the singular and in the plural. It is always α in Classical Greek (Smyth §202).

Masculine/Feminine (first/second declension)

In the plural, the vocative and the nominative are always identical. In the singular, the vocative and the nominative are identical except in the following instances.

• Masculine nouns in α(ς), ου	n-1d	-	νεανία
• Masculine nouns in α(ς), ας	n-1e	-	σατανᾶ
• Masculine nouns in η(ς), ου	n-1f		
Stem is τη(ς)[1]		α	προφῆτα
Other n-1f stems		η	-
• Masculine nouns in η(ς), η	n-1g	-	Μανασσῆ
• Masculine nouns in ο(ς), ου	n-2a	ε (usually)	λόγε
• Feminine nouns in ο(ς), ου	n-2b	ε (usually)	ὁδέ

Third declension nouns

The vocative is the bare stem of the word for masculine and feminine (e.g., πάτερ). If the final consonant cannot stand at the end of a Greek word, it will drop off (§19). Words are also open to ablaut (§4; cf. LaSor §21.415).

---

[1]   Cf. Smyth §226.

First Declension Nouns

All stems in the first declension end in either α or η. Most are feminine, a few masculine, and none are neuter. The plurals of all forms are identical. For accent rules see especially §28.12e-f.

n-1a

Definition: Feminine nouns with stems ending in εα, ια, or ρα and a genitive in ας

n/v sg	-	ὥρα		*n/v pl*	ι	ὧραι
gen sg	ς	ὥρας		*gen pl*	ων	ὡρῶν
dat sg	ι[1]	ὥρᾳ		*dat pl*	ις	ὥραις
acc sg	ν	ὥραν		*acc pl*	νς[2]	ὥρας

Comments

The α is consistent throughout the singular. If any letter other than ρ precedes the final α, the genitive and dative singular would have had an η (n-1c).

There are five exceptions in this class; they all end in ρα but follow the n-1c declension pattern: μάχαιρα, πλήμμυρα, πρῷρα, σάπφιρα, σπεῖρα. These are listed at n-1c.

The following words are also classified as n-1a nouns but do not end in εα, ια, or ρα: Ἅννα, Εὕα, Ἱεροσόλυμα, Ἰωάνα, Ἰωάννα, Μάρθα, Νύμφα, Ῥεβέκκα, στοά.

Listing   (total: 402)

ἀγαθοποιΐα	ἀγγελία	ἄγκυρα	ἀγνεία	ἄγνοια
ἀγνωσία	ἀγορά	ἄγρα	ἀγρυπνία	ἀγωνία
ἀδιαφθορία	ἀδικία	ἀηδία	ἀθανασία	αἱματεκχυσία
αἰσχρολογία	αἰτία	αἰχμαλωσία	ἀκαθαρσία	ἀκαταστασία
ἀκρασία	ἀκρίβεια	ἀκροβυστία	ἀλαζονεία	ἀλεκτοροφωνία
ἀλήθεια	ἁμαρτία	ἀναίδεια	ἀναλογία	ἀνεγκλησία
ἀνθρακιά	Ἅννα[3]	ἄνοια	ἀνομία	ἀντιλογία
ἀντιμισθία	Ἀντιόχεια	ἀπείθεια	ἀπιστία	ἀποκαραδοκία
Ἀπολλωνία	ἀπολογία	ἀπορία	ἀποστασία	ἀποτομία
ἀπουσία	Ἀπφία	ἀπώλεια	ἀρά	Ἀραβία

---

[1]   The final stem vowel lengthens and the iota subscripts.

[2]   ν drops out when immediately followed by σ (§24.4).

[3]   A transliterated name and yet declinable (Lk 2:36; cf. *BDF* §53.3).

ἀρεσκεία	Ἀριμαθαία	ἀσέβεια	ἀσέλγεια	ἀσθένεια
Ἀσία	ἀσιτία	ἀσφάλεια	ἀσωτία	ἀτιμία
Ἀττάλεια	αὐτάρκεια	ἀφειδία	ἀφθαρσία	ἀφθονία
ἀφθορία	Ἀχαΐα	βασιλεία	Βέροια	Βηθαβαρά[1]
Βηθανία	βία	Βιθυνία	βλασφημία	βοήθεια
Γαλατία	Γαλιλαία	Γαλλία[2]	γενεά	γενεαλογία
γερουσία	Γόμορρα[3]	γυμνασία	γωνία	Δαλματία
δειλία	δεισιδαιμονία	διακονία	διάνοια	διασπορά
διαφθορά	διγαμία	διδασκαλία	διερμηνεία	διετία
δικαιοκρισία	διχοστασία	δοκιμασία	δουλεία	δυσεντερία[4]
δυσφημία	δωρεά	δωροφορία	ἐγκράτεια	ἐθελοθρησκία
εἰδέα	εἰδωλολατρία	εἰλικρίνεια	ἐκκλησία	ἐκτένεια
ἐλαία	ἐλαφρία	ἐλευθερία	ἐμπορία	ἐνέδρα
ἐνέργεια	ἔννοια	ἐξουσία	ἐπαγγελία	ἐπαρχεία
ἐπιείκεια	ἐπιθυμία	ἐπικουρία	ἐπιμέλεια	ἐπίνοια
ἐπιποθία	ἐπιτιμία	ἐπιφάνεια	ἐπιχορηγία	ἐργασία
ἐρημία	ἐριθεία	ἑρμηνεία	ἑσπέρα	ἑτοιμασία
Εὕα[5]	εὐγλωττία	εὐγλωττία	εὐδία	εὐδοκία
εὐεργεσία	εὐκαιρία	εὐλάβεια	εὐλογία	εὔνοια
Εὐοδία	εὐοχία	εὐποιΐα	εὐπορία	εὐπρέπεια
εὐσέβεια	εὐτραπελία	εὐφημία	εὐχαριστία	εὐωδία
εὐωχία	ἐφημερία	ἔχθρα	ζευκτηρία	ζημία
ἡγεμονία	ἡλικία	ἡμέρα	ἡσυχία	θεά
θεοσέβεια	θεραπεία	Θεσσαλία	θεωρία	θήρα
θρησκεία	θύρα	θυσία	ἰδέα	Ἰδουμαία
ἱερατεία	Ἱεροσόλυμα[6]	ἱκετηρία	Ἰουδαία	Ἰουλία

---

[1] Alternate form of Βηθανία.

[2] Alternate form of Γαλατία.

[3] The word occurs four times in the N.T., twice as Γόμορρα (nominative singular feminine) and once as Γομόρρας (genitive singular feminine). It also occurs once (Mt 10:15) as Γομόρρων, which is a genitive plural neuter from an alternate form Γόμορρα, ων, τά (n-2c, cf. BDF §57). If this form would have been feminine, the ultima would have had a circumflex (ῶν). The accent given shows the editors preference for the neuter form. A v.l. in Mk 6:11 has Γομόρροις, showing a second declension stem.

[4] Hellenistic form of δυσεντέριον (n-2c; Acts 28:8).

[5] A transliterated name "Eve" (Εὕα, 1 Tim 2:13; Εὕαν, 2 Cor 11:3).

[6] There are three forms of this word. Ἱεροσόλυμα, τά is n-2c used as a neuter plural. Ἱεροσόλυμα, ἡ is a first declension feminine (n-1a) found at Mt 2:3. Ἱερουσαλήμ, ἡ is an indeclinable form (n-3g[2], note the change of breathing) used at Acts 15:4 (v.l. 20:16). Cf. BAGD §56.1. The forms that appear in our text are Ἱεροσολύμοις, Ἱεροσολύμων, Ἱεροσόλυμα.

Ἰταλία	Ἰωάνα[1]	Ἰωάννα[2]	καθέδρα	Καισάρεια
κακία	κακόθεια	κακοπάθεια	κακοπαθία[3]	καλοκαγαθία
Καππαδοκία	καραδοκία	καρδία	καταλαλιά	κατάρα
κατηγορία	κατήφεια	κατοικία	Κεγχρεαί	κειρία
κενοδοξία	κενοφωνία[4]	κεραία	κιθάρα	Κιλικία
Κλαυδία	κληρονομία	κλισία	κοιλία	κοινωνία
κολακεία	κολυμβήθρα	κολωνία	κοπρία	κουστωδία
κυβεία[5]	κυρία	λαλιά	Λαοδίκεια	Λασαία[6]
Λασέα	λατρεία	λειτουργία	Λέκτρα	λέπρα
λίτρα	λογεία	λογομαχία	λοιδορία	Λυδία
Λυκαονία	Λυκία	Λύστρα[7]	λυχνία	μαγεία
μαθήτρια	Μακεδονία	μακροθυμία	μαλακία	μανία
Μάρθα	Μαρία	μαρτυρία	ματαιολογία	μεθοδεία
μεσημβρία	Μεσοποταμία	μετάνοια	μετοικεσία	μήτρα
μισθαποδοσία	μνεία	μοιχεία	Μυσία	μωρία
μωρολογία	νεομηνία	νηστεία	νομοθεσία	νοσσιά
νουθεσία	νουμηνία[8]	Νύμφα[9]	ξενία	ὁδοιπορία
οἰκετεία	οἰκία	οἰκοδομία	οἰκονομία	οἰνοφλυγία
ὀλιγοπιστία	ὁλοκληρία	ὁμιλία	ὁμολογία	ὀπτασία
ὀπώρα	ὀργυιά	ὁρκωμοσία	ὁροθεσία	οὐρά
οὐσία	ὀφθαλμοδουλία	ὀψία[10]	παιδεία	παλιγγενεσία
Παμφυλία	πανοπλία	πανουργία	παραγγελία	παραμυθία
παρανομία	παραφρονία	παραχειμασία	παρηγορία	παρθενία
παροικία	παροιμία	παρουσία	παρρησία	πατριά
πεῖρα	πενθερά	Πέραια	περικεφαλαία	περισσεία

---

1   Alternate form of Ἰωάννα at Lk 3:27.

2   This form of the word with double ν occurs at Lk 8:3 and Lk 24:10. *BAGD* lists as Ἰωάν(ν)α. Cf. *BDF* §40, 55.1c, *MH* 102.

3   Alternate form of κακοπάθεια.

4   Has an alternate form καινοφωνία in 1 Tim 6:20 and 2 Tim 2:16.

5   Has an alternate form κυβία.

6   Has an alternate form Λασέα occurring only as v.l. at Acts 27:8.

7   Has an accusative Λύστραν (Acts 14:6,21; 16:1; cf. 27:5), but the dative is second declension plural: Λύστροις (Acts 14:8; 16:2; 2 Tim 3:11). We have listed it under both categories. Cf. *BDF* §57; *MH* 1:48, 2:147, and discussion at n-2c.

8   Contracted form of νεομηνία.

9   Has a variant Νυμφᾶς. A woman's name occurring in the N.T. only at Col 4:15 in the accusative Νύμφαν, either from the feminine Νύμφα (Attic Νύμφη, ης), or from the masculine Νυμφᾶς, ᾶς (n-1e). *BAGD* suggests it is a shortened form of Νυμφόδωρος. See the discussion there (listed as Νύμφαν) and *BDF* §125.

10   Really an adjective ὄψιος (a-1a[1]).

περιστερά	πέτρα	πήρα	πιθανολογία	πικρία
Πισιδία	πλατεῖα	πλεονεξία	πλευρά	πληροφορία
ποία	πολιτεία	πολυλογία	πολυπλήθεια	πονηρία
πορεία	πορία[1]	πορνεία	πορφύρα	πραγματεία
πρασιά	πραϋπάθεια	πρεσβεία	προθεσμία	προθυμία
πρόνοια	προσδοκία	προσφορά	προσωπολημψία	προσωπολημψία[2]
προφητεία	πρωΐα	πρωτοκαθεδρία	πρωτοκλισία	πτωχεία
πυρά	ῥᾳδιουργία	Ῥεβέκκα	ῥομφαία	ῥυπαρία
Σαμάρεια	Σαμαρία[3]	Σάρρα	σειρά	Σελεύκεια
σκηνοπηγία	σκιά	σκληροκαρδία	σκοτία	σοφία
Σπανία	σπορά	στεῖρα	στενοχωρία	στοά
στρατεία	στρατιά	συγγένεια	συγκυρία	συκομορέα
συμποσία[4]	συμφωνία	συνήθεια	συνοδία	συνορία
συντέλεια	συντυχία	συνωμοσία	Σύρα	Συρία
σωτηρία	ταλαιπωρία	τεκνογονία	τιμωρία	τριετία
τροχιά	τρυμαλία	ὑδρία	υἱοθεσία	ὑπερηφανία
ὑπόνοια	φαντασία	φαρμακεία	φθορά	Φιλαδέλφεια[5]
φιλαδελφία[6]	φιλανθρωπία	φιλαργυρία	φιλία	φιλονεικία[7]
φιλοξενία	φιλοσοφία	Φρυγία	φυτεία	χαρά
χήρα	χρεία	χρηστολογία	χώρα	ψευδομαρτυρία
ὥρα	ὠφέλεια			

---

1   Alternate form of πορεία.
2   Alternate form of προσωπολημψία.
3   Alternate form of Σαμάρεια.
4   Alternate form of συμπόσιον (n-2c) occurring as a v.l. (D) at Mk 6:39.
5   "Philadelphia"
6   "Brotherly love"
7   BAGD lists as φιλον(ε)ικία. Occurs only at Lk 22:24 with the ε.

n-1b

Definition: Feminine nouns with stems ending in η and a genitive in ης

n/v sg	‾	γραφή		*n/v pl*	ι	γραφαί
gen sg	ς	γραφῆς		*gen pl*	ων	γραφῶν
dat sg	ι[1]	γραφῇ		*dat pl*	ις	γραφαῖς
acc sg	ν	γραφήν		*acc pl*	νς[2]	γραφάς

Comments

The η is consistent throughout the singular.

Listing   (total: 248)

Ἀβιληνή	ἀγαθωσύνη	ἀγάπη	ἀγέλη	ἁγιωσύνη
ἀγκάλη	ἀγωγή	ἀδελφή	αἰσχύνη	ἀκοήἀλόη
ἀμοιβή	ἀναβολή	ἀνάγκη	ἀναστροφή	ἀνατολή
ἀνοχή	ἀξίνη	ἀπαρχή	ἀπάτη	ἀπειλή
ἀποβολή	ἀπογραφή	ἀποδοχή	ἀποθήκη	ἀποστολή
ἀρετή	ἁρπαγή	ἀρχή	ἀστραπή	ἀσχημοσύνη
αὐγή	αὐλή	ἁφή	ἀφορμή	ἀφροσύνη
βελόνη	Βερνίκη	βοή	βολή	βοτάνη
βουλή	βροντή	βροχή	γαλήνη	γενετή
γνώμη	γραφή	δαπάνη	Δέρβη	δέσμη
διαθήκη	διαπαρατριβή	διαστολή	διαταγή	διατροφή
διδαχή	δικαιοσύνη	δίκη	δοκιμή	δούλη
δοχή	δραχμή	δυσμή	ἐγκοπή	εἰρήνη
ἐκβολή	ἐκδοχή	ἐκκοπή[3]	ἐκλογή	ἐλεημοσύνη
ἐμπαιγμονή	ἐμπλοκή	ἐντολή	ἐντροπή	ἐξοχή
ἑορτή	ἐπεισαγωγή	ἐπιβουλή	ἐπιγραφή	ἐπιλησμονή
ἐπισκοπή	ἐπιστήμη	ἐπιστολή	ἐπιστροφή	ἐπισυναγωγή
ἐπιταγή	ἐπιτροπή	Εὐνίκη	εὐσχημοσύνη	εὐφροσύνη
εὐχή	ζύμη	ζωή	ζώνη	ἡδονή
θέρμη[4]	Θεσσαλονίκη	θήκη	ἱερωσύνη	Ἰόππη
καλάμη	Κανδάκη	καταβολή	καταδίκη	καταλλαγή
καταστολή	καταστροφή	κατατομή	κεφαλή	Κλαύδη[5]

---

[1]   The final stem vowel lengthens and the iota subscripts.

[2]   ν drops out when immediately followed by σ (§24.4).

[3]   Alternate form of ἐγκοπή.

[4]   Alternate form of θέρμα, ης, ἡ (n-1c).

[5]   Alternate form of Καῦδα (n-3g[2]). See there for discussion.

κλίνη	κλοπή	κοίτη	Κολασσαί[1]	Κολοσσαί[2]
κόμη	κοπή	κραιπάλη[3]	κραυγή	Κρήτη
κριθή	κρύπτη	Κυρήνη	κώμη	λήθη
Λιβύη	λίμνη	λόγχη	λύπη	Μαγδαληνή
μάμμη	μάχη	μεγαλωσύνη	μέθη	Μελίτη[4]
μετοχή	μηλωτή	Μιτυλήνη	μνήμη	μομφή
μονή	μορφή	νεφέλη	νίκη	νομή
νύμφη	ὀδύνη	ὀθόνη	οἰκοδομή	οἰκουμένη
ὀμίχλη	ὀπή	ὀργή	ὀρμή	ὀσμή
ὀφειλή	παιδίσκη	πάλη	παραβολή	παραδιατριβή
παραθήκη	παρακαταθήκη	παρακοή	παραλλαγή	παρασκευή
παραφροσύνη	παρεμβολή	πέδη	πεισμονή	πεντηκοστή
Πέργη	περιοχή	περιτομή	πηγή	πλάνη
πληγή	πλησμονή	πλοκή	πνοή	ποίμνη
πόρνη	προκοπή	προσαγωγή	προσευχή	προσκοπή
πυγμή	πύλη	ῥέδη	ῥιπή	Ῥόδη
ῥοπή	ῥύμη	Ῥώμη	σαγήνη	Σαλμώνη
Σαλώμη	Σαμοθράκη	σαργάνη	σελήνη	σιγή
σκάφη	σκευή	σκηνή	σπουδή	σταφυλή
στέγη	στιγμή	στολή	συγγνώμη	συναγωγή
συνδρομή	συνοχή	Συντύχη	συστροφή	σφαγή
σχολή	σωφροσύνη	ταβέρναι[5]	ταπεινοφροσύνη	ταραχή
ταφή	τελευτή	τέχνη	τιμή	τροπή
τροφή	τρυφή	ὕλη	ὑπακοή	ὑπερβολή
ὑπεροχή	ὑπομονή	ὑποστολή	ὑποταγή	φάτνη
φήμη	φιάλη	φίλη[6]	Φοίβη	Φοινίκη
φυγή	φυλακή	φυλή	φωνή	χλόη
χολή	ψυχή	ὠδή		

---

[1] Alternate form of Κολοσσαί listed as a plural: Κολασσαί, ῶν, τά.

[2] Listed as plural: Κολοσσαί, ῶν, τά.

[3] Has an alternate form κρεπάλη.

[4] Has an alternate form Μελιτήνη.

[5] Is listed as a plural form, ταβέρναι, ῶν, αἱ. It is formed from the Latin meaning "tavern, shop." It occurs in the N.T. only at Acts 28:15 in the name "Three Taverns" (Τριῶν Ταβερνῶν), a place to which Christians came to visit Paul at the beginning of his Roman imprisonment.

[6] Formed from the adjective φίλος.

n-1c

Definition: Feminine nouns with stems ending in α (where the preceding letter is not ε, ι, or ρ) and a genitive in ης.

n/v sg	-	δόξα	n/v pl	ι	δόξαι
gen sg	ς	δόξης	gen pl	ων	δοξῶν
dat sg	ι[1]	δόξῃ	dat pl	ις	δόξαις
acc sg	ν	δόξαν	acc pl	νς[2]	δόξας

Comments

The final stem vowel changes to η in the genitive and dative singular. There are five words ending in ρα that normally would be n-1a nouns, but are declined like n-1c nouns: μάχαιρα, πλήμμυρα, πρῷρα, σάπφιρα, σπεῖρα.

Listing (total: 38)

Ἀθῆναι[3]	ἄκανθα	βασίλισσα	γάγγραινα	Γάζα[4]
γάζα[5]	γέεννα	γλῶσσα	δόξα	Δρούσιλλα
ἐπιοῦσα[6]	ἔχιδνα	θάλασσα	Θέκλα	θέρμα[7]
θύελλα	μάχαιρα	μεμβράνα	μέριμνα	πλήμμυρα
Πρίσκα	Πρίσκιλλα[8]	πρύμνα	πρῷρα	πτέρνα
ῥίζα	Σάπφιρα	Σμύρνα[9]	σμύρνα[10]	Σουσάννα[11]
σπεῖρα	Συράκουσαι	Συροφοινίκισσα	τράπεζα	Τρύφαινα
Τρυφῶσα	Φοινίκισσα[12]	χάλαζα		

---

1. The final stem vowel lengthens and the iota subscripts.
2. ν drops out when immediately followed by σ (§24.4).
3. Athens had several sections and therefore was referred to in the plural.
4. One of the Philistine cities; Acts 8:26.
5. "Treasury"; Acts 8:27.
6. Formed from the participle of ἔπειμι.
7. *BAGD* lists as θέρμα (n-1c) and θέρμη (n-1b). It occurs only in Acts 28:3 as θέρμης; the accent showing the editors' preference for θέρμα (otherwise it would have been θερμῆς).
8. Πρίσκιλλα (Acts 18:2, 18, 26) is the diminutive form of Πρίσκα (Rom 16:3, 19; 2 Tim 4:19).
9. "Smyrna"
10. "Myrrh"
11. Can have genitive in ας (n-1a) or ης (n-1c). It appears in the N.T. only in nominative (Lk 8:3).
12. A v.l. to Mk 7:26 has Σύρα Φοινίκισσα instead of Συροφοινίκισσα, "the Syrophoenician woman."

n-1d

Definition: Masculine nouns with stems ending in α(ς) and a genitive in ου.

nom sg	ς[1]	νεανίας	*n/v pl*	ι	νεανίαι
gen sg	ου[2]	νεανίου	*gen pl*	ων	νεανιῶν
dat sg	ι[3]	νεανίᾳ	*dat pl*	ις	νεανίαις
acc sg	ν	νεανίαν	*acc pl*	νς[4]	νεανίας
voc sg	–	νεανία			

Comments

All but four of the words in this category are proper names.

Listing   (total: 28)

Ἀδρίας	Αἰνέας	Ἀμασίας	Ἀνανίας	Ἀνδρέας
Βαραχίας	Ἑζεκίας	Ζαχαρίας	Ἡλίας	Ἡσαίας
Ἰερεμίας	Ἰεχονίας	Ἰωνάθας	Ἰωσίας	Λυσανίας
Λυσίας	Μαθθίας[5]	Ματθίας	Ματταθίας[6]	Μεσσίας
μητραλῴας	νεανίας	Ὀζίας	Οὐρίας	Ὀχοζίας
πατραλῴας[7]	πατρολῴας	Σιμαίας		

---

[1]   First declension masculine nouns use the alternate ς ending in the nominative singular.

[2]   First declension masculine nouns do not use the ς for the genitive singular as does the feminine in order to avoid confusion with the nominative singular. n-1d nouns borrow the second declension case ending ου. This applies to n-1f nouns (Smyth §225).

[3]   The final stem vowel lengthens and the iota subscripts.

[4]   ν drops out when immediately followed by σ (§24.4).

[5]   Alternate form of Ματθίας.

[6]   Has an indeclinable form Ματταθά (n-3g[2]).

[7]   Alternate form of πατρολῴας.

n-1e

Definition: Masculine nouns with stems ending in α(ς) and a genitive in α

nom sg	ς[1]	σατανᾶς
gen sg	-[2]	σατανᾶ
dat sg	ι[3]	σατανᾷ
acc sg	ν	σατανᾶν
voc sg	-	σατανᾶ

Comments

None of the words in this category appear in the plural in the New Testament. They are mostly proper nouns.

Listing (total: 35)

Ἀγρίππας	Ἄννας	Ἀντιπᾶς	Ἀρέτας	Ἀρτεμᾶς
Βαραββᾶς	Βαριωνᾶς[4]	Βαρναβᾶς	βαρσα(β)βᾶς[5]	βορρᾶς[6]
Δημᾶς	Ἐλύμας	Ἐπαφρᾶς	Ἑρμᾶς	Θευδᾶς
Θωμᾶς	Ἰούδας	Ἰουνιᾶς	Ἰωνᾶς	Καϊάφας
Κηφᾶς	Κλεοπᾶς	Κλωπᾶς	κορβανᾶς	Λουκᾶς
μαμωνᾶς	Νυμφᾶς[7]	Ὀλυμπᾶς	Παρμενᾶς	Πατροβᾶς
Σατανᾶς[8]	Σίλας[9]	Σκευᾶς	Στεφανᾶς[10]	χουζᾶς

---

[1] First declension masculine nouns use the alternate ς ending in the nominative singular.

[2] First declension masculine nouns do not use the ς for the genitive singular as does the feminine in order to avoid confusion with the nominative singular. n-1e nouns do not use any case ending.

[3] The final stem vowel lengthens and the iota subscripts.

[4] Also has an indeclinable form Βαριωνᾶ; cf. Mt 16:17 and the v.l. in Jn 1:42.

[5] The text as a geminate β in Acts 1:23 and a single β in Acts 15:22. In both passages there are variants to the opposite.

[6] βορρᾶς is actually a contract noun (n-1h; Smyth §227) with the stem *βορρεα. It appears in the N.T. only twice (Lk 13:29; Rev 21:13), both times in the genitive βορρᾶ, whereas the genitive of a contract noun is βορροῦ. It is therefore listed as an n-1e and n-1h.

[7] Alternate form of Νύμφα (n-1a). See there for a discussion.

[8] Has an indeclinable form Σατάν; cf. n-3g(2).

[9] BAGD says it can be accented Σιλᾶς (cf. BDF §53.2).

[10] BAGD suggests Στεφανᾶς may be a short form of Στεφανηφόρος or an alternate form of Στέφανος. Cf. BDF §125.1.

n-1f

Definition:　　Masculine nouns with stems ending in η(ς) and a genitive in ου

nom	ς[1]	προφήτης		*n/v*	ι	προφῆται
gen	ου[2]	προφήτου		*gen*	ων	προφητῶν
dat	ι[3]	προφήτῃ		*dat*	ις	προφήταις
acc	ν	προφήτην		*acc*	νς[4]	προφήτας
voc	α η[5]	προφῆτα				

Listing　(total: 139)

ᾅδης	ἀδικοκρίτης	ἀκροατής	ἀνδραποδιστής	ἀποστάτης
Ἀρεοπαγίτης	ἀρσενοκοίτης	ἀρχιληστής	ἀρχιτελώνης	Ἀσιάρχης
αὐλητής	αὐτόπτης	βαπτιστής	βασανιστής	βιαστής
βουλευτής	Γαλάτης	γνώστης	γογγυστής	δανειστής[6]
δανιστής	δεσμώτης	δεσπότης	διερμηνευτής	δικαστής
διώκτης	δότης	δυνάστης	ἐθνάρχης	εἰδωλολάτρης
ἑκατοντάρχης	Ἐλαμίτης	Ἑλληνιστής	ἐμπαίκτης	ἐξορκιστής
ἐπενδύτης	ἐπιθυμητής	ἐπιστάτης	ἐπόπτης	ἐργάτης
ἑρμηνευτής	εὐαγγελιστής	εὐεργέτης	Εὐφράτης	ἐφευρετής
ζηλωτής	Ἡρῴδης	θεριστής	Ἰαμβρῆς[7]	Ἰάννης
ἰδιώτης	Ἱεροσολυμίτης	Ἰορδάνης	Ἰσκαριώτης	Ἰσραηλίτης
Ἰωάννης[8]	καθηγητής	Κανανίτης	καρδιογνώστης	καταφρονητής
κερματιστής	κλέπτης	κοδράντης[9]	κολλυβιστής	κριτής
κτίστης	κυβερνήτης	Λευίτης	ληστής	λυτρωτής
μαθητής	μαργαρίτης	μεριστής	μεσίτης	μετρητής
μιμητής	μισθαποδότης	ναύτης	Νικολαΐτης	Νινευίτης
νομοθέτης	ξέστης	οἰκέτης	οἰκοδεσπότης	οἰνοπότης

---

[1]　First declension masculine nouns use the alternate ς ending in the nominative singular.

[2]　First declension masculine nouns do not use ς for the genitive singular as do the feminine in order to avoid confusion with the nominative singular. They borrow the second declension case ending ου (cf. n-1d).

[3]　The final stem vowel lengthens and the iota subscripts.

[4]　ν drops out when immediately followed by σ (§24.4).

[5]　If the stem of the word ends in τη, the vocative is α. If the n-1f noun ends in anything else, the vocative is η.

[6]　Alternate form of δανιστής.

[7]　Has a variant μαμβρῆς; cf. 2 Tim 3:8.

[8]　On the spelling cf. *BDF* §40; 55.1c; *MH* 102.

[9]　Cf. *BDF* §41.2.

ὀλεθρευτής[1]	ὀλοθρευτής	ὀφειλέτης	παιδευτής	παραβάτης
πατριάρχης	πλανήτης	πλεονέκτης	πλήκτης	ποιητής
πολιτάρχης	πολίτης	πρεσβύτης[2]	προδότης	προσαίτης
προσκυνητής	προσωπολήμπτης	προσωπολήπτης[3]	προφήτης	πρωτοστάτης
σαλπιστής	Σαμαρίτης	Σκύθης	στασιαστής	στρατιώτης
στρατοπεδάρχης[4]	συζητητής	συμμαθητής	συμμιμητής	συμπολίτης
συμφυλέτης	συνηλικιώτης	συντεχνίτης	συστασιαστής	τελειωτής
τελώνης	τετράρχης[5]	τετραάρχης[6]	τεχνίτης	τιμιότης
τολμητής	τραπεζίτης	ὑβριστής	ὑπηρέτης	ὑποκριτής
φαιλόνης	φελόνης[7]	φρεναπάτης	χάρτης	χρεοφειλέτης[8]
χρεωφειλέτης[9]	ψευδοπροφήτης	ψεύστης	ψιθυριστής	

n-1g

Definition: Masculine nouns with stems ending in η(ς) and a genitive in η

nom sg	ς[10]	Μανασσῆς
gen sg	-[11]	Μανασσῆ
dat sg	ι[12]	Μανασσῆ
acc sg	-	Μανασσῆ
voc sg	-	Μανασσῆ

Listing (total: 2)

Μανασσῆς[13]   Ἰωσῆς[14]

---

[1] Alternate form of ὀλοθρευτής.

[2] πρεσβευτής is conjectured in Phlm 9; cf. *BAGD*.

[3] Alternate form of προσωπολήμπτης (Acts 10:34).

[4] V.l. at Acts 28:16 as a dative singular. Could also be στρατοπέδαρχος, ου, ὁ (n-2a).

[5] Has an alternate form τετραάρχης. The word occurs four times in the N.T. In *UBS* it is always with αα (Mt 14:1; Lk 3:19; 9:7; Acts 13:1). *BAGD* lists the word with one α.

[6] Alternate form of τετράρχης.

[7] Alternate form of φαιλόνης.

[8] Has alternate forms: χρεωφειλέτης, χρεοφιλέτης.

[9] Alternate form of χρεοφειλέτης.

[10] First declension masculine nouns use the alternate ς ending in the nominative singular.

[11] First declension masculine nouns do not use ς for the genitive singular as do the feminines in order to avoid confusion with the nominative singular. n-1g nouns do not use any case ending.

[12] The iota subscripts.

[13] *BAGD* says its accusative is Μανασσῆ (which does not occur in the N.T.). It also has an indeclinable form Μανασσῆ (n-3g[2]).

[14] Ἰωσῆς (n-1g) does have a n-3c[2] form (cf. *BAGD*). The n-1g form does not occur in the N.T.

n-1h

Definition: First declension contract nouns

		*μναα	*συκεα	*Ἑρμεα
nom sg	- ς[1]	μνᾶ, ἡ	συκῆ, ἡ	Ἑρμῆς, ὁ
gen sg	ς ου	μνᾶς	συκῆς	Ἑρμοῦ[2]
dat sg	ι[3]	μνᾷ	συκῇ	Ἑρμῇ
acc sg	ν	μνᾶν	συκῆν	Ἑρμῆν
voc sg	-	μνᾶ	συκῆ	Ἑρμῆ
n/v pl	ι	μναῖ	συκαί	Ἑρμαῖ
gen pl	ων	μνῶν	συκῶν	Ἑρμῶν
dat pl	ις	μναῖς	συκαῖς	Ἑρμαῖς
acc pl	νς[4]	μνᾶς	συκᾶς	Ἑρμᾶς

Comments

Contract nouns in α or η are from stems in εα or αα and therefore undergo contraction. On contracts of the first and second declension, see Smyth §227, *BDF* §45, *MH* 119-120, and LaSor §21.224. Except for the accents, μνᾶ is declined like n-1a, συκῆ like n-1b, and Ἑρμῆς like n-1f. On the irregular accents see Smyth §56.

Listing   (total: 6)

Ἀπελλῆς, οῦ, ὁ   βορρᾶς, ᾶ, ὁ[5]   γῆ, γῆς, ἡ[6]   Ἑρμῆς, οῦ, ὁ   μνᾶ, ᾶς, ἡ
συκῆ, ῆς, ἡ

Non-Biblical examples like γῆ are γαλῆ (‹*γαλεα   or *γαλεη) and ἀδελφιδῆ (‹*αδελφιδεα   or *αδελφιδεη).

---

1   The feminine uses no ending; the masculine uses the alternate ς.

2   The masculine borrows the second declension ending in order to avoid confusion with the nominative singular.

3   The final stem vowel lengthens and the iota subscripts.

4   ν drops out when immediately followed by σ (§24.4).

5   βορρᾶς, -ᾶ, ὁ is also a contract noun that was declined in the classical period according to the n-1d pattern: βορρᾶς, βορροῦ, βορρᾷ, βορρᾶν. In the N.T. it occurs only in the genitive as βορρᾶ (Lk 13:29; Rev 21:13), which is the n-1e declension pattern. We have therefore also listed it as a n-1e and a n-1h noun.

6   *γεα or *γαα.

Second Declension Nouns

All stems in the second declension end in o (except the two stems in n-2e that end in εω). Most are masculine; neuter and feminine are also present.

n-2a

Definition: Masculine nouns with stems ending in o(ς)

nom sg	ς	λόγος		*n/v pl*	ι	λόγοι
gen sg	o	λόγου		*gen pl*	ων	λόγων
dat sg	ι[1]	λόγῳ		*dat pl*	ις	λόγοις
acc sg	ν	λόγον		*acc pl*	νς[2]	λόγους
voc sg	ε[3]	λόγε				

Comments

Words followed with an asterisk can be either masculine (n-2a) or feminine (n-2b). They are listed in both categories. On "common gender" see Smyth §198.

Listing   (total: 470)

Ἄγαβος	ἄγαμος*	ἄγγελος	ἁγιασμός	ἁγνισμός
ἀγρός	ἀδελφός	ἀετός	αἰγιαλός	αἶνος
αἰχμάλωτος	ἀλάβαστρος*[4]	Ἀλέξανδρος	ἀλλοτριεπίσκοπος	Ἀλφαῖος
ἀμνός	ἀμπελουργός	Ἀμπλιᾶτος	ἀναβαθμός	Ἀνδρόνικος
ἀνδροφόνος	ἄνεμος	ἀνεψιός	ἀνθρωποκτόνος	ἄνθρωπος
ἀνθύπατος	ἀντίδικος	ἀντίχριστος	ἀπαρτισμός	ἀπελεγμός
ἀπελεύθερος	ἀπόστολος	Ἄππιος[5]	Ἄραβοι[6]	ἀργυροκόπος
ἄργυρος	ἀριθμός	Ἀρίσταρχος	Ἀριστόβουλος	ἄρκος*[7]
ἄρκτος*	ἁρμός	ἁρπαγμός	ἄρτος	ἀρχάγγελος

---

[1]   The final stem vowel lengthens and the ι subscripts.

[2]   ν drops out when immediately followed by σ, and the final o of the stem is lengthened to ου to compensate for the loss (§24.4).

[3]   ε is the normal case ending for the vocative of n-2a nouns.

[4]   Has a neuter form: ἀλάβαστρον, ου, τό (n-2c).

[5]   Occurs only in the name Ἀππίου φόρον, "Forum of Appius." It was a market station established by Appius Claudius Caecus in 312 B.C. It has been transliterated and apparently given a second declension genitive ending.

[6]   V.l. for Ἄραβες in Acts 2:11. *BAGD* say it may be mistakenly formed from the genitive plural Ἀράβων.

[7]   ἄρκος can be feminine (n-2b). Occurs in the N.T. only at Rev 13:2, where its gender is not clear. It is listed in both categories.

Ἀρχέλαος	ἀρχηγός	Ἄρχιππος	ἀρχισυνάγωγος	ἀρχιτρίκλινος
Ἀσιανός	ἀσκός	ἀσπασμός	Ἀσύγκριτος	Αὐγοῦστος
αὐλός	ἀφανισμός	ἀφρός	Ἀχαϊκός	βαθμός
βαπτισμός	Βαρθολομαῖος	Βαρτιμαῖος	βασανισμός	βασιλίσκος
βάτος[1]	βάτος*[2]	βάτραχος	βήρυλλος*	βίος
Βλάστος	βόθρος	βόθυνος	βόρβορος	βουνός
βρόχος	βρυγμός	βυθός	βωμός	Γάϊος
γάμος	γεωργός	γνόφος	γογγυσμός	γόμος
δακτύλιος	δάκτυλος	δεξιολάβος	δέσμιος	δεσμός
Δημήτριος	δημιουργός	δῆμος	διάδοχος	διάκονος*
διαλογισμός	διαμερισμός	διδάσκαλος	Δίδυμος	Διονύσιος
Διόσκουροι[3]	διωγμός	δόλος	δοῦλος	δρόμος
Ἑβραῖος	ἑκατόνταρχος[4]	ἐλεγμός	ἔλεγχος	Ἐλισαῖος
Ἐλισσαῖος[5]	ἐμπαιγμός	ἔμπορος	ἐνιαυτός	ἐνταφιασμός
Ἐπαίνετος	ἔπαινος	Ἐπαφρόδιτος	Ἐπικούρειος	ἐπισιτισμός
ἐπίσκοπος	ἐπίτροπος	Ἔραστος	ἔριφος[6]	ἑταῖρος
Εὔβουλος	εὐνοῦχος	Εὔτυχος	Ζακχαῖος	Ζεβεδαῖος
ζῆλος[7]	ζόφος	ζυγός[8]	ἥλιος	ἧλος
Ἡρῳδιανοί[9]	ἦχος[10]	Θαδδαῖος	θάμβος[11]	θάνατος
θεμέλιος	θεολόγος	θεός*[12]	Θεόφιλος	θερισμός
θησαυρός	θόρυβος	θρῆνος	θρόμβος	θρόνος

---

[1] βάτος, ου, ὁ meaning "bath," occurs in the N.T. only at Lk 16:6.

[2] βάτος, οῦ, ἡ meaning "thornbush" is usually feminine (n-2b) except at Mk 12:26, where it is masculine, and so we have listed it here as well.

[3] The "Dioscuri," the twin sons of Zeus, Castor and Pollux.

[4] Also formed as a n-1f noun: ἑκατοντάρχης, ου, ὁ.

[5] Alternate form of Ἐλισαῖος.

[6] The texts vary between ἔριφος and ἐρίφιον (n-2c).

[7] ζῆλος, ου, ὁ has a third declension form ζῆλος, ους, τό (n-3d[2b]). It occurs 16 times in the N.T., always using the genitive ου and never ους. It occurs twice in the neuter, at 2 Cor 9:2 (ζῆλος) and Phil 3:6 (ζῆλος; v.l. at Acts 5:17). We have listed it at n-3d(2b) as well.

[8] Also formed as ζυγόν, οῦ, τό (n-2c) as in Attic. Occur six times in the N.T. and all can be masculine, three must be (Mt 11:29, 30; Acts 15:10).

[9] Ἡρῳδιανοί, ῶν, οἱ, the "Herodians," hence plural.

[10] Also formed as ἦχος, ἤχους, τό (n-3d[2b]). Occurs four times in the N.T., three as masculine (Lk 4:37; Acts 2:2; Heb 12:19) and once as neuter (Lk 21:25) (ἤχους). Cf. Funk §2021.2, BDF §50.

[11] Also has a n-3d(2b) form: θάμβος, ους, τό.

[12] The stem is actually *θεσο. The intervocalic σ dropped out before the Koine period. The vowels do not contract (§25.5b). Generally, θεός uses the nominative for the vocative singular (Smyth §233). However, in Mt 27:46 it occurs twice as θεέ and elsewhere as θεός.

θυμός	θυρεός	θυρωρός* [1]	Ἰάϊρος	Ἰάκωβος
ἰατρός	ἱερόσυλος	ἱλασμός	ἱματισμός	ἰός
Ἰουδαϊσμός	Ἰούλιος	Ἰοῦστος	ἵππος	κάβος
κάδος	καθαρισμός	καιρός	κάλαμος	κάμηλος* [2]
κάμιλος	Καναναῖος	καπνός	Κάρπος [3]	καρπός [4]
κατακλυσμός	καταρτισμός	κατάσκοπος	κατήγορος	κέραμος
κῆνσος	κῆπος	κηπουρός	κιθαρῳδός	κίνδυνος
κλάδος	Κλαύδιος	κλαυθμός	κληρονόμος	κλῆρος
κλίβανος	κοινωνός*	κόκκος	κόλπος	κονιορτός
κοπετός	κόπος	Κορίνθιος	Κορνήλιος	κόρος
κόσμος	Κούαρτος	κόφινος	κράβαττος	κράββατος [5]
κρημνός	Κρίσπος	κρύσταλλος	κυλισμός	Κύπριος
Κυρηναῖος	Κυρήνιος [6]	κύριος	κῶμος	Λάζαρος
λαός	Λεββαῖος	λειτουργός	λῆρος	λίβανος
λιβανωτός	Λιβερτῖνος	Λιβυστῖνος	λίθος	λιμός*
Λίνος	λογισμός	λόγος	λοίδορος	λοιμός
Λούκιος	λύκος	λύχνος	μάγος	μαζός
Μαθθαῖος [7]	μακαρισμός	Μάλχος	Μᾶρκος	μάρμαρος
μασθός	μαστός	Ματθαῖος	μέθυσος	μερισμός
Μῆδος	μηρός	μιασμός	μίσθιος	μισθός
μισθωτός	μόδιος	μοιχός	μολυσμός	μόσχος
μόχθος	μυελός	μῦθος	μύλος	μῶμος
Ναζωραῖος	ναός	Νάρκισσος	ναύκληρος	νεανίσκος
νεοσσός [8]	νεφρός	νεωκόρος	Νικόδημος	Νικόλαος
νομοδιδάσκαλος	νόμος	νοσσός	νότος	νυμφίος
νῶτος	ὄγκος	ὁδηγός	ὀδυρμός	οἰκιακός
οἰκοδόμος	οἰκονόμος	οἶκος	οἰκτιρμός	οἶνος
ὄλεθρος	ὄλυνθος	ὄμβρος	ὅμιλος	ὀνειδισμός
Ὀνήσιμος	Ὀνησίφορος	ὄνος*	ὄρθρος	ὅρκος
ὄρος [9]	οὐρανός	Οὐρβανός	ὀφθαλμός	ὀχετός

---

[1] Can be either masculine (n-2a) or feminine (n-2b), depending upon the gender of the "doorkeeper." There are no examples of the feminine in the N.T.

[2] Occurs five times in the N.T. as a feminine, once as a masculine (n-2a, Lk 18:25).

[3] "Karpus," a Christian named in 2 Tim 4:13.

[4] "Fruit"

[5] Alternate form of κράβαττος.

[6] BAGD says it is "more correctly Κυρίνιος" in Lk 2:2.

[7] Alternate form of Ματθαῖος.

[8] Alternate form of νοσσός.

[9] "Boundary," not "mountain" (ὄρος, ους, τό, n-3d[2b]).

ὄχλος	πάγος	παιδαγωγός	παράδεισος	παράκλητος
παραπικρασμός	παρθένος*	Πάρθοι[1]	παροξυσμός	παροργισμός
Πάτμος	Παῦλος	πειρασμός	πενθερός	Πέτρος
πηλός	Πιλᾶτος	πλόος[2]	πλοῦτος[3]	πόλεμος
πόνος	Πόντιος	Πόντος[4]	πόντος[5]	Πόπλιος
πορισμός	Πόρκιος	πόρνος	ποταμός	Ποτίολοι[6]
πότος	προσήλυτος	Πρόχορος	πύργος	πυρετός
Πύρρος	πῶλος	ῥαβδοῦχος	ῥαντισμός	Ῥοῦφος
ῥύπος	σαββατισμός	Σαδδουκαῖος	σάκκος	σάλος
σάρδινος[7]	Σαῦλος	σειρός	σεισμός	Σεκοῦνδος
Σέργιος	σίδηρος	σικάριος	Σιλουανός	σιρός
σῖτος	σκηνοποιός	σκοπός	σκορπίος	σμάραγδος
σπίλος	σπόγγος	σπόρος	σταυρός	στεναγμός
Στέφανος[8]	στέφανος[9]	στηριγμός	στόμαχος	στρατηγός
στρατοπέδορχος[10]	στῦλος	συγκοινωνός	σύζυγος	σύμβουλος
συμπρεσβύτερος	συναιχμάλωτος	σύνδεσμος	σύνδουλος	συνέδριος[11]
σύνεδρος	συνέκδημος	συνεπίσκοτος	συνεργός	Σύρος
Σώπατρος	Σωσίπατρος	σωφρονισμός	τάραχος	ταῦρος
τάφος	Τέρτιος	Τέρτουλλος[12]	Τέρτυλλος	Τιβέριος
Τιμαῖος	Τιμόθεος	Τίτιος	τίτλος	Τίτος
τοῖχος	τόκος	τόπος	τράγος	τράχηλος
τρίβολος	τρόμος	τρόπος	Τρόφιμος	τροχός
τύπος	Τύραννος[13]	τύραννος[14]	Τύριος	Τυχικός

---

1   Πάρθοι, ων, οἱ, the "Parthians."

2   The uncontracted form of πλοῦς (n-3e[4]).

3   Occurs fourteen times in the masculine, and eight times as a neuter without any change in form from the masculine (2 Cor 8:2; Eph 1:17; 2:7; 3:8, 16; Phil 4:19; Col 1:27; 2:2).

4   "Pontus" is the name for the Black Sea.

5   "Sea" occurs only as a v.l. in Rev 18:17.

6   Ποτίολοι, ων, οἱ. "Puteoli" (Acts 28:13).

7   A later form of σάρδιον (n-2c).

8   "Stephen"

9   "Crown"

10 Also has a n-1f form, στρατοπεδάρχης, ου, ὁ.

11 BAGD say this word occurs as an error for σύνεδρος as a v.l. at Acts 5:35. In D συνέδριον (n-2c) is in v. 34.

12 Alternate form of Τέρτυλλος, which BAGD says occurs in the subscription to Philemon. It is not listed in NA[26].

13 "Tyrannus," an Ephesian, Acts 19:9.

14 τύραννος with a small τ ("tyrant") appears only as a v.l. reading (Acts 5:39).

ὑάκινθος	ὑετός	υἱός[1]	Ὑμέναιος	ὕμνος
ὕπνος	ὑπογραμμός	ὑσσός	φάγος	φανός
φαρισαῖος	φάρμακος	Φῆστος	φθόγγος	φθόνος
Φίλητος	Φιλιππήσιος	Φίλιπποι[2]	Φίλιππος[3]	Φιλόλογος
φιλόσοφος	φόβος	φόνος	φόρος	φόρτος[4]
Φορτουνᾶτος	φραγμός	Φύγελος[5]	φωλεός	φωτισμός
Χαλδαῖος	χαλινός	χαλκός	χείμαρρος[6]	χειραγωγός
χιλίαρχος	χοῖρος	χορός	χόρτος	χρηματισμός
Χριστιανός	Χριστός	χρόνος	χρυσόλιθος	χρυσόπρασος
χρυσός	χωρισμός	χῶρος[7]	ψαλμός	ψευδάδελφος
ψευδαπόστολος	ψευδοδιδάσκαλος	ψευδόχριστος	ψιθυρισμός	ὦμος

n-2b

Definition: Feminine nouns with stems ending in ο(ς)

nom sg	ς	ὁδός		*n/v* pl	ι	ὁδοί
gen sg	ο	ὁδοῦ		*gen* pl	ων	ὁδῶν
dat sg	ι[8]	ὁδῷ		*dat* pl	ις	ὁδοῖς
acc sg	ν	ὁδόν		*acc* pl	νς[9]	ὁδούς
voc sg	ε[10]	ὁδέ				

Comments

The inflection pattern is identical to the n-2a pattern. The nouns are merely feminine, as will be indicated in the text by the definite article or modifier.

Words followed with an asterisk can be either masculine (n-2a) or feminine (n-2b). We have listed the words in both categories.

---

[1] See Smyth §285.

[2] "Philippi," listed as a plural.

[3] "Philip"

[4] V.l. for φορτίον (n-2c) at Acts 27:10.

[5] Occurs as Φύγελλος in T.R.

[6] Alternate form of the contract noun χειμάρρους (n-2d). See there for comment.

[7] Acts 27:12 meaning "the northwest." χῶρος meaning "place" does not occur in the N.T.

[8] The final stem vowel lengthens and the iota subscripts.

[9] ν drops out when immediately followed by σ, and the final stem vowel is lengthened to compensate for the loss (§24.4).

[10] ε is the normal case ending for the vocative of n-2b nouns.

Listing   (total: 67)

ἄβυσσος	ἄγαμος*	ἀγριέλαιος	Ἄζωτος	Αἴγυπτος
ἀλάβαστρος*[1]	ἀμέθυσος[2]	ἀμέθυστος	ἄμμος	ἄμπελος
ἄρκος*[3]	ἄρκτος*[4]	Ἀσσος	ἄψινθος[5]	βάσανος
βάτος*[6]	βήρυλλος*	βίβλος	βύσσος	Δαμασκός
διάκονος*	διάλεκτος[7]	διέξοδος	διέξοδος	δοκός
εἴσοδος	ἔξοδος	Ἔφεσος	θεός*[8]	θυρωρός
καλλιέλαιος	κάμηλος*[9]	κάμινος	κέδρος	κιβωτός
Κνίδος	κοινωνός*	κόπρος	Κόρινθος	Κύπρος
ληνός	λιμός*	Μίλητος	νάρδος	νῆσος
νόσος	ὁδός	ὄνος*	παρθένος*	Πάφος
Πέργαμος[10]	ῥάβδος	Ῥόδος	Σάμος	σάπφιρος
σορός	σποδός	στάμνος[11]	συκάμινος	Ταρσός
τρίβος	τροφός	Τύρος	ὕαλος[12]	ὕσσωπος[13]
χίος	ψῆφος			

---

[1]   Is both feminine (n-2b), masculine (n-2a), and neuter (ἀλάβαστρον; n-2c). It is listed in all three categories.

[2]   Alternate form of ἀμέθυστος.

[3]   See discussion in n-2a.

[4]   Alternate form of ἄρκος.

[5]   Can be masculine (n-2a) or feminine (n-2b). The masculine does not occur in the N.T. Has an alternate neuter form: ἀψίνθιον, ου, τό (n-2c).

[6]   βάτος, οῦ, ἡ meaning "thornbush" is usually feminine (n-2b), except at Mk 12:26, where it is masculine. It is feminine in Attic Greek, masculine in Hellenistic (cf. BDF §49.1). βάτος meaning "bath" is masculine (n-2a).

[7]   Smyth (232b) says διάλεκτος is properly an adjective.

[8]   The stem is actually *θεσο. The intervocalic σ dropped out before the Koine period. The vowels do not contract (§25.5c).

[9]   Occurs five times in the N.T. as a feminine, once as a masculine (n-2a, Lk 18:25).

[10]   Has a neuter form Πέργαμον, ου, τό (n-2c). The word occurs at Rev 1:11 and 2:12, and gender cannot be decided (cf. BAGD).

[11]   Occurs in the N.T. only at Heb 9:5. Here it is feminine as in Attic, although it can also be masculine as in Doric and LXX (n-2a).

[12]   BAGD says usually feminine, rarely masculine. The gender of the word in the N.T. cannot be determined (Rev 21:18,21).

[13]   ὕσσωπος can be all three genders. BAGD says the neuter appears in our literature only in ms. B (Jn 19:29; Heb 9:19). M-H (p.124) says it is "indeterminate," citing Thackeray 146.

n-2c

Definition: Neuter nouns with stems ending in o(v)

n/v sg	v	ἔργον	*n/v pl*	α	ἔργα
gen sg	o	ἔργου	*gen pl*	ων	ἔργων
dat sg	ι[1]	ἔργῳ	*dat pl*	ις	ἔργοις
acc sg	v	ἔργον	*acc pl*	α	ἔργα

Listing　(total: 232)

ἀγγεῖον	ἄγκιστρον	αἰσθητήριον	ἀκροατήριον	ἀκροθίνιον
ἄκρον	ἀλάβαστρον[2]	ἄλευρον	ἄμμον	ἀμφίβληστρον
ἄμφοδον	ἄμωμον	ἀνάγαιον	ἄνηθον	ἀντίλυτρον
ἀποστάσιον	ἀργύριον	ἄριστον	ἀρνίον	ἄροτρον
ἀσσάριον	ἄστρον	ἄχυρον	ἀψίνθιον[3]	βάιον
βαλλάντιον	βιβλαρίδιον	βιβλίον	βραβεῖον	γαζοφυλάκιον[4]
γενέσια[5]	γεώργιον	γλωσσόκομον	Γόμορρα[6]	γυναικάριον
δαιμόνιον	δάκρυον[7]	δάνειον[8]	δεῖπνον	δένδρον[9]
δεσμωτήριον	δηνάριον	δίδραχμον	δίκτυον	δοκίμιον
δρέπανον	δυσεντέριον	δωδεκάφυλον	δῶρον	ἐγκαίνια[10]
εἰδωλεῖον	εἴδωλον	ἔλαιον	ἐμπόριον	ἔνεδρον
ἐνύπνιον	ἐπικεφάλαιον	ἔργον	ἔριον	ἐρίφιον[11]
ἑρπετόν	ἔσοπτρον	εὐαγγέλιον	ζιζάνιον	ζυγόν[12]

---

[1]　The final stem vowel lengthens and the iota subscripts.

[2]　Also has a masculine (n-2a) and a feminine (n-2b) form (ἀλάβαστρος).

[3]　Has alternate form ἄψινθος (n-2b).

[4]　BAGD lists as γαζοφυλακεῖον and γαζοφυλάκιον as a variant preferred by BDF §13. It occurs in the N.T. at Mk 12:41,43, Lk 21:3, and Jn 8:20. Every time our texts have -άκιον.

[5]　γενέσια, ίων, τά. "Birthday celebration."

[6]　Γόμορρα, ων, τά. See discussion of Γόμορρα at n-1a.

[7]　Has a third declension form (δάκρυ, δάκρυος, τό, n-3e[1]), which accounts for the dative plural δάκρυσι (Lk 7:38, 44; Smyth §285).

[8]　Appears in the N.T. only as δάνειον (Mt 18:27). It can also be written as δάνιον.

[9]　See Smyth §285.

[10]　This word is listed as a plural, meaning "Festival of Lights," "Hanukkah." ἐγκαίνια, ίων, τά.

[11]　The texts vary between ἐρίφιον and ἔριφος (n-2a).

[12]　BAGD lists it under ζυγός, οῦ, ὁ (entry #2), as the word in Rev 6:5. The Attic is τὸ ζυγόν.

ζῷον	ἡδύοσμον	ἡμιώριον[1]	ἡμίωρον[2]	θέατρον
θεῖον	θεμέλιον[3]	θηρίον	θυγάτριον[4]	θυμιατήριον
θυσιαστήριον	ἱερόν	Ἱεροσόλυμα[5]	Ἰκόνιον	ἱλαστήριον
Ἰλλυρικόν	ἱμάτιον	ἱστίον	ἰχθύδιον	κατοικητήριον
κέντρον	κεράμιον	κεράτιον	κεφάλαιον	κηρίον
κιβώριον	κιννάμωμον	κλινάριον	κλινίδιον	κολλούριον[6]
κόπριον	κοράσιον	κρανίον	κράσπεδον	κρίνον
κριτήριον	κύμβαλον	κύμινον	κυνάριον	κῶλον
λάχανον	λέντιον	λίνον	λόγιον	λουτρόν
λύτρον	μάκελλον	μαρτύριον	μεθόριον	μελισσ(ε)ῖον[7]
μεσονύκτιον	μεσότοιχον	μέτρον	μέτωπον	μίλιον
μνημεῖον	μνημόσυνον	Μύρα[8]	μύρον[9]	μυστήριον
νησίον	νοσσίον	νυχθήμερον	ξύλον	ὀθόνιον
οἰκητήριον	ὀνάριον	ὅπλον	ὅριον	ὄρνεον
ὀστέον[10]	ὀψάριον	ὀψώνιον	παιδάριον	παιδίον
πανδοχεῖον	παραμύθιον	Πάταρα	περιβόλαιον	Πέργαμον[11]
πετεινόν[12]	πήγανον	πηδάλιον	πινακίδιον	πλοιάριον
πλοῖον	ποίμνιον	ποτήριον	πραιτώριον	πρεσβυτέριον
προαύλιον	προβάτιον	πρόβατον	προσάββατον	προσκεφάλαιον
προσφάγιον	πρόσωπον	πρωτοτόκια[13]	πτερύγιον	πτύον

---

[1] Occurs only at Rev 8:1. Our texts have this form; *BAGD* lists the alternate form ἡμίωρον. See *MH* 280, 341.

[2] Alternate form of ἡμιώριον.

[3] Has an alternate form θεμέλιος, ου, ὁ (n-2a). Its only occurrence in the N.T. as a neuter is at Acts 16:26.

[4] Diminutive of θυγάτηρ.

[5] Ἱεροσόλυμα, ων, τά. Discussed at n-1a.

[6] Has an alternate form κολλύριον that we have not listed.

[7] V.l. at Lk 24:42 in T.R.

[8] Μύρα, ων, τά. Has a rare feminine variant (Μύραν), in Acts 27:5, which is not listed in our texts.

[9] "Ointment"

[10] Has a n-2d form (ὀστοῦν) that is the contracted form of ὀστέον. The word occurs five times in the N.T. Four times it is in the uncontracted form (Mt 23:27; Lk 24:39; Heb 11:22; variant in Eph 5:30). The fifth time it appears as the contract ὀστοῦν (Jn 19:36).

[11] Can be either neuter (n-2c) or feminine (Πέργαμος, ου, ἡ, n-2b). It occurs in Rev 1:11 in the accusative Πέργαμον, and in Rev 2:12 in the dative Περγάμῳ.

[12] *BAGD* lists πετεινόν as the neuter substantive form of the adjective πετεινός, ή, όν, which would be a-1a(2a).

[13] πρωτοτόκια, ων, τά, meaning "birthright."

Ῥήγιον	σάββατον[1]	σανδάλιον	σάρδιον	Σάρεπτα[2]
σάτον	σημεῖον	σημικίνθιον[3]	σιμικίνθιον	σιτίον
σιτομέτριον	σκάνδαλον	σκύβαλον	σκῦλον	Σόδομα[4]
σουδάριον	σπήλαιον	σπλάγχνον	στάδιον	στοιχεῖον
στρατόπεδον	στρουθίον	σῦκον	συμβούλιον	συμπόσιον
συνέδριον	σύσσημον	σφάγιον	σφυδρόν	σφυρόν
σχοινίον	τάλαντον	ταμεῖον	ταμιεῖον[5]	τεκμήριον
τεκνίον	τέκνον	τελωνεῖον[6]	τελώνιον	τετράδιον
τόξον	τοπάζιον	τρίστεγον	τρύβλιον	Τρωγύλλιον
ὑπερῷον	ὑποζύγιον	ὑπολήνιον	ὑποπόδιον	φάρμακον[7]
φόβητρον[8]	φόρον	φορτίον	φραγέλλιον	φρύγανον
φυλακτήριον	φύλλον	χαλκίον	χαλκολίβανον[9]	χειρόγραφον
χρυσίον	χωρίον	ψιχίον	ψωμίον	ᾠόν
ὠτάριον	ὠτίον			

n-2d

Definition: Second declension contract nouns with stems ending in εο or οο

nom sg	ςν	χειμάρρους (εος)	ὀστοῦν (εον)
gen sg	ο	χειμάρρου	ὀστοῦ
dat sg	ι[10]	χειμάρρῳ	ὀστῷ
acc sg	ν	χειμάρρουν	ὀστοῦν

---

1   Has a dative plural form σάββασιν (instead of σάββατοις) formed by analogy to third declension neuter nouns with stems ending in τ (n-3c[4,5]): *σαββατ + σι. Cf. *BDF* §52.

2   Σάρεπτα, ων, τά. Cf. *BDF* §56.2; Lk 4:26.

3   Alternate form of σμικίνθιον.

4   Σόδομα, ων, τά. In the LXX it is declined as a neuter (*BDF* §57).

5   Uncontracted and older form of ταμεῖον, used as a v.l. at Mt 24:26 (cf. *BDF* §31.2).

6   An itacistic spelling for τελώνιον (cf. *BAGD*).

7   *BAGD* lists it only as a variant of Rev 9:21, but our texts prefer it is the correct reading.

8   Can also be φόβηθρον. Occurs in the N.T. only at Lk 21:11 as φόβητρα.

9   Can be either neuter (n-2c) or masculine (χαλκολίβανος, ου, ὁ; n-2a). Occurs in the N.T. only in the dative χαλκλιβάνῳ with no modifiers (Rev 1:15; 2:18). We list it arbitrarily as a n-2c.

10   The final stem vowel lengthens and the iota subscripts.

n/v pl	ι	α	χείμαρροι[1]	ὀστᾶ[2]	(ὀστέα)[3]
gen pl	ων		χειμάρρων	ὀστῶν	(ὀστέων)
dat pl	ις		χειμάρροις	ὀστοῖς	
acc pl	νς[4]	α	χειμάρρους	ὀστᾶ	

Comments

Contract nouns end in οο or εο. εα contracts to α (Smyth §235). νοῦς, πλοῦς, and χοῦς ("dust") were second declension contract nouns, but by the time of the Koine, they had shifted to the third. See n-3e for discussion. On contract nouns see Smyth §235, *BDF* §45, *MH* 120-121.

Listing   (total: 2)

ὀστοῦν[5]   χειμάρρους[6]

Other examples of nouns in this category found in *BAGD* but not in the N.T. are Εὔπλους and χνοῦς.

n-2e

Definition: Nouns with stems ending in εω(ς)   ("Attic" declension)

n/v sg	ς	Κῶς	Ἀπολλῶς
gen sg	-[7]	Κῶ	Ἀπολλῶ
dat sg	ι	Κῷ	-
acc sg	- ν	Κῶ[8]	Ἀπολλῶ(ν)[9]

---

[1]   The stem ο evidently drops out (εο + ι ‣ οι).

[2]   The stem ending evidently switches from εο to εα, to which is added the alternate α ending in the neuter (εα + α ‣ εα). ε + α contract to α instead of to η. Cf. LaSor §21.332.

[3]   In the N.T. the plural of ὀστοῦν occurs only in uncontracted forms.

[4]   ν drops out when immediately followed by σ (§24.4).

[5]   Stem ends in εο. Has a n-2c form that is the uncontracted form of the word (ὀστέον, ου, τό). The word occurs five times in the N.T. Four times it is in the uncontracted form (Mt 23:27; Lk 24:39; Heb 11:22; v.l. in Eph 5:30). The fifth time it appears as the contract ὀστοῦν (Jn 19:36).

[6]   Stem ends in οο. Has a n-2a form (χείμαρρος). The word occurs in the N.T. only at Jn 18:1, where it is χειμάρρου, which can be either n-2d or n-2a. *BAGD* says the contract form is preferred in the LXX, Philo, and Josephus, so we have included it as a n-2d form.

[7]   ς is not used in order to differentiate the genitive from the nominative.

[8]   T.R. has Κῶν in Acts 21:1 (cf. 1 Macc 15:23).

[9]   The final ν is included in 1 Cor 4:6 and Titus 3:13; it is omitted in Acts 19:1 (cf. Smyth §238d).

Comments

These stems originally ended in o and were preceded by a long vowel. They then underwent a "transfer of quality" (§7.7), whereby the relative lengths of two vowels are exchanged. The words in this category originally had stems ending with a long vowel and o. The long would become short, and the o lengthened to ω (νηος ‣ νεώς). The vocative is the same as the nominative (Smyth §237). There is no example of the plural in the N.T.

For discussion see Smyth §237-8, *MH* 121, *BDF* §44, and Robertson, 260. For adjectives of the Attic declension see a-5a.

Listing[1]   (total: 2)

Ἀπολλῶς, ὁ[2]   Κῶς, ἡ

Third Declension Nouns

Stems ending in a vowel belong to the first or second declension. Stems ending in a consonant (including ι and Ϝ) belong to the third declension.

Because the stem ends in a consonant, when it joins with a case ending beginning with a consonant, those two consonants often create a significant change. This is especially true in the nominative singular and the dative plural, where the case ending often begins with a σ.

To find the noun stem, drop the genitive case ending. The stem has often been obscured in the nominative singular.

The case endings used for the third declension are actually quite similar to those used in the first and second declensions. See "Case Endings" on pp. 164f. for a discussion.

---

[1]   The only other example of this declension listed in *BAGD* is ἅλως, ἅλω (or ἅλωος, probably in imitation of n-2a nouns), ἡ, which also has a n-3f(1a) form (ἅλων, -ωνος, ἡ).

[2]   Short for Ἀπολλώνιος (Acts 18:24 D; Cf. *BDF* §125.1).

n-3a

Definition: Stems ending in a labial (π β φ)

n-3a(1)   Stems ending in π

n-3a(2)   Stems ending in β

n-3a(3)   Stems ending in φ

		π	β
n/v sg	ς[1]	λαῖλαψ	ἄραψ
gen sg	ος	λαίλαπος	ἄραβος
dat sg	ι	λαίλαπι	ἄραβι
acc sg	α	λαίλαπα	ἄραβα
n/v pl	ες	λαίλαπες	ἄραβες
gen pl	ων	λαιλάπων	ἀράβων
dat pl	σι(ν)[2]	λαίλαψι(ν)	ἄραψι(ν)
acc pl	ας	λαίλαπας	ἄραβας

Comments

There are no n-3a(3) nouns in the New Testament. All the words are masculine except λαῖλαψ, ἡ.

n-3a(1)   **Stems ending in π**   (total: 5)

Αἰθίοψ   κώνωψ   λαῖλαψ, ἡ   μώλωψ   σκόλοψ

n-3a(2)   **Stems ending in β**   (total: 2)

Ἄραψ   λίψ

n-3b

Definition: Stems ending in a velar (κ γ χ)

n-3b(1)   Stems ending in κ

n-3b(2)   Stems ending in γ

n-3b(3)   Stems ending in χ

---

[1]   The labial of the stem and the σ of the case ending are written as a ψ (§22.1).
       λαιλαπ + σ ᐅ λαῖλαψ; αραβ + σ ᐅ ἄραψ. λαιλαπ + σι ᐅ λαίλαψι; αραβ + σι ᐅ ἄραψι(ν).

[2]   See footnote for the nominative singular.

		n-3b(1)	n-3b(2)	n-3b(3)
		κ	γ	χ
n/v sg	ς[1]	σάρξ	σάλπιγξ	θρίξ[2]
gen sg	ος	σαρκός	σάλπιγγος	τριχός
dat sg	ι	σαρκί	σάλπιγγι	τριχί
acc sg	α	σάρκα	σάλπιγγα	τρίχα
n/v pl	ες	σάρκες	σάλπιγγες	τρίχες
gen pl	ων	σαρκῶν	σαλπίγγων	τριχῶν
dat pl	σι(ν)[3]	σαρξί(ν)	σάλπιγξι(ν)	θριξί(ν)
acc pl	ας	σάρκας	σάλπιγγας	τρίχας

Comments

All words in this category are feminine unless indicated. See *MH* 130f.

n-3b(1)   **Stems ending in κ**   (total: 19)

ἀλώπηξ[4]	ἄνθραξ, ὁ	γυνή[5]	δεσμοφύλαξ, ὁ	θώραξ, ὁ
κῆρυξ, ὁ	κίλιξ, ὁ	κόραξ, ὁ	ὄρνιξ	πίναξ
πλάξ	σάρξ	σκώληξ, ὁ	Φῆλιξ	Φοῖνιξ[6]
φοῖνιξ, ὁ[7]	φύλαξ, ὁ	χάραξ, ὁ	χοῖνιξ	

n-3b(2)   **Stems ending in γ**   (total: 8)

αἴξ, ὁ ἡ[8]	ἅρπαξ, ὁ[9]	λάρυγξ, ὁ	μάστιξ	πτέρυξ
σάλπιγξ	φάραγξ	φλόξ		

---

[1] The velar of the stem and the σ of the case ending are written as a ξ (§22.2).
σαρκ + σ ⟩ σάρξ; σαλπιγγ + σ ⟩ σάλπιγξ; τριχ + σ ⟩ θρίξ
σαρκ + σι ⟩ σαρξί; σάλπιγγ + σ ⟩ σάλπιγξι; τρικ + σι ⟩ θριξί

[2] For a discussion of the switch from θ to τ in the nominative singular and the dative plural see below.

[3] See the discussion of the nominative singular.

[4] The genitive ἀλώπεκος shows that the final stem vowel is actually an ε. In the nominative singular, the ε lengthens as if it were undergoing strong vowel gradation (§4; cf. n-3f, Funk §1621.3).

[5] The genitive is γυναικός. The nominative singular lengthens the final stem vowel and loses the final ικ. This is reminiscent of vowel gradation, although the η ⟩ αι shift is not a normal pattern (cf. §4). Has a vocative γυναί. (Cf. Smyth §285; LaSor §21.5133; Funk §1621.1.) Its full paradigm is, γυνή, γυναικός, γυναικί, γυναῖκα, γύναι; γυναῖκες, γυναικῶν, γυναιξῖ(ν), γυναῖκας.

[6] "Phoenix," a seaport on Crete (Acts 27:12).

[7] φοῖνιχ, also accented φοίνιξ, can mean "palm tree" (Jn 12:13) or its branches (Rev 7:9), and "phoenix," the mythical Egyptian bird (which does not occur in the N.T.).

[8] Can be either masculine of feminine.

[9] *BAGD* lists it initially as an adjective (ἅρπαξ, αγος), "ravenous," occurring in Mt 7:15 (λύκοι ἅρπαγες), and then as a substantive "robber," occurring at Lk 18:11, 1 Cor 5:10-11; 6:10.

n-3b(3)   **Stems ending in χ**   (total: 3)

θρίξ, (τριχός[1])   σαρδόνυξ, ὁ   ψίξ

n-3c

Definition: Stems ending in a dental

n-3c(1)   Stems ending in τ (but not ματ or ντ)

n-3c(2)   Stems ending in δ

n-3c(3)   Stems ending in θ

n-3c(4)   Stems ending in ματ

n-3c(5)   Stems ending in ντ

   n-3c(5a)   With ς in the nominative singular

   n-3c(5b)   With no ending in the nominative singular

n-3c(6)   Miscellaneous stems

   n-3c(6a)   Stems ending ας

   n-3c(6b)   Stems ending in ρ

   n-3c(6c)   Stems ending in ς

   n-3c(6d)   Irregular stems

The n-3c category is extensive and somewhat complicated. We have therefore divided the category into three subcategories, 1-3, 4-5, and 6. The main point to remember in this category is that a dental drops out when immediately followed by a σ (§25.2). See *MH* 131-134.

n-3c(1-3)

n-3c(1)   Stems ending in τ

n-3c(2)   Stems ending in δ

n-3c(3)   Stems ending in θ

---

[1]   The stem is really *θριχ. Since Greek did not like two aspirates (θ, χ) close together, whenever the χ is present the θ deaspirates to τ. The θ reappears whenever the χ becomes ξ, because of the σ of the case ending (§15.6).

		n-3c(1)	*n-3c(2)*	*n-3c(3)*
nom sg	ς[1]	χάρις	ἐλπίς	ὄρνις
gen sg	ος	χάριτος	ἐλπίδος	ὄρνιθος
dat sg	ι	χάριτι	ἐλπίδι	ὄρνιθι
acc sg	α ν	χάριν[2]	ἐλπίδα	ὄρνιθα
voc sg	-	χάρι	ἐλπί	ὄρνι
nom pl	ες	χάριτες	ἐλπίδες	ὄρνιθες
gen pl	ων	χαρίτων	ἐλπίδων	ὀρνίθων
dat pl	σι(ν)[3]	χάρισι(ν)	ἐλπίσι(ν)	ὄρνισι(ν)
acc pl	ας	χάριτας	ἐλπίδας	ὄρνιθας

Comments

A dental drops out when immediately followed by a σ (§25.2). This explains the changes in the nominative singular and the dative plural.

n-3c(1)	**Stems ending in τ (but not in ματ (n-3c[4]) or ντ (n-3c[5]))** (total: 47)			
ἁγιότης	ἁγνότης	ἀδελφότης	ἀδηλότης	ἁδρότης
αἰσχρότης	ἀκαθάρτης	ἁπλότης	ἀφελότης	βραδύτης
γέλως, ὁ[4]	γόης, ὁ	γυμνότης	ἑνότης	ἐσθής
εὐθύτης	θειότης	θεότης	ἱδρώς, ὁ	ἱκανότης
ἱλαρότης	ἰσότης	Ἰωσῆς, ὁ[5]	καθαρότης	καινότης
Κρής, ὁ	κυριότης	λαμπρότης	ματαιότης	μεγαλειότης
νεότης	νύξ[6]	ὁμοιότης	ὁσιότης	παλαιότης
πένης, ὁ	πιότης	πλάνης	πραότης[7]	πραΰτης
σεμνότης	σής, ὁ	σκληρότης	τελειότης	χάρις
χρηστότης	χρώς, ὁ[8]			

---

1   A dental (τ δ θ) drops out when immediately followed by σ (§22.3).
     *χαριτ + σ ‣ χάρις; *ελπιδ + σ ‣ ἐλπίς; *ορνιθ + σ ‣ ὄρνις
     *χαριτ + σι ‣ χάρισι(ν); *ελπιδ + σ ‣ ἐλπίσι(ν); *ορνιθ + σ ‣ ὄρνισι(ν)

2   Occurs forty-four times, twice as χάριτα (Acts 24:27; Jude 4).

3   See the changes that occur in the nominative singular.

4   See Smyth §285.

5   Has an alternate form with genitive in ῆ (n-1g) that does not occur in the N.T.

6   Funk lists νύξ as a n-3b(1) noun, stems ending in κ (§1621.2). But the stem appears to end in τ, and in the nominative singular and dative plural the τ drops out and the σ joins with the κ forming ξ.

7   Alternate form of πραΰτης.

8   See Smyth §285.

n-3c(2)   **Stems ending in δ**   (total: 58)

ἀκρίς	Ἀντιπατρίς	Ἄρτεμις	ἀσπίς	ἀτμίς
βολίς	Δάμαρις	δισμυριάς	Δορκάς	Ἑβραΐς
Ἑλλάς	ἐλπίς	ἔρις	Ἡρῳδιάς	θυρίς
ἴασπις	ἰκμάς	ἶρις	Ἰωσῆς[1]	κεφαλίς
κλείς	λαμπάς	λεπίς	Λωΐς	μερίς
μοιχαλίς	μυριάς	νῆστις[2]	παγίς	παῖς[3]
παραστάτις	παροψίς	πατρίς	Περσίς	πινακίς
πορφυρόπωλις	πούς, ὁ[4]	πρεσβῦτις	προστάτις	προφῆτις
Πτολεμαΐς	ῥαφίς	ῥυτίς	Σαμαρῖτις	σανίς
σπιλάς	σπυρίς[5]	στιβάς	στοιβάς[6]	συγγενίς
σφραγίς	τετράπουν[7]	Τιβεριάς	Τραχωνῖτις	Τρῳάς
ὑπολαμπάς	χιλιάς	χλαμύς		

n-3c(3)   **Stems ending in θ**   (total: 1)
ὄρνις[8]

n-3c(4-5)

n-3c(4)   Stems ending in ματ.

n-3c(5a)   Stems ending in ντ (with σ in the nominative singular).

n-3c(5b)   Stems ending in ντ (with no ending in the nominative singular).

---

[1]   V.l. in Mt 13:55. Also can be formed as a n-1g noun.

[2]   Can also be formed as a n-3c(5a) form. See there for a discussion.

[3]   Can be either masculine or feminine, depending upon the gender of the "youth" or "slave" (*BAGD* §2). It is predominantly masculine in the N.T.

[4]   The stem is *ποδ. When the δ drops out because it is followed by the σ of the nominative singular or dative plural (§22.3), the preceding stem vowel o can lengthen in order to compensate for that lose (o ‣ ου, §3.5). πούς, ποδός, ποδί, πόδα; πόδες, ποδῶν, ποσί(ν), πόδας.

  This will hold true for the compounds Ἀγαθόπους, δασύπους, and πολύπους, none of which occur in the N.T., as well as τετράπουν, which does occur in the N.T. Cf. LaSor §21.4114, Funk §1631.

[5]   Has an alternate form σφυρίς, which occurs as a v.l. at Acts 17:12.

[6]   Alternate form of στιβάς at Mk 11:8 in T.R.

[7]   τετράπουν, ποδος. *BAGD* lists as an a-3a adjective, τετράπους, ουν (i.e., a contract adjective of two terminations). It is always used as a substantive. It occurs three times in the N.T., always as a neuter (τετράποδα, Acts 10:12, 11:6; τετραπόδων, Rom 1:23). Cf. πούς.

[8]   Can be either masculine or feminine. Occurs only in parallel sayings as ὄρνις (Mt 23:37; Lk 13:34). Also formed as ὄρνιξ, ὄρνιχος, ὁ (ἡ), n-3b(1); cf. *BDF* §47.4. See Smyth §285.

		n-3c(4)	*n-3c(5a)*	*n-3c(5b)*
n/v sg	ς -	ὄνομα, τό[1]	ὀδούς, ὁ[2]	ἄρχων, ὁ[3]
gen sg	ος	ὀνόματος	ὀδόντος	ἄρχοντος
dat sg	ι	ὀνόματι	ὀδόντι	ἄρχοντι
acc sg	-	ὄνομα	ὀδόντα	ἄρχοντα
n/v pl	ες α	ὀνόματα	ὀδόντες	ἄρχοντες
gen pl	ων	ὀνομάτων	ὀδόντων	ἀρχόντων
dat pl	σι[4]	ὀνόμασι(ν)	ὀδοῦσι(ν)	ἄρχουσι(ν)
acc pl	ας α	ὀνόματα	ὀδόντας	ἄρχοντας

Comments

The words in these two classes both end in τ. The τ will drop out in the nominative singular and the dative plural because of the σ of the case ending (§22.3). n-3c(5) nouns have a ντ that will also drop out before the σ and the preceding stem vowel will be lengthened (ο ‣ ου) in order to compensate for the loss either through compensatory lengthening (§24.4) or ablaut (cf. n-3f nouns).

n-3c(4)   **Stems ending in ματ**   (total: 157)

All the words in this class are neuter.

ἀγνόημα	ἀδίκημα	αἷμα	αἴνιγμα	αἴτημα
αἰτίαμα[5]	αἰτίωμα	ἀλίσγημα	ἁμάρτημα	ἀνάθεμα
ἀνάθημα	ἀντάλλαγμα	ἀνταπόδομα	ἄντλημα	ἀπαύγασμα
ἀπόκριμα	ἀποσκίασμα	ἄρμα	ἄρωμα	ἀσθένημα
βάπτισμα	βδέλυγμα	βῆμα	βλέμμα	βούλημα
βρῶμα	γένημα	γέννημα	γράμμα	δεῖγμαδέρμα
διάδημα	διανόημα	διάστημα	διάταγμα	δικαίωμα
διόρθωμα	δόγμα	δόμα	δῶμα	δώρημα
ἔγκλημα	ἑδραίωμα	ἔκτρωμα	ἕλιγμα	ἔνδειγμα
ἔνδυμα	ἐνέργημα	ἔνταλμα	ἐξέραμα	ἐπάγγελμα
ἐπερώτημα	ἐπίβλημα	ἐπικάλυμμα	ζήτημα	ἥττημα

---

[1] No ending is used, and the τ drops off because it cannot stand at the end of a word (§19.1).

[2] Both a dental (τ) and a ν drop out when followed immediately by σ (§22.3; §24.4). The preceding vowel is lengthened to compensate for the loss (ο ‣ ου; §3.5; §24.4).

[3] No case ending is utilized. The τ drops off because it cannot stand at the end of the word (§19.1), and the ο undergoes ablaut (ο ‣ ω; §3.3). This is not compensatory lengthening, since if it were the ο would have lengthened to ου (§3.5).

[4] A dental (τ) and the ντ combination drop out when followed immediately by σ (§22.3), and the preceding vowel can be lengthened in order to compensate for the loss (§24.4).

[5] Alternate form of αἰτίωμα, occurring as a v.l. at Acts 25:7.

θαῦμα	θέλημα	θρέμμα	θυμίαμα	ἴαμα
ἱεράτευμα	κάθαρμα	κάλυμμα	κατάθεμα	κατάκριμα
καταλείμμα	κατάλυμα	κατανάθεμα[1]	καταπέτασμα	κατάστημα
κατόρθωμα	καῦμα	καύχημα	κέλευσμα	κέρμα
κήρυγμα	κλάσμα	κλέμμα	κλῆμα	κλίμα
κρίμα	κτῆμα	κτίσμα	κύλισμα[2]	κῦμα
λεῖμμα	μεσουράνημα	μίασμα	μίγμα	μίσθωμα
μνῆμα	νόημα	νόμισμα	νόσημα	οἴκημα
ὁλοκαύτωμα	ὄμμα	ὁμοίωμα	ὄνομα	ὅραμα
ὅρμημα	ὀφείλημα	ὀχύρωμα	πάθημα	παράπτωμα
περικάθαρμα	περίσσευμα	περίψημα	πλάσμα	πλέγμα
πλήρωμα	πνεῦμα	ποίημα	πολίτευμα	πόμα
πρᾶγμα	πρόκριμα	πρόσκομμα	πτύσμα	πτῶμα
ῥᾳδιούργημα	ῥάπισμα	ῥῆγμα	ῥῆμα	σέβασμα
σκέπασμα	σκήνωμα	σπέρμα	στέμμα	στερέωμα
στίγμα	στόμα	στράτευμα	σύντριμμα	σχῆμα
σχίσμα	σῶμα	τάγμα	τραῦμα	τρῆμα
τρύπημα[3]	ὑπόδειγμα	ὑπόδημα	ὑπόλειμμα	ὑστέρημα
ὕψωμα	φάντασμα	φίλημα	φρόνημα	φύραμα
χάραγμα	χάρισμα	χάσμα	χόρτασμα	χρῆμα
χρῖσμα	ψεῦσμα			

n-3c(5a)   **Stems ending in ντ (using ς in the nom. sing.)**   (total: 5)

n-3c(5a) nouns use the ς for the nominative singular, and the stem vowel undergoes compensatory lengthening (ο › ου; §3.5) when the τ of the stem is dropped because of the σ (§22.3). All nouns in this category are masculine. Note the vowel gradation from the strong form in the nominative singular (e.g., η) to the weak grade elsewhere (e.g., ε; cf. n-3f).

ἱμάς, άντος   Κλήμης, μεντος
Κρήσκης, κεντος   ὀδούς, όντος[4]
Πούδης, δεντος

---

[1]   Alternate form of κατάθεμα, occurring as a v.l.

[2]   Alternate form of κυλισμός (n-2a).

[3]   *BAGD* lists it only as a v.l. at Mt 19:24, but our texts use it.

[4]   All other n-3c(5) words undergo strong vowel gradation in the nominative singular (ο › ω). ὀδούς lengthens its stem vowel in compensation (ο › ου).

n-3c(5b)   **Stems ending in ντ (with no ending in the nom. sg.)**   (total: 8)

n-3c(5b) nouns do not use an ending in the nominative singular, and the stem vowel undergoes ablaut (ο ‣ ω; §3.3; n-3f) when the τ of the stem is dropped because it cannot stand at the end of a word (§19.1). All nouns in this category are masculine.

ἄρχων   γέρων   δράκων   θεράπων   λέων
Σαλωμών[1]   Σολομών[2]   Φλέγων

n-3c(6)

Definition: Miscellaneous neuter nouns. These nouns may or may not end in a dental as do the other n-3c nouns, but they decline as if they do. They are neuters of various classes that have assimilated to the dental pattern. See *BDF* §46.

n-3c(6a)   Nouns ending ας

n-3c(6b)   Nouns ending in ρ

n-3c(6c)   Nouns ending in ς

n-3c(6d)   Irregular stems

		n-3c(6a)	n-3c(6b)	n-3c(6c)	n-3c(6c)
n/v sg	ς -	τέρας, τό[3]	ὕδωρ, τό[4]	φῶς, τό[5]	οὖς, τό[6]
gen sg	ος	τέρατος	ὕδατος	φωτός	ὠτός
dat sg	ι	τέρατι	ὕδατι	φωτί	ὠτί
acc sg	-	τέρας	ὕδωρ	φῶς	οὖς
n/v pl	α	τέρατα	ὕδατα	φῶτα	ὦτα
gen pl	ων	τεράτων	ὑδάτων	φώτων	ὤτων
dat pl	σι(ν)[7]	τέρασι(ν)	ὕδασι(ν)	-	ὠσί(ν)
acc pl	α	τέρατα	ὕδατα	φῶτα	ὦτα

---

[1]   Alternate form of Σολομών.

[2]   Also has a n-3f(1a) formation, Σολομών, ῶνος, ὁ. It keeps ω throughout: Σολομῶντος.

[3]   A dental (τ) drops out when immediately followed by σ (§22.3). *τερατ + σ ‣ τέρας; *τερατ + σι ‣ τέρασι(ν).

[4]   The stem actually ends in ρ that appears whenever a case ending is not used. But the ρ is replaced by a τ whenever an ending is used, assimilating to the n-3c pattern.

[5]   A dental (τ) drops out when followed immediately by σ (§22.3). *φωτ + σ ‣ φῶς

[6]   The stem is *ωτ. The dental (τ) drops out because it is followed immediately by the σ of the case ending (§22.3), and the preceding vowel is shifted to ου (§3.5). *ωτ + σ ‣ ωσ ‣ οὖς

[7]   See footnote for the nominative singular.

n-3c(6d)

		γάλα, τό	γόνυ, τό [2]	μέλι, τό	κρέας, τό [3]
n/v sg	ς -[1]	γάλα, τό	γόνυ, τό [2]	μέλι, τό	κρέας, τό [3]
gen sg	ος	γάλακτος	γόνατος	μέλιτος	κρέως [4]
dat sg	ι	-	-	-	-
acc sg	-	γάλα	γόνυ	μέλι	κρέας
n/v pl	α	-	γόνατα	-	κρέα
gen pl	ων	-	-	-	-
dat pl	σι(ν)	-	γόνασι(ν) [5]	-	-
acc pl	α	-	γόνατα	-	κρέα

Comments

These words are classified more by the ending in the nominative singular than by their stem ending. All the words in this category are neuter, so their nominative and accusative forms match. In this category we are following Funk (§172).

n-3c(6a)   **Nouns ending in ας**   (total: 4)
ἅλας[6]   κέρας   πέρας   τέρας

n-3c(6b)   **Nouns ending in ρ**   (total: 3)
ὄναρ[7]   ὕδωρ, ὕδατος[8]   φρέαρ, φρέατος

n-3c(6c)   **Nouns ending in ς**   (total: 2)
οὖς, ὠτός[9]   φῶς, φωτός
See also στέαρ, στέατος.

n-3c(6d)   **Irregular stems**   (total: 4)
γάλα, ακτος   γόνυ, γόνατος   μέλι, ιτος   κρέας, κρέως
Their stems all end in τ.[10] γάλα and γόνυ are discussed in Smyth (§285).

---

[1]   When no case ending is used, the τ and the κ drop out since they cannot stand at the end of a word (§19.1).

[2]   The stem actually ends in Ϝ (Funk §1720.1; cf. δόρυ), which is visible in the nominative and accusative singular.

[3]   Occurs in the N.T. only at Rom 14:21 and 1 Cor 8:13, both times as κρέα. You can think of the stem as ending in ατ.

[4]   κρέως is irregular. κρέας later developed a genitive κρέατος, possibly in imitation of stems ending in μα (n-3c[4]).

[5]   A dental (τ) drops out when immediately followed by σ (§22.3). *γονατ + σι › γόνασι.

[6]   Occurs as ἅλα (accusative singular instead of ἅλας) in Mk. 9:50. BAGD explains this is by analogy to n-3c(4) type nouns such as σῶμα, σώματος ... σῶμα. Has replaced ἅλς (n-3f[2a]).

[7]   Occurs only in the nominative and accusative (BAGD). In the N.T. it occurs only in the expression κατ' ὄναρ (six times).

[8]   See Smyth §253b, 285.

[9]   See the paradigm for its different forms. Its stem is *ωτ (Smyth §285).

[10]   In BAGD see also οἰνόμελι, οἰνομέλιτος and δόρυ, δόρατος (Funk §172.1).

n-3d

Definition	Stems ending in ς
n-3d(1)	Stems ending in ας
n-3d(2)	Stems ending in ες
n-3d(3)	Stems ending in ος

		n-3d(1)	*n-3d(2)*	*n-3d(2)*	*n-3d(3)*
nom sg	-	γῆρας, τό	γένος, τό[1]	Σωσθένης, ὁ[2]	αἰδώς, ἡ
gen sg	ος	γήρους[3]	γένους[4]	Σωσθένους	αἰδοῦς[5]
dat sg	ι	γήρει[6]	γένει[7]	Σωσθένει	αἰδοῖ
acc sg	- ν	γῆρας	γένος	Σωσθένην[8]	αἰδῶ
n/v pl	α	-	γένη[9]	-	-
gen pl	ων	-	γενῶν[10]	-	-
dat pl	σι(ν)[11]	-	γένεσι(ν)	-	-
acc pl	α[12]	-	γένη	-	-

---

[1] The final stem vowel undergoes qualitative vowel gradation (i.e., ablaut, §4), changing from ε to o. No case ending is used.

[2] The final stem vowel is lengthened (ε › η) in the nominative singular (i.e., strong vowel gradation; §4). Elsewhere you will find the usual contractions (cf. Funk §1970.1).

[3] The word has an alternate genitive γήρως listed by *BAGD*, which is in imitation of n-3d(2b) nouns.

[4] *γενεσ + ος › γενεος › γένους.

[5] *αιδοσ + ος › αιδοος › αἰδοῦς.

[6] The stem vowel changes to ε in imitation of n-3d(2) nouns. The only occurrence of γῆρας is in Luke 1:36 as γήρει. One would expect the dative to be γήρᾳ, and in fact this form is found in the T.R. of the verse and 1 Clem 10:7. Evidently γῆρας was assimilating to the pattern of n-3d(2) nouns.

[7] *γενεσ + ι › γένει.

[8] Borrows the ν ending from the first declension. (The ν can be omitted.) Actually, it has also borrowed the α from the final stem of first declension nouns as well. The intervocalic sigma drops out (§25.5), and the ε of the stem and the α of the borrowed ending contract to η: Σωσθενεσ + αν › Σωσθενεαν › Σωσθένην (*BDF* §46.1). The other two masculine names in this class appear only in the nominative.

[9] *γενεσ + α › γενεα › γένη.

[10] *γενεσ + ων › γενεων › γενῶν.

[11] The σ of the stem and the σ of the case ending simplify to a single σ (§25.1).

[12] In the accusative plural, contract nouns use the same ending as the nominative regardless of the noun's gender (Smyth §263a).

Comments

The contractions are normal. The final σ drops out when the case ending begins with a vowel and is therefore intervocalic (e.g., γενεσος ‣ γενεος ‣ γένους; §25.5). On this category see Smyth §263ff., *MH* 138-140.

n-3d(1)   **Stems ending in ας** (total: 1)

γῆρας, τό

n-3d(2)   **Stems ending in ες** (total: 65)

All words in this category are neuter except for the three masculine names Διοτρέφης, Ἑρμογένης, and Σωσθένης.[1]

In all cases, when the case ending is added, the σ of the stem becomes intervocalic and drops out (§25.5). In the nominative and vocative singular, the final stem vowel undergoes ablaut (§4) changing from ε to ο (LaSor §21.1532).

Sometimes, some of the genitive plurals do not contract their stem ε with the ω of the genitive plural case ending such as ὄρος (ὀρῶν; ὀρέων). See *BDF* §48.

ἄγγος	ἄνθος	βάθος	βάρος	βέλος
βρέφος	γένος	γλεῦκος	δέος[2]	Διοτρέφης, ὁ
δίψος	ἔδαφος	ἔθνος	ἔθος	εἶδος
ἔλεος[3]	ἕλκος	ἔπος	Ἑρμογένης, ὁ	ἔτος
ζεῦγος	ζῆλος[4]	ἦθος	ἦχος[5]	θάμβος[6]
θάρσος	θέρος	ἴχνος	κάρφος	κέρδος
κῆτος	κλέος[7]	κράτος	κτῆνος	μέγεθος
μέλος	μέρος	μῆκος	νέφος	νῖκος
ὄνειδος	ὄξος	ὄρος[8]	ὄφελος	πάθος
πέλαγος	πένθος	πλάτος	πλῆθος	ῥάκος
σκέλος	σκεῦος	σκῆνος	σκότος	στῆθος
στρῆνος	Σωσθένης, ὁ	τάχος	τεῖχος	τέλος
ὕψος	φέγγος	χεῖλος[9]	ψεῦδος	ψῦχος

---

[1] In each of these three names, the final stem vowel is lengthened (ε ‣ η) to their strong grade (§4) in the nominative singular.

[2] The stem is *δειο. The ι drops and the ε will not contract (Smyth §265, 285).

[3] The stem is *ελεε. The first ε will not contract.

[4] ζῆλος has a n-2a form. It occurs 16 times in the N.T., always using the genitive ου and never ους. It occurs twice in the neuter, at 2 Cor 9:2 (ζῆλος) and Phil 3:6 (ζῆλος; v.l. at Acts 5:17). We have listed it at n-2a as well.

[5] Also formed as ἦχος, ου, ὁ (n-2a). See there for discussion.

[6] Also formed as a masculine noun: θάμβος, ου, ὁ (n-2a).

[7] The stem is *κλεε. The first ε will not contract.

[8] The genitive plural will sometimes not contract and form ὀρέων (Rev 6:15; *BDF* §48).

[9] The genitive plural will sometimes not contract and form χειλέων (Heb 13:15; *BDF* §48).

n-3d(3)   **Stems ending in ος**   (total: 1)
αἰδώς, ἡ[1]

n-3e

Definition: Stems ending in a semi-vowel (F ι)

n-3e(1)   Stems ending in F

n-3e(2)   Stems ending in αF

n-3e(3)   Stems ending in εF

n-3e(4)   Stems ending in οF

n-3e(5)   Stems ending in ι

   n-3e(5a)   Stems ending in ι (no ablaut)

   n-3e(5b)   Stems ending in ι (with ablaut)

n-3e(6)   Stems ending in οι

			n-3e(1)	*n-3e(2)*	*n-3e(3)*[2]	*n-3e(4)*[3]
nom sg	ς		ἰχθύς	ναῦς	βασιλεύς[4]	νοῦς[5]
gen sg	ος		ἰχθύος	νεώς	βασιλέως[6]	νοός
dat sg	ι		ἰχθύϊ	νηΐ	βασιλεῖ	νοΐ
acc sg	α	ν	ἰχθύν	ναῦν	βασιλέα[7]	νοῦν
voc sg	-		ἰχθύ	ναῦ	βασιλεῦ	νοῦ
n/v pl	ες		ἰχθύες	νῆες	βασιλεῖς	νόες
gen pl	ων		ἰχθύων	νεῶν	βασιλέων	νοῶν
dat pl	σι(ν)		ἰχθύσι(ν)	ναυσί(ν)	βασιλεῦσι(ν)	νουσί(ν)
acc pl	ας	ες[8]	ἰχθύας	ναῦς	βασιλεῖς	νόας

---

1   This is the only ος stem in Attic Greek (Smyth §266; cf. Funk §1970.2).

2   These nouns all end in εF. The F becomes the vowel υ when the case ending begins with a consonant. It will drop out when the case ending begins with a vowel; in this case, the ε of the stem will contract regularly with the vowel of the case ending. Smyth §278.

3   These nouns all end in οF. The F becomes the vowel υ when the case ending begins with a consonant. It will drop out when the case ending begins with a vowel; in this case, the ο of the stem will contract regularly with the vowel of the case ending. Smyth §278.

4   If ευς is preceded by a vowel, there can be contraction in the genitive singular and the accusative singular and plural (Smyth §276).

5   In Classical Greek νοῦς was a second declension contract noun (n -2d) from the stem *voo. It was declined, νοῦς, νοῦ, νῷ, νοῦν, νοῦ; νοῖ, νῶν, νοῖς, νοῦς.

6   In the genitive singular, the normal ος has been lengthened to ως; cf. LaSor §21.541

7   n-3e(3) nouns use α for the accusative singular.

8   The ες ending was borrowed from the nominative plural (Smyth §272).

		n-3e(5a)	n-3e(5b)	n-3e(6)[1]
nom sg	ς -	νῆστις	πόλις	πειθώ
gen sg	ος	-	πόλεως[2]	πειθοῦς
dat sg	ι	-	πόλει	πειθοῖ[3]
acc sg	ν -	-	πόλιν	πειθώ
voc sg	-		πόλι	πειθοῖ
n/v pl	ες	-	πόλεις	-
gen pl	ων	-	πόλεων	-
dat pl	σι(ν)	-	πόλεσι(ν)	-
acc pl	ες[4]	νήστεις	πόλεις	-

Comments

All the words in this category are masculine or feminine. They exhibit a large variety in contraction, sometimes resisting contraction altogether. The accusative singular is formed with ν except for n-3e(3). Nouns with genitives in εων or εως allow an acute on the antepenult (e.g., πόλεως). The long ultima would normally prevent this (§28.8.1). On this category see Smyth §268-279, *MH* 140-143.

These words all originally ended in a semi-vowel (§11.22). Following are two general guidelines. There are a few exceptions, but not in n-3e(3) and n-3e(5b) nouns.

1. If the case ending begins with a consonant, the F will become the vowel υ. If the case ending begins with a vowel, the F will drop out completely (LaSor §13.373).

2. If the stem ends in ι̯, the ι̯ will either become an ι, or it will undergo ablaut and change into a different vowel. It becomes ε before vowels and in the dative plural.

---

[1] On this category (stems in οι̯) see Smyth §279. There is no plural in Classical Greek. The ι drops if the case ending begins with a vowel. In the nominative singular no case ending is used and the ο shifts to ω. πειθώ is the only word in this category in the N.T. Even though it is feminine, the accusative is the same form as the nominative as if it were neuter.

[2] See comments on the genitive singular βασιλέως. Funk (§2001.3) has a different explanation for the genitive of πόλις. He says that it uses the stem *πολη̯ο (as seen in Homer), and the η̯ο have under gone a transfer of quantity (§7.7) so that η became ε and ο became ω.

[3] See discussion of this word below.

[4] The ες ending was borrowed from the nominative plural (Smyth §272).

n-3e(1)   **Stems ending in ϝ** (total: 11)

ἀχλύς, ἡ   βότρυς, ὁ   δάκρυ, τό[1]   ἰσχύς, ἡ   ἰχθύς, ὁ[2]
ὀσφῦς, ἡ   ὀφρῦς, ἡ   πῆχυς, ὁ[3]   Στάχυς, ὁ[4]   στάχυς, ὁ[5]
ὗς, ἡ

n-3e(2)   **Stems ending in αϝ** (total: 1)

ναῦς,[6] ἡ

n-3e(3)   **Stems ending in εϝ** (total: 24)

All words in this category are masculine.

Ἀλεξανδρεύς   ἁλιεύς   Ἀντιοχεύς   ἀρχιερεύς   βηρεύς
βασιλεύς[7]   βυρσεύς   γναφεύς   γραμματεύς   γονεύς
Θεσσαλονικεύς   ἱερεύς   ἱππεύς   καταγγελεύς   κεραμεύς
Κολασσαεύς   Κολοσσαεύς[8]   Λαοδικεύς   Νηρεύς   πανδοχεύς
Ταρσεύς   φαρμακεύς   φονεύς   χαλκεύς

See also ἀναγωγεύς, γονεῖς, τροφεύς, φαρμακεύς (v.l.), φθορεύς.

---

[1]   δάκρυ appears in three different forms in the N.T.: δάκρυον; δακρύων; δάκρυσιν. The first two are from the second declension noun δάκρυον, ου, τό (n-2c) while the third is from the third declension δάκρυ, υος, τό (n-3e[1]). No case ending is used in the nominative singular. The dative plural appears in Lk 7:38,44. Cf. BDF §52, Funk §1990.2.

[2]   Can also be accented ἰχθῦς (BDF §13; cf. Smyth §273).

[3]   πῆχυς, πήχεως occurs in the N.T. only in the forms πῆχυν and πηχῶν. The ϝ becomes υ in the nominative and accusative singular, and ε elsewhere. Therefore, the genitive plural is a contraction of εων. In other words, it is formed like stems in ι except that you find υ in the nominative and accusative singular (Funk §200.3).

[4]   "Stachys" (Rom 16:9).

[5]   "Head" or "ear" (of grain).

[6]   From the stem *νηϝ, in which the η subsequently lost its length changing to ε. There is an α to ε shift (as in the genitive), possibly due to some confusion among the Greek dialects. Cf. LaSor §21. 5531.

[7]   From the stem *βασιληϝ. The ϝ became short υ, and both vowels underwent "transfer of quality" (§7.7), in which the η became short (ε) and the υ became long.

[8]   Alternate form of Κολασσαεύς (n-3e[3]). Also spelled Κολοσαεύς and Κολασαεύς

n-3e(4)   **Stems ending in o**F (total: 4)

All words in this category are masculine.

βοῦς[1]   νοῦς[2]   πλοῦς[3]   χοῦς[4]

n-3e(5a)   **Stems ending in ι (no ablaut)**   (total: 1)

νῆστις[5]

n-3e(5b)   **Stems ending in ι (with ablaut)**   (total: 191)

All the words in this category are feminine except ὄφις, which is masculine, and
σίναπι, which is neuter. The category is discussed by *BDF* §52, *MH* 127, 142, and
Funk §2002.1).

ἀγαλλίασις	ἀγανάκτησις	ἀθέτησις	ἄθλησις	αἴνεσις
αἵρεσις	αἴσθησις	ἄλυσις	ἅλωσις	’Αμφίπολις
ἀνάβλεψις	ἀνάγνωσις	ἀνάδειξις	ἀναίρεσις	ἀνακαίνωσις
ἀνάκρισις	ἀνάλημψις	ἀνάλυσις	ἀνάμνησις	ἀνάπαυσις
ἀνάστασις	ἀνάχυσις	ἀνάψυξις	ἄνεσις	ἄνοιξις
ἀνταπόδοσις	ἀντίθεσις	ἀντίλημψις	ἀπάντησις	ἀπέκδυσις
ἀπόδειξις	ἀπόθεσις	ἀποκάλυψις	ἀποκατάστασις	ἀπόκρισις
ἀπόλαυσις	ἀπολύτρωσις	ἀπόχρησις	αὔξησις	ἄφεσις
ἄφιξις	βάσις	βεβαίωσις	βίωσις	βρῶσις
γένεσις	γέννησις	γνῶσις	δάμαλις	δέησις
Δεκάπολις	δέρρις	διάγνωσις	διαίρεσις	διάκρισις
διήγησις	δικαίωσις	διόρθωσις	δόσις	δύναμις
δύσις	ἔγερσις	ἔκβασις	ἐκδίκησις	ἐκζήτησις
ἐκπλήρωσις	ἔκστασις	ἔλεγξις	ἔλευσις	ἔνδειξις

---

[1]   Has an accusative plural form βούς. Whereas the F normally drops out when the case
ending begins with a vowel, in this case the F remained as an υ and the α of the case
ending was dropped (cf. LaSor §21.5541). βοFας ‣ βουας ‣ βούς.

Can be either masculine or feminine depending upon whether it is an ox or a cow.

[2]   Smyth (§235) lists νοῦς as a second declension contract noun from *νοο.

[3]   πλοῦς originally was a second declension contract adjective (Smyth §290a), which by
the time of the Koine period had switched to a third declension noun. Its uncontracted form is πλόος.

[4]   Its uncontracted form is χόος. It occurs in the accusative as χοῦν. Cf. discussion in
BAGD.

[5]   νῆστις can be either masculine or feminine. It can have a genitive in ιος (Ionic,
n-3e[5a]) or ιδος (Attic, n-3c[2]). *BAGD* says it is properly an adjective. See also μῆνις,
ιος (or ιδος), ἡ.

Occurs in the N.T. only in the form νήστεις (Mt 15:32; Mk 8:3; cf. *BDF* §47.3, *MH* 132,
Funk §1990.1).

The form in the N.T. evidently is from the Ionic, since the δ has been dropped.

ἔνδυσις	ἐνδόμησις[1]	ἐνδώμησις	ἐνθύμησις	ἔντευξις
ἐξανάστασις	ἕξις	ἐπανόρθωσις	ἔπαυλις	ἐπίγνωσις
ἐπίθεσις	ἐπίλυσις	ἐπιπόθησις	ἐπίστασις	ἐπισύστασις
ἐπιχείρησις	ἐρήμωσις	ζήτησις	θέλησις	θλῖψις
ἴασις	Ἱεράπολις	καθαίρεσις	κάκωσις	κατάβασις
κατάκρισις	κατάνυξις	κατάπαυσις	κατάρτισις	κατασκήνωσις
κατάσχεσις	κατοίκησις	καῦσις	καύχησις	κίνησις
κλάσις	κλῆσις	κοίμησις	κόλασις	κρίσις
κτίσις	κυβέρνησις	κωμόπολις	λῆμψις	λῆψις[2]
λύσις	λύτρωσις	μέμψις	μετάθεσις	μετάλημψις
μητρόπολις	μόρφωσις	Νεάπολις	νέκρωσις	Νικόπολις
ὁμοίωσις	ὅρασις	ὄρεξις	ὄσφρησις	ὄφις, ὁ
ὄψις	πανήγυρις	παράβασις	παράδοσις	παράκλησις
παρατήρησις	πάρδαλις	πάρεσις	πεποίθησις	περίθεσις
περιποίησις	πήρωσις	πίστις	ποίησις	πόλις
πόσις	πρᾶξις	πρόγνωσις	πρόθεσις[3]	προσκαρτέρησις
πρόσκλησις	πρόσκλισις	πρόσλημψις	πρόσληψις[4]	πρόσχυσις
πρόφασις	πτόησις	πτῶσις	πύρωσις	πώρωσις
ῥύσις	Σάρδεις	σεμίδαλις	σίναπι[5]	στάσις
συγκατάθεσις	σύγχυσις	συζήτησις	συμφώνησις	συνάντησις
συνείδησις	σύνεσις	Σύρτις	τάξις	ταπείνωσις
τελείωσις	τήρησις	ὕβρις	ὑπάντησις	ὕπαρξις
ὑπόκρισις	ὑπόμνησις	ὑπόστασις	ὑποτύπωσις	ὑστέρησις
φανέρωσις	φάσις	φρόνησις	φύσις	φυσίωσις
χρῆσις				

n-3e(6) Stems ending in οι (total: 1)

πειθώ, ἡ[6]

See also ἠχώ (*BDF* §50).

---

[1] Alternate form of ἐνδώμησις.

[2] Alternate form of λῆμψις, occurring only as a v.l. at Phil 4:15.

[3] *BAGD* lists this word as found only in ms. D of Mt 12:4 (Mk 2:26; Lk 6:4). Our texts include it as the correct reading.

[4] Alternate form of πρόσλημψις that occurs only as a v.l. at Rom 11:15.

[5] σίναπι, σινάπεως. Only occurs in the N.T. in the genitive. Apparently no ending was used in the nominative singular and the ι stayed vocalic iota. It is the only neuter in this category.

[6] πειθώ is a difficult word. It occurs only at 1 Cor 2:4 either as πειθοῖς or πειθοῖ, and could be formed from the adjective πειθός, ή, όν (a-1a[2a]). See there for the discussion. On the n-3e(6) category see Smyth §279.

n-3f

Definition: Stems showing different degrees of ablaut (nasal and liquid)

n-3f(1)   Stems ending in ν

n-3f(2)   Stems ending in a liquid (λ ρ)

n-3f(1)

Definition: Stems ending in ν showing different degrees of ablaut

n-3f(1a)   Stems ending in ν showing no ablaut

n-3f(1b)   Stems ending in ν showing strong and weak ablaut

n-3f(1c)   Stems ending in ν showing strong and zero ablaut

		n-3f(1a)	*n-3f(1b)*	*n-3f(1b)*	*n-3f(1c)*
n/v sg	-	αἰών	ἡγεμών	ποιμήν	κύων
gen sg	ος	αἰῶνος	ἡγεμόνος	ποιμένος	κυνός
dat sg	ι	αἰῶνι	ἡγεμόνι	ποιμένι	κυνί
acc sg	α -	αἰῶνα	ἡγεμόνα	ποιμένα	κυνά
n/v pl	ες	αἰῶνες	ἡγεμόνες	ποιμένες	κύνες
gen pl	ων	αἰῶνων	ἡγεμόνων	ποιμένων	κυνῶν
dat pl	σι(ν)[1]	αἰῶσι(ν)	ἡγεμόσι(ν)	ποιμέσι(ν)	κυσίν
acc pl	ας	αἰῶνας	ἡγεμόνας	ποιμένας	κύνας

Comments

These words do not use a case ending in the nominative singular, and the final stem ν is lost before the σ of the dative plural without compensatory lengthening (Smyth §250b, 250N). On this category see Smyth §259-261, *MH* 134-136.

The strong/weak grades can be either η/ε or ω/ο. The strong grade is always visible in the nominative singular. The weak and zero grades are visible in all other forms. For a detailed discussion of ablaut see §4. For other nouns undergoing ablaut see n-3c(5) nouns, and ἀλώπηξ (n-3b[1]).

n-3f(1a)   Stems ending in ν showing no ablaut   (total: 40)

Most of the words in this subcategory have the stem vowel ω. A few stems in αν, εν, and ιν have assimilated to this pattern. All words are masculine except for six feminine and one neuter.

---

[1]   The stem ν drops out when followed immediately by a σ (§24.4). There is no compensatory lengthening; cf. n-3f(1b).

ἀγών	αἰών	ἄλων, ἡ	ἀμπελών	ἀρραβών
ἀρτέμων	Ἀσσάρων	ἀφεδρών	Βαβυλών, ἡ	Γαλλίων
δεῖνα[1]	ἐλαιών	Ἕλλην[2]	εὐρακύλων	εὐροκλύδων[3]
ζήνων	Ἡρῳδίων	καύσων	κεντυρίων	κλύδων
κοιτών	λεγιών, ἡ	μεγιστάν	μέλαν, τό[4]	μήν[5]
Μνάσων	μυλών	Νέρων	νυμφών	πύθων
πυλών	Σαλαμίς, ἡ[6]	Σαρών[7]	Σιδών, ἡ	Σίμων
Σολομών[8]	Τίμων	χειμών	χιτών	ὠδίν, ἡ[9]

n-3f(1b)   Stems ending in ν showing a strong and weak grade   (total: 22)

Words in this subclass have a strong grade in the nominative singular (ω, η) and a weak grade (ο, ε) elsewhere. Cf. similar adjectives at a-4b(1).

Most stems in this class end in ω. ἀρχιποίμην, λιμήν, ποιμήν, and φρήν have stems in η, where the others have ω, and ε where the others have ο. Words are masculine unless marked otherwise.

ἀλαζών	Ἀπολλύων	ἀρχιποίμην	ἀρχιτέκτων	βραχίων
γείτων, ὁ ἡ	δαίμων	εἰκών, ἡ	ἡγεμών	Ἰάσων
κανών	λιμήν[10]	Μακεδών	ποιμήν[11]	σιαγών, ἡ

---

[1] δεῖνα is listed in *BAGD* as a noun (δεῖνα, ὁ ἡ τό). In Classical Greek is was an indefinite pronoun used when you did not want to specifically identify someone. It was declined δεῖνα, δεῖνος, δεῖνι, δεῖνα and always occurs with the article. Cf. Smyth §336.

In our literature it is always used as a masculine. In the N.T. it is used only at Mt 26:18 when Jesus tells his disciples to got to Jerusalem πρὸς τὸν δεῖνα (accusative singular masculine).

[2] Ἕλλην and μήν have a long η where the others have ω, and a short ε where the others have ο. Ἕλλην, Ἕλληνος, Ἕλληνι, Ἕλληνα; Ἕλληνες, Ἑλλήνων, Ἕλλησι(ν), Ἕλληνας.

[3] Alternate form of εὐρακύλων.

[4] Its accusative singular is μέλαν since it is neuter. Is actually the neuter of μέλας ("black"), meaning "ink."

[5] See footnote on Ἕλλην.

[6] The stem is actually *Σαλαμιν as is seen in the genitive Σαλαμῖνος. The final ν disappears when followed by the σ of the nominative singular and the dative plural case endings (§24.4; cf. *BDF* §57). ὠδίν also has a stem in ιν. For similar words outside the N.T., see ἀκτις and ῥίς (Funk §1870.4-5).

[7] *BAGD* say that the accent cannot be determined.

[8] Has a n-3c(5b) form, Σολομῶν, ῶντος.

[9] See footnote on Σαλαμίς.

[10] Occurs only in the name Καλοί Λιμένες, and some do not list it as a separate word.

[11] The stem is *ποιμην. In the dative plural it occurs in the zero grade thereby loosing the final stem vowel: › ποιμν + σι. In order for the word to be pronounceable, the ν becomes vocalic (§5), thereby being replaced by α: › ποιμασι. But because the other words in this classification with an η in the nominative singular form their dative plural with an ε, the α becomes an ε (by analogy): › ποιμέσι.

The same holds true for φρήν: *φρην › φρεν + σιν › φρεσίν.

σινδών, ἡ   τέκτων   τρυγών, ἡ   Φιλήμων   φρήν, ἡ[1]
χαλκηδών   χιών, ἡ

n-3f(1c)   **Stems ending in ν showing a strong and zero grade**   (total: 2)

The strong grade appears in the nominative singular and the zero grade elsewhere.

ἀρήν, ἀρνός, ὁ[2] κύων, κυνός, ὁ[3]

n-3f(2)

Definition: Stems ending in a liquid (λ ρ) showing different degrees of ablaut

n-3f(2a)   Stems ending in a liquid showing no ablaut
n-3f(2b)   Stems ending in a liquid showing strong and weak ablaut
n-3f(2c)   Stems ending in a liquid showing strong, weak, and zero ablaut

		n-3f(2a)	n-3f(2b)	n-3f(2b)
nom sg	-	σωτήρ	ῥήτωρ[4]	ἀστήρ
gen sg	ος	σωτῆρος	ῥήτορος	ἀστέρος
dat sg	ι	σωτῆρι	ῥήτορι	ἀστέρι
acc sg	α	σωτῆρα	ῥήτορα	ἀστέρα
voc sg	-	σῶτερ	ῥῆτορ	ἄστερ
n/v pl	ες	σωτῆρες	ῥήτορες	ἀστέρες
gen pl	ων	σωτήρων	ῥητόρων	ἀστέρων
dat pl	σι(ν)	σωτῆρσι(ν)	ῥήτορσι(ν)	ἀστράσι(ν)
acc pl	ας	σωτῆρας	ῥήτορας	ἀστέρας

		n-3f(2c)			
nom sg	-	ἀνήρ	θυγάτηρ	πατήρ	μήτηρ
gen sg	ος	ἀνδρός	θυγατρός	πατρός	μητρός
dat sg	ι	ἀνδρί	θυγατρί	πατρί	μητρί
acc sg	α	ἄνδρα	θυγατέρα	πατέρα	μητέρα
voc sg	-	ἄνερ	θύγατερ	πάτερ	μῆτερ

---

[1] See footnote on ποιμήν.

[2] ἀρήν appears in the N.T. only in the accusative plural ἄρνας (Lk 10:3). The dative plural would be ἀρνάσι(ν) (Funk §1890.3; Smyth §285).

[3] See Smyth §285.

[4] The strong vowel pattern is found in the nominative singular, and the weak grade is found elsewhere.

n/v pl	ες	ἄνδρες	θυγατέρες	πατέρες	μητέρες
gen pl	ων	ἄνδρων	θυγατέρων	πατέρων	μητέρων
dat pl	σι(ν)[1]	ἀνδράσι(ν)	θυγατρασί(ν)	πατράσι(ν)	μητράσι(ν)
acc pl	ας	ἄνδρας	θυγατέρας	πατέρας	μητέρας

Comments

n-3f(2a) nouns maintain the strong vowel grade throughout. n-3f(2b) and n-3f(2c) nouns contain words that undergo qualitative ablaut. This means that the final stem vowel can switch between its strong grade (seen here as the long vowels ω and η), its weak grade (seen here as their corresponding short vowels o and ε), or its zero grade, which means that the vowel drops out altogether. For a detailed discussion see §4 and Funk §181. The strong grade is seen in the nominative singular, and the weak and zero grades are seen elsewhere. The accent is recessive in the vocative (Smyth §262). The interconsonantal ρ become vocalic (ρ ‣ ρα) in the dative plural.

n-3f(2a)   Stems ending in a liquid showing no ablaut   (total: 14)

All the stems in this category end with ρ. (The only exception in the New Testament is ἅλς.

All words are masculine unless indicated.

ἅλς[2]	αὐτόχειρ[3]	Καῖσαρ[4]	μάρτυς[5]	νιπτήρ
ποδινιπτήρ	πρωτόμαρτυς[6]	πῦρ, τό[7]	στατήρ	σωτήρ
φωστήρ	χαρακτήρ	χείρ, ἡ[8]	ψευδόμαρτυς[9]	

---

[1]   When a ρ occurs between two consonants, which it does here because the stem vowel has been lost, it can "develop" a vowel to aid in pronunciation (§5.5). In this case, an α is developed after the ρ. πατηρ ‣ πατρσι ‣ πατράσι.

[2]   The only stem ending in λ in *BAGD* (Funk §1821.4). In Attic Greek it is declined ἅλς, ἁλός, ἁλί, ἅλα, ἅλες, ἁλῶν, ἁλσί(ν), ἅλας. It is being replaced by ἅλας, which is a n-3c(6a) formation. It occurs in the N.T. only as a v.l. at Mk 9:49.

[3]   *BAGD* does not give its gender. The word could be either masculine or feminine in classical Greek. Has a dative plural αὐτοχερσί, evidently going to a weak grade by analogy to n-3f(b) words (ει ‣ ε). It appears in the N.T. only as αὐτόχειρες (Acts 27:19). See footnote to χείρ.

[4]   Transliterated from Latin and assimilated to this pattern.

[5]   The stem is *μαρτυρ. The final ρ is dropped before the σ of the nominative singular as well as the dative plural (e.g. μάρτυσιν; cf. Funk §1821.3). None of the other stems in this class use a σ for the nominative singular, except the compounds of μάρτυς (πρωτόμαρτυς, ψευδόμαρτυς; cf. Smyth §285).

[6]   See footnote on μάρτυς.

[7]   Has an accusative singular πῦρ since the word is neuter, and the accusative must agree with the nominative. This is the only neuter in this category. See Smyth §285

[8]   χείρ has a dative plural χερσί(ν). The stem vowel has evidently shifted to its weak grade (ει ‣ ε) by analogy to the words in n-3f(2b). Funk §1821.2, Smyth §285.

[9]   See footnote on μάρτυς.

n-3f(2b)   **Stems ending in a liquid showing strong and weak**
                 ablaut   (total: 13)

These stems will show a strong grade in the nominative singular (ω η) and the corresponding weak grade elsewhere (o ε). All these words are masculine.

ἀήρ and ἀστήρ have final stem vowels in ε while the others end in o.

ἀήρ	ἀλέκτωρ	ἀστήρ	δειπνοκλήτωρ	κατήγωρ
κοσμοκράτωρ	κτήτωρ	Νικάνωρ	παντοκράτωρ	πράκτωρ
προπάτωρ	ῥήτωρ	σπεκουλάτωρ		

n-3f(2c)   **Stems ending in a liquid showing strong, weak, and zero**
                 ablaut   (total: 5)

ἀνήρ, ὁ[1]   γαστήρ, ἡ[2]   θυγάτηρ, ἡ   μήτηρ, η   πατήρ, ὁ

In all five stems, the nominative singular does not use a case ending and shows a strong grade (η). The zero grade is seen in the genitive and dative singular, and the dative plural, where the vowel has completely dropped out. The weak grade is seen elsewhere (ε).

n-3g

Definition: Irregularly declined and indeclinable stems

n-3g(1)   Irregularly and partially declined stems

n-3g(2)   Indeclinable stems

Comments

Most of these words were borrowed from other languages, especially Hebrew, Aramaic, and Latin, and therefore do not change their form in order to remain true to their original pronunciation. Most are proper nouns. On names in general see *BDF* §36-42, §53-58, and *MH* 143-155.

---

[1]   ἀνήρ shows the zero grade everywhere except in the nominative and vocative singular. Since dropping the vowel results in a νρ cluster that is difficult to pronounce, the word develops an epenthetic δ: *ανηρ + oσ › ανρος › ἀνδρός (§18.3). This particular example is discussed in "Introduction to Consonantal Changes" (§10)

[2]   Declined like θυγάτηρ.

n-3g(1) **Irregularly and partially declined stems** (total: 13)

nom sg	Ζηνᾶς, ὁ	Ζεύς, ὁ	Ἰησοῦς, ὁ[1]	Λευίς[2]	Μωϋσῆς, ὁ[3]
gen sg	Ζηνᾶς	Διός	Ἰησοῦ	Λευί	Μωϋσέως[4]
dat sg	Ζηνᾶς	Διΐ	Ἰησοῦ	Λευί	Μωϋσεῖ[5]
acc sg	Ζηνᾶν	Δία	Ἰησοῦν	Λευίν	Μωϋσῆν[6]
voc sg	-	Ζεῦ	Ἰησοῦ	-	-

nom sg	Λύδδα, ἡ		Θυάτειρα[7]	Λυστρά
gen sg	Λύδδας[8]		Θυατείρων	-
dat sg	-		Θυατείροις	-
acc sg	Λύδδα[9]		Θυάτειρα	Λύστραν

Listing

Ἀκύλας[10]   Γολγοθᾶ[11]   Ζηνᾶς   Ζεύς[12]   Θυάτειρα[13]

---

[1] ς is added in the nominative and ν in the accusative (Funk §206.2).

[2] When the N.T. refers to the Λευί of the O.T., the word is indeclinable (n-3g[2]). When it refers to a N.T. person, it is partially declined (n-3g[1]): Λευίς; Λευίν (Lk 3:24, 29; Heb 7:9, 9; Rev 7:7). ς is added in the nominative and ν in the accusative (Funk §206.2). Cf. *BDF* §55, *MH* 146.

[3] See discussion of the alternate form Μωσῆς, below.

[4] Declines as if the stem ended in ε and uses a lengthened case ending (ε + ως).

[5] Occurs eight times in this form, and once as Μωϋσῆ.

[6] Occurs four times in this form, and once as Μωϋσέα.

[7] This word is used as a plural.

[8] Can also be Λύδδης (Funk §206.5; *BDF* §56.2).

[9] Can also be Λύδδαν (Funk §206.5; *BDF* §56.2).

[10] Ἀκύλας, ὁ is indeclinable except that it has an accusative in αν (cf. Ζηνᾶς). Ἀκύλας occurs three times in the nominative and three times in the accusative.

[11] Γολγοθᾶ, ἡ, is indeclinable except that it has an accusative in αν (cf. Ζηνᾶς). Γολγοθᾶ occurs two times in the nominative (Mt 27:33 [Γολγοθᾶ]; Jn 19:17 [Γολγοθα; no accent]) and in Mk 15:22 as an accusative: UBS⁴ accents as Γολγοθᾶν (n-1h); NA²⁶ accents as Γολγοθάν, which is not the correct accent for a contract noun. *BDF* §39.6 lists as -ᾶ.

[12] Δίς never occurs in the nominative, and hence the different root Ζεύς and Ζεῦ. See Smyth §285 and *LS*.

[13] *BAGD* has Θυάτιρα. Our texts (and WH) have ει in all the four verses it occurs in the N.T. (Acts 16:14; Rev 1:11; 2:18,24.). It is plural with an accusative in αν (cf. *BDF* §57).

| Θυάτιρα[1] | Ἰησοῦς | Λευίς | Λύδδα[2] | Λύστρα[3] |
| Μωσῆς[4] | Μωϋσῆς[5] | Χερούβ[6] | | |

n-3g(2)   Indeclinable stems   (total: 245)

Ἀαρών	Ἀβαδδών, ὁ	ἀββά	Ἄβελ, ὁ	Ἀβιά, ὁ
Ἀβιαθάρ, ὁ	Ἀβιούδ, ὁ	Ἀβραάμ, ὁ	Ἀγάρ, ἡ	Ἀδάμ, ὁ
Ἀδδί, ὁ	Ἀδμίν, ὁ	Ἀζώρ, ὁ	Αἰνών, ἡ	Ἀκελδαμάχ[7]
ἀλληλουϊά	ἄλφα, τό	Ἀμιναδάβ, ὁ	Ἀμών, ὁ[8]	Ἀμώς, ὁ
Ἀράμ, ὁ	Ἀρμαγεδών[9]	Ἀρνί, ὁ	Ἀρφαξάδ, ὁ	Ἀσά[10]
Ἀσάφ, ὁ	Ἀσήρ, ὁ	Ἀχάζ, ὁ	Ἀχάς, ὁ[11]	Ἀχίμ, ὁ
Βάαλ, ὁ	Βαλαάμ, ὁ	Βαλάκ, ὁ	βάρ, ὁ	Βαράκ, ὁ
Βαριωνᾶ, ὁ	Βεεζεβούλ, ὁ[12]	Βελιάρ, ὁ	Βενιαμίν, ὁ[13]	Βεώρ, ὁ
Βηθεσδά, ἡ[14]	Βηθζαθά, ἡ	Βηθλέεμ, ἡ	Βηθσαϊδά(ν), ἡ[15]	Βηθφαγή, ἡ
Βοανηργές	Βόες, ὁ[16]	Βόοζ, ὁ[17]	Βόος, ὁ[18]	Βοσόρ, ὁ[19]

---

[1] Alternate form of Θυάτειρα. See footnote above.

[2] Λύδδα occurs in Acts 9:38 in the genitive Λύδδας; in the extra Biblical literature the form Λύδδης is also attested. Its accusative form is Λύδδα (which in extra-Biblical literature and the variants to Acts 9:32 and 25 also appears as Λύδδαν), which "functions as an indecl. form or a neut. pl."(*BAGD*,481). Cf. Funk §206.5.

[3] Can be either neuter (n-2c) or feminine (n-1a). When it is plural it is neuter (Λύστροις: Acts 14:8; 16:2; 2 Tim 3:11). When it is singular it is feminine (Λύστραν: Acts 14:6,21; 16:1 (v.l. in Acts 27:5). We have listed the word under both categories. Cf. Funk §206.5, *BDG* §57.

[4] Alternate form of Μωϋσῆς in the T.R. (cf. *BDG* §38, §53.1; *MH* 86f.).

[5] Funk (§206.3) says it is declined in the LXX as Μωυσῆς, Μωυσῆ, Μωυσῇ, Μωυσῆν. Rahlfs edition does not include a diaeresis.

[6] Χερούβ, τό/ὁ is indeclinable, except that the plural is in imitation of the Hebrew. In the literature we find the forms Χερουβείν, Χερουβίν, Χερουβείμ, and Χερουβίμ. It is most often in the plural neuter. It is found in the N.T. only at Heb 9:5 as Χερουβίν. *BAGD* lists as a neuter. Cf. Funk §206.6.

[7] Transliteration from the Aramaic (Acts 1:19). There are several variant spellings.

[8] Alternate form of Ἀμώς, used as a v.l. at Mt 1:10.

[9] *BAGD* list as Ἀρμαγεδδών. Occurs only at Rev 16:16, which in our text has a single δ.

[10] Alternate form of Ἀσάφ.

[11] Alternate form of Ἀχάζ.

[12] Has variant spellings of Βεελζεβούβ and Βεελζεβούλ.

[13] Can also be written Βενιαμείν, but not so in our texts.

[14] Alternate form of Βηθζαθά, used as a v.l. at Jn 5:2.

[15] It is written this way five times, and twice with the final ν, as Βηθσαϊδάν (Mk 6:45; 8:22).

[16] The name "Boaz" is written Βόες in Mt 1:5 and Βόος in Lk 3:32.

[17] Alternate form of Βόος, a v.l. at Luke 3:32.

[18] The name "Boaz" is written Βόες in Mt 1:5 and Βόος in Lk 3:32.

[19] *BAGD* list is as a v.l. at 2 Peter 2:15, but our texts include it as the preferred reading.

Γαββαθᾶ	Γαβριήλ, ὁ	Γάδ, ὁ	Γαμαλιήλ, ὁ	Γεδεών, ὁ
Γεθσημανί	Γεννησαρέτ, ἡ	Γώγ, ὁ	Δαβίδ, ὁ[1]	Δαλμανουθά, ἡ
Δάν, ὁ	Δανιήλ, ὁ	Δαυίδ, ὁ	Ἔβερ, ὁ	Ἐλεάζαρ, ὁ
Ἐλιακίμ, ὁ[2]	Ἐλιέζερ, ὁ	Ἐλιούδ, ὁ	Ἐλισάβετ, ἡ	Ἐλμαδάμ, ὁ
Ἐλμωδάμ[3]	ἐλωι[4]	Ἐμμανουήλ, ὁ	Ἐμμώρ, ὁ	Ἐνώς, ὁ
Ἐνώχ, ὁ	Ἐσλί, ὁ	Ἐσρώμ, ὁ	Ἐφραίμ, ὁ	ἐφφαθά
Ζαβουλών, ὁ	Ζάρα, ὁ	ζαφθάνι[5]	Ζοροβαβέλ, ὁ	ηλι[6]
Ἡλί[7]	Ἤρ, ὁ	Ἠσαῦ, ὁ	θάβιτα[8]	Θαμάρ, ἡ
Θάρα, ὁ	Ἰακώβ, ὁ	Ἰανναί, ὁ	Ἰάρετ, ὁ	Ἰαχίν, ο
Ἰεζάβελ, ἡ	Ἰεριχώ, ἡ	Ἰερουσαλήμ, ἡ[9]	Ἰεσσαί, ὁ	Ἰεφθάε, ὁ
Ἰσαάκ, ὁ	Ἰσαχάρ, ὁ	Ἰσκαριώθ, ὁ	Ἰσραήλ, ὁ	Ἰσσαχάρ, ὁ
Ἰωαθάμ, ὁ	Ἰωανάν, ὁ	Ἰωᾶς, ὁ	Ἰώβ, ὁ	Ἰωβήδ, ὁ
Ἰωδά, ὁ	Ἰωήλ, ὁ	Ἰωνμ, ὁ	Ἰωράμ, ὁ	Ἰωρίμ, ὁ
Ἰωσαφάτ, ὁ	Ἰωσήφ, ὁ	Ἰωσήχ, ὁ	ἰῶτα, τό	Κάϊν, ὁ
Καϊνάμ, ὁ[10]	Καϊνάν, ὁ[11]	Κανά, ἡ	Καπερναούμ[12]	Καφαρναούμ, ἡ
Καῦδα[13]	Κεδρών, ὁ	Κίς, ὁ	Κλαῦδα[14]	κορβᾶν
Κόρε, ὁ	κοῦμ	κοῦμι[15]	Κωσάμ, ὁ	λαμα[16]
Λάμεχ, ὁ	λεμά	Λευί, ὁ[17]	Λώτ, ὁ	Μάαθ, ὁ
Μαγδαλά[18]	Μαγαδάν, ἡ	Μαγεδών[19]	Μαγώγ, ὁ	Μαδιάμ, ὁ

---

[1] Alternate form of Δαυίδ.

[2] Also spelled Ἐλιακείμ.

[3] Alternate form of Ἐλμαδάμ.

[4] Aramaic for "my God" in Mk 15:34 (parallel in Mt 27:46 has ηλι). *UBS* includes no accent. *BAGD* accents ἐλωΐ

[5] D's reading for σαβαχθανι at Mt 27:46 and Mk 15:34.

[6] "My God." Jesus' cry on the cross; Mt 27:46. *UBS* has no accent (Ηλι ηλι); *NA* lists as ηλι ηλι; *BAGD* lists as ἠλί. Parallel in Mk 15:34 has ἐλωι.

[7] The name "Heli."

[8] Alternate form of ῥαβιθά, occurring as a v.l. in D at Mk 5:41.

[9] See discussion at n-1(a).

[10] Καϊνάμ occurs twice in the N.T., both times with the final μ. See the alternate Καϊνάν.

[11] Alternate form of Καϊνάμ, used as a v.l. at Luke 3:36, 37.

[12] Alternate form of Καφαρναούμ.

[13] This word has three forms. Καῦδα (n-3g[2]), which is preferred by the UBS text. Κλαῦδα (n-3g[2]), which is the form listed in *BAGD*. Κλαύδη (n-1b) is behind the v.l. in Acts 27:16; Κλαύδην in the T.R. It is the name of an island, occurring the N.T. only at Acts 27:16 as an accusative Καῦδα.

[14] Alternate form of Καῦδα, occurring as a v.l. at Acts 27:16.

[15] Alternate form of κοῦμ.

[16] Aramaic

[17] See discussion on Λευίς at n-3g(1).

[18] Alternate form for Μαγαδάν, used in T.R. in Mt 15:39, v.l. in Mk 8:10.

[19] Alternate form of Ἀρμαγεδών, v.l. at Rev 16:16.

Μαθθάτ[1]	Μαθουσάλα, ὁ	Μαϊνάν, ὁ[2]	Μαλελεήλ, ὁ	Μαναήν, ὁ
μάννα, τό	μαρὰν ἀθᾶ[3]	μαράνα θᾶ [4]	Μαριάμ, ἡ	Ματθάν, ὁ
Ματθάτ, ὁ	Ματταθά, ὁ	Μελεά, ὁ	Μελχί, ὁ	Μελχισέδεκ, ὁ
Μεννά, ὁ	Μιχαήλ, ὁ	Μολόχ, ὁ	Ναασσών, ὁ	Ναγγαί, ὁ
Ναζαρά, ἡ	Ναζαρέθ, ἡ	Ναζαρέτ, ἡ	Ναθάμ, ὁ	Ναθάν[5]
Ναθαναήλ, ὁ	Ναιμάν, ὁ	Ναΐν, ἡ	Ναούμ, ὁ	Ναχώρ, ὁ
Νεεμάν[6]	Νευης[7]	Νεφθαλίμ, ὁ	Νηρί, ὁ	Νίγερ, ὁ
Νινευή, ἡ[8]	Νινευΐ, ἡ[9]	Νῶε, ὁ	πάσχα, τό	Ῥαάβ, ἡ
ῥαββί	ῥαββονί[10]	ῥαββουνί[11]	ῥαβιθά[12]	Ῥαγαύ, ὁ
Ῥαιφάν, ὁ[13]	ῥακά	Ῥαμά, ἡ	ῥαχά[14]	Ῥαχάβ, ἡ
Ῥαχήλ, ἡ	Ῥεμφάν[15]	Ῥεφάν[16]	Ῥησά, ὁ	Ῥοβοάμ, ὁ
Ῥομφά, ὁ[17]	Ῥουβήν, ὁ	Ῥούθ, ἡ	σαβαχθάνι	Σαβαώθ
Σαδώκ, ὁ	Σαλά, ὁ	Σαλαθιήλ, ὁ	Σαλήμ, ἡ	Σαλίμ, τό
Σαλμών, ὁ	Σαμουήλ, ὁ	Σαμφουρειν[18]	Σαμψών, ὁ	Σαούλ, ὁ
Σαρούχ[19]	Σατάν, ὁ[20]	Σεμεΐν, ὁ	Σερούχ, ὁ	Σήθ, ὁ
Σήμ, ὁ	σίκερα, τό	Σιλωάμ, ὁ	Σινά	Σιχάρ[21]

---

[1] Alternate form of Ματθάτ.

[2] Alternate form of Μεννά.

[3] Another way that the Aramaic μαράνα θᾶ can be understood.

[4] μαρὰν ἀθᾶ is an Aramaic phrase meaning "(Our) Lord has come." If it is divided μαράνα θᾶ it means "(Our) Lord, come!" (1 Cor 16:22). UBS has no accent and divides it the second way.

[5] Alternate form of Ναθάμ.

[6] Alternate form of Ναιμάν.

[7] The name of the rich man in the parable in P⁷⁵. Another spelling is Νινευης.

[8] Alternate form of Νινευίτης (n-1f).

[9] Alternate form of Νινευίτης (n-1f).

[10] Alternate form of ῥαββουνί.

[11] Alternate forms include ῥαββουνεί, ῥαββονί, ῥαββονεί. Cf. also ῥαββί.

[12] Cf. BAGD.

[13] Occurs at Acts 7:43. Alternate forms include Ῥομφά (BAGD), Ῥαιφάν, Ῥεμφάν, Ῥομφάν, Ῥεμφά, Ῥομφά, Ῥεφάν.

[14] Alternate form of ῥακά.

[15] Alternate form of Ῥαιφάν.

[16] Alternate form of Ῥαιφάν.

[17] Alternate form of Ῥαιφάν at Acts 7:43. Listed as such by BAGD.

[18] No accent is listed in BAGD. Occurs in D of Jn 11:54.

[19] Alternate form for Σερούχ in the T.R.

[20] Has a genitive Σατανός in imitation of declinable third declension nouns in a variant of Lk 11:18 (P⁷⁵).

[21] Alternate form of Συχάρ.

Σιχέμ[1]   Σιών, ἡ   Σκαριώθ, ὁ[2]   Σκαριώτης[3]   Συμεών, ὁ
Συχάρ, ἡ   Συχέμ[4]   Ταβιθά, ἡ   ταλιθά[5]   Φάλεκ, ὁ
Φανουήλ, ὁ   Φαραώ, ὁ   Φαρές, ὁ   Χανάαν, ἡ   χαρράν, ἡ
Χοραζίν, ἡ   Χωραζίν[6]   Ὠβήδ   ὡσαννά   Ὡσηέ, ὁ[7]

Introduction to Adjectives

There are several ways to divide adjectives. Some divide on the same basis as nouns: vowel stems; consonantal stems. Our initial division is based on whether the adjective has a separate form for the feminine or if the masculine and feminine use the same form. The next subdivision is based on whether the adjectives use first and second declension endings, or first and third.

The standard way of referring to adjectives is to use "1," "2," and "3" to indicate declension. For example, "2-1-2" adjectives use second declension endings for the masculine (i.e., the first number), first declension endings for the feminine (i.e., the second number), and second declension endings for the neuter (i.e., the third number. "3-3" means the adjective uses the same third declension endings for the masculine and feminine (i.e., the first number), and third declension endings for the neuter (i.e., the second number).

Following this scheme we have five basic divisions of adjectives.

a-1   Adjectives using three endings (2-1-2)

a-2   Adjectives using three endings (3-1-3)

a-3   Adjectives using two endings (2-2)

a-4   Adjectives using two endings (3-3)

a-5   Irregular and indeclinable stems

How each of these classes is subdivided differs from class to class. Sometimes the deciding factor is the nominative singular ending used in the feminine or even neuter. Other times it is a difference in the word's stem (as is true of nouns).

Adjectives use the same case endings as nouns. See the introduction to nouns for a discussion of case endings. We will not list the case endings on the adjective paradigms.

---

1   Alternate form of Συχέμ.

2   Alternate form of Ἰσχαριώθ.

3   Alternate form of Ἰσκαριώθ used as a v.l. (D) in Mt 10:4; 26:14; Mk 14:10.

4   BAGD list it as a v.l. in Acts 7:16, but our texts include it as the preferred reading. Is masculine, although BAGD do not list it as such.

5   ταλιθά is not a Greek word, but a Greek transliteration of the Aramaic for "little girl."

6   Alternate form of Χοραζίν.

7   Occurs only at Rom 9:25 and is accented in this manner. It can also be accented Ὡσῆε.

Some words are listed in their plural form (e.g., τριακόσιοι). When a nominative neuter form is explained, the corresponding accusative is not. When the dative plural masculine form is explained, its corresponding neuter is not. We should also be reminded that stems using first and second declension endings actually end in a vowel. The vowel is not part of the case ending.

Outline of Adjectives

a-1 Adjectives

Definition: Adjectives using three endings (2-1-2)

a-1a   Uncontracted stems
  a-1a(1)   Uncontracted stems (feminine in α)
  a-1a(2a)   Uncontracted stems (feminine in η; neuter in ον)
  a-1a(2b)   Uncontracted stems (feminine in η, neuter in ο)
a-1b   Contracted stems (3-1-3)

Comments

Masculine adjectives are declined like λόγος (n-2a), neuter adjectives like ἔργον (n-2c)–except for a-1a(2b) that have the nominative and accusative singular in ο–feminine adjectives in α like ὥρα (n-1a), and feminine adjectives in η like γραφή (n-1b). There is no α ‣ η shift in a-1 adjectives. The accent in the nominative and genitive plural feminine is the same as the masculine (i.e., not ἅγίαι, ἁγιῶν).

a-1a(1)

Definition: Uncontracted stems using three endings (2-1-2) with the feminine in α

nom sg	ἅγιος	ἁγία	ἅγιον
gen sg	ἁγίου	ἁγίας	ἁγίου
dat sg	ἁγίῳ	ἁγίᾳ	ἁγίῳ
acc sg	ἅγιον	ἁγίαν	ἅγιον
voc sg	ἅγιε	ἁγία	ἅγιον
n/v pl	ἅγιοι	ἅγιαι	ἅγια
gen pl	ἁγίων	ἁγίων	ἁγίων
dat pl	ἁγίοις	ἁγίαις	ἁγίοις
acc pl	ἁγίους	ἁγίας	ἅγια

Comments

Every stem ends in a vowel. Preceding that vowel will be either ε, ι, or ρ (otherwise they would be a-1a[2a] adjectives). Most regular comparative and superlative adjectives belong to this category. Lexicons do not list most of these forms as separate words. We have listed them in a separate section following a-1a(1) adjectives.

Listing (total: 137, not including comparatives and superlatives)

ἅγιος	ἄγριος	Ἀθηναῖος	αἴγειος	Αἰγύπτιος
αἰσχρός	αἴτιος	ἀκρογωνιαῖος	ἀλλότριος	ἀμφότεροι
ἀναγκαῖος	ἄξιος	ἀργύρεος[1]	ἄρειος	ἀριστερός
ἄρτιος	ἀρχαῖος	ἀστεῖος	αὐστηρός	αὐχμηρός
βέβαιος	Βεροιαῖος	βίαιος	βλαβερός	βλητέος[2]
Γαλιλαῖος	γνήσιος	γυναικεῖος	Δερβαῖος	δεξιός
δευτεραῖος	δεύτερος	δημόσιος	διακόσιοι	δίκαιος
δισχίλιοι	δόλιος	ἑκούσιος	ἐλαφρός	ἐλεύθερος
ἐναντίος	ἐνεός	ἐννεός[3]	ἐντόπιος	ἐξακόσιοι
ἐπιτήδειος	ἑπτακισχίλιοι	ἐρυθρός	ἕτερος	Ἐφεσῖνος
Ἐφέσιος	ἐχθρός	ἡμέτερος	ἤπιος	θαυμάσιος
θεῖος	ἴδιος	ἱερός	ἱλαρός	Ἰουδαῖος
ἰσχυρός	Ἰτουραῖος	καθαρός	κραταιός	κρυφαῖος

---

[1] Uncontracted form of ἀργυροῦς (a-1b).

[2] Is actually the only N.T. example of a specific pattern (*BDF* §65.3). Occurs only as a nominative singular neuter βλητέον (Lk 5:38).

[3] Alternate form of ἐνεός.

κρύφιος	λαμπρός	λεῖος	λεπρός	λιπαρός
λόγιος	μακάριος	μακρός	μάταιος[1]	μεγαλεῖος
μικρός	μύριοι[2]	μυρίος[3]	μωρός	νεκρός
νέος	νήπιος	νηφαλέος[4]	νηφάλιος	νωθρός
ξηρός	οἶος	ὀκνηρός	ὅμοιος	ὁποῖος
ὄρθριος	ὅσιος	ὄψιος[5]	παλαιός	παραθαλάσσιος
παραπλήσιος	πατρῷος	πενιχρός	πεντακισχίλιοι	πεντακόσιοι
περαιτέρος	πικρός	Πισίδιος	πλούσιος[6]	ποῖος[7]
πονηρός	πυρρός	ῥυπαρός	Ῥωμαῖος	σαπρός
Σιδώνιος	σκληρός	σκολιός	Σμυρναῖος	σπουδαῖος
στερεός	ταλαντιαῖος	τέλειος	τεταρταῖος	τετρακισχίλιοι
τίμιος	τριακόσιοι	τρισχίλιοι	ὑγρός	ὑμέτερος
ὑπεναντίος	ὕστερος	φανερός	φοβερός	χάλκεος[8]
Χαναναῖος	χίλιοι	χλιαρός	χλωρός	χρύσεος[9]
ψυχρός	ὡραῖος			

Comparative and Superlative Adjectives

Adjectives are said to have three "degrees": positive, comparative, superlative. For example, "good," "better," "best." Technically, the comparative degree compares one against one and the superlative compares one against more than one. In Hellenistic Greek the superlative was dropping out of use and in many cases was being used with the same sense as a comparative. This is called its "elative" use. On comparatives and superlatives see *BDF* §60-62, Smyth §313-324, *MH* 164-167, Robertson, 276-281, Funk §240-45. *acCordance* reports there are 198 comparative adjectives and thirty-nine superlative adjectives.

Comparative and superlative adjectives can be formed by adding certain endings to the masculine stem of the adjective or to the adverb. (There are compar-

---

[1]   Can be an adjective with two terminations, as in Attic (a-3a; Titus 3:9; Jas 1:26; a-3b[1]). However it can have a distinct feminine form (a-1a[1]), as in 1 Cor 15:17 and 1 Pet 1:18.

[2]   10,000

[3]   "Innumerable."

[4]   A later form of νηφάλιος.

[5]   Occurs mostly substantivally (n-1a).

[6]   ι is added to the stem *πλουτ in the formation of the adjective. τι ᛫ σι (§26.10).

[7]   An interrogative pronoun.

[8]   Uncontracted form of χαλκοῦς (a-1b).

[9]   Uncontracted form of χρυσοῦς (a-1b).

ative adverbs but they are discussed elsewhere.) There are in fact two sets of endings; the first is regular and the second irregular.

Comparative		Superlative	
τερος, α, ον	a-1a(1)	τατος, η, ον	a-1a(2a)
(ι)ων, ον	a-4b(1)	ιστος, η, ον	a-1a(2a)

The stem vowel o is lengthened to ω if the preceding syllable is short (e.g., νέος › νεώτερος; LaSor §15.14; Smyth §314).

Following are all the regularly formed comparatives that occur in the New Testament (cf. *MH* 165). While most of these forms are not listed in lexicons, the ones with asterisks are listed in *BAGD*. We have listed all these forms in the *Index*.

ἀλυπότερος	ἀναγκαιότερος	ἀνεκτότερος	ἀνώτερος[1]	ἀσθενέστερος
ἀτιμότερος	βαρύτερος	βεβαιότερος	δεισιδαιμονέστερος	
διαφορώτερος	διπλότερος	ἐλαχιστότερος	ἐλεεινότερος	ἐντιμότερος
ἐξώτερος*	ἐσώτερος*	εὐγενέστερος	εὐκοπώτερος	ἰσχυρότερος
καινότερος	κατώτερος*	μακαριώτερος	μειζότερος[2]	μικρότερος
νεώτερος	περισσότερος*	πολυτιμότερος	πονηρότερος	πρεσβύτερος*
πρότερος*	σοφώτερος	σπουδαιότερος	τελειότερος	τομώτερος
ὕστερος	ὑψηλότερος	φρονιμώτερος		

Following are all the regularly formed superlatives that occur in the New Testament. They are a-1a(2a) stems and are listed there as well.

ἁγιώτατος	ἀκριβέστατος	κράτιστος*	τιμιώτατος

Following is a chart of the irregularly formed comparatives and superlatives (cf. Smyth §319 for more details).

Positive	Comparative	Superlative
ἀγαθός, ή, όν	βελτίων, ον[3]	-
	κρείττων, ον[4]	
ἔξω (adverb)	ἐξώτερος, α, ον	-
ἔσω (adverb)	ἐσώτερος, α, ον	-
_[5]	ἥσσων, ον	-

---

[1]   In our literature used only in the neuter as an adverb (ἀνώτερον).

[2]   An irregular formation from μέγας. The comparative μείζων was losing its comparative force and so μειζότερος was also used for the comparative (*BAGD*).

[3]   Used only adverbially in the N.T. (2 Tim 1:18; Acts 10:28 v.l.).

[4]   Also κρείσσων. Formed from κρατύς but functions as the comparative of ἀγαθός. Its superlative is κράτιστος, α, ον.

[5]   No positive degree.

κακός, ή, όν	χείρων, ον	-
κάτω (adverb)	κατώτερος, α, ον	-
μέγας, μεγάλη, μέγα	μείζων, ον[1]	-
	μειζότερος, α, ον[2]	μέγιστος, α, ον
μικρός, α, ον	μικρότερος, α, ον	-
	ἐλάσσων, ον[3]	-
	ἐλαχιστότερος	ἐλάχιστος, η, ον[4]
πολύς, πολλή, πολύ	πλείων, πλεῖον	πλεῖστος, η, ον
πρό(prep.)	πρότερος, α, ον	πρῶτος, η, ον[5]
_[6]	ὕστερος	-
ὕψι (adverb)	-	ὕψιστος, η, ον

a-1a(2a)

Definition: Uncontracted stems using three endings (2-1-2) with the feminine in η and neuter in ον

nom sg	ἀγαθός	ἀγαθή	ἀγαθόν
gen sg	ἀγαθοῦ	ἀγαθῆς	ἀγαθοῦ
dat sg	ἀγαθῷ	ἀγαθῇ	ἀγαθῷ
acc sg	ἀγαθόν	ἀγαθήν	ἀγαθόν
voc sg	ἀγαθέ	ἀγαθή	ἀγαθόν
n/v pl	ἀγαθοί	ἀγαθαί	ἀγαθά
gen pl	ἀγαθῶν	ἀγαθῶν	ἀγαθῶν
dat pl	ἀγαθοῖς	ἀγαθαῖς	ἀγαθοῖς
acc pl	ἀγαθούς	ἀγαθάς	ἀγαθά

Comment

Every stem ends in a vowel. Preceding that vowel will be any letter except ε, ι, or ρ. The middle passive participle morpheme μενο/η belongs to this category (cf. §90).

---

[1]   Here is the paradigm of μείζων. The first column is masc./fem., the second neuter.

nom sg	μείζων	μεῖζον	*nom pl*	μείζονες, μείζους	μείζονα, μείζω
gen sg	μείζονος	μείζονος	*gen pl*	μειζόνων	μειζόνων
dat sg	μείζονι	μείζονι	*dat pl*	μείζοσι(ν)	μείζοσι(ν)
acc sg	μείζονα, μείζω	μεῖζον	*acc pl*	μείζονας, μείζους	μείζονα, μείζω

[2]   μείζων was losing its comparative force, so μειζότερος was used in its place (3 Jn 4).

[3]   Used as a comparative of μικρός.

[4]   From the superlative ἐλάχιστος was formed the comparative ἐλαχιστότερος, Eph 3:8.

[5]   πρῶτος is an a-1a(2a) adjective.

[6]   No positive degree.

Regularly formed superlative adjectives belong to this category. See the full discussion after a-1a(1) above. Following are all the regularly formed superlatives that occur in the New Testament: ἁγιώτατος, ἀκριβέστατος, κράτιστος, τιμιώτατος. For a listing of irregularly formed superlatives and a discussion of comparatives and superlatives in general see a-1a(1). All superlatives are followed with an asterisk below.

Listing   (total: 217)

ἀγαθός	ἀγαπητός	ἁγιώτατος*	ἁγνός	Ἀδραμυττηνός
αἱρετικός	ἀκάνθινος	ἀκριβέστατος*	Ἀλεξανδρῖνος	ἀληθινός
ἀλυκός	ἀμαράντινος	ἀνατολικός	ἀνθρώπινος	ἀνωτερικός
ἁπαλός	ἀργός	ἀρεστός	ἀρκετός	αὐτόματος
βασιλικός	βδελυκτός	βιωτικός	βύσσινος	Γαδαρηνός
Γαλατικός	γεννητός	Γερασηνός	Γεργεσηνός[1]	γνωστός
γραπτός	γυμνός	Δαμασκηνός	δειλός	δεινός
δέκατος	δεκτός	δερμάτινος	δῆλος	διδακτικός
διδακτός	διπλόος[2]	δυνατός	δωδέκατος	ἕβδομος
Ἑβραϊκός	ἐθνικός	εἰρηνικός	ἕκαστος	ἐκλεκτός
ἕκτος	ἐλάχιστος*	ἐλεεινός	ἐλεφάντινος	Ἑλληνικός
ἐμός	ἔνατος	ἑνδέκατος	ἐξουσιαστικός	ἐπαρχικός
ἑσπερινός	ἔσχατος	εὐλογητός	ζεστός	ἡλίκος
θαυμαστός	θνητός	θύϊνος	ἱκανός	Ἰουδαϊκός
ἱππικός	ἴσος	Ἰταλικός	καθημερινός	καθολικός
καινός	κακός	καλός	Καλοί Λιμένες[3]	καταμόνας[4]
κενός	κεραμικός	κλητός	κοινός	κοινωνικός
κόκκινος	κοσμικός	κράτιστος*	κρίθινος	κριτικός
κρυπτός	κυλλός	κυριακός	κωφός	λαξευτός
λειτουργικός	λεπτός	Λευιτικός	λευκοβύσσινος[5]	λευκός
λίθινος	λογικός	λοιπός	μαλακός	μέγας[6]
μέγιστος*[7]	μέσος[8]	μεστός	μόνος	μουσικός
μυλικός	μύλινος	μυλωνικός	Ναζαρηνός	νεωτερικός
νόθος	νομικός	ξένος	ξύλινος	ὄγδοος

---

[1]   Alternate form of Γερασηνός.

[2]   Uncontracted form of διπλοῦς (a-1b).

[3]   The "Fair Havens" harbor (Acts 27:8). We have also listed the two words separately (see καλός [a-1a(2a)] and λιμήν [n-3f(1b)]).

[4]   Our text has two words, κατὰ μόνας (Mk 4:10; Lk 9:18).

[5]   V.l. of βύσσινον λευκόν at Rev 19:14.

[6]   See discussion below.

[7]   Irregular superlative of μέγας.

[8]   The stem is *μεθ, to which is added ια to form the adjective (μεθια ‣ μεσο; §26.4).

ὀλίγος	ὅλος	ὀνικός	ὀπτός	ὀρατός
ὀργίλος	ὀρεινός	ὀρθός	ὀρθρινός	ὀρφανός
ὅσος	ὀστράκινος	παθητός	Πακατιανός	πάμπολυς[1]
παραλυτικός[2]	πατρικός	πεδινός	πεζός	πειθός[3]
πέμπτος	πεντεκαιδέκατος	περισσός	πηλίκος[4]	πιθός[5]
πιστικός	πιστός	πλαστός	πλεῖστος*[6]	πνευματικός
πνικτός	ποδαπός[7]	ποικίλος	πολύς[8]	Ποντικός
πόσος[9]	ποταπός	πρᾶος[10]	προβατικός	προφητικός
πρωϊνός	πρῶτος*[11]	πτωχός	πυκνός	πύρινος
Ῥωμαϊκός	σαρκικός	σάρκινος	σεβαστός	σεμνός
σηρικός[12]	σιδήρεος[13]	σιρικός	σιτευτός	σιτιστός
σκοτεινός	σμαράγδινος	σός	σοφός	στενός
Στοϊκός	στυγητός	Στωϊκός[14]	συνεκλεκτός	συνετός
συστατικός	σωματικός	τακτός	ταπεινός	ταχινός
τεσσαρεσκαιδέκατος	τέταρτος	τετρακόσιοι	τετραπλόος[15]	τιμιώτατος*
τομός	τρίτος	τρίχινος	τυφλός	τυφωνικός
ὑακίνθινος	ὑάλινος	ὑδρωπικός	ὑφαντός	ὑψηλός

---

[1] Cf. πολύς.

[2] Used only as a masculine noun (n-2a) in the N.T.

[3] πειθός is a difficult word. It occurs only at 1 Cor 2:4 either as πειθοῖς or πειθοῖ.

If it is the former as our texts have decided, then it is a dative plural from the second declension adjective πειθός, ή, όν (a-1a[2a]). If it is the latter, then it is a dative singular from the third declension noun πειθοῖ.

If it is a third declension noun, then it is the only example of a noun stem ending in οι in the N.T. Since our texts prefer the reading πειθοῖς, we have categorized the word as the adjective; however, the word is listed at n-3e(6) as well. See *BAGD* on πειθός, Funk §2021.2, and *BDF* §47.4 for a discussion and references.

[4] A correlative pronoun used in the N.T. as an interrogative (*BDF* §304). In Classical Greek, the feminine form was drawn from πραΰς. It seems to vacillate between being 3-1-3 and 3-3.

[5] Alternate form of πειθός.

[6] Irregular superlative of πολύς.

[7] An interrogative pronoun. Alternate form of ποταπός. ποδαπός does not occur in the N.T.

[8] See *Special Paradigms* below.

[9] An interrogative pronoun.

[10] In our literature it occurs only as a v.l. at Mt 11:29 (cf. πραΰς, a-2b). See Smyth §311.c for the full paradigm.

[11] Superlative formed from πρό.

[12] Alternate form of σιρικός.

[13] Uncontracted form of σιδηροῦς (a-1b).

[14] Alternate form of Στοϊκός.

[15] Uncontracted form of τετραπλοῦς (a-1b).

φαῦλος   φθαρτός   φθινοπωρινός   φίλος   φυσικός

φωτεινός   χαλεπός   χοϊκός   χρήσιμος   χρηστός

χωλός   ψυχικός

Special Paradigms

The stem of πολύς is *πολλ;[1] the stem of μέγας is *μεγαλ. Both are declined like
ἀγαθός (a-1a[2a]), except for the four cases underlined below that appear to be
third declension (cf. ταχύς, a-2b). In both words the stem simplifies by losing a λ.
In the nominative/accusative neuter, no case ending is used.

nom	<u>μέγας</u>	μεγάλη	<u>μέγα</u>	μεγάλοι	μεγάλαι	μεγάλα
gen	μεγάλου	μεγάλης	μεγάλου	μεγάλων	μεγάλων	μεγάλων
dat	μεγάλῳ	μεγάλῃ	μεγάλῳ	μεγάλοις	μεγάλαις	μεγάλοις
acc	<u>μέγαν</u>	μεγάλην	<u>μέγα</u>	μεγάλους	μεγάλας	μεγάλα

In the nominative/accusative singular, πολύ behaves as if Ϝ were added to the
abbreviated stem. It is therefore declined just like ταχύς (a-2b). *πολλ ▸ πολ + Ϝ +
σ ▸ πολύς. *πολλ ▸ πολ + Ϝ + ν ▸ πολύν. *πολλ ▸ πολ + Ϝ ▸ πολύ.

nom	<u>πολύς</u>	πολλή	<u>πολύ</u>	πολλοί	πολλαί	πολλά
gen	πολλοῦ	πολλῆς	πολλοῦ	πολλῶν	πολλῶν	πολλῶν
dat	πολλῷ	πολλῇ	πολλῷ	πολλοῖς	πολλαῖς	πολλοῖς
acc	<u>πολύν</u>	πολλήν	<u>πολύ</u>	πολλούς	πολλάς	πολλά

a-1a(2b)

Definition: Uncontracted stems using three endings (2-1-2) with the feminine in η and neuter in ο

nom sg	οὗτος	αὕτη	τοῦτο
gen sg	τούτου	ταύτης	τούτου
dat sg	τούτῳ	ταύτῃ	τούτῳ
acc sg	τοῦτον	ταύτην	τοῦτο
n/v pl	οὗτοι	αὗται	ταῦτα
gen pl	τούτων	τούτων	τούτων
dat pl	τούτοις	ταύταις	τούτοις
acc pl	τούτους	ταύτας	ταῦτα

---

[1]   Technically it is *πολϜο (Smyth §311.b).

Comment

These words are declined just like a-1a(2a) adjectives, except that in the nominative and accusative singular neuter they use o and not ov.

Listing (total: 17)

ἀλλήλων	ἄλλος	αὐτός[1]	ἑαυτοῦ [2]	ἐκεῖνος
ἐμαυτοῦ[3]	ὁ, ἡ, τό	ὅδε[4]	ὅς, ἥ, ὅ[5]	ὅσπερ[6]
ὅστις[7]	οὗτος[8]	σεαυτοῦ[9]	τηλικοῦτος[10]	τοιόσδε[11]
τοιοῦτος[12]	τοσοῦτος[12]			

Special Paradigms

The **definite article** is declined as follows. Basically, the article is the case endings plus and initial τ, except in the nominative where there can be rough breathing.

nom	ὁ	ἡ	τό	οἱ	αἱ	τά
gen	τοῦ	τῆς	τοῦ	τῶν	τῶν	τῶν
dat	τῷ	τῇ	τῷ	τοῖς	ταῖς	τοῖς
acc	τόν	τήν	τό	τούς	τάς	τά

---

[1] The key to differentiating between αὐτός and οὗτος is that the former always begins with αυ and smooth breathing.

[2] ἑαυτοῦ, ἧς, οὗ. Third person singular masculine and feminine, and plural of all genders, reflexive pronoun. A reflexive pronoun refers back to the subject and therefore can never occur in the nominative. In Classical Greek for the plural you find ἡμῶν αὐτῶν and ὑμῶν αὐτῶν for first and second person. These forms can still be seen in Hellenistic Greek (Funk §2570.3, BDF §288.1).

[3] ἐμαυτοῦ, ἧς. First person singular masculine and feminine reflexive pronoun. A reflexive pronoun refers back to the subject and therefore can never occur in the nominative. No neuter form.

[4] ὅδε, ἥδε, τόδε. The first element of the word is declined just like the definite article. The second part remains unchanged.

[5] See *Special Paradigms* below. ὅς γε can be written ὅσγε.

[6] The first part of the word declines just like the relative pronoun while the second half remains unchanged.

[7] See *Special Paradigms* below.

[8] Each form begins with either a τ or rough breathing. If the case ending has an o class vowel, there will be an o following the initial τ; if the case ending has an ε class vowel, there will be an α following the initial τ.

[9] σεαυτοῦ, ἧς. Second person singular, masculine and feminine, reflexive pronoun. A reflexive pronoun refers back to the subject and therefore can never occur in the nominative. No neuter form.

[10] Fluctuates between a-1a(2a) and a-1a(2b).

[11] τοιόσδε, τοιάδε, τοιόνδε. Declined like the relative pronoun except that it has α in the feminine instead of η. It occurs in the N.T. only once, at 2 Pet 1:17 in the genitive singular feminine τοιᾶσδε.

[12] Fluctuates between a-1a(2a) and a-1a(2b).

The **relative pronoun** always begins with rough breathing and always has an accent. Its stem is *σϝο (cf. §27.3).

nom	ὅς	ἥ	ὅ	οἵ	αἵ	ἅ
gen	οὗ	ἧς	οὗ	ὧν	ὧν	ὧν
dat	ᾧ	ᾗ	ᾧ	οἷς	αἷς	οἷς
acc	ὅν	ἥν	ὅ	οὕς	ἅς	ἅ

The first half of **ὅστις** declines just like the relative pronoun (a-1a[2b]) and the second half declines just like τίς (a-4b[2]). The neuter is often written ὅ τί in order to differentiate it from the conjunction ὅτι. We have listed it as an a-1a(2b) adjective because it functions as an indefinite relative. The genitive singular occurs, apparently in a second declension form, in the expression ἕως ὅτου five times in the New Testament.

nom	ὅστις	ἥτις	ὅτι	οἵτινες	αἵτινες	ἅτινα
gen	οὗτινος	ἧστινος	οὗτινος	ὧντινων	ὧντινων	ὧντινων
dat	ᾧτινι	ᾗτινι	ᾧτινι	οἷστισι(ν)	αἷστισι(ν)	οἷστισι(ν)
acc	ὅντινα	ἥντινα	ὅτι	οὕστινας	ἅστινας	ἅτινα

a-1b

Definition: Contract adjectives using three endings (2-1-2)

nom sg	ἁπλοῦς	ἁπλῆ	ἁπλοῦν
gen sg	ἁπλοῦ	ἁπλῆς	ἁπλοῦ
dat sg	ἁπλῷ	ἁπλῇ	ἁπλῷ
acc sg	ἁπλοῦν	ἁπλῆν	ἁπλοῦν
n/v pl	ἁπλοῖ	ἁπλαῖ	ἁπλᾶ
gen pl	ἁπλῶν	ἁπλῶν	ἁπλῶν
dat pl	ἁπλοῖς	ἁπλαῖς	ἁπλοῖς
acc pl	ἁπλοῦς	ἁπλᾶς	ἁπλᾶ

Comment

All the stems in this category actually end in εο or οο (e.g. *ἁπλεο + ς ⟩ ἁπλοῦς), evidently shifting to εα in the feminine (with εα ⟩ η in the singular and εα ⟩ α in the plural; cf. LaSor §22.211). The circumflex is evidence of the contraction. The only time you see a significant change due to contraction is in the nominative and accusative singular, masculine and neuter. See *MH* 156; Smyth §290.

In Koine Greek there is a class of contract adjectives whose stems end in ρε that therefore would make the final vowel in the feminine singular an α and not an η (πορφυροῦς, σιδηροῦς).

It is common to see texts switch between contracted and uncontracted forms of the same word (*BDF* §45). On accents see Smyth §56, §290.c. Many barytones in this category have a recessive accent (LaSor §212).

Listing   (total: 8)

ἁπλοῦς	ἀργυροῦς[1]	διπλοῦς	πορφυροῦς[2]	σιδηροῦς[3]
τετραπλοῦς	χαλκοῦς	χρυσοῦς[4]		

a-2 Adjectives

Definition: Adjectives using three endings (3-1-3)

a-2a   Stems ending in ν(τ)

a-2b   Stems ending in F

Comment

All these words have stems ending in a consonant (cf. a-4). The adjectives in this category use third declension case endings in the masculine and neuter, and first declension in the feminine. Unlike a-1 adjectives, the feminine can undergo the α ‣ η shift in the singular. See *MH* 158-161.

---

[1]   Contracted form of ἀργύρεος (a-1a[2a]).

[2]   Contracted form of πορφύρεος (a-3a), preferred in Attic, LXX, and Josephus (*BAGD*). Our texts use the contracted form as seen by the accent: πορφυροῦν.

[3]   Contracted form of σιδήρεος (a-1a[2a]).

[4]   Occurs as χρυσῆν (accusative singular feminine) in Rev 1:13. Uncontracted forms appear as variants at Rev 2:1 (χρυσέων), 4:4 (χρυσέους), and 5:8 (χρυσέας). χρυσᾶν (feminine singular) is found in Rev 1:13 instead of the usual χρυσῆν. *BAGD* says this is by analogy to ἀργυρᾶν (cf.*BDF* §45; *MH* 120-21).

a-2a

Definition:	Stems ending in ντ using three endings (3-1-3)		
nom sg	πᾶς[1]	πᾶσα[2]	πᾶν[3]
gen sg	παντός	πάσης	παντός
dat sg	παντί	πάσῃ	παντί
acc sg	πάντα	πᾶσαν	πᾶν
n/v pl	πάντες	πᾶσαι	πάντα
gen pl	πάντων	πασῶν	πάντων
dat pl	πᾶσι(ν)[1]	πάσαις	πᾶσι(ν)
acc pl	πάντας	πάσας	πάντα

Comment

The masculine is declined like n-2a, the feminine like n-1a, and the neuter like n-2c. To this category belongs the active participle morphemes ντ (ων, ουσα, ον; σας, σασα, σαν) and οτ (ως, υία, ος; §90). All the stems end in ντ except for εἷς and compounds, which end in ν. See Smyth on stems in ν (§298) and on stems in ντ (§299).

μέλας does not really belong in this category because its stem ends in ν, like a-4b(2) adjectives. However, unlike a-4b(2) adjectives that are 3-3, μέλας is a 3-1-3 adjective, so we placed it here.

ἄκων and ἑκών are actually from a different pattern (Smyth §235b, Funk §2370.1), but they are declined just like the present participle.

Listing   (total: 9)

ἄκων	ἅπας	εἷς, μία, ἕν[4]	ἑκών	μέλας[4]
μηδείς[5]	οὐδείς[6]	οὐθείς[7]	πᾶς	

---

[1]   The stem in the masculine/neuter is *παντ. The ντ disappears when followed immediately by the σ in the nominative singular and the dative plural, and the preceding vowel is lengthened in compensation for the loss of the ντ (§24.4c). *παντ + σ ‣ πανσ ‣ πας ‣ πᾶς. *παντ + σι ‣ πανσι ‣ πασι ‣ πᾶσι.

[2]   The stem of πᾶς is *παντ. The feminine adds ια to *παντ, τι forms σ (§26.10; Smyth §295), ν drops out before σ, the preceding vowel is lengthened in compensation (§24.4), and the adjective follows the first declension pattern (n-1c).

[3]   No ending is used in the nominative and accusative singular neuter. Since τ cannot stand at the end of a Greek word it is dropped (§19.1).

[4]   See *Special Paradigms* below.

[5]   μηδείς, μηδεμία, μηδέν. See the discussion of εἷς in *Special Paradigms* below.

[6]   οὐδείς, οὐδεμία, οὐδέν. See the discussion of εἷς in *Special Paradigms* below.

[7]   οὐθείς, οὐθεμία, οὐθέν. A later form of οὐδείς (οὐθενός; genitive singular masculine; twice), οὐθέν (five times). See the discussion of εἷς in *Special Paradigms* below.

Special Paradigms

εἷς, μία, ἕν.   The masculine and neuter use the stem *εν that loses the ν when the case ending σ is added. The ε lengthens to ει in compensation for the loss (§24.4). The feminine is formed from the stem *σμ that subsequently loses its initial σ (cf. §25.6), ια is added, which becomes μία.

nom sg	εἷς	μία	ἕν
gen sg	ἑνός	μιᾶς	ἑνός
dat sg	ἑνί	μιᾷ	ἑνί
acc sg	ἑνά	μίαν	ἕν

μέλας.   The stem of μέλας is *μελαν. In the nominative singular (masculine) and dative plural (masculine and neuter), the ν drops off because of the σ of the case ending (§24.4). In the nominative and accusative singular neuter no case ending is used. In the feminine the stem is altered by adding ι after the ν. The ι and ν undergo metathesis (§17), and the ι becomes ι. *μελαν + ι + α ‣ μελαινα ‣ μέλαινα. The neuter form μέλαν functions as a neuter noun (n-3f[1a]), and we have listed it as such.

nom	μέλας	μέλαινα	μέλαν	μέλανες	μέλαιναι	μέλανα
gen	μέλανος	μελαίνης	μέλανος	μελάνων	μελαινῶν	μελάνων
dat	μέλανι	μελαίνῃ	μέλανι	μέλασι(ν)	μελαίναις	μέλασι(ν)
acc	μέλανα	μέλαιναν	μέλαν	μέλανας	μελαίνας	μέλανα

a-2b

Definition: Stems ending in Ϝ using three endings (3-1-3)

nom sg	ταχύς	ταχεῖα	ταχύ[1]
gen sg	ταχέως[2]	ταχείας	ταχέως
dat sg	ταχεῖ	ταχείᾳ	ταχεῖ
acc sg	ταχύν	ταχεῖαν	ταχύ
n/v pl	ταχεῖς	ταχεῖαι	ταχέα
gen pl	ταχέων	ταχειῶν	ταχέων
dat pl	ταχέσι(ν)	ταχείαις	ταχέσι(ν)
acc pl	ταχεῖς	ταχείας	ταχέα

---

[1]   The nominative and accusative singular use no ending. We are left with basically the bare stem, and Ϝ has changed to vocalic υ.

[2]   The genitive singular is formed by analogy to n-3e(5b) nouns. The Attic εος can appear as a v.l. (*BDF* §46.3).

Comment

The stem ends in F. F changes to vocalic υ if the case ending begins with a consonant, to ε if the case ending begins with a vowel. The masculine is declined somewhat like πόλις (n-3e[5b]). The feminine stem is formed by adding ι to the stem *ταχF. F becomes ε (see above), and ει form ει: *ταχF + ι ‣ ταχει ‣ ταχει + α ‣ ταχεῖα (Funk §2300.2). See Smyth §296-297.

Listing (total: 13)

βαθύς	βαρύς	βραδύς	βραχύς	γλυκύς
εὐθύς[1]	ἥμισυς	θῆλυς	ὀξύς	πλατύς
πραΰς	ταχύς[2]	τραχύς		

a-3 Adjectives

Definition: Adjectives using two endings (2-2)

a-3a   Stems consistently using two endings

a-3b(1)   Stems alternating between two (2-2) and three (2-1-2) endings (feminine in α)

a-3b(2)   Stems alternating between two (2-2) and three (2-1-2) endings (feminine in η)

Comment

2-2 adjectives use the same set of endings for the masculine and feminine, and a different set of endings for the neuter. As always the masculine and neuter will have the same forms in the genitive and dative. See *MH* 156-158.

a-3a

Definition   Stems consistently using two endings (2-2)

	masculine/feminine	*neuter*
nom sg	ἁμαρτωλός	ἁμαρτωλόν
gen sg	ἁμαρτωλοῦ	ἁμαρτωλοῦ
dat sg	ἁμαρτωλῷ	ἁμαρτωλῷ
acc sg	ἁμαρτωλόν	ἁμαρτωλόν
voc sg	ἁμαρτωλέ	ἁμαρτωλόν

---

[1]   Not the adverb εὐθύς.

[2]   Its comparative is τάχιον and its superlative is τάχιστα.

n/v pl	ἁμαρτωλοί	ἁμαρτωλά
gen pl	ἁμαρτωλῶν	ἁμαρτωλῶν
dat pl	ἁμαρτωλοῖς	ἁμαρτωλοῖς
acc pl	ἁμαρτωλούς	ἁμαρτωλά

Comment

The masculine/feminine are declined like λόγος (n-2a) and the neuter like δῶρον (n-2c).

Listing   (total: 338)

ἀγαθοεργός	ἀγαθοποιός	ἀγενεαλόγητος	ἄγναφος	ἄγνωστος
ἀγοραῖος	ἀγράμματος	ἀδάπανος	ἄδηλος	ἀδιάκριτος
ἀδιάλειπτος	ἄδικος	ἀδόκιμος	ἄδολος	ἀδύνατος
ἄζυμος	ἀθέμιτος	ἄθεος	ἄθεσμος	ἀθῷος
ἀΐδιος	αἰφνίδιος	ἀκάθαρτος	ἄκακος	ἄκαρπος
ἀκατάγνωστος	ἀκατακάλυπτος	ἀκατάκριτος	ἀκατάλυτος	ἀκατάπαστος
ἀκατάπαυστος	ἀκατάστατος	ἀκατάσχετος	ἀκέραιος	ἄκρατος
ἀλάλητος	ἄλαλος	ἀλλόφυλος	ἄλογος	ἄλυπος
ἀμάραντος	ἀμάρτυρος	ἁμαρτωλός	ἄμαχος	ἄμεμπτος
ἀμέριμνος	ἀμετάθετος	ἀμετακίνητος	ἀμεταμέλητος	ἀμετανόητος
ἄμετρος	ἀμίαντος	ἀμώμητος	ἄμωμος	ἀναίτιος
ἄναλος	ἀναμάρτητος	ἀναντίρρητος	ἀνάξιος	ἀνάπειρος[1]
ἀνάπηρος[2]	ἀναπολόγητος	ἀναρίθμητος	ἀνέγκλητος	ἀνεκδιήγητος
ἀνεκλάλητος	ἀνέκλειπτος	ἀνεκτός	ἀνέλεος[3]	ἀνένδεκτος
ἀνεξεραύνητος[4]	ἀνεξίκακος	ἀνεξιχνίαστος	ἀνεπαίσχυντος	ἀνεπίλημπτος
ἀνεύθετος	ἀνήμερος	ἀνθρωπάρεσκος	ἄνιπτος	ἀνόητος
ἄνομος	ἀνόνητος[5]	ἀνόσιος	ἀντίτυπος	ἄνυδρος
ἀνυπόκριτος	ἀνυπότακτος	ἀόρατος	ἀπαίδευτος	ἀπαράβατος
ἀπαρασκεύαστος	ἀπείραστος	ἄπειρος	ἀπέραντος	ἀπερίτμητος
ἄπιστος	ἀπόβλητος	ἀπόδεκτος	ἀπόδημος	ἀπόκρυφος
ἀποσυνάγωγος	ἀπρόσιτος	ἀπρόσκοπος	ἄπταιστος	ἄραφος
ἄρρητος	ἄρρωστος	ἀρτιγέννητος	ἀρχιερατικός	ἀσάλευτος
ἄσβεστος	ἄσημος	ἄσιτος	ἄσοφος	ἄσπιλος
ἄσπονδος	ἀστήρικτος	ἄστοργος	ἀσύμφωνος	ἀσύνετος

---

[1]   Occurs at Lk 14:31 and 21. *BAGD* lists the alternate ἀνάπηρος as the preferred reading.

[2]   Alternate form of ἀνάπειρος.

[3]   Occurs at Jas 2:13, where T.R. reads ἀνίλεως (n-2e).

[4]   Can be spelled ἀνεξερεύνητος.

[5]   V.l. for ἀνόητος at 1 Tim 6:9.

ἀσύνθετος	ἄτακτος	ἄτεκνος	ἄτιμος	ἄτομος
ἄτοπος	αὐθαίρετος	αὐτοκατάκριτος	αὐτόφωρος	ἄφαντος
ἄφθαρτος	ἀφιλάγαθος	ἀφιλάργυρος	ἄφωνος	ἀχάριστος
ἀχειροποίητος	ἀχρεῖος	ἄχρηστος	ἄψυχος	βάρβαρος
βαρύτιμος	βασίλειος	βέβηλος	βλάσφημος	βοηθός
βρώσιμος	γενέθλιος	γνώριμος	δευτερόπρωτος	διάβολος
διάφορος	δίγαμος	διθάλασσος	δίλογος	δίστομος
δίψυχος	δόκιμος	δυσβάστακτος	δυσερμήνευτος	δύσκολος
δυσνόητος	ἔγγυος[1]	ἐγκάθετος	ἔγκυος	εἰδωλόθυτος
εἰρηνοποιός	ἔκγονος	ἔκδηλος	ἔκδικος	ἔκδοτος
ἔκθαμβος	ἔκθετος	ἔκτρομος	ἔκφοβος	ἔμφοβος
ἔμφυτος	ἐνάλιος	ἔνδικος	ἔνδοξος	ἔννομος
ἔννυχος	ἔνοχος	ἔντιμος	ἔντρομος	ἔξυπνος
ἐπάρατος	ἐπάρχειος	ἐπαυτόφωρος[2]	ἐπίγειος	ἐπιθανάτιος
ἐπικατάρατος	ἐπίλοιπος	ἐπίορκος	ἐπιούσιος	ἐπιπόθητος
ἐπίσημος	ἐπουράνιος	ἔρημος[3]	ἑτερόγλωσσος	εὐάρεστος
εὔθετος	εὔθυμος	εὔκαιρος	εὔκοπος	εὐμετάδοτος
εὐπάρεδρος	εὐπερίσπαστος	εὐπερίστατος	εὐπρόσδεκτος	εὐπρόσεδρος
εὐρύχωρος	εὔσημος	εὔσπλαγχνος	εὔφημος	εὐχάριστος
εὔχρηστος	εὐώνυμος	ἐφήμερος	ἤρεμος	ἡσύχιος
θανάσιμος	θανατηφόρος	θεοδίδακτος	θεοδίδακτος	θεομάχος
θεόπνευστος	θρησκός	ἱερόθυτος	ἰσάγγελος	ἰσότιμος
ἰσόψυχος	κακοποιός	κακοῦργος	καλοδιδάσκαλος	καρποφόρος
κατάδηλος	κατάλαλος	κατάλοιπος	καταχθόνιος	κατείδωλος
κενόδοξος	λιθόστρωτος	μακροχρόνιος	ματαιολόγος	μελίσσιος
μεμψίμοιρος	μέτοχος	μογγιλάλος[4]	μογιλάλος	μονόφθαλμος
νεόφυτος	οἰκουργός	οἰκουρός[5]	ὀκταήμερος	ὀλέθριος
ὀλιγόπιστος	ὀλιγόψυχος	ὁλόκληρος	ὁμότεχνος	οὐράνιος
ὄψιμος	πανοῦργος	παράδοξος	παράλιος	παράσημος
παρείσακτος	παρεπίδημος	πάροικος	πάροινος	
πατροπαράδοτος	περίεργος	περίλυπος	περίοικος	περιούσιος
περίχωρος[6]	πλάνος	πολύλαλος	πολυποίκιλος	πολύσπλαγχνος

---

[1] *BAGD* lists it as an adjective (ἔγγυος, ον; a-3a) used only as a noun in the N.T. (Heb 7:22). This is its only occurrence in the N.T.

[2] ἐπαυτοφώρῳ (Jn 8:4 v.l.) is from the adjective ἐπαυτόφωρος, ον, "(caught) in the act." See *BAGD* on αὐτόφωρος.

[3] ἔρημος is frequently used as a feminine noun (n-2b).

[4] Alternate form of μογιλάλος, used as a v.l. at Mk 7:32.

[5] Alternate form of οἰκουργός.

[6] Predominantly used as a substantive, often with an understood γῆ.

πολυεύστλαγχνος	πολύτιμος	πορφύρεος[1]	ποταμοφόρητος	πρόγονος
πρόδηλος	πρόδρομος	πρόθυμος	πρόϊμος	πρόσκαιρος
πρόσπεινος	πρόσφατος	πρώϊμος[2]	πρωτότοκος	σητόβρωτος
σκληροτράχηλος	σκωληκόβρωτος	σπερμολόγος	σπόριμος	συγκληρονόμος
συμμέτοχος	σύμμορφος	σύμφορος	σύμφυτος	σύμφωνος
σύμψυχος	σύντροφος[3]	σύσσωμος	σωτήριος	ταλαίπωρος
τετράγωνος	τετράμηνος	τρίμηνος	ὕπανδρος	ὑπέρακμος
ὑπερήφανος	ὑπέρογκος	ὑπήκοος	ὑπόδικος	φιλάγαθος
φιλάδελφος	φίλανδρος	φιλάργυρος	φίλαυτος	φιλήδονος
φιλόθεος	φιλόνεικος[4]	φιλόξενος	φιλόστοργος	φιλότεκνος
φλύαρος	φρόνιμος	φωσφόρος	χειροποίητος	
χρυσοδακτύλιος	ψευδολόγος	ψευδώνυμος	ὠφέλιμος	

a-3b

In this category are adjectives with stems alternating between two (2-2) and three (2-1-2) endings. The subcategories are determined by whether the feminine ends in α (a-3b[1]) or η (a-3b[2]). These adjectives are often written in lexicons with the feminine in brackets to indicate the possibility of fluctuation (e.g., αἰώνιος, (α), ον).

a-3b(1)

Definition: Stems alternating between two (2-2) and three (2-1-2) endings (feminine in α)

Comment

Stems in this category may be declined just like the a-3a pattern, or at times they may use a separate form in the feminine. In this case, the feminine will be declined like ἁγία (a-1a[1]), retaining the α all the way through the singular.

Listing   (total: 5)

αἰώνιος	ἑδραῖος	κόσμιος	οἰκεῖος	παρόμοιος

---

[1]   Uncontracted form of πορφυροῦς (a-1b). See discussion there.
[2]   Alternate form of πρόϊμος.
[3]   Can also be a masculine noun (n-2a).
[4]   *BAGD* list as φιλόν(ε)ικος. In the N.T. it occurs only at 1 Cor 11:16, spelled in our texts with the ε.

a-3b(2)

Definition: Stems alternating between two (2-2) and three (2-1-2) endings (feminine in η)

Comment

Stems in this category may be declined just like the a-3a pattern, or at times they may use a separate form in the feminine. In this case, the feminine will be declined like ἀγαθή (a-1a[2a]), retaining the η all the way through the feminine singular.

Listing   (total: 3)

ἕτοιμος   πτηνός   σκυθρωπός

a-4 Adjectives

Definition: Adjectives using two endings (3-3)

a-4a	Stems ending in ες
a-4b	Stems ending in (o)ν
a-4b(1)	Stems ending in oν
a-4b(2)	Stems ending in ν
a-4c	Miscellaneous 3-3 stems

Comments

Adjectives in this category use one set of endings when they modify a masculine or a feminine word, and another set of endings when they modify a neuter word. In both cases they follow third declension noun patterns since all the stems end in a consonant (cf. a-2). See *MH* 161-162.

ἵλεως, ων is a 3-3 adjective, but we have listed it as a-5a. See there for reasons.

a-4a

Definition: Stems ending in ες

	masculine/feminine	*neuter*
nom sg	ἀληθής[1]	ἀληθές[2]
gen sg	ἀληθοῦς	ἀληθοῦς
dat sg	ἀληθεῖ	ἀληθεῖ
acc sg	ἀληθῆ[3]	ἀληθές
nom pl	ἀληθεῖς	ἀληθῆ
gen pl	ἀληθῶν	ἀληθῶν
dat pl	ἀληθέσι(ν)[4]	ἀληθέσι(ν)
acc pl	ἀληθεῖς	ἀληθῆ

Comment

The stems in this category all end in εσ. This means that when a case ending is added which begins with a vowel, the σ becomes intervocalic, drops out, and the final stem vowel contracts with the initial vowel of the case ending (§25.5). For example, ἀληθεσ + ος ‣ ἀληθεος ‣ ἀληθοῦς.

In the masculine/feminine, these words are declined like Σωσθένης (n-3d[2a]); in the neuter like γένος (n-3d[2b]), except in the nominative and accusative singular.

Listing   (total: 66)

ἀβαρής	ἀγενής	αἰσχροκερδής	ἀκλινής	ἀκρατής
ἀκριβής	ἀληθής	ἀλλογενής	ἀλυσιτελής	ἀμαθής
ἀνωφελής	ἀπειθής	ἀσεβής	ἀσθενής	ἀσφαλής
αὐθάδης	αὐτάρκης	ἀφανής	ἀψευδής	γραώδης
δαιμονιώδης	διαυγής	διαφανής	διετής	διηνεκής
διοπετής	ἐγκρατής	εἰλικρινής	ἑκατονταετής	ἐκτενής
ἐμφανής	ἐναργής	ἐνδεής	ἐνεργής	ἐπιεικής
ἐπισφαλής	ἐπιφανής	εὐγενής	εὐλαβής	εὐπειθής
εὐσεβής	ἡμιθανής	θειώδης	θεοσεβής	θεοστυγής
ἱεροπρεπής	μεγαλοπρεπής	μονογενής	ὁλοτελής	ὁμοιοπαθής
παντελής	περικρατής	πετρώδης	πλήρης[5]	ποδήρης

---

[1] No ending is used, and the final stem vowel undergoes ablaut (ε ‣ η; §4).

[2] No ending is used in the nominative or accusative singular but the final stem vowel is not altered, differentiating the masculine/feminine from the neuter.

[3] ἀληθες + α ‣ ἀληθεα ‣ ἀληθῆ.

[4] In all three genders the σ of the stem and the σ of the case ending simplify (§25.1).

[5] πλήρης is sometimes indeclinable, normally when it would be in the genitive.

πολυτελής   πρηνής   προπετής   προσφιλής   συγγενής[1]
συμπαθής   τεσσερακονταετής   τεσσερακονταετής[2]
τρεῖς[3]   ὑγιής   ψευδής

Special Paradigms

τρεῖς. The stem *τρεσ is declined as follows. It uses ες in both the nominative and accusative masculine/feminine.

nom pl	τρεῖς	τρία
gen pl	τριῶν	τριῶν
dat pl	τρισί(ν)[4]	τρισί(ν)
acc pl	τρεῖς	τρία

a-4b(1)

Definition: Stems ending in ον

nom sg	ἄφρων[5]	ἄφρον[6]
gen sg	ἄφρονος	ἄφρονος
dat sg	ἄφρονι	ἄφρονι
acc sg	ἄφρονα	ἄφρον
nom pl	ἄφρονες	ἄφρονα
gen pl	ἀφρόνων	ἀφρόνων
dat pl	ἄφροσι(ν)[7]	ἄφροσι(ν)
acc pl	ἄφρονας	ἄφρονα

Comment

The masculine/feminine are declined like ἡγεμών (n-3f[1b]); the neuter as well except for the nominative and accusative. The vowel is in its strong grade in the nominative singular, and its weak grade elsewhere (cf. n-3f[1b]).

---

[1]   In our literature only used substantivally.

[2]   Alternate form of τεσσερακονταετής. In our texts always occurs as "τεσσε-" (Acts 7:23, 13:18).

[3]   See *Special Paradigms* below.

[4]   The σ of the stem and the σ of the case ending simplify (§25.1).

[5]   No ending is used, and the final stem vowel undergoes ablaut (ο › ω; §4).

[6]   No ending is used in the nominative/accusative singular but the final stem vowel is not altered, differentiating the masculine/feminine from the neuter.

[7]   The σ of the stem and the σ of the case ending simplify (§25.1).

This category includes comparatives in (ι)ων. See the discussion of comparatives at a-1a(1). Comparatives are included below and followed with an asterisk.

Listing   (total: 26)

ἀνελεήμων	ἀσχήμων	ἄφρων	βελτίων*	δεισιδαίμων
ἑκατον	ταπλασίων	ἐλάσσων*	ἐλάττων¹	ἐλεήμων
ἐπιστήμων	ἑπταπλασίων	εὐσχήμων	ἥσσων*	ἥττων²
κρείσσων*³	κρείττων*⁴	μείζων*⁵	οἰκτίρμων	ὁμόφρων
πλείων*⁶	πολλαπλασίων	σώφρων	ταπεινόφρων	φιλόφρων
χείρων*				

a-4b(2)

Definition: Stems ending in ν

nom sg	τίς⁷	τί⁸
gen sg	τίνος	τίνος
dat sg	τίνι	τίνι
acc sg	τίνα	τί
nom pl	τίνες	τίνα
gen pl·	τίνων	τίνων
dat pl	τίσι(ν)⁹	τίσι(ν)
acc pl	τίνας	τίνα

---

1   Alternate form of ἐλάσσων.

2   Alternate form of ἥσσων.

3   See κρείττων.

4   Appears as both κρείττων and κρείσσων, from the stem *κρατυ. In the formation of the comparative, different Greek dialects developed the word differently, thus resulting in two possible spellings in the Koine: κρείσσων (four times), κρείττων (fifteen times).

5   The paradigm of μείζων is given on p. 221.

6   Comparative of πολύς. Has an alternate contracted form πλέων, πλέον (ειω · εω; Lk 3:13; Jn 21:15; Acts 15:28). Cf. *BDF* §30.2, *MH* 82.

7   The final stem ν drops out when immediately followed by a σ (§24.4).

8   No ending is used in the nominative/accusative singular, and the ν drops off since it cannot stand at the end of a Greek word (§19.1). Funk (§1510.1) says the stem in these places is *τι; we assume he means *τιν modified to *τι because there is no ending.

9   The final stem ν drops out when immediately followed by a σ (§24.4).

Comments

See μέλας (*μελαν) at a-2a and εἷς at a-2a.

Listing (total: 2)

τίς[1]   τὶς[2]

a-4c

Definition: Miscellaneous 3-3 stems

nom sg	ἄρσην	ἄρσεν
gen sg	ἄρσενος	ἄρσενος
dat sg	ἄρσενι	ἄρσενι
acc sg	ἄρσενα	ἄρσεν
nom pl	τέσσαρες	τέσσαρα
gen pl	τεσσάρων	τεσσάρων
dat pl	τέσσαρσι(ν)	τέσσαρσι(ν)
acc pl	τέσσαρας[3]	τέσσαρα

Comments

τέσσαρες does not occur in the singular but is much more common that ἄρσην, so we have mixed the paradigms.

BAGD lists ἀμήτωρ, genitive -ορος, without further indication. Funk (§2370.41) and Smyth (§291a) list it as ἀμήτωρ, ορ, genitive ορος. They also list ἀπάτωρ, ορ, genitive ορος. *MH* (162) lists as "Miscellaneous (Mainly One Termination)." Smyth (§312) lists as "Adjectives of one ending." The stems evidently end in ρ (cf. n-3c[6b] nouns). They retain ρ outside the nominative, unlike ὕδωρ (n-3c[6b]). Each word occurs only once, in the nominative singular, at Heb 7:3.

Listing (total: 5)

ἀμήτωρ, ορος   ἀπάτωρ, ορος   ἄρρην, εν[4]   ἄρσην, εν[5]   τέσσαρες[6]

---

[1] Interrogative pronoun. Will always have the accent on the first syllable.

[2] Indefinite pronoun (enclitic). Usually loses its accent to the following word. When it does have an accent, it is a grave on the last syllable. Apart from accent, it is identical in form to the interrogative pronoun.

[3] Sometimes you will find τέσσαρες (cf. τρεῖς, *BDF* §46.2).

[4] *ἀρρη. Alternate form of ἄρσην.

[5] *ἀρσε. In the nominative singular the ε undergoes ablaut to η; elsewhere the weak grade ε shows. It does not have a consonant stem like the other a-4 adjectives.

[6] τέσσαρ.

a-5 Adjectives

a-5a   Irregular stems
a-5b   Indeclinable stems

a-5a

Definition: Irregular stems

nom	δύο[1]	ἵλεως		
gen	δύο	-		
dat	δυσί	-		
acc	δύο	-		
nom sg	ἐγώ[2]	-	σύ[3]	-
gen sg	ἐμοῦ	μου[4]	σοῦ	σου[5]
dat sg	ἐμοί	μοι	σοί	σοι
acc sg	ἐμέ	με	σέ	σε
nom pl	ἡμεῖς[6]		ὑμεῖς[7]	
gen pl	ἡμῶν		ὑμῶν	
dat pl	ἡμῖν		ὑμῖν	
acc pl	ἡμᾶς		ὑμᾶς	

Comments

These stems are not easily classified.

---

[1]   δύο is only partially inflected and occurs only in the plural.

[2]   From a different stem than the oblique cases.

[3]   Developed from *τϝε.

[4]   These are the "unemphatic" forms. They are written without accents because they are enclitics and are therefore pronounced with the word that follows.

[5]   See footnote on μου.

[6]   The singular and plural forms are derived from different stems. ἡμεῖς appears to be third declension.

[7]   The singular and plural forms are derived from different stems. Probably developed from *ϝυμ or *ϝυσμ (LaSor §23.141). ὑμεῖς appears to be third declension.

Listing (total: 9)

ἀνίλεως¹	ἅρπαξ²	δύο	ἐγώ	Ἑλληνίς³
ἡμεῖς	ἵλεως⁴	σύ	ὑμεῖς	

a-5b

Definition: Indeclinable stems

Comments

Greek can use the alphabet as numbers; alpha is "one," beta is "two," etc. When they are written, the letter can be followed by the prime mark, αʹ, to show that it is acting as a number. We listed the numbers up through "8" (η). (The number "7" is referred to by the stigma ("ϛ"). The Nestle text uses capital letters and the prime mark in book titles. The *UBS* does not include the prime mark. The numerals are listed on pp. 247f.

Listing (total: 34)

αʹ	βʹ	γʹ	δʹ	δέκα
δεκαδύο⁵	δεκαοκτώ	δεκαπέντε	δεκατέσσαρες	δώδεκα
εʹ⁶	ἑβδομήκοντα	ἑβδομηκοντάκις	εἴκοσι	ἑκατόν

---

1   ἵλεως, ων, genitive ω. An adjective of the Attic declension. See ἵλεως. Alternate form of ἀνέλεος (a-3a) used as a v.l. in Jas 2:13 in T.R. as a nominative.

2   *BAGD* lists ἅρπαξ, αγος, as an adjective (but does not show a feminine or neuter form). It occurs in the N.T. as an adjective at Mt 7:15 in the expression λύκοι ἅρπαγες, "ravenous wolves" (cf. Gen 49:27 and similar references in LS). Elsewhere in the N.T. it is used as a masculine substantive meaning "robber" (ἅρπαγες, Lk 18:11, 1 Cor 6:10; ἅρπαξιν, 1 Cor 5:10; ἅρπαξ, 1 Cor 5:11).

   It is declined as a velar stem. LS says it can be declined as an adjective in all three genders but is used mostly as a substantive. It did not fit neatly into any category, so we have listed it here. Smyth (§312) lists it as an adjective of one ending (masculine and feminine use the same form) where the neuter can occur in the oblique cases.

3   *BAGD* lists it initially as an adjective occurring in Acts 17:12 (τῶν Ἑλληνίδων γυναικῶν) and as a feminine substantive (Ἑλληνίς; Mk 7:26). *BAGD* list it as Ἑλληνις, ίδος, ἡ.

4   This is the one example in the N.T. of an adjective from the "Attic" declension; ἀνίλεως does not occur in the N.T. (See n-2e for nouns of the Attic declensions and Smyth §237, Funk §2370.2, *BDF* §44.1, *MH* 121.) From the stem *ιλην, which underwent "transfer of quality" (§7.7) in which the long η became its short ε and the short o became its long ω. It appears in the N.T. only as ἵλεως, in Heb 8:12 and Mt 16:22. It is a 3-3 adjective.

   ἀνίλεως is also an adjective of the Attic declension; it is listed in Bauer but does not occur in the N.T. Has a neuter form in ων. ω is short for accent purposes.

5   Alternate form for δώδεκα.

6   Used for the numeral "5" as a v.l. at Acts 19:9.

ἕνδεκα	ἐνενήκοντα	ἐννέα	ἕξ	ἑξήκοντα
ἑπτά	ζ′[1]	ιβ′[2]	ὀγδοήκοντα	ὀκτώ
πέντε	πεντήκοντα	τέσσαρες	τεσσαράκοντα[3]	τέσσαρες
τεσσεράκοντα[4]	τριάκοντα	χξς′[5]	῝Ω[6]	

Pronouns

Following is a list of pronouns drawn from Funk (§255 - 273; cf. Smyth §325 - 340, BDF §64, MH 178-182).

Pronouns

Personal	ἐγώ (ἡμεῖς)
	σύ (ὑμεῖς)
	αὐτός, ή, ό[7]
Reflexive[8]	ἐμαυτοῦ, ῆς
	σεαυτοῦ, ῆς
	ἑαυτοῦ, ῆς, οῦ[9]
Reciprocal	ἀλλήλων

Pronominal adjectives

Identity	αὐτός, αὐτή, αὐτό		
Possessive	ἐμός, ή, όν	Relative	ὅς, ἥ, ὅ
	σός, σή, σόν		ὅστις, ἥτις, ὅ τι
	ἡμέτερος, α, ον		ὅσος, η, ον
	ὑμέτερος, α, ον		οἷος, α, ον
	ἴδιος, α, ον		ὁποῖος, α, ον
	ἀλλότριος, α, ον		ἡλίκος, η, ον

---

[1] ζ is used for the numeral "7" as v.l. at Rev 13:18. The stigma is used for "6." See χξς′.

[2] Abbreviation for the number "twelve." Our texts have δώδεκα.

[3] Alternate form of τεσσεράκοντα.

[4] See *BAGD*.

[5] The number "666" in Rev 13:18 in T.R. for ἑξακόσιοι (χ′) ἑξήκοντα (ξ′) ἕχ (ς′). See "Comments" to the n-3g(2) discussion on numbers.

[6] *UBS* has no accent; *UBS* adds ῾. Cf. Rev 1:8 (v.l. 11); 21:6; 22:13.

[7] Functions as the personal, intensive, and identity pronouns.

[8] Because reflexive pronouns refer back to the subject, there is no nominative form.

[9] Functions as the reflexive pronoun for third person singular, and all persons in the plural.

Interrogative	τίς, τί	Indefinite[1]	τις, τι
	πόσος, η, ον		ἄλλος, η, ο
	ποῖος, α, ον		ἕτερος, α, ον
	πηλίκος, η, ον		ἕκαστος, η, ον
	ποταπός, ή, όν		ἑκάτερος, α, ον
	πότερος, α, ον[2]		ἀμφότεροι, αι, α
			πολύς, πολλή, πολύ
			ὁ δεῖνα[3]
Demonstrative	ὁ, ἡ, τό		
	οὗτος, αὕτη, τοῦτο		
	ἐκεῖνος, η, ο		
	ὅδε, ἥδε, τόδε		
	τοσοῦτος, τοσαύτη, τοσοῦτο(ν)		
	τοιοῦτος, τοιαύτη, τοιοῦτο(ν)		
	τηλικοῦτος, τηλικαύτη, τηλικοῦτο(ν)		
	τοιόσδε, τοιάδε, τοιόνδε		

Adverbs

Following is a list of adverbs. Comparatives and superlatives are in the second list. The line of distinction between adverbs and other forms of speech can often be difficult to draw. For example, is μόνον the accusative neuter of μόνος functioning adverbially, or has it become set as an adverb? If not μόνον, then how about πρῶτον or ὕστερον?

Following this list we have listed forms that can function adverbially, most of them being accusative neuter. The third list includes comparative and superlative forms that are not normally listed in lexicons.

Forms followed by as asterisk can also function as an improper preposition in the New Testament.[4] On adverbs see *MH* 164-167, *BDF* §102-106, Smyth §341-346, Robertson, 293-303.

---

[1] τις is a true indefinite. The others can function as indefinite pronouns.

[2] Occurs only in the fixed form πότερον.

[3] The Classical indefinite.

[4] Funk (§1400) defines proper prepositions as those that can be compounded with verbs, and improper prepositions as those that never are compounded with verbs and in fact border on adverbs.

Adverbs of the positive degree   (total: 266)

ἀγνῶς	ἀδήλως	ἀδιαλείπτως	ἀδίκως	ἀεί
αἰσχροκερδῶς	ἀκαίρως	ἀκμήν	ἀκριβῶς	ἀκωλύτως
ἀληθῶς	ἀλλαχόθεν	ἀλλαχοῦ	ἄλλως	ἅμα*
ἀμέμπτως	ἀναγκαστῶς	ἀναντιρρήτως	ἀναξίως*	ἀνόμως
ἄντικρυς*	ἀντιπέρα*	ἄνω	ἄνωθεν	ἀνώτερον
ἀξίως	ἅπαξ	ἀπαρτί	ἀπερισπάστως	ἁπλῶς
ἀποτόμως	ἀπροσωπολήμπτως	ἄρτι	ἀσμένως	ἆσσον
ἀσφαλῶς	ἀσώτως	ἀτάκτως	αὔριον	αὐτοῦ
ἄφνω	ἀφόβως	βαρέως	γνησίως	δεινῶς
δεῦρο	δεῦτε	δηλαυγῶς	δήποτε	δήπου
δικαίως	δίς	δυσκόλως	δωρεάν	Ἑβραϊστί
ἐγγύς*	ἐθνικῶς	εἰκῇ	εἶτα	ἑκάστοτε
ἐκεῖ	ἐκεῖθεν	ἐκεῖσε	ἑκουσίως	ἔκπαλαι
ἐκπερισσῶς	ἐκτενῶς	ἐκτός*	Ἑλληνιστί	ἔμπροσθεν*
ἐνθάδε	ἔνθεν	ἐνίοτε	ἐννόμως	ἐντεῦθεν
ἐξαίφνης	ἐξάπινα	ἐξαυτῆς	ἐξέφνης	ἑξῆς
ἔξω*	ἔξωθεν*	ἐπάναγκες	ἐπάνω*	ἐπαύριον
ἔπειτα	ἐπέκεινα*[1]	ἐπιμελῶς	ἑπτάκις	ἐσχάτως
ἔσω*	ἔσωθεν	ἑτέρως	ἔτι	ἑτοίμως
εὖ	εὐαρέστως	εὖγε	εὐθέως	εὐθύμως
εὐθύς	εὐκαίρως	εὐσεβῶς	εὐσχημόνως	εὐτόνως
ἐφάπαξ	ἐχθές	ἤ	ἡδέως	ἤδη
Ἰουδαϊκῶς	ἴσως	καθεξῆς	καθό	καθόλου
καθώς	καθώσπερ	κακῶς	καλῶς	κατέναντι*
κατενώπιον*	κάτω	κενῶς	κρυφῇ	κυκλόθεν
κύκλῳ*[2]	λάθρα	λαμπρῶς	λίαν	Λυκαονιστί
μακράν	μακρόθεν	μακροθύμως	μάτην	μεγάλως
μεταξύ*	μετέπειτα	μετρίως	μηδαμῶς[3]	μηδέποτε
μηδέπω	μηθαμῶς	μηκέτι	μήπω	μόγις
μόλις	νομίμως	νουνεχῶς	νῦν[4]	νυνί
ὅθεν	ὀλίγως	ὅλως	ὁμοθυμαδόν	ὁμοίως
ὁμολογουμένως	ὁμόσε	ὁμοῦ	ὅμως	ὄντως

---

[1]   *BAGD* say it is an adverb that is followed by the genitive. Others list it as an improper preposition.

[2]   In the N.T. κύκλῳ is always used as an improper preposition.

[3]   Has an alternate form μαθαμῶς, which does not occur in the N.T.

[4]   The neuter plural form of the article τά can be written with νῦν as τανῦν (Acts 20:32; 27:22).

ὄπισθεν*	ὀπίσω*[1]	ὅπως[2]	ὀρθῶς	ὁσάκις
ὁσίως	οὗ	οὐ[3]	οὐδαμῶς	οὐδέποτε
οὐδέπω	οὐκέτι	οὐκοῦν	οὔπω	οὐρανόθεν
οὔτε	οὕτως[4]	οὐχί	ὀψέ*	παιδιόθεν
παιδόθεν	πάλαι	πάλιν	παμπληθεί	πανοικεί
πανταχῇ	πανταχόθεν	πανταχοῦ	πάντῃ	πάντοθεν
πάντοτε	πάντως	παραπλησίως	παραυτίκα	παραχρῆμα
παρεκτός*	πεζῇ	πεντάκις	πέραν*	πέριξ
περισσοτέρως	περισσῶς	πέρυσι	πικρῶς	πλήν*
πλησίον*	πλουσίως	πνευματικῶς	πόθεν	πολλάκις
πολυμερῶς	πολυτρόπως	πόρρω*	πόρρωθεν	ποσάκις
ποταπῶς	πότε	ποῦ	πού	προθύμως
προσφάτως	πρωΐ	πρώτως	πώποτε	ῥητῶς
ῥοιζηδόν	Ῥωμαϊστί	σήμερον	σιωπῇ[5]	σπουδαίως
συντόμως	σφόδρα	σφοδρῶς	σχεδόν	σωματικῶς
σωφρόνως	τάχα	ταχέως	ταχύ	τελείως
τηλαυγῶς	τηνικαῦτα	τολμηροτέρως	τότε	τρίς
τυπικῶς	ὑπεράνω*	ὑπερβαλλόντως	ὑπερέκεινα*	ὑπερεκπερισσοῦ
ὑπερεκπερισσῶς	ὑπερλίαν	ὑπερπερισσῶς	ὑποκάτω*	φανερῶς
φειδομένως	φιλανθρώπως	φιλοφρόνως	φρονίμως	φυσικῶς
χαμαί	χθές	χωρίς*	ὧδε	ὡς
ὡσαύτως				

The following are forms that can function adverbially, most of them being accusative neuter. Sometimes you will find them listed as adverbs.

ἀνεκτότερον	βράχυ	δεύτερον	διπλοῦν	δωρεαν[6]
ἔννυχα	ἐνάντιον*	ἔσχατον	ἴδιος[7]	ἴσα
λοιπόν	μακρά	μέσον	μηδέν	μικρόν
μόνον†	ὀλίγον	παραπλήσιον	ἐν παρρησίᾳ	περισσόν
πολύ	πόσῳ	πρότερον	πρῶτον	πυκνά
τετραπλοῦν	τρίτον	ὑπέρ[8]	ὕστερον†	

---

[1] τὸ ὀπίσω can be written as τοὔπισω, but not in the N.T.

[2] Can function as a conjunction.

[3] Including the alternate forms οὐχ and οὐκ.

[4] οὕτως is written in the N.T. with the movable ς 204 times. It is written as οὕτω without the movable ς four times (§6.7).

[5] Formed from the dative of σιωπή.

[6] This is the only feminine in the group; all the others are neuter.

[7] Infrequently used adverbially.

[8] This preposition functions adverbially at 2 Cor 11:23.

Comparatives and superlatives

Many are not listed in lexicons. Some are accusative neuter forms functioning adverbially.

ἀκριβέστερον	ἀνώτερον	βέλτιον	διπλότερον	ἐγγύτερον†
ἐκτενέστερον	ἔλαττον	ἥδιστα†	ἧσσον	κάλλιον†
κατωτέρω†	κομψότερον†	κρεῖσσον	μάλιστα	μᾶλλον†
μεῖζον	μέσον	περαιτέρω†	περισσότερον	πλεῖον
πλείων	πλέον	πορρώτερον¹	πορρωτέρω²	πυκνότερον
σπουδαιοτέρως	τάχιον†	τάχιστα†	τολμηρότερον†	

Particles

ἀλλά	ἀμήν	ἄν	ἄρα	ἆρα
γέ³	δέ	δή	ἐάνπερ	εἰ
εἴπερ	εἴπως	εἴτε	ἤ	ἡνίκα
ἤπερ	ἤτοι	καίτοι	καίτοιγε	μέν
μενοῦν	μενοῦνγε	μέντοι	μή	μηδέ⁴
μήν	μήποτε⁵	μήτι	ναί	νή
ὁπότε	ὅπου	ὅταν	ὅτε	οὖν
ὄφελον⁶	περ	ποτέ	πότερον⁷	πῶς
πώς	τέ	τοιγαροῦν	τοίνυν	ὡσάν
ὡσεί	ὥσπερ	ὡσπερεί	ὥστε	

Conjunctions

A † means that the word is listed in the *Index*. Forms followed by as asterisk can also function as an improper preposition in the New Testament.

γάρ	διό	διόπερ	διότι	ἐάν

---

1   Has a variant form, πορρωτέρω.

2   A v.l. of πορρώτερον at Lk 24:28.

3   Can be joined with others words (καίγε, μήγε, μήτιγε, ὅσγε), although these do not occur in our text. See καίτοιγε, μενοῦνγε.

4   Can function as an adverb or a conjunction.

5   Can function adverbially.

6   See discussion at *BAGD* on its origin.

7   From the adjective πότερος, which is used in our literature only in the fixed form πότερον as an interrogative word in disjunctive questions.

ἐπάν	ἐπεί	ἐπειδή	ἐπειδήπερ	ἕως*[1]
ἵνα	ἱνατί	καθά[2]	καθάπερ[2]	καθότι
καί	καίπερ	μήπου	μήπως	μήτε
ὅτι	οὐδέ	πρίν*		

Prepositions

Forms followed by an asterisk can be classified as an improper preposition.

ἀνά	ἄνευ*	ἀντί	ἀπέναντι*	ἀπό
ἄτερ*	ἄχρι(ς)*[3]	διά[4]	εἵνεκεν*[5]	εἰς
ἐκ[6]	ἐμμέσῳ[7]	ἐν	ἔναντι*	ἐναντίον*[8]
ἕνεκα*[9]	ἕνεκεν*[10]	ἐντός*	ἐνώπιον*	ἐπί
ἐσώτερον[11]	κατά[12]	μετά	μέχρι(ς)*[13]	παρά
περί	πρό	πρός	σύν	ὑπέρ[14]
ὑπό	χάριν			

Interjections

See also ἄγε, ἴδε, ἰδού.

ἔα	οὐά	οὐαί	ὤ

---

[1] Can function as a preposition.

[2] Can function adverbially.

[3] Can function as a conjunction. Occurs forty-six times without the movable ς (ἄχρι) and three times with it (ἄχρις; cf. §6.7).

[4] Can be joined with other words and written as διαπαντός (Lk 24:53; Heb 9:6) and διατί (Mt 9:14; 13:10; Lk 19:23, 31).

[5] See ἕνεκεν.

[6] Also alternate form ἐξ.

[7] ἐν μέσῳ can be written ἐμμέσῳ (cf. *BAGD*), but not in our text.

[8] Accusative singular neuter of ἐναντίος (which is not in the N.T.).

[9] See ἕνεκεν.

[10] Occurs twenty-two times in the form ἕνεκεν, three times as ἕνεκα (Lk 6:22; Acts 19:32; 26:21), and once as εἵνεκεν (2 Cor 3:10).

[11] Accusative singular neuter of ἐσώτερος and can function as an improper preposition.

[12] κατὰ εἷς is written as καθεῖς in a v.l. at Rom 12:5 (cf. *BAGD* on εἷς, 5e).

[13] Can function as a conjunction. It occurs fourteen times without the movable ς (μέχρι) and three times with it (μέχρις; §6.7).

[14] Functions adverbially at 2 Cor 11:23.

Numerals

The following list was drawn from *MH* 167-178 based on usage in the LXX. For others see Smyth (§347-354), *BD* §63.[1]

	Cardinals[2]	Ordinals	Adverbials
1.	εἷς	πρῶτος	ἅπαξ
2.	δύο	δεύτερος	δίς
3.	τρεῖς	τρίτος	τρίς
4.	τέσσαρες	τέταρτος	τετράκις
5.	πέντε	πέμπτος	πεντάκις
6.	ἕξ	ἕκτος	ἑξάκις
7.	ἑπτά	ἕβδομος	ἑπτάκις
8.	ὀκτώ	ὄγδοος	ὀκτάκις
9.	ἐννέα	ἔνατος	ἐνάκις
10.	δέκα	δέκατος	
11.	ἕνδεκα	ἑνδέκατος	
12.	δώδεκα or δεκαδύο	δωδέκατος	
14.	δεκατέσσαρες	τεσσαρεσκαιδέκατος	
15.	δεκαπέντε	πεντεκαιδέκατος	
16.	δέκα ἕξ		
18.	δέκα ὀκτώ or δέκα καὶ ὀκτώ		
20.	εἴκοσι(ν)	εἰκοστός	
30.	τριάκοντα		
40.	τεσσαράκοντα or τεσσεράκοντα		
50.	πεντήκοντα	πεντηκοστός	
60.	ἑξήκοντα		
70.	ἑβδομήκοντα		ἑβδομηκοντάκις
80.	ὀγδοήκοντα		
90.	ἐνενήκοντα		
100.	ἑκατόν	ἑκατοστός	
200.	διακόσιοι		
300.	τριακόσιοι		
400.	τετρακόσιοι	τετρακοσιοστός	
500.	πεντακόσιοι		
600.	ἑξακόσιοι		
1,000.	χίλιοι	χιλιοστός	
2,000.	δισχίλιοι		
3,000.	τρισχίλιοι		
4,000.	τετρακισχίλιοι		
5,000.	πεντακισχίλιοι or χιλιάδες πέντε		
7,000.	χιλιάδες ἑπτά or ἑπτακισχίλιοι		
10,000.	μύριοι or δέκα χιλιάδες		
12,000.	δώδεκα χιλιάδες		
20,000.	εἴκοσι χιλιάδες or δισμύριοι		
50,000.	μυριάδες πέντε		
100,000.	μυριάδες μυριάδων		

---

[1]   These numerals are essential to learn for the Friday afternoon football games often played in Greek classes.

[2]   The cardinals from five through 199 are indeclinable; the rest decline.

Introduction to Principal Parts

We have already discussed our method of subdividing verbs roots based on how the verbal root is modified to form the present tense stem (cf. §33; *BBG*, chapter 20). Following are the eight basic sections. (For more detail see the Table of Contents.)

v-1	Present tense = verbal root	*λυ › λύω › ἔλυσα
v-2	Present tense = verbal root + ι	*βαλ › βάλλω › ἔβαλον
v-3	Present tense = verbal root + ν	*αὐξα › αὐξάνω › αὐξήσω
v-4	Present tense = verbal root + τ	*βαπ › βάπτω › βάψω
v-5	Present tense = verbal root + σκ	*ἀρε › ἀρέσκω › ἀρέσω
v-6	μι verbs	*δο › δίδωμι
v-7	Verbal roots that change their stem vowel	ἀκούω › ἀκήκοα
v-8	Verbs that use more than one verbal root to form their different tense stems	ἐσθίω › φάγομαι

At the beginning of each section we will include a basic discussion and an outline of the subdivisions. Often there will be a chart of morphological changes that will be evident throughout the verbs in that subdivision. These subdivisions can also be subdivided.

As a general rule, we have followed the forms of the words given in *BAGD*, unless they disagree with our text. Several words that *BAGD* says occurs only in the variant readings are now included as the preferred reading in our texts. In one special situation, though, we have modified verbs. When a verb is listed in *BAGD* in a middle or passive form but is not deponent, we have listed it in the active. This way, only the true deponents are listed in the middle or passive form (except, of course, the fifth and sixth principal parts columns).

We have listed all the principal parts that occur in the New Testament, and included others as well. If the formation of the principal parts is in any way irregular, it is explained in the footnotes and usually tied back into our discussions in §30ff. If you want to see more principal parts see *LS*, but realize that the forms may have changed from Attic to Koine.

Compound verbs formed with prepositions have been listed under their verbal (or second) element. They are indicated in the index as "cv-." If the verbal element of the compound verb is not listed as a separate verb in *LS*, we have told you so in the footnotes. However, this may not have much significance. The verb may have existed and it may not be listed, or it may have been a verb at one time that evolved into a verbal morpheme.

Be aware of the types of changes that prepositions can undergo when they are added to another word. σύν can become συλ (συλλαλέω), συγ (συγχράομαι), συμ (συμμαρτυρέω), συρ (ἐπισυρράπτω), or drop out (συζάω). ἐν can become ἐγ (ἐγκρατεύομαι), ἐμ (ἐμπτύω), or ἐλ (ἐλλογάω). μετά can be aspirated to μεθ (μεθίστημι), κατά to καθ (καθίστημι), and ἀπό to ἀφ (ἀφομοιόω).

If the compound is formed another way (e.g., with a noun [ἀγαθοεργέω], adverb [εὐλογέω], or alpha-privative [ἀδυνατέω]), we list the verb as a separate entry. This is the most helpful system since often the nature of a compound verb not formed with a preposition can become tricky to identify. For example, could a first year student locate the root of ἀγαθουργέω? Not without difficulty.

Most of the time the verbal root is easy to identify. However, because the root is technically a theoretical form, and because vowels can change easily, at times we had to make somewhat arbitrary decisions as to what we call the root. For example, is the root of δίδωμι *δο or *δω? As a general rule we chose the short vowel over the long (i.e., the weak grade). Many texts speak of *δο and *δω as two different roots when actually they are the same root change by ablaut (§4). We tried to make decisions that would be the most helpful to students learning Greek while purely academic concerns were secondary.

It is important that you learn to identify the verbal root before trying to understand its principal parts. v-1 type verbs will be easy since the root has not been modified. In the other types of verbs, look either at the aorist or work backwards from the present tense to the verbal root using the description of the category.

Following is a list of items we will *not* discuss in the footnotes of specific verbs.

1. The effects of common morphological rules.

2. Changes described at the beginning of each category.

3. Instructions at the beginning of the section. For example, v-2d words all have liquid futures and aorists unless otherwise stated.

4. The lengthening of final stem vowels before tense formatives and personal endings (e.g., ἀγαπάω ‣ ἠγάπησα).

5. Changes in the final stem consonant in the perfect middle/passive (§46.4).

6. Deaspiration due to reduplication in the perfect (e.g., φεύγω ‣ πέφυγα; §15.5).

7. Changes in prepositions as elements in compound verbs (e.g., συλλαμβάνω ‣ συνελάβανον).

8. If the same change is visible throughout all the principal parts, the change will be explained in the footnote for the present tense stem and will not be repeated for the other stems. For example, καλέω inserts an η after the tense stem in the perfect and aorist passive. This is stated in the footnote to the present tense stem and not repeated for the other three principal parts. You should check the footnote to the present tense before looking at the footnotes to the other tenses.

9. Augmentation and reduplication rules (§31-32).

10. Accents (§28-29).

We *will* discuss the following in footnotes.

1. Difficult changes not readily understandable.
2. Special forms of the tense stems (e.g., liquid futures).
3. Ablaut.
4. Verbal roots.
5. Compound verbs formed with a preposition.

I would be severely remiss if I did not emphasize that Funk's discussions of verbs were a great help in categorizing the verbs. When listing the total number of verbs, we do not include compound verbs.

Class v-1
Present Stem = Verbal Root

v-1 verbs do not alter their verbal root in order to form their present tense stem. This is the largest category of verbs and the most "regular."

v-1a

Verbal roots ending in ι or ϝ

V-1a roots end in ι or υ. The ι and υ originally were consonantal iota (ι) and digamma (ϝ). When these two letters fell out of use, they became iota and upsilon. Because of this change, the iota and upsilon will not undergo any further changes when personal endings and tense formatives are added. What this gives us are "regular" verbs.

v-1a(1)   Roots ending in ι   (total: 4)

κυλίω[1]	κυλίσω	ἐκύλισα	-		κεκύλισμαι	ἐκυλίσθην
πρίω[2]	-	-	-		-	ἐπρίσθην[3]
συνίω[4]	-	-	-		-	-

---

[1]   ἀνακυλίω, ἀποκυλίω, προσκυλίω. Inserts a σ after the stem in the perfect middle/passive and the aorist passive (§46.5). The aorist passive does not occur in the N.T. See *BDF* §101.

[2]   Alternate form of πρίζω (v-2a[1]). διαπρίω.

[3]   Inserts a σ after the stem (§46.5), unless the alternate form πρίζω is preferred (v-2a[1]).

[4]   See discussion at alternate form συνίημι (cv-6a).

χρίω[1]   -   ἔχρισα   -   -   ἐχρίσθην[2]

v-1a(2)   Roots ending in αι   (total: 2)

παίω[3]   -   ἔπαισα   -   -   -
πταίω   -   ἔπταισα   -   -   -

v-1a(3)   Roots ending in ει   (total: 2)

κλείω[4]   κλείσω   ἔκλεισα   -   κέκλεισμαι   ἐκλείσθην
σείω[5]   σείσω   ἔσεισα   -   -   ἐσείσθην[6]

v-1a(4)   Roots ending in υ   (total: 19)

ἀνύω[7]   -   ἤνυσα   -   -   -
ἀρτύω[8]   ἀρτύσω   -   -   ἤρτυμαι   ἠρτύθην
βρύω   -   -   -   -   -
δακρύω   -   ἐδάκρυσα   -   -   -
δεικνύω[9]   -   -   -   -   -
δύω[10]   -   ἔδυσα[11]   δέδυκα   δέδυμαι   ἐδύην[12]

---

[1]   ἐγχρίω, ἐπιχρίω
[2]   Inserts a σ after the stem (§46.5). The aorist passive does not occur in the N.T.
[3]   προσπαίω
[4]   Inserts a σ after the stem in the perfect middle/passive and the aorist passive (§46.5). ἀποκλείω, ἐγκλείω, ἐκκλείω, κατακλείω, συγκλείω
[5]   ἀνασείω, διασείω, ἐπισείω, κατασείω
[6]   Inserts a σ after the stem (§46.5)
[7]   διανύω
[8]   See Smyth §518c. Alternate form of ἀρτύνω.
[9]   ὑποδεικνύω. Alternate form of δείκνυμι at Jn 2:18; see v-3c(2) for discussion of principal parts.
[10]   ἀπεκδύομαι, ἐκδύω, ἐνδύω, ἐπενδύομαι, ἐπιδύω, παρεισδύω. Its alternate form is δύνω, v-3a(1), the category of verbs that adds ν in the present tense. Compound verb can be listed with or without the ν (e.g., παρεισδύνω or παρεισδύ(ν)ω). See BDF §101 on δύειν. See BDF §101.
[11]   Also has a root aorist ἐδύην (§44.2c).
[12]   Also has an athematic second aorist ἔδυν that does not occur in the N.T.

ἕλκω[1]	ἑλκύσω	εἵλκυσα[2]	-	-	εἱλκύσθην[3]
θύω[4]	-	ἔθυσα	-	τέθυμαι	ἐτύθην[5]
ἰσχύω[6]	ἰσχύσω	ἴσχυσα	-	-	ἰσχύθην
καμμύω	-	ἐκάμμυσα	-	-	-
κωλύω[7]	-	ἐκώλυσα	-	-	ἐκωλύθην
λύω[8]	λύσω	ἔλυσα	-	λέλυμαι	ἐλύθην
μεθύω[9]	-	-	-	-	ἐμεθύσθην[10]
μειγνύω[11]	-	-	-	-	-
μηνύω	-	ἐμήνυσα	μεμήνυκα	-	ἐμηνύθην
πτύω[12]	πτύσω	ἔπτυσα	-	-	ἐπτύσθην[13]
ῥύομαι[14]	ῥύσομαι	ἐρρυσάμην[15]	-	-	ἐρρύσθην[16]
φύω[17]	-	-	-	-	ἐφύην[18]
ὠρύομαι	-	-	-	-	-

v-1a(5)   Roots ending in αυ   (total: 3)

θραύω[19]	-	-	-	τέθραυσμαι	ἐθραύσθην

---

1 ἐξέλκω. *σελκυ loses the υ in the present and the initial σ is replaced with rough breathing (§31.5a). Imperfect εἷλκον (ε + σελκυ ‣ εελκυ ‣ εἷλκον). Cf. Funk §482.30.

2 From the root *σελκυ. It therefore receives the syllabic augment, the intervocalic σ drops out, and the vowels contract to ει: ε + *σελκυ ‣ εελκυ ‣ εἵλκυσα (§31.5a; Smyth §431).

3 Inserts a σ after the stem (§46.5). The aorist passive does not occur in the N.T. On the augment see the aorist active.

4 ἐπιθύω

5 The θ of the root (*θυ) deaspirates to a τ because of the θ of the tense formative (§15.8). θυ ‣ εθυθην ‣ ἐτύθην.

6 ἐνισχύω, ἐξισχύω, ἐπισχύω, κατισχύω (imperfect, κατίσχυον).

7 διακωλύω

8 ἀναλύω, ἀπολύω, διαλύω, ἐκλύω, ἐπιλύω, καταλύω, παραλύω

9 Alternate for of μεθύσκω (v-5a). μεθύσκω occurs three times in the N.T. (Lk 12:45, Eph 5:18, 1 Thess 5:7); μεθύω occurs the other five times.

10 Inserts a σ after the stem (§46.5)

11 See μείγνυμι (v-3c[2]).

12 ἐκπτύω, ἐμπτύω

13 Inserts a σ after the stem (§46.5)

14 See BDF §101.

15 For doubling the initial ρ after augment see §31.2b.

16 For doubling the initial ρ after augment see §31.2b. Inserts a σ after the stem (§46.5)

17 ἐκφύω, συμφύω. See BDF §101.

18 Second aorist passive (§47.8).

19 Inserts a σ after the stem in the perfect middle/passive and the aorist passive (§46.5). The aorist passive does not occur in the N.T.

| παύω[1] | παύσω | ἔπαυσα | - | πέπαυμαι | ἐπαύθην[2] |
| ψαύω[3] | ψαύσω | ἔψαυσα | ἔψαυκα | ἔψαυσμαι | ἐψαύσθην |

v-1a(6) Roots ending in ευ (which retain the υ in the present)
(total: 81)

ἀγγαρεύω	ἀγγαρεύσω	ἠγγάρευσα	-	-	-
ἀγορεύω[4]	-	ἠγόρευσα	ἠγόρευκα	ἠγόρευμαι	ἠγορεύθην
ἀγρεύω	-	ἤγρευσα	-	-	-
αἰχμαλωτεύω	-	ᾐχμαλώτευσα	-	-	-
ἀληθεύω	-	-	-	-	-
ἁλιεύω	-	-	-	-	-
ἀνθυπατεύω	-	-	-	-	-
βασιλεύω[5]	βασιλεύσω	ἐβασίλευσα	-	-	-
βατεύω[6]	-	-	-	-	-
βολεύομαι[7]	-	ἐβόλευσα	-	-	-
βουλεύω[8]	βουλεύσω	ἐβούλευσα	-	βεβούλευμαι	-
βραβεύω[9]	-	-	-	-	-
γαμβρεύω[10]	γαμβρεύσω	-	-	-	-
γεύομαι	γεύσομαι	ἐγευσάμην	-	-	-
γυμνητεύω[11]	-	-	-	-	-
γυμνιτεύω	-	-	-	-	-
δεκατεύω[12]	-	-	-	-	-

---

[1] ἀναπαύω, ἐπαναπαύομαι, καταπαύω, συναναπαύομαι.

[2] The aorist passive of παύω does not occur in the N.T., but the future passive does. ἐπαναπαύομαι has a second future passive ἐπαναπαήσομαι (Lk 10:6) and a second aorist passive ἐπανεπάην (Didache). ἀναπαύω as a second future passive ἀναπαήσομαι (Rev 14:13; §47.8) and a second aorist passive ἀνεπάην. Both compounds are formed from the verbal root *πα and not *παυ (BDF §78).

[3] Inserts a σ after the stem in the perfect middle/passive and the aorist passive (§46.5).The perfect middle/passive does not occur in the N.T. ἐπιψαύω, προσψαύω

[4] προσαγορεύω

[5] συμβασιλεύω

[6] ἐμβατεύω. See κενεμβατεύω.

[7] παραβολεύομαι

[8] παραβουλεύομαι, συμβουλεύω. Has an active aorist συνεβούλευσα.

[9] καταβραβεύω

[10] ἐπιγαμβρεύω

[11] Alternate form of γυμνιτεύω.

[12] ἀποδεκατεύω

δεσμεύω	-	-	-	-	-
δουλεύω	δουλεύσω	ἐδούλευσα	δεδούλευκα	-	-
δυναστεύω[1]	-	-	-	-	-
ἑδρεύω[2]					
εἰρηνεύω	εἰρηνεύσω	εἰρήνευσα	-		-
ἐνεδρεύω	-	-	-	-	-
ἑρμηνεύω[3]	-	ἑρμήνευσα[4]	-	-	-
ζηλεύω	-	-	-	-	-
ἡγεμονεύω	-	-	-	-	-
θεραπεύω	θεραπεύσω	ἐθεράπευσα	-	τεθεράπευμαι	ἐθεραπεύθην
θηρεύω	-	ἐθήρευσα	-	-	-
θριαμβεύω	-	ἐθριάμβευσα	-	-	-
ἱερατεύω	-	-	-	-	-
καπηλεύω	-	-	-	-	-
κελεύω[5]	-	ἐκέλευσα	-	-	-
κινδυνεύω	-	-	-	-	-
κενεμβατεύω[6]	-				
κρατεύομαι[7]	-	-	-	-	-
κηδεύω	-	ἐκήδευσα	-	-	-
κυκλεύω	-	ἐκύκλευσα	-	-	-
κινδυνεύω	-	-	-	-	-
κυριεύω[8]	κυριεύσω	ἐκυρίευσα	-		ἐκυριεύθην
λατρεύω	λατρεύσω	ἐλάτρευσα	-	-	-
μαγεύω	μαγεύσω	-	-	-	-
μαθητεύω	-	ἐμαθήτευσα	-	-	ἐμαθητεύθην
μαντεύομαι	-	-	-	-	-
μεθερμηνεύω	-	-	-	-	-
μεσιτεύω	-	ἐμεσίτευσα	-	-	-

---

1 καταδυναστεύω

2 Occurs in the N.T. only as the compound ἐνδρεύω as a present. (The compound παρεδρεύω does not occur in the N.T.). *LS* shows an aorist ἐνήδρευσα, confirming it is a compound verb. ἑδρεύω is not listed in *LS*.

3 διερμηνεύω, μεθερμηνεύω

4 Does not augment (§31.7a).

5 διακελεύω

6 Cf. *BAGD* and βατεύω. This is a conjectured form to explain Col 2:18.

7 ἐγκρατεύομαι. κρατεύομαι is not listed in *LS*.

8 κατακυριεύω

μνημονεύω	-	ἐμνημόνευσα	-	-	-
μνηστεύω	-	-	-	ἐμνήστευμαι[1]	ἐμνηστεύθην
μοιχεύω	μοιχεύσω	ἐμοίχευσα	-	-	ἐμοιχεύθην
νεύω[2]	-	ἔνευσα	-	-	-
νηστεύω	νηστεύσω	ἐνήστευσα	-	-	-
νυκτερεύω[3]	-	-	-	-	-
ὁδεύω[4]	-	ὥδευσα	-	-	-
ὀλεθρεύω[5]	-	ὠλέθρευσα	-	-	ὠλεθρεύθην
ὀλοθρεύω[6]	-	ὠλόθρευσα	-	-	ὠλοθρεύθην
ὀπτεύω[7]	-	ὤπτευσα	-	-	-
παγιδεύω	-	ἐπαγίδευσα	-	-	-
παιδεύω	-	ἐπαίδευσα	-	πεπαίδευμαι	ἐπαιδεύθην
πεζεύω	-	-	-	-	-
περισσεύω[8]	περισσεύσω	ἐπερίσσευσα	-	-	ἐπερισσεύθην
περπερεύομαι	-	-	-	-	-
πιστεύω	πιστεύσω	ἐπίστευσα	πεπίστευκα	πεπίστευμαι	ἐπιστεύθην
πολιτεύομαι	-	ἐπολιτευσάμην	-	πεπολίτευμαι	-
πορεύομαι[9]	πορεύσομαι	-	-	πεπόρευμαι	ἐπορεύθην
πορνεύω[10]	πορνεύσω	ἐπόρνευσα	-	-	-
πραγματεύομαι[11]	-	ἐπραγματευσάμην	-	-	-
πρεσβεύω	πρεσβεύσω	ἐπρέσβευσα	-	-	-
προφητεύω	προφητεύσω	ἐπροφήτευσα	-	-	-
πρωτεύω	-	-	-	-	-
πτωχεύω	-	ἐπτώχευσα	-	-	-

---

[1] Because of the initial consonant cluster, this word is undergoes vocalic and not consonantal reduplication in the perfect (§31.2c). It does, however, have a variant form that does reduplicate (BDF §68; MH 193).

[2] διανεύω, ἐκνεύω, ἐννεύω, ἐπινεύω, κατανεύω, συγκατανεύω

[3] διανυκτερεύω

[4] διοδεύω, συνοδεύω

[5] Alternate form of ὀλοθρεύω. ἐξολεθρεύω is from this root (Acts 3:23), but the simple verb does not occur in the N.T.

[6] Occurs only once in the N.T., as ὀλοθρεύων (Heb 11:28). The alternate form ὀλεθρεύω does not occur in the N.T. as a simple verb.

[7] ἐποπτεύω

[8] ὑπερπερισσεύω

[9] διαπορεύομαι, εἰσπορεύομαι, ἐκπορεύομαι, ἐμπορεύομαι, ἐπιπορεύομαι, παραπορεύομαι, προπορεύομαι, προσπορεύομαι, συμπορεύομαι, συνεκπορεύομαι

[10] ἐκπορνεύω

[11] διαπραγματεύομαι

πυκτεύω	-	-	-	-	-
ῥυπαρεύω	-	-	-	-	ἐρυπαρεύθην
σαλεύω	-	ἐσάλευσα	-	σεσάλευμαι	ἐσαλεύθην
στρατεύομαι[1] -		ἐστρατευσάμην	-	-	-
σωρεύω[2]	σωρεύσω	-	-	σεσώρευμαι	-
τροπεύω[3]	-	-	-	-	-
τοξεύω[4]	-	-	-	-	-
φιλοπρωτεύω -		-	-	-	-
φονεύω	φονεύσω	ἐφόνευσα	-	-	ἐφονεύθην
φυγαδεύω	-	-	-	-	ἐφυγαδεύθην
φυτεύω[5]	-	ἐφύτευσα	-	πεφύτευμαι	ἐφυτεύθην
χρηστεύομαι	-	ἐχρηστευσάμην	-	-	ἐχρηστεύθην

v-1a(7)   Roots ending in ευ (which lose the υ in the present)[6]
(total: 5)

βραδυπλοέω	-	-	-	-	-
πλέω[7]	-	ἔπλευσα	-	-	-
πνέω[8]	-	ἔπνευσα	-	-	-
ῥέω[9]	ῥεύσω	-	-	-	ἐρύην[10]
χέω[11]	χεῶ[12]	ἔχεα[13]	κέχυκα	κέχυμαι	ἐχύθην

---

[1]   ἀντιστρατεύομαι. Always middle deponent. *BAGD* lists as active στρατεύω.

[2]   ἐπισωρεύω

[3]   ἐπιτροπεύω. τροπεύω is not listed in *LS*.

[4]   κατατοξεύω

[5]   μεταφυτεύω

[6]   In the present, these words will contract like a regular ε contract verb. Funk (§3690) lists these verbs as v-1d(2b), roots in ε that do not lengthen (cf. §27.7).

[7]   ἀποπλέω, διαπλέω, ἐκπλέω, καταπλέω, παραπλέω, ὑποπλέω. Root was originally *πλεϝ. The ϝ has been lost without leaving any trace (LaSor §24.2531).

[8]   ἐκπνέω, ἐμπνέω, ὑποπνέω

[9]   Three forms of the root are involved in forming the principal parts of this verb: *ῥε (present; weak form of *ῥευ), *ῥευ (future), and *ῥυ (aorist passive; zero form of *ῥευ). v-7. Funk (§482.5) says the root is *ῥευ, and the other forms are the weak grade. Compound is παραρρέω, where the rough breathing on ῥέω changed to a double ρ. See *LS*.

[10]   Second aorist passive (§47.8).

[11]   The root alternates between *χε and *χυ. Funk (§482.5) says that the root is actually *χευ, and χε and χυ are the weak grade of that root. v-7. There also is another root involved: χυν(ν): the compound ὑπερεκ- appears as ὑπερεκχύννω in Lk 6:38 (listed as v-3a[1]). Compounds are ἐκχέω, ἐπιχέω, καταχέω, συγχέω.

[12]   Attic future (§43.7)

[13]   Non-sigmatic first aorist (§44.5e).

v-1a(8)   **Roots ending in ου**   (total: 3)

ἀκούω[1]	ἀκούσω[2]	ἤκουσα	ἀκήκοα[3]	-	ἠκούσθην[4]
κρούω	-	ἔκρουσα	-	-	-
λούω[5]	-	ἔλουσα	-	λέλουμαι[6]	-

v-1b

Verbal roots ending in a stop (π β φ, κ γ χ, τ δ θ)

Description

v-1b(1)   Roots ending in a labial (π β φ)

v-1b(2)   Roots ending in a velar (κ γ χ)

v-1b(3)   Roots ending in a dental (τ δ θ)

v-1b(4)   Roots ending in a stop (which add ε to form the present)

The variations of the words in these four subcategories are easy to learn. If the root ends in a labial or a velar, in the future and the aorist the final stem consonant will join with the σ of the tense formative and will be written as ψ or ξ respectively. If the root ends in a dental, the dental will drop out.

In the perfect middle/passive of labial roots, the final consonant will totally assimilate to μ because of the initial μ of the personal ending. For the changes in other persons /number cf. §47.5.

In the aorist passive, π, κ, or γ will aspirate to their respective aspirates, and the θ will become σ. There are many examples of ablaut (§4; v-7).

future/aorist

π	+	σ	›	ψ	(§22.1)	κ	+	σ	›	ξ	(§22.2)	τ + σ › σ (§22.3)

$$\pi + \sigma \rightarrow \psi \quad (\S22.1) \qquad \kappa + \sigma \rightarrow \xi \quad (\S22.2) \qquad \tau + \sigma \rightarrow \sigma \quad (\S22.3)$$

$$\beta + \sigma \rightarrow \psi \quad (\S22.1) \qquad \gamma + \sigma \rightarrow \xi \quad (\S22.2) \qquad \delta + \sigma \rightarrow \sigma \quad (\S22.3)$$

$$\phi + \sigma \rightarrow \psi \quad (\S22.1) \qquad \chi + \sigma \rightarrow \xi \quad (\S22.2) \qquad \theta + \sigma \rightarrow \sigma \quad (\S22.3)$$

---

[1]   διακούω, εἰσακούω, ἐπακούω, παρακούω, προακούω, ὑπακούω.

[2]   Some list as ἀκούσομαι.

[3]   Second perfect (§45.5b). One of the few examples of Attic reduplication in the N.T. (§32.6). The first syllable (first vowel and single consonant) is reduplicated, the second stem vowel is lengthened, and ου › ο: *ἀκο › ἀκακο › ἀκηκο (v-7).

[4]   Inserts a σ after the stem (§46.5).

[5]   ἀπολούω. Cf. Smyth §398a.

[6]   Appears in Jn 13:10 in this form; in Heb 10:22 a σ is inserted after the stem (λέλουσμαι: §46.5).

aorist passive

π + θ ‣ φθ (§20.1)   γ + θ ‣ χθ (§20.2)

κ + θ ‣ χθ (§20.2)   θ + θ ‣ σθ (§20.3)

v-1b(1)   Roots ending in a labial (π β φ)   (total: 19)

ἀλείφω[1]	-	ἤλειψα	-	-	ἠλείφθην
βλέπω[2]	βλέψω	ἔβλεψα	-	-	-
γράφω[3]	γράψω	ἔγραψα	γέγραφα[4]	γέγραμμαι	ἐγράφην[5]
θλίβω[6]	-	-	-	τέθλιμμαι	ἐθλίβην[7]
κρύβω[8]	-	-	-	-	-
λάμπω[9]	λάμψω	ἔλαμψα	-	-	-
λείπω[10]	λείψω	ἔλιπον[11]	λέλοιπα[12]	λέλειμμαι	ἐλείφθην
μέμφομαι	-	ἐμεμψάμην	-		
νήφω[13]	-	ἔνηψα	-	-	-
πέμπω[14]	πέμψω	ἔπεμψα	πέπομφα[15]	-	ἐπέμφθην
πρέπω	-	-	-		
σέβω	-	-	-		
σήπω	-	-	σέσηπα[16]	-	
στίλβω	-	-	-		

---

[1]   ἐξαλείφω

[2]   ἀναβλέπω, ἀποβλέπω, διαβλέπω, ἐμβλέπω, ἐπιβλέπω, περιβλέπω, προβλέπω. *BDF* §101.

[3]   ἀπογράφω, ἐγγράφω, ἐπιγράφω, καταγράφω, προγράφω

[4]   Second perfect (§45.5b)

[5]   Second aorist passive (§47.8)

[6]   ἀποθλίβω, συνθλίβω

[7]   Second aorist passive (§47.8). The aorist passive does not occur in the N.T.

[8]   περικρύβω. *BAGD* says that κρύβω is a new formation from the aorist passive ἐκρύβην. κρύβω is not listed in *LS*.

[9]   ἐκλάμπω, ἐπιλάμπω, περιλάμπω

[10]   ἀπολείπω (alternate form of ἀπολιμπάνω, cv-3a[2b]), διαλείπω, ἐγκαταλείπω, ἐκλείπω, ἐπιλείπω, καταλείπω, περιλείπομαι, ὑπολείπω (colloquial form ὑπολιμπάνω, cv-3a[2b]). See *BDF* §101.

[11]   Second aorist (§44.5a). The stem is in the weak grade (ει ‣ ι; §4, v-7). The aorist passive does not occur in the N.T.

[12]   Second perfect (§45.5b). The diphthong has shifted (ει ‣ οι; §4).

[13]   ἀνανήφω, ἐκνήφω

[14]   ἀναπέμπω, ἀποπέμπω, ἐκπέμπω, ἐμπέμπω, μεταπέμπω, προπέμπω, συμπέμπω

[15]   Second perfect (§45.5b). Stem vowel has become ο due to ablaut (§4, v-7). The final π is aspirated to φ (§14.1). The perfect active does not occur in the N.T.

[16]   Second perfect (§45.5b)

στρέφω[1]	στρέψω	ἔστρεψα	-	ἔστραμμαι[2]	ἐστράφην[3]
τρέπω[4]	-	ἔτρεψα	-	τέτραμμαι[5]	ἐτράπην[6]
τρέφω[7]	-	ἔθρεψα	-	τέθραμμαι[8]	ἐτράφην[9]
τρίβω[10]	τρίψω	ἔτριψα	-	τέτριμμαι	ἐτρίβην[11]
τύφω	-	-	-	-	-

v-1b(2)   Roots ending in a velar (κ γ χ)   (total: 34)

ἄγχω[12]	-	ἠγξάμην	-	-	-
ἄγω[13]	ἄξω	ἤγαγον[14]	-	ἦγμαι	ἤχθην
ἄρχω[15]	ἄρξω	ἦρξα	-	-	-
αὔξω[16]	-	-	-	-	ηὐξήθην
βρέχω	-	ἔβρεξα	-	-	-
βρύχω	-	-	-	-	-
δέχομαι[17]	δέξομαι	ἐδεξάμην	-	δέδεγμαι	ἐδέχθην
διώκω[18]	διώξω	ἐδίωξα	-	δεδίωγμαι	ἐδιώχθην

---

1   ἀναστρέφω, ἀποστρέφω, διαστρέφω, ἐκστρέφω, ἐπιστρέφω, καταστρέφω, μεταστρέφω, συναναστρέφω (in our literature only passive, and some therefore list as -ρέφομαι), συστρέφω, ὑποστρέφω.

2   Ablaut shifts stem vowel to α (§4, v-7).

3   Second aorist passive (§47.8). Ablaut shifts the stem vowel to α (§4).

4   ἀνατρέπω, ἀποτρέπω, ἐκτρέπω, ἐντρέπω, ἐπιτρέπω, μετατρέπω, περιτρέπω, προτρέπω

5   Ablaut shifts stem vowel to α (§4, v-7).

6   Ablaut shifts stem vowel to α (§4, v-7). Second aorist passive (§47.8).

7   The root is *θρεφ. When the φ is present, the θ deaspirates to τ (§15.6). When the θ is replaced with another letter, the initial θ returns as in the aorist active. Compounds are ἀνατρέφω, ἐκτρέφω, ἐντρέφω.

8   Ablaut shifts stem vowel to α (§4, v-7).

9   Second aorist passive (§47.8).

10   διατρίβω, συντρίβω

11   Second aorist passive (§47.8)

12   ἀπάγχω

13   ἀνάγω, ἀπάγω, διάγω, εἰσάγω, ἐξάγω, ἐπάγω, ἐπανάγω, ἐπισυνάγω, κατάγω, μετάγω, παράγω, παρεισάγω, περιάγω, προάγω, προσάγω, συνάγω, συναπάγω, ὑπάγω. BDF§101.

14   Receives both reduplication and an augment: *αγ ‣ αγαγ ‣ ἤγαγον (§44.5d). This is different from Attic reduplication (§32.6), where it is not the reduplicated vowel but the original vowel that is lengthened. Second aorist (§44.5a); also has a first aorist form (ἦξα).

15   ἐνάρχομαι, προενάρχομαι, προϋπάρχω, ὑπάρχω.

16   Alternate form of αὐξάνω (v-3a[1]). See there for discussion.

17   ἀναδέχομαι, ἀπεκδέχομαι, ἀποδέχομαι, διαδέχομαι, εἰσδέχομαι, ἐκδέχομαι, ἐνδέχομαι, ἐπιδέχομαι, παραδέχομαι, προσδέχομαι, ὑποδέχομαι

18   ἐκδιώκω, καταδιώκω

εἴκω[1]	-	εἶξα	-	-	-
ἐλέγχω[2]	ἐλέγξω	ἤλεγξα	ἐλήλεγμαι[3]	-	ἠλέγχθην
ἔοικα[4]	-	-	-	-	-
ἐρεύγομαι	ἐρεύξομαι	-	-	-	-
ἔρχομαι[5]	ἐλεύσομαι[6]	ἦλθον[7]	ἐλήλυθα[8]	-	-
εὔχομαι[9]	εὔξομαι	εὐξάμην	-	-	-
ἔχω[10]	ἕξω[11]	ἔσχον[12]	ἔσχηκα[13]	-	-

---

[1] "I yield." ὑπείκω. See ἔοικα below.

[2] διακατελέγχομαι, ἐξελέγχω

[3] Attic reduplication (§32.6)

[4] "To seem likely." A perfect used impersonally as a present from an obsolete present εἴκω (§45.5d; Funk §3880). LS list two verbs, εἴκω. On the first they say, "v. ἔοικα." But the third meaning of the second entry is, ""impers., it is allowable or possible," which sounds as if it may be the root of ἔοικα.

[5] Uses multiple roots with ablaut: *ερχ, *ελευθ (v-7, v-8). ἀνέρχομαι, ἀντιπαρέρχομαι, ἀπέρχομαι, διεξέρχομαι, διέρχομαι, εἰσέρχομαι, ἐξέρχομαι, ἐπέρχομαι, ἐπανέρχομαι, ἐπεισέρχομαι, κατέρχομαι, παρέρχομαι, παρεισέρχομαι, περιέρχομαι, προέρχομαι, προσέρχομαι, συνέρχομαι, συνεισέρχομαι. See BDF §101.

[6] From the root *ελευθ. When a θ is immediately followed by σ, it drops out (§22.3).

[7] The zero grade of the root *ελθευ that loses its vowels (ᐧ ελθ). Second aorist (§44.5a) Can occur with first aorist endings (ἤλθα; §44.5b).

[8] Second perfect (§45.5b). From the root *ελευθ, which loses its ε (ablaut [4]). It undergoes Attic reduplication in which the ελ is reduplicated and the ε is also lengthened, i.e. a double augment (§32.8).

[9] προσεύχομαι

[10] From the root *σεχ. The σ drops off and is replaced with a rough breathing (cf. §31.5a; Smyth §431). But whenever there is another aspirate (such as χ) in the verb, the rough breathing (which is also an aspirate) deaspirates to a smooth breathing. Whenever the second aspirate is lost as it is in the future, the rough breathing will return (§25.6a). See BDF §101.

This also affects compounds. For example, the future of ἀντέχω is ἀνθέξω. Evidently, the τ of the preposition ἀντί aspirates to θ because of the rough breathing in ἔχω, which was also subsequently lost because of the aspirate χ. The "original" θ deaspirates to τ in the present because of the aspirate χ (§15.6). When the χ is lost, the θ returns. The same is true of ἀπέχω and μετέχω.

Augments in the imperfect to εἶχον. Because of the original σ, it received a syllabic augment, the intervocalic σ dropped out and the two vowels contracted: ε + *σεχ ᐧ εεχον ᐧ εἶχον (§25.5). The stem vowel undergoes ablaut (§4, v-7)

ἀνέχω (some list as deponent, ἀνέχομαι), ἀντέχω (some list as a deponent, ἀντέχομαι), ἀπέχω, ἐνέχω, ἐξέχω, ἐπέχω, κατέχω, μετέχω, παρέχω, περιέχω, προέχω, προκατέχω, προσανέχω, προσέχω, συμπεριέχω, συνέχω, ὑπέχω, ὑπερέχω

[11] See explanation in the present for the rough breathing.

[12] Is formed from the zero form of the root *σεχ in which the ε of the root has dropped out due to ablaut (§4), leaving *σχ. The augment is added and a second aorist is formed (§44.5a). Smyth says it is due to syncope (§493c).

[13] Is formed from the zero form of the root (*σεχ ᐧ σχ) to which is added an η (§45.3). Funk (§482.30) says it is from the root *σχη.

ἥκω[1]	ἥξω	ἦξα	-	-	-
λέγω[2]	ἐρῶ[3]	εἶπον[4]	εἴρηκα[5]	εἴρημαι[6]	ἐρρέθην[7]
λέγω[8]	λέξω	ἔλεξα	-	λέλεγμαι	-
λείχω[9]	-	-	-	-	-
μάχομαι[10]	-	-	-	-	-
οἴγω[11]	οἴξω	ἔῳξα[12]	ἔῳγα[13]	ἔῳγμαι	ἐῴχθην[14]

---

[1] ἀνήκω, καθήκω. See BDF §101.

[2] From the root meaning "say." Compounds are ἀντιλέγω, διαλέγομαι, ἐπιλέγω, προλέγω, προσλέγω. Compounds with εἶπον are ἀπεῖπον and προεῖπον. Some list εἶπον and compounds (e.g., προεῖπον) as separate words. See BDF §101.

λέγω uses multiple roots (v-8): *λεγ, *Fεπ, *Fρη (> Fερ; Funk §487.2). Ablaut too (v-7).

[3] From the root *Fερ, in which the F has dropped off (§31.5b; the present was εἴρω). Liquid future (§43.6).

[4] *Fεπ (§31.5b) augments with a syllabic augment, F dropped out, and the vowels contracted (εFεπ > εεπ > ειπ; §31.5b). Second aorist (§44.5a).

[5] *Fρη undergoes vocalic reduplication to form the perfect, the F drops (§31.5b), and the reduplication lengthens in order to compensate (*Fρη > εFρη > ερη > εἴρηκα).

[6] *Fρη undergoes vocalic reduplication to form the perfect, the F drops and the reduplication lengthens in order to compensate for the loss (*Fρη > εFρη > ερη > εἴρημαι).

[7] *Fρη may have shortened to Fρε, the F lost, and the initial ρ doubled after the augment in order to form the aorist passive (*Fρη > Fρε > ρε > ἐρρέθην). There is also a form of the aorist passive ἐρρήθην, in which the root *Fρη was not shortened. Cf. Funk §343.1.

[8] From the root meaning "pick up." Compounds are ἐκλέγομαι, καταλέγω, παραλέγομαι, and συλλέγω. See BDF §101.

[9] ἀπολείχω, ἐπιλείχω

[10] διαμάχομαι

[11] ἀνοίγω, διανοίγω, ἐξανοίγω. ἀνοίγω is an interesting word (see BD §101). On the augment see §31.8, Smyth §431. It is a compound from αν + *Fοιγ, in which F drops out (§31.5b). Because οἴγω only appears in compound, augmentation varies depending upon whether the speaker thought of ἀνοίγω as simple or compound. This accounts for the many different forms of the word. The imperfect is ἤνοιγον in the N.T., augmenting the preposition; in Classical Greek it was ἀνέῳγον (Funk §3372.3; §339.3).

[12] The primary form of the aorist (active/middle) is ἀνέῳξα, in which an ε was augmented before the F of the original root. The F was subsequently lost, the οι lengthened, and the ι subscripted: αν + ε + Fοιγ > ανεοιγ + σα > ἀνέῳξα. Funk (§3372.2) says the stem was augmented with η, F dropped out, and the word underwent "quantitative metathesis" (what we call "transfer of quality" [§7.7]), which means that the length of the η transfers to the οι, η becoming short ε and οι becoming long ῳ (§31.5b). Some say it has double augment (§31.8).

Alternate forms ἤνοιξα and ἠνέῳξα both appear. The former augments only the preposition; the latter augments the preposition and stem. Is a compound form διανοίγω.

[13] Second perfect (§45.5b). See aorist (active/middle) for discussion of the "εῳ."

[14] The main aorist passive of ἀνοίγω is ἀνεῴχθην. See aorist (active/middle) for discussion of the εῳ. The final γ of the stem has aspirated to χ (§14.5). Has three alternate forms: ἠνοίγην (which augments the preposition; second aorist passive, §47.8); ἠνεῴχθην (which augments both the preposition and stem); ἠνοίχθην (which augments the preposition). Cf. MH 189. Funk says that the aorist passive infinitive is "wrongly" augmented, ἀνεῳχθῆναι (Lk 3:21; §3732.3).

ὀρέγω	-	-	-	-	-
πλέκω[1]	-	ἔπλεξα	-	πέπλεγμαι	ἐπλάκην[2]
πνίγω[3]	-	ἔπνιξα	-	-	ἐπνίγην[4]
στέγω	-	-	-	-	-
στήκω	-	-	-	-	-
τήκω	-	-	-	-	ἐτάκην[5]
τίκτω[6]	τέξομαι[7]	ἔτεκον[8]	-	-	ἐτέχθην
τρέχω[9]	-	ἔδραμον[10]	-	-	-
τρώγω	-	-	-	-	-
φεύγω[11]	φεύξομαι	ἔφυγον[12]	πέφευγα[13]	-	-
φθέγγομαι[14]	-	ἐφθεγξάμην	-	-	-
ψύχω[15]	-	ἔψυξα	-	-	ἐψύγην[16]
ψώχω	-	-	-	-	-

v-1b(3)   Roots ending in a dental (τ δ θ)   (total: 19)

The σ that appears at the end of the stem in the perfect middle/passive and aorist passive is not inserted as it is in words like ἀκούω ‣ ἠκούσθην. Rather, a final dental becomes σ when followed by θ (§20.3).

ᾄδω[17]   -   -   -   -   -

---

1   ἐμπλέκω

2   Second aorist passive (§47.8). Stem vowel has become α due to ablaut (§4, v-7).

3   ἀποπνίγω, συμπνίγω

4   Second aorist passive (§47.8).

5   Second aorist passive, which does not occur in the N.T. (§47.8). Stem vowel becomes α (§4, v-7).

6   The root is *τκ. It reduplicates to form the present, and then the τκ undergoes metathesis (§7.6): *τκ ‣ τιτκ ‣ τίκτ.

7   τκ ‣ τεκ + σ ‣ τέξομαι

8   Second aorist (§44.5a). The stem shows the weak grade (τκ ‣ τεκ; §4, v-7).

9   Roots are *θρεχ and *δραμ (v-8; Funk §487.9). Whenever the aspirate χ is present, the τ aspirates to a θ (§15.6). If the χ were altered, the θ would reappear. (Cf. θρεκτός, θρεκτικός) Has compounds εἰστρέχω, ἐπισυντρέχω, κατατρέχω, περιτρέχω, προτρέχω, προστρέχω, συντρέχω, ὑποτρέχω.

10   Uses the root *δραμ. Second aorist (§44.5a).

11   ἀποφεύγω, διαφεύγω, ἐκφεύγω, καταφεύγω. See BDF §101.

12   Stem has undergone ablaut to the weak grade (ευ ‣ ε; §4, v-7). Second aorist (§44.5a)

13   Second perfect (§45.5b), occurring in the N.T. only in the compound verb ἐκφεύγω.

14   ἀποφθέγγομαι

15   ἀναψύχω, ἀποψύχω, ἐκψύχω, καταψύχω. The root is *ψυχ, but the aorist passive is from *φυγ (Funk §482.30; BDF §76.1; 101).

16   Second aorist passive (§47.8).

17   Attic contracted form of ἀείδω.

ἀλήθω	-	-	-	-	-
διδῶ[1]	-	-	-	-	-
ἔθω	-	-	εἴωθα[2]	-	-
ἐρείδω	-	ἤρεισα	-	ἤρεισμαι	-
ἐσθίω[3]	φαγόμαι[4]	ἔφαγον[5]	-	-	-
εὕδω[6]	-	-	-	-	-
ἥδομαι[7]	-	-	-	-	-
κνήθω	-	-	-	-	-
νήθω[8]	-	-	-	-	-
οἶδα[9]	εἰδήσω[10]	ᾔδειν[11]	-	-	-
πείθω[12]	πείσω	ἔπεισα	πέποιθα[13]	πέπεισμαι	ἐπείσθην
πέτομαι[14]	πτήσομαι	ἐπτόμην[15]	-	-	-

1   A by-form of δίδωμι (v-6a), occurring as a v.l. only at Rev 3:9 as διδῶ.

2   A second perfect of an obsolete ἔθω (§45.5d; Funk §3880). Pluperfect is εἰώθειν.

3   Lk 22:30 has ἔσθητε (pres. subj.) from the root *εσθ. κατεσθίω, συνεσθίω. Funk (§487.4) explains that the root is *εδ. To the root was added θι, which was an old way of forming the present tense stem. δ + θ formed σ resulting in ἐσθίω. It has a future ἔδομαι (cf. ἐδεστός). It uses *φαγ in other tenses (v-8). Can be written ἔσθω, both as a simple verb and in compounds (e.g., κατέσθω; cf. BDF §101, MH 238).

4   From the root *φαγ. No tense formative is used in the future (§43.8c).

5   From the root *φαγ. Second aorist (§44.5a).

6   καθεύδω

7   συνήδομαι

8   The root is *νη, and θ was added to form the present tense stem (Smyth §490). Cf. πλήθω (v-1c[2]). νήθω is not listed in LS. See BDF §101.

9   Uses two roots, *οιδ and *ϝιδ (v-8; Funk §487.5). Cf. the Latin "video," in which the ϝ has come over as a "v." ϝιδ is also the root of εἶδον, which we have listed with ὁράω. There is no reduplication and it uses the regular aorist endings without theσ. οἶδα is really a second perfect that through time became used as a present. LaSor says that it might be from a verbal root *ϝεϝιδα in which the digammas dropped out; see future form. Compound is σύνοιδα. It is conjugated as follows: οἶδα, οἶδας, οἶδε(ν), οἴδαμεν, οἴδατε, οἴδασι(ν). See paradigm at §45.5c. An alternate third plural is found at Acts 26:4, ἴσασι(ν), which is a remnant of an older Attic conjugation (Funk §388).

10   From the root *ϝιδ. Reduplicated to form the future (since it probably is an old future perfect), ϝ dropped out, the vowels contracted, and η was inserted (§43.8d): *ϝιδ ⟩ εϝιδ ⟩ ειδ ⟩ εἰδήσω. In Attic it is εἴσομαι. See BDF §101.

11   Actually is an augmented pluperfect that functions as an aorist. From the same root *ϝιδ, but contrary to the future when the ϝ dropped out, the vowels contracted differently to differentiate the two roots.

12   ἀναπείθω. See BDF §101.

13   Second perfect (§45.5b). Has undergone ablaut (ει ⟩ οι; §4, v-7).

14   The root is *πετ. In the future it undergoes metathesis (πετ ⟩ πτε ⟩ πτη [§7.6]), or the ε was lost (§7.2) and an η was inserted (Smyth §493). ἐπιπέτομαι. See BDF §101.

15   Second aorist (§44.5a), which does not occur in the N.T. Has lost its stem vowel due to syncope (§7.2) or ablaut (§4, v-7). Also has a root aorist, ἔπτην (§44.2c), appearing in the compound verb ἐπιπέτομαι. For other forms see LS and Funk (§411).

πίπτω[1]	πεσοῦμαι[2]	ἔπεσον[3]	πέπτωκα[4]	-	-
πρήθω[5]	-	-	-	πέπρησμαι	ἐπρήσθην
σπένδω	-	-	-	-	-
σπεύδω	-	ἔσπευσα	-	-	-
φείδομαι	φείσομαι	ἐφεισάμην	-	-	-
ψεύδομαι	ψεύσομαι	ἐψευσάμην	-	-	-

v-1b(4) Roots ending in a stop, but add ε to form the present[6]
(total: 2)

δοκέω	δόξω	ἔδοξα	-	-	-
ὠθέω[7]	-	ὦσα	-	-	-

v-1c

Verbal roots ending in a liquid/nasal

Description

v-1c(1) Roots ending in a liquid (ρ)

v-1c(2) Roots ending in a nasal (μ, ν)

All futures are liquids unless indicated (§43.3) All aorists are liquids unless indicated (§44.1c).

---

[1] The root is *πτ, which can change to πετ in its strong grade (v-7). We list its root as *πτ, contrary to our custom of using the strong grade, to avoid confusion with πέτομαι, which also has a root *πετ.

    *πτ reduplicates as if it were a μι verb to form the present tense: *πτ ‣ πίπτω.

    ἀναπίπτω, ἀντιπίπτω, ἀποπίπτω, ἐκπίπτω, ἐμπίπτω, ἐπιπίπτω, καταπίπτω, παραπίπτω, περιπίπτω, προσπίπτω, συμπίπτω.

[2] Has both a Doric (§43.8a) and a contract (§43.8b) future, not occurring the in N.T.

[3] Root is *πετ (strong grade). τ drops out when immediately followed by σ (§22.3). Second aorist (§44.5a). Has a first aorist, ἔπεσα, but not in the N.T. (*BDF* §81.3, *MH* 208).

[4] Root is *πτ (zero grade). It reduplicates and inserts an ω before the tense formative much like other words insert an η or σ: *πτ ‣ πεπτ ‣ πέπτωκα.

[5] ἐμπρήθω (alternate form of ἐμπί(μ)πρημι).

[6] In the present, they will behave just like ε contract verbs (cf. Smyth §485).

[7] ἀπωθέω, ἐξωθέω. From the root *Ϝωθε. Imperfect, ὤθουν. In Classical Greek the imperfect was ἐώθουν and the aorist was ἔωσα and ἐώσθην. By the Koine period, the Ϝ has totally dropped out without notice.

v-1c(1)   Roots ending in ρ   (total: 7)

δέρω	-	ἔδειρα[1]	-	-	ἐδάρην[2]
ἱμείρομαι[3]	-	-	-	-	-
μαρτύρομαι[4]	-	ἐμαρτυράμην	-	-	-
ὀμείρομαι	-	-	-	-	-
πτύρω	-	-	-	-	-
σύρω[5]	-	ἔσυρα	-	-	-
φέρω[6]	οἴσω[7]	ἤνεγκα[8]	ἐνήνοχα[9]	ἐνήνεγμαι	ἠνέχθην[10]

v-1c(2)   Roots ending in μ, ν   (total: 22)

αἰσχύνω[11]	-	-	-	ἤσχυμμαι	ᾐσχύνθην
ἀμύνομαι	-	ἠμυνάμην	-	-	-
βαθύνω	-	ἐβάθυνα	-	-	-
βαρύνω[12]	-	ἐβάρυνα	-	-	-
γέμω	-	-	-	-	-

---

[1] Stem vowel becomes ει due to ablaut (§4).

[2] Second aorist passive (§47.8). Stem vowel becomes α due to ablaut (§4). η inserted (§47.7).

[3] V.l. for ὀμείρομαι at 1 Thess 2:8.

[4] διαμαρτύρομαι, προμαρτύρομαι

[5] κατασύρω

[6] φέρω builds its principal parts from three roots: *φερ, *οἰ, *ἐνεκ (v-7, v-8; Funk §487.10). ἀναφέρω, ἀποφέρω, διαφέρω, εἰσφέρω, ἐκφέρω, ἐπιφέρω, καταφέρω, παραφέρω, παρεισφέρω, περιφέρω, προφέρω, προσφέρω, συμφέρω, ὑποφέρω

[7] From the alternate verbal root *οἰ. Is not a liquid future.

[8] Varies between first and second aorist endings (§44.5b). Not a liquid aorist.

*ἐνεκ › ενκ › ενενκ › ενεγκ › ηνεγκ. From the alternate verbal root *ἐνεκ that undergoes reduplication (§44.5d). The stem loses its vowel in its zero grade (§4), reduplicates, the ν becomes γ (§24.2), and the reduplicated ε augments as well. This is not Attic reduplication since it is the reduplicated vowel being lengthened and not the original stem vowel. (Funk says the ε is lost not through ablaut but through syncope (Funk §3440.2; MBG §7.2)

[9] *ἐνεκ › ενοκ › ενενοκ › ενηνοκ › ενηνοχα. The root *ἐνεκ undergoes ablaut (ε › ο; §4), consonantal and vocalic reduplication. The κ is then aspirated to χ (§14). Second perfect (45.5b). Occurs in the N.T. only in the compound προσφέρω.

[10] *ἐνεκ › ηνεκ › ηνεχθην. The root is augmented, and the κ aspirates to χ before the θ (§14 .5).

[11] In our literature αἰσχύνω occurs only in the middle/passive. ἐπαισχύνομαι, καταισχύνω.

[12] καταβαρύνω. Smyth (§518c) says that υνω was added by analogy to verbs in -αινω and -αιρω, assuming a root *βαρ.

γίνομαι[1]	γενήσομαι[2]	ἐγενόμην[3]	γέγονα[4]	γεγένημαι[5]	ἐγενήθην[6]
εὐθύνω[7]	-	εὔθυνα[8]	-	-	-
κλίνω[9]	κλινῶ	ἔκλινα	κέκλικα	-	ἐκλίθην
κρίνω[10]	κρινῶ	ἔκρινα	κέκρικα	κέκριμαι	ἐκρίθην
μεγαλύνω	μεγαλυνῶ	-	-	-	ἐμεγαλύνθην
μένω[11]	μενῶ	ἔμεινα[12]	μεμένηκα[13]	-	-
μηκύνω	-	-	-	-	-
μολύνω	-	ἐμόλυνα	-	-	ἐμολύνθην
ὀξύνω[14]	-	-	-	-	-
ὀτρύνω[15]	-	ὤτρυνα[16]	-	-	-
παχύνω	-	-	-	-	ἐπαχύνθην
πλατύνω	-	-	-	πεπλάτυμμαι	ἐπλατύνθην
πληθύνω[17]	πληθυνῶ	ἐπλήθυνα	-	-	ἐπληθύνθην
πλύνω[18]	πλυνῶ	ἔπλυνα	-	-	-

---

1   γεν ▸ γν ▸ γιγν ▸ γιν ▸ γίνομαι. The verbal root is *γεν. It goes to its zero form (γν), reduplicates to form the present stem (γιγν), the second γ drops off (γιν), and the connecting vowel and personal endings are added. It is not a liquid. ἀπογίνομαι, διαγίνομαι, ἐπιγίνομαι, παραγίνομαι, προγίνομαι, συμπαραγίνομαι. See BDF §101.

2   Is not a liquid future. η added to form tense stem (§43.8d).

3   Second aorist (§44.5a)

4   Stem vowel becomes ο due to ablaut (§4, v-7). Second perfect (§45.5b).

5   η added to form tense stem (§46.6).

6   η added to form tense stem (§47.7).

7   κατευθύνω

8   No augment (§31.4a)

9   ἀνακλίνω, ἐκκλίνω, κατακλίνω, προσκλίνω. κλίνω and κρίνω are from a small class of verbs that lose ν in the perfect and aorist passive tenses (Funk §482.30; §24.11).

10 ἀνακρίνω, ἀνταποκρίνομαι, ἀποκρίνομαι, διακρίνω, ἐγκρίνω, ἐπικρίνω, κατακρίνω, συγκρίνω, συνυποκρίνομαι, ὑποκρίνομαι. κλίνω and κρίνω are from a small class of verbs that lose ν in the perfect and aorist passive tenses (Funk §482.30; §24.11).

11 ἀναμένω, διαμένω, ἐμμένω, ἐπιμένω, καταμένω, παραμένω, περιμένω, προσμένω, συμπαραμένω, ὑπομένω

12 Stem vowel becomes ει due to ablaut (§4, v-7).

13 η added to form tense stem (§45.3).

14 παροξύνω

15 παροτρύνω

16 LS lists an Epic aorist as ὄτρυνα (no augment).

17 Smyth (§490) says the alternate form πλήθω adds θ to form the present tense stem (cf. πίμπλημι). Cf. νήθω, v-1b(3).

18 ἀποπλύνω

σκληρύνω	σκληρυνῶ	ἐσκλήρυνα	-	-	ἐσκληρύνθην
τρέμω	-	-	-	-	-
ὠδίνω[1]	-	-	-	-	-

v-1d

Verbal roots ending in a vowel

Description

v-1d(1a) Roots ending in α (which lengthen the α before a tense formative)

v-1d(1b) Roots ending in α (which do not lengthen the α before a tense formative)

v-1d(2a) Roots ending in ε (which lengthen the ε before a tense formative)

v-1d(2b) Roots ending in ε (which do not lengthen the ε before a tense formative)

v-1d(2c) Roots ending in ε (which lose the ε in the present tense)

v-1d(3) Roots ending in o

v-1d verbs usually called "contract verbs" because their final root vowel contracts with the connecting vowels. They also lengthen their final root vowel before a tense formative (or in the case of the perfect middle/passive, before the personal endings).[2] There are, however, certain verbs that do not lengthen their root vowel, and they have been given separate categories (v-1d[1b]; v-1d[2b]). v-1b(4) verbs insert ε in their present tense stem, making them appear to be ε contract verbs.

There is some variation in v-1d(2b); some verbs do lengthen their final root vowel in some of the tenses. Smyth (§397) gives the following rule. "Verbs in εω of two syllables do not contract ει with o or ω." See also v-1a(7) verbs.

General changes

The root vowels lengthen according to the pattern in §3.3: α ‣ η, ε ‣ η, o ‣ ω.

v-1d(1a) Roots ending in α (which lengthen the α before a tense formative) (total: 62)

ἀγαπάω	ἀγαπήσω	ἠγάπησα	ἠγάπηκα	ἠγάπημαι	ἠγαπήθην

---

[1] συνωδίνω

[2] Contract verbs actually formed their present tense stem by adding ιω to the verbal root and the ι was subsequently lost (Smyth §522).

ἀκροάομαι[1]	-	-	-	-	-
ἀλοάω	-	-	-	-	-
ἀμάω	-	ἤμησα	-	-	-
ἀντάω[2]	ἀντήσω	ἤντησα	ἤντηκα	-	-
ἀπατάω[3]	-	ἠπάτησα	-	-	ἠπατήθην
ἀριστάω	-	ἠρίστησα	-	-	-
ἀρτάω[4]	ἀρτήσα	ἤρτησα	ἤρτηκα	ἤρτημαι	ἠρτήθην
ἀτιμάω[5]	-	ἠτίμησα	-	-	-
βοάω[6]	βοήσω	ἐβόησα	-	-	-
βριμάομαι[7]	-	ἐβριμησάμην	-	-	ἐβριμήθην
γεννάω[8]	γεννήσω	ἐγέννησα	γεγέννηκα	γεγέννημαι	ἐγεννήθην
δαπανάω[9]	δαπανήσω	ἐδαπάνησα	-	-	ἐδαπανήθην
διψάω	διψήσω	ἐδίψησα	-	-	-
δοκάω[10]	-	ἐδόκησα	-	-	-
ἐλεάω[11]	-	-	-	-	-
ἐραυνάω[12]	-	ἠραύνησα	-	-	-
ἐρωτάω[13]	ἐρωτήσω	ἠρώτησα	-	-	ἠρωτήθην
ζάω[14]	ζήσω[15]	ἔζησα	-	-	-

---

1   ἐπακροάομαι (occurs only as an imperfect, ἐπηκροώμην, at Acts 16:25).

2   ἀπαντάω, καταντάω, συναντάω, ὑπαντάω

3   ἐξαπατάω. See φρεναπατάω.

4   ἐξαρτάω

5   See τιμάω.

6   ἀναβοάω, ἐπιβοάω, καταβοάω

7   ἐμβριμάομαι (also ἐμβριμίομαι), although there are no clear examples in the N.T. We find -ωμαι in Mk 14:5 and Jn 11:38.

8   ἀναγεννάω

9   ἐκδαπανάω, προσδαπανάω

10   προσδοκάω. δοκάω is not listed in LS.

11   BAGD says this stem arose through confusion of α and ε contract stems, beginning with the more common ἐλεέω (v-1d[2a]). ἐλεῶντος is found at Rom 9:16.

12   ἐξεραυνάω. ἐρευνάω is the Classical form.

13   διερωτάω, ἐπερωτάω

14   ἀναζάω, συζάω. In Classical Greek there are contract verbs with a long final vowel such as ζήω from the root *ζη (cf. χρήομαι). Most have fully assimilated to the -αω pattern except for ζάω and χράομαι (Funk §3691). BAGD list them as α contracts. ι is added to *ζη to form ζάω. In the present it is conjugated as ζῶ, ζῇς, ζῇ, ζῶμεν, ζῆτε, ζῶσιν(ν). χράομαι is conjugated χρῶμαι, χρᾶσαι, χρᾶται, χρώμεθα, χρᾶσθε, χρῶνται. χρῶ is the present middle imperative. Their imperfect is as follows. Active: ἔζων, ἔζης, ἔζη, ἐζῶμεν, ἐζῆτε, ἔζων. Middle/passive: ἐχρώμην, ἐχρῶ, ἐχρᾶτο, ἐχρώμεθα, ἐχρᾶσθε, ἐχρῶντο (Funk §4031). See BDF §101.

15   Some list the future as ζήσομαι.

ἡττάομαι	-	-	-	ἥττημαι	ἡττήθην
ἱστάω[1]	-	-	-	-	-
καυχάομαι[2]	καυχήσομαι	ἐκαυχησάμην	-	κεκαύχημαι	-
κοιμάω	-	-	-	κεκοίμημαι	ἐκοιμήθην
κολλάω[3]	-	-	-	-	ἐκολλήθην
κολυμβάω[4]	-	ἐκολύμβησα	-	-	-
κομάω	-	-	-	-	-
κτάομαι	κτήσομαι	ἐκτησάμην	-	κέκτημαι	-
λακάω[5]	-	ἐλάκησα	-	-	-
λικμάω	λικμήσω	-	-	-	-
λογάω[6]	-	-	-	-	-
μασάομαι	-	-	-	-	-
μελετάω[7]	-	ἐμελέτησα	-	-	-
μεριμνάω[8]	μεριμνήσω	ἐμερίμνησα	-	-	-
μνάομαι	-	-	-	μέμνησμαι[9]	-
μοιχάω[10]	-	-	-	-	-
μυκάομαι[11]	-	ἐμυκησάμην	-	-	-
μωμάομαι	-	ἐμωμησάμην	-	-	ἐμωμήθην
ναρκάω[12]	ναρκήσω	ἐνάρκησα	-	-	-
νικάω[13]	νικήσω	ἐνίκησα	νενίκηκα	-	ἐνικήθην
ξυράω[14]	ξυρήσομαι	ἐξύρησα	-	ἐξύρημαι	-
ὀδυνάω	-	-	-	-	-

---

[1] συνιστάω. Cf. ἵστημι (v-6a).

[2] ἐγκαυχάομαι, κατακαυχάομαι

[3] προσκολλάω

[4] ἐκκολυμβάω

[5] See *BDF* §101.

[6] ἐλλογάω

[7] προμελετάω

[8] προμεριμνάω

[9] σ is inserted after the stem (§46.5).

[10] See *BDF* §101.

[11] From the root *μυκ. α is added to form the present tense stem (Smyth §486).

[12] καταναρκάω

[13] ὑπερνικάω

[14] *BAGD* says there are three roots involved. From *ξυρ comes ξύρωνται, ξυρήσονται, ξυρήσωνται, and ἐξύρημαι. In 1 Cor 11:6 is the form ξυρᾶσθαι. Our texts accent it ξυρᾶσθαι, which means it is a present middle infinitive from the root *ξυρα. *BAGD* prefers ξύρασθαι, which means it is an aorist middle infinitive from the root*ξυρ. See discussion there for the arguments. See *BDF* §101.

ὁράω¹	ὄψομαι	ὠψάμην²	ἑώρακα³	-	ὤφθην
		εἶδον⁴			
ὁρμάω	-	ὥρμησα	-	-	-
πηδάω⁵	-	ἐπήδησα	-	-	-
πειράω	-	-	-	-	-
πιμπλάω⁶	-	-	-	-	-
πλανάω⁷	πλανήσω	ἐπλάνησα	-	πεπλάνημαι	ἐπλανήθην
σιγάω	-	ἐσίγησα	-	σεσίγημαι	-
σιωπάω	σιωπήσω	ἐσιώπησα	-	-	-
σκιρτάω	-	ἐσκίρτησα	-	-	-
σπαταλάω	-	ἐσπατάλησα	-	-	-
συλάω	-	ἐσύλησα	-	-	-
τελευτάω	τελευτήσω	ἐτελεύτησα	τετελεύτηκα	-	-
τιμάω⁸	τιμήσω	ἐτίμησα	-	τετίμημαι	-
τολμάω⁹	τολμήσω	ἐτόλμησα	-	-	-
τρυγάω	τρυγήσω	ἐτρύγησα	-	-	-

---

1 ἀφοράω, ἐφοράω, καθοράω, παροράω, προοράω, συνοράω, ὑπεροράω. See BDF §101.

 ἴδε and ἰδού are often listed as a separate words. εἶδον is also often listed as a separate word.

 ὁράω is in the process of being replaced by βλέπω, θεωρέω, and ὀπτάνομαι, a present formed from the same root as the aorist passive ὤφθην (Funk §487.6).

 The imperfect is ἑώρων from the root *Ϝορα (§31.5b; Smyth §431). Either the stem has received a double augment (εϜορα ‣ εϜωρα) and the intervocalic Ϝ was dropped (§27.4a, §31.8, §32.7), or it was augmented with η and the two vowels have undergone "quantitative metathesis" (§17), in which the η becomes its short ε and the ο becomes its long ω (*Ϝορα ‣ ηϜορα ‣ ηορα ‣ ἑώρων; Funk §3372.2). Cf. ἀνοίγω (‣ ἀνέῳξα; cv-1b[2]).

 The future and aorist passive are from the alternate root *ὀπ (v-8).

2 The only occurrence of this aorist is as an aorist middle subjunctive ὄψησθε at Lk 13:28. Most view εἶδον as functioning as the aorist of ὁράω.

3 For explanation of the stem and vocalic reduplication see discussion on the imperfect above. BAGD says that ἑόρακα is possible, in which there has only been one augment. The pluperfect occurs as ἑωράκει.

4 εἶδον is from the root *Ϝιδ (§31.5b, Smyth §431; from which οἶδα was formed). It is a second aorist (§44.5a) that was taking over the function of the aorist of ὁράω. Most list as the aorist of ὁράω.

5 ἀναπηδάω, εἰσπηδάω, ἐκπηδάω

6 ἐμπι(μ)πλάω. πιμπλάω is an alternate form of πί(μ)πλημι. See there for discussion (v-6a). The μ can be omitted, so some list as πί(μ)πλάω. See BDF §101.

7 ἀποπλανάω

8 ἐπιτιμάω. See ἀτιμάω.

9 ἀποτολμάω

τρυφάω[1]	-	ἐτρύφησα	-	-	-
φρεναπατάω[2]	-	-	-	-	-
φυσάω[3]	-	ἐφύσησα	-	-	-
χολάω	-	-	-	-	-
χράομαι[4]	-	ἐχρησάμην	-	κέχρημαι	-
ψηλαφάω	-	ἐψηλάφησα	-	-	-

v-1d(1b)   Roots ending in α (which do not lengthen the α before a tense formative)   (total: 19)

The basic rule is that the α is not lengthened if the root has ε, ι, or ρ immediately before it. There are a few words that do not follow this rule (cf. Smyth §488).

ἀγαλλιάω	-	ἠγαλλίασα	-	-	ἠγαλλιάθην[5]
αἰτιάομαι[6]	-	ἠτιασάμην	-	-	-
ἀράομαι[7]	-	ἠρασάμην	-	ἦραμαι	-
γελάω[8]	γελάσω	ἐγέλασα	-	-	-
δειλιάω	-	ἐδειλίασα	-	-	-
ἐάω[9]	ἐάσω	εἴασα	-	-	ἐάθην
θεάομαι	-	ἐθεασάμην	-	τεθέαμαι	ἐθεάθην
θλάω[10]	-	-	τέθλακα	-	ἐθλάσθην[11]
θυμιάω	-	ἐθυμίασα	-	-	-
ἰάομαι	ἰάσομαι	ἰασάμην	-	ἴαμαι	ἰάθην
κλάω[12]	-	ἔκλασα	-	-	ἐκλάσθην[13]
κονιάω	-	-	-	κεκονίαμαι	-

---

[1]   ἐντρυφάω

[2]   See ἀπατάω.

[3]   ἐμφυσάω

[4]   καταχράομαι, παραχράομαι, συγχράομαι. See discussion on ζάω. The root is *χρα.

[5]   Appears as a variant with a σ inserted after the tense stem (ἠγαλλιάσθην; §46.5).

[6]   προαιτιάομαι. Occurs as a simple verb in variant to Rom 3:9.

[7]   καταράομαι

[8]   καταγελάω

[9]   προσεάω. The root is *σεϝα (§31.5a; Smyth §431). When the ϝ dropped out εα would not contract. When augmented with ε, the σ becomes intervocalic, drops out, and the vowels contract (§25.5). Thus the imperfect is εἴων and the aorist εἴασα. Has an optative ἐάσαι (3 sg.).

[10]   συνθλάω

[11]   Inserts σ after the tense stem (§46.5).

[12]   ἐκκλάω, κατακλάω.

[13]   Inserts σ after the tense stem (§46.5).

κοπιάω	-	ἐκοπίασα	κεκοπίακα	-	-
κρέμαμαι[1]	-	ἐκρέμασα	-	-	ἐκρεμάσθην[2]
πεινάω	πεινάσω	ἐπείνασα	-	-	-
περάω[3]	-	ἐπέρασα	-	-	-
σπάω[4]	σπάσω	ἔσπασα	-	-	ἐσπάσθην[5]
στρηνιάω[6]	-	ἐστρηνίασα	-	-	-
χαλάω	χαλάσω	ἐχάλασα	-	-	ἐχαλάσθην[7]

v-1d(2a)   Roots ending in ε (which lengthen the ε before a tense formative)   (total: 228)

See also v-1b(4) verbs, which add ε to form their present tense stem.

ἀγαθοεργέω[8]	-	-	-	-	-
ἀγαθοποιέω	-	ἠγαθοποίησα	-	-	-
ἀγανακτέω	-	ἠγανάκτησα	-	-	-
ἀγνοέω	-	ἠγνόησα	-	-	-
ἀγραυλέω	-	-	-	-	-
ἀγρυπνέω	-	-	-	-	-
ἀδημονέω	-	-	-	-	-
ἀδικέω	ἀδικήσω	ἠδίκησα	ἠδίκηκα	-	ἠδικήθην
ἀδημονέω	-	-	-	-	-
ἀδυνατέω	ἀδυνατήσω	-	-	-	-
ἀθετέω	ἀθετήσω	ἠθέτησα	-	-	-
ἀθλέω[9]	-	ἤθλησα	ἤθληκα	-	-

---

[1]   *BAGD* lists as κρεμάννυμι, which we list as v-3c(1). It occurs seven times in the N.T., three times in the present as κρεμάμενος (Gal 3:13), κρεμάμενον (Acts 28:4), and κρέμαται (Mt 22:40), none showing the νυ. (v-3c[1] verbs add ννυ to form the present tense stem and drop them elsewhere.) The present in the N.T. seems to be κρεμάω, and therefore we list it as v-1d(1b). It has one compound that *BAGD* lists as ἐκκρεμάννυμι, which occurs once in the N.T. as ἐξεκρέματο (imperfect middle deponent; Lk 19:48). We list the compound at cv-3c(1).

[2]   Inserts σ after the stem (§46.5).

[3]   διαπεράω

[4]   ἀνασπάω, ἀποσπάω, διασπάω, ἐπισπάομαι, περισπάω

[5]   Inserts σ after the tense stem (§46.5).

[6]   καταστρηνιάω

[7]   σ is inserted after the tense stem (§46.5)

[8]   See ἐργέω. Has an uncontracted form ἀγαθοεργεῖν (1 Tim 6:18) and a contracted form ἀγαθουργῶν (Acts 14:17).

[9]   συναθλέω

ἀθυμέω	-	-	-	-	-
αἱμορροέω	-	-	-	-	-
αἱρέω[1]	αἱρήσομαι[2]	εἱλόμην[3]	-	ᾕρημαι	ᾑρέθην
αἰτέω[4]	αἰτήσω	ᾔτησα	ᾔτηκα	ᾔτημαι	-
ἀκηδεμονέω	-	-	-	-	-
ἀκολουθέω[5]	ἀκολουθήσω	ἠκολούθησα	ἠκολούθηκα	-	-
ἀλγέω[6]	-	-	ἤλγηκα	-	-
ἀλληγορέω	-	-	-	-	-
ἀμελέω	-	ἠμέλησα	-	-	-
ἀνθομολογέομαι[7]	-	-	-	-	-
ἀνθρωπέω[8]	-	ἠνθρώπησα	-	-	-
ἀντλέω	-	ἤντλησα	ἤντληκα	-	-
ἀντοφθαλμέω	-	-	-	-	-
ἀπειθέω	-	ἠπείθησα	-	-	-
ἀπειλέω	-	ἀπείλησα	-	-	-
ἀπιστέω	-	ἠπίστησα	-	-	-
ἀπορέω[9]	-	-	ἠπόρηκα	-	ἠπορήθην
ἀργέω[10]	αργήσω	ἤργησα	ἤργηκα	ἤργημαι	ἠργήθην
ἀριθμέω[11]	-	ἠρίθμησα	-	ἠρίθμημαι	-
ἁρμολογέω[12]	-	-	-	-	-
ἀρνέομαι[13]	ἀρνήσομαι	ἠρνησάμην	-	ἤρνημαι	ἠρνήθην
ἀσεβέω	-	ἠσέβησα	-	-	-

---

[1] ἀναιρέω, ἀφαιρέω, διαιρέω, ἐξαιρέω, καθαιρέω, περιαιρέω, προαιρέω. Some list as a deponent, αἱρέομαι. αἱρέω uses two roots, *αιρε and *Ϝελ (v-8). Cf. Funk §487.1. BDF §101.

[2] Has a future form ἑλῶ (liquid future §43.3) in the compound ἀναιρέω (ἀνείλατε in Acts 2:23; ἀνείλαν in Acts 10:39, and ἀνείλατο in Acts 7:21). BAGD says it was formed after the second aorist ἀνεῖλον.

[3] *Ϝελ ‣ εϜελ ‣ εελ ‣ εἱλόμην. From the root *Ϝελ. Second aorist (§44.5a), which received the syllabic augment, the Ϝ dropped out, and the two vowels contracted to ει. BAGD lists εἱλόμην (Heb 11:25) and εἱλάμην (2 Thess 2:13).

[4] ἀπαιτέω, ἐξαιτέω, ἐπαιτέω, παραιτέομαι, προσαιτέω

[5] ἐξακολουθέω, ἐπακολουθέω, κατακολουθέω, παρακολουθέω, συνακολουθέω

[6] ἀπαλγέω

[7] See ὁμολογέω.

[8] ἐνανθρωπέω. ἀνθρωπέω is not listed in LS.

[9] ἐξαπορέω. See BDF §101.

[10] καταργέω. See BDF §101.

[11] καταριθμέω

[12] ασυναρμολογέω

[13] ἀπαρνέομαι

ἀσθενέω	-	ἠσθένησα	ἠσθένηκα	-	-
ἀσκέω	-	-	-	-	-
ἀστατέω	-	-	-	-	-
ἀστοχέω	-	ἠστόχησα	-	-	-
ἀσχημονέω	-	-	-	-	-
ἀτακτέω	-	ἠτάκτησα	-	-	-
αὐθεντέω	-	-	-	-	-
αὐλέω	-	ηὔλησα	-	-	-
αὐχέω	-	-	-	-	-
ἀχέω[1]	-	-	-	-	-
βαρέω[2]	-	ἐβάρησα	-	βεβάρημαι	ἐβαρήθην
βατταλογέω[3]	βατταλογήσω	ἐβατταλόγησα	-	-	-
βλασφημέω	-	ἐβλασφήμησα	-	-	ἐβλασφημήθην
βοηθέω	-	ἐβοήθησα	-	-	-
γαμέω[4]	-	ἐγάμησα[5]	γεγάμηκα	-	ἐγαμήθην
γεωργέω	-	-	-	-	-
γονυπετέω	-	ἐγονυπέτησα	-	-	-
γρηγορέω[6]	-	ἐγρηγόρησα	-	-	-
δειπνέω	δειπνήσω	ἐδείπνησα	-	-	-
δεσμέω[7]	-	-	-	-	-
δημέω[8]	-	ἐδήμησα	-	-	-
δημηγορέω	-	-	-	-	-
διακονέω[9]	διακονήσω	διηκόνησα	-	-	διηκονήθην
δικέω[10]	δικήσω	ἐδίκησα	-	-	-
διχοτομέω	διχοτομήσω	-	-	-	-
δουλαγωγέω	-	-	-	-	-
δυνατέω	δυνατήσω	-	-	-	-

---

[1] προσαχέω

[2] ἐπιβαρέω, καταβαρέω. See *BDF* §101.

[3] Also spelled βαττολογέω.

[4] Smyth (§485) says the root added ε to form all the tenses. See *BDF* §101.

[5] Liquid aorist ἔγημα with a lengthened tense stem vowel (§44.3) in Lk 14:20 and 1 Cor 7:28. Elsewhere it uses the first aorist ἐγάμησα.

[6] διαγρηγορέω

[7] Alternate form of δεσμεύω (v–1a[6]). All of our texts have "ευ-."

[8] ἀποδημέω, ἐκδημέω, ἐνδημέω, ἐπιδημέω. δημέω is not listed in *LS*.

[9] Augmented as a compound (§31.6). Its imperfect is διηκονουν.

[10] ἐκδικέω

δυσφημέω	-	-	-	-	-
δωρέομαι	-	ἐδωρησάμην	-	δεδώρημαι	-
εἰλέω[1]	-	εἴλησα[2]	-	-	-
εἰρηνοποιέω[3]	-	εἰρηνοποίησα	-	-	-
ἐλαττονέω	-	ἠλαττόνησα	-	-	-
ἐλεέω[4]	ἐλεήσω	ἠλέησα	-	ἠλέημαι	ἠλεήθην
ἐργέω[5]	-	ἤργησα	ἤργηκα	-	-
ἑτεροδιδασκαλέω	-	-	-	-	-
ἑτεροζυγέω	-	-	-	-	-
εὐαρεστέω	-	εὐαρέστησα	εὐαρέστηκα	-	-
εὐδοκέω[6]	-	εὐδόκησα[7]	-	-	-
εὐεργετέω	-	-	-	-	-
εὐθυδρομέω	-	εὐθυδρόμησα	-	-	-
εὐθυμέω	-	-	-	-	-
εὐκαιρέω[8]	-	εὐκαίρησα	-	-	-
εὐλαβέομαι	-	-	-	-	ηὐλαβήθην
εὐλογέω[9]	εὐλογήσω	εὐλόγησα	εὐλόγηκα	εὐλόγημαι	εὐλογήθην
εὐνοέω[10]	-	-	-	-	-
εὐπορέω	-	-	-	-	-
εὐπροσωπέω	-	εὐπροσώπησα	-	-	-
εὐσεβέω	-	-	-	-	-
εὐσχημονέω	-	-	-	-	-
εὐφορέω	-	εὐφόρησα	-	-	-
εὐψυχέω	-	-	-	-	-
εὐχαριστέω	-	εὐχαρίστησα	-	-	εὐχαριστήθην
εὐωχέομαι[11]	-	-	-	-	-

---

[1] ἀπειλέω, ἐνειλέω, προσαπειλέω.

[2] ἀπειλέω has an aorist middle that augments the first element of the compound: ἠπειλησαμην. Possibly this is because the second element by itself does not augment; cf. *BDF* §316.

[3] See ποιέω.

[4] Cf. ἐλεάω

[5] ἐνεργέω, συνεργέω, συνυπουργέω. See ἱερουργέω.

[6] συνευδοκέω

[7] Has an augmented form ηὐδόκησα that does not occur in the N.T. (§31.4b).

[8] Its imperfect can be εὐκαίρουν (Mk 6:31) or ηὐκαίρουν (Acts 17:21).

[9] ἐνευλογέω, κατευλογέω

[10] See νοέω.

[11] συνευωχέομαι

ζέω	-	-	-	-	-
ζητέω[1]	ζητήσω	ἐζήτησα	-	-	ἐζητήθην
ζωγρέω	-	-	-	ἐζώγρημαι	-
ζῳογονέω	ζῳογονήσω	-	-	-	-
ζῳοποιέω[2]	ζῳοποιήσω	ἐζῳοποίησα	-	-	ἐζῳοποιήθην
ζωπυρέω[3]	-	ἐζωπύρησα	-	-	-
ἡγέομαι[4]	ἡγήσομαι	ἡγησάμην	-	ἥγημαι	-
ἠχέω[5]	-	ἤχησα	-	ἤχημαι	ἠχήθην
θαμβέω[6]	-	-	-	-	ἐθαμβήθην[7]
θαρρέω[8]	-	ἐθάρρησα	-	-	-
θαρσέω[9]	-	ἐθάρσησα	-	-	-
θεομαχέω	-	-	-	-	-
θεωρέω[10]	θεωρήσω	ἐθεώρησα	-	-	-
θηριομαχέω	-	ἐθηριομάχησα	-	-	-
θορυβέω	-	-	-	-	-
θρηνέω	θρηνήσω	ἐθρήνησα	-	-	-
θροέω	-	-	-	-	ἐθροήθην
θυμέω[11]	θυμήσω	ἐθύμησα	-	-	ἐθυμήθην
θυμομαχέω	-	-	-	-	-
ἱεροσυλέω	-	-	-	-	-
ἱερουργέω[12]	-	-	-	-	-
ἱστορέω[13]	-	ἱστόρησα	-	-	-
κακέω[14]	-	ἐκάκησα	-	-	-

---

1   ἀναζητέω, ἐκζητέω, ἐπιζητέω, συζητέω

2   συζῳοποιέω (› συνεζωοποίησα). See ποιέω.

3   ἀναζωπυρέω

4   διηγέομαι, ἐκδιηγέομαι, ἐξηγέομαι, προηγέομαι

5   ἐξηχέω, κατηχέω

6   ἐκθαμβέω

7   Has an alternative form ἐθαμβώθην (from *θανμο or else the endings have been confused) that is not in the N.T.

8   Cf. *BAGD* for its relationship with θαρσέω.

9   Cf. *BAGD* for its relationship with θαρρέω.

10   ἀναθεωρέω, παραθεωρέω. See *BDF* §101.

11   διενθυμέομαι, ἐνθυμέομαι, ἐπιθυμέω. See also ἀθυμέω, εὐθυμέω. θυμέω is not listed in *LS*.

12   See ἐργέω. ἱερουργέω is the contracted form of ἱερο + ἐργέω.

13   διϊστορέω

14   ἐγκακέω, ἐκκακέω. κακέω is not listed in *LS*.

κακολογέω	-	ἐκακολόγησα	-	-	-
κακοπαθέω[1]	-	-	-	-	ἐκακοπάθησα
κακοποιέω[2]	-	ἐκακοποίησα	-	-	-
κακουχέω[3]	-	-	-	-	-
καλοποιέω[4]	-	-	-	-	-
καρποφορέω	καρποφορήσω	ἐκαρποφόρησα	-	-	-
καρτερέω[5]	-	ἐκαρτέρησα	-	-	-
κατηγορέω	κατηγορήσω	κατηγόρησα	-	-	-
κεντέω[6]	-	ἐκέντησα	-	-	-
κινέω[7]	κινήσω	ἐκίνησα	-	-	ἐκινήθην
κληροδοτέω[8]	-	-	-	-	-
κληρονομέω[9]	κληρονομήσω	ἐκληρονόμησα	κεκληρονόμηκα	-	-
κοινωνέω[10]	κοινωνήσω	ἐκοινώνησα	κεκοινώνηκα	-	-
κοσμέω	-	ἐκόσμησα	-	κεκόσμημαι	-
κρατέω	κρατήσω	ἐκράτησα	κεκράτηκα	κεκράτημαι	-
κυέω[11]	-	ἐκύησα	-	-	-
κυνέω[12]	κυνήσω	ἐκύνησα	-	-	-
λαλέω[13]	λαλήσω	ἐλάλησα	λελάληκα	λελάλημαι	ἐλαλήθην
λατομέω	-	ἐλατόμησα	-	λελατόμημαι	-
λειτουργέω	-	ἐλειτούργησα	-	-	-
λιθοβολέω	-	ἐλιθοβόλησα	-	-	ἐλιθοβολήθην
λογέομαι[14]	-	ἐλογησάμην	-	-	ἐλογήθην
λογομαχέω	-	-	-	-	-
λοιδορέω[15]	-	ἐλοιδόρησα	-	-	-

---

[1] συγκακοπαθέω. See παθέω. κακοπαθέω is not listed in *LS*.
[2] See ποιέω.
[3] συγκακουχέομαι
[4] See ποιέω.
[5] προσκαρτερέω
[6] ἐκκεντέω
[7] μετακινέω, συγκινέω
[8] κατακληροδοτέω
[9] κατακληρονομέω
[10] συγκοινωνέω
[11] ἀποκυέω. See *BDF* §101.
[12] προσκυνέω
[13] ἀπολαλέω, διαλαλέω, ἐκλαλέω, καταλαλέω, προσλαλέω, συλλαλέω.
[14] ἀπολογέομαι, ἐλλογέω. λογέομαι is not listed in *LS*.
[15] ἀντιλοιδορέω

λυπέω[1]	-	ἐλύπησα	λελύπηκα	-	ἐλυπήθην
μακροθυμέω	-	ἐμακροθύμησα	-	-	-
μαρτυρέω[2]	μαρτυρήσω	ἐμαρτύρησα	μεμαρτύρηκα	μεμαρτύρημαι	ἐμαρτυρήθην
μεγαλαυχέω	-	-	-	-	-
μετρέω[3]	-	ἐμέτρησα	-	-	ἐμετρήθην
μετριοπαθέω[4]	-	-	-	-	-
μιμέομαι	μιμήσομαι	ἐμιμησάμην	-	-	-
μισέω	μισήσω	ἐμίσησα	μεμίσηκα	μεμίσημαι	-
μοσχοποιέω[5]	-	ἐμοσχοποίησα	-	-	-
μυέω	-	-	-	μεμύημαι	-
μυθέομαι[6]	-	-	-	-	-
ναυαγέω	-	ἐναυάγησα	-	-	-
νοέω[7]	νοήσω	ἐνόησα	νενόηκα	-	-
νομέω[8]	-	-	-	-	-
νομοθετέω	-	ἐνομοθέτησα	-	νενομοθέτημαι	-
νοσέω	-	-	-	-	-
νουθετέω	νουθετήσω	ἐνουθέτησα	-	-	-
ξενοδοχέω	-	ἐξενοδόχησα	-	-	-
ὁδηγέω	ὁδηγήσω	-	-	-	-
ὁδοιπορέω	-	ὡδοιπόρησα	-	-	-
οἰκέω[9]	οἰκήσω	ᾤκησα	-	-	-
οἰκοδεσποτέω	-	-	-	-	-
οἰκοδομέω[10]	οἰκοδομήσω	ᾠκοδόμησα	-	ᾠκοδόμημαι[11]	οἰκοδομήθην[12]
οἰκονομέω	-	-	οἰκονόμηκα	-	-

---

[1]   συλλυπέω

[2]   ἐπιμαρτυρέω, καταμαρτυρέω, συμμαρτυρέω, συνεπιμαρτυρέω. See also ψευδομαρτυρέω.

[3]   ἀντιμετρέω

[4]   See παθέω.

[5]   See ποιέω.

[6]   παραμυθέομαι

[7]   κατανοέω, μετανοέω, προνοέω, ὑπονοέω. See εὐνοέω.

[8]   παρανομέω. νομέω is not listed in LS.

[9]   ἐνοικέω, ἐγκατοικέω, κατοικέω, παροικέω, περιοικέω, συνοικέω

[10] ἀνοικοδομέω, ἐποικοδομέω, συνοικοδομέω

[11] Occurs as a third singular pluperfect, ᾠκοδόμητο (Lk 4:29), and as infinitive, οἰκοδομῆσθαι (Lk 6:48, showing no reduplication). It can appear in the indicative without reduplication.

[12] BAGD lists the augmented form ᾠκοδομήθην, but it does not augment in the N.T. (Jn 2:20).

ὀκνέω	-	ὤκνησα	-	-	-
ὀλιγωρέω	-	-	-	-	-
ὁμιλέω[1]	-	ὡμίλησα	-	-	-
ὁμολογέω[2]	ὁμολογήσω	ὡμολόγησα	-	-	-
ὁμορέω[3]	-	-	-	-	-
ὀρθοποδέω	-	-	-	-	-
ὀρθοτομέω	-	-	-	-	-
ὁρκέω[4]	ὁρκήσω	ὥρκησα	ὥρκηκα		
ὀρχέομαι	-	ὠρχησάμην	-	-	-
οὐδενέω[5]	-	-	-	-	οὐδενήθην
οὐθενέω[6]	-	οὐθένησα	-	οὐθένημαι	-
ὀχλέω[7]	-	-	-	-	-
ὀχλοποιέω[8]	-	ὠχλοποίησα	-	-	-
παθέω[9]	-	ἐπάθησα	-	-	-
πατέω[10]	πατήσω	ἐπάτησα	-	-	ἐπατήθην
πειθαρχέω	-	ἐπειθάρχησα	-	-	-
πενθέω	πενθήσω	ἐπένθησα	-	-	-
πλεονεκτέω	-	ἐπλεονέκτησα	-	-	ἐπλεονεκτήθην
πληροφορέω	-	ἐπληροφόρησα	-	πεπληροφόρημαι	ἐπληροφορήθην
πλουτέω	-	ἐπλούτησα	πεπλούτηκα	-	-
ποθέω[11]	-	ἐπόθησα	-	-	-
ποιέω[12]	ποιήσω	ἐποίησα	πεποίηκα	πεποίημαι	ἐποιήθην
πολεμέω	πολεμήσω	ἐπολέμησα	-	-	ἐπολεμήθην

---

[1] συνομιλέω

[2] ἐξομολογέω. See ἀνθομολογέομαι.

[3] συνομορέω

[4] ἐπιορκέω. ὁρκέω is not listed in LS.

[5] ἐξουδενέω. Occurs only at Mk 9:12. Has a variant ἐξουδενώθην that shows a root in ο and not ε. οὐδενέω is not listed in LS.

[6] Alternate form of οὐδενέω. ἐξουθενέω. οὐθενέω is not listed in LS.

[7] ἐνοχλέω, παρενοχλέω

[8] See ποιέω.

[9] συμπαθέω. See μετριοπαθέω and κακοπαθέω. παθέω is not listed in LS.

[10] ἐμπεριπατέω, καταπατέω, περιπατέω

[11] ἐπιποθέω

[12] See ἀγαθοποιέω, εἰρηνοποιέω, ζῳοποιέω, κακοποιέω, καλοποιέω, μοσχοποιέω, ὀχλοποιέω. None of these augment as compound verbs. We have listed the following as compounds since they are formed with prepositions: περιποιέω, προσποιέω, συζωοποιέω. See p. 248 for rationale.

πονέω[1]	-	-	-	-	ἐπονήθην
πορέω[2]	-	-	-	-	-
πορθέω	-	ἐπόρθησα	-	-	-
προσωπολημπτέω[3]	-	-	-	-	-
πτοέω	-	-	-	-	ἐπτοήθην
πωλέω	-	ἐπώλησα	-	-	-
σαφέω[4]	-	ἐσάφησα	-	-	-
σκοπέω[5]	σκοπήσω	ἐσκόπησα	-	ἐσκόπημαι	-
στενοχωρέω[6]	-	-	-	-	-
στερέω[7]	-	ἐστέρησα	-	ἐστέρημαι	-
στοιχέω[8]	στοιχήσω	-	-	-	-
στρατολογέω	-	ἐστρατολόγησα	-	-	-
στυγέω[9]	-	-	-	-	-
συκοφαντέω	-	ἐσυκοφάντησα	-	-	-
συλαγωγέω	-	-	-	-	-
σωφρονέω	-	ἐσωφρόνησα	-	-	-
ταλαιπωρέω	-	ἐταλαιπώρησα	-	-	-
τεκνογονέω	-	-	-	-	-
τεκνοτροφέω	-	ἐτεκνοτρόφησα	-	-	-
τετραρχέω[10]	-	-	-	-	-
τηρέω[11]	τηρήσω	ἐτήρησα	τετήρηκα	τετήρημαι	ἐτηρήθην
τιμωρέω	-	-	-	-	ἐτιμωρήθην
τροποφορέω	-	ἐτροποφόρησα	-	-	-
τροφοφορέω	-	ἐτροφοφόρησα	-	-	-
ὑδροποτέω	-	-	-	-	-
ὑμνέω	ὑμνήσω	ὕμνησα	-	-	-
ὑπηρετέω	-	ὑπηρέτησα	-	-	-

---

[1] διαπονέομαι, καταπονέω. πονέω can be middle deponent.

[2] διαπορέω. πορέω is not listed in LS.

[3] The μ can be omitted, προσωπολήπτέω. It occurs once in the N.T. (Jas 2:9) with the μ.

[4] διασαφέω

[5] ἐπισκοπέω, κατασκοπέω. See BDF §101.

[6] See χωρέω.

[7] ἀποστερέω

[8] συστοιχέω

[9] ἀποστυγέω

[10] Some texts spell τετρααχέω, and others list as τετρ(α)αρχέω.

[11] διατηρέω, παρατηρέω, συντηρέω

ὑστερέω[1]	-	ὑστέρησα	ὑστέρηκα	ὑστέρημαι	ὑστερήθην
ὑψηλοφρονέω[2]	-	-	-	-	-
φθονέω	-	ἐφθόνησα	-	-	-
φιλέω[3]	-	ἐφίλησα	πεφίληκα	-	-
φιλοτιμέομαι	-	-	-	-	-
φλυαρέω	-	-	-	-	-
φοβέω[4]	-	-	-	-	ἐφοβήθην
φρονέω[5]	φρονήσω	ἐφρόνησα	-	-	-
φρουρέω	φρουρήσω	-	-	-	-
φωνέω[6]	φωνήσω	ἐφώνησα	-	-	ἐφωνήθην
χαλιναγωγέω	χαλιναγωγήσω	ἐχαλιναγώγησα	-	-	-
χειρέω[7]	-	ἐχείρησα	-	-	-
χειραγωγέω	-	-	-	-	-
χειροτονέω[8]	-	ἐχειροτόνησα	-	κεχειροτόνημαι	ἐχειροτονήθην
χορηγέω[9]	χορηγήσω	ἐγορήγησα	-	-	ἐχορηγήθην
χρονοτριβέω	-	-	-	-	-
χωρέω[10]	χωρήσω	ἐχώρησα	κεχώρηκα	-	-
ψευδομαρτυρέω[11]	-	-	-	-	-
ὠνέομαι	-	ὠνησάμην[12]	-	-	-
ὠφελέω	ὠφελήσω	ὠφέλησα	-	-	ὠφελήθην

v-1d(2b)   Roots ending in ε (which do not lengthen the ε before a tense formative)   (total: 10)

In some cases the ε will lengthen.

αἰνέω[13]	αἰνέσω	ἤνεσα	-	-	-

---

[1]   ἀφυστερέω. See *BDF* §101.

[2]   See φρονέω.

[3]   καταφιλέω

[4]   ἐκφοβέω

[5]   καταφρονέω, παραφρονέω, περιφρονέω, ὑπερφρονέω. See ὑψηλοφρονέω.

[6]   ἀναφωνέω, ἐκφωνέω, ἐμφωνέω, ἐπιφωνέω, καταφωνέω, προσφωνέω, συμφωνέω

[7]   ἐπιχειρέω

[8]   προχειροτονέω

[9]   ἐπιχορηγέω

[10]   ἀναχωρέω, ἀποχωρέω, ἐκχωρέω, συγχωρέω, ὑποχωρέω. See στενοχωρέω.

[11]   Imperfect, ἐψευδομαρτυροῦν (§31.6). Cf. μαρτυρέω.

[12]   Smyth (§529) says ἐπριάμην is used for ἐωνησάμην, from the root *πρια. In the N.T. the word occurs only once, as an aorist middle, ὠνήσατο (Acts 7:16). The root is *Ϝωνε (§31.5b; Smyth §431), which develops into ἐωνούμην, ἐωνήθην. In Koine the initial Ϝ was evidently forgotten. See *BDF* §101.

[13]   ἐπαινέω, παραινέω

ἀκαιρέομαι	-	-	-	-	ἠκαιρέθην
ἀρκέω[1]	-	ἤρκεσα	-	-	ἠρκέσθην[2]
δέω[3]	δήσω	ἔδησα	δέδεκα	δέδεμαι	ἐδέθην
ἐμέω	-	ἤμεσα	-	-	-
καλέω[4]	καλέσω	ἐκάλεσα	κέκληκα	κέκλημαι	ἐκλήθην
λυσιτελέω[5]	-	-	-	-	-
τελεοφορέω[6]	-	-	-	-	-
τελέω[7]	τελέσω	ἐτέλεσα	τετέλεκα	τετέλεσμαι	ἐτελέσθην
φορέω	φορέσω	ἐφόρεσα	πεφόρηκα	-	-

v-1d(2c) Roots ending in ε (which lose the ε in the present tense) (total: 10)

These verbs may appear to insert an η in all tenses except the present, but the η is the lengthened tense vowel that is lost in the present.

βούλομαι[8]	-	-	-	-	ἐβουλήθην
δεῖ[9]	-	-	-	-	-
δέομαι[10]	-	-	-	-	ἐδεήθην
θέλω[11]	θελήσω	ἠθέλησα	-	-	ἠθελήθην

---

[1] ἐπαρκέω

[2] σ inserted after tense stem (§46.5).

[3] καταδέω, περιδέω (pluperfect περιεδέδετο, Jn 11:14), συνδέω, ὑποδέω

[4] ἀντικαλέω, ἐγκαλέω, εἰσκαλέομαι, ἐπικαλέω, μετακαλέω, παρακαλέω, προκαλέω, προσκαλέω, συγκαλέω, συμπαρακαλέω.
   In the last three principal parts, the verbal root *καλ reduces to its zero grade (§4.4c, v-7) and the ε lenghtens to η (§4), or it undergoes metathesis (§7.6).

[5] See τελέω.

[6] See φορέω.

[7] ἀποτελέω, διατελέω, ἐκτελέω, ἐπιτελέω, συντελέω. See λυσιτελέω. Cf. Smyth §409N. The root is *τελεσ. The σ drops out in the perfect active and reappears in the perfect middle/ passive and aorist passive (cf. cf. Smyth §409eN), appearing as if the σ were inserted (§46.5).

[8] Funk lists βούλομαι in this category, but then says the η is inserted in the aorist passive (3:95). He in fact says this for all the forms in this category. We have listed the word as if the η is part of the root and is simply lost (as Funk says) in the present.

[9] The imperfect is ἔδει, and the present subjunctive is δέῃ.

[10] προσδέομαι. The root was originally *δεε and therefore, after the final ε has dropped out, the other ε and the ο connecting vowel do not contract; cf. aorist passive.

[11] The imperfect and aorist augment with an η because the root was originally *εθελ (BDF §66.3, 101).

μέλω[1]	μελήσομαι	ἐμέλησα	-	-	ἐμελήθην
μέλλω[2]	μελλήσω	-	-	-
νέμω[3]	-	-	-	-	ἐνεμήθην
οἶμαι[4]	-	-	-	-
οἴομαι[5]	-	-	-	-	ᾠήθην
οἴχομαι[6]	-	-	-	ᾤχημαι	-

v-1d(3)   Roots ending in o   (total: 104)

ἀκριβόω	-	ἠκρίβωσα	-	-	-
ἀκυρόω	-	ἠκύρωσα	-	-	-
ἀλλοιόω	-	ἠλλοίωσα	-	-	ἠλλοιώθην
ἀλλοτριόω[7]	-	ἠλλοτρίωσα	-	ἠλλοτρίωμαι	-
ἀλόω[8]	-	-	-	-	-
ἀξιόω[9]	ἀξιώσω	ἠξίωσα	-	ἠξίωμαι	ἠξιώθην
ἀρθρόω[10]	-	-	-	-	-
ἀροτριάω	-	-	-	-	-
ἀτιμόω[11]	-	-	-	-	-
ἀχρειόω	-	-	-	ἠχρείωμαι	ἠχρεώθην[12]
βεβαιόω[13]	βεβαιώσω	ἐβεβαίωσα	-	-	ἐβεβαιώθην

---

[1] ἐπιμελέομαι, μεταμέλομαι. The simple verb in the present form is obsolete by the time of the Koine except for the third singular μέλει, which is used both personally and impersonally. μέλει is formed as if the root actually ended in ε, yet has an imperfect ἔμελεν and an imperative μελέτω. Note the presence of the ε in ἐπιμελέομαι but not in μεταμέλομαι. See BDF §101.

[2] In the manuscripts, the augment varies between ε and η (BDF §66.3). It occurs in the following forms: ἔμελλεν (3t); ἔμελλον (3t); ἤμελλεν (11t); ἤμελλον (1t).

[3] ἀπονέμω, διανέμω

[4] An alternate form of οἴομαι. We find both imperfects ᾠόμην and ᾤμην (Smyth §398b). See BDF §101.

[5] *οιε. Contracts to οἶμαι (Jn 21:35), οἰέσθω (Jas 1:7), οἰόμενοι (Phil 1:47).

[6] *οιχε. παροίχομαι. See Smyth (§486) and BDF §101.

[7] ἀπαλλοτριόω

[8] ἀναλόω. Alternate form of ἀναλίσκω (cv-5b). ἀλόω is not listed in LS. See principal parts at ἁλίσκομαι (v-5b).

[9] καταξιόω

[10] διαρθρόω

[11] Alternate form of ἀτιμάω (v-1d[1a]) and ἀτιμάζω (v-2a[1]). In the N.T. it is always the α contract ἀτιμάω (7t).

[12] The ι is evidently absorbed.

[13] διαβεβαιόομαι

βεβηλόω	-	ἐβεβήλωσα	-	-	-
βιόω	-	ἐβίωσα	-	-	-
δεκατόω[1]	-	-	δεδεκάτωκα	δεδεκάτωμαι	-
δηλόω[2]	δηλώσω	ἐδήλωσα	-	δεδήλωμαι	ἐδηλώθην
δικαιόω	δικαιώσω	ἐδικαίωσα	-	δεδικαίωμαι	ἐδικαιώθην
διπλόω	-	ἐδίπλωσα	-	-	-
δολιόω	-	-	-	-	-
δολόω	-	-	-	-	-
δουλόω[3]	δουλώσω	ἐδούλωσα	-	δεδούλωμαι	ἐδουλώθην
δυναμόω[4]	-	ἐδυνάμωσα	-	δεδυνάμωμαι	ἐδυναμώθην
ἐλαττόω	-	ἠλάττωσα	-	ἠλάττωμαι	-
ἐλευθερόω	ἐλευθερώσω	ἠλευθέρωσα	-	-	ἠλευθερώθην
ἑλκόω	-	-	-	εἵλκωμαι[5]	-
ἐναντιόομαι	-	-	-	-	-
ἕπομαι[6]	-	-	-	-	-
ἐρημόω	-	-	-	ἠρήμωμαι	ἠρημώθην
ἐσσόομαι	-	-	-	-	ἡσσώθην
εὐοδόω	-	-	-	-	εὐοδώθην
ζηλόω[7]	ζηλώσω	ἐζήλωσα	-	-	-
ζημιόω	-	-	-	-	ἐζημιώθην
ζυμόω	-	-	-	-	ἐζυμώθην
ἡλόω[8]	-	ἥλωσα	-	-	-
θανατόω	θανατώσω	ἐθανάτωσα	-	-	ἐθανατώθην
θεμελιόω	θεμελιώσω	ἐθεμελίωσα	-	τεθεμελίωμαι	-
θυμόω	-	-	-	-	ἐθυμώθην
ἱκανόω	-	ἱκάνωσα	-	-	-
καινόω[9]	-	-	-	-	-

---

[1] ἀποδεκατόω

[2] προσδηλόω

[3] καταδουλόω

[4] ἐνδυναμόω

[5] The root probably began with a letter that is now lost (cf. Funk §3430.4), possibly σ (§31.5a), which explains the apparently irregular vocalic reduplication. *σελκο › εσελκο › εελκο › εἵλκωμαι. Cf. ἑλκύω, v-1a(4).

[6] The root is *σεπ (§31.5a; Smyth §431). It is augmented with ε, the intervocalic σ drops out, and the vowels contract. Appears in the N.T. only in the compound συνείπετο (Acts 20:4), the imperfect of συνέπομαι.

[7] παραζηλόω

[8] προσηλόω

[9] ἀνακαινόω

κακόω	κακώσω	ἐκάκωσα	-	κεκάκωμαι	-
κατιόω	-	-	-	κεκατίωμαι	-
καυματόω	-	-	-	-	ἐκαυματώθην
καυσόω	-	-	-	-	-
κενόω	κενώσω	ἐκένωσα	-	κεκένωμαι	ἐκενώθην
κεφαλαιόω[1]	-	ἐκεφαλαίωσα	-	-	-
κεφαλιόω	-	ἐκεφαλίωσα	-	-	-
κημόω	κημώσω	-	-	-	-
κληρόω[2]	-	-	-	κεκλήρωμαι	ἐκληρώθην
κοινόω	-	ἐκοίνωσα	κεκοίνωκα	κεκοίνωμαι	-
κολοβόω	-	ἐκολόβωσα	-	κεκολόβωμαι	ἐκολοβώθην
κομβόομαι[3]	-	ἐκομβωσάμην	-	-	-
κραταιόω	-	-	-	-	ἐκραταιώθην
κυκλόω[4]	κυκλώσω	ἐκύκλωσα	-	-	ἐκυκλώθην
κυρόω[5]	-	ἐκύρωσα	-	κεκύρωμαι	-
λυτρόω	-	ἐλύτρωσα	-	-	ἐλυτρώθην
μαστιγόω	μαστιγώσω	ἐμαστίγωσα	-	-	ἐμαστιγώθην
ματαιόω	-	-	-	-	ἐματαιώθην
μεσόω	-	-	-	-	-
μεστόω	-	-	-	μεμέστωμαι	-
μισθόω	-	ἐμισθωσάμην	-	-	-
μονόω	-	-	-	μεμόνωμαι	-
μορφόω[6]	-	-	-	μεμόρφωμαι	ἐμορφώθην
νεκρόω	-	ἐνέκρωσα	-	νενέκρωμαι	-
νεόω[7]	-	ἐνέωσα	-	-	-
ὁμοιόω[8]	ὁμοιώσω	ὡμοίωσα	-	ὡμοίωμαι	ὡμοιώθην
ὀρθόω[9]	ὀρθώσω	ὤρθωσα	-	-	ὠρθώθην
οὐδενόω[10]	-	-	-	-	-

---

1 ἀνακεφαλαιόω
2 προσκληρόω
3 ἐγκομβόομαι
4 περικυκλόω
5 προκυρόω
6 μεταμορφόω, συμμορφόω
7 ἀνανεόω (which some list as a deponent, ἀνανεόομαι).
8 ἀφομοιόω
9 ἀνορθόω, ἐπιδιορθόω
10 ἐξουδενόω. Alternate form of ἐξουθενέω (cv-1d[2a]).

οὐθενόω[1]	-	-	-	-	-
παλαιόω	-	-	πεπαλαίωκα	-	ἐπαλαιώθην
πηρόω	-	-	-	-	-
πιστόω	-	-	-	-	ἐπιστώθην
πληρόω[2]	πληρώσω	ἐπλήρωσα	πεπλήρωκα	πεπλήρωμαι	ἐπληρώθην
πυρόω[3]	-	-	-	πεπύρωμαι	ἐπυρώθην
πωρόω	-	ἐπώρωσα	πεπώρωκα	πεπώρωμαι	ἐπωρώθην
ῥιζόω[4]	-	ἐρίζωσα	-	ἐρρίζωμαι	ἐριζώθην
ῥυπόω	-	ἐρύπωσα	-	-	-
σαρόω	-	ἐσάρωσα	-	σεσάρωμαι	ἐσαρώθην
σημειόω	-	-	-	-	-
σθενόω	σθενώσω	-	-	-	-
σκηνόω[5]	σκηνώσω	ἐσκήνωσα	-	-	-
σκοτόω	-	-	-	ἐσκότωμαι	ἐσκοτώθην
σπαργανόω	-	ἐσπαργάνωσα	-	ἐσπαργάνωμαι	-
σπιλόω	-	-	-	ἐσπίλωμαι	-
στατόω[6]	-	ἐστάτωσα	-	-	-
σταυρόω[7]	σταυρώσω	ἐσταύρωσα	-	ἐσταύρωμαι	ἐσταυρώθην
στερεόω	-	ἐστερέωσα	-	-	ἐστερεώθην
στεφανόω	-	ἐστεφάνωσα	-	ἐστεφάνωμαι	ἐστεφανώθην
στρεβλόω	-	-	-	-	-
ταπεινόω	ταπεινώσω	ἐταπείνωσα	-	τεταπείνωμαι	ἐταπεινώθην
ταρταρόω	-	ἐταρτάρωσα	-	-	-
τελειόω	-	ἐτελείωσα	τετελείωκα	τετελείωμαι	ἐτελειώθην
τεκνόω	-	ἐτέκνωσα	-	-	-
τεφρόω	-	ἐτέφρωσα	-	-	-
τυπόω[8]	-	-	-	τετύπωμαι	-
τυφλόω	-	ἐτύφλωσα	τετύφλωκα	-	-
τυφόω	-	-	-	τετύφωμαι	ἐτυφώθην

---

1 ἐξουθενόω. Alternate form of ἐξουθενέω (cv-1d[2a]). οὐθενόω is not listed in *LS*.
2 ἀναπληρόω, ἀνταναπληρόω, ἐκπληρόω, προσαναπληρόω, συμπληρόω
3 ἐκπυρόω
4 ἐκριζόω
5 ἐπισκηνόω, κατασκηνόω
6 ἀναστατόω. στατόω is not listed in *LS*.
7 ἀνασταυρόω, συσταυρόω
8 ἐντυπόω

ὑπνόω[1]	-	ὕπνωσα	-	-	-
ὑψόω[2]	ὑψώσω	ὕψωσα	-	-	ὑψώθην
φανερόω	φανερώσω	ἐφανέρωσα	πεφανέρωκα	πεφανέρωμαι	ἐφανερώθην
φιμόω	φιμώσω	ἐφίμωσα	πεφίμωκα	πεφίμωμαι	ἐφιμώθην
φραγελλόω	-	ἐφραγέλλωσα	-	-	-
φυσιόω	-	-	-	πεφυσίωμαι	ἐφυσιώθην
χαλινόω	-	-	-	-	-
χαριτόω	-	ἐχαρίτωσα	-	κεχαρίτωμαι	-
χρυσόω	-	-	-	κεχρύσωμαι	-

Class v-2

Present Stem = Verbal Root + ι

v-2 verbs form their present tense stem by adding ι to their verbal root. The ι will then usually modify the final stem consonant in some way. Again, it is important to remember that the addition of ι does not affect any of the other tenses. In discussing the formation of those other tenses, we must go to the verbal root and not to the present tense stem.

As Smyth points out (§623), it is often impossible to determine the exact stem of many of these verbs. In fact, most of the verbs ending in ιζω and αζω do not have stems in δ or γ, but rather were assimilated to the pattern (Smyth §512). Many are denominals (i.e., verbs formed from nouns) that have assimilated to αζω/ιζω by analogy (LaSor §24.2514, Funk §484.10). Since the primary function of this text is to help students learn New Testament Greek and not teach morphology, we will not deal with these intricacies.

Stems ending in γ can be either v-2a or v-2b (by analogy), depending on how the final γ is altered when forming the present tense stem.

v-2a

Verbal roots ending in δ or γ add ι › ζω

v-2a(1)   **Roots ending in δ + ι › αζω / ιζω**   (total: 199)

| present | δ + ι › ζ | (§6.1) |
| future | δ + σ › σ | (§15.3) |

---

[1]   ἀφυπνόω
[2]   ὑπερυψόω

aorist	δ + σ ▸ σ	(§15.3)
perfect (active)	δ + μ ▸ σμ	(§14.3)
perfect (middle/passive)	δ + μ ▸ σμ	(§14.3)
aorist (passive)	δ + θ ▸ σθ	(§13.3)

In the perfect middle/passive and aorist passive these verbs will appear to insert σ after the tense stem (§46.5). Rather, the σ is the altered dental.

All but one of the Attic futures appearing in the New Testament are from this category. All these words end in άζω and ίζω except ἁρμόζω, καθέζομαι, κατακλύζω, ὀλολύζω, and πιέζω.

ἁγιάζω	-	ἡγίασα	-	ἡγίασμαι	ἡγιάσθην
ἀγκαλίζομαι[1]	-	ἠγκάλισα	-	-	-
ἁγνίζω	-	ἥγνισα	ἥγνικα	ἥγνισμαι	ἡγνίσθην
ἀγοράζω[2]	-	ἠγόρασα	-	ἠγόρασμαι	ἠγοράσθην
ἀγωνίζομαι[3]	-	ἠγωνισάμην	-	ἠγώνισμαι	-
ἀθροίζω[4]	-	ἤθροισα	-	ἤθροισμαι	ἠθροίσθην
αἱρετίζω	-	ᾑρέτισα	-	-	-
αἰχμαλωτίζω	-	-	-	-	ᾐχμαλωτίσθην
ἀκμάζω	-	ἤκμασα	-	-	-
ἀλαλάζω	-	-	-	-	-
ἁλίζω[5]	-	-	-	-	ἡλίσθην
ἀναγκάζω	-	ἠνάγκασα	-	-	ἠναγκάσθην
ἀνδρίζομαι	-	-	-	-	-
ἀνεμίζω	-	-	-	-	-
ἀνετάζω	-	-	-	-	-
ἀνταγωνίζομαι[6]	-	-	-	-	-
ἁρμόζω	-	ἥρμοσα	-	ἥρμοσμαι	ἡρμόσθην
ἀρτίζω[7]	ἀρτίσω	ἤρτισα	ἤρτικα	ἤρτισμαι	-
ἀσπάζομαι[8]	-	ἠσπασάμην	-	-	-
ἀσπίζω[9]	-	-	ἤσπικα	-	-

---

[1] ἐναγκαλίζομαι

[2] ἐξαγοράζω

[3] ἀνταγωνίζομαι, ἐπαγωνίζομαι, καταγωνίζομαι, συναγωνίζομαι

[4] ἐπαθροίζω, συναθροίζω

[5] συναλίζω

[6] See γνωρίζω.

[7] ἐξαρτίζω, καταρτίζω, προκαταρτίζω

[8] ἀπασπάζομαι

[9] ὑπερασπίζω

ἀσφαλίζω	-	ἠσφάλισα	-	-	ἠσφαλίσθην
ἀτενίζω	-	ἠτένισα	-	-	-
ἀτιμάζω	-	ἠτίμασα	-	-	ἠτιμάσθην
αὐγάζω[1]	αὐγάσω	ηὔγασα	-	-	-
αὐλίζομαι[2]	-	ηὐλισάμην	ηὔλισμαι	-	ηὐλίσθην
ἀφανίζω[3]	-	-	-	-	ἠφανίσθην
ἀφρίζω[4]	-	-	-	-	-
βαπτίζω[5]	βαπτίσω	ἐβάπτισα	-	βεβάπτισμαι	ἐβαπτίσθην
βασανίζω	-	ἐβασάνισα	-	-	ἐβασανίσθην
βαστάζω	βαστάσω	ἐβάστασα	-	-	-
βιάζω[6]	βιάσομαι	ἐβιασάμην	-	βεβίασμαι	ἐβιάσθην
βιβάζω[7]	βιβάσω	ἐβίβασα	-	-	ἐβιβάσθην
βολίζω	-	ἐβόλισα	-	-	-
βυθίζω	-	-	-	-	ἐβυθίσθην
γαμίζω[8]	-	-	-	-	-
γεμίζω	-	ἐγέμισα	-	-	ἐγεμίσθην
γενεαλογέω	-	-	-	-	-
γνωρίζω[9]	γνωρίσω	ἐγνώρισα	-	-	ἐγνωρίσθην
γογγύζω[10]	γογγύσω	ἐγόγγυσα	-	-	-
γυμνάζω		-	-	γεγύμνασμαι	-
δαιμονίζομαι	-	-	-	-	ἐδαιμονίσθην
δαμάζω	-	ἐδάμασα	-	δεδάμασμαι	-
δανείζω[11]	-	-	-	-	-
δανίζω	-	ἐδάνισα	-	-	-
δειγματίζω[12]	-	ἐδειγμάτισα	-	-	-

---

[1] διαυγάζω, καταυγάζω
[2] συναυλίζομαι is a v.l. for συναλίζω at Acts 1:4; cf. *BAGD*.
[3] See φανίζω.
[4] ἀπαφρίζω, ἐπαφρίζω
[5] ἐμβαπτίζω
[6] παραβιάζομαι
[7] ἀναβιβάζω, ἐμβιβάζω, ἐπιβιβάζω, καταβιβάζω, προβιβάζω, συμβιβάζω
[8] ἐκγαμίζω
[9] ἀναγνωρίζω, διαγνωρίζω. γνωρίζω has an Attic future (§43.7b), but in the N.T. it uses a regular future.
[10] διαγογγύζω
[11] Alternate form of δανίζω. Does not occur in our texts.
[12] παραδειγματίζω

δελεάζω	-	-	-		-
δικάζω[1]	-	ἐδίκασα	-	-	ἐδικάσθην
διστάζω	διστάσω	ἐδίστασα	-	-	-
διχάζω	-	ἐδίχασα	-	-	-
δογματίζω	-	-	-	δεδογμάτισμαι	-
δοκιμάζω[2]	δοκιμάσω	ἐδοκίμασα	-	δεδοκίμασμαι	-
δοξάζω[3]	δοξάσω	ἐδόξασα	-	δεδόξασμαι	ἐδοξάσθην
ἐγγίζω[4]	ἐγγιῶ[5]	ἤγγισα	ἤγγικα	-	-
ἐδαφίζω	ἐδαφιῶ[6]	-	-	-	-
ἐθίζω[7]	-	εἴθισα	-	εἴθισμαι	εἰθίσθην
ἐλπίζω[8]	ἐλπιῶ[9]	ἤλπισα	ἤλπικα	-	-
ἐνυπνιάζομαι	-	-	-	-	ἐνυπνιάσθην
ἐξουσιάζω[10]	-	-	-	-	ἠξουσιάσθην
ἑορτάζω	-	-	-	-	-
ἐπηρεάζω	-	-	-	-	-
ἐργάζομαι[11]	-	ἠργασάμην[12]	-	εἴργασμαι	εἰργάσθην
ἐρεθίζω	-	ἠρέθισα	-	-	-
ἐρίζω[13]	ἐρίσω	-	-	-	-
ἐτάζω[14]	-	ἤτασα	-	-	-
ἑτοιμάζω[15]	ἑτοιμάσω	ἡτοίμασα	ἡτοίμακα	ἡτοίμασμαι	ἡτοιμάσθην

---

[1]   καταδικάζω

[2]   ἀποδοκιμάζω

[3]   ἐνδοξάζομαι, συνδοξάζω

[4]   προσεγγίζω

[5]   Attic future (§43.7b)

[6]   Attic future (§43.7b)

[7]   ἐθίζω is from *σϝεθιδ (Smyth §431), which accounts for the unusual augment. σϝεθιδ ⟩ εσϝεθιδ ⟩ εεθιδ ⟩ ειθιδ ⟩ εἴθισα (§31.5a).

[8]   ἀπελπίζω, προελπίζω

[9]   Attic future (§43.7b)

[10] κατεξουσιάζω. οὐσιάζω was a rare verb, and by the time of the N.T. it was probably not viewed as a compound.

[11] κατεργάζομαι, περιεργάζομαι, προσεργάζομαι.The root is *ϝεργαδ (§31.5b; Smyth §431), which means it can augment with ε, ϝ becomes interconsonantal and drops out, and the two ε's contract to ει (§31.5b). The same holds true for reduplication. The aorist can augment with η, "forgetting" about the original ϝ.

[12] Also augments to εἰργασάμεθα in 2 Jn 8 and κατειργάσατο in Rom 7:8; 15:18; 2 Cor 7:11; 12:12; 1 Pet 4:3 (BDF §67.3). BAGD says προσεργάζομαι can be augmented with either ει or η, but it occurs in the N.T. only with η (Lk 19:16).

[13] καθερίζω

[14] ἀνετάζω, ἐξετάζω

[15] προετοιμάζω

εὐαγγελίζω[1]	-	εὐηγγέλισα	-	εὐηγγέλισμαι	εὐηγγελίσθην
εὐνουχίζω	-	εὐνούχισα	-	-	εὐνουχίσθην
ἐωρίζω[2]	-	-	-	-	-
ἡσυχάζω	-	ἡσύχασα	-	-	-
θαυμάζω[3]	θαυμάσομαι	ἐθαύμασα	-	-	ἐθαυμάσθην
θεατρίζω	-	-	-	-	-
θεματίζω[4]	-	ἐθεμάτισα	-	-	-
θερίζω	θερίσω	ἐθέρισα	-	-	ἐθερίσθην
θηλάζω	-	ἐθήλασα	-	-	-
θησαυρίζω[5]	-	ἐθησαύρισα	-	τεθησαύρισμαι	-
θορυβάζω	-	-	-	-	-
θραυματρίζω	-	-	-	-	-
ἱματίζω	-	-	-	ἱμάτισμαι	-
ἰουδαΐζω	-	-	-	-	-
ἰσχυρίζομαι[6]	-	-	-	-	-
καθαρίζω[7]	καθαριῶ[8]	ἐκαθάρισα	-	κεκαθάρισμαι	ἐκαθαρίσθην[9]
καθέζομαι[10]	-	-	-	-	ἐκαθέσθην
καθίζω[11]	καθίσω[12]	ἐκάθισα	κεκάθικα	-	-
καινίζω[13]	-	ἐκαίνισα	-	κεκαίνισμαι	-
κατοπτρίζω[14]	-	-	-	-	-
καυματίζω	-	ἐκαυμάτισα	-	-	ἐκαυματίσθην
καυστηριάζω	-	-	-	κεκαυστηρίασμαι	-
καυτηριάζω[15]	-	-	-	-	-

---

[1] προευαγγελίζομαι. Augments as a compound verb: εὐηγγιλιζόμην.

[2] μετεωρίζομαι. ἐωρίζω is not listed in LS.

[3] ἐκθαυμάζω

[4] ἀναθεματίζω, καταθεματίζω, καταναθεματίζω

[5] ἀποθησαυρίζω

[6] διϊσχυρίζομαι

[7] Has an alternate form καθερίξω, but it does not appear in the N.T. διακαθαρίζω

[8] Attic future (§43.7b)

[9] Has a v.l. ἐκαθερίσθην (Mk 1:42; 8:3) from καθερίζω (BDF §29.1; MH 67).

[10] παρακαθέζομαι

[11] ἀνακαθίζω, ἐπικαθίζω, παρακαθίζω, περικαθίζω, συγκαθίζω. See BDF §101.

[12] Has an Attic future (καθιῶ; §43.7b) that does not occur in the N.T. (nor compounds).

[13] ἀνακαινίζω, ἐγκαινίζω

[14] See τρίζω.

[15] Alternate form of καυστηριάζω.

κεντρίζω[1]	-	ἐκέντρισα	-	-	ἐκεντρίσθην
κεφαλίζω[2]	-	ἐκεφάλισα	-	-	-
κιθαρίζω	-	-	-	-	-
κλυδωνίζομαι	-	-	-	-	-
κλύζω[3]	-	-	-	-	ἐκλύσθην
κολάζω	κολάσω	ἐκολασάμην	-	-	ἐκολάσθην
κολαφίζω	-	ἐκολάφισα	-	-	-
κομίζω[4]	κομίσομαι[5]	ἐκόμισα	-	-	ἐκομίσθην
κοπάζω	-	ἐκόπασα	-	-	-
κουφίζω	-	-	-	-	-
κραυγάζω[6]	κραυγάσω	ἐκραύγασα	-	-	-
κρημνίζω[7]	-	ἐκρήμνισα	-	-	-
κρυσταλλίζω	-	-	-	-	-
κτίζω	-	ἔκτισα	-	ἔκτισμαι	ἐκτίσθην
λακτίζω	-	-	-	-	-
λιθάζω[8]	λιθάσω	ἐλίθασα	-	-	ἐλιθάσθην
λογίζομαι[9]	-	ἐλογισάμην	-	-	ἐλογίσθην
μακαρίζω	μακαριῶ[10]	ἐμακάρισα	-	-	-
μαστίζω	-	-	-	-	-
μερίζω[11]	μεριῶ[12]	ἐμέρισα	μεμέρικα	μεμέρισμαι	ἐμερίσθην
μεσάζω	-	-	-	-	-
μορφίζω[13]	-	-	-	-	-
μυκτηρίζω[14]	-	-	-	-	-
μυρίζω	-	ἐμύρισα	-	-	-

---

[1] ἐγκεντρίζω
[2] ἀποκεφαλίζω
[3] κατακλύζω
[4] ἐκκομίζω, συγκομίζω
[5] Also has an Attic future κομιοῦμαι (§43.7b; 1 Pet 5:4; v.l. in Col 3:25 and 2 Pet 2:13).
[6] ἀνακραυγάζω
[7] κατακρημνίζω
[8] καταλιθάζω
[9] ἀναλογίζομαι, διαλογίζομαι, συλλογίζομαι, παραλογίζομαι.
[10] Attic future (§43.7b)
[11] διαμερίζω, συμμερίζω (which *BAGD* lists as a deponent).
[12] Attic future (§43.7b)
[13] συμμορφίζω
[14] ἐκμυκτηρίζω

μυωπάζω	-	-	-	-	-
νηπιάζω	-	-	-	-
νομίζω	-	ἐνόμισα	-	-
νοσφίζω	-	ἐνοσφισάμην-	-	-
ξενίζω	-	ἐξένισα	-	-	ἐξενίσθην
ὄζω[1]	-	-	-	-	-
οἰκίζω[2]	οἰκιῶ[3]	ᾤκισα	-	-
ὀλολύζω	-	-	-	-
ὁμοιάζω[4]	-	-	-	-
ὀνειδίζω	-	ὠνείδισα	-	-
ὀνομάζω[5]	-	ὠνόμασα	-	-	ὠνομάσθην
ὁπλίζω[6]	-	ὥπλισα	-	ὥπλισμαι	-
ὀπτρίζω[7]	-	-	-	-	-
ὀργίζω[8]	ὀργιῶ[9]	ὤργισα	-	-	ὠργίσθην
ὀρθρίζω	-	-	-	-	-
ὁρίζω[10]	ὁριῶ[11]	ὥρισα	-	ὥρισμαι	ὁρίσθην
ὁρκίζω[12]	-	-	-	-	-
ὁρμίζω[13]	-	ὥρμισα	-	ὥρμισμαι	ὡρμίσθην
ὀρφανίζω[14]	-	-	-	-	ὠρφανίσθην
ὀχθίζω[15]	-	ὥχθισα	-	-	-
παρρησιάζομαι	παρρησιάσομαι	ἐπαρρησιασάμην	-	-	-
πειράζω[16]	πειράσω	ἐπείρασα	-	πεπείρασμαι	ἐπειράσθην

---

[1] The Doric has ὄσδω, yet there are many examples of the ζ remaining (cf. *LS*, p. 1200).

[2] κατοικίζω, μετοικίζω (has an Attic future, μετοικιῶ; §43.7b).

[3] Attic future (§43.7b) is listed only with compound μετοικίζω.

[4] παρομοιάζω

[5] ἐπονομάζω

[6] καθοπλίζω

[7] κατοπτρίζω. ὀπτρίζω is not listed in *LS*. See other roots in *οπ such as the future and aorist of ὁράω, and ὄπτομαι.

[8] παροργίζω

[9] Attic future (§43.7b)

[10] ἀποδιορίζω, ἀφορίζω, προορίζω

[11] Has an Attic future -οριῶ (Mt 13:49; §43.7b). But a regular future ἀφορίσει also occurs at Mt 25:32.

[12] ἐνορκίζω, ἐξορκίζω

[13] προσορμίζω

[14] ἀπορφανίζω

[15] προσοχθίζω

[16] ἐκπειράζω. See *BDF* §101.

πελεκίζω	-	-	-	πεπελέκισμαι	-
πιάζω[1]	-	ἐπίασα	-	-	ἐπιάσθην
πιέζω	-	-	-	πεπίεσμαι	-
πλεονάζω[2]	-	ἐπλεόνασα	-	-	-
πλουτίζω	-	ἐπλούτισα	-	-	ἐπλουτίσθην
ποντίζω[3]	-	-	-	-	ἐποντίσθην
ποτίζω	-	ἐπότισα	πεπότικα	πεπότισμαι	ἐποτίσθην
πρίζω[4]	-	-	-	-	ἐπρίσθην
πυρράζω	-	-	-	-	-
ῥαβδίζω	-	-	-	-	ἐραβδίσθην
ῥαντίζω	ῥαντιῶ[5]	ἐρράντισα[6]	-	ρεράντισμαι	-
ῥαπίζω	ῥαπίσω	ἐράπισα	-	-	-
ῥιπίζω	-	-	-	-	-
σαλπίζω[7]	σαλπίσω	ἐσάλπισα	-	-	-
σεβάζομαι	-	-	-	-	ἐσεβάσθην
σεληνιάζομαι	-	-	-	-	-
σινιάζω	-	ἐσινίασα	-	-	-
σκανδαλίζω	-	ἐσκανδάλισα	-	ἐσκανδάλισμαι	ἐσκανδαλίσθην
σκευάζω[8]	σκευάσω	ἐσκεύασα	-	ἐσκεύασμαι	ἐσκευάσθην
σκιάζω[9]	-	ἐσκίασα	-	-	-
σκορπίζω[10]	-	ἐσκόρπισα	-	-	ἐσκορπίσθην
σκοτίζομαι[11]	-	-	-	ἐσκότισμαι	ἐσκοτίσθην
σμυρνίζω	-	-	-	ἐσμύρνισμαι	-
σοφίζω[12]	-	ἐσόφισα	-	σεσόφισμαι	-

---

[1] ὑποπιάζω and ὑπωπιάζω. Alternate forms; the ο has lengthened to ω. ὑπωπιάζω is used in our texts. See *BDF* §101.

[2] ὑπερπλεονάζω

[3] καταποντίζω

[4] Alternate form of πρίω; cf. v–1a(1) for discussion.

[5] Attic future (§43.7b)

[6] On the doubled ρ cf. §31.2b.

[7] In Classical Greek the root was *σαλπιγγ, as seen in the aorist ἐσάλπιγξα (Smyth §510).

[8] ἀνασκευάζω, ἀποσκευάζω (which some list as ἀποσκευάζομαι), ἐπισκευάζομαι, κατασκευάζω, παρασκευάζω

[9] ἐπισκιάζω, κατασκιάζω

[10] διασκορπίζω

[11] Occurs only in the passive in the N.T. Some list as σκοτίζω.

[12] κατασοφίζομαι

σπλαγχνίζομαι	-	-	-	-	ἐσπλαγχνίσθην
σπουδάζω	σπουδάσω	ἐσπούδασα	-	-	-
στεγάζω[1]	-	ἐστέγασα	-	-	-
στομίζω[2]	-	-	-	-	-
στυγνάζω	-	ἐστύγνασα	-	-	-
σφραγίζω[3]	-	ἐσφράγισα	-	ἐσφράγισμαι	ἐσφραγίσθην
σχηματίζω[4]	σχηματίσω	ἐσχημάτισα	-	-	-
σχίζω	σχίσω	ἔσχισα	-	-	ἐσχίσθην
σχολάζω	-	ἐσχόλασα	-	-	-
σῴζω[5]	σώσω	ἔσωσα	σέσωκα	σέσωσμαι	ἐσώθην[6]
σωφρονίζω	-	-	-	-	-
ταφιάζω[7]	-	ἐταφίασα	-	-	-
τραυματίζω	-	ἐτραυμάτισα	-	τετρατμάτισμαι	ἐτραυματίσθην
τραχηλίζω	-	-	-	τετραχήλισμαι	-
τρίζω[8]	-	-	-	-	-
τυμπανίζω	-	-	-	-	ἐτυμπανίσθην
τυρβάζω	-	-	-	-	-
ὑβρίζω[9]	-	ὕβρισα	-	-	ὑβρίσθην
ὑλίζω[10]	-	-	-	-	-
ὑπνίζω[11]	ὑπνίσω	-	-	-	-
φανίζω[12]	φανίσω	ἐφάνισα	-	-	ἐφανίσθην
φαντάζω	-	-	-	-	-
φημίζω[13]	-	ἐφήνισα	-	-	ἐφημίσθην
φλογίζω	-	-	-	-	-

---

[1]　ἀποστεγάζω

[2]　ἀποστομίζω, ἐπιστομίζω. στομίζω is not listed in L$\dot{S}$.

[3]　κατασφραγίζω

[4]　μετασχηματίζω, συσχηματίζω

[5]　ἀνασῴζω, διασῴζω, ἐκσῴζω. Roots are *σω and *σωι (Smyth §508a), but it functions as if the root were *σω(ι)δ.

[6]　Normally σωδ + θ ꞏ σωσθ, but here the σ drops out.

[7]　ἐνταφιάζω. ταφιάζω is not listed in LS.

[8]　See κατοπτρίζω.

[9]　ἐνυβρίζω

[10]　διϋλίζω

[11]　ἐξυπνίζω

[12]　ἐμφανίζω. See ἀφανίζω.

[13]　διαφημίζω

φορτίζω[1]	-	-	-	πεφόρτισμαι	-
φράζω	-	ἔφρασα	-	-	-
φροντίζω	-	-	-	-	-
φυλακίζω	-	-	-	-	-
φωτίζω	φωτίσω[2]	ἐφώτισα	-	πεφώτισμαι	ἐφωτίσθην
χαρίζομαι	χαρίσομαι	ἐχαρισάμην	-	κεχάρισμαι	ἐχαρίσθην
χειμάζω[3]	χειμάσω	ἐχείμασα	κεχείμακα	-	-
χειρίζω[4]	-	ἐχειρισάμην	-	κεχείρισμαι	-
χλευάζω[5]	-	-	-	-	-
χορτάζω	-	ἐχόρτασα	-	-	ἐχορτάσθην
χρήζω	-	-	-	-	-
χρηματίζω	χρηματίσω	ἐχρημάτισα	-	κεχρημάτισμαι	ἐχρηματίσθην
χρονίζω	χρονίσω[6]	-	-	-	-
χωρίζω[7]	χωρίσω	ἐχώρισα	-	κεχώρισμαι	ἐχωρίσθην
ψηφίζω[8]	-	ἐψήφισα	-	-	ἐψηφίσθην
ψωμίζω	-	ἐψώμισα	-	-	-
ὠτίζομαι[9]	-	ὠτισάμην	-	-	-

v-2a(2)   Roots ending in γ + ι ‣ ζ[10]   (total: 7)

The original formation was κι/χι and then by analogy γι/τι (Smyth §651, Funk §932.3). The γ becomes ξ in the future and the aorist when added to the σ of the tense formatives. It reappears in the perfect, but becomes χ before the θ of the aorist passive.

present	γ + ι ‣ ζ	(§26.2)
future	γ + σ ‣ ξ	(§22.2)
aorist (active)	γ + σ ‣ ξ	(§22.2)
aorist (passive)	γ + θ ‣ χθ	(§20.2)

---

[1]   ἀποφορτίζομαι, συμφορτίζω

[2]   Has an Attic future φωτιῶ that does not occur in the N.T. (§43.7b).

[3]   παραχειμάζω

[4]   διαχειρίζω, προχειρίζω

[5]   διαχλευάζω

[6]   Has an Attic future χρονιῶ that does not occur in the N.T. (v.l. Rev 22:5; §43.7b).

[7]   ἀποχωρίζω, διαχωρίζω

[8]   καταψηφίζομαι, συμψηφίζω, συγκαταψηφίζομαι

[9]   ἐνωτίζομαι. ὠτίζομαι is not listed in LS.

[10]   Funk (§484.11) says that not all of these verbs actually end in γ, but they all behave as if they do.

ἁρπάζω[1]	ἁρπάσω	ἥρπασα	ἥρπακα	-	ἡρπάσθην[2]
κράζω[3]	κράξω	ἔκραξα[4]	κέκραγα[5]	-	-
νυστάζω	-	ἐνύσταξα	-	-	-
παίζω[6]	παίξω	ἔπαιξα	-	-	ἐπαίχθην
στενάζω[7]	στενάξω	ἐστέναξα	-	-	-
στηρίζω[8]	στηρίξω[9]	ἐστήριξα[10]	-	ἐστήριγμαι	ἐστηρίχθην
σφάζω[11]	σφάξω	ἔσφαξα	-	ἔσφαγμαι	ἐσφάγην[12]

v-2b

Verbal roots ending in a velar (κ γ χ) add ι ▸ σσω   (total: 24)

Since ι is added to form the present tense stem, the combination of κ or χ with ι forms σσ. By analogy, πλάσσω (*πλατ) forms its tense stems as a velar.[13]

present	velar + ι ▸ σσ	(§26.3)
future	velar + σ ▸ ξ	(§22.2)
aorist (active)	velar + σ ▸ ξ	(§22.2)
perfect (middle/passive)	velar + μ ▸ γμ	(§21.2)
aorist (passive)	velar + θ ▸ χθ	(§20.2)

---

1. *ἁρπαγ. διαρπάζω. Funk §484.10. The root is *ἁρπαγ, so we have listed it as a v-2a(2) verb. However, the principal parts, except for the present, seem to be formed from a dental root where the final consonant drops off (v-2a[1]). See the σ in the aorist passive stem, typical of dental stems.

2. Has a second aorist passive ἡρπάγην (2 Cor 12:2,4; §47.8) and second future passive ἁρπαγήσομαι (1 Thess 4:17; §47.8). These show that the root actually ends in γ.

3. ἀνακράζω, ἐπικράζω. See *BDF* §101.

4. ἀνακράζω shows a first (ἀνέκραξαν) and second aorist (ἀνέκραγον) at Lk 23:18 as two possible readings. Has an alternate second aorist ἔκραγον (Acts 24:21; *BDF* §75).

5. Second perfect (§45.5b).

6. ἐμπαίζω. See *BDF* §101.

7. ἀναστενάζω, συστενάζω

8. ἐπιστηρίζω

9. *BAGD* lists an Attic future στηριῶ (§43.7b; does not occur in the N.T.) and a future built from the stem that appears to be a dental: στηρίσω (*BDF* §71; *MH* 259).

10. Has a first aorist ἐστήρισα as if it were from a dental stem (ἐστήρισεν [Lk 9:51; cf. LaSor §24.2512); στήρισον [Rom 3:2]). Funk §484.11.

11. κατασφάζω. *BAGD* lists it also possibly as κατασφάττω. It occurs only at Lk 19:27 as κατασφάξατε.

12. Second aorist passive (§47.8).

13. Smyth (§516) says that none of these verbs can be derived from roots in γι or δι but rather roots were assimilated to this pattern. Funk (§484.2) says that the roots end in κ or χ and by analogy some roots in γ or τ.

ἀλλάσσω[1]	ἀλλάξω	ἤλλαξα	-	ἤλλαγμαι	ἤλλάγην[2]
βδελύσσομαι	-	-	-	ἐβδέλυγμαι	-
δράσσομαι[3]	-	-	-	-	-
ἐλίσσω	ἐλίξω	-	-	-	ἐλίχθην
κηρύσσω[4]	κηρύξω	ἐκήρυξα	-	κεκήρυγμαι	ἐκηρύχθην
μάσσω[5]	-	ἔμαξα	-	-	ἐμάγην[6]
νύσσω[7]	-	ἔνυξα	-	-	ἐνύγην[8]
ὀρύσσω[9]	-	ὤρυξα	-	-	ὠρύγην[10]
πατάσσω	πατάξω	ἐπάταξα	-	-	-
πλάσσω[11]	-	ἔπλασα[12]	πέπλακα[13]	-	ἐπλάσθην[14]
πλήσσω[15]	-	ἔπληξα	-	πέπληγμαι	ἐπλήγην[16]
πράσσω[17]	πράξω	ἔπραξα	πέπραχα[18]	πέπραγμαι	ἐπράχθην
πτύσσω[19]	-	ἔπτυξα	-	-	-
πυρέσσω	-	-	-	-	-
ῥήσσω[20]	-	-	-	-	-
σπαράσσω[21]	-	ἐσπάραξα	-	-	-

---

[1] ἀπαλλάσσω, ἀποκαταλλάσσω, διαλλάσσομαι, καταλλάσσω, μεταλλάσσω, συναλλάσσω

[2] Second aorist passive (§47.8).

[3] *δραγ

[4] προκηρύσσω

[5] ἀπομάσσω, ἐκμάσσω

[6] Second aorist passive, which does not occur in the N.T. (§47.8).

[7] κατανύσσομαι

[8] Second aorist passive (§47.8).

[9] διορύσσω, ἐξορύσσω

[10] Second aorist passive, which does not occur in the N.T. (§47.8). διορύσσω forms a first aorist infinitive διορυχθῆναι (Mt 24:43; Lk 12:39).

[11] From the root *πλατ that follows this pattern by analogy (see Smyth §515a).

[12] *πλατ + σ ‣ πλασ (§22.3).

[13] From the root *πλατ, but replaces the τ with a κ by analogy to the other verbs in this category.

[14] *πλατ + σ ‣ πλασ (§22.3). Has a second aorist in Classical Greek, ἐπλήγην (§44.5a).

[15] ἐκπλήσσω, ἐπιπλήσσω

[16] Second aorist passive (§47.8).

[17] ἀναπράσσω

[18] Second perfect (§45.5b). The final γ aspirated to χ.

[19] *πτυγ. ἀναπτύσσω

[20] διαρήσσω, προσρήσσω. A later form of ῥήγνυμι. You can find ῥήσσω and ῥήγνυμι (v-3c[2]) in the compounds (διαρήγνυμι, προσρήγνυμι). See ῥήγνυμι for principal parts.

[21] συσπαράσσω

ταράσσω[1]	-	ἐτάραξα	-	τετάραγμαι	ἐταράχθην
τάσσω[2]	τάξομαι	ἔταξα	τέταχα[3]	τέταγμαι	ἐτάχθην[4]
τινάσσω[5]	-	ἐτίναξα	-	-	-
τυλίσσω[6]	-	ἐτύλιξα	-	τετύλιγμαι	-
φράσσω	-	ἔφραξα	-	-	ἐφράγην[7]
φρίσσω	-	ἔφριξα	πέφρικα	-	-
φρυάσσω	-	ἐφρύαξα	-	-	-
φυλάσσω[8]	φυλάξω	ἐφύλαξα	πεφύλαχα[9]	-	ἐφυλάχθην

v-2c

Verbal roots ending in a digamma (Ϝ)   (total: 2)

When Ϝ and ι join, they form ι, as seen in the present tense of all roots below. Ϝ becomes vocalic υ in all the other tenses.[10]

καίω[11]	καύσω	ἔκαυσα	-	κέκαυμαι	ἐκαύθην[12]
κλαίω[13]	κλαύσω[14]	ἔκλαυσα	-	-	-

---

[1]   διαταράσσω, ἐκταράσσω, συνταράσσω. Root is *ταραχ (cf. ταραχή).

[2]   ἀνατάσσομαι, ἀντιτάσσω, ἀποτάσσω, διατάσσω, ἐπιδιατάσσομαι, ἐπιτάσσω, προτάσσω, προστάσσω, συντάσσω, ὑποτάσσω

[3]   Second perfect (§45.5b), occurring only in the compound διατάσσω (διατέταχα).

[4]   Has a second aorist passive (-ταγην; §47.8). ὑποτάσσω appears only as a second aorist, but διατάσσω appears as both a first and second aorist.

[5]   ἀποτινάσσω, ἐκτινάσσω

[6]   ἐντυλίσσω

[7]   Second aorist passive (§47.8).

[8]   διαφυλάσσω. Smyth (§513) lists the root as *φυλακ (cf. φυλακή).

[9]   πεφύλαχα could be listed as a second perfect (§45.5b) as does Funk (§3870), but the root is *φυλακ and κκα could have simplified to κα and then aspirated to χα. We have listed it as a first perfect since the sound of κα and χα are similar.

[10]   The two words in this category are basically v-1a types. Cf. Smyth §519-20.

[11]   *καϜ. Compounds are ἐκκαίω, κατακαίω.

[12]   Has a second aorist passive (§47.2) ἐκάην, appearing three times in Rev 8:7 as κατεκάη, and a second future passive (§47.7) κατακαήσεται, appearing in 1 Cor 3:15 (variant in 2 Pet 3:10). A first future passive (κατακαυθήσεται) also occurs in Rev 18:8. Stem vowel shifts from αι ᐳ αυ (§4, v-7).

[13]   *κλαϜ.

[14]   BAGD lists it both as active and deponent (κλαύσομαι).

v-2d

Verbal roots ending in a liquid or nasal

v-2d(1)   Roots ending in a liquid (λ)

v-2d(2)   Roots ending in a liquid (αρ)

v-2d(3)   Roots ending in a liquid (ερ)

v-2d(4)   Roots ending in a nasal (αν)

v-2d(5)   Roots ending in a nasal (εν)

v-2d(6)   Roots adding νι to the verbal root to form the present tense stem

Liquids and nasals are often (improperly) called "liquids." They do have similarities, but they are distinctly different sounds. (The term "lingual" is sometimes use for λ, ρ, and ν because they use the tongue in their pronunciation.) Their most obvious similarity is that their futures follow the liquid pattern by adding not σ but εσ. When the connecting vowel is added, the σ becomes intervocalic, drops out, and the ε of the tense formative and the connecting vowel contract (§43.3). Except for the accent, these words in the future therefore behave as if they were ε contracts. They also have liquid aorists in that α and not σα functions as the tense formative.

The stem vowels in this category are flexible. To understand them properly you might want to review the discussion of ablaut (§4). We will *not* footnote ablaut since it is so frequent.

The present undergoes significant changes. When ι is added to λ (v-2d[1]), they produce λλ (§26.6). In the other four classes, ι becomes vocalic ι, and the final stem consonant and the ι undergo metathesis (e.g., *αρ + ι › αρι › αιρ › αἴρω; §7.6; §26.7).[1] (ὀφείλω follows the pattern of the latter four classes.) Therefore, when looking at the tenses other than the present, remember that the λλ or the ι is a factor only in the present. It does not have to be accounted for in the other tenses.

All of the following words have liquid futures and liquid aorists unless otherwise indicated(§43.6). Stems in ν change to μ in the perfect middle/passive because of the μ (§24.8).

---

[1] αρι › αιρ; ερι › ειρ; ανι › αιν; ενι › ειν. Smyth (§519) and LaSor (§24.2553) say that the ι drops and the preceding vowel is lengthened to compensate. Funk (§484.40) says in the case of ανι/αρι, ι is inserted (epenthesis) and the ι dropped. In the case of ενι/ερι, the ι is dropped and the preceding vowel is lengthened in compensation. Morphology is not an exact science, and all three explanations achieve the same result.

v-2d(1) Roots ending in a λ + ι (total: 13)

ἀγγέλλω[1]	ἀγγελῶ	ἤγγειλα	ἤγγελκα	ἤγγελμαι	ἠγγέλην[2]
ἅλλομαι[3]	-	ἡλάμην[4]	-	-	-
βάλλω[5]	βαλῶ	ἔβαλον[6]	βέβληκα	βέβλημαι	ἐβλήθην[7]
ἐποκέλλω[8]	-	ἐπώκειλα	-	-	-
θάλλω[9]	-	ἔθαλον[10]	-	-	-
κέλλω[11]	-	ἔκειλα	-	-	-
ὀφείλω[12]	-	ὤφελον[13]	-	-	-
σκύλλω	-	-	-	ἔσκυλμαι	-
στέλλω[14]	στελῶ	ἔστειλα	ἔσταλκα	ἔσταλμαι	ἐστάλην[15]
σφάλλω	-	-	-	-	ἐσφάλην[16]
τέλλω[17]	τελῶ	ἔτειλα	τέταλκα	τέταλμαι	-
τίλλω	τιλῶ	ἔτιλα	τέτιλκα	-	ἐτίλθην[18]
ψάλλω	ψαλῶ	-	-	-	-

---

[1] ἀναγγέλλω, ἀπαγγέλλω, διαγγέλλω, ἐξαγγέλλω, ἐπαγγέλλομαι, καταγγέλλω, παραγγέλλω, προεπαγγέλλομαι, προκαταγγέλλω

[2] Second aorist passive (§47.8)

[3] ἀνάλλομαι, ἐνάλλομαι, ἐξάλλομαι, ἐφάλλομαι. See BDF §101.

[4] The compound ἐφάλλομαι has a second aorist (§44.5a), ἐφαλόμην, based on ἡλόμην.

[5] In explaining its principal parts you can postulate the stem vowel goes to its zero grade and the η is inserted (*βαλ ‣ βλ ‣ βλη; §4, v-7). You can also postulate metathesis (§7.6) whereby βαλ ‣ βλα and then the α lengthens (βλα ‣ βλη). ἀμφιβάλλω, ἀναβάλλω, ἀντιβάλλω, ἀποβάλλω, διαβάλλω, ἐκβάλλω, ἐμβάλλω, ἐπιβάλλω, καταβάλλω, μεταβάλλω, παραβάλλω, παρεμβάλλω, περιβάλλω, προβάλλω, συμβάλλω, ὑπερβάλλω, ὑποβάλλω.

[6] Second aorist (§44.5a).

[7] Smyth says it is from the root *βελε (§128a). See footnote on present tense.

[8] See discussion at κέλλω.

[9] ἀναθάλλω. See BDF §101.

[10] Second aorist (§44.5a).

[11] ἐπικέλλω, ἐποκέλλω. κέλλω and ὀκέλλω in Classical Greek have the same basic meaning, as do the two compounds built on them, ἐπικέλλω and ἐποκέλλω. The only occurrence of the words is as ἐπέκειλαν at Acts 27:41, thus preferring ἐπικέλλω. There is a v.l. ἐπώκειλαν.

[12] προσοφείλω. ὀφείλω has a root ending in λ, but unlike the other roots in the class λι do not form λλ. As is true of v-2d(2-5) verbs, the λ and ι metathesize (*οφελ + ι ‣ οφελι ‣ ὀφείλω). The iota, therefore, does not come into consideration in the aorist.

[13] Second aorist (§44.5.a). LS shows a first aorist, ὠφείλησα. Neither occurs in the N.T.

[14] ἀποστέλλω, διαστέλλω, ἐξαποστέλλω, ἐπιστέλλω, καταστέλλω, συναποστέλλω, συστέλλω, ὑποστέλλω. Stem vowel shifts ε ‣ ει ‣ α (§4, v-7).

[15] Second aorist passive (§47.8).

[16] Second aorist passive, which does not occur in the N.T. (§47.8).

[17] ἀνατέλλω, ἐντέλλω, ἐξανατέλλω. Stem vowel shifts ε ‣ ει ‣ α (§4, v-7).

[18] Also has a second aorist ἐτίλην (§44.5a), neither of which occurs in the N.T.

v-2d(2)   Roots ending in αρ + ι   (total: 3)

αἴρω¹	ἀρῶ	ἦρα	ἦρκα	ἦρμαι	ἤρθην
καθαίρω²	-	ἐκάθαρα	-	κεκάθαρμαι	-
χαίρω³	χαρήσομαι⁴	-	-	-	ἐχάρην⁵

v-2d(3)   Roots ending in ερ + ι   (total: 7)

ἐγείρω⁶	ἐγερῶ	ἤγειρα	-	ἐγήγερμαι⁷	ἠγέρθην
κείρω	-	ἔκειρα	-	-	-
οἰκτείρω⁸	-	-	-	-	-
οἰκτίρω	οἰκτιρήσω⁹	-	- ·	-	-
πείρω¹⁰	-	ἔπειρα	-	πέπαρμαι	ἐπάρην¹¹
σπείρω¹²	-	ἔσπειρα	-	ἔσπαρμαι	ἐσπάρην¹³
φθείρω¹⁴	φθερῶ	ἔφθειρα	-	ἔφθαρμαι	ἐφθάρην¹⁵

v-2d(4)   Roots ending in αν + ι   (total: 21)

βασκαίνω	-	ἐβάσκανα	-	-	-
εὐφραίνω	-	ηὔφρανα	-	-	ηὐφράνθην
θερμαίνω	-	-	-	-	-
λευκαίνω	-	ἐλεύκανα	-	-	-

---

1   ἀπαίρω, ἐξαίρω, ἐπαίρω (in N.T. only as passive), μεταίρω, συναίρω, ὑπεραίρω. On the augment see §31.5d.

2   διακαθαίρω, ἐκκαθαίρω. καθαίρω is not a compound verb; cf. καθαρίζω. See *BDF* §101.

3   προσχαίρω, συγχαίρω (its future is not deponent, συγχαρήσω).

4   η is inserted after the tense stem (§43.8d). It is not a liquid future (except for the compound καταχαροῦμαι, which does not occur in the N.T.).

5   Second aorist passive (§47.8).

6   διεγείρω, ἐξεγείρω, ἐπεγείρω, συνεγείρω. See *BDF* §101.

7   Attic reduplication (§32.6). The initial vowel and consonant double, and the second vowel is lengthened (εγερ ‣ εγεγερ ‣ ἐγήγερμαι; v-7).

8   Alternate form of οἰκτίρω. See *BDF* §101.

9   Instead of the expected liquid future, it inserts an η as if it were an ε contract stem (§43.8d).

10   περιπείρω

11   Second aorist passive (§47.8).

12   διασπείρω, ἐπισπείρω. Stem vowel shifts ε ‣ ει ‣ α (§4; v-7).

13   Second aorist passive (§47.8).

14   διαφθείρω, καταφθείρω. Stem vowel shifts ε ‣ ει ‣ α (§4; v-7).

15   Second aorist passive (§47.8).

λυμαίνω	-	ἐλύμανα	-	-	-
μαίνομαι[1]	-	-	-	-	-
μαραίνω	-	-	-	μεμάραμμαι	ἐμαράνθην
μιαίνω	μιανῶ	ἐμίανα	-	μεμίαμμαι[2]	ἐμιάνθην
μωραίνω	-	ἐμώρανα	-	-	ἐμωράνθην
ξαίνω	ξανῶ	ἔξηνα[3]	-	ἔξασμαι	ἐξάνθην
ξηραίνω	-	ἐξήρανα	-	ἐξήραμμαι	ἐξηράνθην
πικραίνω[4]	πικρανῶ	ἐπίκρανα	-	-	ἐπικράνθην
ποιμαίνω	ποιμανῶ	ἐποίμανα	-	-	-
ῥαίνω[5]	ῥανῶ	ἔρρανα	-	ἔρραμμαι[6]	ἐρράνθην
ῥυπαίνω	-	-	-	-	ἐρυπάνθην[7]
σαίνω	-	-	-	-	-
σημαίνω	-	ἐσήμανα	-	-	-
σιαίνομαι[8]	-	-	-	-	-
ὑγιαίνω	-	-	-	-	-
ὑφαίνω[9]	-	-	-	-	-
φαίνω[10]	φανοῦμαι	ἔφανα	-	-	ἐφάνην[11]

v-2d(5)   Roots ending in εν + ι   (total: 2)

κτείνω[12]	κτενῶ	ἔκτεινα	-	-	ἐκτάνθην
τείνω[13]	τενῶ	ἔτεινα	-	-	-

---

[1] ἐμμαίνομαι
[2] In Classical Greek it could insert a σ (μεμίασμαι, §46.5), but does not in the N.T.
[3] Lengthens the stem vowel.
[4] παραπικραίνω
[5] περιραίνω. On doubling the ρ see §31.2b.
[6] In Classical Greek it could insert a σ (ἔρρασμμαι, §46.6), but does not in the N.T.
[7] ρ can double after augment (§31.2b). It occurs in the N.T. only as ῥυπανθήτω (Rev 22:1).
[8] V.l. for σαίω at 1 Thess 3:3; cf. BAGD.
[9] See φαίνω.
[10] ἀναφαίνω, ἐπιφαίνω. See ὑφαίνω.
[11] Second aorist passive (§47.8).
[12] ἀποκτείνω. Is used interchangeably with -κτέννω (Mt 10:28; Mk 12:5; Lk 12:4; 2 Cor 3:6 v.l.; Rev 6:11; cf. BDF §73). Stem vowel shifts ε ‣ ει ‣ α (§4; v-7).
[13] ἐκτείνω, ἐπεκτείνομαι, παρατείνω, προτείνω, ὑπερεκτείνω

Class v-3

Present Tense Stem = Verbal Root + ν

v-3 verbs form their present tense stem by adding ν (or some variation) to their verbal root. v-3a verbs add ν if the root ends in a vowel, αν if the root ends in a consonant. (A small subclass of the latter also insert a ν into the present tense stem.) v-3b stems add νε to form the present. v-3c stems add νυ if the root ends in a consonant, ννυ if the root ends in a vowel.

In the future and aorist (active/middle), the vowels are somewhat flexible. Verbs that end in a short vowel will normally lengthen it, just like contract verbs. Stems ending in a consonant will add a vowel (normally η) before the σ of the tense formative. η can also be added in the formation of the other tense stems. v-3a(1) and v-3a(2b) mostly use second aorists. On this category see Smyth §523-525.

v-3a

Present Tense Stem = Verbal Root + (α)ν

v-3a(1)   Roots ending in a vowel add ν   (total: 13)

Most of the aorists in this category are second aorists (§44.5a), so we will not footnote this information.

ἀποκτέννω[1]	-	-	-	-
αὐξάνω[2]	αὐξήσω	ηὔξησα	-	ηὐξήθην
βλαστάνω[3]	-	ἐβλάστησα	-	-
βραδύνω[4]	-	-	-	-
δάκνω	-	-	-	ἐδήχθην[5]
δύνω[6]	-	ἔδυν[7]	δέδυκα	δέδυμαι	ἐδύην[8]

[1] Alternate form of ἀποκτείνω (cv-2d[5]). See there for principal parts. ἀποκτέννω does not fit cleanly into any category. The stem ends in -εν, not a vowel, but it adds ν to form the present tense stem.

[2] συναυξάνω, ὑπεραυξάνω. The verbal root also formed its present tense stem without modification as αὔξω, as seen in αὔξει (Eph 2:21; Col 2:19; cf. v-1). All forms in the N.T. show the α (or a lengthened η). The longer form was becoming predominate in the Koine period. See *BD* §101.

[3] ἐκβλαστάνω. See *BD* §101.

[4] See δύνω.

[5] Stem vowel shifts α › η (§4, v-7).

[6] ἐνδύνω. See βραδύνω and the discussion of the alternate δύω (v-1a[4]).

[7] Only aorist in N.T. is ἔδυ (from the second aorist ἔδυν; Mk 1:32), with the variant ἔδυσεν (from the first aorist ἔδυσα).

[8] Second aorist passive, which does not occur in the N.T. (§47.8).

ἱστάνω¹   -   -   -   -   -

κάμνω   -   ἔκαμον   κέκμηκα²   -   -

πίνω³   πίομαι⁴   ἔπιον   πέπωκα⁵   -   ἐπόθην⁶

τέμνω⁷   -   ἔτεμον   τέτμηκα   τέτμημαι   ἐτμήθην

τίνω⁸   τίσω⁹   -   -   -   -

φθάνω¹⁰   -   ἔφθασα   -   -   -

χύννω¹¹   -   -   -   -   -

v-3a(2a)   Roots ending in a consonant add αν (without modification)   (total: 4)

Most of the aorists in this category are second aorists (§44.5a), so we will not foot-note this information.

αἰσθάνομαι   -   ἠσθόμην   -   -   -

ἁμαρτάνω¹²   ἁμαρτήσω¹³   ἥμαρτον¹⁴   ἡμάρτηκα¹⁵   -   -

---

1   ἀποκαθιστάνω (alternate form of ἀποκαθίστημι, cv-6a), καθιστάνω (alternate form of καθιστήμι [cv-6a]), παριστάνω, συνιστάνω (cf. ἵστημι, v-6a). ἱστάνω is an alternate form of ἵστημι (v-6a). See there for principal parts.

2   Root is *καμ. Has reduced to its zero grade (§4.4c, v-7) and an η inserted after the tense stem (§45.3). It can also be explained with metathesis (*καμ ‣ κμα ‣ κμη; §7.6). The perfect active does not occur in the N.T.

3   καταπίνω, συμπίνω. There are two roots, *πι and *πο (‣ πω in the perfect; Smyth §529; Funk §487.8). See BDF §101.

4   There is no indication that this is a future stem (§43.8c).

5   Stem vowel becomes ω due to ablaut (§4, v-7).

6   Stem vowel becomes ο due to ablaut (§4, v-7).

7   περιτέμνω, συντέμνω. η is inserted after the tense stem in the perfect active (§45.3), perfect middle/passive (§646.), and the aorist passive (§47.7). Smyth (§492) explains the tense stems with metathesis (*τεμ ‣ τμε ‣ τμη; §7.6). Perhaps ablaut (§4, v-7).

8   ἀποτίνω. Root is *τινϝ. ϝ is dropped in Attic (Smyth §523.N2).

9   See BAGD for discussion of the alternate form τείσω.

10   προφθάνω. See BDF §101.

11   The alternate form χέω is listed as a v-1a(7) verb with compounds ἐκχέω, ἐπιχέω, καταχέω, and συγχέω. However, the same root can form the present χύννω (v-3a[1]). Compounds formed from the root can use either χέω or χύννω. See BDF §101.

ἐκχύννω, συγχύννω, ὑπερεκχύννω. συνχύννω/συνχέω occurs as συγχύννεται (Acts 21:31; v.l. συγχύνεται), συνέχεον (Acts 21:27; uncontracted from -χε + ον), συνέχυννεν (Acts 9:22; T.R. has συνέχυννεν), συνέχεα (v.l. at Acts 21:27), συγκέχυμαι (Acts 19:32; συγκεχυμένη as v.l. at Acts 19:29), and συνεχύθην (not in the N.T.).

12   προαμαρτάνω

13   η inserted after the tense stem (§43.8d).

14   Has a first aorist ἡμάρτησα, in which an η is inserted after the tense stem. In the N.T. it is used only in non-indicative forms.

15   η inserted after the tense stem (§45.3).

βλαστάνω   -   ἐβλάστησα[1] -   -   -

ὀπτάνομαι[2]   -   -   -   -   -

v-3a(2b)   Roots ending in a consonant add αν (with an epenthetic ν)   (total: 8)

If the vowel in the final syllable is short, a ν is inserted (epenthesis, §7.9) before the final stem consonant. This ν is in turn subject to change according to the rules, depending upon what the following stem consonant is. If the consonant is a labial (τ δ θ), the ν will become a μ (e.g., λαμβάνω; §24.1). If it is a velar (κ γ χ), the ν will become a γ (e.g., λαγχάνω; §24.2).

All these verbs have second aorists.

θιγγάνω[3]   -   ἔθιγον   -   -   -

λαγχάνω[4]   -   ἔλαχον   -   -   -

λαμβάνω[5]   λήμψομαι[6]   ἔλαβον   εἴληφα[7]   εἴλημμαι[8]   ἐλήμφθην[9]

λανθάνω[10]   -   ἔλαθον   -   λέλησμαι[11]   -

λιμπάνω[12]   -   -   -   -   -

---

[1]   η inserted after the tense stem (§44.5c).

[2]   Formed from the same stem as the aorist passive of ὁράω: ὤφθην (*οπ).

[3]   *θιγ ‣ θινγαν ‣ θιγγάνω (§24.2)

[4]   *λαχ ‣ λανχαν ‣ λαγχάνω (§24.2)

[5]   *λαβ ‣ λανβαν ‣ λαμβάνω (§24.1).   See BDF §101. ἀναλαμβάνω, ἀντιλαμβάνω, ἀπολαμβάνω, ἐπιλαμβάνομαι, καταλαμβάνω, μεταλαμβάνω, παραλαμβάνω, προλαμβάνω, προσαναλαμβάνω, προσλαμβάνω, συλλαμβάνω, συναντιλαμβάνομαι, συμπαραλαμβάνω, συμπεριλαμβάνω, ὑπολαμβάνω

[6]   Stem vowel has shifted (α ‣ η; §4, v-7).

[7]   *λαβ ‣ ειλαβ ‣ ειληβ ‣ εἴληφα. The stem has vocalic rather than consonantal reduplication, the stem vowel becomes η due to ablaut (§4), and the final stem stop (β) is aspirated to φ. It is a second perfect (§45.5b) and therefore uses no κ.

It is possible the verbal root originally was Ϝελαβ or σελαβ. It would have therefore received the vocalic reduplication (ε), the intervocalic Ϝ or σ would have dropped out, and the two ε's would have contracted. In the aorist (active and passive), the stem behaves as if it originally had been *λαβ.

The μ is retained in the perfect middle/passive and aorist passive.

[8]   *λαβ ‣ ειλαβ ‣ ειληβ ‣ ειληφ (§21.1) ‣ εἴλαμμαι

[9]   *λαβ ‣ ελαβ ‣ εληβ ‣ εληνβ ‣ ελημβ ‣ ελημφ (§20.1) ‣ ἐλήμφθην

[10] *λαθ ‣ λανθάνω. Compounds are ἐκλανθάνομαι, ἐπιλανθάνομαι.

[11] *λαθ ‣ λεληθμαι ‣ λέλησμαι

Root is *λαθ. The stem vowel becomes η due to ablaut (§4, v-7), and the dental (θ) assimilates to σ when followed by μ (§22.3).

[12] ἀπολιμπάνω, διαλιμπάνω, ὑπολιμπάνω. Colloquial form of λείπω (v-1b[1]). It usually occurs in compound verbs.

μανθάνω[1]   -   ἔμαθον   μεμάθηκα[2] -   -
πυνθάνομαι[3] -   ἐπυθόμην   -   -   -
τυγχάνω[4]   τεύξω   ἔτυχον   τέτευχα[5] -   -

v-3b

Verbal roots add νε (total: 1)

ἱκνέομαι[6]   ἵξομαι   ἱκόμην[7]   -   -   -

v-3c

Verbal roots ending in a vowel add (ν)νυ

v-3c(1)   Roots ending in a vowel add ννυ   (total: 10)

All aorist (active/middle) are first aorists. Many of the forms insert σ after the stem in the perfect middle/passive and the aorist passive (§46.5); we will not indicate this information in the footnotes. They appear to be μι verbs in that they use the alternate personal ending μι, but they lack the other characteristics.

ἀμφιέννυμι[8] -   -   -   ἠμφίεσμαι   -
ζβέννυμι[9]   -   -   -   -   -
ζώννυμι[10]   ζώσω   ἔζωσα   -   ἔζωσμαι   -

---

1   *μαθ › μανθ + ανω. Compound is καταμανθάνω.
2   η is inserted after the tense stem (§45.3).
3   *πυθ › πυνθάνομαι (no change)
4   *τυγ › τυνχ + ανω. Stem vowel changes ε › ευ (§4, v-7) in the future active/middle and perfect active. ἐντυγχάνω, ἐπιτυγχάνω, παρατυγχάνω, συντυγχάνω, ὑπερεντυγχάνω. See BDF §101.
5   Second perfect (§45.5b). Has another form, τέτυχα, at Heb 8:6.
6   Behaves in the present like an ε contract verb. ἀφικνέομαι, διϊκνέομαι, ἐφικνέομαι
7   Second aorist (§44.5a).
8   Can be formed ἀμφιάζω (v-2a[1]) and ἀμφιέζω. See BDF §101.
9   Alternate form of σβέννυμι.
10   ἀναζώννυμι, διαζώννυμι, περιζώννυμι, ὑποζώννυμι (which has a present participle ὑποζωννύς). περιζωννύω is also listed in BAGD in which the verbal root has followed the usually thematic formation. There is no present or imperfect of this word in the N.T. Jn 21:18 has ἐζώννυες from the thematic conjugation. The simple verb occurs elsewhere only at Acts 12:8 (ζῶσαι). See BDF §101.

κεράννυμι[1]	-	ἐκέρασα	-	κεκέρασμαι	ἐκράθην[2]
κορέννυμι	-	-	-	κεκόρεσμαι	ἐκορέσθην
κρεμάννυμι[3]	-	ἐκρέμασα	-	-	ἐκρεμάσθην
πετάννυμι[4]	-	ἐπέτασα	-	-	-
ῥώννυμι	-	-	-	ἔρρωμαι[5]	-
σβέννυμι	σβέσω	ἔσβεσα	-	-	ἐσβέσθην[6]
στρωννύμι[7]	-	ἔστρωσα	-	ἔστρωμαι	ἐστρώθην

v-3c(2)   Roots ending in a consonant add νυ   (total: 10)

All are first aorists. Some have presents in -υω, e.g., δείκνυμι and δεικνύω. They use the alternate personal ending μι, but they do not reduplicate in the present as μι verbs do.

ἄγνυμι[8]	ἐάξω[9]	ἔαξα	-	-	ἐάγην[10]
δείκνυμι[11]	δείξω	ἔδειξα	δέδειχα[12]	δέδειγμαι	ἐδείχθην
ἐλαύνω[13]	-	ἤλασα	ἐλήλακα[14]	-	-

---

1   συγκεράννυμι. Alternate spelling for κρέμαμαι (v-1d[1b]). κρεμάννυμι is preferred by BAGD (see below). See discussion of κρέμαμαι at v-1d(1b). See BDF §101.

2   The root is *κερα. The stem reduces to its zero form: *κερα ‣ κρα ‣ ἐκράθην (§4.4c).

3   Job 26:7 has κρεμάζω. The present of the form κρεμάννυμι does not appear in the Greek Bible (BAGD). Compound is ἐκκρεμάννυμι. The only occurrence of this compound is ἐξεκρέματο (imperfect middle; Lk 19:48), which is closer to the stem as seen in Job 26:7 than κρεμάννυμι. See discussion of κρέμαμαι at v-1d(1b). BDF §101.

4   ἐκπετάννυμι. BAGD lists the pluperfect form as ἐκπεπετάκειν, but it does not occur in the N.T.

5   Doubles the initial ρ after augment (§31.2b). See BDF §101.

6   Can insert a σ after the tense stem, but not in the N.T. (§46.5).

7   BAGD list it as στρώννυμι and στρωννύω (v-1a[4]). The only N.T. occurrence of the first principal part is the imperfect ἐστρώννυον and the compound ὑπεστρώννυον (Lk 19:36). Compounds are καταστρώννυμι, ὑποστρώννυμι (ὑποστρωννύω).

8   The root is Ϝαγ. When the augment is added the Ϝ drops out but the two vowels will not contract (ε + Ϝαγ ‣ εαγ; §31.5b, Smyth §431). κατάγνυμι. See BDF §101.

9   Funk (§3372.3) says that the future "is augmented (wrongly)." Cf. §43.8e. See note on present for explanation of augment.

10   Second aorist passive (§47.8).

11   ἀναδείκνυμι, ἀποδείκνυμι, ἐνδείκνυμι, ἐπιδείκνυμι, ὑποδείκνυμι. The alternate form δεικνύω (v-1a[4]) formed from the thematic conjugation is found in Jn 2:18.

12   Second perfect, which does not appear in the N.T. (§45.5b). Stem κ has aspirated to χ (§14.1).

13   ἀπελαύνω, συνελαύνω. From the root *ελα. Adds νυ to form the present, and then undergoes metathesis resulting in ἐλαύνω (Funk §485.40; Smyth §128).

14   Root is *ελα, which undergoes Attic reduplication (§32.6). The stem reduplicates and the second vowel lengthens: *ελα ‣ ελελα ‣ ἐλήλακα.

ζεύγνυμι[1]	-	ἔζευξα	-	-	-
μείγνυμι[2]	-	-	-	-	-
μίγνυμι[3]	-	ἔμιξα	-	μέμιγμαι	ἐμίγην[4]
ὄλλυμι[5]	ὀλέσω[6]	ὤλεσα[7]	ὀλῶλα[8]	-	-
ὀμνύω[9]	-	ὤμοσα[10]	ὀμώμοκα[11]	-	ὠμόθην[12]
πήγνυμι[13]	-	ἔπηξα	-	-	-
ῥήγνυμι[14]	ῥήξω	ἔρρηξα[15]	ἔρρηγα[16]	-	ἐράγην[17]

---

[1] συζεύγνυμι

[2] See μίγνυμι.

[3] συναναμίγνυμι. Can also be formed μείγνυμι (ἔμειξα, μέμειγμαι, ἐμείγην) or μειγνύω (v-1a[4]). In the N.T. μίγνυμι is always preferred over μείγνυμι (4t).

[4] Stem vowel becomes ι due to ablaut (§4). Second aorist passive (§47.8).

[5] The root is *ολ. When the νυ is added to form the present tense stem, the ν totally assimilates to λ (reverse assimilation (§13.3). *ολ + νυ + μι ‣ ὄλλυμι. ἀπόλλυμι, συναπόλλυμι. See BDF §101.

[6] ε is inserted after the tense stem; normally an η is used (§43.8d). Also has a liquid future: ἀπολῶ (1 Cor 1:19; §43.3).

[7] ε is inserted after the tense stem (§44.5c). Also has a second aorist ἀπωλόμην (§44.5a).

[8] Second perfect (§45.3). Attic reduplication, in which the stem is reduplicated and the original stem vowel lengthened: *ολ ‣ ολολα ‣ ολωλα (v-7; §32.6).
BAGD lists a first perfect ἀπολώλεκα (which inserts an ε after the tense stem; §45.3), but it does not occur in the N.T.

[9] On ὄμνυμι cf. Smyth §488a; v-3c(2). See BDF §101.

[10] The root is *ομ, which augments the vowel and inserts an ο after the tense stem (§44.5c). Funk §485.42, Smyth §486.

[11] Attic reduplication (§32.6).

[12] Can insert a σ after the tense stem (ὠμόσθην; §46.5). The sixth principal part does not occur in the N.T.

[13] προσπήγνυμι. See BDF §101.

[14] *Ϝρηγ. Has a thematic form ῥήσσει (v-2b) in Mk 9:18 (v.l. in Mt 9:17; BDF §101; MH 403). διαρήσσω, περιρήγνυμι, προσρήσσω, συρρήγνυμι.
The doubling of the initial ρ varies among compounds and among passages (e.g., δια(ρ)ρήγνυμι).

[15] BAGD lists the aorist as ἔρ(ρ)ηξα. The only augmented form has ρρ (Lk 9:42). The compound διαρήγνυμι has double ρ (Mt 26:65; Acts 14:14) while περιρήγνυμι (Acts 16:22) and προσρήγνυμι (Lk 6:48,49) augment with a single ρ (cf. §31.2b).

[16] Second perfect, which does not appear in the N.T. (§45.5b).

[17] Second aorist passive, which does not appear in the N.T. (§47.8). The stem vowel shifts η ‣ α (§4, v-7).

v-3d

Verbal roots add νι   (total: 2)

Cf. Funk (§485.7) and Smyth (§523h).

βαίνω[1]	βήσομαι[2]	ἔβην[3]	βέβηκα[4]	-	-
κερδαίνω[5]	κερδήσω[6]	ἐκέρδησα[7]	-	-	ἐκερδήθην[8]

Class v-4

Present Tense Stem = Verbal Root + τ

All the verbal roots in this category end in π.[9] They add τ to form their present tense stem. The π is open to substantial changes in the other tenses. These are the same types of changes as we find in other roots ending in a labial (v-1b[1]). Some of these verbs have alternate forms in -έω (e.g., ῥιπτέω). Total: 19.

future	π + σ › ψ	(§22.1)		
aorist (active)	π + σ › ψ	(§22.1)		
perfect (middle/passive)	π + μ › μμ	(§21.1)		
aorist (passive)	π + θ › φθ	(§20.1)		

ἄπτω[10]	-	ἦψα	-	-	ἥφθην
ἀστράπτω[11]	-	ἤστραψα	-	-	-

---

[1]   The root is *βα, which lengthens to *βη in three of the tense stems (§4, v-7). The word always occurs in compound verbs in the N.T. LaSor says it properly belongs in v-3a(1) (i.e., ν is added to form the present tense stem).

ἀναβαίνω, ἀποβαίνω, διαβαίνω, ἐκβαίνω, ἐμβαίνω, ἐπιβαίνω, καταβαίνω, μεταβαίνω, παραβαίνω, προβαίνω, προσαναβαίνω, συγκαταβαίνω, συμβαίνω, συναναβαίνω, ὑπερβαίνω

[2]   α lengthens to η before tense formative.

[3]   The root *βα reduces to its zero form (βα › β). Root aorist (§44.2c).

[4]   α lengthens to η before tense formative.

[5]   ἐπικερδαίνω. See *BDF* §101.

[6]   Stem vowel lengthens to η before the tense formative.

[7]   Stem vowel lengthens to η before the tense formative. Has an liquid aorist ἐκέρδανα (1 Cor 9:21; §44.1c). The other fourteen times in the N.T. it uses a first aorist.

[8]   Stem vowel lengthens to η before the tense formative.

[9]   A few have assimilated from other roots. Funk (§932.8) says all the roots are labial roots.

[10]   ἀνάπτω, καθάπτω, περιάπτω

[11]   ἐξαστράπτω, περιαστράπτω

βάπτω[1]	βάψω	ἔβαψα	-	βέβαμμαι	-
βλάπτω[2]	-	ἔβλαψα	-	-	ἐβλάφθην[3]
θάλπω	-	-	-	-	-
θάπτω[4]	-	ἔθαψα	-	-	ἐτάφην[5]
θρύπτω[6]	-	-	-	-	-
καλύπτω[7]	καλύψω	ἐκάλυψα	-	κεκάλυμμαι	ἐκαλύφθην
κάμπτω[8]	κάμψω	ἔκαμψα	-	-	-
κλέπτω	κλέψω	ἔκλεψα	-	-	ἐκλάπην[9]
κόπτω[10]	κόψω	ἔκοψα	-	κέκομμαι	ἐκόπην[11]
κρύπτω[12]	κρύψω	ἔκρυψα	-	κέκρυμμαι	ἐκρύβην[13]
κύπτω[14]	-	ἔκυψα	-	-	-
νίπτω[15]	-	ἔνιψα	-	-	-
ῥάπτω[16]	-	-	-	-	-
ῥίπτω[17]	-	ἔρριψα	-	ἔρριμμαι	ἐρρίθην[18]

---

[1] ἐμβάπτω

[2] Smyth says the root is *βλαβ (§505).

[3] Has a second aorist form ἐβλάβην.

[4] συνθάπτω

[5] Second aorist passive (§47.8). The root is *θαπ. ἐθάπην shifts to ἐτάφην because of a transfer of aspiration: θ deaspirates to τ and π aspirates to φ (§14.6; cf. §15.8). It is not clear why the aspiration is transferred.

[6] συνθρύπτω

[7] Root is *καλυβ (cf. καλύβη). ἀνακαλύπτω, ἀποκαλύπτω, ἐπικαλύπτω, κατακαλύπτω, παρακαλύπτω, περικαλύπτω, συγκαλύπτω

[8] ἀνακάμπτω, συγκάμπτω

[9] Second aorist passive, which does not appear in the N.T. (§47.8).

[10] ἀνακόπτω, ἀποκόπτω, ἐγκόπτω, ἐκκόπτω, κατακόπτω, προκόπτω, προσκόπτω

[11] Second aorist passive (§47.8).

[12] BAGD says that it can form its present κρύπω as if it were a v-1 verb; there are no examples in the N.T. Compounds are ἀποκρύπτω, ἀνακρύπτω, ἐγκρύπτω. Cf. περικρύβω.

[13] Second aorist passive (§47.8).

[14] ἀνακύπτω, κατακύπτω, παρακύπτω, συγκύπτω

[15] ἀπονίπτω. A form developed later as ἀπονίζω. Appears only once in the N.T. as ἀπενίψατο (Mt 27:24).

[16] ἐπιράπτω, ἐπισυρράπτω

[17] *ῥιφ (Smyth §505; BDF §101). ἀπορίπτω, ἐπιρίπτω. In Acts 22:23, ε is inserted after the tense stem: ῥιπτούντων (ε + ο ‧ ου). Compound is ἀπορίπτω. BAGD lists as -(ρ)ρ, which occurs only once in the N.T. as ἀπορίψαντας (Acts 27:43). BAGD also lists a second aorist that does not occur in the N.T. (ἀπερίθην). BAGD also lists the imperfect as ἐ(ρ)ρίπτουν; the imperfect does not occur in the N.T. BAGD lists the compound ἐπι- as ἐπι(ρ)ρίπτω. It occurs only with a single ρ (Lk 19:35; 1 Pet 5:7); the aorist passive ἐπερρίθην does not occur.

[18] Also has a second aorist passive ἐρρίφην, which does not appear in the N.T. (§47.8).

σκάπτω[1]   σκάψω   ἔσκαψα   -   ἔσκαμμαι   ἐσκάφην[2]
σκέπτομαι[3] σκέψομαι ἐσκεψάμην -   -   -
τύπτω   -   -   -   -   -

Class v-5

Present Tense Stem = Verbal Root + (ι)σκ

Some vowel stems lengthen their final vowel before σκ. Some consonant stems will undergo ablaut, lose their stem vowel, and add η or ω before σκ. There also are a few examples of reduplication to form the present tense stem. Adding ισκ to consonantal stems was a later development (Smyth §526d). If the stem ends in a stop, it is dropped (e.g., *δακ ‣ διδάσκω). Two vowel stems add ισκ contrary to the rule (θνῇσκω, μιμνῇσκομαι).

v-5a   Roots ending in a vowel add σκ   (total: 17)

ἀρέσκω   ἀρέσω   ἤρεσα   -   -   -
βιβρώσκω[4] -   -   βέβρωκα   βέβρωμαι   ἐβρώθην
βόσκω   -   -   -   -   -
γαμίσκω[5]   -   -   -   -   -
γηράσκω   -   ἐγήρασα   γεγήρακα   -   -
γινώσκω[6]   γνώσομαι   ἔγνων[7]   ἔγνωκα   ἔγνωσμαι[8] ἐγνώσθην[9]
διδάσκω[10] διδάξω   ἐδίδαξα   -   -   ἐδιδάχθην
διδύσκω[11] -   -   -   -   -

---

[1] κατασκάπτω

[2] Second aorist passive, which does not appear in the N.T. (§47.8).

[3] ἐπισκέπτομαι

[4] The verbal root is *βρω, which reduplicates to form the present tense stem (§32.4).

[5] Alternate form of γαμίζω (v-2a[1]). In our texts γαμίζω is always used.

[6] *γνο ‣ γιγνοσκω ‣ γινοσκω ‣ γινώσκω. The verbal root is *γνο. It reduplicates to form the present tense stem, the second γ drops out, and the stem vowel lengthens. ἀναγινώσκω, διαγινώσκω, ἐπιγινώσκω, καταγινώσκω, προγινώσκω

[7] Root aorist (§44.2c). See there for its paradigm, and at §96.

[8] σ is inserted after the tense stem (§46.5).

[9] σ is inserted after the tense stem (§46.5).

[10] The root is *δακ. κ drops out when immediately followed by σκ (see Introduction; Smyth §99, 526d).

[11] ἐνδιδύσκω. διδύσκω is a later form of ἐνδύω. διδύσκω is not listed in LS.

θνῄσκω[1]	θανοῦμαι[2]	ἔθανον[3]	τέθνηκα[4]	-	-
ἱλάσκομαι[5]	-	-	-	-	ἱλάσθην[6]
μεθύσκω[7]	-	-	-	-	ἐμεθύσθην[8]
μιμνῄσκομαι[9]	μνήσω	ἔμνησα	-	μέμνημαι	ἐμνήσθην[10]
πάσχω[11]	-	ἔπαθον[12]	πέπονθα[13]	-	-
πιπράσκω[14]	-	-	πέπρακα	πέπραμαι	ἐπράθην
φάσκω	-	-	-	-	-
φαύσκω[15]	φαύσω	-	-	-	-
φώσκω[16]	-	-	-	-	-

v-5b   Roots ending in a consonant add ισκ   (total: 2)

Stems ending in α/ο may lengthen to α/ω before σκ.

ἁλίσκομαι[17]	-	ἥλωσα	-	-	ἡλώθην

---

[1] The verbal root is *θαν. In the present and perfect active it reduces to its zero form (§4.4c, v-7) and inserts an η after the stem: *θαν ‣ θν ‣ θνη. (Smyth, §492, says the stem undergoes metathesis, *θαν ‣ θνα.) Contrary to the pattern it adds ισκ and not σκ. The ι subsequently subscripts. Cf. μιμνῄσκομαι. Compounds are ἀποθνῄσκω, συναποθνῄσκω.

[2] Liquid future (§43.3).

[3] Second aorist (§44.5a).

[4] *θαν ‣ θν ‣ θνη ‣ θεθνατα ‣ τέθνηκα. Or, *θαν ‣ θνα ‣ θνη (§7.6). Does not occur in the N.T.

[5] See *BDF* §101.

[6] σ is inserted after the tense stem (§46.5).

[7] Alternate form of μεθύω. See v-1a(4) for discussion.

[8] σ is inserted after the tense stem (§46.5).

[9] The verbal root is *μνη, which reduplicates to form the present tense stem. Contrary to the regular pattern, the present tense stem adds ισκ and not σκ; the ι subsequently subscripts (cf. θνῄσκω). The simple verb is a passive deponent in the N.T., but active in compound verbs and in the other tense stems. ἀναμιμνῄσκω, ἐπαναμιμνῄσκω, ὑπομιμνῄσκω

[10] σ is inserted after the tense stem (§46.5).

[11] There are two roots, *παθ and *πενθ (Smyth §529; v-8). Funk says they are *παθ and *πονθ (§487.7). When σκ is added, the θ is lost before the σ (§22.3) and its aspiration passed to κ, which becomes χ (§14.1). παθσκω ‣ πασσκω ‣ πασσχω ‣ πάσχω. Has a contract future that does not occur in the N.T. Compounds are προπάσχω, συμπάσχω.

[12] Second aorist (§44.5a).

[13] Second perfect (§45.5b).

[14] The verbal root is *πρα, which reduplicates to form the present tense stem. *BDF* §101.

[15] ἐπιφαύσκω. φώσκω normally occurs in compounds.

[16] ἐπιφώσκω. See *BDF* §101.

[17] ἀναλίσκω (cf. ἀναλόω, cv-1d[3]), καταναλίσκω, συναλίσκομαι. Cf. ἁλόω (v-1d[3]). ω is inserted after the stem in the aorist stems (§44.5c). See *BDF* §101.

εὑρίσκω[1]   εὑρήσω[2]   εὗρον[3]   εὕρηκα[4]   -   εὑρέθην[5]

Class v-6
Athematic (μι) Verbs

μι verbs are easy to learn. See the discussion at §40.4. v-3c(1) and v-3c(2) verbs can be classified as μι verbs that do not reduplicate. But also included in their formation of the present tense stem is the addition of (ν)νυ. We have therefore categorized them as v-3 words. For further discussion see *BDF* §92-100.

The vowels change their length frequently (§4) and we will not footnote those changes.

v-6a   Athematic verbs that reduplicate to form their present tense stem   (total: 8)

In order to find the verbal root from the present stem, cross out the reduplicated letters; the next consonant (or consonant cluster) and vowel are the root. μι verbs often have alternate forms in -άω or -άνω.

δίδωμι[6]	δώσω	ἔδωκα[7]	δέδωκα[8]	δέδομαι	ἐδόθην
ἵημι[9]	ἥσω	ἧκα[10]	εἷκα[11]	ἕωμαι[12]	εἵθην

---

1   *ευρ. ἀνευρίσκω.

2   η is inserted after the tense stem (§43.8d).

3   Second aorist (§44.5a). ἀνευρίσκω uses first aorist endings at Lk 2:16 (ἀνεῦραν).

4   η is inserted after the tense stem (§45.3).

5   ε is inserted after the tense stem (§47.7).

6   δίδωμι is the paradigmatic verb used in §41ff. See there for peculiarities. ἀναδίδωμι, ἀνταποδίδωμι, ἀποδίδωμι, διαδίδωμι, ἐκδίδωμι, ἐπιδίδωμι, μεταδίδωμι, παραδίδωμι, προδίδωμι, προσδίδωμι

7   κ aorist using κα and not σα as the tense formative (§44.1d).

8   Occurs three times in the pluperfect δεδώκειν, all without the initial vocalic reduplication (Mk 14:44; Lk 19:15; Jn 11:57).

9   *σε ‣ σισημι ‣ ισημι ‣ ἵημι. The verbal root is *σε (§31.5a; Smyth §431). When it is reduplicated to σισε, the first σ is replaced by rough breathing (§25.6b), and the second σ is interconsonantal and therefore drops out (§25.4), leaving the ι of the reduplication and the ε of the verbal root, which lengthens to η. (Funk says the roots are *η and *ε [§3733.4]). Occurs in the N.T. only in compounds: ἀνίημι, ἀφίημι, ἐναφίημι, καθίημι, παρίημι, συνίημι (also συνίω, v-1a[1]). The paradigm of ἀφίημι is given at §96.

10   κ aorist using κα and not σα as the tense formative (§44.1d).

11   Also ἕωκα.

12   Inserts an ω after the stem (§46.6).

ἵστημι¹	στήσω	ἔστησα	ἔστηκα²	ἔσταμαι	ἐστάθην
κίχρημι³	-	ἔχρησα	-	-	-
ὀνίνημι⁴	-	ὤνησα	-	-	-
πίμπλημι⁵	-	ἔπλησα	-	πέπλησμαι⁶	ἐπλήσθην⁷
πίμπρημι⁸	-	ἔπρησα	-	-	ἐπρήσθην⁹
τίθημι¹⁰	θήσω	ἔθηκα¹¹	τέθεικα¹²	τέθειμαι	ἐτέθην¹³

1   ἵστημι is the paradigmatic verb used in §41ff. See there for peculiarities. The verbal root is *στα. It reduplicates to form the present tense; the initial σ drops off and is replaced by rough breathing (§25.6b). *στα ‣ σιστημι ‣ ἵστημι. The aorist therefore has smooth breathing since there is no reduplication in that tense. On the augment cf. §31.5a. The verbal root could also form the present tense as a v-3a(1) verb: ἱστάνω (notice the breathing carried over from the athematic formation). In our texts only at Rom 3:31 (ἱστάνομεν); cf BDF §93; MH 202. Cf. ἀποκαθιστάνω. See BDF §101.

     ἀνίστημι, ἀνθίστημι, ἀντικαθίστημι, ἀποκαθίστημι, ἀφίστημι, διίστημι, ἐνίστημι, ἐξίστημι, ἐξανίστημι, ἐφίστημι, ἐπανίστημι, καθίστημι, κατεφίσταμαι, μεθίστημι (has a by-form μεθιστάνω that does not occur in the N.T.), παρίστημι, περιΐστημι, προΐστημι, συνίστημι (also συνιστάω, cv-1d[1a]; συνιστάνω, cv-3a[1]), συνεφίστημι

     BAGD lists three forms of συνίστημι: συνίστημι (four times in N.T.; v-6a); συνιστάνω (seven times; v-3a[1]); συνιστάω (three times in T.R.; v-1d[1a]; but our text reads συνίσταντες in 2 Cor 6:4 with a v.l. of συνιστῶντες). Four times BAGD does not commit itself: συνέστηκεν (Col 1:17); συνεστῶσα (2 Pet 3:5; perf. ptcp. fem.); συνεστήσατε (2 Cor 7:11); συνεστῶτας (Lk 9:32). This is a good example of how the different formation patterns were overlapping in the Koine period.

2   κ aorist (§44.1d). Never occurs in the N.T.

3   Root is *χρη. Just as in the perfect, when two successive aspirates occur due to reduplication, the first deaspirates (χ ‣ κ; §15.1).

4   *ονη ‣ ονονημι ‣ ὀνίνημι. The verbal root is *ονη. It reduplicates to form the present tense, but the original ο becomes ι in imitation of the other μι verbs that use ι in their reduplication (Funk §3450.2).

5   *πλα ‣ πιπλημι ‣ πίμπλημι. The verbal root is *πλα. After reduplication, it can develop an epenthetic μ (Funk §3450.3). πί(μ)πλημι. ἐμπίμπλημι, listed as ἐμπί(μ)πλημι by BAGD. Only occurrence in the present in our texts is ἐμπιμπλῶν (Acts 14:17). Has an alternate form ἐπι(μ)πλάω.

6   σ is inserted after the tense stem (§46.5).

7   σ is inserted after the tense stem (§46.5).

8   *πρα ‣ πιπρημι ‣ πίμπρημι. The verbal root is *πρα. After reduplication, it can develop an epenthetic μ (Funk §3450.3). πί(μ)πρημι. ἐμπίμπρημι, καταπίμπρημι. BAGD lists it as ἐμπί(μ)πρημι. In our texts, it occurs in the present only as the variant ἐμπιπρᾶσθαι (Acts 28:6).

9   σ is inserted after the tense stem, but not in the N.T. (§46.5).

10   τίθημι is the paradigmatic verb used in §41ff. See there for peculiarities. ἀνατίθημι, ἀντιδιατίθημι, ἀποτίθημι, διατίθημι, ἐκτίθημι, ἐντίθημι, ἐπιτίθημι, κατατίθημι, μετατίθημι, παρατίθημι, περιτίθημι, προτίθημι, προστίθημι, προσανατίθημι, συντίθημι, συνεπιτίθημι, συγκατατίθημι, ὑποτίθημι

11   κ aorist using κα and not σα as the tense formative (§44.1d).

12   Stem vowel becomes ει due to ablaut (§4).

13   θε ‣ εθεθην ‣ ἐτέθην. The stem aspirate (θ) deaspirates to τ because of the θ of the tense formative (§15.8; Smyth §125c).

v-6b   Athematic verbs that do not reduplicate to form their present tense stem   (total: 7)

Even though five of the words end in regular deponent endings, they are classified as μι verbs because they follow the athematic conjugation (i.e., no connecting vowel.

δύναμαι[1]	δυνήσομαι[2]	-	-	-	ἠδυνήθην[3]
εἰμί[4]	ἔσομαι	ἤμην[5]	-	-	-
εἶμι[6]	-	-	-	-	-
κάθημαι[7]	καθήσομαι	-	-	-	-
κεῖμαι[8]	-	-	-	-	-
στάμαι[9]	-	-	-	-	-
φημί[10]	-	ἔφη[11]	-	-	-

---

[1]   The imperfect augments with η or ε (cf. §41.3ff.). See *BDF* §101.

[2]   Lengthens stem vowel as if it were an α contract verb.

[3]   Lengthens stem vowel as if it were an α contract verb. Augments irregularly with an η and not an ε. Has a form in which σ is inserted after the tense stem and the stem α is not lengthened: ἠδυνάσθην (does not occur in the N.T.; §46.3).

[4]   "I am." Its paradigm is given at §96. ἄπειμι (imperfect, ἀπῇεσαν), εἴσειμι, ἔνειμι, ἔξειμι, ἔπειμι, πάρειμι, συμπάρειμι, σύνειμι. See *BDF* §98.

Its root is *εσ. It is athematic in the present, deponent in the future, and uses a mixture of active and middle/passive endings in the imperfect (cf. Smyth §770; Funk §371-3710, §378, §405-4050).

σύνειμι can be from εἰμί and εἶμι. σύνειμι from εἰμί means "to be with" (Lk 9:18; Acts 22:11). σύνειμι from εἶμι means "to come together" (Lk 8:4).

ἔνι is a shortened form of ἔνεστιν, which is from ἔνειμι. It occurs in our literature always with a negative as οὐκ ἔνι (1 Cor 6:5; Gal 3:28 (3t); Col 3:11; Jas 1:17).

ἔξεστι is a third person singular impersonal verb from the unused ἔξειμι.

[5]   ἤμην is an imperfect. See discussion in Smyth §771.

[6]   "I will go." Used as a future of ἔρχομαι in Attic, and as a v.l. at Jn 7:34. On σύνειμι see footnote on εἰμί. For its paradigm see §96.

[7]   συγκάθημαι

[8]   ἀνάκειμαι, ἀντίκειμαι, ἀπόκειμαι, ἐπίκειμαι, κατάκειμαι, παράκειμαι, περίκειμαι, πρόκειμαι, σύγκειμαι, συνανάκειμαι, ὑπόκειμαι

[9]   ἐπίσταμαι. στάμαι is not listed in *LS*.

[10]   σύμφημι

[11]   ἔφη occurs forty-three times in the N.T., over half of the sixty-six times φημί occurs. It can be either imperfect or second aorist (cf. *BAGD* p. 856).

Class v-7

Verbal Roots that Change their Stem Vowel (total: 41)

The words listed here have already been listed in categories v-1 through v-6. In the index they are listed as belonging to one of these. But for ease of memorization and understanding, we have collected the verbs in the New Testament that change their stem vowel in the formation of their principal parts (§4).[1] These changes can normally be explained through ablaut (§4). There are, however, various other reasons as well. Roots that undergo ablaut tend to use the strong grade in the present tense (Smyth §502).

ἀκούω	ἀκούσω	ἤκουσα	ἀκήκοα	-	ἠκούσθην	v-1a(8)
βαίνω	βήσομαι	ἔβην	βέβηκα	-	-	v-3d
βάλλω	βαλῶ	ἔβαλον	βέβληκα	βέβλημαι	ἐβλήθην	v-2d(1)
γίνομαι	γενήσομαι	ἐγενόμην	γέγονα	γεγένημαι	ἐγενήθην	v-1c(2)
δάκνω	-	-	-	-	ἐδήχθην	v-3a(1)
ἐγείρω	ἐγερῶ	ἤγειρα	-	ἐγήγερμαι	ἠγέρθην	v-2d(3)
ἔρχομαι	ἐλεύσομαι	ἦλθον	ἐλήλυθα	-	-	v-1b(2)
ἔχω	ἕξω	ἔσχον	ἔσχηκα	-	-	v-1b(2)
θνῄσκω	θανοῦμαι	ἔθανον	τέθνηκα	-	-	v-5a
καίω	καύσω	ἔκαυσα	-	κέκαυμαι	ἐκαύθην	v-2c
καλέω	καλέσω	ἐκάλεσα	κέκληκα	κέκλημαι	ἐκλήθην	v-1d(2b)
κάμνω	-	ἔκαμον	κέκμηκα	-	-	v-3a(1)
κτείνω	κτενῶ	ἔκτεινα	-	-	ἐκτάνθην	v-2d(5)
λαμβάνω	λήμψομαι	ἔλαβον	εἴληφα	εἴλημμαι	ἐλήμφθην	v-3a(2b)
λανθάνω	-	ἔλαθον	-	λέλησμαι	-	v-3a(2b)
λέγω	ἐρῶ	εἶπον	εἴρηκα	εἴρημαι	ἐρρέθην	v-1b(2)
λείπω	λείψω	ἔλιπον	λέλοιπα	λέλειμμαι	ἐλείφθην	v-1b(1)
μένω	μενῶ	ἔμεινα	μεμένηκα	-	-	v-1c(2)
ὄλλυμι	ὀλέσω	ὤλεσα	ὀλώλα	-	-	v-3c(2)
πείθω	πείσω	ἔπεισα	πέποιθα	πέπεισμαι	ἐπείσθην	v-1b(3)
πέμπω	πέμψω	ἔπεμψα	πέπομφα	-	ἐπέμφθην	v-1b(1)
πέτομαι	πτήσομαι	ἐπτόμην	-	-	-	v-1b(3)
πίνω	πίομαι	ἔπιον	πέπωκα	-	ἐπόθην	v-3a(1)

---

[1]   We have included all six examples of Attic reduplication (§32.6) since the stem vowel is lengthened. We have not included verbs that lengthen their final stem vowel before tense forlatives or pdrsonal endings (v-1d) nor theμι verbs. We have included a few that can be explained by multiple roots (v-8).

πίπτω	πεσοῦμαι	ἔπεσον	πέπτωκα	-	-	v-1b(3)
πλέκω	-	ἔπλεξα	-	πέπλεγμαι	ἐπλάκην	v-1b(2)
ῥέω	ῥεύσω	-	-	-	ἐρύην	v-1a(7)
ῥήγνυμι	ῥήξω	ἔρρηξα	ἔρρηγα	-	ἐράγην	v-3c(2)
σπείρω	-	ἔσπειρα	-	ἔσπαρμαι	ἐσπάρην	v-2d(3)
στέλλω	στελῶ	ἔστειλα	ἔσταλκα	ἔσταλμαι	ἐστάλην	v-2d(1)
στρέφω	στρέψω	ἔστρεψα	-	ἔστραμμαι	ἐστράφην	v-1b(1)
τέλλω	τελῶ	ἔτειλα	τέταλκα	τέταλμαι	-	v-2d(1)
τέμνω	-	ἔτεμον	τέτμηκα	τέτμημαι	ἐτμήθην	v-3a(1)
τήκω	-	-	-	-	ἐτάκην	v-1b(2)
τίκτω	τέξομαι	ἔτεκον	-	-	ἐτέχθην	v-1b(2)
τρέπω	-	ἔτρεψα	-	τέτραμμαι	ἐτράπην	v-1b(1)
τρέφω	-	ἔθρεψα	-	τέθραμμαι	ἐτράφην	v-1b(1)
τυγχάνω	τεύξω	ἔτυχον	τέτευχα	-	-	v-3a(2b)
φέρω	οἴσω	ἤνεγκα	ἐνήνοχα	ἐνήνεκμαι	ἠνέχθην	v-1c(1)
φεύγω	φεύξομαι	ἔφυγον	πέφευγα	-	-	v-1b(2)
φθείρω	φθερῶ	ἔφθειρα	-	ἔφθαρμαι	ἐφθάρην	v-2d(3)
χέω	χεῶ	ἔχεα	κέχυκα	κέχυμαι	ἐχύθην	v-1a(7)

Class v-8

Verbs Using More than One Verbal Root (total: 9)

The words listed here have already been listed in categories v-1 through v-6. In the index they are listed as belonging to one of these. But for ease of memorization and understanding, we have collected here all the verbs in the New Testament that use more than one verbal root in the formation of their principal parts. This does not include verbs whose roots undergo ablaut (v-7).

Actually, one verb does not use several verbal roots. For some reason or another, a verbal root was used only in certain tenses. Another verbal root was likewise restricted to other tenses. Eventually, verbal roots that were compatible in meaning with another verbal root would become associated with the other, and in fact would contribute to which tenses the other root functioned in. For example, the root behind ἔρχομαι was restricted for use just in the present tense, while the root *ελευθ in various forms was restricted to the future, aorist active/middle, and perfect active. Therefore, due to the nature of things, ἔρχομαι and ἦλθον came to be regarded as the same verb using different roots.

Cf. also πίνω (v-3a[1]) and ὠνέομαι (v-1d[2a]).

αἱρέω[1]	αἱρήσομαι	εἱλόμην	-	ᾕρημαι	ᾑρέθην
ἔρχομαι[2]	ἐλεύσομαι	ἦλθον	ἐλήλυθα	-	-
ἐσθίω[3]	φάγομαι	ἔφαγον	-	-	-
λέγω[4]	ἐρῶ	εἶπον	εἴρηκα	εἴρημαι	ἐρρέθην
οἶδα[5]	εἰδήσω	ᾔδειν	-	-	-
ὁράω[6]	ὄψομαι	ὠψάμην εἶδον	ἑώρακα	-	ὤφθην
πάσχω[7]	-	ἔπαθον	πέπονθα	-	-
τρέχω[8]	-	ἔδραμον	-	-	-
φέρω[9]	οἴσω	ἤνεγκα	ἐνήνοχα	ἐνήνεκμαι	ἠνέχθην

[1]	v-1d(2a)	*αιρε, *Ϝελ
[2]	v-1b(2)	*ερχ, *ελευθ
[3]	v-1b(3)	*εδ, *φαγ
[4]	v-1b(2)	*λεγ, *Ϝερ, *Ϝεπ
[5]	v-1b(3)	*οιδ, *Ϝιδ
[6]	v-1d(1a)	*Ϝορα, *οπ, *Ϝιδ
[7]	v-5a	*παθ, *πενθ
[8]	v-1b(2)	*θρεχ, *δραμ
[9]	v-1c(1)	*φερ, *οι, *ενεκ

Index

Αἰγύπτιος	a-1a(1)	ἄκακος	a-3a	ἄλαλος	a-3a
Αἴγυπτος	n-2b	ἄκανθα	n-1c	ἅλας	n-3c(6a)
ἀίδιος	a-3a	ἀκάνθινος	a-1a(2a)	ἀλγέω	v-1d(2a)
αἰδώς	n-3d(3)	ἄκαρπος	a-3a	ἀλείφω	v-1b(1)
Αἰθίοψ	n-3a(1)	ἀκατάγνωστος	a-3a	ἀλεκτοροφωνία	n-1a
αἷμα	n-3c(4)	ἀκατακάλυπτος	a-3a	ἀλέκτωρ	n-3f(2b)
αἱματεκχυσία	n-1a	ἀκατάκριτος	a-3a	Ἀλεξανδρεύς	n-3e(3)
αἱμορροέω	v-1d(2a)	ἀκατάλυτος	a-3a	Ἀλεξανδρῖνος	a-1a(2a)
Αἰνέας	n-1d	ἀκατάπαστος	a-3a	Ἀλέξανδρος	n-2a
αἴνεσις	n-3e(5b)	ἀκατάπαυστος	a-3a	ἄλευρον	n-2c
αἰνέω	v-1d(2b)	ἀκαταστασία	n-1a	ἀλήθεια	n-1a
αἴνιγμα	n-3c(4)	ἀκατάστατος	a-3a	ἀληθεύω	v-1a(6)
αἶνος	n-2a	ἀκατάσχετος	a-3a	ἀληθής	a-4a
Αἰνών	n-3g(2)	Ἀκελδαμάχ	n-3g(2)	ἀληθινός	a-1a(2a)
αἴξ	n-3b(2)	ἀκέραιος	a-3a	ἀλήθω	v-1b(3)
αἵρεσις	n-3e(5b)	ἀκηδεμονέω	v-1d(2a)	ἀληθῶς	adverb
αἱρετίζω	v-2a(1)	ἀκηδεμονέω	v-1d(2	ἁλιεύς	n-3e(3)
αἱρετικός	a-1a(2a)	ἀκλινής	a-4a	ἁλιεύω	v-1a(6)
αἱρέω	v-1d(2a); v-8	ἀκμάζω	v-2a(1)	ἁλίζω	v-2a(1)
αἴρω	v-2d(2)	ἀκμήν	adverb	ἀλίσγημα	n-3c(4)
αἰσθάνομαι	v-3a(2a)	ἀκοή	n-1b	ἁλίσκομαι	v-5b
αἴσθησις	n-3e(5b)	ἀκολουθέω	v-1d(2a)	ἀλλά	particle
αἰσθητήριον	n-2c	ἀκούω	v-1a(8); v-7	ἀλλάσσω	v-2b
αἰσχροκερδής	a-4a	ἀκρασία	n-1a	ἀλλαχόθεν	adverb
αἰσχροκερδῶς	adverb	ἀκρατής	a-4a	ἀλλαχοῦ	adverb
αἰσχρολογία	n-1a	ἄκρατος	a-3a	ἀλληγορέω	v-1d(2a)
αἰσχρός	a-1a(1)	ἀκρίβεια	n-1a	ἀλληλουϊά	n-3g(2)
αἰσχρότης	n-3c(1)	ἀκριβέστατος	a-1a(2a)	ἀλλήλων	a-1a(2b)
αἰσχύνη	n-1b	ἀκριβής	a-4a	ἀλλογενής	a-4a
αἰσχύνω	v-1c(2)	ἀκριβόω	v-1d(3)	ἀλλοιόω	v-1d(3)
αἰτέω	v-1d(2a)	ἀκριβῶς	adverb	ἄλλομαι	v-2d(1)
αἴτημα	n-3c(4)	ἀκρίς	n-3c(2)	ἄλλος	a-1a(2b)
αἰτία	n-1a	ἀκροάομαι	v-1d(1a)	ἀλλοτριεπίσκοπος	n-2a
αἰτιάομαι	v-1d(1b)	ἀκροατήριον	n-2c	ἀλλότριος	a-1a(1)
αἰτίαμα	n-3c(4)	ἀκροατής	n-1f	ἀλλοτριόω	v-1d(3)
αἴτιος	a-1a(1)	ἀκροβυστία	n-1a	ἀλλόφυλος	a-3a
αἰτίωμα	n-3c(4)	ἀκρογωνιαῖος	a-1a(1)	ἄλλως	adverb
αἰφνίδιος	a-3a	ἀκροθίνιον	n-2c	ἀλοάω	v-1d(1a)
αἰχμαλωσία	n-1a	ἄκρον	n-2c	ἄλογος	a-3a
αἰχμαλωτεύω	v-1a(6)	Ἀκύλας	n-3g(1)	ἀλόη	n-1b
αἰχμαλωτίζω	v-2a(1)	ἀκυρόω	v-1d(3)	ἀλόω	v-1d(3)
αἰχμάλωτος	n-2a	ἀκωλύτως	adverb	ἅλς	n-3f(2a)
αἰών	n-3f(1a)	ἄκων	a-2a	ἀλυκός	a-1a(2a)
αἰώνιος	a-3b(1)	ἄλα	see ἅλας	ἄλυπος	a-3a
ἀκαθαρσία	n-1a	ἀλάβαστρος	n-2a; n-2b	ἀλυπότερος	a-1a(1)
ἀκαθάρτης	n-3c(1)	ἀλάβαστρον	n-2c	ἄλυσις	n-3e(5b)
ἀκάθαρτος	a-3a	ἀλαζονεία	n-1a	ἀλυσιτελής	a-4a
ἀκαιρέομαι	v-1d(2b)	ἀλαζών	n-3f(1b)	ἄλφα	n-3g(2)
ἀκαίρως	adverb	ἀλαλάζω	v-2a(1)	Ἀλφαῖος	n-2a
		ἀλάλητος	a-3a	ἅλων	n-3f(1a)

ἀλώπηξ	n-3b(1)	ἄμωμος	a-3a	ἀνακλίνω	cv-1c(2)
ἅλωσις	n-3e(5b)	Ἀμών	n-3g(2)	ἀνακόπτω	cv-4
ἅμα	adverb	Ἀμώς	n-3g(2)	ἀνακράζω	cv-2a(2)
ἀμαθής	a-4a	ἄν	particle	ἀνακραυγάζω	cv-2a(1)
ἀμαράντινος	a-1a(2a)	ἀνά	prep.	ἀνακρίνω	cv-1c(2)
ἀμάραντος	a-3a	ἀναβαθμός	n-2a	ἀνάκρισις	n-3e(5b)
ἁμαρτάνω	v-3a(2a)	ἀναβαίνω	cv-3d	ἀνακυλίω	cv-1a(1)
ἁμάρτημα	n-3c(4)	ἀναβάλλω	cv-2d(1)	ἀνακύπτω	cv-4
ἁμαρτία	n-1a	ἀναβιβάζω	cv-2a(1)	ἀναλαμβάνω	cv-3a(2b)
ἀμάρτυρος	a-3a	ἀναβλέπω	cv-1b(1)	ἀνάλημψις	n-3e(5b)
ἁμαρτωλός	a-3a	ἀνάβλεψις	n-3e(5b)	ἀναλίσκω	cv-5b
Ἀμασίας	n-1d	ἀναβοάω	cv-1d(1a)	ἀνάλλομαι	cv-2d(1)
ἄμαχος	a-3a	ἀναβολή	n-1b	ἀναλογία	n-1a
ἀμάω	v-1d(1a)	ἀνάγαιον	n-2c	ἀναλογίζομαι	cv-2a(1)
ἀμέθυσος	n-2b	ἀναγγέλλω	cv-2d(1)	ἄναλος	a-3a
ἀμέθυστος	n-2b	ἀναγεννάω	cv-1d(1a)	ἀναλόω	cv-1d(3)
ἀμελέω	v-1d(2a)	ἀναγινώσκω	cv-5a	ἀνάλυσις	n-3e(5b)
ἄμεμπτος	a-3a	ἀναγκάζω	v-2a(1)	ἀναλύω	cv-1a(4)
ἀμέμπτως	adverb	ἀναγκαῖος	a-1a(1)	ἀναμάρτητος	a-3a
ἀμέριμνος	a-3a	ἀναγκαιότερος	a-1a(1)	ἀναμένω	cv-1c(2)
ἀμετάθετος	a-3a	ἀναγκαστῶς	adverb	ἀναμιμνήσκω	cv-5a
ἀμετακίνητος	a-3a	ἀνάγκη	n-1b	ἀνάμνησις	n-3e(5b)
ἀμεταμέλητος	a-3a	ἀναγνωρίζω	cv-2a(1)	ἀνανεόω	cv-1d(3)
ἀμετανόητος	a-3a	ἀνάγνωσις	n-3e(5b)	ἀνανήφω	cv-1b(1)
ἄμετρος	a-3a	ἀνάγω	cv-1b(2)	Ἀνανίας	n-1d
ἀμήν	particle	ἀναδείκνυμι	cv-3c(2)	ἀναντίρρητος	a-3a
ἀμήτωρ	a-4c	ἀνάδειξις	n-3e(5b)	ἀναντιρρήτως	adverb
ἀμίαντος	a-3a	ἀναδέχομαι	cv-1b(2)	ἀνάξιος	a-3a
Ἀμιναδάβ	n-3g(2)	ἀναδίδωμι	cv-6a	ἀναξίως	adverb
ἄμμον	n-2c	ἀναζάω	cv-1d(1a)	ἀνάπαυσις	n-3e(5b)
ἄμμος	n-2b	ἀναζητέω	cv-1d(2a)	ἀναπαύω	cv-1a(5)
ἀμνός	n-2a	ἀναζώννυμι	cv-3c(1)	ἀναπείθω	cv-1b(3)
ἀμοιβή	n-1b	ἀναζωπυρέω	cv-1d(2a)	ἀνάπειρος	a-3a
ἄμπελος	n-2b	ἀναθάλλω	cv-2d(1)	ἀναπέμπω	cv-1b(1)
ἀμπελουργός	n-2a	ἀνάθεμα	n-3c(4)	ἀναπηδάω	cv-1d(1a)
ἀμπελών	n-3f(1a)	ἀναθεματίζω	cv-2a(1)	ἀνάπηρος	a-3a
Ἀμπλιᾶτος	n-2a	ἀναθεωρέω	cv-1d(2a)	ἀναπίπτω	cv-1b(3)
ἀμύνομαι	v-1c(2)	ἀνάθημα	n-3c(4)	ἀναπληρόω	cv-1d(3)
ἀμφιάζω	see ἀμφιέννυμι	ἀναίδεια	n-1a	ἀναπολόγητος	a-3a
		ἀναίρεσις	n-3e(5b)	ἀναπράσσω	cv-2b
ἀμφιβάλλω	cv-2d(1)	ἀναιρέω	cv-1d(2a)	ἀναπτύσσω	cv-2b
ἀμφίβληστρον	n-2c	ἀναίτιος	a-3a	ἀνάπτω	cv-4
ἀμφιέζω	see ἀμφιέννυμι	ἀνακαθίζω	cv-2a(1)	ἀναρίθμητος	a-3a
		ἀνακαινίζω	cv-2a(1)	ἀνασείω	cv-1a(3)
ἀμφιέννυμι	v-3c(1)	ἀνακαινόω	cv-1d(3)	ἀνασκευάζω	cv-2a(1)
Ἀμφίπολις	n-3e(5b)	ἀνακαίνωσις	n-3e(5b)	ἀνασπάω	cv-1d(1b)
ἄμφοδον	n-2c	ἀνακαλύπτω	cv-4	ἀνάστασις	n-3e(5b)
ἀμφότεροι	a-1a(1)	ἀνακάμπτω	cv-4	ἀναστατόω	cv-1d(3)
ἀμώμητος	a-3a	ἀνάκειμαι	cv-6b	ἀνασταυρόω	cv-1d(3)
ἄμωμον	n-2c	ἀνακεφαλαιόω	cv-1d(3)	ἀναστενάζω	cv-2a(2)

ἀναστρέφω	cv-1b(1)	ἀνήρ	n-3f(2c)	ἀντιλέγω	cv-1b(2)
ἀναστροφή	n-1b	ἀνθίστημι	cv-6a	ἀντίλημψις	n-3e(5b)
ἀνασῴζω	cv-2a(1)	ἀνθομολογέομαι	v-1d(2a)	ἀντιλογία	n-1a
ἀνατάσσομαι	cv-2b	ἄνθος	n-3d(2)	ἀντιλοιδορέω	cv-1d(2a)
ἀνατέλλω	cv-2d(1)	ἀνθρακιά	n-1a	ἀντίλυτρον	n-2c
ἀνατίθημι	cv-6a	ἄνθραξ	n-3b(1)	ἀντιμετρέω	cv-1d(2a)
ἀνατολή	n-1b	ἀνθρωπάρεσκος	a-3a	ἀντιμισθία	n-1a
ἀνατολικός	a-1a(2a)	ἀνθρωπέω	v-1d(2a)	Ἀντιόχεια	n-1a
ἀνατρέπω	cv-1b(1)	ἀνθρώπινος	a-1a(2a)	Ἀντιοχεύς	n-3e(3)
ἀνατρέφω	cv-1b(1)	ἀνθρωποκτόνος	n-2a	ἀντιπαρέρχομαι	cv-1b(2)
ἀναφαίνω	cv-2d(4)	ἄνθρωπος	n-2a	Ἀντιπᾶς	n-1e
ἀναφέρω	cv-1c(1)	ἀνθυπατεύω	v-1a(6)	Ἀντιπατρίς	n-3c(2)
ἀναφωνέω	cv-1d(2a)	ἀνθύπατος	n-2a	ἀντιπέρα	adverb
ἀνάχυσις	n-3e(5b)	ἀνίημι	cv-6a	ἀντιπίπτω	cv-1b(3)
ἀναχωρέω	cv-1d(2a)	ἀνίλεως	a-5a	ἀντιστρατεύομαι	cv-1a(6)
ἀνάψυξις	n-3e(5b)	ἄνιπτος	a-3a	ἀντιτάσσω	cv-2b
ἀναψύχω	cv-1b(2)	ἀνίστημι	cv-6a	ἀντίτυπος	a-3a
ἀνδραποδιστής	n-1f	Ἅννα	n-1a	ἀντίχριστος	n-2a
Ἀνδρέας	n-1d	Ἅννας	n-1e	ἀντλέω	v-1d(2a)
ἀνδρίζομαι	v-2a(1)	ἀνόητος	a-3a	ἄντλημα	n-3c(4)
Ἀνδρόνικος	n-2a	ἄνοια	n-1a	ἀντοφθαλμέω	v-1d(2a)
ἀνδροφόνος	n-2a	ἀνοίγω	cv-1b(2)	ἄνυδρος	a-3a
ἀνεγκλησία	n-1a	ἀνοικοδομέω	cv-1d(2a)	ἀνυπόκριτος	a-3a
ἀνέγκλητος	a-3a	ἄνοιξις	n-3e(5b)	ἀνυπότακτος	a-3a
ἀνεκδιήγητος	a-3a	ἀνομία	n-1a	ἀνύω	v-1a(4)
ἀνεκλάλητος	a-3a	ἄνομος	a-3a	ἄνω	adverb
ἀνέκλειπτος	a-3a	ἀνόμως	adverb	ἄνωθεν	adverb
ἀνεκτός	a-3a	ἀνόνητος	a-3a	ἀνωτερικός	a-1a(2a)
ἀνεκτότερος	a-1a(1)	ἀνορθόω	cv-1d(3)	ἀνώτερον	adverb
ἀνελεήμων	a-4b(1)	ἀνόσιος	a-3a	ἀνώτερος	a-1a(1)
ἀνέλεος	a-3a	ἀνοχή	n-1b	ἀνωφελής	a-4a
ἀνεμίζω	v-2a(1)	ἀνταγωνίζομαι	cv-2a(1)	ἀξίνη	n-1b
ἄνεμος	n-2a	ἀντάλλαγμα	n-3c(4)	ἄξιος	a-1a(1)
ἀνένδεκτος	a-3a	ἀνταναπληρόω	cv-1d(3)	ἀξιόω	v-1d(3)
ἀνεξεραύνητος	a-3a	ἀνταποδίδωμι	cv-6a	ἀξίως	adverb
ἀνεξίκακος	a-3a	ἀνταπόδομα	n-3c(4)	ἀόρατος	a-3a
ἀνεξιχνίαστος	a-3a	ἀνταπόδοσις	n-3e(5b)	ἀπαγγέλλω	cv-2d(1)
ἀνεπαίσχυντος	a-3a	ἀνταποκρίνομαι	cv-1c(2)	ἀπάγχω	cv-1b(2)
ἀνεπίλημπτος	a-3a	ἀντάω	v-1d(1a)	ἀπάγω	cv-1b(2)
ἀνέρχομαι	cv-1b(2)	ἀντέχω	cv-1b(2)	ἀπαίδευτος	a-3a
ἄνεσις	n-3e(5b)	ἀντί	prep.	ἀπαίρω	cv-2d(2)
ἀνετάζω	cv-2a(1)	ἀντιβάλλω	cv-2d(1)	ἀπαιτέω	cv-1d(2a)
ἄνευ	prep.	ἀντιδιατίθημι	cv-6a	ἀπαλγέω	cv-1d(2a)
ἀνεύθετος	a-3a	ἀντίδικος	n-2a	ἀπαλλάσσω	cv-2b
ἀνευρίσκω	cv-5b	ἀντίθεσις	n-3e(5b)	ἀπαλλοτριόω	cv-1d(3)
ἀνέχω	cv-1b(2)	ἀντικαθίστημι	cv-6a	ἀπαλός	a-1a(2a)
ἀνεψιός	n-2a	ἀντικαλέω	cv-1d(2b)	ἀπαντάω	cv-1d(1a)
ἄνηθον	n-2c	ἀντίκειμαι	cv-6b	ἀπάντησις	n-3e(5b)
ἀνήκω	cv-1b(2)	ἄντικρυς	adverb	ἄπαξ	adverb
ἀνήμερος	a-3a	ἀντιλαμβάνω	cv-3a(2b)	ἀπαράβατος	a-3a

ἀπαρασκεύαστος	a-3a	ἀπογράφω	cv-1b(1)	ἀπολούω	cv-1a(8)
ἀπαρνέομαι	cv-1d(2a)	ἀποδείκνυμι	cv-3c(2)	ἀπολύτρωσις	n-3e(5b)
ἀπαρτί	adverb	ἀπόδειξις	n-3e(5b)	ἀπολύω	cv-1a(4)
ἀπαρτισμός	n-2a	ἀποδεκατεύω	cv-1a(6)	ἀπομάσσω	cv-2b
ἀπαρχή	n-1b	ἀποδεκατόω	cv-1d(3)	ἀπονέμω	cv-1d(2c)
ἅπας	a-2a	ἀπόδεκτος	a-3a	ἀπονίπτω	cv-4
ἀπασπάζομαι	cv-2a(1)	ἀποδέχομαι	cv-1b(2)	ἀποπέμπω	cv-1b(1)
ἀπατάω	v-1d(1a)	ἀποδημέω	cv-1d(2a)	ἀποπίπτω	cv-1b(3)
ἀπάτη	n-1b	ἀπόδημος	a-3a	ἀποπλανάω	cv-1d(1a)
ἀπάτωρ	a-4c	ἀποδίδωμι	cv-6a	ἀποπλέω	cv-1a(7)
ἀπαύγασμα	n-3c(4)	ἀποδιορίζω	cv-2a(1)	ἀποπλύνω	cv-1c(2)
ἀπαφρίζω	cv-2a(1)	ἀποδοκιμάζω	cv-2a(1)	ἀποπνίγω	cv-1b(2)
ἀπείθεια	n-1a	ἀποδοχή	n-1b	ἀπορέω	v-1d(2a)
ἀπειθέω	v-1d(2a)	ἀπόθεσις	n-3e(5b)	ἀπορία	n-1a
ἀπειθής	a-4a	ἀποθήκη	n-1b	ἀπορίπτω	cv-4
ἀπειλέω	v-1d(2a)	ἀποθησαυρίζω	cv-2a(1)	ἀπορρίπτω	see
ἀπειλή	n-1b	ἀποθλίβω	cv-1b(1)		ἀπορίπτω
ἄπειμι	cv-6b	ἀποθνήσκω	cv-5a	ἀπορφανίζω	cv-2a(1)
ἀπεῖπον	cv-1b(2);	ἀποκαθιστάνω	cv-3a(1)	ἀποσκευάζω	cv-2a(1)
	see λέγω	ἀποκαθίστημι	cv-6a	ἀποσκίασμα	n-3c(4)
ἀπείραστος	a-3a	ἀποκαλύπτω	cv-4	ἀποσπάω	cv-1d(1b)
ἄπειρος	a-3a	ἀποκάλυψις	n-3e(5b)	ἀποστασία	n-1a
ἀπεκδέχομαι	cv-1b(2)	ἀποκαραδοκία	n-1a	ἀποστάσιον	n-2c
ἀπεκδύομαι	cv-1a(4)	ἀποκαταλλάσσω	cv-2b	ἀποστάτης	n-1f
ἀπέκδυσις	n-3e(5b)	ἀποκατάστασις	n-3e(5b)	ἀποστεγάζω	cv-2a(1)
ἀπελαύνω	cv-3c(2)	ἀπόκειμαι	cv-6b	ἀποστέλλω	cv-2d(1)
ἀπελεγμός	n-2a	ἀποκεφαλίζω	cv-2a(1)	ἀποστερέω	cv-1d(2a)
ἀπελεύθερος	n-2a	ἀποκλείω	cv-1a(3)	ἀποστολή	n-1b
Ἀπελλῆς	n-1h	ἀποκόπτω	cv-4	ἀπόστολος	n-2a
ἀπελπίζω	cv-2a(1)	ἀπόκριμα	n-3c(4)	ἀποστοματίζω	cv-2a(1)
ἀπέναντι	prep.	ἀποκρίνομαι	cv-1c(2)	ἀποστρέφω	cv-1b(1)
ἀπέραντος	a-3a	ἀπόκρισις	n-3e(5b)	ἀποστυγέω	cv-1d(2a)
ἀπερισπάστως	adverb	ἀποκρύπτω	cv-4	ἀποσυνάγωγος	a-3a
ἀπερίτμητος	a-3a	ἀπόκρυφος	a-3a	ἀποτάσσω	cv-2b
ἀπέρχομαι	cv-1b(2)	ἀποκτείνω	cv-2d(5)	ἀποτελέω	cv-1d(2b)
ἀπέχω	cv-1b(2)	ἀποκτέννω	v-3a(1)	ἀποτίθημι	cv-6a
ἀπιστέω	v-1d(2a)	ἀποκυέω	cv-1d(2a)	ἀποτινάσσω	cv-2b
ἀπιστία	n-1a	ἀποκυλίω	cv-1a(1)	ἀποτίνω	cv-3a(1)
ἄπιστος	a-3a	ἀπολαλέω	cv-1d(2a)	ἀποτολμάω	cv-1d(1a)
ἁπλότης	n-3c(1)	ἀπολαμβάνω	cv-3a(2b)	ἀποτομία	n-1a
ἁπλοῦς	a-1b	ἀπόλαυσις	n-3e(5b)	ἀποτόμως	adverb
ἁπλῶς	adverb	ἀπολείπω	cv-1b(1)	ἀποτρέπω	cv-1b(1)
ἀπό	prep.	ἀπολείχω	cv-1b(2)	ἀπουσία	n-1a
ἀποβαίνω	cv-3d	ἀπολιμπάνω	cv-3a(2b)	ἀποφέρω	cv-1c(1)
ἀποβάλλω	cv-2d(1)	ἀπόλλυμι	cv-3c(2)	ἀποφεύγω	cv-1b(2)
ἀποβλέπω	cv-1b(1)	Ἀπολλύων	n-3f(1b)	ἀποφθέγγομαι	cv-1b(2)
ἀπόβλητος	a-3a	Ἀπολλωνία	n-1a	ἀποφορτίζομαι	cv-2a(1)
ἀποβολή	n-1b	Ἀπολλῶς	n-2e	ἀπόχρησις	n-3e(5b)
ἀπογίνομαι	cv-1c(2)	ἀπολογέομαι	cv-1d(2a)	ἀποχωρέω	cv-1d(2a)
ἀπογραφή	n-1b	ἀπολογία	n-1a	ἀποχωρίζω	cv-2a(1)

ἀποψύχω	cv-1b(2)	ἁρμός	n-2a	ἀσεβής	a-4a
Ἄππιος	n-3g(1)	ἀρνέομαι	v-1d(2a)	ἀσέλγεια	n-1a
ἀπρόσιτος	a-3a	Ἀρνί	n-3g(2)	ἄσημος	a-3a
ἀπρόσκοπος	a-3a	ἀρνίον	n-2c	Ἀσήρ	n-3g(2)
ἀπροσωπολήμπτως	adverb	ἀροτριάω	v-1d(3)	ἀσθένεια	n-1a
ἄπταιστος	a-3a	ἄροτρον	n-2c	ἀσθενέστερος	a-1a(1)
ἅπτω	v-4	ἁρπαγή	n-1b	ἀσθενέω	v-1d(2a)
Ἀπφία	n-1a	ἁρπαγμός	n-2a	ἀσθένημα	n-3c(4)
ἀπωθέω	cv-1b(4)	ἁρπάζω	v-2a(2)	ἀσθενής	a-4a
ἀπώλεια	n-1a	ἅρπαξ	a-5a	Ἀσία	n-1a
ἀρά	n-1a	ἀρραβών	n-3f(1a)	Ἀσιανός	n-2a
ἄρα	particle	ἄρρην	a-4c	Ἀσιάρχης	n-1f
ἆρα	particle	ἄρρητος	a-3a	ἀσιτία	n-1a
Ἀραβία	n-1a	ἄρρωστος	a-3a	ἄσιτος	a-3a
Ἄραβοι	n-2a	ἀρσενοκοίτης	n-1f	ἀσκέω	v-1d(2a)
Ἀράμ	n-3g(2)	ἄρσην	a-4c	ἀσκός	n-2a
ἀράομαι	v-1d(1b)	ἀρτάω	v-1d(1a)	ἀσμένως	adverb
ἄραφος	a-3a	Ἀρτεμᾶς	n-1e	ἄσοφος	a-3a
Ἄραψ	n-3a(2)	Ἄρτεμις	n-3c(2)	ἀσπάζομαι	v-2a(1)
ἀργέω	v-1d(2a)	ἀρτέμων	n-3f(1a)	ἀσπασμός	n-2a
ἀργός	a-1a(2a)	ἄρτι	adverb	ἀσπίζω	v-2a(1)
ἀργύρεος	a-1a(1)	ἀρτιγέννητος	a-3a	ἄσπιλος	a-3a
ἀργύριον	n-2c	ἀρτίζω	v-2a(1)	ἀσπίς	n-3c(2)
ἀργυροκόπος	n-2a	ἄρτιος	a-1a(1)	ἄσπονδος	a-3a
ἄργυρος	n-2a	ἄρτος	n-2a	ἀσσάριον	n-2c
ἀργυροῦς	a-1b	ἀρτύω	v-1a(4)	Ἀσσάρων	n-3f(1a)
ἄρειος	a-1a(1)	Ἀρφαξάδ	n-3g(2)	ἆσσον	adverb
Ἀρεοπαγίτης	n-1f	ἀρχάγγελος	n-2a	Ἄσσος	n-2b
ἀρεσκεία	n-1a	ἀρχαῖος	a-1a(1)	ἀστατέω	v-1d(2a)
ἀρέσκω	v-5a	Ἀρχέλαος	n-2a	ἀστεῖος	a-1a(1)
ἀρεστός	a-1a(2a)	ἀρχή	n-1b	ἀστήρ	n-3f(2b)
Ἀρέτας	n-1e	ἀρχηγός	n-2a	ἀστήρικτος	a-3a
ἀρετή	n-1b	ἀρχιερατικός	a-3a	ἄστοργος	a-3a
ἀρήν	n-3f(1c)	ἀρχιερεύς	n-3e(3)	ἀστοχέω	v-1d(2a)
ἀριθμέω	v-1d(2a)	ἀρχιληστής	n-1f	ἀστραπή	n-1b
ἀριθμός	n-2a	ἀρχιποίμην	n-3f(1b)	ἀστράπτω	v-4
Ἀριμαθαία	n-1a	Ἄρχιππος	n-2a	ἄστρον	n-2c
Ἀρίσταρχος	n-2a	ἀρχισυνάγωγος	n-2a	Ἀσύγκριτος	n-2a
ἀριστάω	v-1d(1a)	ἀρχιτέκτων	n-3f(1b)	ἀσύμφωνος	a-3a
ἀριστερός	a-1a(1)	ἀρχιτελώνης	n-1f	ἀσύνετος	a-3a
Ἀριστόβουλος	n-2a	ἀρχιτρίκλινος	n-2a	ἀσύνθετος	a-3a
ἄριστον	n-2c	ἄρχω	v-1b(2)	ἀσφάλεια	n-1a
ἀρκετός	a-1a(2a)	ἄρχων	n-3c(5b)	ἀσφαλής	a-4a
ἀρκέω	v-1d(2b)	ἄρωμα	n-3c(4)	ἀσφαλίζω	v-2a(1)
ἄρκος	n-2a; n-2b	Ἀσά	n-3g(2)	ἀσφαλῶς	adverb
ἄρκτος	n-2a; n-2b	ἀσάλευτος	a-3a	ἀσχημονέω	v-1d(2a)
ἅρμα	n-3c(4)	Ἀσάφ	n-3g(2)	ἀσχημοσύνη	n-1b
Ἁρμαγεδών	n-3g(2)	ἄσβεστος	a-3a	ἀσχήμων	a-4b(1)
ἁρμόζω	v-2a(1)	ἀσέβεια	n-1a	ἀσωτία	n-1a
ἁρμολογέω	v-1d(2a)	ἀσεβέω	v-1d(2a)	ἀσώτως	adverb

ἀτακτέω	v-1d(2a)	ἀφελότης	n-3c(1)	Βάαλ	n-3g(2)
ἄτακτος	a-3a	ἄφεσις	n-3e(5b)	Βαβυλών	n-3f(1a)
ἀτάκτως	adverb	ἀφή	n-1b	βαθμός	n-2a
ἄτεκνος	a-3a	ἀφθαρσία	n-1a	βάθος	n-3d(2)
ἀτενίζω	v-2a(1)	ἄφθαρτος	a-3a	βαθύνω	v-1c(2)
ἄτερ	prep.	ἀφθονία	n-1a	βαθύς	a-2b
ἀτιμάζω	v-2a(1)	ἀφθορία	n-1a	βαίνω	v-3d; v-7
ἀτιμάω	v-1d(1a)	ἀφίημι	cv-6a	βάϊον	n-2c
ἀτιμία	n-1a	ἀφικνέομαι	cv-3b	Βαλαάμ	n-3g(2)
ἄτιμος	a-3a	ἀφιλάγαθος	a-3a	Βαλάκ	n-3g(2)
ἀτιμότερος	a-1a(1)	ἀφιλάργυρος	a-3a	βαλλάντιον	n-2c
ἀτιμόω	v-1d(3)	ἄφιξις	n-3e(5b)	βάλλω	v-2d(1); v-7
ἀτμίς	n-3c(2)	ἀφίστημι	cv-6a	βαπτίζω	v-2a(1)
ἄτομος	a-3a	ἄφνω	adverb	βάπτισμα	n-3c(4)
ἄτοπος	a-3a	ἀφόβως	adverb	βαπτισμός	n-2a
Ἀττάλεια	n-1a	ἀφομοιόω	cv-1d(3)	βαπτιστής	n-1f
αὐγάζω	v-2a(1)	ἀφοράω	cv-1d(1a)	βάπτω	v-4
αὐγή	n-1b	ἀφορίζω	cv-2a(1)	βάρ	n-3g(2)
Αὔγουστος	n-2a	ἀφορμή	n-1b	Βαραββᾶς	n-1e
αὐθάδης	a-4a	ἀφρίζω	v-2a(1)	Βαράκ	n-3g(2)
αὐθαίρετος	a-3a	ἀφρός	n-2a	Βαραχίας	n-1d
αὐθεντέω	v-1d(2a)	ἀφροσύνη	n-1b	βάρβαρος	a-3a
αὐλέω	v-1d(2a)	ἄφρων	a-4b(1)	βαρέω	v-1d(2a)
αὐλή	n-1b	ἀφυπνόω	cv-1d(3)	βαρέως	adverb
αὐλητής	n-1f	ἀφυστερέω	cv-1d(2a)	Βαρθολομαῖος	n-2a
αὐλίζομαι	v-2a(1)	ἄφωνος	a-3a	Βαριησοῦς	n-3g(1)
αὐλός	n-2a	Ἀχάζ	n-3g(2)	Βαριωνᾶ	n-3g(2)
αὐξάνω	v-3a(1)	Ἀχαΐα	n-1a	Βαριωνᾶς	n-1e
αὔξησις	n-3e(5b)	Ἀχαϊκός	n-2a	Βαρναβᾶς	n-1e
αὔξω	v-1b(2)	ἀχάριστος	a-3a	βάρος	n-3d(2)
αὔριον	adverb	Ἀχάς	n-3g(2)	βαρσα(β)βᾶς	n-1e
αὐστηρός	a-1a(1)	ἀχειροποίητος	a-3a	Βαρτιμαῖος	n-2a
αὐτάρκεια	n-1a	ἀχέω	v-1d(2a)	βαρύνω	v-1c(2)
αὐτάρκης	a-4a	Ἀχίμ	n-3g(2)	βαρύς	a-2b
αὐτοκατάκριτος	a-3a	ἀχλύς	n-3e(1)	βαρύτερος	a-1a(1)
αὐτόματος	a-1a(2a)	ἀχρεῖος	a-3a	βαρύτιμος	a-3a
αὐτόπτης	n-1f	ἀχρειόω	v-1d(3)	βασανίζω	v-2a(1)
αὐτός	a-1a(2b)	ἄχρηστος	a-3a	βασανισμός	n-2a
αὐτοῦ	adverb	ἄχρι	prep.; conj.	βασανιστής	n-1f
αὐτόφωρος	a-3a	ἄχρις	see ἄχρι	βάσανος	n-2b
αὐτόχειρ	n-3f(2a)	ἄχυρον	n-2c	βασιλεία	n-1a
αὐχέω	v-1d(2a)	ἀψευδής	a-4a	βασίλειος	a-3a
αὐχμηρός	a-1a(1)	ἄψινθος	n-2b	βασιλεύς	n-3e(3)
ἀφαιρέω	cv-1d(2a)	ἀψίνθιον	n-2c	βασιλεύω	v-1a(6)
ἀφανής	a-4a	ἄψυχος	a-3a	βασιλικός	a-1a(2a)
ἀφανίζω	v-2a(1)			βασιλίσκος	n-2a
ἀφανισμός	n-2a			βασίλισσα	n-1c
ἄφαντος	a-3a	**βῆτα**		βάσις	n-3e(5b)
ἀφεδρών	n-3f(1a)			βασκαίνω	v-2d(4)
ἀφειδία	n-1a	β	a-5b	βαστάζω	v-2a(1)

βατεύω	v-1a(6)	βλαστάνω	v-3a(1)	βρυγμός	n-2a
βάτος ("bush")	n-2a; n-2b	Βλάστος	n-2a	βρύχω	v-1b(2)
βάτος ("bath")	n-2a	βλασφημέω	v-1d(2a)	βρύω	v-1a(4)
βάτραχος	n-2a	βλασφημία	n-1a	βρῶμα	n-3c(4)
βατταλογέω	v-1d(2a)	βλάσφημος	a-3a	βρώσιμος	a-3a
βδέλυγμα	n-3c(4)	βλέμμα	n-3c(4)	βρῶσις	n-3e(5b)
βδελυκτός	a-1a(2a)	βλέπω	v-1b(1)	βυθίζω	v-2a(1)
βδελύσσομαι	v-2b	βλητέος	a-1a(1)	βυθός	n-2a
βέβαιος	a-1a(1)	Βοανηργές	n-3g(2)	βυρσεύς	n-3e(3)
βεβαιότερος	a-1a(1)	βοάω	v-1d(1a)	βύσσινος	a-1a(2a)
βεβαιόω	v-1d(3)	Βόες	n-3g(2)	βύσσος	n-2b
βεβαίωσις	n-3e(5b)	βοή	n-1b	βωμός	n-2a
βέβηλος	a-3a	βοήθεια	n-1a		
βεβηλόω	v-1d(3)	βοηθέω	v-1d(2a)		
Βεεζεβούλ	n-3g(2)	βοηθός	a-3a	**γάμμα**	
Βελιάρ	n-3g(2)	βόθρος	n-2a		
βελόνη	n-1b	βόθυνος	n-2a	γ	a-5b
βέλος	n-3d(2)	βολεύομαι	v-1a(6)	Γαββαθά	n-3g(2)
βελτίων	a-4b(1)	βολή	n-1b	Γαβριήλ	n-3g(2)
Βενιαμίν	n-3g(2)	βολίζω	v-2a(1)	γάγγραινα	n-1c
Βερνίκη	n-1b	βολίς	n-3c(2)	Γάδ	n-3g(2)
Βέροια	n-1a	Βόοζ	n-3g(2)	Γαδαρηνός	a-1a(2a)
Βεροιαῖος	a-1a(1)	Βόος	n-3g(2)	Γάζα ("Gaza")	n-1c
Βεώρ	n-3g(2)	βόρβορος	n-2a	γάζα ("treasury")	n-1c
Βηθαβαρά	n-1a	βορρᾶς	n-1e; n-1h	γαζοφυλάκιον	n-2c
Βηθανία	n-1a	βόσκω	v-5a	Γάϊος	n-2a
Βηθεσδά	n-3g(2)	Βοσόρ	n-3g(2)	γάλα	n-3c(6d)
Βηθζαθά	n-3g(2)	βοτάνη	n-1b	Γαλάτης	n-1f
Βηθλέεμ	n-3g(2)	βότρυς	n-3e(1)	Γαλατία	n-1a
Βηθσαϊδά(ν)	n-3g(2)	βουλευτής	n-1f	Γαλατικός	a-1a(2a)
Βηθφαγή	n-3g(2)	βουλεύω	v-1a(6)	γαλήνη	n-1b
βῆμα	n-3c(4)	βουλή	n-1b	Γαλιλαία	n-1a
βηρεύς	n-3e(3)	βούλημα	n-3c(4)	Γαλιλαῖος	a-1a(1)
βήρυλλος	n-2a; n-2b	βούλομαι	v-1d(2c)	Γαλλία	n-1a
βία	n-1a	βουνός	n-2a	Γαλλίων	n-3f(1a)
βιάζω	v-2a(1)	βοῦς	n-3e(4)	Γαμαλιήλ	n-3g(2)
βίαιος	a-1a(1)	βραβεῖον	n-2c	γαμβρεύω	v-1a(6)
βιαστής	n-1f	βραβεύω	v-1a(6)	γαμέω	v-1d(2a)
βιβάζω	v-2a(1)	βραδύνω	v-3a(1)	γαμίζω	v-2a(1)
βιβλαρίδιον	n-2c	βραδυπλοέω	v-1a(7)	γαμίσκω	v-5a
βιβλίον	n-2c	βραδύς	a-2b	γάμος	n-2a
βίβλος	n-2b	βραδύτης	n-3c(1)	γάρ	conj.
βιβρώσκω	v-5a	βραχίων	n-3f(1b)	γαστήρ	n-3f(2c)
Βιθυνία	n-1a	βραχύς	a-2b	γέ	particle
βίος	n-2a	βρέφος	n-3d(2)	Γεδεών	n-3g(2)
βιόω	v-1d(3)	βρέχω	v-1b(2)	γέεννα	n-1c
βίωσις	n-3e(5b)	βριμάομαι	v-1d(1a)	Γεθσημανί	n-3g(2)
βιωτικός	a-1a(2a)	βροντή	n-1b	γείτων	n-3f(1b)
βλαβερός	a-1a(1)	βροχή	n-1b	γελάω	v-1d(1b)
βλάπτω	v-4	βρόχος	n-2a	γέλως	n-3c(1)

γεμίζω	v-2a(1)	γονεύς	n-3e(3)	δανιστής	n-1f
γέμω	v-1c(2)	γόνυ	n-3c(6d)	δαπανάω	v-1d(1a)
γενεά	n-1a	γονυπετέω	v-1d(2a)	δαπάνη	n-1b
γενεαλογέω	v-2a(1)	γράμμα	n-3c(4)	Δαυίδ	n-3g(2)
γενεαλογία	n-1a	γραμματεύς	n-3e(3)	δέ	particle
γενέθλιος	a-3a	γραπτός	a-1a(2a)	δέησις	n-3e(5b)
γενέσια	n-2c	γραφή	n-1b	δεῖ	v-1d(2c)
γένεσις	n-3e(5b)	γράφω	v-1b(1)	δεῖγμα	n-3c(4)
γενετή	n-1b	γραώδης	a-4a	δειγματίζω	v-2a(1)
γένημα	n-3c(4)	γρηγορέω	v-1d(2a)	δείκνυμι	v-3c(2)
γεννάω	v-1d(1a)	γυμνάζω	v-2a(1)	δεικνύω	v-1a(4)
γέννημα	n-3c(4)	γυμνασία	n-1a	δειλία	n-1a
Γεννησαρέτ	n-3g(2)	γυμνητεύω	v-1a(6)	δειλιάω	v-1d(1b)
γέννησις	n-3e(5b)	γυμνιτεύω	v-1a(6)	δειλός	a-1a(2a)
γεννητός	a-1a(2a)	γυμνός	a-1a(2a)	δεῖνα	n-3f(1a)
γένος	n-3d(2)	γυμνότης	n-3c(1)	δεινός	a-1a(2a)
Γερασηνός	a-1a(2a)	γυναικάριον	n-2c	δεινῶς	adverb
Γεργεσηνός	a-1a(2a)	γυναικεῖος	a-1a(1)	δειπνέω	v-1d(2a)
γερουσία	n-1a	γυνή	n-3b(1)	δειπνοκλήτωρ	n-3f(2b)
γέρων	n-3c(5b)	Γώγ	n-3g(2)	δεῖπνον	n-2c
γεύομαι	v-1a(6)	γωνία	n-1a	δεισιδαιμονέστερος	a-1a(1)
γεωργέω	v-1d(2a)			δεισιδαιμονία	n-1a
γεώργιον	n-2c			δεισιδαίμων	a-4b(1)
γεωργός	n-2a	**δέλτα**		δέκα	a-5b
γῆ	n-1h			δεκαδύο	a-5b
γῆρας	n-3d(1)	δ	a-5b	δεκαοκτώ	a-5b
γηράσκω	v-5a	Δαβίδ	n-3g(2)	δεκαπέντε	a-5b
γίνομαι	v-1c(2); v-7	δαιμονίζομαι	v-2a(1)	Δεκάπολις	n-3e(5b)
γινώσκω	v-5a	δαιμόνιον	n-2c	δεκατέσσαρες	a-5b
γλεῦκος	n-3d(2)	δαιμονιώδης	a-4a	δεκατεύω	v-1a(6)
γλυκύς	a-2b	δαίμων	n-3f(1b)	δέκατος	a-1a(2a)
γλῶσσα	n-1c	δάκνω	v-3a(1); v-7	δεκατόω	v-1d(3)
γλωσσόκομον	n-2c	δάκρυ	n-3e(1)	δεκτός	a-1a(2a)
γναφεύς	n-3e(3)	δάκρυον	n-2c	δελεάζω	v-2a(1)
γνήσιος	a-1a(1)	δακρύω	v-1a(4)	δένδρον	n-2c
γνησίως	adverb	δακτύλιος	n-2a	δεξιολάβος	n-2a
γνόφος	n-2a	δάκτυλος	n-2a	δεξιός	a-1a(1)
γνώμη	n-1b	Δαλμανουθά	n-3g(2)	δέομαι	v-1d(2c)
γνωρίζω	v-2a(1)	Δαλματία	n-1a	δέος	n-3d(2)
γνώριμος	a-3a	δαμάζω	v-2a(1)	Δερβαῖος	a-1a(1)
γνῶσις	n-3e(5b)	δάμαλις	n-3e(5b)	Δέρβη	n-1b
γνώστης	n-1f	Δάμαρις	n-3c(2)	δέρμα	n-3c(4)
γνωστός	a-1a(2a)	Δαμασκηνός	a-1a(2a)	δερμάτινος	a-1a(2a)
γογγύζω	v-2a(1)	Δαμασκός	n-2b	δέρρις	n-3e(5b)
γογγυσμός	n-2a	Δάν	n-3g(2)	δέρω	v-1c(1)
γογγυστής	n-1f	δανείζω	v-2a(1)	δεσμεύω	v-1a(6)
γόης	n-3c(1)	δάνειον	n-2c	δεσμέω	v-1d(2a)
Γολγοθᾶ	n-3g(1)	δανειστής	n-1f	δέσμη	n-1b
Γόμορρα	n-1a; n-2c	δανίζω	v-2a(1)	δέσμιος	n-2a
γόμος	n-2a	Δανιήλ	n-3g(2)	δεσμός	n-2a

δεσμοφύλαξ	n-3b(1)	διακελεύω	cv-1a(6)	διασπορά	n-1a
δεσμωτήριον	n-2c	διακονέω	v-1d(2a)	διαστέλλω	cv-2d(1)
δεσμώτης	n-1f	διακονία	n-1a	διάστημα	n-3c(4)
δεσπότης	n-1f	διάκονος	n-2a; n-2b	διαστολή	n-1b
δεῦρο	adverb	διακόσιοι	a-1a(1)	διαστρέφω	cv-1b(1)
δεῦτε	adverb	διακούω	cv-1a(8)	διασῴζω	cv-2a(1)
δευτεραῖος	a-1a(1)	διακρίνω	cv-1c(2)	διαταγή	n-1b
δευτερόπρωτος	a-3a	διάκρισις	n-3e(5b)	διάταγμα	n-3c(4)
δεύτερος	a-1a(1)	διακωλύω	cv-1a(4)	διαταράσσω	cv-2b
δέχομαι	v-1b(2)	διαλαλέω	cv-1d(2a)	διατάσσω	cv-2b
δέω	v-1d(2b)	διαλέγομαι	cv-1b(2)	διατελέω	cv-1d(2b)
δή	particle	διαλείπω	cv-1b(1)	διατηρέω	cv-1d(2a)
δηλαυγῶς	adverb	διάλεκτος	n-2b	διατί	see διά; prep.
δῆλος	a-1a(2a)	διαλιμπάνω	cv-3a(2b)		
δηλόω	v-1d(3)	διαλλάσσομαι	cv-2b	διατίθημι	cv-6a
Δημᾶς	n-1e	διαλογίζομαι	cv-2a(1)	διατρίβω	cv-1b(1)
δημέω	v-1d(2a)	διαλογισμός	n-2a	διατροφή	n-1b
δημηγορέω	v-1d(2a)	διαλύω	cv-1a(4)	διαυγάζω	cv-2a(1)
Δημήτριος	n-2a	διαμαρτύρομαι	cv-1c(1)	διαυγής	a-4a
δημιουργός	n-2a	διαμάχομαι	cv-1b(2)	διαφανής	a-4a
δῆμος	n-2a	διαμένω	cv-1c(2)	διαφέρω	cv-1c(1)
δημόσιος	a-1a(1)	διαμερίζω	cv-2a(1)	διαφεύγω	cv-1b(2)
δηνάριον	n-2c	διαμερισμός	n-2a	διαφημίζω	cv-2a(1)
δήποτε	adverb	διανέμω	cv-1d(2c)	διαφθείρω	cv-2d(3)
δήπου	adverb	διανεύω	cv-1a(6)	διαφθορά	n-1a
διά	prep.	διανόημα	n-3c(4)	διάφορος	a-3a
διαβαίνω	cv-3d	διάνοια	n-1a	διαφορώτερος	a-1a(1)
διαβάλλω	cv-2d(1)	διανοίγω	cv-1b(2)	διαφυλάσσω	cv-2b
διαβεβαιόομαι	cv-1d(3)	διανυκτερεύω	cv-1a(6)	διαχειρίζω	cv-2a(1)
διαβλέπω	cv-1b(1)	διανύω	cv-1a(4)	διαχλευάζω	cv-2a(1)
διάβολος	a-3a	διαπαντός	see διά; prep.	διαχωρίζω	cv-2a(1)
διαγγέλλω	cv-2d(1)			διγαμία	n-1a
διαγίνομαι	cv-1c(2)	διαπαρατριβή	n-1b	δίγαμος	a-3a
διαγινώσκω	cv-5a	διαπεράω	cv-1d(1b)	διδακτικός	a-1a(2a)
διαγνωρίζω	cv-2a(1)	διαπλέω	cv-1a(7)	διδακτός	a-1a(2a)
διάγνωσις	n-3e(5b)	διαπονέομαι	cv-1d(2a)	διδασκαλία	n-1a
διαγογγύζω	cv-2a(1)	διαπορεύομαι	cv-1a(6)	διδάσκαλος	n-2a
διαγρηγορέω	cv-1d(2a)	διαπορέω	cv-1d(2a)	διδάσκω	v-5a
διάγω	cv-1b(2)	διαπραγματεύομαι	cv-1a(6)	διδαχή	n-1b
διαδέχομαι	cv-1b(2)	διαπρίω	cv-1a(1)	δίδραχμον	n-2c
διάδημα	n-3c(4)	διαρθρόω	cv-1d(3)	Δίδυμος	n-2a
διαδίδωμι	cv-6a	διαρπάζω	cv-2a(2)	διδύσκω	v-5a
διάδοχος	n-2a	διαρήγνυμι	see διαρήσσω	διδῶ	v-1b(3)
διαζώννυμι	cv-3c(1)			δίδωμι	v-6a; v-7
διαθήκη	n-1b	διαρήσσω	cv-2b	διεγείρω	cv-2d(3)
διαίρεσις	n-3e(5b)	διασαφέω	cv-1d(2a)	διενθυμέομαι	cv-1d(2a)
διαιρέω	cv-1d(2a)	διασείω	cv-1a(3)	διεξέρχομαι	cv-1b(2)
διακαθαίρω	cv-2d(2)	διασκορπίζω	cv-2a(1)	διέξοδος	n-2b
διακαθαρίζω	cv-2a(1)	διασπάω	cv-1d(1b)	διερμηνεία	n-1a
διακατελέγχομαι	cv-1b(2)	διασπείρω	cv-2d(3)	διερμηνευτής	n-1f

διερμηνεύω	cv-1a(6)	διψάω	v-1d(1a)	δυσεντερία	n-1a
διέρχομαι	cv-1b(2)	δίψος	n-3d(2)	δυσεντέριον	n-2c
διερωτάω	cv-1d(1a)	δίψυχος	a-3a	δυσερμήνευτος	a-3a
διετής	a-4a	διωγμός	n-2a	δύσις	n-3e(5b)
διετία	n-1a	διώκτης	n-1f	δύσκολος	a-3a
διηγέομαι	cv-1d(2a)	διώκω	v-1b(2)	δυσκόλως	adverb
διήγησις	n-3e(5b)	δόγμα	n-3c(4)	δυσμή	n-1b
διηνεκής	a-4a	δογματίζω	v-2a(1)	δυσνόητος	a-3a
διθάλασσος	a-3a	δοκάω	v-1d(1a)	δυσφημέω	v-1d(2a)
διϊκνέομαι	cv-3b	δοκέω	v-1b(4)	δυσφημία	n-1a
διΐστημι	cv-6a	δοκιμάζω	v-2a(1)	δύω	v-1a(4)
διϊστορέω	cv-1d(2a)	δοκιμασία	n-1a	δώδεκα	a-5b
διϊσχυρίζομαι	cv-2a(1)	δοκιμή	n-1b	δωδέκατος	a-1a(2a)
δικάζω	v-2a(1)	δοκίμιον	n-2c	δωδεκάφυλον	n-2c
δικαιοκρισία	n-1a	δόκιμος	a-3a	δῶμα	n-3c(4)
δίκαιος	a-1a(1)	δοκός	n-2b	δωρεά	n-1a
δικαιοσύνη	n-1b	δόλιος	a-1a(1)	δωρεάν	adverb
δικαιόω	v-1d(3)	δολιόω	v-1d(3)	δωρέομαι	v-1d(2a)
δικαίωμα	n-3c(4)	δόλος	n-2a	δώρημα	n-3c(4)
δικαίως	adverb	δολόω	v-1d(3)	δῶρον	n-2c
δικαίωσις	n-3e(5b)	δόμα	n-3c(4)	δωροφορία	n-1a
δικαστής	n-1f	δόξα	n-1c		
δικέω	v-1d(2a)	δοξάζω	v-2a(1)		
δίκη	n-1b	Δορκάς	n-3c(2)	**ἒ ψιλόν**	
δίκτυον	n-2c	δόσις	n-3e(5b)		
δίλογος	a-3a	δότης	n-1f	ἐ	a-5b
διό	conj.	δουλαγωγέω	v-1d(2a)	ἔα	interjection
διοδεύω	cv-1a(6)	δουλεία	n-1a	ἐάν	conj.
Διονύσιος	n-2a	δουλεύω	v-1a(6)	ἐάνπερ	particle
διόπερ	conj.	δούλη	n-1b	ἑαυτοῦ	a-1a(2b)
διοπετής	a-4a	δοῦλος	a-1a(2a)	ἐάω	v-1d(1b)
διόρθωμα	n-3c(4)	δοῦλος	n-2a	ἑβδομήκοντα	a-5b
διόρθωσις	n-3e(5b)	δουλόω	v-1d(3)	ἑβδομηκοντάκις	a-5b
διορύσσω	cv-2b	δοχή	n-1b	ἕβδομος	a-1a(2a)
Διόσκουροι	n-2a	δράκων	n-3c(5b)	Ἔβερ	n-3g(2)
διότι	conj.	δράσσομαι	v-2b	Ἑβραϊκός	a-1a(2a)
Διοτρέφης	n-3d(2)	δραχμή	n-1b	Ἑβραῖος	n-2a
διπλόος	a-1a(2a)	δρέπανον	n-2c	Ἑβραΐς	n-3c(2)
διπλότερος	a-1a(1)	δρόμος	n-2a	Ἑβραϊστί	adverb
διπλοῦς	a-1b	Δρούσιλλα	n-1c	ἐγγίζω	v-2a(1)
διπλόω	v-1d(3)	δύναμαι	v-6b	ἐγγράφω	cv-1b(1)
δίς	adverb	δύναμις	n-3e(5b)	ἔγγυος	a-3a
δισμυριάς	n-3c(2)	δυναμόω	v-1d(3)	ἐγγύς	adverb
διστάζω	v-2a(1)	δυναστεύω	v-1a(6)	ἐγγύτερον	adverb
δίστομος	a-3a	δυνάστης	n-1f	ἐγείρω	v-2d(3); v-7
δισχίλιοι	a-1a(1)	δυνατέω	v-1d(2a)	ἔγερσις	n-3e(5b)
διϋλίζω	cv-2a(1)	δυνατός	a-1a(2a)	ἐγκάθετος	a-3a
διχάζω	v-2a(1)	δύνω	v-3a(1)	ἐγκαίνια	n-2c
διχοστασία	n-1a	δύο	a-5a	ἐγκαινίζω	cv-2a(1)
διχοτομέω	v-1d(2a)	δυσβάστακτος	a-3a	ἐγκακέω	cv-1d(2a)

ἐγκαλέω	cv-1d(2b)
ἐγκαταλείπω	cv-1b(1)
ἐγκατοικέω	cv-1d(2a)
ἐγκαυχάομαι	cv-1d(1a)
ἐγκεντρίζω	cv-2a(1)
ἐγκλείω	cv-1a(3)
ἔγκλημα	n-3c(4)
ἐγκομβόομαι	cv-1d(3)
ἐγκοπή	n-1b
ἐγκόπτω	cv-4
ἐγκράτεια	n-1a
ἐγκρατεύομαι	cv-1a(6)
ἐγκρατής	a-4a
ἐγκρίνω	cv-1c(2)
ἐγκρύπτω	cv-4
ἔγκυος	a-3a
ἐγχρίω	cv-1a(1)
ἐγώ	a-5a
ἐδαφίζω	v-2a(1)
ἔδαφος	n-3d(2)
ἑδραῖος	a-3b(1)
ἑδραίωμα	n-3c(4)
ἐδρεύω	v-1a(6)
Ἐζεκίας	n-1d
ἐθελοθρησκία	n-1a
ἐθίζω	v-2a(1)
ἐθνάρχης	n-1f
ἐθνικός	a-1a(2a)
ἐθνικῶς	adverb
ἔθνος	n-3d(2)
ἔθος	n-3d(2)
ἔθω	v-1b(3)
εἰ	particle
εἰδέα	n-1a
εἶδον	see ὁράω; v-1d(1a)
εἶδος	n-3d(2)
εἰδωλεῖον	n-2c
εἰδωλόθυτος	a-3a
εἰδωλολατρία	n-1a
εἰδωλολάτρης	n-1f
εἴδωλον	n-2c
εἰλέω	v-1d(2a)
εἰκῇ	adverb
εἴκοσι	a-5b
εἴκω	v-1b(2)
εἰκών	n-3f(1b)
εἰλικρίνεια	n-1a
εἰλικρινής	a-4a
εἰμί ("I am")	v-6b

εἶμι ("I will go")	v-6b
εἵνεκεν	prep.
εἴπερ	particle
εἶπον	see λέγω; v-1b(2)
εἴπως	particle
εἰρηνεύω	v-1a(6)
εἰρήνη	n-1b
εἰρηνικός	a-1a(2a)
εἰρηνοποιέω	v-1d(2a)
εἰρηνοποιός	a-3a
εἰς	prep.
εἷς, μία, ἕν	a-2a
εἰσάγω	cv-1b(2)
εἰσακούω	cv-1a(8)
εἰσδέχομαι	cv-1b(2)
εἴσειμι	cv-6b
εἰσέρχομαι	cv-1b(2)
εἰσκαλέομαι	cv-1d(2b)
εἴσοδος	n-2b
εἰσπηδάω	cv-1d(1a)
εἰσπορεύομαι	cv-1a(6)
εἰστρέχω	cv-1b(2)
εἰσφέρω	cv-1c(1)
εἶτα	adverb
εἴτε	particle
εἴωθα	see ἔθω; v-1b(3)
ἐκ	prep.
ἕκαστος	a-1a(2a)
ἑκάστοτε	adverb
ἑκατόν	a-5b
ἑκατονταετής	a-4a
ἑκατονταπλασίων	a-4b(1)
ἑκατοντάρχης	n-1f
ἑκατόνταρχος	n-2a
ἐκβαίνω	cv-3d
ἐκβάλλω	cv-2d(1)
ἔκβασις	n-3e(5b)
ἐκβλαστάνω	cv-3a(1)
ἐκβολή	n-1b
ἐκγαμίζω	cv-2a(1)
ἔκγονος	a-3a
ἐκδαπανάω	cv-1d(1a)
ἐκδέχομαι	cv-1b(2)
ἔκδηλος	a-3a
ἐκδημέω	cv-1d(2a)
ἐκδίδωμι	cv-6a
ἐκδιηγέομαι	cv-1d(2a)
ἐκδικέω	cv-1d(2a)

ἐκδίκησις	n-3e(5b)
ἔκδικος	a-3a
ἐκδιώκω	cv-1b(2)
ἔκδοτος	a-3a
ἐκδοχή	n-1b
ἐκδύω	cv-1a(4)
ἐκεῖ	adverb
ἐκεῖθεν	adverb
ἐκεῖνος	a-1a(2b)
ἐκεῖσε	adverb
ἐκζητέω	cv-1d(2a)
ἐκζήτησις	n-3e(5b)
ἐκθαμβέω	cv-1d(2a)
ἔκθαμβος	a-3a
ἐκθαυμάζω	cv-2a(1)
ἔκθετος	a-3a
ἐκκαθαίρω	cv-2d(2)
ἐκκαίω	cv-2c
ἐκκακέω	cv-1d(2a)
ἐκκεντέω	cv-1d(2a)
ἐκκλάω	cv-1d(1b)
ἐκκλείω	cv-1a(3)
ἐκκλησία	n-1a
ἐκκλίνω	cv-1c(2)
ἐκκολυμβάω	cv-1d(1a)
ἐκκομίζω	cv-2a(1)
ἐκκοπή	n-1b
ἐκκόπτω	cv-4
ἐκκρεμάννυμι	cv-3c(1)
ἐκλαλέω	cv-1d(2a)
ἐκλάμπω	cv-1b(1)
ἐκλανθάνομαι	cv-3a(2b)
ἐκλέγομαι	cv-1b(2)
ἐκλείπω	cv-1b(1)
ἐκλεκτός	a-1a(2a)
ἐκλογή	n-1b
ἐκλύω	cv-1a(4)
ἐκμάσσω	cv-2b
ἐκμυκτηρίζω	cv-2a(1)
ἐκνεύω	cv-1a(6)
ἐκνήφω	cv-1b(1)
ἑκούσιος	a-1a(1)
ἑκουσίως	adverb
ἔκπαλαι	adverb
ἐκπειράζω	cv-2a(1)
ἐκπέμπω	cv-1b(1)
ἐκπερισσῶς	adverb
ἐκπετάννυμι	cv-3c(1)
ἐκπηδάω	cv-1d(1a)
ἐκπίπτω	cv-1b(3)

ἐκπλέω	cv-1a(7)	ἐλαχιστότερος	a-1a(1)	ἐμβριμάομαι	cv-1d(1a)
ἐκπληρόω	cv-1d(3)	ἐλεάω	v-1d(1a)	ἐμέω	v-1d(2b)
ἐκπλήρωσις	n-3e(5b)	Ἐλεάζαρ	n-3g(2)	ἐμμαίνομαι	cv-2d(4)
ἐκπλήσσω	cv-2b	ἐλεγμός	n-2a	Ἐμμανουήλ	n-3g(2)
ἐκπνέω	cv-1a(7)	ἔλεγξις	n-3e(5b)	Ἐμμαοῦς	n-3g(1)
ἐκπορεύομαι	cv-1a(6)	ἔλεγχος	n-2a	ἐμμένω	cv-1c(2)
ἐκπορνεύω	cv-1a(6)	ἐλέγχω	v-1b(2)	ἐμμέσῳ	prep.
ἐκπτύω	cv-1a(4)	ἐλεεινός	a-1a(2a)	Ἐμμώρ	n-3g(2)
ἐκπυρόω	cv-1d(3)	ἐλεεινότερος	a-1a(1)	ἐμός	a-1a(2a)
ἐκριζόω	cv-1d(3)	ἐλεέω	v-1d(2a)	ἐμπαιγμονή	n-1b
ἔκστασις	n-3e(5b)	ἐλεημοσύνη	n-1b	ἐμπαιγμός	n-2a
ἐκστρέφω	cv-1b(1)	ἐλεήμων	a-4b(1)	ἐμπαίζω	cv-2a(2)
ἐκσῴζω	cv-2a(1)	ἔλεος	n-3d(2)	ἐμπαίκτης	n-1f
ἐκταράσσω	cv-2b	ἐλευθερία	n-1a	ἐμπέμπω	cv-1b(1)
ἐκτείνω	cv-2d(5)	ἐλεύθερος	a-1a(1)	ἐμπεριπατέω	cv-1d(2a)
ἐκτελέω	cv-1d(2b)	ἐλευθερόω	v-1d(3)	ἐμπι(μ)πλάω	cv-1d(1a)
ἐκτένεια	n-1a	ἔλευσις	n-3e(5b)	ἐμπίμπλημι	cv-6a
ἐκτενής	a-4a	ἐλεφάντινος	a-1a(2a)	ἐμπίμπρημι	cv-6a
ἐκτενῶς	adverb	Ἐλιακίμ	n-3g(2)	ἐμπίπτω	cv-1b(3)
ἐκτίθημι	cv-6a	ἕλιγμα	n-3c(4)	ἐμπλέκω	cv-1b(2)
ἐκτινάσσω	cv-2b	Ἐλιέζερ	n-3g(2)	ἐμπλοκή	n-1b
ἕκτος	a-1a(2a)	Ἐλιούδ	n-3g(2)	ἐμπνέω	cv-1a(7)
ἐκτός	adverb	Ἐλισάβετ	n-3g(2)	ἐμπορεύομαι	cv-1a(6)
ἐκτρέπω	cv-1b(1)	Ἐλισαῖος	n-2a	ἐμπορία	n-1a
ἐκτρέφω	cv-1b(1)	ἑλίσσω	v-2b	ἐμπόριον	n-2c
ἔκτρομος	a-3a	ἕλκος	n-3d(2)	ἔμπορος	n-2a
ἔκτρωμα	n-3c(4)	ἑλκόω	v-1d(3)	ἐμπρήθω	cv-1b(3)
ἐκφέρω	cv-1c(1)	ἕλκω	v-1a(4)	ἔμπροσθεν	adverb
ἐκφεύγω	cv-1b(2)	Ἑλλάς	n-3c(2)	ἐμπτύω	cv-1a(4)
ἐκφοβέω	cv-1d(2a)	Ἕλλην	n-3f(1a)	ἐμφανής	a-4a
ἔκφοβος	a-3a	Ἑλληνικός	a-1a(2a)	ἐμφανίζω	cv-2a(1)
ἐκφύω	cv-1a(4)	Ἑλληνίς	a-5a	ἔμφοβος	a-3a
ἐκφωνέω	cv-1d(2a)	Ἑλληνιστής	n-1f	ἐμφυσάω	cv-1d(1a)
ἐκχέω	cv-1a(7)	Ἑλληνιστί	adverb	ἔμφυτος	a-3a
ἐκχύννω	cv-3a(1)	ἐλλογάω	cv-1d(1a)	ἐμφωνέω	cv-1d(2a)
ἐκχωρέω	cv-1d(2a)	ἐλλογέω	cv-1d(2a)	ἐν	prep.
ἐκψύχω	cv-1b(2)	Ἐλμαδάμ	n-3g(2)	ἐναγκαλίζομαι	cv-2a(1)
ἑκών	a-2a	Ἐλμωδάμ	n-3g(2)	ἐνάλιος	a-3a
ἐλαία	n-1a	ἐλπίζω	v-2a(1)	ἐνάλλομαι	cv-2d(1)
ἔλαιον	n-2c	ἐλπίς	n-3c(2)	ἐνανθρωπέω	cv-1d(2a)
ἐλαιών	n-3f(1a)	Ἐλύμας	n-1e	ἔναντι	prep.
Ἐλαμίτης	n-1f	ἔλωι	n-3g(2)	ἐναντίον	prep.
ἐλάσσων	a-4b(1)	ἐμαυτοῦ	a-1a(2b)	ἐναντιόομαι	v-1d(3)
ἐλάττων	a-4b(1)	ἐμβαίνω	cv-3d	ἐναντίος	a-1a(1)
ἐλαττονέω	v-1d(2a)	ἐμβάλλω	cv-2d(1)	ἐναργής	a-4a
ἐλαττόω	v-1d(3)	ἐμβαπτίζω	cv-2a(1)	ἐνάρχομαι	cv-1b(2)
ἐλαύνω	v-3c(2); v-7	ἐμβάπτω	cv-4	ἔνατος	a-1a(2a)
ἐλαφρία	n-1a	ἐμβατεύω	cv-1a(6)	ἐναφίημι	cv-6a
ἐλαφρός	a-1a(1)	ἐμβιβάζω	cv-2a(1)	ἐνδεής	a-4a
ἐλάχιστος	a-1a(2a)	ἐμβλέπω	cv-1b(1)	ἔνδειγμα	n-3c(4)

ἐνδείκνυμι	cv-3c(2)	ἐνοικέω	cv-1d(2a)	ἐξαπατάω	cv-1d(1a)
ἔνδειξις	n-3e(5b)	ἐνορκίζω	cv-2a(1)	ἐξάπινα	adverb
ἔνδεκα	a-5b	ἐνότης	n-3c(1)	ἐξαπορέω	cv-1d(2a)
ἐνδέκατος	a-1a(2a)	ἐνοχλέω	cv-1d(2a)	ἐξαποστέλλω	cv-2d(1)
ἐνδέχομαι	cv-1b(2)	ἔνοχος	a-3a	ἐξαρτάω	cv-1d(1a)
ἐνδημέω	cv-1d(2a)	ἔνταλμα	n-3c(4)	ἐξαρτίζω	cv-2a(1)
ἐνδιδύσκω	cv-5a	ἐνταφιάζω	cv-2a(1)	ἐξαστράπτω	cv-4
ἔνδικος	a-3a	ἐνταφιασμός	n-2a	ἐξαυτῆς	adverb
ἐνδόμησις	n-3e(5b)	ἐντέλλω	cv-2d(1)	ἐξεγείρω	cv-2d(3)
ἐνδοξάζομαι	cv-2a(1)	ἐντεῦθεν	adverb	ἔξειμι	cv-6b
ἔνδοξος	a-3a	ἔντευξις	n-3e(5b)	ἐξελέγχω	cv-1b(2)
ἐνδρεύω	cv-1a(6)	ἐντίθημι	cv-6a	ἐξέλκω	cv-1a(4)
ἔνδυμα	n-3c(4)	ἔντιμος	a-3a	ἐξέραμα	n-3c(4)
ἐνδυναμόω	cv-1d(3)	ἐντιμότερος	a-1a(1)	ἐξεραυνάω	cv-1d(1a)
ἐνδύνω	cv-3a(1)	ἐντολή	n-1b	ἐξέρχομαι	cv-1b(2)
ἔνδυσις	n-3e(5b)	ἐντόπιος	a-1a(1)	ἔξεστι	cv-6b
ἐνδύω	cv-1a(4)	ἐντός	prep.	ἐξετάζω	cv-2a(1)
ἐνδώμησις	n-3e(5b)	ἐντρέπω	cv-1b(1)	ἐξέφνης	adverb
ἐνέδρα	n-1a	ἐντρέφω	cv-1b(1)	ἐξέχω	cv-1b(2)
ἐνεδρεύω	cv-1a(6)	ἔντρομος	a-3a	ἐξηγέομαι	cv-1d(2a)
ἔνεδρον	n-2c	ἐντροπή	n-1b	ἐξήκοντα	a-5b
ἐνειλέω	cv-1d(2a)	ἐντρυφάω	cv-1d(1a)	ἐξῆς	adverb
ἔνειμι	cv-6b	ἐντυγχάνω	cv-3a(2b)	ἐξηχέω	cv-1d(2a)
ἕνεκα	prep.	ἐντυλίσσω	cv-2b	ἕξις	n-3e(5b)
ἕνεκεν	prep.	ἐντυπόω	cv-1d(3)	ἐξίστημι	cv-6a
ἐνενήκοντα	a-5b	ἐνυβρίζω	cv-2a(1)	ἐξισχύω	cv-1a(4)
ἐνεός	a-1a(1)	ἐνυπνιάζομαι	v-2a(1)	ἔξοδος	n-2b
ἐνέργεια	n-1a	ἐνύπνιον	n-2c	ἐξολεθρεύω	cv-1a(6)
ἐνεργέω	cv-1d(2a)	ἐνώπιον	prep.	ἐξομολογέω	cv-1d(2a)
ἐνέργημα	n-3c(4)	Ἐνώς	n-3g(2)	ἐξορκίζω	cv-2a(1)
ἐνεργής	a-4a	ἐνωτίζομαι	cv-2a(1)	ἐξορκιστής	n-1f
ἐνευλογέω	cv-1d(2a)	Ἐνώχ	n-3g(2)	ἐξορύσσω	cv-2b
ἐνέχω	cv-1b(2)	ἐξ	see ἐκ;	ἐξουδενέω	cv-1d(2a)
ἐνθάδε	adverb		prep.	ἐξουδενόω	cv-1d(3)
ἔνθεν	adverb	ἔξ	a-5b	ἐξουθενέω	cv-1d(2a)
ἐνθυμέομαι	cv-1d(2a)	ἐξαγγέλλω	cv-2d(1)	ἐξουθενόω	cv-1d(3)
ἐνθύμησις	n-3e(5b)	ἐξαγοράζω	cv-2a(1)	ἐξουσία	n-1a
ἔνι	see ἔνειμι;	ἐξάγω	cv-1b(2)	ἐξουσιάζω	v-2a(1)
	cv-6b	ἐξαιρέω	cv-1d(2a)	ἐξουσιαστικός	a-1a(2a)
ἐνιαυτός	n-2a	ἐξαίρω	cv-2d(2)	ἐξοχή	n-1b
ἐνίοτε	adverb	ἐξαιτέω	cv-1d(2a)	ἐξυπνίζω	cv-2a(1)
ἐνίστημι	cv-6a	ἐξαίφνης	adverb	ἔξυπνος	a-3a
ἐνισχύω	cv-1a(4)	ἐξακολουθέω	cv-1d(2a)	ἔξω	adverb
ἐννέα	a-5b	ἐξακόσιοι	a-1a(1)	ἔξωθεν	adverb
ἐννεός	a-1a(1)	ἐξαλείφω	cv-1b(1)	ἐξωθέω	cv-1b(4)
ἐννεύω	cv-1a(6)	ἐξάλλομαι	cv-2d(1)	ἐξώτερος	a-1a(1)
ἔννοια	n-1a	ἐξανάστασις	n-3e(5b)	ἔοικα	v-1b(2)
ἔννομος	a-3a	ἐξανατέλλω	cv-2d(1)	ἑορτάζω	v-2a(1)
ἐννόμως	adverb	ἐξανίστημι	cv-6a	ἑορτή	n-1b
ἔννυχος	a-3a	ἐξανοίγω	cv-1b(2)	ἐπαγγελία	n-1a

ἐπαγγέλλομαι	cv-2d(1)	ἐπερώτημα	n-3c(4)	ἐπικρίνω	cv-1c(2)
ἐπάγγελμα	n-3c(4)	ἐπέχω	cv-1b(2)	ἐπιλαμβάνομαι	cv-3a(2b)
ἐπάγω	cv-1b(2)	ἐπηρεάζω	v-2a(1)	ἐπιλάμπω	cv-1b(1)
ἐπαγωνίζομαι	cv-2a(1)	ἐπί	prep.	ἐπιλανθάνομαι	cv-3a(2b)
ἐπαθροίζω	cv-2a(1)	ἐπιβαίνω	cv-3d	ἐπιλέγω	cv-1b(2)
Ἐπαίνετος	n-2a	ἐπιβάλλω	cv-2d(1)	ἐπιλείπω	cv-1b(1)
ἐπαινέω	cv-1d(2b)	ἐπιβαρέω	cv-1d(2a)	ἐπιλείχω	cv-1b(2)
ἔπαινος	n-2a	ἐπιβιβάζω	cv-2a(1)	ἐπιλησμονή	n-1b
ἐπαίρω	cv-2d(2)	ἐπιβλέπω	cv-1b(1)	ἐπίλοιπος	a-3a
ἐπαισχύνομαι	cv-1c(2)	ἐπίβλημα	n-3c(4)	ἐπίλυσις	n-3e(5b)
ἐπαιτέω	cv-1d(2a)	ἐπιβοάω	cv-1d(1a)	ἐπιλύω	cv-1a(4)
ἐπακολουθέω	cv-1d(2a)	ἐπιβουλή	n-1b	ἐπιμαρτυρέω	cv-1d(2a)
ἐπακούω	cv-1a(8)	ἐπιγαμβρεύω	cv-1a(6)	ἐπιμέλεια	n-1a
ἐπακροάομαι	cv-1d(1a)	ἐπίγειος	a-3a	ἐπιμελέομαι	cv-1d(2c)
ἐπάν	conj.	ἐπιγίνομαι	cv-1c(2)	ἐπιμελῶς	adverb
ἐπάναγκες	adverb	ἐπιγινώσκω	cv-5a	ἐπιμένω	cv-1c(2)
ἐπανάγω	cv-1b(2)	ἐπίγνωσις	n-3e(5b)	ἐπινεύω	cv-1a(6)
ἐπαναμιμνήσκω	cv-5a	ἐπιγραφή	n-1b	ἐπίνοια	n-1a
ἐπαναπαύομαι	cv-1a(5)	ἐπιγράφω	cv-1b(1)	ἐπιορκέω	cv-1d(2a)
ἐπανέρχομαι	cv-1b(2)	ἐπιδείκνυμι	cv-3c(2)	ἐπίορκος	a-3a
ἐπανίστημι	cv-6a	ἐπιδέχομαι	cv-1b(2)	ἐπιοῦσα	n-1c
ἐπανόρθωσις	n-3e(5b)	ἐπιδημέω	cv-1d(2a)	ἐπιούσιος	a-3a
ἐπάνω	adverb	ἐπιδιατάσσομαι	cv-2b	ἐπιπέτομαι	cv-1b(3)
ἐπάρατος	a-3a	ἐπιδίδωμι	cv-6a	ἐπιπίπτω	cv-1b(3)
ἐπαρκέω	cv-1d(2b)	ἐπιδιορθόω	cv-1d(3)	ἐπιπλήσσω	cv-2b
ἐπαρχεία	n-1a	ἐπιδύω	cv-1a(4)	ἐπιποθέω	cv-1d(2a)
ἐπάρχειος	a-3a	ἐπιείκεια	n-1a	ἐπιπόθησις	n-3e(5b)
ἐπαρχικός	a-1a(2a)	ἐπιεικής	a-4a	ἐπιπόθητος	a-3a
ἔπαυλις	n-3e(5b)	ἐπιεικία	see	ἐπιποθία	n-1a
ἐπαύριον	adverb		ἐπιείκεια;	ἐπιπορεύομαι	cv-1a(6)
ἐπαυτόφωρος	a-3a		n-1a	ἐπιράπτω	cv-4
Ἐπαφρᾶς	n-1e	ἐπιζητέω	cv-1d(2a)	ἐπιρίπτω	cv-4
ἐπαφρίζω	cv-2a(1)	ἐπιθανάτιος	a-3a	ἐπιρράπτω	see
Ἐπαφρόδιτος	n-2a	ἐπίθεσις	n-3e(5b)		ἐπιράπτω;
ἐπεγείρω	cv-2d(3)	ἐπιθυμέω	cv-1d(2a)		cv-4
ἐπεί	conj.	ἐπιθυμητής	n-1f	ἐπιρρίπτω	see
ἐπειδή	conj.	ἐπιθυμία	n-1a		ἐπιρίπτω;
ἐπειδήπερ	conj.	ἐπιθύω	cv-1a(4)		cv-4
ἐπεῖδον	see ἐποράω;	ἐπικαθίζω	cv-2a(1)	ἐπισείω	cv-1a(3)
	cv-1d(1a)	ἐπικαλέω	cv-1d(2b)	ἐπίσημος	a-3a
ἔπειμι	cv-6b	ἐπικάλυμμα	n-3c(4)	ἐπισιτισμός	n-2a
ἐπεισαγωγή	n-1b	ἐπικαλύπτω	cv-4	ἐπισκέπτομαι	cv-4
ἐπεισέρχομαι	cv-1b(2)	ἐπικατάρατος	a-3a	ἐπισκευάζομαι	cv-2a(1)
ἔπειτα	adverb	ἐπίκειμαι	cv-6b	ἐπισκηνόω	cv-1d(3)
ἐπέκεινα	adverb	ἐπικέλλω	cv-2d(1)	ἐπισκιάζω	cv-2a(1)
ἐπεκτείνομαι	cv-2d(5)	ἐπικερδαίνω	cv-3d	ἐπισκοπέω	cv-1d(2a)
ἐπενδύομαι	cv-1a(4)	ἐπικεφάλαιον	n-2c	ἐπισκοπή	n-1b
ἐπενδύτης	n-1f	Ἐπικούρειος	n-2a	ἐπίσκοπος	n-2a
ἐπέρχομαι	cv-1b(2)	ἐπικουρία	n-1a	ἐπισπάομαι	cv-1d(1b)
ἐπερωτάω	cv-1d(1a)	ἐπικράζω	cv-2a(2)	ἐπισπείρω	cv-2d(3)
				ἐπίσταμαι	cv-6b

ἐπίστασις	n-3e(5b)	ἔπος	n-3d(2)	ἔσω	adverb
ἐπιστάτης	n-1f	ἐπουράνιος	a-3a	ἔσωθεν	adverb
ἐπιστέλλω	cv-2d(1)	ἑπτά	a-5b	ἐσώτερος	a-1a(1)
ἐπιστήμη	n-1b	ἑπτάκις	adverb	ἐτάζω	v-2a(1)
ἐπιστήμων	a-4b(1)	ἑπτακισχίλιοι	a-1a(1)	ἑταῖρος	n-2a
ἐπιστηρίζω	cv-2a(2)	ἑπταπλασίων	a-4b(1)	ἑτερόγλωσσος	a-3a
ἐπιστολή	n-1b	Ἔραστος	n-2a	ἑτεροδιδασκαλέω	v-1d(2b)
ἐπιστομίζω	cv-2a(1)	ἐραυνάω	v-1d(1a)	ἑτεροζυγέω	v-1d(2a)
ἐπιστρέφω	cv-1b(1)	ἐργάζομαι	v-2a(1)	ἕτερος	a-1a(1)
ἐπιστροφή	n-1b	ἐργασία	n-1a	ἑτέρως	adverb
ἐπισυνάγω	cv-1b(2)	ἐργάτης	n-1f	ἔτι	adverb
ἐπισυναγωγή	n-1b	ἐργέω	v-1d(2a)	ἑτοιμάζω	v-2a(1)
ἐπισυντρέχω	cv-1b(2)	ἔργον	n-2c	ἑτοιμασία	n-1a
ἐπισυρράπτω	cv-4	ἐρεθίζω	v-2a(1)	ἕτοιμος	a-3b(2)
ἐπισύστασις	n-3e(5b)	ἐρείδω	v-1b(3)	ἑτοίμως	adverb
ἐπισφαλής	a-4a	ἐρεύγομαι	v-1b(2)	ἔτος	n-3d(2)
ἐπισχύω	cv-1a(4)	ἐρευνάω	see	εὖ	adverb
ἐπισχωρεύω	cv-1a(6)		ἐραυνάω;	Εὕα	n-1a
ἐπιταγή	n-1b		v-1d(1a)	εὐαγγελίζω	v-2a(1)
ἐπιτάσσω	cv-2b	ἐρημία	n-1a	εὐαγγέλιον	n-2c
ἐπιτελέω	cv-1d(2b)	ἔρημος	a-3a	εὐαγγελιστής	n-1f
ἐπιτήδειος	a-1a(1)	ἐρημόω	v-1d(3)	εὐαρεστέω	v-1d(2a)
ἐπιτίθημι	cv-6a	ἐρήμωσις	n-3e(5b)	εὐάρεστος	a-3a
ἐπιτιμάω	cv-1d(1a)	ἐρίζω	v-2a(1)	εὐαρέστως	adverb
ἐπιτιμία	n-1a	ἐριθεία	n-1a	Εὔβουλος	n-2a
ἐπιτρέπω	cv-1b(1)	ἔριον	n-2c	εὖγε	adverb
ἐπιτροπεύω	cv-1a(6)	ἔρις	n-3c(2)	εὐγενέστερος	a-1a(1)
ἐπιτροπή	n-1b	ἐρίφιον	n-2c	εὐγενής	a-4a
ἐπίτροπος	n-2a	ἔριφος	n-2a	εὐγλωττία	n-1a
ἐπιτυγχάνω	cv-3a(2b)	Ἑρμᾶς	n-1e	εὐδία	n-1a
ἐπιφαίνω	cv-2d(4)	ἑρμηνεία	n-1a	εὐδοκέω	v-1d(2a)
ἐπιφάνεια	n-1a	ἑρμηνευτής	n-1f	εὐδοκία	n-1a
ἐπιφανής	a-4a	ἑρμηνεύω	v-1a(6)	εὕδω	v-1b(3)
ἐπιφαύσκω	cv-5a	Ἑρμῆς	n-1h	εὐεργεσία	n-1a
ἐπιφέρω	cv-1c(1)	Ἑρμογένης	n-3d(2)	εὐεργετέω	v-1d(2a)
ἐπιφωνέω	cv-1d(2a)	ἑρπετόν	n-2c	εὐεργέτης	n-1f
ἐπιφώσκω	cv-5a	ἐρυθρός	a-1a(1)	εὔθετος	a-3a
ἐπιχειρέω	cv-1d(2a)	ἔρχομαι	v-1b(2);	εὐθέως	adverb
ἐπιχείρησις	n-3e(5b)		v-7; v-8	εὐθυδρομέω	v-1d(2a)
ἐπιχέω	cv-1a(7)	ἐρωτάω	v-1d(1a)	εὐθυμέω	v-1d(2a)
ἐπιχορηγέω	cv-1d(2a)	ἐσθής	n-3c(1)	εὔθυμος	a-3a
ἐπιχορηγία	n-1a	ἐσθίω	v-1b(3); v-8	εὐθύμως	adverb
ἐπιχρίω	cv-1a(1)	ἔσθω	see ἐσθίω	εὐθύνω	v-1c(2)
ἐπιψαύω	cv-1a(5)	Ἑσλί	n-3g(2)	εὐθύς	a-2b
ἐποικοδομέω	cv-1d(2a)	ἔσοπτρον	n-2c	εὐθύς	adverb
ἐποκέλλω	cv-2d(1)	ἑσπέρα	n-1a	εὐθύτης	n-3c(1)
ἕπομαι	v-1d(3)	ἑσπερινός	a-1a(2a)	εὐκαιρέω	v-1d(2a)
ἐπονομάζω	cv-2a(1)	Ἑσρώμ	n-3g(2)	εὐκαιρία	n-1a
ἐποπτεύω	cv-1a(6)	ἑσσόομαι	v-1d(3)	εὔκαιρος	a-3a
ἐπόπτης	n-1f	ἔσχατος	a-1a(2a)	εὐκαίρως	adverb
		ἐσχάτως	adverb		

εὔκοπος	a-3a	εὐφροσύνη	n-1b	ζέω	v-1d(2a)
εὐκοπώτερος	a-1a(1)	εὐχαριστέω	v-1d(2a)	ζηλεύω	v-1a(6)
εὐλάβεια	n-1a	εὐχαριστία	n-1a	ζῆλος, ου	n-2a
εὐλαβέομαι	v-1d(2a)	εὐχάριστος	a-3a	ζῆλος, ους	n-3d(2)
εὐλαβής	a-4a	εὐχή	n-1b	ζηλόω	v-1d(3)
εὐλογέω	v-1d(2a)	εὔχομαι	v-1b(2)	ζηλωτής	n-1f
εὐλογητός	a-1a(2a)	εὔχρηστος	a-3a	ζημία	n-1a
εὐλογία	n-1a	εὐψυχέω	v-1d(2a)	ζημιόω	v-1d(3)
εὐμετάδοτος	a-3a	εὐωδία	n-1a	Ζηνᾶς	n-3g(1)
Εὐνίκη	n-1b	εὐώνυμος	a-3a	ζήνων	n-3f(1a)
εὐνοέω	v-1d(2a)	εὐωχέομαι	v-1d(2a)	ζητέω	v-1d(2a)
εὔνοια	n-1a	εὐωχία	n-1a	ζήτημα	n-3c(4)
εὐνουχίζω	v-2a(1)	ἐφάλλομαι	cv-2d(1)	ζήτησις	n-3e(5b)
εὐνοῦχος	n-2a	ἐφάπαξ	adverb	ζιζάνιον	n-2c
Εὐοδία	n-1a	Ἐφεσῖνος	a-1a(1)	Ζοροβαβέλ	n-3g(2)
εὐοδόω	v-1d(3)	Ἐφέσιος	a-1a(1)	ζόφος	n-2a
εὐοχία	n-1a	Ἔφεσος	n-2b	ζυγός	n-2a
εὐπάρεδρος	a-3a	ἐφευρετής	n-1f	ζυγόν	n-2c
εὐπειθής	a-4a	ἐφημερία	n-1a	ζύμη	n-1b
εὐπερίσπαστος	a-3a	ἐφήμερος	a-3a	ζυμόω	v-1d(3)
εὐπερίστατος	a-3a	ἐφικνέομαι	cv-3b	ζωγρέω	v-1d(2a)
εὐποιΐα	n-1a	ἐφίστημι	cv-6a	ζωή	n-1b
εὐπορέω	v-1d(2a)	ἐφοράω	cv-1d(1a)	ζώνη	n-1b
εὐπορία	n-1a	Ἐφραΐμ	n-3g(2)	ζώννυμι	v-3c(1)
εὐπρέπεια	n-1a	ἐφφαθά	n-3g(2)	ζωννύω	see
εὐπρόσδεκτος	a-3a	ἐχθές	adverb		ζώννυμι
εὐπρόσεδρος	a-3a	ἔχθρα	n-1a	ζωογονέω	v-1d(2a)
εὐπροσωπέω	v-1d(2a)	ἐχθρός	a-1a(1)	ζῷον	n-2c
εὐρακύλων	n-3f(1a)	ἔχιδνα	n-1c	ζωοποιέω	v-1d(2a)
εὑρίσκω	v-5b	ἔχω	v-1b(2); v-7	ζωπυρέω	v-1d(2a)
εὐροκλύδων	n-3f(1a)	ἐωρίζω	v-2a(1)		
εὐρύχωρος	a-3a	ἕως	conj; prep.		
εὐσέβεια	n-1a				
εὐσεβέω	v-1d(2a)			## ἦτα	
εὐσεβής	a-4a				
εὐσεβῶς	adverb			ἤ	particle
εὔσημος	a-3a	## ζῆτα		ἤ	adverb
εὔσπλαγχνος	a-3a			ἡγεμονεύω	v-1a(6)
εὐσχημονέω	v-1d(2a)	ζ	a-5b	ἡγεμονία	n-1a
εὐσχημόνως	adverb	Ζαβουλών	n-3g(2)	ἡγεμών	n-3f(1b)
εὐσχημοσύνη	n-1b	Ζακχαῖος	n-2a	ἡγέομαι	v-1d(2a)
εὐσχήμων	a-4b(1)	Ζάρα	n-3g(2)	ἡδέως	adverb
εὐτόνως	adverb	ζαφθάνι	n-3g(2)	ἤδη	adverb
εὐτραπελία	n-1a	Ζαχαρίας	n-1d	ἤδιστα	adverb
Εὔτυχος	n-2a	ζάω	v-1d(1a)	ἥδομαι	v-1b(3)
εὐφημία	n-1a	ζβέννυμι	v-3c(1)	ἡδονή	n-1b
εὔφημος	a-3a	Ζεβεδαῖος	n-2a	ἡδύοσμον	n-2c
εὐφορέω	v-1d(2a)	ζεστός	a-1a(2a)	ἦθος	n-3d(2)
εὐφραίνω	v-2d(4)	ζεύγνυμι	v-3c(1)	ἥκω	v-1b(2)
Εὐφράτης	n-1f	ζεῦγος	n-3d(2)	ηλι ("My God")	n-3g(2)
		ζευκτηρία	n-1a	Ἠλί ("Heli")	n-3g(2)
		Ζεύς	n-3g(1)	Ἠλίας	n-1d

ἡλικία	n-1a	θανατηφόρος	a-3a	Θεσσαλονικεύς	n-3e(3)
ἡλίκος	a-1a(2a)	θάνατος	n-2a	Θεσσαλονίκη	n-1b
ἥλιος	n-2a	θανατόω	v-1d(3)	Θευδᾶς	n-1e
ἧλος	n-2a	θάπτω	v-4	θεωρέω	v-1d(2a)
ἡλόω	v-1d(3)	Θάρα	n-3g(2)	θεωρία	n-1a
ἡμεῖς	a-5a	θαρρέω	v-1d(2a)	θήκη	n-1b
ἡμέρα	n-1a	θαρσέω	v-1d(2a)	θηλάζω	v-2a(1)
ἡμέτερος	a-1a(1)	θάρσος	n-3d(2)	θῆλυς	a-2b
ἡμιθανής	a-4a	θαῦμα	n-3c(4)	θήρα	n-1a
ἥμισυς	a-2b	θαυμάζω	v-2a(1)	θηρεύω	v-1a(6)
ἡμιώριον	n-2c	θαυμάσιος	a-1a(1)	θηριομαχέω	v-1d(2a)
ἡμίωρον	n-2c	θαυμαστός	a-1a(2a)	θηρίον	n-2c
ἡνίκα	particle	θεά	n-1a	θησαυρίζω	v-2a(1)
ἤπερ	particle	θεάομαι	v-1d(1b)	θησαυρός	n-2a
ἤπιος	a-1a(1)	θεατρίζω	v-2a(1)	θιγγάνω	v-3a(2b)
Ἥρ	n-3g(2)	θέατρον	n-2c	θλάω	v-1d(1b)
ἤρεμος	a-3a	θεῖον	n-2c	θλίβω	v-1b(1)
Ἡρῴδης	n-1f	θεῖος	a-1a(1)	θλῖψις	n-3e(5b)
Ἡρῳδιανοί	n-2a	θειότης	n-3c(1)	θνήσκω	v-5a; v-7
Ἡρῳδιάς	n-3c(2)	θειώδης	a-4a	θνητός	a-1a(2a)
Ἡρῳδίων	n-3f(1a)	Θέκλα	n-1c	θορυβάζω	v-2a(1)
Ἡσαΐας	n-1d	θέλημα	n-3c(4)	θορυβέω	v-1d(2a)
Ἡσαῦ	n-3g(2)	θέλησις	n-3e(5b)	θόρυβος	n-2a
ἥσσων	a-4b(1)	θέλω	v-1d(2c)	θραυματρίζω	v-2a(1)
ἡσυχάζω	v-2a(1)	θεματίζω	v-2a(1)	θραύω	v-1a(5)
ἡσυχία	n-1a	θεμέλιον	n-2c	θρέμμα	n-3c(4)
ἡσύχιος	a-3a	θεμέλιος	n-2a	θρηνέω	v-1d(2a)
ἤτοι	particle	θεμελιόω	v-1d(3)	θρῆνος	n-2a
ἡττάομαι	v-1d(1a)	θεοδίδακτος	a-3a	θρησκεία	n-1a
ἥττημα	n-3c(4)	θεολόγος	n-2a	θρησκός	a-3a
ἥττων	a-4b(1)	θεομαχέω	v-1d(2a)	θριαμβεύω	v-1a(6)
ἠχέω	v-1d(2a)	θεομάχος	a-3a	θρίξ	n-3b(3)
ἦχος, ἤχου, ὁ	n-2a	θεόπνευστος	a-3a	θροέω	v-1d(2a)
ἦχος, ἤχους, τό	n-3d(2)	θεός	n-2a; n-2b	θρόμβος	n-2a
		θεοσέβεια	n-1a	θρόνος	n-2a
		θεοσεβής	a-4a	θρύπτω	v-4

θῆτα

		θεοστυγής	a-4a	Θυάτειρα	n-3g(1)
θᾶ	see μαράνα θᾶ; n-3g(2)	θεότης	n-3c(1)	Θυάτιρα	n-3g(1)
		Θεόφιλος	n-2a	θυγάτηρ	n-3f(2c)
		θεραπεία	n-1a	θυγάτριον	n-2c
θάβιτα	n-3g(2)	θεραπεύω	v-1a(6)	θύελλα	n-1c
Θαδδαῖος	n-2a	θεράπων	n-3c(5b)	θύϊνος	a-1a(2a)
θάλασσα	n-1c	θερίζω	v-2a(1)	θυμέω	v-1d(2a)
θάλλω	v-2d(1)	θερισμός	n-2a	θυμίαμα	n-3c(4)
θάλπω	v-4	θεριστής	n-1f	θυμιατήριον	n-2c
Θαμάρ	n-3g(2)	θέρμα	n-1c	θυμιάω	v-1d(1b)
θαμβέω	v-1d(2a)	θερμαίνω	v-2d(4)	θυμομαχέω	v-1d(2a)
θάμβος, ου, ὁ	n-2a	θέρμη	n-1b	θυμός	n-2a
θάμβος, ους, τό	n-3d(2)	θέρος	n-3d(2)	θυμόω	v-1d(3)
θανάσιμος	a-3a	Θεσσαλία	n-1a	θύρα	n-1a

θυρεός	n-2a	ἱερόσυλος	n-2a	Ἰσαχάρ	n-3g(2)
θυρίς	n-3c(2)	ἱερουργέω	v-1d(2a)	Ἰσκαριώθ	n-3g(2)
θυρωρός	n-2a; n-2b	Ἰερουσαλήμ	n-3g(2)	Ἰσκαριώτης	n-1f
θυσία	n-1a	ἱερωσύνη	n-1b	ἴσος	a-1a(2a)
θυσιαστήριον	n-2c	Ἰεσσαί	n-3g(2)	ἰσότης	n-3c(1)
θύω	v-1a(4)	Ἰεφθάε	n-3g(2)	ἰσότιμος	a-3a
Θωμᾶς	n-1e	Ἰεχονίας	n-1d	ἰσόψυχος	a-3a
θώραξ	n-3b(1)	ἵημι	v-6a; v-7	Ἰσραήλ	n-3g(2)
		Ἰησοῦς	n-3g(1)	Ἰσραηλίτης	n-1f
ἰῶτα		ἱκανός	a-1a(2a)	Ἰσσαχάρ	n-3g(2)
		ἱκανότης	n-3c(1)	ἱστάνω	v-3a(1)
		ἱκανόω	v-1d(3)	ἱστάω	v-1d(1a)
Ἰάϊρος	n-2a	ἱκετηρία	n-1a	ἵστημι	v-6a; v-7
Ἰακώβ	n-3g(2)	ἰκμάς	n-3c(2)	ἱστίον	n-2c
Ἰάκωβος	n-2a	ἱκνέομαι	v-3b	ἱστορέω	v-1d(2a)
ἴαμα	n-3c(4)	Ἰκόνιον	n-2c	ἰσχυρίζομαι	v-2a(1)
Ἰαμβρῆς	n-1f	ἱλαρός	a-1a(1)	ἰσχυρός	a-1a(1)
Ἰανναί	n-3g(2)	ἱλαρότης	n-3c(1)	ἰσχυρότερος	a-1a(1)
Ἰάννης	n-1f	ἱλάσκομαι	v-5a	ἰσχύς	n-3e(1)
ἰάομαι	v-1d(1b)	ἱλασμός	n-2a	ἰσχύω	v-1a(4)
Ἰάρετ	n-3g(2)	ἱλαστήριον	n-2c	ἴσως	adverb
ἴασις	n-3e(5b)	ἵλεως	a-5a	Ἰταλία	n-1a
ἴασπις	n-3c(2)	Ἰλλυρικόν	n-2c	Ἰταλικός	a-1a(2a)
Ἰάσων	n-3f(1b)	ἱμάς	n-3c(5a)	Ἰτουραῖος	a-1a(1)
ἰατρός	n-2a	ἱματίζω	v-2a(1)	ἰχθύδιον	n-2c
Ἰαχίν	n-3g(2)	ἱμάτιον	n-2c	ἰχθύς	n-3e(1)
ιβ	a-5b	ἱματισμός	n-2a	ἴχνος	n-3d(2)
ἴδε	see ὁράω; v-1d(1a)	ἱμείρομαι	v-1c(1)	Ἰωαθάμ	n-3g(2)
		ἵνα	conj.	Ἰωανάν ("Joanan")	n-3g(2)
ἰδέα	n-1a	ἱνατί	conj.	Ἰωάνα ("John")	n-1a
ἴδιος	a-1a(1)	Ἰόππη	n-1b	Ἰωάννα ("Joanna")	n-1a
ἰδιώτης	n-1f	Ἰορδάνης	n-1f	Ἰωάννης ("John")	n-1f
ἰδού	see ὁράω; v-1d(1a)	ἰός	n-2a	Ἰωάς	n-3g(2)
Ἰδουμαία	n-1a	Ἰουδαία	n-1a	Ἰώβ	n-3g(2)
ἱδρώς	n-3c(1)	ἰουδαΐζω	v-2a(1)	Ἰωβήδ	n-3g(2)
Ἰεζάβελ	n-3g(2)	Ἰουδαϊκός	a-1a(2a)	Ἰωδά	n-3g(2)
Ἰεράπολις	n-3e(5b)	Ἰουδαϊκῶς	adverb	Ἰωήλ	n-3g(2)
ἱερατεία	n-1a	Ἰουδαῖος	a-1a(1)	Ἰωνάθας	n-1d
ἱεράτευμα	n-3c(4)	Ἰουδαϊσμός	n-2a	Ἰωνάμ	n-3g(2)
ἱερατεύω	v-1a(6)	Ἰούδας	n-1e	Ἰωνᾶς	n-1e
Ἰερεμίας	n-1d	Ἰουλία	n-1a	Ἰωράμ	n-3g(2)
ἱερεύς	n-3e(3)	Ἰούλιος	n-2a	Ἰωρίμ	n-3g(2)
Ἰεριχώ	n-3g(2)	Ἰουνιᾶς	n-1e	Ἰωσαφάτ	n-3g(2)
ἱερόθυτος	a-3a	Ἰοῦστος	n-2a	Ἰωσῆς	n-3c(1); n-1g
ἱερόν	n-2c	ἱππεύς	n-3e(3)		
ἱεροπρεπής	a-4a	ἱππικός	a-1a(2a)	Ἰωσήφ	n-3g(2)
ἱερός	a-1a(1)	ἵππος	n-2a	Ἰωσήχ	n-3g(2)
Ἱεροσόλυμα	n-1a; n-2c	ἶρις	n-3c(2)	Ἰωσίας	n-1d
Ἱεροσολυμίτης	n-1f	Ἰσαάκ	n-3g(2)	ἰῶτα	n-3g(2)
ἱεροσυλέω	v-1d(2a)	ἰσάγγελος	a-3a		

κάππα

κάβος	n-2a
κἀγώ	crasis
κάδος	n-2a
καθά	conj.
καθαίρεσις	n-3e(5b)
καθαιρέω	cv-1d(2a)
καθαίρω	v-2d(2)
καθάπερ	conj.
καθάπτω	cv-4
καθαρίζω	v-2a(1)
καθαρισμός	n-2a
κάθαρμα	n-3c(4)
καθαρός	a-1a(1)
καθαρότης	n-3c(1)
καθέδρα	n-1a
καθέζομαι	v-2a(1)
καθεῖς	see κατά; prep.
καθεξῆς	adverb
καθερίζω	see καθαρίζω; v-2a(1)
καθεύδω	cv-1b(3)
καθηγητής	n-1f
καθήκω	cv-1b(2)
κάθημαι	v-6b
καθημέραν	see ἡμέρα; n-1a
καθημερινός	a-1a(2a)
καθίζω	v-2a(1)
καθίημι	cv-6a
καθιστάνω	cv-3a(1)
καθίστημι	cv-6a
καθό	adverb
καθολικός	a-1a(2a)
καθόλου	adverb
καθοπλίζω	cv-2a(1)
καθοράω	cv-1d(1a)
καθότι	conj.
καθώς	adverb
καθώσπερ	adverb
καί	conj.
Καϊάφας	n-1e
καίγε	see γέ; particle
Κάϊν	n-3g(2)
Καϊνάμ	n-3g(2)
Καϊνάν	n-3g(2)
καινίζω	v-2a(1)

καινός	a-1a(2a)
καινότερος	a-1a(1)
καινότης	n-3c(1)
καινοφωνία	see κενοφωνία; n-1a
καινόω	v-1d(3)
καίπερ	conj.
καιρός	n-2a
Καῖσαρ	n-3f(2a)
Καισάρεια	n-1a
καίτοι	particle
καίτοιγε	particle
καίω	v-2c; v-7
κἀκεῖ	crasis
κἀκεῖθεν	crasis
κἀκεῖνος	crasis
κακέω	v-1d(2a)
κακία	n-1a
κακοήθεια	n-1a
κακολογέω	v-1d(2a)
κακοπάθεια	n-1a
κακοπαθέω	v-1d(2a)
κακοπαθία	n-1a
κακοποιέω	v-1d(2a)
κακοποιός	a-3a
κακός	a-1a(2a)
κακοῦργος	a-3a
κακουχέω	v-1d(2a)
κακόω	v-1d(3)
κακῶς	adverb
κάκωσις	n-3e(5b)
καλάμη	n-1b
κάλαμος	n-2a
καλέω	v-1d(2b); v-7
καλλιέλαιος	n-2b
κάλλιον	adverb
καλοδιδάσκαλος	a-3a
Καλοί Λιμένες	see καλός (a-1a[2a]) and λιμήν (n-3f[1b])
καλοκαγαθία	n-1a
καλοποιέω	v-1d(2a)
καλός	a-1a(2a)
κάλυμμα	n-3c(4)
καλύπτω	v-4
καλῶς	adverb
κάμηλος	n-2a; 2b
κάμιλος	n-2a

κάμινος	n-2b
καμμύω	v-1a(4)
κάμνω	v-3a(1); v-7
κἀμέ	crasis
κἀμοί	crasis
κάμπτω	v-4
κἄν	crasis
Κανά	n-3g(2)
Κανααῖος	n-2a
Κανανίτης	n-1f
Κανδάκη	n-1b
κανών	n-3f(1b)
Καπερναούμ	n-3g(2)
καπηλεύω	v-1a(6)
καπνός	n-2a
Καππαδοκία	n-1a
καραδοκία	n-1a
καρδία	n-1a
καρδιογνώστης	n-1f
Κάρπος ("Karpus")	n-2a
καρπός ("fruit")	n-2a
καρποφορέω	v-1d(2a)
καρποφόρος	a-3a
καρτερέω	v-1d(2a)
κάρφος	n-3d(2)
κατά	prep.
καταβαίνω	cv-3d
καταβάλλω	cv-2d(1)
καταβαρέω	cv-1d(2a)
καταβαρύνω	cv-1c(2)
κατάβασις	n-3e(5b)
καταβιβάζω	cv-2a(1)
καταβοάω	cv-1d(1a)
καταβολή	n-1b
καταβραβεύω	cv-1a(6)
καταγγελεύς	n-3e(3)
καταγγέλλω	cv-2d(1)
καταγελάω	cv-1d(1b)
καταγινώσκω	cv-5a
κατάγνυμι	cv-3c(2)
καταγράφω	cv-1b(1)
κατάγω	cv-1b(2)
καταγωνίζομαι	cv-2a(1)
καταδέω	cv-1d(2b)
κατάδηλος	a-3a
καταδικάζω	cv-2a(1)
καταδίκη	n-1b
καταδιώκω	cv-1b(2)
καταδουλόω	cv-1d(3)
καταδυναστεύω	cv-1a(6)

κατάθεμα	n-3c(4)	κατάπαυσις	n-3e(5b)	καταχέω	cv-1a(7)
καταθεματίζω	cv-2a(1)	καταπαύω	cv-1a(5)	καταχθόνιος	a-3a
καταισχύνω	cv-1c(2)	καταπέτασμα	n-3c(4)	καταχράομαι	cv-1d(1a)
κατακαίω	cv-2c	καταπίμπρημι	cv-6a	καταψηφίζομαι	cv-2a(1)
κατακαλύπτω	cv-4	καταπίνω	cv-3a(1)	καταψύχω	cv-1b(2)
κατακαυχάομαι	cv-1d(1a)	καταπίπτω	cv-1b(3)	κατείδωλος	a-3a
κατάκειμαι	cv-6b	καταπλέω	cv-1a(7)	κατέναντι	adverb
κατακλάω	cv-1d(1b)	καταπονέω	cv-1d(2a)	κατενώπιον	adverb
κατακλείω	cv-1a(3)	καταποντίζω	cv-2a(1)	κατεξουσιάζω	cv-2a(1)
κατακληροδοτέω	cv-1d(2a)	κατάρα	n-1a	κατεργάζομαι	cv-2a(1)
κατακληρονομέω	cv-1d(2a)	καταράομαι	cv-1d(1b)	κατέρχομαι	cv-1b(2)
κατακλίνω	cv-1c(2)	καταργέω	cv-1d(2a)	κατέσθω	see
κατακλύζω	cv-2a(1)	καταριθμέω	cv-1d(2a)		κατεσθίω
κατακλυσμός	n-2a	καταρτίζω	cv-2a(1)	κατεσθίω	cv-1b(3)
κατακολουθέω	cv-1d(2a)	κατάρτισις	n-3e(5b)	κατευθύνω	cv-1c(2)
κατακόπτω	cv-4	καταρτισμός	n-2a	κατευλογέω	cv-1d(2a)
κατακρημνίζω	cv-2a(1)	κατασείω	cv-1a(3)	κατεφίσταμαι	cv-6a
κατάκριμα	n-3c(4)	κατασκάπτω	cv-4	κατέχω	cv-1b(2)
κατακρίνω	cv-1c(2)	κατασκευάζω	cv-2a(1)	κατηγορέω	v-1d(2a)
κατάκρισις	n-3e(5b)	κατασκηνόω	cv-1d(3)	κατηγορία	n-1a
κατακύπτω	cv-4	κατασκήνωσις	n-3e(5b)	κατήγορος	n-2a
κατακυριεύω	cv-1a(6)	κατασκιάζω	cv-2a(1)	κατήγωρ	n-3f(2b)
καταλαλέω	cv-1d(2a)	κατασκοπέω	cv-1d(2a)	κατήφεια	n-1a
καταλαλιά	n-1a	κατάσκοπος	n-2a	κατηχέω	cv-1d(2a)
κατάλαλος	a-3a	κατασοφίζομαι	cv-2a(1)	κατιόω	v-1d(3)
καταλαμβάνω	cv-3a(2b)	καταστέλλω	cv-2d(1)	κατισχύω	cv-1a(4)
καταλέγω	cv-1b(2)	κατάστημα	n-3c(4)	κατοικέω	cv-1d(2a)
κατάλειμμα	n-3c(4)	καταστολή	n-1b	κατοίκησις	n-3e(5b)
καταλείπω	cv-1b(1)	καταστρέφω	cv-1b(1)	κατοικητήριον	n-2c
καταλιθάζω	cv-2a(1)	καταστρηνιάω	cv-1d(1b)	κατοικία	n-1a
καταλλαγή	n-1b	καταστροφή	n-1b	κατοικίζω	cv-2a(1)
καταλλάσσω	cv-2b	καταστρώννυμι	cv-3c(1)	κατοπτρίζω	cv-2a(1)
κατάλοιπος	a-3a	κατασύρω	cv-1c(1)	κατόρθωμα	n-3c(4)
κατάλυμα	n-3c(4)	κατασφάζω	cv-2a(2)	κάτω	adverb
καταλύω	cv-1a(4)	κατασφάττω	cv-2a(2);	κατώτερος	a-1a(1)
καταμανθάνω	cv-3a(2b)		see σφάζω	κατωτέρω	adverb
καταμαρτυρέω	cv-1d(2a)	κατασφραγίζω	cv-2a(1)	Καῦδα	n-3g(2)
καταμένω	cv-1c(2)	κατάσχεσις	n-3e(5b)	καῦμα	n-3c(4)
καταμόνας	a-1a(2a)	κατατίθημι	cv-6a	καυματίζω	v-2a(1)
κατανάθεμα	n-3c(4)	κατατομή	n-1b	καυματόω	v-1d(3)
καταναθεματίζω	cv-2a(1)	κατατοξεύω	cv-1a(6)	καῦσις	n-3e(5b)
καταναλίσκω	cv-5b	κατατρέχω	cv-1b(2)	καυσόω	v-1d(3)
καταναρκάω	cv-1d(1a)	καταυγάζω	cv-2a(1)	καυστηριάζω	v-2a(1)
κατανεύω	cv-1a(6)	καταφέρω	cv-1c(1)	καύσων	n-3f(1a)
κατανοέω	cv-1d(2a)	καταφεύγω	cv-1b(2)	καυτηριάζω	v-2a(1)
καταντάω	cv-1d(1a)	καταφθείρω	cv-2d(3)	καυχάομαι	v-1d(1a)
κατάνυξις	n-3e(5b)	καταφιλέω	cv-1d(2a)	καύχημα	n-3c(4)
κατανύσσομαι	cv-2b	καταφρονέω	cv-1d(2a)	καύχησις	n-3e(5b)
καταξιόω	cv-1d(3)	καταφωνέω	cv-1d(2a)	Καφαρναούμ	n-3g(2)
καταπατέω	cv-1d(2a)	καταφρονητής	n-1f	Κεγχρεαί	n-1a

κέδρος	n-2b	κιθάρα	n-1a	Κλωπᾶς	n-1e
Κεδρών	n-3g(2)	κιθαρίζω	v-2a(1)	κνήθω	v-1b(3)
κεῖμαι	v-6b	κιθαρῳδός	n-2a	Κνίδος	n-2b
κειρία	n-1a	Κιλικία	n-1a	κοδράντης	n-1f
κείρω	v-2d(3)	κίλιξ	n-3b(1)	κοιλία	n-1a
κέλευσμα	n-3c(4)	κινδυνεύω	v-1a(6)	κοιμάω	v-1d(1a)
κελεύω	v-1a(6)	κίνδυνος	n-2a	κοίμησις	n-3e(5b)
κέλλω	v-2d(1)	κινέω	v-1d(2a)	κοινός	a-1a(2a)
κενεμβατεύω	v-1a(6)	κίνησις	n-3e(5b)	κοινόω	v-1d(3)
κενοδοξία	n-1a	κιννάμωμον	n-2c	κοινωνέω	v-1d(2a)
κενόδοξος	a-3a	Κίς	n-3g(2)	κοινωνία	n-1a
κενός	a-1a(2a)	κίχρημι	v-6a	κοινωνικός	a-1a(2a)
κενοφωνία	n-1a	κλάδος	n-2a	κοινωνός	n-2a; n-2b
κενόω	v-1d(3)	κλαίω	v-2c	κοίτη	n-1b
κεντέω	v-1d(2a)	κλάσις	n-3e(5b)	κοιτών	n-3f(1a)
κεντρίζω	v-2a(1)	κλάσμα	n-3c(4)	κόκκινος	a-1a(2a)
κέντρον	n-2c	Κλαῦδα	n-3g(2)	κόκκος	n-2a
κεντυρίων	n-3f(1a)	Κλαύδη	n-1b	κολάζω	v-2a(1)
κενῶς	adverb	Κλαυδία	n-1a	κολακεία	n-1a
κεραία	n-1a	Κλαύδιος	n-2a	κόλασις	n-3e(5b)
κεραμεύς	n-3e(3)	κλαυθμός	n-2a	Κολασσαεύς	n-3e(3)
κεραμικός	a-1a(2a)	κλάω	v-1d(1b)	Κολασσαί	n-1b
κεράμιον	n-2c	κλείς	n-3c(2)	κολαφίζω	v-2a(1)
κέραμος	n-2a	κλείω	v-1a(3)	κολλάω	v-1d(1a)
κεράννυμι	v-3c(1)	κλέμμα	n-3c(4)	κολλούριον	n-2c
κέρας	n-3c(6a)	Κλεοπᾶς	n-1e	κολλυβιστής	n-1f
κεράτιον	n-2c	κλέος	n-3d(2)	κολλύριον	see
κερδαίνω	v-3d; v-7	κλέπτης	n-1f		κολλούριον
κέρδος	n-3d(2)	κλέπτω	v-4	κολοβόω	v-1d(3)
κέρμα	n-3c(4)	κλῆμα	n-3c(4)	Κολοσσαεύς	n-3e(3)
κερματιστής	n-1f	Κλήμης	n-3c(5a)	Κολοσσαί	n-1b
κεφάλαιον	n-2c	κληροδοτέω	v-1d(2a)	κόλπος	n-2a
κεφαλαιόω	v-1d(3)	κληρονομέω	v-1d(2a)	κολυμβάω	v-1d(1a)
κεφαλή	n-1b	κληρονομία	n-1a	κολυμβήθρα	n-1a
κεφαλίζω	v-2a(1)	κληρονόμος	n-2a	κολωνία	n-1a
κεφαλιόω	v-1d(3)	κλῆρος	n-2a	κομάω	v-1d(1a)
κεφαλίς	n-3c(2)	κληρόω	v-1d(3)	κομβόομαι	v-1d(3)
κηδεύω	v-1a(6)	κλῆσις	n-3e(5b)	κόμη	n-1b
κημόω	v-1d(3)	κλητός	a-1a(2a)	κομίζω	v-2a(1)
κῆνσος	n-2a	κλίβανος	n-2a	κομψότερον	adverb
κῆπος	n-2a	κλίμα	n-3c(4)	κονιάω	v-1d(1b)
κηπουρός	n-2a	κλινάριον	n-2c	κονιορτός	n-2a
κηρίον	n-2c	κλίνη	n-1b	κοπάζω	v-2a(1)
κήρυγμα	n-3c(4)	κλινίδιον	n-2c	κοπετός	n-2a
κῆρυξ	n-3b(1)	κλίνω	v-1c(2)	κοπή	n-1b
κηρύσσω	v-2b	κλισία	n-1a	κοπιάω	v-1d(1b)
κῆτος	n-3d(2)	κλοπή	n-1b	κόπος	n-2a
Κηφᾶς	n-1e	κλύδων	n-3f(1a)	κοπρία	n-1a
κιβώριον	n-2c	κλυδωνίζομαι	v-2a(1)	κόπριον	n-2c
κιβωτός	n-2b	κλύζω	v-2a(1)	κόπρος	n-2b

κόπτω	v-4	κρίνον	n-2c	κυριακός	a-1a(2a)
κόραξ	n-3b(1)	κρίνω	v-1c(2)	κυριεύω	v-1a(6)
κοράσιον	n-2c	κρίσις	n-3e(5b)	κύριος	n-2a
κορβᾶν	n-3g(2)	Κρίσπος	n-2a	κυριότης	n-3c(1)
κορβανᾶς	n-1e	κριτήριον	n-2c	κυρόω	v-1d(3)
Κόρε	n-3g(2)	κριτής	n-1f	κύων	n-3f(1c)
κορέννυμι	v-3c(1)	κριτικός	a-1a(2a)	κῶλον	n-2c
Κορίνθιος	n-2a	κρούω	v-1a(8)	κωλύω	v-1a(4)
Κόρινθος	n-2b	κρύβω	v-1b(1)	κώμη	n-1b
Κορνήλιος	n-2a	κρύπτη	n-1b	κωμόπολις	n-3e(5b)
κόρος	n-2a	κρυπτός	a-1a(2a)	κῶμος	n-2a
κοσμέω	v-1d(2a)	κρύπτω	v-4	κώνωψ	n-3a(1)
κοσμικός	a-1a(2a)	κρυσταλλίζω	v-2a(1)	Κώς	n-2e
κόσμιος	a-3b(1)	κρύσταλλος	n-2a	Κωσάμ	n-3g(2)
κοσμοκράτωρ	n-3f(2b)	κρυφαῖος	a-1a(1)	κωφός	a-1a(2a)
κόσμος	n-2a	κρυφῇ	adverb
Κούαρτος	n-2a	κρύφιος	a-1a(1)
κούμ	n-3g(2)	κτάομαι	v-1d(1a)

λάμβδα

κοῦμι	n-3g(2)	κτείνω	v-2d(5); v-7		
κουστωδία	n-1a	κτῆμα	n-3c(4)	λαγχάνω	v-3a(2b)
κουφίζω	v-2a(1)	κτῆνος	n-3d(2)	Λάζαρος	n-2a
κόφινος	n-2a	κτήτωρ	n-3f(2b)	λάθρα	adverb
κράβαττος	n-2a	κτίζω	v-2a(1)	λαῖλαψ	n-3a(1)
κράββατος	n-2a	κτίσις	n-3e(5b)	λακάω	v-1d(1a)
κράζω	v-2a(2)	κτίσμα	n-3c(4)	λακτίζω	v-2a(1)
κραιπάλη	n-1b	κτίστης	n-1f	λαλέω	v-1d(2a)
κρανίον	n-2c	κυβεία	n-1a	λαλιά	n-1a
κράσπεδον	n-2c	κυβέρνησις	n-3e(5b)	λαμά	n-3g(2)
κραταιός	a-1a(1)	κυβερνήτης	n-1f	λαμβάνω	v-3a(2b); v-7
κραταιόω	v-1d(3)	κυέω	v-1d(2a)	Λάμεχ	n-3g(2)
κρατεύομαι	v-1a(6)	κυκλεύω	v-1a(6)	λαμπάς	n-3c(2)
κρατέω	v-1d(2a)	κυκλόθεν	adverb	λαμπρός	a-1a(1)
κράτιστος	a-1a(2a)	κυκλόω	v-1d(3)	λαμπρότης	n-3c(1)
κράτος	n-3d(2)	κύκλῳ	adverb	λαμπρῶς	adverb
κράτιστος	a-1a(2a)	κύλισμα	n-3c(4)	λάμπω	v-1b(1)
κραυγάζω	v-2a(1)	κυλισμός	n-2a	λανθάνω	v-3a(2b); v-7
κραυγή	n-1b	κυλίω	v-1a(1)		
κρέας	n-3d(1)	κυλλός	a-1a(2a)	λαξευτός	a-1a(2a)
κρείσσων	a-4b(1)	κῦμα	n-3c(4)	Λαοδίκεια	n-1a
κρείττων	a-4b(1)	κύμβαλον	n-2c	Λαοδικεύς	n-3e(3)
κρέμαμαι	v-1d(1b)	κύμινον	n-2c	λαός	n-2a
κρεμάννυμι	v-3c(1)	κυνάριον	n-2c	λάρυγξ	n-3b(2)
κρημνίζω	v-2a(1)	κυνέω	v-1d(2a)	Λασαία	n-1a
κρημνός	n-2a	Κύπριος	n-2a	Λασέα	n-1a
Κρής	n-3c(1)	Κύπρος	n-2b	λατομέω	v-1d(2a)
Κρήσκης	n-3c(5a)	κύπτω	v-4	λατρεία	n-1a
Κρήτη	n-1b	Κυρηναῖος	n-2a	λατρεύω	v-1a(6)
κριθή	n-1b	Κυρήνη	n-1b	λάχανον	n-2c
κρίθινος	a-1a(2a)	Κυρήνιος	n-2a	Λεββαῖος	n-2a
κρίμα	n-3c(4)	κυρία	n-1a	λεγιών	n-3f(1a)

λέγω	v-1b(2); v-7; v-8	λιπαρός	a-1a(1)	**μῦ**	
λέγω	v-1b(2)	λίτρα	n-1a		
λεῖμμα	n-3c(4)	λίψ	n-3a(2)	Μάαθ	n-3g(2)
λεῖος	a-1a(1)	λογάω	v-1d(1a)	Μαγδαλά	n-3g(2)
λείπω	v-1b(1); v-7	λογεία	n-1a	Μαγαδάν	n-3g(2)
λειτουργέω	v-1d(2a)	λογέομαι	v-1d(2a)	Μαγδαληνή	n-1b
λειτουργία	n-1a	λογίζομαι	v-2a(1)	Μαγεδών	n-3g(2)
λειτουργικός	a-1a(2a)	λογικός	a-1a(2a)	μαγεία	n-1a
λειτουργός	n-2a	λόγιον	n-2c	μαγεύω	v-1a(6)
λείχω	v-1b(2)	λόγιος	a-1a(1)	μάγος	n-2a
Λέκτρα	n-1a	λογισμός	n-2a	Μαγώγ	n-3g(2)
λεμά	n-3g(2)	λογομαχέω	v-1d(2a)	Μαδιάμ	n-3g(2)
λέντιον	n-2c	λογομαχία	n-1a	μαζός	n-2a
λεπίς	n-3c(2)	λόγος	n-2a	μαθητεύω	v-1a(6)
λέπρα	n-1a	λόγχη	n-1b	μαθητής	n-1f
λεπρός	a-1a(1)	λοιδορέω	v-1d(2a)	μαθήτρια	n-1a
λεπτός	a-1a(2a)	λοιδορία	n-1a	Μαθθαῖος	n-2a
Λευί	n-3g(2)	λοίδορος	n-2a	Μαθθάτ	n-3g(2)
Λευίς	n-3g(1)	λοιμός	n-2a	Μαθθίας	n-1d
Λευίτης	n-1f	λοιπός	a-1a(2a)	Μαθουσάλα	n-3g(2)
Λευιτικός	a-1a(2a)	Λουκᾶς	n-1e	Μαϊνάν	n-3g(2)
λευκαίνω	v-2d(4)	Λούκιος	n-2a	μαίνομαι	v-2d(4)
λευκοβύσσινος	a-1a(2a)	λουτρόν	n-2c	μακαρίζω	v-2a(1)
λευκός	a-1a(2a)	λούω	v-1a(8)	μακάριος	a-1a(1)
λέων	n-3c(5b)	Λύδδα	n-3g(1)	μακαρισμός	n-2a
λήθη	n-1b	Λυδία	n-1a	μακαριώτερος	a-1a(1)
λῆμψις	n-3e(5b)	Λυκαονία	n-1a	Μακεδονία	n-1a
ληνός	n-2b	Λυκαονιστί	adverb	Μακεδών	n-3f(1b)
λῆρος	n-2a	Λυκία	n-1a	μάκελλον	n-2c
ληστής	n-1f	λύκος	n-2a	μακράν	adverb
λῆψις	n-3e(5b)	λυμαίνω	v-2d(4)	μακρόθεν	adverb
λίαν	adverb	λύνω	v-1c(2)	μακροθυμέω	v-1d(2a)
λίβανος	n-2a	λυπέω	v-1d(2a)	μακροθυμία	n-1a
λιβανωτός	n-2a	λύπη	n-1b	μακροθύμως	adverb
Λιβερτῖνος	n-2a	Λυσανίας	n-1d	μακρός	a-1a(1)
Λιβύη	n-1b	Λυσίας	n-1d	μακροχρόνιος	a-3a
Λιβυστῖνος	n-2a	λύσις	n-3e(5b)	μαλακία	n-1a
λιθάζω	v-2a(1)	λυσιτελέω	v-1d(2b)	μαλακός	a-1a(2a)
λίθινος	a-1a(2a)	Λύστρα	n-3g(1)	Μαλελεήλ	n-3g(2)
λιθοβολέω	v-1d(2a)	λύτρον	n-2c	μάλιστα	adverb
λίθος	n-2a	λυτρόω	v-1d(3)	μᾶλλον	adverb
λιθόστρωτος	a-3a	λύτρωσις	n-3e(5b)	Μάλχος	n-2a
λικμάω	v-1d(1a)	λυτρωτής	n-1f	μάμμη	n-1b
λιμήν	n-3f(1b)	λυχνία	n-1a	μαμωνᾶς	n-1e
λίμνη	n-1b	λύχνος	n-2a	Μαναήν	n-3g(2)
λιμός	n-2a; n-2b	λύω	v-1a(4)	μανασσῆ	n-3g(2)
λιμπάνω	v-3a(2b)	Λωΐς	n-3c(2)	Μανασσῆς	n-1g
λίνον	n-2c	Λώτ	n-3g(2)	μανθάνω	v-3a(2b)
Λίνος	n-2a			μανία	n-1a
				μάννα	n-3g(2)

μαντεύομαι	v-1a(6)	μεθιστάνω	cv-3a(1)	μέσος	a-1a(2a)
μαραίνω	v-2d(4)	μεθίστημι	cv-6a	μεσότοιχον	n-2c
μαρὰν ἀθὰ	n-3g(2)	μεθοδεία	n-1a	μεσουράνημα	n-3c(4)
μαράνα θᾶ	n-3g(2)	μεθόριον	n-2c	μεσόω	v-1d(3)
μαργαρίτης	n-1f	μεθύσκω	v-5a	Μεσσίας	n-1d
Μάρθα	n-1a	μέθυσος	n-2a	μεστός	a-1a(2a)
Μαρία	n-1a	μεθύω	v-1a(4)	μεστόω	v-1d(3)
Μαριάμ	n-3g(2)	μείγνυμι	v-3c(2); v-7	μετά	prep.
Μᾶρκος	n-2a	μειγνύω	v-1a(4)	μεταβαίνω	cv-3d
μάρμαρος	n-2a	μειζότερος	a-1a(1)	μεταβάλλω	cv-2d(1)
μαρτυρέω	v-1d(2a)	μείζων	a-4b(1)	μετάγω	cv-1b(2)
μαρτυρία	n-1a	μέλαν	n-3f(1a)	μεταδίδωμι	cv-6a
μαρτύριον	n-2c	μέλας	a-2a	μετάθεσις	n-3e(5b)
μαρτύρομαι	v-1c(1)	Μελεά	n-3g(2)	μεταίρω	cv-2d(2)
μάρτυς	n-3f(2a)	μέλει	see μέλω;	μετακαλέω	cv-1d(2b)
μασάομαι	v-1d(1a)		v-1d(2c)	μετακινέω	cv-1d(2a)
μασθός	n-2a	μελισσ(ε)ῖον	n-2c	μεταλαμβάνω	cv-3a(2b)
μάσσω	v-2b	μελετάω	v-1d(1a)	μετάλημψις	n-3e(5b)
μαστιγόω	v-1d(3)	μέλι	see μέλω	μεταλλάσσω	cv-2b
μαστίζω	v-2a(1)	μελίσσιος	a-3a	μεταμέλομαι	cv-1d(2c)
μάστιξ	n-3b(2)	Μελίτη	n-1b	μεταμορφόω	cv-1d(3)
μαστός	n-2a	Μελιτήνη	see Μελίτη	μετανοέω	cv-1d(2a)
ματαιολογία	n-1a	μέλλω	v-1d(2c)	μετάνοια	n-1a
ματαιολόγος	a-3a	μέλος	n-3d(2)	μεταξύ	adverb
μάταιος	a-1a(1)	Μελχί	n-3g(2)	μεταπέμπω	cv-1b(1)
ματαιότης	n-3c(1)	Μελχισέδεκ	n-3g(2)	μεταστρέφω	cv-1b(1)
ματαιόω	v-1d(3)	μέλω	v-1d(2c)	μετασχηματίζω	cv-2a(1)
μάτην	adverb	μεμβράνα	n-1c	μετατίθημι	cv-6a
Μαθθαῖος	n-2a	μέμφομαι	v-1b(1)	μετατρέπω	cv-1b(1)
Μαθθάν	n-3g(2)	μεμψίμοιρος	a-3a	μεταφυτεύω	cv-1a(6)
Μαθθάτ	n-3g(2)	μέμψις	n-3e(5b)	μετέπειτα	adverb
Μαθθίας	n-1d	μέν	particle	μετέχω	cv-1b(2)
Ματταθά	n-3g(2)	Μεννά	n-3g(2)	μετεωρίζομαι	cv-2a(1)
Ματταθίας	n-1d	μενοῦν	particle	μετοικεσία	n-1a
μάχαιρα	n-1c	μενοῦνγε	particle	μετοικίζω	cv-2a(1)
μάχη	n-1b	μέντοι	particle	μετοχή	n-1b
μάχομαι	v-1b(2)	μένω	v-1c(2); v-7	μέτοχος	a-3a
μεγαλαυχέω	v-1d(2a)	μερίζω	v-2a(1)	μετρέω	v-1d(2a)
μεγαλεῖος	a-1a(1)	μέριμνα	n-1c	μετρητής	n-1f
μεγαλειότης	n-3c(1)	μεριμνάω	v-1d(1a)	μετριοπαθέω	v-1d(2a)
μεγαλοπρεπής	a-4a	μερίς	n-3c(2)	μετρίως	adverb
μεγαλύνω	v-1c(2)	μερισμός	n-2a	μέτρον	n-2c
μεγάλως	adverb	μεριστής	n-1f	μέτωπον	n-2c
μεγαλωσύνη	n-1b	μέρος	n-3d(2)	μέχρι	prep.; conj.
μέγας	a-1a(2a)	μεσάζω	v-2a(1)	μέχρις	see μέχρι
μέγεθος	n-3d(2)	μεσημβρία	n-1a	μή	particle
μεγιστάν	n-3f(1a)	μεσιτεύω	v-1a(6)	μήγε	see γέ; part.
μέγιστος	a-1a(2a)	μεσίτης	n-1f	μηδαμῶς	adverb
μεθερμηνεύω	cv-1a(6)	μεσονύκτιον	n-2c	μηδέ	particle
μέθη	n-1b	Μεσοποταμία	n-1a	μηδείς	a-2a

μηδέποτε	adverb	μνημεῖον	n-2c	Μυσία	n-1a
μηδέπω	adverb	μνήμη	n-1b	μυστήριον	n-2c
Μῆδος	n-2a	μνημονεύω	v-1a(6)	μυωπάζω	v-2a(1)
μηθαμῶς	adverb	μνημόσυνον	n-2c	μώλωψ	n-3a(1)
μηκέτι	adverb	μνηστεύω	v-1a(6)	μωμάομαι	v-1d(1a)
μῆκος	n-3d(2)	μογγιλάλος	a-3a	μῶμος	n-2a
μηκύνω	v-1c(2)	μογιλάλος	a-3a	μωραίνω	v-2d(4)
μηλωτή	n-1b	μόγις	adverb	μωρία	n-1a
μήν	particle	μόδιος	n-2a	μωρολογία	n-1a
μήν	n-3f(1a)	μοιχαλίς	n-3c(2)	μωρός	a-1a(1)
μηνύω	v-1a(4)	μοιχάω	v-1d(1a)	Μωσῆς	n-3g(1)
μήποτε	particle	μοιχεία	n-1a	Μωϋσῆς	n-3g(1)
μήπου	conj.	μοιχεύω	v-1a(6)		
μήπω	adverb	μοιχός	n-2a		
μήπως	conj.	μόλις	adverb	$ν\hat{υ}$	
μηρός	n-2a	Μολόχ	n-3g(2)		
μήτε	conj.	μολύνω	v-1c(2)	Νααςσών	n-3g(2)
μήτηρ	n-3f(2c)	μολυσμός	n-2a	Ναγγαί	n-3g(2)
μήτι	particle	μομφή	n-1b	Ναζαρά	n-3g(2)
μήτιγε	see γέ; part.	μορφίζω	v-2a(1)	Ναζαρέθ	n-3g(2)
μήτρα	n-1a	μονή	n-1b	Ναζαρέτ	n-3g(2)
μητραλῴας	n-1d	μονογενής	a-4a	Ναζαρηνός	a-1a(2a)
μητρόπολις	n-3e(5b)	μόνον	adverb	Ναζωραῖος	n-2a
μιαίνω	v-2d(4)	μόνος	a-1a(2a)	Ναθάμ	n-3g(2)
μίασμα	n-3c(4)	μονόφθαλμος	a-3a	Ναθαναήλ	n-3g(2)
μιασμός	n-2a	μονόω	v-1d(3)	ναί	particle
μίγμα	n-3c(4)	μορφή	n-1b	Ναιμάν	n-3g(2)
μίγνυμι	v-3c(2)	μορφόω	v-1d(3)	Ναθάν	n-3g(2)
μικρός	a-1a(1)	μόρφωσις	n-3e(5b)	Ναΐν	n-3g(2)
μικρότερος	a-1a(1)	μοσχοποιέω	v-1d(2a)	ναός	n-2a
Μίλητος	n-2b	μόσχος	n-2a	Ναούμ	n-3g(2)
μίλιον	n-2c	μουσικός	a-1a(2a)	νάρδος	n-2b
μιμέομαι	v-1d(2a)	μόχθος	n-2a	ναρκάω	v-1d(1a)
μιμητής	n-1f	μυελός	n-2a	Νάρκισσος	n-2a
μιμνήσκομαι	v-5a	μυέω	v-1d(2a)	ναυαγέω	v-1d(2a)
μισέω	v-1d(2a)	μυθέομαι	v-1d(2a)	ναύκληρος	n-2a
μισθαποδοσία	n-1a	μῦθος	n-2a	ναῦς	n-3e(2)
μισθαποδότης	n-1f	μυκάομαι	v-1d(1a)	ναύτης	n-1f
μίσθιος	n-2a	μυκτηρίζω	v-2a(1)	Ναχώρ	n-3g(2)
μισθός	n-2a	μυλικός	a-1a(2a)	νεανίας	n-1d
μισθόω	v-1d(3)	μύλινος	a-1a(2a)	νεανίσκος	n-2a
μίσθωμα	n-3c(4)	μύλος	n-2a	Νεάπολις	n-3e(5b)
μισθωτός	n-2a	μυλών	n-3f(1a)	Νεεμάν	n-3g(2)
Μιτυλήνη	n-1b	μυλωνικός	a-1a(2a)	νεκρός	a-1a(1)
Μιχαήλ	n-3g(2)	Μύρα	n-2c	νεκρόω	v-1d(3)
μνᾶ	n-1h	μυριάς	n-3c(2)	νέκρωσις	n-3e(5b)
μνάομαι	v-1d(1a)	μυρίζω	v-2a(1)	νέμω	v-1d(2c)
Μνάσων	n-3f(1a)	μύριοι	a-1a(1)	νεομηνία	n-1a
μνεία	n-1a	μυρίος	a-1a(1)	νέος	a-1a(1)
μνῆμα	n-3c(4)	μύρον	n-2c	νεοσσός	n-2a

νεότης	n-3c(1)	νόμισμα	n-3c(4)	**ὂ μικρόν**	
νεόφυτος	a-3a	νομοδιδάσκαλος	n-2a		
νεόω	v-1d(3)	νομοθεσία	n-1a	ὁ, ἡ, τό	a-1a(2b)
Νέρων	n-3f(1a)	νομοθετέω	v-1d(2a)	ὀγδοήκοντα	a-5b
Νευης	n-3g(2)	νομοθέτης	n-1f	ὄγδοος	a-1a(2a)
νεύω	v-1a(6)	νόμος	n-2a	ὄγκος	n-2a
νεφέλη	n-1b	νοσέω	v-1d(2a)	ὄδε	a-1a(2b)
Νεφθαλίμ	n-3g(2)	νόσημα	n-3c(4)	ὁδεύω	v-1a(6)
νέφος	n-3d(2)	νόσος	n-2b	ὁδηγέω	v-1d(2a)
νεφρός	n-2a	νοσσία	n-1a	ὁδηγός	n-2a
νεωκόρος	n-2a	νοσσίον	n-2c	ὁδοιπορέω	v-1d(2a)
νεωτερικός	a-1a(2a)	νοσσός	n-2a	ὁδοιπορία	n-1a
νεώτερος	a-1a(1)	νοσφίζω	v-2a(1)	ὁδός	n-2b
νή	particle	νότος	n-2a	ὀδούς	n-3c(5a)
νήθω	v-1b(3)	νουθεσία	n-1a	ὀδυνάω	v-1d(1a)
νηπιάζω	v-2a(1)	νουθετέω	v-1d(2a)	ὀδύνη	n-1b
νήπιος	a-1a(1)	νουμηνία	n-1a	ὀδυρμός	n-2a
Νηρεύς	n-3e(3)	νουνεχῶς	adverb	Ὀζίας	n-1d
Νηρί	n-3g(2)	νοῦς	n-3e(4)	ὄζω	v-2a(1)
νησίον	n-2c	νυκτερεύω	v-1a(6)	ὅθεν	adverb
νῆσος	n-2b	Νύμφα	n-1a	ὀθόνη	n-1b
νηστεία	n-1a	Νυμφᾶς	n-1e	ὀθόνιον	n-2c
νηστεύω	v-1a(6)	νύμφη	n-1b	οἴγω	v-1b(2)
νῆστις, ιος	n-3e(5a)	νυμφίος	n-2a	οἶδα	v-1b(3); v-8
νῆστις, ιδος	n-3c(2)	νυμφών	n-3f(1a)	οἰκεῖος	a-3b(1)
νηφαλέος	a-1a(1)	νῦν	adverb	οἰκετεία	n-1a
νηφάλιος	a-1a(1)	νυνί	adverb	οἰκέτης	n-1f
νήφω	v-1b(1)	νύξ	n-3c(1)	οἰκέω	v-1d(2a)
Νίγερ	n-3g(2)	νύσσω	v-2b	οἴκημα	n-3c(4)
Νικάνωρ	n-3f(2b)	νυστάζω	v-2a(2)	οἰκητήριον	n-2c
νικάω	v-1d(1a)	νυχθήμερον	n-2c	οἰκία	n-1a
νίκη	n-1b	Νῶε	n-3g(2)	οἰκιακός	n-2a
Νικόδημος	n-2a	νωθρός	a-1a(1)	οἰκίζω	v-2a(1)
Νικολαΐτης	n-1f	νῶτος	n-2a	οἰκοδεσποτέω	v-1d(2a)
Νικόλαος	n-2a			οἰκοδεσπότης	n-1f
Νικόπολις	n-3e(5b)			οἰκοδομέω	v-1d(2a)
νῖκος	n-3d(2)	**ξῖ**		οἰκοδομή	n-1b
Νινευή	n-3g(2)			οἰκοδομία	n-1a
Νινευΐ	n-3g(2)			οἰκοδόμος	n-2a
Νινευίτης	n-1f	ξαίνω	v-2d(4)	οἰκονομέω	v-1d(2a)
νιπτήρ	n-3f(2a)	ξενία	n-1a	οἰκονομία	n-1a
νίπτω	v-4	ξενίζω	v-2a(1)	οἰκονόμος	n-2a
νοέω	v-1d(2a)	ξενοδοχέω	v-1d(2a)	οἶκος	n-2a
νόημα	n-3c(4)	ξένος	a-1a(2a)	οἰκουμένη	n-1b
νόθος	a-1a(2a)	ξέστης	n-1f	οἰκουργός	a-3a
νομέω	v-1d(2a)	ξηραίνω	v-2d(4)	οἰκουρός	a-3a
νομή	n-1b	ξηρός	a-1a(1)	οἰκτείρω	v-2d(3)
νομίζω	v-2a(1)	ξύλινος	a-1a(2a)	οἰκτιρμός	n-2a
νομικός	a-1a(2a)	ξύλον	n-2c	οἰκτίρμων	a-4b(1)
νομίμως	adverb	ξυράω	v-1d(1a)	οἰκτίρω	v-2d(3)

οἶμαι	v-1d(2c)	ὁμοίωσις	n-3e(5b)	ὀργυιά	n-1a
οἰνοπότης	n-1f	ὁμολογέω	v-1d(2a)	ὀρέγω	v-1b(2)
οἶνος	n-2a	ὁμολογία	n-1a	ὀρεινός	a-1a(2a)
οἰνοφλυγία	n-1a	ὁμολογουμένως	adverb	ὄρεξις	n-3e(5b)
οἴομαι	v-1d(2c)	ὁμορέω	v-1d(2a)	ὀρθοποδέω	v-1d(2a)
οἷος	a-1a(1)	ὁμόσε	adverb	ὀρθός	a-1a(2a)
οἱοσδηποτοῦν	see οἷος	ὁμότεχνος	a-3a	ὀρθοτομέω	v-1d(2a)
οἴχομαι	v-1d(2c)	ὁμοῦ	adverb	ὀρθόω	v-1d(3)
ὀκνέω	v-1d(2a)	ὁμόφρων	a-4b(1)	ὀρθρίζω	v-2a(1)
ὀκνηρός	a-1a(1)	ὅμως	adverb	ὀρθρινός	a-1a(2a)
ὀκταήμερος	a-3a	ὄναρ	n-3c(6b)	ὄρθριος	a-1a(1)
ὀκτώ	a-5b	ὀνάριον	n-2c	ὄρθρος	n-2a
ὀλεθρευτής	n-1f	ὀνειδίζω	v-2a(1)	ὀρθῶς	adverb
ὀλεθρεύω	v-1a(6)	ὀνειδισμός	n-2a	ὀρίζω	v-2a(1)
ὀλέθριος	a-3a	ὄνειδος	n-3d(2)	ὅριον	n-2c
ὄλεθρος	n-2a	Ὀνήσιμος	n-2a	ὀρκέω	v-1d(2a)
ὀλιγοπιστία	n-1a	Ὀνησίφορος	n-2a	ὀρκίζω	v-2a(1)
ὀλιγόπιστος	a-3a	ὀνικός	a-1a(2a)	ὅρκος	n-2a
ὀλίγος	a-1a(2a)	ὀνίνημι	v-6a; v-7	ὀρκωμοσία	n-1a
ὀλιγόψυχος	a-3a	ὄνομα	n-3c(4)	ὁρμάω	v-1d(1a)
ὀλιγωρέω	v-1d(2a)	ὀνομάζω	v-2a(1)	ὁρμή	n-1b
ὀλίγως	adverb	ὄνος	n-2a; n-2b	ὅρμημα	n-3c(4)
ὄλλυμι	v-3c(2); v-7	ὄντως	adverb	ὁρμίζω	v-2a(1)
ὀλοθρευτής	n-1f	ὄξος	n-3d(2)	ὄρνεον	n-2c
ὀλοθρεύω	v-1a(6)	ὀξύνω	v-1c(2)	ὄρνιξ	n-3b(1)
ὁλοκαύτωμα	n-3c(4)	ὀξύς	a-2b	ὄρνις	n-3c(3)
ὁλοκληρία	n-1a	ὀπή	n-1b	ὁροθεσία	n-1a
ὁλόκληρος	a-3a	ὄπισθεν	adverb	ὅρος ("boundary")	n-2a
ὀλολύζω	v-2a(1)	ὀπίσω	adverb	ὄρος ("mountain")	n-3d(2)
ὅλος	a-1a(2a)	ὁπλίζω	v-2a(1)	ὀρύσσω	v-2b
ὁλοτελής	a-4a	ὅπλον	n-2c	ὀρφανίζω	v-2a(1)
Ὀλυμπᾶς	n-1e	ὁποῖος	a-1a(1)	ὀρφανός	a-1a(2a)
ὄλυνθος	n-2a	ὁπότε	particle	ὀρχέομαι	v-1d(2a)
ὅλως	adverb	ὅπου	particle	ὅς	a-1a(2b)
ὄμβρος	n-2a	ὀπτάνομαι	v-3a(2a)	ὁσάκις	adverb
ὁμείρομαι	v-1c(1)	ὀπτασία	n-1a	ὅσγε	see ὅς
ὁμιλέω	v-1d(2a)	ὀπτασία	n-1a	ὅσιος	a-1a(1)
ὁμιλία	n-1a	ὀπτεύω	v-1a(6)	ὁσιότης	n-3c(1)
ὅμιλος	n-2a	ὀπτός	a-1a(2a)	ὁσίως	adverb
ὁμίχλη	n-1b	ὀπτρίζω	v-2a(1)	ὀσμή	n-1b
ὄμμα	n-3c(4)	ὀπώρα	n-1a	ὅσος	a-1a(2a)
ὀμνύω	v-3c(2)	ὅπως	adverb	ὅσπερ	a-1a(2b)
ὁμοθυμαδόν	adverb	ὅραμα	n-3c(4)	ὀστέον	n-2c
ὁμοιάζω	v-2a(1)	ὅρασις	n-3e(5b)	ὅστις	a-1a(2b)
ὁμοιοπαθής	a-4a	ὁρατός	a-1a(2a)	ὀστοῦν	n-2d
ὅμοιος	a-1a(1)	ὁράω	v-1d(1a); v-8	ὀστράκινος	a-1a(2a)
ὁμοιότης	n-3c(1)			ὄσφρησις	n-3e(5b)
ὁμοιόω	v-1d(3)	ὀργή	n-1b	ὀσφῦς	n-3e(1)
ὁμοίωμα	n-3c(4)	ὀργίζω	v-2a(1)	ὅταν	particle
ὁμοίως	adverb	ὀργίλος	a-1a(2a)	ὅτε	particle

ὅτι	conj.	ὀχύρωμα	n-3c(4)	πανταχόθεν	adverb
ὀτρύνω	v-1c(2)	ὀψάριον	n-2c	πανταχοῦ	adverb
οὖ	adverb	ὀψέ	adverb	παντελής	a-4a
οὐ	adverb	ὀψία	n-1a	πάντη	adverb
οὐά	interjection	ὄψιμος	a-3a	πάντοθεν	adverb
οὐαί	interjection	ὄψιος	a-1a(1)	παντοκράτωρ	n-3f(2b)
οὐδαμῶς	adverb	ὄψις	n-3e(5b)	πάντοτε	adverb
οὐδέ	conj.	ὀψώνιον	n-2c	πάντως	adverb
οὐδείς	a-2a			παρά	prep.
οὐδενέω	v-1d(2a)			παραβαίνω	cv-3d
οὐδενόω	v-1d(3)	**πῖ**		παραβάλλω	cv-2d(1)
οὐδέποτε	adverb			παράβασις	n-3e(5b)
οὐδέπω	adverb	παγιδεύω	v-1a(6)	παραβάτης	n-1f
οὐθείς	a-2a	παγίς	n-3c(2)	παραβιάζομαι	cv-2a(1)
οὐθενέω	v-1d(2a)	πάγος	n-2a	παραβολεύομαι	cv-1a(6)
οὐθενόω	v-1d(3)	πάθημα	n-3c(4)	παραβολή	n-1b
οὐκέτι	adverb	παθητός	a-1a(2a)	παραβουλεύομαι	cv-1a(6)
οὐκοῦν	adverb	πάθος	n-3d(2)	παραγγελία	n-1a
οὖν	particle	παιδαγωγός	n-2a	παραγγέλλω	cv-2d(1)
οὔπω	adverb	παιδάριον	n-2c	παραγίνομαι	cv-1c(2)
οὐρά	n-1a	παιδεία	n-1a	παράγω	cv-1b(2)
οὐράνιος	a-3a	παιδευτής	n-1f	παραδειγματίζω	cv-2a(1)
οὐρανόθεν	adverb	παιδεύω	v-1a(6)	παράδεισος	n-2a
οὐρανός	n-2a	παιδιόθεν	adverb	παραδέχομαι	cv-1b(2)
Οὐρβανός	n-2a	παιδίον	n-2c	παραδιατριβή	n-1b
Οὐρίας	n-1d	παιδίσκη	n-1b	παραδίδωμι	cv-6a
οὖς	n-3c(6c)	παιδόθεν	adverb	παράδοξος	a-3a
οὐσία	n-1a	παίζω	v-2a(2)	παράδοσις	n-3e(5b)
οὔτε	adverb	παῖς	n-3c(2)	παραζηλόω	cv-1d(3)
οὗτος	a-1a(2b)	παθέω	v-1d(2a)	παραθαλάσσιος	a-1a(1)
οὕτω	see οὕτως	παίω	v-1a(2)	παραθεωρέω	cv-1d(2a)
οὕτως	adverb	Πακατιανός	a-1a(2a)	παραθήκη	n-1b
οὐχ	see οὐ	πάλαι	adverb	παραινέω	cv-1d(2b)
οὐχί	adverb	παλαιός	a-1a(1)	παραιτέομαι	cv-1d(2a)
ὀφειλέτης	n-1f	παλαιότης	n-3c(1)	παρακαθέζομαι	cv-2a(1)
ὀφειλή	n-1b	παλαιόω	v-1d(3)	παρακαθίζω	cv-2a(1)
ὀφείλημα	n-3c(4)	πάλη	n-1b	παρακαλέω	cv-1d(2b)
ὀφείλω	v-2d(1)	παλιγγενεσία	n-1a	παρακαλύπτω	cv-4
ὄφελον	particle	πάλιν	adverb	παρακαταθήκη	n-1b
ὄφελος	n-3d(2)	παμπληθεί	adverb	παράκειμαι	cv-6b
ὀφθαλμοδουλία	n-1a	πάμπολυς	a-1a(2a)	παράκλησις	n-3e(5b)
ὀφθαλμός	n-2a	Παμφυλία	n-1a	παράκλητος	n-2a
ὄφις	n-3e(5b)	πανδοχεῖον	n-2c	παρακοή	n-1b
ὀφρῦς	n-3e(1)	πανδοχεύς	n-3e(3)	παρακολουθέω	cv-1d(2a)
ὀχετός	n-2a	πανήγυρις	n-3e(5b)	παρακούω	cv-1a(8)
ὀχθίζω	v-2a(1)	πανοικεί	adverb	παρακύπτω	cv-4
ὀχλέω	v-1d(2a)	πανοπλία	n-1a	παραλαμβάνω	cv-3a(2b)
ὀχλοποιέω	v-1d(2a)	πανουργία	n-1a	παραλέγομαι	cv-1b(2)
ὄχλος	n-2a	πανοῦργος	a-3a	παράλιος	a-3a
Ὀχοζίας	n-1d	πανταχῇ	adverb	παραλλαγή	n-1b

παραλογίζομαι	cv-2a(1)	παρέρχομαι	cv-1b(2)	παχύνω	v-1c(2)
παραλυτικός	a-1a(2a)	πάρεσις	n-3e(5b)	πέδη	n-1b
παραλύω	cv-1a(4)	παρέχω	cv-1b(2)	πεδινός	a-1a(2a)
παραμένω	cv-1c(2)	παρηγορία	n-1a	πεζεύω	v-1a(6)
παραμυθέομαι	cv-1d(2a)	παρθενία	n-1a	πεζός	a-1a(2a)
παραμυθία	n-1a	παρθένος	n-2a; n-2b	πεζῇ	adverb
παραμύθιον	n-2c	Πάρθοι	n-2a	πειθαρχέω	v-1d(2a)
παρανομέω	cv-1d(2a)	παρίημι	cv-6a	πειθός	a-1a(2a)
παρανομία	n-1a	παριστάνω	cv-3a(1)	πείθω	v-1b(3); v-7
παραπικραίνω	cv-2d(4)	παρίστημι	cv-6a	πειθώ	n-3e(6)
παραπικρασμός	n-2a	πάροδος	n-2b	πεινάω	v-1d(1b)
παραπίπτω	cv-1b(3)	Παρμενᾶς	n-1e	πεῖρα	n-1a
παραπλέω	cv-1a(7)	παροικέω	cv-1d(2a)	πειράζω	v-2a(1)
παραπλήσιος	a-1a(1)	παροικία	n-1a	πειρασμός	n-2a
παραπλησίως	adverb	πάροικος	a-3a	πείρω	v-2d(3)
παραπορεύομαι	cv-1a(6)	παροιμία	n-1a	πειράω	v-1d(1a)
παράπτωμα	n-3c(4)	πάροινος	a-3a	πεισμονή	n-1b
παραρρέω	cv-1a(7); see ῥέω	παροίχομαι	cv-1d(2c)	πέλαγος	n-3d(2)
		παρομοιάζω	cv-2a(1)	πελεκίζω	v-2a(1)
παράσημος	a-3a	παρόμοιος	a-3b(1)	πέμπτος	a-1a(2a)
παρασκευάζω	cv-2a(1)	παροξύνω	cv-1c(2)	πέμπω	v-1b(1); v-7
παρασκευή	n-1b	παροξυσμός	n-2a	πένης	n-3c(1)
παραστάτις	n-3c(2)	παροράω	cv-1d(1a)	πενθερά	n-1a
παρατείνω	cv-2d(5)	παροργίζω	cv-2a(1)	πενθερός	n-2a
παρατηρέω	cv-1d(2a)	παροργισμός	n-2a	πενθέω	v-1d(2a)
παρατήρησις	n-3e(5b)	παροτρύνω	cv-1c(2)	πένθος	n-3d(2)
παρατίθημι	cv-6a	παρουσία	n-1a	πενιχρός	a-1a(1)
παρατυγχάνω	cv-3a(2b)	παροψίς	n-3c(2)	πεντάκις	adverb
παραυτίκα	adverb	παρρησία	n-1a	πεντακισχίλιοι	a-1a(1)
παραφέρω	cv-1c(1)	παρρησιάζομαι	v-2a(1)	πεντακόσιοι	a-1a(1)
παραφρονέω	cv-1d(2a)	πᾶς	a-2a	πέντε	a-5b
παραφρονία	n-1a	πάσχα	n-3g(2)	πεντεκαιδέκατος	a-1a(2a)
παραφροσύνη	n-1b	πάσχω	v-5a; v-7	πεντήκοντα	a-5b
παραχειμάζω	cv-2a(1)	Πάταρα	n-2c	πεντηκοστή	n-1b
παραχειμασία	n-1a	πατάσσω	v-2b	πεποίθησις	n-3e(5b)
παραχράομαι	cv-1d(1a)	πατέω	v-1d(2a)	περ	particle
παραχρῆμα	adverb	πατήρ	n-3f(2c)	Πέραια	n-1a
πάρδαλις	n-3e(5b)	Πάτμος	n-2a	περαιτέρος	a-1a(1)
παρεδρεύω	cv-1a(6)	πατραλῴας	n-1d	περαιτέρω	adverb
πάρειμι	cv-6b	πατριά	n-1a	πέραν	adverb
παρεισάγω	cv-1b(2)	πατριάρχης	n-1f	πέρας	n-3c(6a)
παρείσακτος	a-3a	πατρικός	a-1a(2a)	περάω	v-1d(1b)
παρεισδύω	cv-1a(4)	πατρίς	n-3c(2)	Πέργαμον	n-2c
παρεισέρχομαι	cv-1b(2)	Πατροβᾶς	n-1e	Πέργαμος	n-2b
παρεισφέρω	cv-1c(1)	πατρολῴας	n-1d	Πέργη	n-1b
παρεκτός	adverb	πατροπαράδοτος	a-3a	περί	prep.
παρεμβάλλω	cv-2d(1)	πατρῷος	a-1a(1)	περιάγω	cv-1b(2)
παρεμβολή	n-1b	Παῦλος	n-2a	περιαιρέω	cv-1d(2a)
παρενοχλέω	cv-1d(2a)	παύω	v-1a(5); v-7	περιάπτω	cv-4
παρεπίδημος	a-3a	Πάφος	n-2b	περιαστράπτω	cv-4

περιβάλλω	cv-2d(1)	περιτρέχω	cv-1b(2)	πιστόω	v-1d(3)
περιβλέπω	cv-1b(1)	περιφέρω	cv-1c(1)	πλανάω	v-1d(1a)
περιβόλαιον	n-2c	περιφρονέω	cv-1d(2a)	πλάνη	n-1b
περιδέω	cv-1d(2b)	περίχωρος	a-3a	πλάνης	n-3c(1)
περιεργάζομαι	cv-2a(1)	περίψημα	n-3c(4)	πλανήτης	n-1f
περίεργος	a-3a	περπερεύομαι	v-1a(6)	πλάνος	a-3a
περιέρχομαι	cv-1b(2)	Περσίς	n-3c(2)	πλάξ	n-3b(1)
περιέχω	cv-1b(2)	πέρυσι	adverb	πλάσμα	n-3c(4)
περιζώννυμι	cv-3c(1)	πετάννυμι	v-3c(1)	πλάσσω	v-2b
περιζωννύω	v-3c(1); see ζώννυμι	πετεινόν	n-2c	πλαστός	a-1a(2a)
		πέτομαι	v-1b(3); v-7	πλατεῖα	n-1a
περίθεσις	n-3e(5b)	πέτρα	n-1a	πλάτος	n-3d(2)
περιΐστημι	cv-6a	Πέτρος	n-2a	πλατύνω	v-1c(2)
περικάθαρμα	n-3c(4)	πετρώδης	a-4a	πλατύς	a-2b
περικαθίζω	cv-2a(1)	πήγανον	n-2c	πλέγμα	n-3c(4)
περικαλύπτω	cv-4	πηγή	n-1b	πλείων	a-4b(1)
περίκειμαι	cv-6b	πήγνυμι	v-3c(2)	πλεῖστος	a-1a(2a)
περικεφαλαία	n-1a	πηδάλιον	n-2c	πλέκω	v-1b(2); v-7
περικρατής	a-4a	πηδάω	v-1d(1a)	πλέον	see πολύς; a-1a(2a)
περικρύβω	cv-1b(1)	πηλίκος	a-1a(2a)		
περικυκλόω	cv-1d(3)	πηλός	n-2a	πλεονάζω	v-2a(1)
περιλάμπω	cv-1b(1)	πήρα	n-1a	πλεονεκτέω	v-1d(2a)
περιλείπομαι	cv-1b(1)	πηρόω	v-1d(3)	πλεονέκτης	n-1f
περίλυπος	a-3a	πήρωσις	n-3e(5b)	πλεονεξία	n-1a
περιμένω	cv-1c(2)	πῆχυς	n-3e(1)	πλευρά	n-1a
πέριξ	adverb	πιάζω	v-2a(1)	πλέω	v-1a(7)
περιοικέω	cv-1d(2a)	πιέζω	v-2a(1)	πληγή	n-1b
περίοικος	a-3a	πιθανολογία	n-1a	πλῆθος	n-3d(2)
περιούσιος	a-3a	πιθός	a-1a(2a)	πληθύνω	v-1c(2)
περιοχή	n-1b	πικραίνω	v-2d(4)	πλήκτης	n-1f
περιπατέω	cv-1d(2a)	πικρία	n-1a	πλήμμυρα	n-1c
περιπείρω	cv-2d(3)	πικρός	a-1a(1)	πλήν	adverb
περιπίπτω	cv-1b(3)	πικρῶς	adverb	πλήρης	a-4a
περιποιέω	cv-1d(2a)	Πιλᾶτος	n-2a	πληροφορέω	v-1d(2a)
περιποίησις	n-3e(5b)	πιμπλάω	v-1d(1a)	πληροφορία	n-1a
περιραίνω	cv-2d(4)	πίμπλημι	v-6a	πληρόω	v-1d(3)
περιρήγνυμι	cv-3c(2)	πίμπρημι	v-6a	πλήρωμα	n-3c(4)
περισπάω	cv-1d(1b)	πινακίδιον	n-2c	πλησίον	adverb
περισσεία	n-1a	πινακίς	n-3c(2)	πλησμονή	n-1b
περίσσευμα	n-3c(4)	πίναξ	n-3b(1)	πλήσσω	v-2b
περισσεύω	v-1a(6)	πίνω	v-3a(1); v-7	πλοιάριον	n-2c
περισσός	a-1a(2a)	πιότης	n-3c(1)	πλοῖον	n-2c
περισσότερος	a-1a(1)	πιπράσκω	v-5a	πλοκή	n-1b
περισσοτέρως	adverb	πίπτω	v-1b(3); v-7	πλόος	n-2a
περισσῶς	adverb	Πισιδία	n-1a	πλοῦς	n-3e(4)
περιστερά	n-1a	Πισίδιος	a-1a(1)	πλούσιος	a-1a(1)
περιτέμνω	cv-3a(1)	πιστεύω	v-1a(6)	πλουσίως	adverb
περιτίθημι	cv-6a	πιστικός	a-1a(2a)	πλουτέω	v-1d(2a)
περιτομή	n-1b	πίστις	n-3e(5b)	πλουτίζω	v-2a(1)
περιτρέπω	cv-1b(1)	πιστός	a-1a(2a)	πλοῦτος	n-2a

πλύνω	v-1c(2)	πονηρότερος	a-1a(1)	πρᾶος	a-1a(2a)
πνεῦμα	n-3c(4)	πόνος	n-2a	πραότης	n-3c(1)
πνευματικός	a-1a(2a)	ποντίζω	v-2a(1)	πρασιά	n-1a
πνευματικῶς	adverb	Ποντικός	a-1a(2a)	πράσσω	v-2b
πνέω	v-1a(7)	Πόντιος	n-2a	πραϋπάθεια	n-1a
πνίγω	v-1b(2)	Πόντος ("Pontus")	n-2a	πραΰς	a-2b
πνικτός	a-1a(2a)	πόντος ("sea")	n-2a	πραΰτης	n-3c(1)
πνοή	n-1b	Πόπλιος	n-2a	πρέπω	v-1b(1)
ποδαπός	a-1a(2a)	πορεία	n-1a	πρεσβεία	n-1a
ποδήρης	a-4a	πορεύομαι	v-1a(6)	πρεσβεύω	v-1a(6)
ποδινιπτήρ	n-3f(2a)	πορέω	v-1d(2a)	πρεσβυτέριον	n-2c
πόθεν	adverb	πορθέω	v-1d(2a)	πρεσβύτερος	a-1a(1)
ποθέω	v-1d(2a)	πορία	n-1a	πρεσβύτης	n-1f
ποία	n-1a	πορισμός	n-2a	πρεσβῦτις	n-3c(2)
ποιέω	v-1d(2a)	Πόρκιος	n-2a	πρήθω	v-1b(3)
ποίημα	n-3c(4)	πορνεία	n-1a	πρηνής	a-4a
ποίησις	n-3e(5b)	πορνεύω	v-1a(6)	πρίζω	v-2a(1)
ποιητής	n-1f	πόρνη	n-1b	πρίν	conj; prep
ποικίλος	a-1a(2a)	πόρνος	n-2a	Πρίσκα	n-1c
ποιμαίνω	v-2d(4)	πόρρω	adverb	Πρίσκιλλα	n-1c
ποιμήν	n-3f(1b)	πόρρωθεν	adverb	πρίω	v-1a(1)
ποίμνη	n-1b	πορρωτέρω	adverb	πρό	prep.
ποίμνιον	n-2c	πορφύρα	n-1a	προάγω	cv-1b(2)
ποῖος	a-1a(1)	πορφύρεος	a-3a	προαιρέω	cv-1d(2a)
πολεμέω	v-1d(2a)	πορφυρόπωλις	n-3c(2)	προαιτιάομαι	cv-1d(1b)
πόλεμος	n-2a	πορφυροῦς	a-1b	προακούω	cv-1a(8)
πόλις	n-3e(5b)	ποσάκις	adverb	προαμαρτάνω	cv-3a(2a)
πολιτάρχης	n-1f	πόσις	n-3e(5b)	προαύλιον	n-2c
πολιτεία	n-1a	πόσος	a-1a(2a)	προβαίνω	cv-3d
πολίτευμα	n-3c(4)	ποταμός	n-2a	προβάλλω	cv-2d(1)
πολιτεύομαι	v-1a(6)	ποταμοφόρητος	a-3a	προβατικός	a-1a(2a)
πολίτης	n-1f	ποταπός	a-1a(2a)	προβάτιον	n-2c
πολλάκις	adverb	ποταπῶς	adverb	πρόβατον	n-2c
πολλαπλασίων	a-4b(1)	πότε	adverb	προβιβάζω	cv-2a(1)
πολυεύστλαγχνος	a-3a	ποτέ	particle	προβλέπω	cv-1b(1)
πολύλαλος	a-3a	πότερον	particle	προγίνομαι	cv-1c(2)
πολυλογία	n-1a	ποτήριον	n-2c	προγινώσκω	cv-5a
πολυμερῶς	adverb	ποτίζω	v-2a(1)	πρόγνωσις	n-3e(5b)
πολυπλήθεια	n-1a	Ποτίολοι	n-2a	πρόγονος	a-3a
πολυποίκιλος	a-3a	πότος	n-2a	προγράφω	cv-1b(1)
πολύς	a-1a(2a)	ποῦ	adverb	πρόδηλος	a-3a
πολύσπλαγχνος	a-3a	πού	adverb	προδίδωμι	cv-6a
πολυτελής	a-4a	Πούδης	n-3c(5a)	προδότης	n-1f
πολύτιμος	a-3a	πούς	n-3c(2)	πρόδρομος	a-3a
πολυτιμότερος	a-1a(1)	πρᾶγμα	n-3c(4)	προεῖπον	cv-1b(2);
πολυτρόπως	adverb	πραγματεία	n-1a		see
πόμα	n-3c(4)	πραγματεύομαι	v-1a(6)		προλέγω
πονέω	v-1d(2a)	πραιτώριον	n-2c	προελπίζω	cv-2a(1)
πονηρία	n-1a	πράκτωρ	n-3f(2b)	προενάρχομαι	cv-1b(2)
πονηρός	a-1a(1)	πρᾶξις	n-3e(5b)	προεπαγγέλλομαι	cv-2d(1)

προέρχομαι	cv-1b(2)	προσδαπανάω	cv-1d(1a)	προσρήσσω	cv-2b
προετοιμάζω	cv-2a(1)	προσδέομαι	cv-1d(2c)	προστάσσω	cv-2b
προευαγγελίζομαι	cv-2a(1)	προσδέχομαι	cv-1b(2)	προστάτις	n-3c(2)
προέχω	cv-1b(2)	προσδηλόω	cv-1d(3)	προστίθημι	cv-6a
προηγέομαι	cv-1d(2a)	προσδίδωμι	cv-6a	προστρέχω	cv-1b(2)
πρόθεσις	n-3e(5b)	προσδοκάω	cv-1d(1a)	προσφάγιον	n-2c
προθεσμία	n-1a	προσδοκία	n-1a	πρόσφατος	a-3a
προθυμία	n-1a	προσεάω	cv-1d(1b)	προσφάτως	adverb
πρόθυμος	a-3a	προσεγγίζω	cv-2a(1)	προσφέρω	cv-1c(1)
προθύμως	adverb	προσεδρεύω	cv-1a(6)	προσφιλής	a-4a
πρόϊμος	a-3a	προσεργάζομαι	cv-2a(1)	προσφορά	n-1a
προΐστημι	cv-6a	προσέρχομαι	cv-1b(2)	προσφωνέω	cv-1d(2a)
προκαλέω	cv-1d(2b)	προσευχή	n-1b	προσχαίρω	cv-2d(2)
προκαταγγέλλω	cv-2d(1)	προσεύχομαι	cv-1b(2)	πρόσχυσις	n-3e(5b)
προκαταρτίζω	cv-2a(1)	προσέχω	cv-1b(2)	προσψαύω	cv-1a(5)
προκατέχω	cv-1b(2)	προσηλόω	cv-1d(3)	προσωπολημπτέω	v-1d(2a)
πρόκειμαι	cv-6b	προσήλυτος	n-2a	προσωπολήμπτης	n-1f
προκηρύσσω	cv-2b	πρόσκαιρος	a-3a	προσωπολημψία	n-1a
προκοπή	n-1b	προσκαλέω	cv-1d(2b)	προσωποληπτέω	v-1d(2a)
προκόπτω	cv-4	προσκαρτερέω	cv-1d(2a)	προσωπολήπτης	n-1f
πρόκριμα	n-3c(4)	προσκαρτέρησις	n-3e(5b)	προσωποληψία	n-1a
προκυρόω	cv-1d(3)	προσκεφάλαιον	n-2c	πρόσωπον	n-2c
προλαμβάνω	cv-3a(2b)	προσκληρόω	cv-1d(3)	προτάσσω	cv-2b
προλέγω	cv-1b(2)	πρόσκλησις	n-3e(5b)	προτείνω	cv-2d(5)
προμαρτύρομαι	cv-1c(1)	προσκλίνω	cv-1c(2)	πρότερος	a-1a(1)
προμελετάω	cv-1d(1a)	πρόσκλισις	n-3e(5b)	προτίθημι	cv-6a
προμεριμνάω	cv-1d(1a)	προσκολλάω	cv-1d(1a)	προτρέπω	cv-1b(1)
προνοέω	cv-1d(2a)	πρόσκομμα	n-3c(4)	προτρέχω	cv-1b(2)
πρόνοια	n-1a	προσκοπή	n-1b	προϋπάρχω	cv-1b(2)
προοράω	cv-1d(1a)	προσκόπτω	cv-4	πρόφασις	n-3e(5b)
προορίζω	cv-2a(1)	προσκυλίω	cv-1a(1)	προφέρω	cv-1c(1)
προπάσχω	cv-5a	προσκυνέω	cv-1d(2a)	προφητεία	n-1a
προπάτωρ	n-3f(2b)	προσκυνητής	n-1f	προφητεύω	v-1a(6)
προπέμπω	cv-1b(1)	προσλαλέω	cv-1d(2a)	προφήτης	n-1f
προπετής	a-4a	προσλαμβάνω	cv-3a(2b)	προφητικός	a-1a(2a)
προπορεύομαι	cv-1a(6)	προσλέγω	cv-1b(2)	προφῆτις	n-3c(2)
πρός	prep.	πρόσλημψις	n-3e(5b)	προφθάνω	cv-3a(1)
προσάββατον	n-2c	πρόσληψις	n-3e(5b)	προχειρίζω	cv-2a(1)
προσαγορεύω	cv-1a(6)	προσμένω	cv-1c(2)	προχειροτονέω	cv-1d(2a)
προσάγω	cv-1b(2)	προσορμίζω	cv-2a(1)	Πρόχορος	n-2a
προσαγωγή	n-1b	προσοφείλω	cv-2d(1)	πρύμνα	n-1c
προσαιτέω	cv-1d(2a)	προσοχθίζω	cv-2a(1)	πρωΐ	adverb
προσαίτης	n-1f	προσπαίω	cv-1a(2)	πρωΐα	n-1a
προσαναβαίνω	cv-3d	πρόσπεινος	a-3a	πρώϊμος	a-3a
προσαναλαμβάνω	cv-3a(2b)	προσπήγνυμι	cv-3c(2)	πρωϊνός	a-1a(2a)
προσαναπληρόω	cv-1d(3)	προσπίπτω	cv-1b(3)	πρῷρα	n-1c
προσανατίθημι	cv-6a	προσποιέω	cv-1d(2a)	πρωτεύω	v-1a(6)
προσανέχω	cv-1b(2)	προσπορεύομαι	cv-1a(6)	πρωτοκαθεδρία	n-1a
προσαπειλέω	cv-1d(2a)	προσρήγνυμι	see	πρωτόμαρτυς	n-3f(2a)
προσαχέω	cv-1d(2a)		προσρήσσω	πρωτοκλισία	n-1a

πρῶτος	a-1a(2a)
πρῶτον	adverb
πρωτοστάτης	n-1f
πρωτοτόκια	n-2c
πρωτότοκος	a-3a
πρώτως	adverb
πταίω	cv-1a(2)
πτέρνα	n-1c
πτερύγιον	n-2c
πτέρυξ	n-3b(2)
πτηνός	a-3b(2)
πτοέω	v-1d(2a)
πτόησις	n-3e(5b)
Πτολεμαΐς	n-3c(2)
πτύον	n-2c
πτύρω	v-1c(1)
πτύσμα	n-3c(4)
πτύσσω	v-2b
πτύω	v-1a(4)
πτῶμα	n-3c(4)
πτῶσις	n-3e(5b)
πτωχεία	n-1a
πτωχεύω	v-1a(6)
πτωχός	a-1a(2a)
πυγμή	n-1b
πύθων	n-3f(1a)
πυκνός	a-1a(2a)
πυκτεύω	v-1a(6)
πύλη	n-1b
πυλών	n-3f(1a)
πυνθάνομαι	v-3a(2b)
πῦρ	n-3f(2a)
πυρά	n-1a
πύργος	n-2a
πυρέσσω	v-2b
πυρετός	n-2a
πύρινος	a-1a(2a)
πυρόω	v-1d(3)
πυρράζω	v-2a(1)
πυρρός	a-1a(1)
Πύρρος	n-2a
πύρωσις	n-3e(5b)
πωλέω	v-1d(2a)
πῶλος	n-2a
πώποτε	adverb
πωρόω	v-1d(3)
πώρωσις	n-3e(5b)
πῶς	particle
πώς	particle

ῥῶ

Ῥαάβ	n-3g(2)
ῥαββί	n-3g(2)
ῥαββονί	n-3g(2)
ῥαββουνί	n-3g(2)
ῥαβδίζω	v-2a(1)
ῥάβδος	n-2b
ῥαβδοῦχος	n-2a
ῥαβιθά	n-3g(2)
Ῥαγαύ	n-3g(2)
ῥαδιούργημα	n-3c(4)
ῥαδιουργία	n-1a
ῥαίνω	v-2d(4)
Ῥαιφάν	n-3g(2)
ῥακά	n-3g(2)
ῥάκος	n-3d(4)
Ῥαμά	n-3g(2)
ῥαντίζω	v-2a(1)
ῥαντισμός	n-2a
ῥαπίζω	v-2a(1)
ῥάπισμα	n-3c(4)
ῥάπτω	v-4
ῥαφίς	n-3c(2)
ῥαχά	n-3g(2)
Ῥαχάβ	n-3g(2)
Ῥαχήλ	n-3g(2)
Ῥεβέκκα	n-1a
ῥέδη	n-1b
Ῥεμφάν	n-3g(2)
Ῥεφάν	n-3g(2)
ῥέω	v-1a(7); v-7
Ῥήγιον	n-2c
ῥῆγμα	n-3c(4)
ῥήγνυμι	v-3c(2); v-7
ῥῆμα	n-3c(4)
Ῥησά	n-3g(2)
ῥήσσω	v-2b
ῥήτωρ	n-3f(2b)
ῥητῶς	adverb
ῥίζα	n-1c
ῥιζόω	v-1d(3)
ῥιπή	n-1b
ῥιπίζω	v-2a(1)
ῥίπτω	v-4
ῥιπτέω	see ῥίπτω
Ῥοβοάμ	n-3g(2)
Ῥόδη	n-1b
Ῥόδος	n-2b
ῥοιζηδόν	adverb

Ῥομφά	n-3g(2)
ῥομφαία	n-1a
ῥοπή	n-1b
Ῥουβήν	n-3g(2)
Ῥούθ	n-3g(2)
Ῥοῦφος	n-2a
ῥύμη	n-1b
ῥύομαι	v-1a(4)
ῥυπαίνω	v-2d(4)
ῥυπαρεύω	v-1a(6)
ῥυπαρία	n-1a
ῥυπαρός	a-1a(1)
ῥύπος	n-2a
ῥυπόω	v-1d(3)
ῥύσις	n-3e(5b)
ῥυτίς	n-3c(2)
Ῥωμαϊκός	a-1a(2a)
Ῥωμαῖος	a-1a(1)
Ῥωμαϊστί	adverb
Ῥώμη	n-1b
ῥώννυμι	v-3c(1)

σίγμα

σαβαχθάνι	n-3g(2)
Σαβαώθ	n-3g(2)
σαββατισμός	n-2a
σάββατον	n-2c
σαγήνη	n-1b
Σαδδουκαῖος	n-2a
Σαδώκ	n-3g(2)
σαίνω	v-2d(4)
σάκκος	n-2a
Σαλά	n-3g(2)
Σαλαθιήλ	n-3g(2)
Σαλαμίς	n-3f(1a)
σαλεύω	v-1a(6)
Σαλήμ	n-3g(2)
Σαλίμ	n-3g(2)
Σαλμών	n-3g(2)
Σαλμώνη	n-1b
σάλος	n-2a
σάλπιγξ	n-3b(2)
σαλπίζω	v-2a(1)
σαλπιστής	n-1f
Σαλώμη	n-1b
Σαλωμών	n-3c(5b)
Σαμάρεια	n-1a
Σαμαρία	n-1a

Σαμαρίτης	n-1f	Σερούχ	n-3g(2)	Σκαριώτης	n-3g(2)
Σαμαρῖτις	n-3c(2)	Σήθ	n-3g(2)	σκάφη	n-1b
Σαμοθράκη	n-1b	Σήμ	n-3g(2)	σκέλος	n-3d(2)
Σάμος	n-2b	σημαίνω	v-2d(4)	σκέπασμα	n-3c(4)
Σαμουήλ	n-3g(2)	σημεῖον	n-2c	σκέπτομαι	v-4
Σαμφουρειν	n-3g(2)	σημειόω	v-1d(3)	σκευάζω	v-2a(1)
Σαμψών	n-3g(2)	σήμερον	adverb	Σκευᾶς	n-1e
σανδάλιον	n-2c	σημικίνθιον	n-2c	σκευή	n-1b
σανίς	n-3c(2)	σήπω	v-1b(1)	σκεῦος	n-3d(2)
Σαούλ	n-3g(2)	σηρικός	a-1a(2a)	σκηνή	n-1b
σαπρός	a-1a(1)	σής	n-3c(1)	σκηνοπηγία	n-1a
Σάπφιρα	n-1c	σητόβρωτος	a-3a	σκηνοποιός	n-2a
σάπφιρος	n-2b	σθενόω	v-1d(3)	σκῆνος	n-3d(2)
σαργάνη	n-1b	σιαγών	n-3f(1b)	σκηνόω	v-1d(3)
Σάρδεις	n-3e(5b)	σιαίνομαι	v-2d(4)	σκήνωμα	n-3c(4)
σάρδινος	n-2a	σιγάω	v-1d(1a)	σκιά	n-1a
σάρδιον	n-2c	σιγή	n-1b	σκιάζω	v-2a(1)
σαρδόνυξ	n-3b(3)	σιδήρεος	a-1a(2a)	σκιρτάω	v-1d(1a)
Σάρεπτα	n-2c	σίδηρος	n-2a	σκληροκαρδία	n-1a
σαρκικός	a-1a(2a)	σιδηροῦς	a-1b	σκληρός	a-1a(1)
σάρκινος	a-1a(2a)	Σιδών	n-3f(1a)	σκληρότης	n-3c(1)
σάρξ	n-3b(1)	Σιδώνιος	a-1a(1)	σκληροτράχηλος	a-3a
Σαρούχ	n-3g(2)	Σιχάρ	n-3g(2)	σκληρύνω	v-1c(2)
σαρόω	v-1d(3)	σικάριος	n-2a	σκολιός	a-1a(1)
Σάρρα	n-1a	σίκερα	n-3g(2)	σκόλοψ	n-3a(1)
Σαρών	n-3f(1a)	Σίλας	n-1e	σκοπέω	v-1d(2a)
Σατάν	n-3g(2)	Σιλουανός	n-2a	σκοπός	n-2a
Σατανᾶς	n-1e	Σιλωάμ	n-3g(2)	σκορπίζω	v-2a(1)
σάτον	n-2c	Σιμαίας	n-1d	σκορπίος	n-2a
Σαῦλος	n-2a	σμικίνθιον	n-2c	σκοτεινός	a-1a(2a)
σαφέω	v-1d(2a)	Σίμων	n-3f(1a)	σκοτία	n-1a
σβέννυμι	v-3c(1)	Σινά	n-3g(2)	σκοτίζομαι	v-2a(1)
σεαυτοῦ	a-1a(2b)	σίναπι	n-3e(5b)	σκότος	n-3d(2)
σεβάζομαι	v-2a(1)	σινδών	n-3f(1b)	σκοτόω	v-1d(3)
σέβασμα	n-3c(4)	σινιάζω	v-2a(1)	σκύβαλον	n-2c
σεβαστός	a-1a(2a)	σιρικός	a-1a(2a)	Σκύθης	n-1f
σέβω	v-1b(1)	σιρός	n-2a	σκυθρωπός	a-3b(2)
σειρά	n-1a	σιτευτός	a-1a(2a)	σκύλλω	v-2d(1)
σειρός	n-2a	σιτίον	n-2c	σκῦλον	n-2c
σεισμός	n-2a	σιτιστός	a-1a(2a)	σκωληκόβρωτος	a-3a
σείω	v-1a(3)	σιτομέτριον	n-2c	σκώληξ	n-3b(1)
Σεκοῦνδος	n-2a	σῖτος	n-2a	σμαράγδινος	a-1a(2a)
Σελεύκεια	n-1a	Σιχέμ	n-3g(2)	σμάραγδος	n-2a
σελήνη	n-1b	Σιών	n-3g(2)	Σμύρνα ("Smyrna")	n-1c
σεληνιάζομαι	v-2a(1)	σιωπάω	v-1d(1a)	σμύρνα ("myrrh")	n-1c
Σεμεΐν	n-3g(2)	σιωπῇ	adverb	Σμυρναῖος	a-1a(1)
σεμίδαλις	n-3e(5b)	σκανδαλίζω	v-2a(1)	σμυρνίζω	v-2a(1)
σεμνός	a-1a(2a)	σκάνδαλον	n-2c	Σόδομα	n-2c
σεμνότης	n-3c(1)	σκάπτω	v-4	Σολομῶν, ῶνος	n-3f(1a)
Σέργιος	n-2a	Σκαριώθ	n-3g(2)	Σολομῶν, ῶντος	n-3c(5b)

σορός	n-2b	στέγη	n-1b	στρουθίον	n-2c
σός	a-1a(2a)	στέγω	v-1b(2)	στρώννυμι	v-3c(1)
σουδάριον	n-2c	στεῖρα	n-1a	στρωννύω	see
Σουσάννα	n-1c	στέλλω	v-2d(1); v-7		στρώννυμι
σοφία	n-1a	στέμμα	n-3c(4)	στυγέω	v-1d(2a)
σοφίζω	v-2a(1)	στεναγμός	n-2a	στυγητός	a-1a(2a)
σοφός	a-1a(2a)	στενάζω	v-2a(2)	στυγνάζω	v-2a(1)
σοφώτερος	a-1a(1)	στενός	a-1a(2a)	στῦλος	n-2a
Σπανία	n-1a	στενοχωρέω	v-1d(2a)	Στωϊκός	a-1a(2a)
σπαράσσω	v-2b	στενοχωρία	n-1a	σύ	a-5a
σπαργανόω	v-1d(3)	στερεός	a-1a(1)	συγγένεια	n-1a
σπαταλάω	v-1d(1a)	στερεόω	v-1d(3)	συγγενής	a-4a
σπάω	v-1d(1b)	στερέω	v-1d(2a)	συγγενίς	n-3c(2)
σπεῖρα	n-1c	στερέωμα	n-3c(4)	συγγνώμη	n-1b
σπείρω	v-2d(3); v-7	Στεφανᾶς	n-1e	συγκάθημαι	cv-6b
σπεκουλάτωρ	n-3f(2b)	Στέφανος ("Stephen")	n-2a	συγκαθίζω	cv-2a(1)
σπένδω	v-1b(3)	στέφανος ("crown")	n-2a	συγκακοπαθέω	cv-1d(2a)
σπέρμα	n-3c(4)	στεφανόω	v-1d(3)	συγκακουχέομαι	cv-1d(2a)
σπερμολόγος	a-3a	στῆθος	n-3d(2)	συγκαλέω	cv-1d(2b)
σπεύδω	v-1b(3)	στήκω	v-1b(2)	συγκαλύπτω	cv-4
σπήλαιον	n-2c	στηριγμός	n-2a	συγκάμπτω	cv-4
σπιλάς	n-3c(2)	στηρίζω	v-2a(2)	συγκαταβαίνω	cv-3d
σπίλος	n-2a	στιβάς	n-3c(2)	συγκατάθεσις	n-3e(5b)
σπιλόω	v-1d(3)	στίγμα	n-3c(4)	συγκατανεύω	cv-1a(6)
σπλαγχνίζομαι	v-2a(1)	στιγμή	n-1b	συγκατατίθημι	cv-6a
σπλάγχνον	n-2c	στίλβω	v-1b(1)	συγκαταψηφίζομαι	cv-2a(1)
σπόγγος	n-2a	στοά	n-1a	σύγκειμαι	cv-6b
σποδός	n-2b	στοιβάς	n-3c(2)	συγκεράννυμι	cv-3c(1)
σπορά	n-1a	Στοϊκός	a-1a(2a)	συγκινέω	cv-1d(2a)
σπόριμος	a-3a	στοιχεῖον	n-2c	συγκλείω	cv-1a(3)
σπόρος	n-2a	στοιχέω	v-1d(2a)	συγκληρονόμος	a-3a
σπουδάζω	v-2a(1)	στολή	n-1b	συγκοινωνέω	cv-1d(2a)
σπουδαῖος	a-1a(1)	στόμα	n-3c(4)	συγκοινωνός	n-2a
σπουδαιότερος	a-1a(1)	στοματίζω	v-2a(1)	συγκομίζω	cv-2a(1)
σπουδαίως	adverb	στόμαχος	n-2a	συγκρίνω	cv-1c(2)
σπουδή	n-1b	στομίζω	v-2a(1)	συγκύπτω	cv-4
σπυρίς	n-3c(2)	στρατεία	n-1a	συγκυρία	n-1a
στάδιον	n-2c	στράτευμα	n-3c(4)	συγχαίρω	cv-2d(2)
στάμαι	v-6b	στρατεύομαι	v-1a(6)	συγχέω	cv-1a(7)
στάμνος	n-2b	στρατηγός	n-2a	συγχράομαι	cv-1d(1a)
στασιαστής	n-1f	στρατιά	n-1a	συγχύννω	cv-3a(1)
στάσις	n-3e(5b)	στρατιώτης	n-1f	σύγχυσις	n-3e(5b)
στατήρ	n-3f(2a)	στρατολογέω	v-1d(2a)	συγχωρέω	cv-1d(2a)
στατόω	v-1d(3)	στρατοπεδάρχης	n-1f	συζάω	cv-1d(1a)
σταυρός	n-2a	στρατοπέδαρχος	n-2a	συζεύγνυμι	cv-3c(2)
σταυρόω	v-1d(3)	στρατόπεδον	n-2c	συζητέω	cv-1d(2a)
σταφυλή	n-1b	στρεβλόω	v-1d(3)	συζήτησις	n-3e(5b)
Στάχυς	n-3e(1)	στρέφω	v-1b(1); v-7	συζητητής	n-1f
στάχυς	n-3e(1)	στρηνιάω	v-1d(1b)	σύζυγος	n-2a
στεγάζω	v-2a(1)	στρῆνος	n-3d(2)	συζωοποιέω	cv-1d(2a)

συκάμινος	n-2b	σύμφορος	a-3a	συνεῖδον	see
συκῆ	n-1h	συμφορτίζω	cv-2a(1)		συνοράω;
συκομορέα	n-1a	συμφυλέτης	n-1f		cv-1d(1a)
σῦκον	n-2c	σύμφυτος	a-3a	σύνειμι	cv-6b
συκοφαντέω	v-1d(2a)	συμφύω	cv-1a(4)	σύνειμι	cv-6b
συλαγωγέω	v-1d(2a)	συμφωνέω	cv-1d(2a)	συνεισέρχομαι	cv-1b(2)
συλάω	v-1d(1a)	συμφώνησις	n-3e(5b)	συνέκδημος	n-2a
συλλαλέω	cv-1d(2a)	συμφωνία	n-1a	συνεκλεκτός	a-1a(2a)
συλλαμβάνω	cv-3a(2b)	σύμφωνος	a-3a	συνεκπορεύομαι	cv-1a(6)
συλλέγω	cv-1b(2)	συμψηφίζω	cv-2a(1)	συνελαύνω	cv-3c(2)
συλλογίζομαι	cv-2a(1)	σύμψυχος	a-3a	συνεπιμαρτυρέω	cv-1d(2a)
συλλυπέω	cv-1d(2a)	σύν	prep.	συνεπίσκοτος	n-2a
συμβαίνω	cv-3d	συνάγω	cv-1b(2)	συνεπιτίθημι	cv-6a
συμβάλλω	cv-2d(1)	συναγωγή	n-1b	συνέπομαι	cv-1d(3)
συμβασιλεύω	cv-1a(6)	συναγωνίζομαι	cv-2a(1)	συνεργέω	cv-1d(2a)
συμβιβάζω	cv-2a(1)	συναθλέω	cv-1d(2a)	συνεργός	n-2a
συμβουλεύω	cv-1a(6)	συναθροίζω	cv-2a(1)	συνέρχομαι	cv-1b(2)
συμβούλιον	n-2c	συναίρω	cv-2d(2)	συνεσθίω	cv-1b(3)
σύμβουλος	n-2a	συναιχμάλωτος	n-2a	σύνεσις	n-3e(5b)
Συμεών	n-3g(2)	συνακολουθέω	cv-1d(2a)	συνετός	a-1a(2a)
συμμαθητής	n-1f	συναλίζω	cv-2a(1)	συνευδοκέω	cv-1d(2a)
συμμαρτυρέω	cv-1d(2a)	συναλίσκομαι	cv-5b	συνευωχέομαι	cv-1d(2a)
συμμερίζω	cv-2a(1)	συναλλάσσω	cv-2b	συνεφίστημι	cv-6a
συμμέτοχος	a-3a	συναναβαίνω	cv-3d	συνέχω	cv-1b(2)
συμμιμητής	n-1f	συνανάκειμαι	cv-6b	συνήδομαι	cv-1b(3)
συμμορφίζω	cv-2a(1)	συναναμίγνυμι	cv-3c(2)	συνήθεια	n-1a
σύμμορφος	a-3a	συναναπαύομαι	cv-1a(5)	συνηλικιώτης	n-1f
συμμορφόω	cv-1d(3)	συναναστρέφω	cv-1b(1)	συνθάπτω	cv-4
συμπαθέω	cv-1d(2a)	συναντάω	cv-1d(1a)	συνθλάω	cv-1d(1b)
συμπαθής	a-4a	συνάντησις	n-3e(5b)	συνθλίβω	cv-1b(1)
συμπαραγίνομαι	cv-1c(2)	συναντιλαμβάνομαι		συνθρύπτω	cv-4
συμπαρακαλέω	cv-1d(2b)		cv-3a(2b)	συνίημι	cv-6a
συμπαραλαμβάνω	cv-3a(2b)	συναπάγω	cv-1b(2)	συνιστάνω	cv-3a(1)
συμπαραμένω	cv-1c(2)	συναποθνήσκω	cv-5a	συνιστάω	cv-1d(1a)
συμπάρειμι	cv-6b	συναπόλλυμι	cv-3c(2)	συνίστημι	cv-6a
συμπάσχω	cv-5a	συναποστέλλω	cv-2d(1)	συνίω	v-1a(1)
συμπέμπω	cv-1b(1)	συναρμολογέω	cv-1d(2a)	συνοδεύω	cv-1a(6)
συμπεριέχω	cv-1b(2)	συναρπάζω	cv-2a(2)	συνοδία	n-1a
συμπεριλαμβάνω	cv-3a(2b)	συναυλίζομαι	cv-2a(1)	σύνοιδα	cv-1b(3)
συμπίνω	cv-3a(1)	συναυξάνω	cv-3a(1)	συνοικέω	cv-1d(2a)
συμπίπτω	cv-1b(3)	σύνδεσμος	n-2a	συνοικοδομέω	cv-1d(2a)
συμπληρόω	cv-1d(3)	συνδέω	cv-1d(2b)	συνομιλέω	cv-1d(2a)
συμπνίγω	cv-1b(2)	συνδοξάζω	cv-2a(1)	συνομορέω	cv-1d(2a)
συμπολίτης	n-1f	σύνδουλος	n-2a	συνοράω	cv-1d(1a)
συμπορεύομαι	cv-1a(6)	συνδρομή	n-1b	συνορία	n-1a
συμποσία	n-1a	συνεγείρω	cv-2d(3)	συνοχή	n-1b
συμπόσιον	n-2c	συνέδριον	n-2c	συνταράσσω	cv-2b
συμπρεσβύτερος	n-2a	συνέδριος	n-2a	συντάσσω	cv-2b
συμφέρω	cv-1c(1)	σύνεδρος	n-2a	συντέλεια	n-1a
σύμφημι	cv-6b	συνείδησις	n-3e(5b)	συντελέω	cv-1d(2b)

συντέμνω	cv-3a(1)	σχεδόν	adverb	τάραχος	n-2a
συντεχνίτης	n-1f	σχῆμα	n-3c(4)	Ταρσεύς	n-3e(3)
συντηρέω	cv-1d(2a)	σχηματίζω	v-2a(1)	Ταρσός	n-2b
συντίθημι	cv-6a	σχίζω	v-2a(1)	ταρταρόω	v-1d(3)
συντόμως	adverb	σχίσμα	n-3c(4)	τάσσω	v-2b
συντρέχω	cv-1b(2)	σχοινίον	n-2c	ταῦρος	n-2a
συντρίβω	cv-1b(1)	σχολάζω	v-2a(1)	ταφή	n-1b
σύντριμμα	n-3c(4)	σχολή	n-1b	ταφιάζω	v-2a(1)
σύντροφος	a-3a	σῴζω	v-2a(1)	τάφος	n-2a
συντυγχάνω	cv-3a(2b)	σῶμα	n-3c(4)	τάχα	adverb
Συντύχη	n-1b	σωματικός	a-1a(2a)	ταχέως	adverb
συντυχία	n-1a	σωματικῶς	adverb	ταχινός	a-1a(2a)
συνυποκρίνομαι	cv-1c(2)	Σώπατρος	n-2a	τάχιον	adverb
συνυπουργέω	cv-1d(2a); see ἐργέω	σωρεύω	v-1a(6)	τάχιστα	adverb
		Σωσθένης	n-3d(2)	τάχος	n-3d(2)
συνωδίνω	cv-1c(2)	Σωσίπατρος	n-2a	ταχύ	adverb
συνωμοσία	n-1a	σωτήρ	n-3f(2a)	ταχύς	a-2b
Σύρα	n-1a	σωτηρία	n-1a	τέ	particle
Συράκουσαι	n-1c	σωτήριος	a-3a	τείνω	v-2d(5)
Συρία	n-1a	σωφρονέω	v-1d(2a)	τεῖχος	n-3d(2)
Σύρος	n-2a	σωφρονίζω	v-2a(1)	τεκμήριον	n-2c
Συροφοινίκισσα	n-1c	σωφρονισμός	n-2a	τεκνίον	n-2c
συρρήγνυμι	cv-3c(2)	σωφρόνως	adverb	τεκνογονέω	v-1d(2a)
Σύρτις	n-3e(5b)	σωφροσύνη	n-1b	τεκνογονία	n-1a
σύρω	v-1c(1)	σώφρων	a-4b(1)	τέκνον	n-2c
συσπαράσσω	cv-2b			τεκνοτροφέω	v-1d(2a)
σύσσημον	n-2c			τεκνόω	v-1d(3)
σύσσωμος	a-3a	**ταῦ**		τέκτων	n-3f(1b)
συστασιαστής	n-1f			τέλειος	a-1a(1)
συστατικός	a-1a(2a)	ταβέρναι	n-1b	τελειότερος	a-1a(1)
συσταυρόω	cv-1d(3)	Ταβιθά	n-3g(2)	τελειότης	n-3c(1)
συστέλλω	cv-2d(1)	τάγμα	n-3c(4)	τελειόω	v-1d(3)
συστενάζω	cv-2a(2)	τακτός	a-1a(2a)	τελείως	adverb
συστοιχέω	cv-1d(2a)	ταλαιπωρέω	v-1d(2a)	τελείωσις	n-3e(5b)
συστρατιώτης	n-1f	ταλαιπωρία	n-1a	τελειωτής	n-1f
συστρέφω	cv-1b(1)	ταλαίπωρος	a-3a	τελεοφορέω	v-1d(2b)
συστροφή	n-1b	ταλαντιαῖος	a-1a(1)	τελευτάω	v-1d(1a)
συσχηματίζω	cv-2a(1)	τάλαντον	n-2c	τελευτή	n-1b
Συχάρ	n-3g(2)	ταλιθά	n-3g(2)	τελέω	v-1d(2b)
Συχέμ	n-3g(2)	ταμεῖον	n-2c	τέλλω	v-2d(1); v-7
σφαγή	n-1b	ταμιεῖον	n-2c	τέλος	n-3d(2)
σφάγιον	n-2c	τανῦν	see νῦν; adverb	τελωνεῖον	n-2c
σφάζω	v-2a(2)			τελώνης	n-1f
σφάλλω	v-2d(1)	τάξις	n-3e(5b)	τελώνιον	n-2c
σφόδρα	adverb	ταπεινός	a-1a(2a)	τέμνω	v-3a(1); v-7
σφοδρῶς	adverb	ταπεινοφροσύνη	n-1b	τέρας	n-3c(6a)
σφραγίζω	v-2a(1)	ταπεινόφρων	a-4b(1)	Τέρτιος	n-2a
σφραγίς	n-3c(2)	ταπεινόω	v-1d(3)	Τέρτουλλος	n-2a
σφυδρόν	n-2c	ταπείνωσις	n-3e(5b)	Τέρτυλλος	n-2a
σφυρόν	n-2c	ταράσσω	v-2b	τεσσαράκοντα	a-5b
		ταραχή	n-1b		

τεσσαρακονταετής	a-4a	τοιγαροῦν	particle	τρίτος	a-1a(2a)
τεσσερακονταετής	a-4a	τοίνυν	particle	τρίχινος	a-1a(2a)
τέσσαρες	a-4c	τοιόσδε	a-1a(2b)	τρόμος	n-2a
τεσσαρεσκαιδέκατος		τοιοῦτος	a-1a(2b)	τροπεύω	v-1a(6)
	a-1a(2a)	τοῖχος	n-2a	τροπή	n-1b
τεσσεράκοντα	a-5b	τόκος	n-2a	τρόπος	n-2a
τετραάρχης	n-1f	τολμάω	v-1d(1a)	τροποφορέω	v-1d(2a)
τεταρταῖος	a-1a(1)	τολμηρότερον	adverb	τροφή	n-1b
τέταρτος	a-1a(2a)	τολμηροτέρως	adverb	Τρόφιμος	n-2a
τετράγωνος	a-3a	τολμητής	n-1f	τροφός	n-2b
τετράδιον	n-2c	τομός	a-1a(2a)	τροφοφορέω	v-1d(2a)
τετρακισχίλιοι	a-1a(1)	τομώτερος	a-1a(1)	τροχιά	n-1a
τετρακόσιοι	a-1a(1)	τοξεύω	v-1a(6)	τροχός	n-2a
τετράμηνος	a-3a	τόξον	n-2c	τρύβλιον	n-2c
τετραπλόος	a-1a(2a)	τοπάζιον	n-2c	τρυγάω	v-1d(1a)
τετραπλοῦς	a-1b	τόπος	n-2a	τρυγών	n-3f(1b)
τετράπους	n-3c(2)	τοσοῦτος	a-1a(2b)	τρυμαλία	n-1a
τετραρχέω	v-1d(2a)	τότε	adverb	τρύπημα	n-3c(4)
τετράρχης	n-1f	τοὐναντίον	crasis	Τρύφαινα	n-1c
τεφρόω	v-1d(3)	τοὔνομα	crasis	τρυφάω	v-1d(1a)
τέχνη	n-1b	τοὔπισω	see ὀπίσω; prep.	τρυφή	n-1b
τεχνίτης	n-1f			Τρυφῶσα	n-1c
τήκω	v-1b(2); v-7	τράγος	n-2a	Τρῳάς	n-3c(2)
τηλαυγῶς	adverb	τράπεζα	n-1c	Τρωγύλλιον	n-2c
τηλικοῦτος	a-1a(2b)	τραπεζίτης	n-1f	τρώγω	v-1b(2)
τηνικαῦτα	adverb	τραῦμα	n-3c(4)	τυγχάνω	v-3a(2b); v-7
τηρέω	v-1d(2a)	τραυματίζω	v-2a(1)		
τήρησις	n-3e(5b)	τραχηλίζω	v-2a(1)	τυλίσσω	v-2b
Τιβεριάς	n-3c(2)	τράχηλος	n-2a	τυμπανίζω	v-2a(1)
Τιβέριος	n-2a	τραχύς	a-2b	τυπικῶς	adverb
τίθημι	v-6a; v-7	Τραχωνῖτις	n-3c(2)	τύπος	n-2a
τίκτω	v-1b(2); v-7	τρεῖς	a-4a	τυπόω	v-1d(3)
τίλλω	v-2d(1)	Τρεῖς Ταβέρναι	see ταβέρναι; n-1b	τύπτω	v-4
Τιμαῖος	n-2a			Τύραννος	n-2a
τιμάω	v-1d(1a)	τρέμω	v-1c(2)	τύραννος	n-2a
τιμή	n-1b	τρέπω	v-1b(1); v-7	τυρβάζω	v-2a(1)
τίμιος	a-1a(1)	τρέφω	v-1b(1); v-7	Τύριος	n-2a
τιμιότης	n-1f	τρέχω	v-1b(2); v-8	Τύρος	n-2b
τιμιώτατος	a-1a(2a)	τρῆμα	n-3c(4)	τυφλός	a-1a(2a)
Τιμόθεος	n-2a	τριάκοντα	a-5b	τυφλόω	v-1d(3)
Τίμων	n-3f(1a)	τριακόσιοι	a-1a(1)	τυφόω	v-1d(3)
τιμωρέω	v-1d(2a)	τρίβολος	n-2a	τύφω	v-1b(1)
τιμωρία	n-1a	τρίβος	n-2b	τυφωνικός	a-1a(2a)
τινάσσω	v-2b	τρίβω	v-1b(1)	Τυχικός	n-2a
τίνω	v-3a(1)	τριετία	n-1a		
τίς	a-4b(2)	τρίζω	v-2a(1)		
τὶς	a-4b(2)	τρίμηνος	a-3a	ὐ ψιλόν	
Τίτιος	n-2a	τρίς	adverb		
τίτλος	n-2a	τρίστεγον	n-2c	ὑακίνθινος	a-1a(2a)
Τίτος	n-2a	τρισχίλιοι	a-1a(1)	ὑάκινθος	n-2a
				ὑάλινος	a-1a(2a)

ὕαλος	n-2b	ὑπερλίαν	adverb	ὑποπνέω	cv-1a(7)
ὑβρίζω	v-2a(1)	ὑπερνικάω	cv-1d(1a)	ὑποπόδιον	n-2c
ὕβρις	n-3e(5b)	ὑπέρογκος	a-3a	ὑπόστασις	n-3e(5b)
ὑβριστής	n-1f	ὑπεροράω	cv-1d(1a)	ὑποστέλλω	cv-2d(1)
ὑγιαίνω	v-2d(4)	ὑπεροχή	n-1b	ὑποστολή	n-1b
ὑγιής	a-4a	ὑπερπερισσεύω	cv-1a(6)	ὑποστρέφω	cv-1b(1)
ὑγρός	a-1a(1)	ὑπερπερισσῶς	adverb	ὑποστρώννυμι	cv-3c(1)
ὑδρία	n-1a	ὑπερπλεονάζω	cv-2a(1)	ὑποστρωννύω	see
ὑδροποτέω	v-1d(2a)	ὑπερυψόω	cv-1d(3)		ὑποστρώννυμι
ὑδρωπικός	a-1a(2a)	ὑπερφρονέω	cv-1d(2a)	ὑποταγή	n-1b
ὕδωρ	n-3c(6b)	ὑπερῷον	n-2c	ὑποτάσσω	cv-2b
ὑετός	n-2a	ὑπέχω	cv-1b(2)	ὑποτίθημι	cv-6a
υἱοθεσία	n-1a	ὑπήκοος	a-3a	ὑποτρέχω	cv-1b(2)
υἱός	n-2a	ὑπηρετέω	v-1d(2a)	ὑποτύπωσις	n-3e(5b)
ὕλη	n-1b	ὑπηρέτης	n-1f	ὑποφέρω	cv-1c(1)
ὑλίζω	v-2a(1)	ὑπνίζω	v-2a(1)	ὑποχωρέω	cv-1d(2a)
ὑμεῖς	a-5a	ὕπνος	n-2a	ὑπωπιάζω	see πιάζω;
Ὑμέναιος	n-2a	ὑπνόω	v-1d(3)		cv-2a(1)
ὑμέτερος	a-1a(1)	ὑπό	prep.	ὗς	n-3e(1)
ὑμνέω	v-1d(2a)	ὑποβάλλω	cv-2d(1)	ὑσσός	n-2a
ὕμνος	n-2a	ὑπογραμμός	n-2a	ὕσσωπος	n-2b
ὑπάγω	cv-1b(2)	ὑπόδειγμα	n-3c(4)	ὑστερέω	v-1d(2a)
ὑπακοή	n-1b	ὑποδείκνυμι	cv-3c(2)	ὑστέρημα	n-3c(4)
ὑπακούω	cv-1a(8)	ὑποδεικνύω	cv-1a(4)	ὑστέρησις	n-3e(5b)
ὕπανδρος	a-3a	ὑποδέχομαι	cv-1b(2)	ὕστερον	adverb
ὑπαντάω	cv-1d(1a)	ὑποδέω	cv-1d(2b)	ὕστερος	a-1a(1)
ὑπάντησις	n-3e(5b)	ὑπόδημα	n-3c(4)	ὑφαίνω	v-2d(4)
ὕπαρξις	n-3e(5b)	ὑπόδικος	a-3a	ὑφαντός	a-1a(2a)
ὑπάρχω	cv-1b(2)	ὑποζύγιον	n-2c	ὑψηλός	a-1a(2a)
ὑπείκω	cv-1b(2)	ὑποζώννυμι	cv-3c(1)	ὑψηλότερος	a-1a(1)
ὑπεναντίος	a-1a(1)	ὑποκάτω	adverb	ὑψηλοφρονέω	v-1d(2a)
ὑπέρ	prep.	ὑπόκειμαι	cv-6b	ὕψιστος	a-1a(2a)
ὑπεραίρω	cv-2d(2)	ὑποκρίνομαι	cv-1c(2)	ὕψος	n-3d(2)
ὑπέρακμος	a-3a	ὑπόκρισις	n-3e(5b)	ὑψόω	v-1d(3)
ὑπεράνω	adverb	ὑποκριτής	n-1f	ὕψωμα	n-3c(4)
ὑπερασπίζω	cv-2a(1)	ὑπολαμβάνω	cv-3a(2b)		
ὑπεραυξάνω	cv-3a(1)	ὑπολαμπάς	n-3c(2)		
ὑπερβαίνω	cv-3d	ὑπόλειμμα	n-3c(4)	φῖ	
ὑπερβαλλόντως	adverb	ὑπολείπω	cv-1b(1)		
ὑπερβάλλω	cv-2d(1)	ὑπολήνιον	n-2c	φάγος	n-2a
ὑπερβολή	n-1b	ὑπολιμπάνω	cv-3a(2b)	φαιλόνης	n-1f
ὑπερέκεινα	adverb	ὑπολύνω	cv-1c(2)	φαίνω	v-2d(4)
ὑπερεκπερισσοῦ	adverb	ὑπομένω	cv-1c(2)	Φάλεκ	n-3g(2)
ὑπερεκπερισσῶς	adverb	ὑπομιμνήσκω	cv-5a	φανερός	a-1a(1)
ὑπερεκτείνω	cv-2d(5)	ὑπόμνησις	n-3e(5b)	φανερόω	v-1d(3)
ὑπερεκχύννω	cv-3a(1)	ὑπομονή	n-1b	φανερῶς	adverb
ὑπερεντυγχάνω	cv-3a(2b)	ὑπονοέω	cv-1d(2a)	φανέρωσις	n-3e(5b)
ὑπερέχω	cv-1b(2)	ὑπόνοια	n-1a	φανίζω	v-2a(1)
ὑπερηφανία	n-1a	ὑποπιάζω	cv-2a(1)	φανός	n-2a
ὑπερήφανος	a-3a	ὑποπλέω	cv-1a(7)	Φανουήλ	n-3g(2)
				φαντάζω	v-2a(1)

φαντασία	n-1a	φίλημα	n-3c(4)	φράζω	v-2a(1)
φάντασμα	n-3c(4)	Φιλήμων	n-3f(1b)	φράσσω	v-2b
φάραγξ	n-3b(2)	Φίλητος	n-2a	φρέαρ	n-3c(6b)
Φαραώ	n-3g(2)	φιλία	n-1a	φρεναπατάω	v-1d(1a)
Φαρές	n-3g(2)	Φιλιππήσιος	n-2a	φρεναπάτης	n-1f
Φαρισαῖος	n-2a	Φίλιπποι ("Philippi")	n-2a	φρήν	n-3f(1b)
φαρμακεία	n-1a	Φίλιππος ("Philip")	n-2a	φρίσσω	v-2b
φαρμακεύς	n-3e(3)	φιλόθεος	a-3a	φρονέω	v-1d(2a)
φάρμακον ("poison")	n-2c	Φιλόλογος	n-2a	φρόνημα	n-3c(4)
φάρμακος ("poisoner")	n-2a	φιλονεικία	n-1a	φρόνησις	n-3e(5b)
φάσις	n-3e(5b)	φιλόνεικος	a-3a	φρόνιμος	a-3a
φάσκω	v-5a	φιλοξενία	n-1a	φρονιμώτερος	a-1a(1)
φάτνη	n-1b	φιλόξενος	a-3a	φρονίμως	adverb
φαῦλος	a-1a(2a)	φιλοπρωτεύω	v-1a(6)	φροντίζω	v-2a(1)
φαύσκω	v-5a	φίλος	a-1a(2a)	φρουρέω	v-1d(2a)
φέγγος	n-3d(2)	φιλοσοφία	n-1a	φρυάσσω	v-2b
φείδομαι	v-1b(3)	φιλόσοφος	n-2a	φρύγανον	n-2c
φειδομένως	adverb	φιλόστοργος	a-3a	Φρυγία	n-1a
φελόνης	n-1f	φιλότεκνος	a-3a	φυγαδεύω	v-1a(6)
φέρω	v-1c(1); v-7; v-8	φιλοτιμέομαι	v-1d(2a)	Φύγελος	n-2a
		φιλοφρόνως	adverb	φυγή	n-1b
φεύγω	v-1b(2); v-7	φιλόφρων	a-4b(1)	φυλακή	n-1b
Φῆλιξ	n-3b(1)	φιμόω	v-1d(3)	φυλακίζω	v-2a(1)
φήμη	n-1b	Φλέγων	n-3c(5b)	φυλακτήριον	n-2c
φημί	v-6b	φλογίζω	v-2a(1)	φύλαξ	n-3b(1)
φημίζω	v-2a(1)	φλόξ	n-3b(2)	φυλάσσω	v-2b
Φῆστος	n-2a	φλυαρέω	v-1d(2a)	φυλή	n-1b
φθάνω	v-3a(1)	φλύαρος	a-3a	φύλλον	n-2c
φθαρτός	a-1a(2a)	φοβερός	a-1a(1)	φύραμα	n-3c(4)
φθέγγομαι	v-1b(2)	φοβέω	v-1d(2a)	φυσάω	v-1d(1a)
φθείρω	v-2d(3); v-7	φόβητρον	n-2c	φυσικός	a-1a(2a)
φθινοπωρινός	a-1a(2a)	φόβος	n-2a	φυσικῶς	adverb
φθόγγος	n-2a	Φοίβη	n-1b	φυσιόω	v-1d(3)
φθονέω	v-1d(2a)	Φοινίκη	n-1b	φύσις	n-3e(5b)
φθόνος	n-2a	Φοινίκισσα	n-1c	φυσίωσις	n-3e(5b)
φθορά	n-1a	Φοῖνιξ ("Phoenix")	n-3b(1)	φυτεία	n-1a
φιάλη	n-1b	φοῖνιξ ("palm tree")	n-3b(1)	φυτεύω	v-1a(6)
φιλάγαθος	a-3a	φονεύς	n-3e(3)	φύω	v-1a(4)
Φιλαδέλφεια	n-1a	φονεύω	v-1a(6)	φωλεός	n-2a
φιλαδελφία	n-1a	φόνος	n-2a	φωνέω	v-1d(2a)
φιλάδελφος	a-3a	φορέω	v-1d(2b)	φωνή	n-1b
φίλανδρος	a-3a	φόρον	n-2c	φῶς	n-3c(6c)
φιλανθρωπία	n-1a	φόρος	n-2a	φώσκω	v-5a
φιλανθρώπως	adverb	φορτίζω	v-2a(1)	φωστήρ	n-3f(2a)
φιλαργυρία	n-1a	φορτίον	n-2c	φωσφόρος	a-3a
φιλάργυρος	a-3a	φόρτος	n-2a	φωτεινός	a-1a(2a)
φίλαυτος	a-3a	Φορτουνᾶτος	n-2a	φωτίζω	v-2a(1)
φιλέω	v-1d(2a)	φραγέλλιον	n-2c	φωτισμός	n-2a
φίλη	n-1b	φραγελλόω	v-1d(3)		
φιλήδονος	a-3a	φραγμός	n-2a		

χῖ

χαίρω	v-2d(2)
χάλαζα	n-1c
χαλάω	v-1d(1b)
Χαλδαῖος	n-2a
χαλεπός	a-1a(2a)
χαλιναγωγέω	v-1d(2a)
χαλινός	n-2a
χαλινόω	v-1d(3)
χάλκεος	a-1a(1)
χαλκεύς	n-3e(3)
χαλκηδών	n-3f(1b)
χαλκίον	n-2c
χαλκολίβανον	n-2c
χαλκός	n-2a
χαλκοῦς	a-1b
χαμαί	adverb
Χανάαν	n-3g(2)
Χαναναῖος	a-1a(1)
χαρά	n-1a
χάραγμα	n-3c(4)
χαρακτήρ	n-3f(2a)
χάραξ	n-3b(1)
χαρίζομαι	v-2a(1)
χάριν	prep.
χάρις	n-3c(1)
χάρισμα	n-3c(4)
χαριτόω	v-1d(3)
χαρράν	n-3g(2)
χάρτης	n-1f
χάσμα	n-3c(4)
χεῖλος	n-3d(2)
χειμάζω	v-2a(1)
χείμαρρος	n-2a
χειμάρρους	n-2d
χειμών	n-3f(1a)
χείρ	n-3f(2a)
χειραγωγέω	v-1d(2a)
χειραγωγός	n-2a
χειρέω	v-1d(2a)
χειρίζω	v-2a(1)
χειρόγραφον	n-2c
χειροποίητος	a-3a
χειροτονέω	v-1d(2a)
χείρων	a-4b(1)
Χερούβ	n-3g(1)
χέω	v-1a(7); v-7
χήρα	n-1a
χθές	adverb

χιλίαρχος	n-2a
χιλιάς	n-3c(2)
χίλιοι	a-1a(1)
χίος	n-2b
χιτών	n-3f(1a)
χιών	n-3f(1b)
χλαμύς	n-3c(2)
χλευάζω	v-2a(1)
χλιαρός	a-1a(1)
χλόη	n-1b
χλωρός	a-1a(1)
χξς	a-5b
χοϊκός	a-1a(2a)
χοῖνιξ	n-3b(1)
χοῖρος	n-2a
χολάω	v-1d(1a)
χολή	n-1b
χόος	see χούς
Χοραζίν	n-3g(2)
χορηγέω	v-1d(2a)
χορός	n-2a
χορτάζω	v-2a(1)
χόρτασμα	n-3c(4)
χόρτος	n-2a
χουζᾶς	n-1e
χοῦς	n-3e(4)
χράομαι	v-1d(1a)
χρεία	n-1a
χρεοφειλέτης	n-1f
χρεωφειλέτης	n-1f
χρή	v-1d(2a)
χρῄζω	v-2a(1)
χρῆμα	n-3c(4)
χρηματίζω	v-2a(1)
χρηματισμός	n-2a
χρήσιμος	a-1a(2a)
χρῆσις	n-3e(5b)
χρηστεύομαι	v-1a(6)
χρηστολογία	n-1a
χρηστός	a-1a(2a)
χρηστότης	n-3c(1)
χρῖσμα	n-3c(4)
Χριστιανός	n-2a
Χριστός	n-2a
χρίω	v-1a(1)
χρονίζω	v-2a(1)
χρόνος	n-2a
χρονοτριβέω	v-1d(2a)
χρύσεος	a-1a(1)
χρυσίον	n-2c

χρυσοδακτύλιος	a-3a
χρυσόλιθος	n-2a
χρυσόπρασος	n-2a
χρυσός	n-2a
χρυσοῦς	a-1b
χρυσόω	v-1d(3)
χρώς	n-3c(1)
χύννω	v-3a(1)
χωλός	a-1a(2a)
χώρα	n-1a
Χωραζίν	n-3g(2)
χωρέω	v-1d(2a)
χωρίζω	v-2a(1)
χωρίον	n-2c
χωρίς	adverb
χωρισμός	n-2a
χῶρος	n-2a

ψῖ

ψάλλω	v-2d(1)
ψαλμός	n-2a
ψαύω	v-1a(5)
ψευδάδελφος	n-2a
ψευδαπόστολος	n-2a
ψευδής	a-4a
ψευδοδιδάσκαλος	n-2a
ψευδολόγος	a-3a
ψεύδομαι	v-1b(3)
ψευδομαρτυρέω	v-1d(2a)
ψευδομαρτυρία	n-1a
ψευδόμαρτυς	n-3f(2a)
ψευδοπροφήτης	n-1f
ψεῦδος	n-3d(2)
ψευδόχριστος	n-2a
ψευδώνυμος	a-3a
ψεῦσμα	n-3c(4)
ψεύστης	n-1f
ψηλαφάω	v-1d(1a)
ψηφίζω	v-2a(1)
ψῆφος	n-2b
ψιθυρισμός	n-2a
ψιθυριστής	n-1f
ψίξ	n-3b(3)
ψιχίον	n-2c
ψυχή	n-1b
ψυχικός	a-1a(2a)
ψῦχος	n-3d(2)
ψυχρός	a-1a(1)

ψύχω	v-1b(2)
ψωμίζω	v-2a(1)
ψωμίον	n-2c
ψώχω	v-1b(2)

ὦ μέγα

Ὦ ("Omega")	a-5b
ὦ	interjection
Ὠβήδ	n-3g(2)
ὧδε	adverb
ᾠδή	n-1b
ὠδίν	n-3f(1a)
ὠδίνω	v-1c(2)
ὠθέω	v-1b(4)
ὦμος	n-2a
ὠνέομαι	v-1d(2a)
ᾠόν	n-2c
ὥρα	n-1a
ὡραῖος	a-1a(1)
ὠρύομαι	v-1a(4)
ὡς	adverb
ὡσάν	particle
ὡσαννά	n-3g(2)
ὡσαύτως	adverb
ὡσεί	particle
Ὡσηέ	n-3g(2)
ὥσπερ	particle
ὡσπερεί	particle
ὥστε	particle
ὠτάριον	n-2c
ὠτίζομαι	v-2a(1)
ὠτίον	n-2c
ὠφέλεια	n-1a
ὠφελέω	v-1d(2a)
ὠφέλιμος	a-3a